Macroeconomics for managers

Macroeconomics for managers

Michael K. Evans

Blackwell
Publishing

350 Main Street, Malden, MA 02148-5020, USA
108 Cowley Road, Oxford OX4 1JF, UK
550 Swanston Street, Carlton, Victoria 3053, Australia

First published 2004 by Blackwell Publishing Ltd

Library of Congress Cataloging-in-Publication Data

Evans, Michael K.

Macroeconomics for managers / Michael K. Evans.
p. cm.
Includes bibliographical references and index.

 ISBN 1-4051-0144-X (hardcover : alk. paper) – 1-4051-0145-8 (pbk. : alk. paper)
 1. Managerial economics. 2. Macroeconomics. I. Evans, Michael K.

 HD30.22.E85 2003
 339/.024/68–21

                                                                    2002156369

A catalogue record for this title is available from the British Library.

Set in 10/12$\frac{1}{2}$ Book Antiqua
by Newgen Imaging Systems (P) Ltd, Chennai, India
Printed and bound in the United Kingdom
by TJ International, Padstow, Cornwall

For further information on
Blackwell Publishing, visit our website:
http://www.blackwellpublishing.com

Contents

Preface and Acknowledgments

The focus of macroeconomics has changed dramatically since I first taught this subject in 1962. Then, crude Keynesian economics – the use of simplistic rules of fiscal stimulus – and the Phillips curve – the tradeoff between inflation and unemployment – reigned supreme, and virtually all mainstream economists thought macroeconomic performance could be optimized by pushing the right buttons and pulling the right levers. After the US economy fell flat on its face in the 1970s, with four recessions in 12 years, two bouts of double-digit inflation, double-digit unemployment rates, and a prime rate as high as $21\frac{1}{2}\%$, existing theory was scrapped, and replaced by the doctrine of rational expectations, including the mantra that fine tuning would never work, and the best policies were a full-employment balanced budget and equilibrium short-term interest rates set at the growth rate of nominal GDP. More recently, macroeconomics has focused on the difference between short-term and long-term explanations for changes in real GDP, inflation, and the unemployment rate. Debate still rages in certain quarters between the "new classical" economists, who think all markets clear quickly in the absence of government intervention, and the "new Keynesian" economists, who think some markets clear very slowly or not at all. Yet while these debates are of great interest to certain academics, they are generally ignored by business managers, the audience for whom this book is addressed.

I have always thought that macroeconomics should be approached as an empirical discipline: theories that are not supported by the facts should be discarded. The problem with this approach, of course, is that the "facts" frequently change. Human beings are not machines, and they often react differently when the same situation is repeated. In some cases, they learn by their past mistakes. In other cases, the "facts" are not really the same because underlying conditions have changed. Thus promulgating even simple rules that are designed to improve economic performance may have unintended consequences.

The modern study of macroeconomics began with John Maynard Keynes, who sought to cure the Great Depression while saving capitalism and democracy. Even today, governments rise and fall – some at the voting booth, some through revolution – when governments cannot provide conditions that reasonably approximate full employment, price stability, and a rising standard of living. Of course they are not always successful, but that is not really the message imparted here. Governments will keep these goals in mind, and will implement changes in monetary, fiscal, trade, and regulatory policies if they are not met. Business managers should be aware of how these policies are likely to change – and how that will affect their sales and profits.

Many recessions are caused entirely or primarily by exogenous shocks: wars, energy crises, major strikes, or terrorist attacks. Obviously macroeconomists cannot be expected to predict these variables: indeed, any economist who accurately predicted the 9/11 terrorist attack probably would have been detained indefinitely for prolonged questioning. That is not the only reason that macroeconomists have never been able to predict *any* of the recessions in the US economy, but it is a contributing factor. That pattern is likely to continue in the future. Indeed, if private and public sector economists widely agreed that a recession was about to start, policy shifts would probably be taken to reduce if not entirely eliminate the likelihood of an actual downturn.

Nonetheless, macroeconomics can offer valuable advice and guidance even if it provides no hint of when these shocks will strike next. Based on how consumers, businesses, and government policymakers react to these shocks, managers are often able to determine how they should alter their own business plans. Often, the biggest business mistakes are not made because of inability to foresee these shocks, but the inability to adjust to them once they have occurred.

Recent macroeconomic textbooks have tended to focus more on the long-run determinants of the economy, relegating short-term fluctuations to a less prominent position: I do not follow that practice. To a certain extent, that may have been due to a lingering belief that we do not have business cycles any more. The 2001 recession exposed this hypothesis as a cruel mirage. The recession itself was quite mild; on an annual basis, real GDP rose slightly in 2001, and the unemployment rate increased less than 2%, the smallest gain in any official recession. Nonetheless, the decline of 50% in the S&P 500 index and 75% in the Nasdaq composite index could not be so easily ignored, and set the stage for an extended period of sluggish growth. As capital spending failed to recover, and as the trade deficit widened at record rates, more and more economists – and politicians – became concerned that the US could be headed down the path of extended stagnation that plagued Europe and Japan in the 1990s. As this is being written, no one knows what course the US economy will follow in the next several years and decades, but the 2001 experience has made it clear that the "best and the brightest" still do not know what macroeconomic policies to use to generate optimal performance.

In part that is because consumers and business executives react differently to the same changes in fiscal policy at different times. Recent evidence shows that while consumers spent 80% to 90% of the Reagan tax cuts, they spent only 20% to 25% of the Bush tax cuts.[1] Similarly, the investment tax credit spurred investment in the early to mid 1960s and again in the late 1970s, but a 30% "bonus depreciation" adjustment in late 2001 hardly boosted capital spending at all in 2002. Results of this sort cause most macroeconomists to take a decidedly dim view about the short-term benefits of fiscal policy stimulus.

Because of results of this sort, very few macroeconomists still think that models can be used for policy purposes, and this textbook does not contain a section on that topic. Many years ago, it was widely believed that macro-economic models could be used to improve forecast accuracy, but that concept has also disappeared. Especially telling, in my view, has been the inability to predict the downturns of 1991 and 2001, when the excess baggage of misleading Keynesian nostrums had been widely discarded, and proliferation of inexpensive computer time permitted exhaustive testing of a wide variety of alternative hypotheses and models. The fact that these recessions were caused primarily by exogenous shocks reemphasizes the degree to which unforeseen shocks are likely to buffet the US – and the world – economies from time to time in the future.

If macroeconomic analysis cannot be used for policy prescriptions, and it cannot be expected to predict recessions in the future, how can a study of macroeconomics benefit business managers? This text addresses the following questions and attempts to supply relevant answers.

- What are the current economic data telling us right now? How can they best be monitored and related to my company sales and profit outlook? To what extent do various components of the leading indicators supply an accurate view of the near future?
- What moves are the Federal Reserve – and the central banks in other major countries – likely to take in the near future, and how will that affect business conditions?
- The ratio of the Federal budget to GDP has recently changed from a 2% surplus to a 3% deficit. How will that affect interest rates, inflation, productivity growth – and how will changes in those variables affect my business situation?
- To what extent do international fluctuations affect my business – and to what extent is the US economy still the "straw that stirs the drink"? What factors will determine whether an increasing proportion of manufacturing activity will move to foreign locations – and where should my company be setting up new plants?
- What linkages between interest rates and major components of consumption and investment are most likely to hold in the future, and will enable me to gauge the response of changes in interest rates, whether or not they are caused by the central bank?
- The next time a recession starts, will it be short and mild, or long and severe? And perhaps even more importantly, will the recovery be robust or stagnant? What will that mean for monetary and fiscal policy, and how will it affect my business?

There are many other relevant questions that can be asked, and hopefully can be answered, by the material found in this text. While respectfully drawing on the theoretical developments in macroeconomics that have been made by others, I have sought to infuse this text with a more empirical flavor and offer a valuable guide for business managers.

Most of this material was developed when I was teaching macroeconomics at the Kellogg Graduate School of Management at Northwestern University. In developing the course material, my perception indicated that while there were several useful macroeconomic texts for the academic market, none of them – including my own previous text – adequately addressed the issue of how business managers and executives can use macroeconomic data and information to improve the performance of their businesses. This book is the outcome of those efforts. For those who prefer the more traditional treatment of certain key economic topics, such as consumption, investment, and inflation, that material has been retained in appendixes to some chapters. Also, the IS/LM diagram and Mundell-Fleming model are covered for optional reading; in my opinion they still offer a useful groundwork for explaining how the economy actually works. Yet most of the exposition focuses on how managers and executives should react to unexpected changes in key economic variables. After all, if changes in the economy are expected, presumably there won't be any need to alter those business plans.

Notes

1. For a summary of these results, see "History Casts Doubt on Efficacy of Tax Cuts," *Wall Street Journal*, November 11, 2002, p. 2.

Acknowledgments

I would like to thank Al Bruckner at Blackwell Publishing, who originally suggested this approach, and Seth Ditchik and Elizabeth Wald, who carried the project to its fruition. Numerous students at Kellogg improved this material, but in particular I would like to thank Michael Locke and Michael Sununu for many helpful comments. Nicholas Stadtmiller also read an early draft and offered a number of useful comments. Finally, as always, I would like to thank Susan Carroll for standing by me in good times and bad and serving as a constant source of inspiration and encouragement.

Michael K. Evans
Boca Raton, Florida
November, 2002

part I
Introductory concepts

The first three chapters of this book discuss the basic concepts of macroeconomics. The first chapter provides a brief introduction and roadmap of what lies ahead in the remainder of this book. While it is often stated that macroeconomists have a great deal of difficulty agreeing on basic concepts – a condition that often stems from differing political viewpoints – there is nonetheless a common core of principles to which virtually all macroeconomists currently subscribe. These are presented in chapter 1, followed by a discussion of why policy disagreements so often occur in this field. It is important to distinguish between the rules of macroeconomic relationships that invariably reoccur, and the policies that are advanced to improve the state of the economy based on whether one espouses a liberal or conservative point of view. Thus, for example, during the 2001 recession and sluggish 2002 recovery, almost all economists agreed that some fiscal stimulus was desirable, but opinion was sharply split about whether this should take the form of increased government spending or tax reduction; and, if the latter, whose taxes should be cut the most. These discussions and disagreements will presumably continue in the future; it is the role of the macroeconomist to set the ground rules so that the arguments are at least based on a common set of assumptions. The groundwork laid in the first chapter should alert managers to spot macroeconomic arguments that are based on spurious reasoning or political opinions, as opposed to those that will help them direct the future course of their businesses.

Chapters 2 and 3 provide a brief discussion of the most important concepts used in macroeconomics, and briefly investigate some of the more important issues in measuring these concepts. This latter area may appear to be arcane to some, yet it is important to realize that if the government statistics say the unemployment rate is falling when it is actually rising, or the rate of inflation is declining when it is actually increasing, a set of seriously misguided policies could be implemented that will have adverse effects on the economy in later years.

The macroeconomic framework is built on the concept of double-entry bookkeeping: the amount that economic agents want to purchase is balanced by the amount that is produced. Besides serving as a useful explanation of how the economy functions, this methodology should help to insure that the statistics are accurate, since both sides must balance. When complete statistics are available, that is invariably the case. However, since some of these statistics are based on tax records and various statistical surveys that are not fully available until three to five years later, preliminary data are sometimes misleading. Managers should be aware when current economic results are likely to contain errors that could affect their business in the future. Some of the more likely sources of these errors are also discussed in chapters 2 and 3.

chapter one
The importance of macroeconomics

Introduction

Macroeconomic events and policies affect the daily lives of almost everyone, especially business managers. Whether your company offers financial services, produces cyclical consumer or capital goods, or is at the cutting edge of fast-breaking technology, it is not immune to events that unfold in the economy.

Virtually all political leaders of capitalist countries want their economies to grow rapidly at full employment with low, stable inflation and rising stock prices. The global track record of the past two decades has improved with respect to keeping inflation low, but outside the US growth in most regions of the world has been below average. As various measures are implemented to improve economic performance, companies around the globe must alter their own business strategies.

Trying to forecast the future is a hazardous occupation. After having tried to predict the economy and monitoring other forecasters for four decades, it has become obvious that no one ever gets it right all the time. Failure to forecast creates a planning void that leads to suboptimal decisions. It is not possible to predict truly exogenous events, such as energy shocks or terrorist attacks. Nonetheless, it is vitally important to know how the economy will react to these shocks once they do occur. Macroeconomics can provide useful answers to these questions. It can also alert managers to upcoming endogenous shifts in the economy.

Even if the sales of your company are not directly affected by the twists and turns in the economy – and many dot.com companies belatedly realized that they were not isolated from the business cycle – the ability to construct an optimal capital structure is vital for every corporation. Managers must understand how much to borrow, when to borrow, and the appropriate debt/equity mix. A clear understanding of the macroeconomic factors that determine financial market prices is also essential for successful business management.

While all branches of economics are evolving disciplines, that is particularly true for macroeconomics. To a certain extent, all social sciences are a blend of "art" and "science." The "science" consists of various relationships that hold if other things remain the same, often known as **ceteris paribus**. For example, if personal income rises, consumers will spend more, ceteris paribus – that is, assuming no change in monetary conditions, the stock of wealth, or consumer attitudes. If interest rates decline and expectations about future sales and profitability remain the same, firms will invest more. If the cost of production rises and demand does not decline, prices will also rise, and so on.

However, economics is not a laboratory science, and in most cases, other things are changing. If personal income rises because workers receive bigger pay increases, that might boost inflation, hence raising interest rates, which would off-set the gain in income. Under those circumstances, consumption might not rise at all. If interest rates decline, capital spending might also fall for a while because the drop in interest rates reflects a decrease in loan demand because of an ongoing recession. As a consequence, the results indicated by theory must invariably be examined in the context of what else is changing in the economy.

The "art" of interpreting the facts occurs when there is no clear-cut conclusion. For example, will a capital gains tax cut raise or lower tax revenues? If a smaller budget deficit is desired, is this goal better accomplished with spending cuts or tax increases? What determines the personal saving rate? Is the economy better off with a stronger or a weaker dollar? Should the budget surplus be spent on tax cuts for the rich or medical care benefits for the poor?

Furthermore, macroeconomics will never be an exact science because of the critical role of expectations. Consumer spending is based in part on what individuals think their income will be in the future. Purchases of capital goods depend on expected future profitability and the expected real rate of interest, measured as the current rate minus the expected rate of inflation. Financial market decisions are based almost entirely on expectations about future changes in profits, inflation, and government policies. Thus it is virtually impossible to explain how the overall economy functions without making explicit assumptions about how expectations will be affected by changes in policies. Also, it is not possible to generate useful forecasts without providing accurate guesses about how expectations will change in the future.

In addition to the problems posed by changing expectations, though, macro-economics is unusually vulnerable to personal opinions masquerading as facts that affect all of our daily lives. The issues of whether or not someone has a job, the interest rate at which one can borrow to purchase a car or home, how much income will rise – and how much of it will be taxed away – are all part of macroeconomics. Hence opinions and emotions often run deeper here than in other social sciences; and in macroeconomics more than microeconomics.

One other critical difference exists between economics and other disciplines, and for that matter between social and physical sciences generally. Suppose the National Weather Service can accurately predict that a major hurricane will soon strike the East Coast. Low-lying areas can be evacuated, and buildings can be boarded up, but nothing can be done to divert the hurricane. However, suppose the economics profession can accurately predict that a sharp rise in the inflation rate will occur if current policies are continued. The central bank can raise interest rates and curtail the expansion of credit, and Congress and the President can vote to reduce expenditures. If such steps are taken, the increase in inflation probably will not occur. Indeed, many economists believe that timely action by the monetary and fiscal authorities in 1994 held inflation at 3% even though forecasters and financial market investors expected it to increase that year.

Individuals learn from the past and correct their mistakes, so their behavior patterns often tend to shift over time. That has led some economists to argue that there are no stable theoretical relationships that can be used for forecasting. It is generally true that consumers react differently to an economic phenomenon after it has become familiar. Consumer reactions to tax cuts, changes in monetary policy, and energy shocks have varied considerably over the past 30 years.

Yet many stable patterns in consumer and business behavior have lasted over decades and even generations, and can be used to form the core of macroeconomic theory. Many of the empirical relationships among macroeconomic variables, while far from "perfect" and subject to change, provide links strong enough to improve our understanding of how the economy works. They can be used for accurate forecasts, and can serve as the basis for intelligent policy decisions. While expectations do change, they are not formed in a vacuum but in most cases are tied to underlying economic relationships.

Besides providing the underlying relationships that form the foundation of modern macroeconomics, these theories should be empirically verified. Thus as each topic is introduced, the relevant facts and figures are presented, and key economic relationships are shown empirically as well as theoretically. Even for those who do not choose to use formal models, empirical implementation reinforces the viewpoint, found throughout this text, that if a theory cannot be empirically verified, it probably does not explain how the real world actually works.

Empirical testing is an important tool for obtaining the answers to questions for positive economics – what actually happens. Such decisions can be compared to normative economics – what ought to be – where there are no "right" answers. For example, it is not clear how much a democratic society should tax the "rich" to provide a decent standard of living for the "poor." Taking such points into consideration, this chapter also offers a brief discussion of why macroeconomists are more likely to disagree than their counterparts in microeconomics. Finally, after discussing these methodological issues, the chapter concludes with a roadmap for this book.

1.1 What is macroeconomics?

Macroeconomics is the study of aggregate economic relationships. It focuses on the interrelationships between aggregate economic variables: real output, the rate of inflation, the growth rate, employment and unemployment, interest rates, the value of the currency, and major components of aggregate demand and income.

Macroeconomic relationships explain the aggregate behavior of economic agents – individuals and firms – for various levels of income, assets, liquidity, interest rates, relative prices, and other economic variables.

Any economy consists of *purchasers* of goods and services, and *producers* of those goods and services. In the aggregate, consumers and businesses who purchase goods and services are the same economic agents as the employees and firms who produce these items. However, most consumers and businesses produce only one good or service, whereas they purchase a large variety of different goods and services. Thus, in the short run, planned purchases may not be the same as planned production, whereas in the long run they are always equal unless government forces interfere with market activity.

The key long-run relationships of macroeconomics explain consumer spending, purchases of capital goods, exports and imports, the cost and availability of debt and equity capital, the value of the currency, inflation, employment and unemployment, wage rates, profit margins, productivity, and the maximum sustainable growth rate of the economy. The growth rate determines the maximum amount of goods and services that can be produced in the long run. In the short run, planned purchases may be either more or less than total maximum production. If planned purchases exceed maximum production, inflation will usually rise as the market uses higher prices as a rationing device. If planned purchases fall below maximum production, the unemployment rate will rise. If the long-term growth rate of the economy remains sluggish, either there will not be enough jobs for those desiring employment, or the available work will be divided among more people, resulting in a declining standard of living.

The principal macroeconomic goals of any society are to provide a job for everyone who wants to work, keep the rate of inflation low and stable, and generate rapid growth in productivity and the standard of living. In the long run, virtually all economists agree that markets clear unless they are constrained or reversed by government policies that prohibit market prices – including interest rates and foreign exchange rates – from reaching equilibrium values. The long-run equilibrium relations that form the core of macroeconomics are well defined and can be stated rigorously; the policy prescriptions are also well defined. In the short run, however, markets adjust at different rates, so the short-run impact of changes in the economy may be different than the long-run impact. Thus when outside forces, known as exogenous shocks, temporarily derail the economy from its long-term optimal path, the appropriate government policies may be different in the short run than in the long run. These policies can be divided into the following categories.

- **Monetary policy** consists of decisions made by the central bank to change the cost and availability of money and credit, the cost of money being the rate of interest. In the 1980s and 1990s, changes in monetary policy were the most common method used to affect economic activity. In the long run, changes in monetary policy affect the rate of inflation but not the real growth rate. In the short run, however, various markets take different amounts of time to return to equilibrium following an exogenous shock. As a result, changes in monetary policy affect output as well as prices. The adjustment time often varies because of changes in expectations, which in general cannot be predicted accurately.

- **Fiscal policy** consists of changes in tax rates or government spending programs to influence the state of the economy. In the 1960s and the 1970s, fiscal policy was used to try and regulate short-run changes in output and inflation, but the results were generally counterproductive, so these methods are not used very often – although the Bush tax cut was accelerated by issuing rebate checks during the third quarter of 2001 because of the ongoing recession that year. In the long run, the major role played by fiscal policy is to determine the growth rate of the economy by influencing the growth rates of labor, capital, and technology.
- **Trade policy** consists of decisions to determine the level of tariffs and quotas on imports, and subsidies on exports, that affect the size of the net export balance. It also includes various measures used to influence the value of the currency. Restrictions on foreign trade may appear to benefit certain domestic industries, but blunting foreign competition and forcing consumers to accept a smaller choice of goods at higher prices reduces the standard of living in the long run.
- **Regulatory policy** consists of issuing government standards that influence the performance of the economy in order to accomplish stated regulatory goals. These include requirements for cleaner air or water, occupational safety and health standards, consumer product safety, and equal opportunity laws. Although these are also determined by the President and Congress, and may impose substantial costs on businesses and consumers, they are not considered part of fiscal policy because they do not usually involve significant changes in government spending programs.

The amount of aggregate purchases and production, and the relationships between these two sides of the economy, determine output, interest rates, inflation, employment and unemployment, the net export balance, value of the currency, and the long-term growth rate. To the extent that outcome is not deemed satisfactory, monetary, fiscal, trade, and regulatory policies are used to improve the economic situation, consistent with various political goals determined by elected representatives.

In the past, some economists and policymakers believed that the real growth rate and the standard of living could be enhanced by printing more money, boosting government spending, or reducing the value of the currency. During periods of slack capacity and excess labor, these policies can boost the growth rate *in the short run*. In the long run, though, the growth rate or the standard of living cannot be boosted by such measures; only the rate of inflation is increased, which generally tends to reduce the standard of living. To that extent, macroeconomic policies generally produce more desirable results than occurred during much of the twentieth century. In particular, business cycle recessions in the US are now far less frequent than was the case before 1982.

1.2 Links between macroeconomics and microeconomics

At one time, macroeconomics and microeconomics used to be considered separate disciplines: one determined how the overall economy changed, while the other explained the behavior of individual consumers and firms. However, this artificial distinction pleased few economists. After all, if individual consumers base their purchasing decisions on income, assets, liquidity, interest rates, and other variables, then at the aggregate level, total consumption should be related to the same variables in some fashion that approximates the weighted average of individual decisions. Similarly, decisions of individual firms about how much to invest, how many workers to employ, and how to determine prices for individual products and services should be based on the same factors at both the micro and the macro level.

Thus it is now generally recognized that the core theories of economics for consumer, business, and financial market behavior are based on a common set of assumptions and principles. Nonetheless, the linkages between these two disciplines are not always straightforward. In particular, the following factors should be taken into consideration.

- *Rigidities* – markets do not always clear immediately, and the response time varies for different markets. In particular, macroeconomic markets such as labor markets may take much longer to clear than microeconomic markets for commodities or services such as steel or airline travel.
- *Liquidity* – individual economic agents may be constrained in their purchases, so short-run spending decisions are not always based on long-run expected income.
- *Knowledge* – since information is expensive to obtain, lack of knowledge may lead to markets that do not clear, since one party (the seller) may know more than the other party (the buyer).
- *Expectations* – microeconomics markets are invariably based on the presumption that when price rises, the quantity demanded falls and the quantity supplied rises. However, if expectations change, rising prices may be accompanied by an increase in demand for a while (buy it now before it becomes even more expensive), which will defer a return to equilibrium indefinitely. That is particularly true in financial markets.

In an attempt to link microeconomics and macroeconomics, and also to strip away inessential assumptions, some macroeconomists start with two basic premises: private sector economic agents will always try to maximize their utility at any given time, and in the long run all markets clear unless prohibited from doing so by government action. Perhaps it seems difficult to argue with these assumptions. Yet because some markets do not clear for several years, it is important for macroeconomics to explain what happens in the interim.

Many markets do not clear instantaneously; prices and wages may adjust slowly after demand has changed. Wages are usually determined only once a year or, in the case of some union contracts, only once every three years. Thus the demand and supply of labor may not be in equilibrium for an extended period of time. Many individuals will accept unemployment for an extended period of time rather than accept a substantial reduction in their wage or salary, or an unpleasant or unfamiliar job.

Microeconomists acknowledge that acquiring knowledge is not costless and in many cases is quite expensive. Thus, even in the closest approximation to perfectly competitive markets that clear instantaneously, namely financial and commodities markets, lack of knowledge may result in disequilibrium situations for quite some time, such as when financial market "bubbles" occur. At the macroeconomic level, knowledge may not only be expensive to obtain but may not be available at all. If economic agents are able to make only partially informed decisions, markets may not clear for an extended period.

Expectations play a major role in determining consumption, investment, interest rates, and foreign exchange rates, but these are based on "best guesses" and are often incorrect. As a result, expectations can change significantly as additional knowledge becomes available. That could cause financial market prices and interest rates to fluctuate sharply even if underlying economic conditions actually remained unchanged. For example, interest rates might rise sharply based on the expectation that inflation was increasing; if that did not happen, interest rates would then decline to their previous levels. In this case, a substantial fluctuation in interest rates would occur even though the actual rate of inflation remained unchanged.

The world is clearly dynamic, and the underlying linkages do change over time. Hence the accepted macroeconomic theory of 25 or 50 years ago has little bearing on the current situation. The major issue is whether these changes are rapid enough to defeat intelligent estimation of short-term fluctuations, or whether the changes are gradual enough that stable empirical linkages can be established. We assume the latter assumption better represents reality.

Macroeconomics is not simply an aggregated version of microeconomics. The **fallacy of composition** states that what is true for individuals may not be true in the aggregate. For example, if everyone tries to boost their real income by raising wages and prices, aggregate real income probably would not rise at all.

Because decisions by different households are driven by different economic factors, strict aggregation sometimes gives the wrong answers. At any given level of income, some consumers choose to save a substantial part of their income, while some prefer not to save anything. Some owners of businesses are inveterate risk-takers, willing to plunge headlong into expansion, while others are content to grow at a much more modest pace.

For all these reasons, the study of macroeconomics is much more than a replication of microeconomics on an aggregate level. To develop the key structural relationships of macroeconomics, it is appropriate to take into account those macroeconomic factors that may inhibit or preclude consumers and businesses from maximizing utility, or forces that may keep markets from clearing.

1.3 Current core of macroeconomic theory

At the January 1997 meetings of the American Economic Association, several prominent macroeconomists were asked to present brief papers attempting to answer the question, *"Is there a core of practical macroeconomics that we should all believe?"* It is not surprising that each of the five economists answered the question positively. What is perhaps more surprising is that all of them basically agreed on what is included in that core.[1]

The fact that five macroeconomists, no matter how distinguished, can agree on this core does not necessarily settle the matter; other macroeconomists who were not invited to participate in the symposium may have had different views. Nonetheless, we think this core does represent the mainstream thinking of macroeconomics in the late 1990s and early 2000s, and is also in line with the views represented in this textbook. The principal points of this core are as follows:

1. All of the major components of aggregate demand – consumption, investment, and net exports – are negatively related to the real interest rate, which is defined as the nominal interest rate minus the expected rate of inflation.
2. In the short run, movements in economic activity are dominated by changes in aggregate demand, while in the long run, the economy tends to return to a steady-state growth path.
3. The long-run growth rate is determined by (a) the ratio of investment to GDP, and (b) the degree to which fiscal, trade, and regulatory policies encourage the spread of free markets and technical innovation and invention.
4. The central bank controls the *nominal short-term* interest rate, but the *real long-term* interest rate affects aggregate demand. Long-term interest rates are determined in large part on the expected future rate of inflation.
5. Economic agents have forward-looking expectations, which means they base their decisions on what they expect to happen in the future, as contrasted to simpler extrapolations of the past. Of course, their predictions are not always accurate, but people learn from past mistakes and adjust their expectations accordingly. As a result, unexpected changes in monetary and fiscal policy are likely to have a larger impact on the economy than expected changes, and permanent changes in those policies will generally have a larger impact than temporary changes.
6. Changes in monetary policy affect both output and prices in the short run, but only prices in the long run. There is no long-run tradeoff between unemployment and inflation.

7. Changes in monetary policy affect real output with a shorter lag than inflation. Because monetary policy is transmitted through a variety of methods,
   and because the lags are variable, the short-term impact of monetary policy
   often cannot be predicted accurately. In particular, there are many important dimensions of monetary policy that are not captured by interest rates
   alone: credit conditions, the yield spread, changes in equity market prices,
   and changes in other tangible asset prices are all important.

8. In the short run, wages are based on predetermined variables, which means
   they react to changes in the economy only with a substantial lag. In the long
   run, the real wage is equal to the marginal productivity of labor, while the
   nominal wage is determined by monetary factors.

9. Federal government budget deficits can be financed either by selling Treasury
   securities to the central bank, which is akin to printing money and is inflationary, or by selling them to the private sector, which will raise real interest
   rates and hence reduce real growth. Hence an increase in the cyclically adjusted
   deficit reduces the long-term growth rate, whereas a decline in the deficit boosts
   that growth rate.

10. Markets clear and economic agents attempt to maximize their utility, subject
    to short-term rigidities and adjustments, liquidity constraints, and incorrect
    expectations. Nonetheless, labor markets may not clear for many years, lead-
    ing to extended periods of high unemployment even though the rest of the
    economy appears to be in equilibrium.

These "core" statements lie between the beliefs of the strict monetarists on the
one hand, who think that only money matters, and the older school of thought –
an offshoot of Keynesian economics – that once claimed monetary factors did
not matter at all. They also lie between the strict rational expectationalists,
who claim the core of macroeconomics is essentially unstable because economic
agents are always reacting to new information, and the older school of thought,
which claimed expectations were either exogenous or a simple extrapolation of
the past.

1.4 Macroeconomics – an empirical discipline

The methodological approach used in this text demonstrates the empirical relevance of the theories that are presented. At a minimum, the theoretical relationships
set forth must agree with the facts. Theories that are unsupported by the facts are
generally not considered further.

However, economics is not a laboratory science, because several variables are
usually changing at the same time, including the underlying conditions that one
would hold constant in a controlled experiment. Thus economists often qualify
these statements by appending the phrase **ceteris paribus**, meaning "other things
being equal." If real interest rates rose, for example, capital spending might still

increase if the expected level of sales also rose. Hence the correct statement is that investment and real interest rates are negatively correlated, ceteris paribus. Similar comments apply to the relationship between consumption and income, wages and prices, and bond prices and stock prices. In all these cases, a strong positive correlation is observed – assuming that the other factors affecting these variables are all unchanged.

Because underlying conditions do keep changing, so the "paribus" is not "ceteris," empirical testing in economics often becomes complicated. Several alternative theories often appear to support the available facts. In such cases, further data and testing are needed to determine which of these competing theories is most likely to be correct.

Students sometimes complain that macroeconomics is a difficult subject because "everything seems to be changing at the same time." That may indeed be the case. Yet failure to understand these multiple linkages generally leads to examples of the Law of Unintended Consequences. Policies designed, for example, to boost aggregate demand might end up boosting inflation instead; or they might raise short-term demand at the expense of reducing the long-term growth rate in productivity. It does not make sense to consider a change in output in isolation without also considering how it would affect inflation, interest rates, productivity, and other key macroeconomic variables.[2]

Part of the "everything is changing" syndrome reflects the difference between *ex ante* magnitudes, which economic agents plan to do, and *ex post* magnitudes, which is what actually does happen. An exogenous increase in income may cause consumers to plan an increase in expenditures, but those plans may cause businesses to raise their prices. In that case, the monetary authorities could restrict credit and boost interest rates, which would offset the planned increase in consumer spending. It might seem that an increase in income had no impact on consumer spending; yet the *ex ante* plans did call for such an increase, which was offset by changes in other economic developments. In this case, the problem is solved by realizing that consumer spending is a function of both income and monetary conditions.

Even if the facts appear to agree with a particular hypothesis, that does not necessarily mean such a theory is correct. The tradeoff between inflation and unemployment appeared to be supported by empirical data from several countries and different time periods, yet the underlying theory was incorrect and the apparent stability of the empirical relationship ultimately collapsed. From 1992 through 2000, the US economy simultaneously enjoyed falling unemployment and a declining inflation rate.

There are many other examples of empirical relationships failing to stand the test of time. Before World War II, inflation generally moved with the business cycle; now it is usually countercyclical. Robust empirical relationships relating the money supply to interest rates and income disappeared after the deregulation of the banking sector and the increased importance of international capital flows. The value of the dollar used to rise in recessions and fall during expansions; now the opposite usually occurs.

In these and many other cases, mere agreement between the available data and the proposed theory were insufficient to verify such a theory. Nonetheless, demonstrating that the data do indeed agree with any proposed theory is a necessary, if not sufficient, condition for using that theory to explain the economy.

1.5   The importance of policy applications

The same changes in policy, such as a given change in income tax rates, often have widely differing effects on the economy because (a) economic agents react differently, (b) the underlying economic conditions are different, and (c) the reaction of the monetary authorities is different. However, that does not mean the effect of a change in tax rates is unpredictable. Instead, the importance of each of these three factors must be assessed separately to determine the effect on the economy. It would be a serious mistake to assume that because similar policies often generate different results, one cannot determine the impact of policy changes, implying they should not be used at all.

Expectations of both policymakers and private sector economic agents certainly take past errors into account. Perhaps the best-known switch over the past 25 years has occurred in the area of monetary policy. It used to be thought that the monetary authorities, when faced with signs of higher inflation, would fail to tighten policy soon enough because they feared it would prematurely end the expansion. Once Fed Chairman Paul Volcker demonstrated in the early 1980s that was no longer the case, economic agents now assume the Fed will institute contractionary measures at the first signs of higher inflation. Not only did monetary policy change, but the expectations of consumers and businesses also changed.

Some economists claim that changes in monetary, fiscal, and trade policies affect the economy only when they are unexpected. That is more likely to be true in financial markets, where traders and investors search diligently for all available information and quickly incorporate it in market prices, so only unexpected changes move the market. However, consumers and businesses react negatively to a rise in interest rates whether it was expected or not. When the dollar declines, net exports improve whether it was expected or not.

Changes in government policy that come as a complete surprise – such as the imposition of wage and price controls by Richard Nixon in August 1971 – are the rare exception. Most of the time, changes in monetary and fiscal policy are not made in a vacuum but reflect what is already happening in the economy. In particular, when faced with certain economic signals, the monetary authorities will invariably react in a predictable fashion. If the economy is growing rapidly at full employment and inflationary expectations start to increase, the Fed will tighten. If the economy is heading into a recession, the Fed will ease. During recessions, the

Federal budget surplus will shrink – or the deficit will increase – even if spending and tax policies do not change; in addition, previous experience has shown that recessions are likely to be accompanied by tax cuts and increased spending programs. No one knows in advance precisely how government policy will change in respect to a particular economic situation, but most of the general moves can be foreseen.

Thus it is important to take into account the general state of the economy at the time when policy changes occur. The impact of a tax cut, for example, is generally quite different depending on whether monetary policy eased, remained neutral, or tightened when the tax cut was implemented. The impact of a tax cut would also vary substantially depending on whether the economy was in a boom or a recession, or whether inflation was rising or falling. A temporary tax increase when the economy is at overfull employment would generally be beneficial; a tax increase in the middle of a recession would make the downturn even more serious.

Macroeconomists agree that short-term fluctuations in output and inflation can be influenced by appropriate use of monetary policy, whereas maximizing the long-term growth rate is a function of fiscal, trade, and regulatory policies. One of the principal aims of this text is to explain when changes in these policies are likely to be implemented, how economic agents are likely to react to those changes, and how they will affect the economy.

1.6 Positive and normative economics: why macroeconomists disagree

Positive economics refers to statements about what actually does occur – at least under ceteris paribus conditions. When the price of a good drops, consumers will demand more. When income rises, consumption rises. When interest rates rise, investment declines.

Normative economics refers to what should be, which varies depending on the political viewpoints of the individual. In many cases, economists disagree about the degree of income or wealth inequality; some think the free market should decide these issues, while others believe that great squalor should not coexist in the midst of great wealth. This leads to heated discussions about the optimal degree of taxes, transfer payments, and government regulation. For example, economists remain deeply divided on whether the 2001 tax cut of the Bush Administration was beneficial because it shortened the recession by boosting consumer spending, or whether the money was wasted and should have been spent on higher medical care benefits and aid to education.

In some cases, the blinding light of actual events has settled arguments that used to verge on the normative. Economists no longer believe that long-term growth can be boosted by bigger increases in the money supply, that the performance of the economy can be enhanced by fine tuning, that a weak dollar is good for America (as once proclaimed by Jimmy Carter's Treasury Secretary, Michael Blumenthal), that the government can control the tradeoff between inflation and unemployment, that increasing the deficit boosts the growth rate, that raising both government spending and taxes by the same amount raises real GDP, or that devaluing the currency boosts the long-term growth rate. Perhaps these ideas sound far-fetched today; but at one time they were all part of mainstream economic doctrine.

However, many aspects of normative economics are still debated as vigorously as ever. There are no right or wrong answers to how much of "my" income should be taken by the government to benefit "you." Most of these disagreements in macro-economics are not presented on such a personal level; instead, massive amounts of research, bound in impressive-looking reports, are offered as allegedly impeccable evidence supporting one side or the other. In these reports, normative issues are not argued on moral, ethical, or social grounds; both sides of the case present their arguments in terms of what "actually" happens, as opposed to what should happen to benefit various sectors of society. The courts are now filled with "junk science" in many disciplines, but economics lends itself particularly well to these types of specious arguments.

Part of the problem occurs because economics is not a laboratory science with controlled experiments; the ceteris paribus conditions seldom remain the same. The 1962–4 Kennedy-Johnson tax cuts were followed by an actual budget surplus, while the 1982–4 Reagan tax cuts, which reduced rates by about the same percentage, were followed by a huge budget deficit. An income tax increase in 1968 was followed by higher inflation and a recession, while an income tax increase in 1993 was followed by a boom and lower inflation. Those who wish to pick and choose from alternative evidence to support their predetermined conclusions thus have a wide range of options. In fact, it is meaningless to offer any blanket statement about whether tax cuts raise or lower the budget deficit, or whether tax increases enhance or retard economic growth, since it obviously depends on what happens to government spending and monetary policy.

Political differences often fuel bitter debates among economists. In recent years, liberals have "proven" that a capital gains tax cut would boost the deficit and leave the growth rate unchanged; conservatives have "proven" that such a tax cut would reduce the deficit and boost the growth rate. Liberals have found that an increase in the minimum wage does not raise unemployment; conservatives have found precisely the opposite.

Expressed in such terms, these are not just normative arguments. For example, the normative argument for boosting the minimum wage would say that in this land of plenty, everyone deserves a living wage; the normative argument against it would claim it is not the job of the government to redistribute income. However, one seldom hears these arguments. Instead, the debate is couched on whether a hike in the minimum wage actually boosts the unemployment rate among the unskilled. It becomes not just an argument about what ought to be, but in the minds of the economists involved, an argument about what "is."

Occasionally indisputable empirical results can still generate major disagreements. The degree of income inequality in the US economy widened in the 1990s.

To liberals, that was a clear sign that redistributive policies should be expanded, and high marginal tax rates should be raised rather than reduced. To conservatives, it was a clear sign that "a rising tide lifts all boats," since many of the people with large incomes were previously poor, so high marginal tax rates should be cut further to encourage incentives and improve the work ethic.

Sometimes economists can agree on the end result but disagree about the intervening path. When inflation is above desired levels, it can be reduced by tighter monetary policies. Yet economists still argue about whether expectations change in the near term, eliminating excess inflation in a year or less; or whether it will take several years, with an unnecessary and costly increase in the rate of unemployment in the interim. Should the monetary authorities follow gradualism or go "cold turkey"? This argument raged for decades. When put to the test, the answer actually turned out to be some of both: in 1981–2, the rate of inflation fell from 13% to 4% in a year and a half, but at the cost of a severe recession. Leading economists who had argued that inflation could decline no faster than 1% per year turned out to be wrong – but those who claimed inflation could be conquered without any intervening recession were also wrong.

One problem that often arises in these discussions is the confusion of cause and effect. This fallacy is often referred to in economics as **ergo**, which is shorthand for the Latin phrase, post hoc, ergo propter hoc – after this, therefore because of this. Many times the problem occurs because two or more variables change simultaneously. For example, consumption will rise when income rises; but the gain in income may well have occurred because consumers decided to spend more. Capital spending will rise when the rate of capacity utilization rises; but that rate may have risen precisely because firms ordered more capital goods. The value of the dollar usually rises in the beginning of a recovery following a drop in the trade deficit; yet the improvement in net exports was due to lower imports because of the recession, while the rise in the dollar reflects an improvement in the expected rate of return. The apparent claim that a shrinking trade deficit boosts the dollar is fallacious. Indeed, the dollar rose sharply during the latter half of the 1990s even as the trade deficit zoomed to a record high proportion of GDP.

Yet even without erroneous logic, flawed statistical and econometric methods are too often used to produce incorrect results. With today's high-powered personal computers and readily available databases, hundreds of alternative regression equations can be calculated in a few minutes, and by the law of large numbers, one or more of these random correlations is likely to give the result desired on ad hoc or political grounds.

This tendency led to a series of articles in the 1980s with titles such as "Who Will Take the 'Con' out of Econometrics?" Even in the 1960s, economists joked that the correct pronunciation of "econometrics" ought to be "economist's tricks." With today's high-powered tools, econometricians are often accused of "torturing the data until they confess."

The combination of political biases, logical fallacies, and data mining have produced bitter arguments among macroeconomists, each of whom manages to buttress the argument at hand with reams of statistical data. No economist is immune to these errors. Nonetheless, the aim of this book is to present theories that are both empirically robust and supported by facts in the appropriate historical concept – and then apply these theories to current economic problems, policies, and solutions.

1.7   Roadmap of this book

A full understanding of how the economy functions requires an explanation of the complete core model of macroeconomics. However, the key linkages cannot all be introduced at the same time; the building blocks must be introduced in order. Nonetheless, it is useful to know in advance some of the key issues facing macroeconomists today.

Since "you can't tell the players without a scorecard," the first task is to describe the key components of macroeconomic activity, including *gross domestic product* in current and constant (chained) dollars, *national* and *personal income,* and the various measures of *inflation* and *unemployment.* Some of the problems inherent in recent data are also introduced, serving as a guide to the unwary. These topics are covered in chapters 2 and 3.

Part II of the book covers the major components of aggregate demand, including the joint determination of output and interest rates under the assumptions that (a) capacity constraints do not exist, and (b) prices are fixed. These unrealistic assumptions are dropped as soon as possible. Nonetheless, the concept of equilibrium in the goods market and the assets market under stable prices is a useful starting point to explain how output and interest rates are determined in the short run.

Consumption accounts for about two-thirds of GDP and, in the long run, consumer demand drives the economy, so the consumption function is first examined in chapter 4. Chapter 5 presents the functions for fixed investment, plus a brief introduction to the determinants of net exports. All these components of aggregate demand depend significantly on the real rate of interest, so the determination of interest rates and an introduction to monetary policy are covered in chapter 6. Chapter 7 explains the joint determination of income and interest rates using the IS/LM diagram; for those who do not wish to emphasize the theoretical approach, this chapter can be skipped without loss of continuity.

Part III proceeds to discard the unrealistic assumptions about the lack of capacity constraints and fixed price levels, and concentrates on the principal elements of aggregate supply. Chapter 8 focuses on the principal causes of inflation. In the long run, inflation is a monetary phenomenon. In the short run, monetary factors remain important, but exogenous shocks and labor market costs are also key factors. There is, however, no reason why inflation must rise as the economy approaches full employment; the so-called Phillips curve is discredited.

In the 1990s, almost all industrialized countries discovered how to keep inflation under control. However, the problem of high unemployment has not been solved so easily; most countries except for the US suffered a rising unemployment rate during that decade. Chapter 9 discusses why high unemployment persists, and explains why the recent unemployment rate is so much higher in Europe, Latin America, and most of Asia than in the US.

Short-run fluctuations in the unemployment rate are closely tied to changes in real GDP, but long-run levels of unemployment are more closely related to the overall productive capacity of the economy. Chapter 10 derives the production function, which represents the maximum amount that can be produced by any given economy for the current levels of labor input, capital stock, and technology. Whereas changes in monetary policy are the principal factor influencing short-term changes in output, the long-term growth rate is more closely tied to fiscal policy, and some of the principal linkages between productivity and fiscal policy are also discussed in this chapter.

The building blocks of the domestic model are now in place, but the impact of the international sector has not yet been examined; this is discussed in part IV. Chapter 11 presents the basic determinants of net exports and the value of the currency. A brief appendix to the chapter summarizes the theory of comparative advantage and the modern theory of international trade. Chapter 12 turns to a discussion of international financial markets, and the effect of foreign exchange rates on domestic economic activity. Chapter 13 introduces the Mundell-Fleming model, which is the extension of the IS/LM model to the foreign sector and provides a method of joint determination for output, interest rates, net exports, and the value of the currency. This chapter can also be skipped without loss of continuity. Chapter 14 then presents several case studies in international trade, explaining why some countries have prospered and others have slumped – including the recent debacle in southeast Asia.

Part V of the book examines the short-run cyclical behavior of the economy. While the US has suffered only two mild recessions since 1982, the rest of the world has not been so fortunate; cyclical fluctuations still remain a major part of the worldwide economic landscape. Chapter 15 discusses the major causes and characteristics of business cycles. Chapter 16 explains the cyclical mechanisms that influence capital spending, housing, inventory investment, and purchases of consumer durables. Chapter 17 presents an examination of cyclical fluctuations in financial markets, which used to occur with approximately the same frequency as cycles in the real sector. More recently, however, financial market cycles have occurred more often, while real cycle business sectors have occurred less often. The factors that determine fluctuations in the stock market are analyzed, and the 1999–2002 stock market bubble and collapse are discussed.

Part VI provides a more detailed analysis of macroeconomic policy issues. Chapter 18 presents an outline of optimal fiscal policies now and for the future, including various aspects of tax reform. Chapter 19 discusses the optimal rules for monetary policy. The book concludes with a brief survey of forecasting methods in chapter 20.

KEY TERMS AND CONCEPTS

Ceteris Paribus	Microeconomics
Empirical Discipline	Monetary Policy
Ergo	Normative and Positive Economics
Fallacy of Composition	Regulatory Policy
Fiscal Policy	Trade Policy
Macroeconomics	

SUMMARY

- Macroeconomics is the study of aggregate economic relationships.
- In the long run, all markets clear unless they are constrained by government forces. The long-run equilibrium relations that form the core of macroeconomics are generally accepted and can be stated rigorously.
- In the short run, various markets adjust at different rates, so the short-run impact of changes in the economy may be different than the long-run impact.
- The macroeconomic goals of any society are to provide full employment, low and stable inflation, and rapid growth in productivity and the standard of living.
- Although microeconomics and macroeconomics used to be considered as separate disciplines, it is now realized that the core theories of economics for consumer, business, and financial market behavior are based on a common set of assumptions and principles.
- The core approach to macroeconomics is based on short-term fluctuations around a long-term trend. Short-term fluctuations are caused by various shocks, both endogenous and exogenous. These departures from equilibrium are due to various rigidities in the economic system, but if the appropriate monetary, trade, and fiscal policies are implemented, the economy will return to its

long-term trend growth rate in a year or two. If they are not, however, the economy could remain well below its maximum productive potential indefinitely.
- Virtually all macroeconomists agree that changes in monetary policy influence both output and prices in the short run, but only inflation in the long run. However, they disagree about the timing and mechanism by which changes in monetary policy are transmitted to the real sector.
- Long-run growth is related to the growth in the labor force, capital stock, and the level of technology. The key policy variable that influences these factors is fiscal policy.
- Inappropriate monetary, trade, and fiscal policies that are used to stimulate output temporarily in the short run usually boost inflation and diminish the level of output in the long run.
- Economists now agree that private sector economic agents take expectations of future events into account when planning their current activity.
- Macroeconomics is an empirical discipline. Theories that cannot be verified empirically are eventually discarded. However, the fact that a given theory appears to agree with the facts does not necessarily serve as a verification. It is necessary to determine whether that theory can generate accurate forecasts.

- Macroeconomics is an applied discipline. Abstract theories based on unrealistic assumptions that provide inaccurate results in the real world are of no use in macroeconomics. Furthermore, any useful theory must be able to explain what economic policies are likely to be implemented under certain circumstances, and how they affect the economy.
- Macroeconomists often disagree on appropriate policies. That is not only because of normative judgments about what ought to be, but arguments about how the economy actually reacts to changes in given policies. Often these high-sounding arguments mask personal prejudices or are fronts for special interest groups. Thus examining what happens after these policies have been applied often sheds a great deal of light on the correct underlying theory.

QUESTIONS AND PROBLEMS

1. In 2001 and 2002, political opinion was bitterly divided between the Republicans, who wanted to cut high marginal personal income tax rates and offer retroactive benefits to corporations by canceling the alternative minimum tax, and the Democrats, who wanted to offer a $300 rebate to those who paid no income tax, extend unemployment benefits, and institute prescription drug benefits for the poor.
   (A) How would you "prove" the Republican case if you were a lobbyist for General Motors?
   (B) How would you "prove" the Democrats' case if you were a lobbyist for the Urban Institute?
   (C) Suppose you had no political biases in either direction. What data would you want to examine before forming any conclusion?
   (D) How would your answer change if this question appeared on an exam, and you thought your professor was more liberal than you?
2. In his 1964 presidential campaign, Barry Goldwater argued that a reduction in both government spending and taxes would boost economic growth. His views were disparaged by most economists and he was overwhelmingly defeated. The winner of that election, Lyndon Johnson, initially cut spending and taxes, returning the government budget to surplus, and the economy prospered. Later, he raised spending and taxes, and the economy plunged into recession.
   (A) Based on positive economics only – i.e., ignoring your political persuasion – do you think there is enough evidence to support the Goldwater position?
   (B) If your answer to (A) is yes, why do you think the overwhelming majority of economists opposed his plan? If your answer is no, explain what other factors would be required to explain what really did happen.
   (C) In 1981 and 1982, the Reagan Administration boosted spending and cut taxes, and shortly thereafter the economy entered an extended period of expansion. Was that the correct fiscal program to undertake?

(D) In 1993, the Clinton Administration reduced spending and raised taxes, and the economy entered another extended period of expansion. Was that the correct fiscal program to undertake? If so, how does that compare with your answer to (C)?

(E) It should be clear from the answers to (A)–(D) that factors other than fiscal policy are responsible for determining economic performance. Indeed, those factors will be discussed in the remainder of this book. At this point, based on the material in this chapter, what other factors need to be considered?

3. Which of the following statements (a) are true under conditions of ceteris paribus, (b) represent the fallacy of composition, (c) represent the fallacy of "ergo," (d) cannot be determined without further information?

(A) In the later stages of business cycle expansions, it is observed that interest rates rise, and the ratio of capital spending to GDP also rises. That is because higher interest rates lead to an increase in capital spending.

(B) If someone decides to save 10% of his income instead of 5%, his personal saving will increase. Thus if everyone in the economy decides to save 10% of their income instead of 5%, the national saving rate will rise.

(C) A reduction in the capital gains tax rate will boost stock prices. That in turn will increase the growth rate, sending stock prices still higher. As a result, personal and corporate income tax receipts will rise enough to offset the decline in capital gains tax revenue, so the tax cut will "pay for itself."

(D) An increase in the money supply will initially boost the real growth rate, but in the long run will leave the growth rate unchanged but raise the inflation rate.

(E) An increase in the minimum wage will boost real growth because the lowest paid workers will have more to spend, hence raising total consumption.

(F) A decrease in the top marginal tax rate bracket will boost real growth because consumers with the highest income will have more to spend, hence raising total consumption.

(G) A decrease in the corporate income tax rate will boost real growth because that will stimulate corporate earnings, hence boosting investment and total GDP.

(H) During recessions, imports decline because of the reduction in purchasing power. That improves the trade balance, which strengthens the value of the dollar the following year.

4. Which of the following are examples of fiscal policy, monetary policy, trade policy, regulatory policy – or some combination?

(A) Increase of 30% on steel tariffs to "rescue" the depressed steel industry.

(B) Federal Open Market Committee (FOMC) votes to reduce the Federal funds rate from 3% to 2%.

(C) Congress votes to reduce all personal income tax rates by 10%.

(D) In response to the increased deficit caused by a 10% tax cut, the FOMC votes to raise the Federal funds rate back from 2% to 3%.

(E) Government passes a "gas guzzling" tax, boosting prices of new motor vehicles that get less than 15 mpg by 10%.

(F) Because of agricultural shortages, government imposes an export ban on soybeans.

(G) Treasury Secretary says "a weak dollar is good for America." The value of the dollar drops 20%, and in reaction to the higher inflation, the FOMC boosts the funds rate from 6% to 8%.

(H) President decides to implement a new economic program that includes (a) personal income tax cuts, (b) corporate income tax cuts, (c) excise tax cuts, (d) increase in government spending, (e) devaluation of the dollar, (f) directive to FOMC to hold interest rates at below-equilibrium levels, and (g) wage and price controls. (Note: if this example sounds far-fetched, that is precisely the economic program implemented by Richard Nixon on August 15, 1971.)

Appendix: thumbnail sketch of the development of macroeconomics

One hallmark of all important disciplines is that they are constantly changing, adapting to new information that encourages practitioners to examine historical information in a different light and correct past errors. In the case of macroeconomics, though, the shift has been extreme. Most students will presumably wish to focus on the current theory. Yet for those who studied macroeconomics earlier, used older textbooks, or were exposed to past discussions of policy analysis, a brief historical review of the major strands of economic thought may be appropriate.

Before the Great Depression of the 1930s, macroeconomics did not receive much attention, and most of the emphasis on what is now called "macro" was relegated to the monetary sector. It was assumed that the economy was usually in equilibrium at full employment, and any deviations from that level were short-lived, so the economy would return to equilibrium in a short time. Most economists accepted Say's Law, which stated that "supply creates its own demand" – in equilibrium, an increase in production would always be balanced by purchasers of those additional goods and services.

The Great Depression shattered all these illusions. It was clear the economy was not working the way it should, but few knew how to fix a broken system. The publication of *The General Theory of Employment, Interest, and Money* in 1936 by John Maynard Keynes provided a new perspective, although many of these ideas had been presented to the British government for over a decade. Keynes claimed that since individual firms and consumers were not spending enough to boost the economy to full employment, the government should do the job by spending more; the resulting increase in the deficit did not matter. He also said that further easing in monetary policy, such as a decline in interest rates or an increase in the money supply, would not work during times of depression; this represented a switch from previous thinking, when changes in monetary policy were thought to be the principal method of guiding the economy back to full employment. Finally, Keynes said that unemployment remained high because of "sticky" wages, which meant that employees refused to take pay cuts even if they lost their jobs and could not find alternative employment. His suggestion at the time was to boost prices, hence reducing real wages while holding nominal wages constant.

A year later, John Hicks authored an article entitled *Mr. Keynes and the Classics*, in which he argued that Keynes's "new solution" was not a general theory at all, but merely a special case of the depression. In that article, Hicks introduced the concept of the interaction between fiscal and monetary policy, known as the IS/LM diagram, which still remains a cornerstone for understanding macroeconomics. Hicks attempted to provide a balanced role for both monetary and fiscal policy.

The depression scenario was soon rendered moot by the enormous buildup in armaments used to fight World War II. After the war, most economists gradually switched to the Keynesian viewpoint that fiscal policy was much more important than monetary policy for controlling the economy. Only Milton Friedman and his followers at the Chicago school were left to argue that monetary factors were important or, in their words, that "money matters."

While Keynes forever changed the way in which macroeconomists think, and his work was arguably the most influential analysis of the century, many of his claims were eventually proven to be incorrect, or at least superseded by more recent events. The personal saving rate does not rise as income rises over time, so it is not necessary for the government to boost its spending over time to save the economy from ever-widening depressions. Monetary policy is an increasingly important determinant of the economy, in part because of the increasing use of credit and the rise in the aggregate debt/income ratio. Finally, while markets eventually do clear, that fact alone certainly does not guarantee full employment.

The rate of inflation was not deemed an important issue during the Depression years, but after World War II, when the economy remained near full employment, Keynesians reached the conclusion that one of the dangers of full employment was that it boosted inflation. Based on empirical evidence referred to as the "Phillips curve," most economists claimed there was a clearly defined and readily measurable tradeoff between the unemployment rate and the inflation rate. For the US economy, the tradeoff was allegedly about 1 to 1, meaning that a decrease in the unemployment rate from 5% to 4% (say) could be accomplished if one were willing to permit the inflation rate to rise from 2% to 3%. Conversely, in order to reduce the inflation rate by 1%, it would be necessary to raise the unemployment rate by 1%. Such changes could be accomplished by a judicious use of both monetary and fiscal policy, which became known as "fine tuning" the economy.

Even during the 1950s and 1960s, it gradually became obvious that many of the Keynesian dictums were inaccurate. The major breakthrough occurred in 1957 with the appearance of *A Theory of the Consumption Function* by Milton Friedman. This work introduced the concept of the permanent income hypothesis, which said consumers base their spending patterns on expected, or permanent income, rather than current income alone. Keynes had always stressed the important role of expectations for capital spending, but not for consumption. Friedman said it also applied to individuals and provided both theoretical and empirical support for the hypothesis that the percentage gap between consumption and income does not rise as the economy expands. Furthermore, the economy performed just as well when the ratio of government spending to GDP was declining as when it was rising. As a result, ever-increasing government spending was not necessary to keep the economy functioning at full employment. In addition, higher interest rates and lower growth in the money supply had a noticeable impact on real growth in the short run and inflation in the long run.

Another major setback to Keynesian economics occurred in the late 1960s, when the tradeoff between inflation and unemployment disintegrated because both inflation and unemployment rose at the same time. Milton Friedman and Edmund Phelps had both predicted the demise of the Phillips curve ahead of time, so once it actually occurred, their theories received greater acceptance. That led to the reinstatement of monetary policy as one of the principal determinants of the economy. Friedman's comments, which were given as his Presidential Address to the American Economic Association (AEA) annual meetings at the end of 1967, are still read and discussed vigorously.

The inability of the economics profession to predict double-digit inflation, let alone the combination of double-digit inflation and double-digit unemployment, called for a complete reevaluation of macroeconomics. Not only did Keynesian "fine tuning" fall into disfavor and disuse, but some even claimed that macroeconomics as a discipline was incapable of predicting what would happen in the future.

The most notable blast at Keynesian economics was offered by Robert Lucas and Thomas Sargent, two of the major developers of the theory of rational expectations. They claimed:[3]

That these predictions [of the 1970s] were wildly incorrect and the doctrine on which they were based is fundamentally flawed are now simple matters of fact, involving no novelties in economic theory. The task now facing contemporary students of the business cycle is to sort through the wreckage . . . . Our first and most important point is that existing Keynesian macroeconometric models cannot provide reliable guidances in the formulation of monetary, fiscal, or other types of policy [because] of a sound theoretical or econometric basis . . . there is no hope that minor or even major modification of these models will lead to significant improvement in their reliability. . . . [P]olicies that affect behavior mainly because their consequences cannot be correctly diagnosed, such as monetary instability and deficit financing, have the capacity only to disrupt. The deliberate provision of misinformation cannot be used in a systematic way to improve the economic environment.

Harsh words, indeed. Much of the criticism was deserved, as Keynesian econometric models of the 1960s contained faulty linkages that generated bad forecasts and worse advice. Those incorrect links needed to be expunged from the body of macroeconomics and replaced with more accurate explanations. On the other hand, that hardly means macroeconomics has nothing to offer the profession and the economy at large. Mancur Olson, in his "Distinguished Lecture on Economics in Government" published in 1996, stated:[4]

> It is very important indeed that economists, inside government and out, get things right. When we are wrong, we do a lot of harm. When we are right – and have the clarity needed to prevail against the special interests and the quacks – we make an extraordinary contribution to the amelioration of poverty and the progress of humanity.

That is very much the spirit in which macroeconomics is approached in this text. Lucas and Sargent sounded a well-deserved wakeup call to a macroeconomics profession that was in danger of becoming obsolete. On the other hand, changes made in this field over the past 30 years have rebuilt macroeconomics to the position where economic performance, following many of these principles, has been much improved, and advice given by macroeconomists with no ax to grind does improve economic welfare.

Even during the era of widespread acceptance of the Keynesian framework of macroeconomics, many theorists were concerned because those theories were not developed from a microeconomic base. The links between micro and macro were established by several economists; the leaders were Edmund Phelps and Robert Lucas, who integrated rational expectations into the explanation of both micro- and macroeconomics.

Lucas and Sargent correctly pointed out that economic agents react differently to exogenous changes based on previous experience. One key example of this was the different reactions to the energy shocks of the past 30 years. When energy prices rose the first time, the general reaction was that while it was a complete surprise, it was unlikely to reoccur in the future. Thus outside of reducing other expenditures when gasoline prices rose, economic agents made few other adjustments. When the second energy shock occurred, the reaction was completely different: many now thought higher energy prices would become a regular occurrence, so consumers chose more energy-efficient houses, cars, and appliances, while investors in the energy patch viewed this as a great opportunity to benefit from ever-increasing energy prices. In fact nothing of the sort happened – in part because of the conservation measures taken after the second shock. By the time the third energy shock occurred in 1990, it was considered a yawner, not worthy of any adjustment in behavior patterns. Similarly, the tripling of crude oil prices in 2000 had very little impact on the economy.

Another major development in macroeconomics has been that, because business cycles have become milder and less frequent, emphasis has shifted toward trying to determine the long-run determinants of productivity, taking into consideration long-term planning horizons for both consumers and investors. This development has also branched out into what is generally known as supply-side economics, which stresses the importance of monetary, trade, and fiscal policies for increasing maximum real growth rather than determining the components of aggregate demand.

One corollary of supply-side economics is that monetary policy should be used to control the rate of inflation and short-term fluctuations in real output, while fiscal policy should be used to boost productivity growth. Supply-side economics also stresses that more emphasis should be placed on boosting the long-term growth rate of productivity, and short-term fine tuning should be avoided.

A malignant spur of supply-side economics, which claims that the deficit can actually be reduced by cutting broad-based tax rates because of some allegedly enormous feedback effect, has been fixed in the minds of the general public as "supply-side economics," but that has never been the case and is not believed by most supply-side economists.

By the end of 2000, the US economy had completed almost 10 years of uninterrupted expansion – and for the first time had accomplished this without any increase in the rate of inflation. Indeed, except for the mild 1990–91 recession that was caused at least in part by the Iraqi invasion of Kuwait, the US economy had not undergone a recession since 1982. The growth rate of productivity also rebounded, although not as much as was initially reported. The US economy also functioned much better than in Europe and Japan, whereas for most of the post-WWII period, the opposite was true. While the 2001 recession started in March, it was brief and mild, and partial evidence suggests the economy was recovering enough during the summer months that an actual recession probably would not have been declared if not for the slump in economic activity following the terrorist attacks of 9/11.

Nonetheless, the continuing double-digit unemployment rates in Europe, the lack of growth in Japan, continuing problems in Latin America, the inability of the former Soviet Union countries to prosper, and the collapse of many countries in southeast Asia all continue to emphasize that while the US economy has moved closer to optimal performance, that clearly is not the case for much of the rest of the world.

Relative to the state of the profession 30 years ago, macroeconomists have learned the following important facts.

- The important economic tradeoff is not between inflation and unemployment, but between inflation and productivity. When inflation is high, most of the incentives to improve productivity are absent, so higher costs are matched by higher prices instead of better methods of producing and distributing goods and services. When that occurs, the standard of living falls. Indeed, *even in the short run, low unemployment rates need not lead to higher inflation.*

- Inflation will generally remain low and stable – excluding exogenous shocks – when economic agents expect it to remain low and stable. Thus a credible monetary policy is the starting point of successful economic behavior. Almost all free-market economies are now governed by this hypothesis.
- Productivity and the standard of living will grow more rapidly as the government's share of GDP declines. It is government spending rather than the tax rate that is the single most important fiscal policy variable. Milton Friedman pointed this out 40 years ago, but many economists ignored it or did not believe it until recently.
- On an international basis, a strong correlation exists between the proportion of GDP that is saved and invested and the growth rate of that economy. However, in the short run, a rise in the investment ratio caused by higher inflation – such as investing in real estate as an inflation hedge – does not boost productivity. An increase in the saving and investment rate benefits the economy only in an environment of low, stable inflation.
- The path to a successful economy consists of a credible monetary policy that keeps inflation low, a credible fiscal policy that minimizes the growth rate of government spending, a credible trade policy that keeps the value of the currency near its equilibrium value and encourages free trade, and a credible regulatory policy that encourages invention and innovation while minimizing the heavy hand of overregulation. In a capitalistic society, those are the primary requirements: the rest is more or less window-dressing.

Notes

1. These results are briefly reported in the Papers and Proceedings of the *American Economic Review*, May 1997, pp. 230–46. The five economists are Robert M. Solow of MIT, John B. Taylor of Stanford, Martin Eichenbaum of Northwestern, Alan S. Blinder of Princeton, and Olivier Blanchard of MIT. Solow is best known for his work on growth models in the 1950s; the other four are of more recent vintage.
2. A prime recent example of the Law of Unintended Consequences occurred when the Clinton Administration, in 1993, passed a law stating that salaries over $1 million were not deductible as a business expense. As a result, compensation of top executives switched to stock options, which eventually created massive fraud, a stock market bubble, the 2001 recession, and sluggish growth during the following recovery.
3. Robert E. Lucas, Jr. and Thomas J. Sargent, "After Keynesian Macroeconomics," in Preston J. Miller, ed., *The Rational Expectations Revolution* (MIT Press, 1994), p. 6. This article originally appeared in the *Federal Reserve Bank of Minneapolis Quarterly Review*, Spring 1979.
4. Mancur Olson, Jr., "Distinguished Lecture on Economics in Government: Big Bills Left on the Sidewalk: Why Some Nations are Rich, and Others Poor," *Journal of Economic Perspectives*, Spring 1996, pp. 21–2.

chapter two

National income and product accounts (NIPA)

Introduction

Macroeconomics without data provides few real-life answers. Thus it is important at the outset to introduce the principal empirical concepts of macroeconomics, and show how they are measured.

It is difficult to talk intelligently about "unemployment," "inflation," "real growth," "money supply," or "interest rates" without some idea of what these terms are, their approximate magnitudes, and what they represent. This chapter introduces the national income and product accounts (NIPA), which contain data for the various components of aggregate demand and income. The next chapter discusses other key components of economic data: inflation, employment and unemployment, productivity, and various measures of labor costs. The definitions of other important economic concepts such as the money supply, foreign exchange rates, industrial production, the rate of capacity utilization, and various interest rates are deferred to the appropriate chapters when the theory of these variables is discussed.

2.1 How the national income and product accounts are constructed

The **national income and product accounts** (NIPA) are the framework used to measure and report the key measures of macroeconomic activity for total demand and production. These data are prepared by the Bureau of Economic Analysis (BEA), part of the Commerce Department. The key concepts examined in this chapter include:

- **Gross Domestic Product** (GDP): the total amount of goods and services that are *purchased* for final use and are produced by labor and capital located in the US. That specifically excludes **intermediate goods and services**, which are used as inputs for the production of other goods and services. It also excludes goods and services that are produced elsewhere, even if they are purchased and used in the US.

- **National Income** (NI): the total amount of income paid to the factors of production, which are wages and salaries, supplements (fringe benefits), corporate profits, unincorporated business income, rental income, and net interest.
- **Personal Income** (PI): the total amount of income received by individuals, whether earned or not (i.e., including transfer payments). However, realized capital gains are excluded.
- **Disposable Income** (DI): personal income minus personal income taxes.
- **Personal Outlays** (POUT): consumption plus interest on consumer loans plus individual transfer payments to foreigners.
- **Personal Saving** (SP): disposable income minus personal outlays.

A Double-Entry Bookkeeping System

The data that measure GDP, NI, PI, and other important macroeconomic aggregates are all included in NIPA. The NIPA data are designed so the total amount of final goods and services purchased equals the total amount paid to the factors of production, including depreciation and indirect business taxes. Total GDP is also equal to the sum of *value added* at each stage of production.

The NIPA system of macroeconomic data is a **double-entry bookkeeping system** that equilibrates the total amount purchased for final use – aggregate demand – with the total payments to those factors that produce these items. That means every item included in aggregate demand – every good or service that is purchased for final use – is also equal to a combination of entries in aggregate income that sum to the total purchase price. Except for a relatively small statistical discrepancy, the value of all items of final demand is matched by payments to the factors that produced them.

National income includes only those factors that are directly paid in the production of any good or service. The total list of factor payments also includes depreciation and indirect business taxes. These payments are reflected in the final price of the product but not in the cost of production, and serve as links between NI and GDP. The other principal link between NI and GDP is known as net factor income, which adjusts for the fact that profits of domestic corporations earned abroad are not part of domestic demand; this point is discussed in section 2.4.

Based on the definition of GDP and NI, if an individual or business buys some item that is not produced – that is, purchases an item that already exists – it is not part of GDP. Similarly, if someone receives income based on a transaction that does not have some corresponding productive activity – such as the increase in the value of an existing asset – that income is not included in NI. Only the commissions on selling that product or asset would be included in GDP and NI.

In order to be included in NIPA, the amount spent on purchasing a good or service, or the income payment received, must be balanced by a transaction on the other side of the accounts. Some examples of transactions that show up as one type of transaction without any balancing items, and hence are not part of GDP or NI, are described in section 2.7.

2.2   Components of GDP: final goods and services

One of the keys to understanding the NIPA system is that, with the single exception of inventory investment, aggregate demand consists exclusively of **final goods and services**, which means items purchased by final users. Items that are used to produce other goods and services are not included in GDP. Final goods and services are grouped into four major categories: consumption (C), investment (I), net exports (F), and government purchases (G). The GDP, or aggregate demand identity, is written as:

$$C + I + F + G = GDP.$$

Consumption consists of items purchased by individuals for final use, and is often divided into durable goods, nondurable goods, and services. Durable goods are those that last more than three years, mostly motor vehicles, furniture, appliances, and home electronic equipment. Nondurable goods are those used up immediately, such as food, gasoline, and household cleaning supplies; clothing is actually in an intermediate category, but it is listed with nondurables.

Investment is divided into three major categories: capital spending, residential construction (housing), and inventory investment. **Capital spending** consists of purchases of new machinery and structures by businesses. **Residential construction** includes the construction of new housing units, major additions and alterations, and brokerage commissions. Construction of a new home is recorded in GDP at the time it is built, not when it is purchased; at the time of purchase, only the brokerage commission is included in GDP. **Inventory investment** represents the difference between production and sales, and is explained below in greater detail.

Net exports equal exports minus imports. Exports are purchases of domestically produced goods and services by any foreign purchaser, whether or not they are final purchases. For example, a ton of steel sold to a domestic automobile manufacturer is not part of GDP; the same ton of steel sold to a foreign purchaser is an export. Imports are purchases of any good or services by US economic agents produced abroad, whether or not they are final purchases.

Imports are subtracted from GDP. If someone buys an imported car, consumption and imports rise by almost the same amount. The only parts of the transaction that boost GDP are transportation and distribution costs, wholesale and retail sales margins, and the sales tax (indirect business taxes).

Government Purchases and Other Expenditures

Government purchases are goods and services purchased for final use, just as is the case for consumption and investment. Purchases are usually listed separately for Federal defense purchases, Federal nondefense purchases, and state and local government purchases. At the state and local government level, most purchases are either wages and salaries or construction. At the Federal level, most purchases are for national defense.

At the Federal level, purchases are much smaller than government expenditures. About two-thirds of the Federal budget represents **transfer payments**, which are payments made to individuals without any services performed, and hence are not included in GDP. Transfer payments also include interest on the national debt and payments to state and local governments known as grants-in-aid.

Most of the items included in aggregate demand seem logical. When a consumer buys a new car, a loaf of bread, or pays a utility bill, each of these purchases is part of consumption. When a business purchases a new machine, that is part of investment. When a foreign company buys an airplane made in the US, that is an export, and when a consumer buys a car made in Japan, that is an import. When the Federal government buys a missile, or state and local governments pay salaries to schoolteachers or police officers, these are part of government purchases. Some of the more unusual inclusions and exclusions are discussed in section 2.5.

Inventory Investment: An Exception to the Rule

Inventory investment is the one exception to the rule that GDP consists only of goods and services purchased for final use. This category is an accounting concept created because NIPA data are reported for a given time period. When NIPA data show that consumer purchases of (say) household appliances are $50 billion, that means per unit of time, usually one quarter. Otherwise the concept of GDP becomes meaningless; it might mean all the goods and services produced and sold since the beginning of the nation.

The NIPA figures are reported every quarter on an annual rate basis, which means actual annual expenditures are equal to an average of the four quarterly numbers, not the sum. Some series, such as personal income and consumption, are reported on a monthly basis, also at annual rates. The NIPA data are also seasonally adjusted, which means the regular seasonal patterns are removed from the data. Otherwise (for example) the figures would show a huge increase in discretionary consumer spending every December.

Sometimes a business might purchase goods it plans to use later in the production process, or sell to a final user, but those events have not yet happened. The factor payments for these goods have already been made, so there must be an equivalent entry on the product side of NIPA. Such goods are classified as inventory investment for that particular time period. For example, suppose a car dealer receives a shipment of 500 cars in one quarter but sells only 400 (assume for this purpose that stocks were zero before that shipment). Eventually, the other 100 cars will also be sold. From a NIPA viewpoint, those 100 cars must be included in GDP because they have already been produced, so to balance that production on the demand side, they are categorized as inventory investment. The same general argument can be made for apparel purchased for eventual sale by a department store, parts purchased by a machine tool factory, or any situation where raw materials, parts, or finished goods are planned to be used or sold in the future.

Table 2.1 Components of aggregate demand (2001 values*)

Component	Current $	Chained $
Total gross domestic product	10,082	9,215
Consumption	6,987	6,377
Durables	836	932
Nondurables	2,041	1,870
Services	4,110	3,595
Investment	1,586	1,575
Capital spending	1,202	1,255
Structures	325	271
Equipment	877	988
Residential construction	445	374
New homes	253	217
Other residential	192	157
Inventory investment	−60	−61
Net exports	−349	−416
Exports	1,034	1,076
Imports	1,383	1,492
Government purchases	1,858	1,640
Federal defense	400	366
Federal nondefense	228	205
State and local	1,230	1,069

* All figures in billions of current dollars
Source: Bureau of Economic Analysis (BEA), which is part of the Commerce Department. Updates for these and many other figures can be obtained regularly on their website, www.bea.gov. That website will direct you to several major categories, including one for national income and product accounts. The next click down brings you to a list of over 100 tables, which permit you to select the particular NIPA category desired. Historical data are also provided for all these variables on both a quarterly and annual basis. This website is comprehensive, easy to use, and the data can easily be downloaded into a standard spreadsheet.

These figures were current at the time of printing. However, by the time you are reading this, they will have been revised. A similar comment applies to all NIPA data given in this text.

Relative Size of the Major Components of GDP

The major categories of GDP are summarized in table 2.1, which shows that consumption is about two-thirds of GDP, fixed investment is slightly less than one-sixth of GDP, and government purchases are slightly more than one-sixth of GDP. Net exports could be either positive or negative, but in recent years have been as much as −5% of GDP. Inventory investment is generally less than 1% of GDP in absolute value, but generally accounts for more than half of the total fluctuations in GDP during recessions. It also serves an important role in equilibrating demand and income in the short run, and hence cannot be ignored even though it appears to be only a minuscule proportion of total GDP.

You will also note that while the current dollar components sum to GDP, the chained dollar components do not. This is not an arithmetic error, but occurs because of the use of the chained deflator, which is explained later in this chapter.

MANAGER'S BRIEFCASE: INTERPRETING THE GDP STATISTICS

On the last Friday of the first month of each quarter, the BEA releases its advance estimates of GDP for the previous quarter. These figures are revised the following month, and revised again in two months' time. Also, the numbers are revised the following July, and are revised again every five years when the benchmarks are recalculated. Nonetheless, the advance estimate garners the lion's share of the attention. What should you look for?

First, most of the headlines will focus on the growth rate in what used to be called constant dollars and are now called chained dollars, and the increase in the implicit GDP deflator; this disaggregation is covered in the following chapter. The data for the implicit GDP deflator can essentially be disregarded; the key numbers are the amount that real GDP has risen.

It is usually important to distinguish between the change in inventory investment and the change in all other components of GDP, known as final sales. For example, if real GDP were to rise at an annual rate of 4% (about $100 billion at 2002 levels), check to see how much of that gain was accounted for by inventory investment. If most of the gain was caused by unintended inventory stockpiling, real growth in the following quarter is likely to be smaller. On the other hand, if real GDP rose at an annual rate of only 2% but inventory investment fell $50 billion, so that final sales rose $100 billion, the economy would probably be well on its way toward recovery even though 2% is generally considered an anemic growth rate.

Sometimes big gains or losses occur in government purchases, especially in decennial census years, when extra employees are hired for that purpose. Such gains should be subtracted from the growth rate; private sector gains will probably provide a better indicator of how fast the economy is changing.

Another key area to check is the gain or loss in net exports. If real growth is strong because imports did not rise very much, that may mean firms expect slower growth ahead, so they have cut back on their imports. In this case, domestic private sector final sales probably represents the best estimate of the underlying growth rate. That number is equivalent to total consumption plus total fixed investment in chained dollars.

continued

MANAGER'S BRIEFCASE (*continued*)

A good example of the pitfalls that can occur by taking the GDP figures at face value can be seen in 2000.2. Real GDP had risen at an annual rate of only 2.6% in the first quarter, but then accelerated to 4.8% in the second quarter, according to the BEA.[1] That might seem as if the economy was accelerating – *but precisely the opposite was true; it was decelerating and in fact was heading into recession.* Here's what happened.

In 2000.1, real GDP rose $53 billion. However, in that quarter, inventory investment fell $47 billion, net exports fell $29 billion, and government purchases fell $4 billion. Hence domestic private sector final sales rose $132 billion, or a very rapid 7.0% annual rate. In 2000.2, by comparison, inventory investment rose $46 billion, net exports fell $26 billion, and government purchases rose $18 billion, which means *domestic private sector final sales* rose only $70 billion, or only about half as much as the previous quarter. Whenever examining the overall GDP figures, it is useful for managers to look at this measure of economic activity as well. A correct interpretation of the GDP figures would have shown that the slowdown was already underway.

CASE STUDY 2.1   SHIFTING SHARES OF GDP IN THE POST-WWII PERIOD

Since the end of World War II, the composition of GDP has undergone several changes, as shown in figures 2.1 and 2.2. In the early postwar years, defense expenditures for the Korean War boosted the ratio of government purchases to GDP sharply, offset by a decline in the ratio of consumption to GDP, which was accomplished partially by credit controls and diversion of production facilities from domestic to military motor vehicles. After the Korean War, the decline in Federal government purchases was offset by a large increase in state and local government purchases. During the 1960s and 1970s, the ratio of capital spending to GDP increased rapidly, spurred in part by the investment tax credit and other changes in the tax laws designed to stimulate capital formation.

A major shift occurred after 1980. The combination of another major income tax cut, the decline in interest rates, and deregulation of the banking sector that opened new avenues of credit availability boosted the ratio of consumer spending to GDP. The ratio of capital spending and housing to GDP declined slightly, but the biggest change occurred in the ratio of net exports to GDP, which fell sharply as the value of the dollar swung from undervalued to overvalued. That decline was reversed later in the decade, when the dollar returned to its equilibrium value.

During the 1990s, the booming stock market caused a rise in the ratio of both consumer and capital spending to GDP; that was offset by a further marked decline in ratios of both Federal and state and local government spending to GDP. Also, the ratio of net exports to GDP dropped sharply as the US economy grew

continued

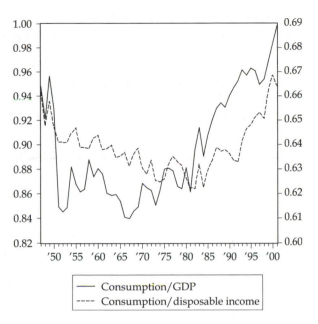

Figure 2.1   Ratio of consumption to disposable income and total GDP (all figures are in current dollars)
Source: Bureau of Economic Analysis website, www.bea.gov

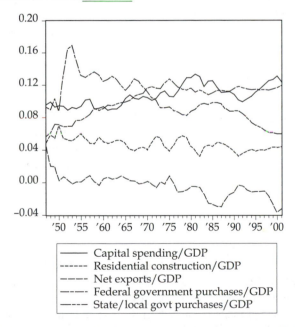

Figure 2.2   Ratio of other components of final demand (excluding inventory investment) to GDP
Source: Bureau of Economic Analysis website, www.bea.gov

CASE STUDY 2.1 (*continued*)

faster than the rest of the world, and more manufacturing activity was transferred to foreign locations.

As discussed in chapters 4 and 5, the consumption and capital spending ratios are negatively correlated with the real rate of interest, defined as the nominal rate minus the expected rate of inflation. The net export ratio is negatively correlated with the value of the dollar, but the relative growth rates of the US and the rest of the world are also important.

2.3 Differences between final and intermediate goods and services

Intermediate goods and services are those items purchased by businesses that are not included in GDP. In some cases, the same item that would be included in final demand if purchased by a consumer may not be included if purchased by a business, and an item would be included in GDP if purchased by a foreign buyer but not a domestic buyer

Most intermediate goods are easily identified. When an auto manufacturer buys steel, plastics, batteries, tires, and so on, it is purchasing intermediate goods that will be used in the production of motor vehicles. The same general nomenclature holds for office supplies – paper clips, manila folders, etc. – which are considered intermediate goods. However, note that any purchase of capital goods used for the productive process, whether on the plant floor or in the office, is considered part of investment. Thus computers are investment, computer programs (software) are investment, but blank computer discs and CD ROMs are intermediate goods.[2]

Intermediate goods and services are not counted in GDP because that would result in double-counting. For example, it would mean counting the steel that was used in manufacturing an automobile twice – once when the steel itself was produced, and a second time when the automobile itself was sold.

Defining and Determining Intermediate Services

The distinction between final and intermediate often becomes murkier in the area of services. If business employees take an airline trip for business reasons, that trip is an intermediate service. Yet if they take the *same trip* for personal reasons, it is a final purchase, and hence is part of consumption. Obviously there will be some arbitrary decisions, such as when the trip is half business and half personal. In general, though, purchases of goods and services by businesses are not part of final demand unless they are capital goods. For example, a purchase of a personal computer or telephone system is part of GDP whether it is bought by a business or an individual, but dining at Le Haut Prix is part of final demand only if paid for by an individual and not later included in the expense account.

Differentiating between a business and personal trip on the same airplane may seem to be needless hair-splitting. However, the concept should be clear: if someone travels for business purposes, the reason is presumably to increase the total amount of goods or services sold by that business. In the case of a sales trip, the link is obvious. A trip to a resort area to hear a motivational speech may be less obvious, but theoretically is also designed to boost sales. Hence the factor payments on the other side of the transaction – the amount the airline pays in wages, rents (landing fees), interest, depreciation, and earns in profits – are balanced by the increase in sales of the corporation that incurred the business expense.

Suppose a so-called business trip turns out to be a complete boondoggle, and no additional sales ever result from these expenditures. In that case, the rise in payments to airlines, hotels, restaurants, and rental car companies would be completely offset by the loss in profits of that corporation. There would be no change in GDP, so these expenditures would be correctly classified as intermediate goods and services.

2.4   Components of national income

Aggregate demand always equals aggregate supply on an ex post basis, but there is no corresponding item in NIPA for "Gross National Income." The basic measure of aggregate income in NIPA is national income (NI), which is the amount paid to factors of production. However, it is *not* equivalent to GDP. Several significant items are excluded, primarily net factor income from abroad, depreciation (D), and indirect business taxes (TB). If NFI is net factor income, then $NI = GDP + NFI - D - TB$, plus several small adjustment items.

Net factor income is defined as receipts of foreign factor income received in the US minus payments of US factor income to the rest of the world. This is approximately equal to income of US corporations earned abroad minus income of foreign corporations earned in the US. **Depreciation** is a noncash item representing funds set aside for replacement of plant and equipment when it becomes obsolescent. **Indirect business taxes** are taxes levied on the price or value of the good or service, compared to taxes levied on income. The major indirect business taxes are levied at the state and local level and include sales taxes and real estate taxes; this category also includes customs duties, and "sin taxes" on alcohol, tobacco, and gasoline, some of which are Federal taxes.

National income consists of wages and salaries (W), supplements to wages and salaries (mainly employer-paid contributions to social security and health-care premiums) (S), proprietors' income (net income received by unincorporated businesses) (YP), rental income (R), interest income (IN), and corporate profits (Z). Symbolically this can be written as $NI = W + S + YP + R + IN + Z$. The major

Table 2.2 Components of national income (2001 values)

Component	Value*
Total national income	8,122
Compensation of employees	5,875
Wages and salaries	4,951
Supplements	924
Employer contributions to social insurance	353
Other labor income	571
Proprietors' income	728
Rental income	138
Net interest income	650
Corporate profits (adjusted for IVA and CCA)	732
Pretax operating earnings	670
Corporate income taxes	199
Dividends	410
Retained earnings	61
Inventory valuation adjustment (IVA)	5
Capital consumption adjustment (CCA)	57

* All figures in billions of current dollars
Source: BEA website, www.bea.gov

components of NI, and their recent values, are given in table 2.2. A complete list of key NIPA identities is given in the appendix to this chapter.

Major Components of National Income

As noted above, both sides of the NIPA must be balanced. Theoretically, the total amount of final goods and services purchased must be equal to the amount of income earned in the production of those goods and services. Empirically these do not always match exactly, so there is a statistical discrepancy; historically it has usually been less than 1% of GDP, although it exceeded that percentage starting in 2000.

Wages and salaries are straightforward; they are simply the amount that employees earn. The data are usually considered the most reliable in the NIPA figures because they are taken directly from reports of social security taxes that employers must pay. Bonuses that are included on W-2 forms are also part of wages and salaries. Stock options that are exercised and generate capital gains income are not included in either NI or PI. **Supplements to wages and salaries** consist of compensation to employees they do not receive in their paychecks. The main components are the employer portion of social security taxes, contributions to group healthcare plans, and contributions to private sector pension and retirement plans.

Proprietors' income represents net income received by sole proprietorships, partnerships, and other unincorporated businesses. It is the unincorporated business analog of corporate profits. **Rental income** primarily consists of rents on buildings, although it also includes royalties on tangible assets (e.g., mines) and on intellectual properties (books, patents, etc.).

Net interest income is interest paid by firms that are producing goods and services. It excludes interest paid by governments, since they are not producing anything, and interest paid by consumers, who likewise are not producing anything when they pay interest on a car purchase or other personal loan. While that is a serviceable definition, the BEA actually calculates net interest income in a more roundabout fashion. First, it estimates the total amount of interest income received by individuals. This is divided into two categories: monetary and imputed. Monetary interest income is the interest earned on bank accounts, similar deposits at financial institutions, or directly on debt instruments such as bonds. Imputed interest consists primarily of the interest earned on funds that are paid to life insurance companies and pension plans. The key fact to remember here is that most of net interest income is imputed; the amount of interest income consumers actually receive from savings accounts or debt instruments is a small fraction of the total. For that reason, using this component of income to determine consumer spending may give misleading results.

From total personal interest income, the BEA subtracts interest paid by government and consumers to calculate net interest income. This method often causes significant problems when trying to balance the product and income sides of the NIPA data because imputed interest income is difficult to measure, and revisions equal to as much as 20% of the preliminary data are not uncommon. Theoretically, though, interest income is just another type of payment to the factors of production.

Corporate profits are equal to national income minus payments to labor, rents, and interest payments; unincorporated business income is also excluded. While that definition might seem to be straightforward, several different measures of corporate profits are reported to the public, and they often differ widely. Some of these are discussed in case study 2.3.

CASE STUDY 2.2   SHIFTING PATTERNS OF COMPONENTS OF FACTOR INCOME

Figures 2.3 and 2.4 show how various components of factor income have shifted in the US economy for the post-WWII period. Figure 2.3 shows the ratio of labor and capital income relative to GDP. It may seem odd that *both* of these ratios show a slight increase over time, but the answer is found in figure 2.4, which shows

continued

CASE STUDY 2.2 (*continued*)

Figure 2.3   Comparison of returns to labor and capital as a proportion of GDP (returns to capital include corporate profits, net interest income, net rental income, and depreciation)
Source: BEA website, www.bea.gov

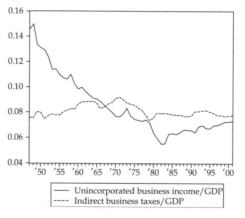

Figure 2.4   Ratios of other components of factor income to GDP
Source: BEA website, www.bea.gov

the remaining components: unincorporated business income and indirect business taxes. The latter has not changed very much as a proportion of GDP, and the shifts that do occur are largely exogenous, reflecting changes in various Federal excise tax rates. Hence the major change in income distribution over the postwar period has been the decline in unincorporated business income.

continued

CASE STUDY 2.2 (*continued*)

To a certain extent, that represents the shrinkage of the relative importance of the farm sector in the overall economy. However, part of it also reflects that the income of independent professional practices, such as physicians, attorneys, and accountants, declined in relative terms from the late 1940s to about 1980; some of this represented the move toward corporations, but it also reflected a slower rate of growth in income. However, over the past two decades, this ratio has risen again, as shown in figure 2.4. For the most part, this reflects the astronomical incomes received by a few lawyers who won the "legal lottery" in the tobacco, asbestos, and other class-action suits.

Figure 2.3 shows a clear negative correlation between the returns to labor and capital. The biggest switch occurred in the early 1970s, when the ratio of returns of labor to capital rose from slightly over 2.0 to 2.5 before declining back to 2.0 at the end of that decade, where it has remained ever since. The finding that returns to labor represent two-thirds of GDP and returns to capital represent one-third of GDP is of long standing and holds not only for the US but most other industrial nations.[3]

What caused the shift in factor proportions around 1970? After a full decade of prosperity, businesses had failed to control costs very carefully, and during the latter half of the 1960s, found it easy to pass them along in the form of higher prices. The 1970 recession ended that practice, but wage rates, based on lagged unemployment, still increased rapidly because the unemployment rate had averaged only 3.7% for the previous four years. It took almost an entire decade for the ratio of employee compensation to returns to capital to return to its long-time historical average of 2.

CASE STUDY 2.3   DIFFERENT MEASURES OF CORPORATE PROFITS

The numbers for corporate profits reported to stockholders are often significantly different from those reported by the BEA for several major reasons. The general rule is that NIPA profits are operating profits and represent payments to factors of production. To the extent that corporate profits reported to stockholders contain items that are not tied to current operations, they differ from the NIPA figures. The principal differences are caused by the following factors:

1. Difference between actual and operating profits. Firms sometimes take massive writeoffs to clear the books and set the stage for more rapid profit growth in the

continued

CASE STUDY 2.3 (*continued*)

future. In most cases, these writeoffs are all booked in a single quarter, which results in unusually large fluctuations in profits. For this reason, most firms also report profits from ongoing operations separately. It is the latter category that is reported in NIPA profits.

2. Adjustment for profits received because the value of existing materials or parts rose, known as **inventory valuation adjustment**, or IVA. If a firm records a profit because the value of its raw materials or other inventories rose, that is not included in NI. Firms generally have the option of choosing different methods for reporting any such gains. If they use the LIFO method – last in, first out – inventory gains will be minimized, and the profits reported to stockholders will be essentially the same as the NIPA definition. However, many firms use FIFO – first in, first out – which means inventory gains are included in profits reported to stockholders, but are not part of NIPA profits.

   The BEA reports this adjustment separately. When commodity prices are rising, IVA is negative, meaning firms are overstating economic profits; when commodity prices are falling, IVA is positive, meaning firms are understating profits to stockholders. For the 1997–9 period, IVA averaged about +$10 billion, since commodity prices were falling during most of that period.

3. Adjustment for the difference between economic and accounting depreciation, known as **capital consumption adjustment**, or CCA. Except for real estate, most firms are able to write off capital expenditures more quickly than would be warranted by economic depreciation or obsolescence. When that happens, accounting depreciation exceeds economic depreciation, so profits reported to stockholders are understated. The BEA subtracts a certain amount from accounting depreciation and adds it to accounting profits to generate the figures for economic depreciation and profits. The figure for corporate CCA was quite large in the late 1990s, averaging over $90 billion per year during that period.

   In 2001.4, the government offered a 30% "bonus depreciation" on certain types of capital equipment purchases during the next three years. As a result, NIPA profits, which included that CCA adjustment, reportedly rose from $687 to $811 billion, while profits without the CCA adjustment fell further, declining from $663 to $626 billion. For the purposes of evaluating stock market investment decisions and monitoring profits generally, the latter figure is more useful.

   The BEA also calculates CCA for proprietors' income and rental income. The CCA for proprietors' income is close to zero, but it has recently been about −$50 billion for rental income. After the tax laws were reformed in 1986, accounting depreciation schedules for rental properties now understate economic depreciation, which means the number of years over which rental property must be depreciated for tax purposes is longer than the useful life without repairs. The attempt to eviscerate what the IRS viewed as abusive tax shelters required

continued

CASE STUDY 2.3 (*continued*)

that depreciation for residential property be written down at a slower rate than economic depreciation. However, these adjustments are not as important and are often ignored when examining the figures for NI and PI.

4. Capital gains are not included in NIPA corporate income because there is no balancing item being produced on the product side of the accounts. We have already noted that capital gains due to the increased value of inventory stocks are not included in profits reported by the BEA. Similarly, profits due to other types of capital gains, notably equities but also including real estate, are excluded from economic profits, even if they are realized. In many cases, realized capital gains are included as part of operating income reported to stockholders, although occasionally they are treated separately as one-time gains. Capital losses, on the other hand, are generally treated as one-time writeoffs and not included in operating income. Capital gains and losses are similarly excluded from personal income, as discussed in section 2.5.

   In 1988, Standard & Poors started to publish data on operating earnings for the S&P 500 companies; figures for earnings reported to shareholders had been published since 1926 on an annual basis, and since 1935 on a quarterly basis. Figure 2.5 shows the unusually large differentials that have occurred in recent years.

   The figures for S&P 500 operating profits and total corporate profits as reported in NIPA track fairly closely, although some differences do occur. However, note that in the 2000–2001 recession, companies took tremendous one-time writeoffs, so that in the second and third quarter of 2001, book profits were only half as large as operating profits.

5. Massive accounting fraud. In mid-2002 it suddenly became clear that many firms had been systematically and fraudulently overstating corporate earnings in order to boost their stock prices and enrich top officers of the corporations with unbelievably generous stock options. As of August 14, 2002, CEOs and CFOs were required to sign an affidavit stating that the financial returns were correct, under penalties of up to 20 years' imprisonment. To the extent that chief executives willfully overstated their corporate earnings, the previous NIPA data was also incorrect and will be revised. Yet in spite of the handful of well-publicized cases of crooked behavior, it is likely that these errors, as egregious as they seemed in individual cases, did not have much effect on the overall corporate profit figure in 2001 of some $670 billion.

   In general, investment decisions are made based on operating profits; few investors – or business managers – are fooled by these one-time writeoffs. However, companies will sometimes claim enormous gains in profits in years following these writeoffs, trying to give the impression that their executives have made tremendous

continued

CASE STUDY 2.3 (*continued*)

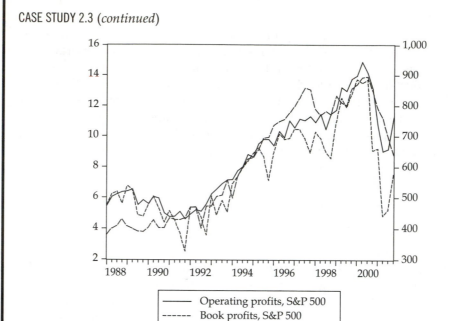

Figure 2.5   Different measures of corporate profits, 1988–2001
Sources: Standard & Poors; BEA website, www.bea.gov

strides in boosting profit margins. Investment analysts and business managers generally should not be misled by gains of this sort, but should base their analysis on operating profits data. Until the 1999–2002 stock market bubble, these sorts of changes had generally been discounted by investors.

The Tradeoff Between Corporate Profits and Net Interest Income

Even if accountants are doing an honest job, corporate profits are difficult to interpret because they depend so critically on the amount set aside for depreciation allowances and paid for interest expense. That is why some financial analysts prefer the concept of EBIDTA – earnings before interest, depreciation, taxes, and amortization. It is claimed that measure provides a better estimate of the pretax return on capital, and is often a more reliable tool in making investment decisions – although outright fraud and deception can fool the most dedicated analyst or statistician.

We emphasize this point because from 1992 through 1997, profits rose sharply as a proportion of GDP, increasing from 6.8% to 10.1%, although this ratio declined again from 1998 through 2001. Many observers assumed that the sharp increase in profit margins reflected superior management techniques, use of the latest technology, sharper control of costs, and similar factors. While that may have been true

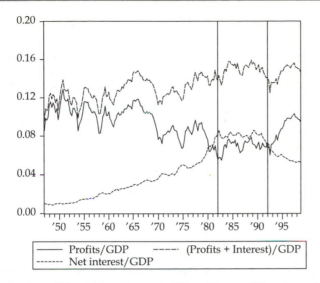

Figure 2.6   Ratio of profits to GDP, net interest income to GDP, and the sum of these two series
Source: BEA website, www.bea.gov

for some individual companies, figure 2.6 shows that the ratio of profits plus net interest income to GDP was no higher in the late 1990s than in the late 1980s. The ratio of depreciation to GDP, not shown separately, was also virtually unchanged over this period. Hence the gain in profit margins was due to lower interest rates. On an aggregate basis, the improvement in cost controls was primarily reflected in lower prices rather than higher margins.

From 1954 through 1982, the ratio of profits to GDP fell, while the ratio of net interest income to GDP rose steadily. These ratios were little changed from 1982 through 1992. After 1992, the profit ratio increased sharply while the net interest income ratio fell rapidly. In all three periods, though, the sum of the two ratios changed very little. Hence the impressive growth in profit margins during the 1990s was largely a mirage – which became apparent to investors only in late 2000 and 2001. Yet some of the financial analysts who championed the use of EBIDTA – and presumably should have known better – were among the biggest cheerleaders claiming that profit margins could rise indefinitely.

Differences Between GDP and GNP

Most economics textbooks written before 1992 did not even contain the term *gross domestic product*. The key measure of aggregate demand used to be *gross national product* (GNP). By definition, GNP is equal to GDP plus net factor income. In most years, net factor income is slightly positive, which means profits earned by US corporations abroad were slightly more than profits earned by foreign corporations in the US. When that occurs, GNP will be slightly larger than GDP. The US was one of the last major countries to switch from reporting GNP to GDP as its principal measure of aggregate economic activity. Why was the switch made?

Consider the example of Coca-Cola and DaimlerChrysler, formerly Daimler-Benz. Coca-Cola is a US corporation, so its total profits are included in national income. Under the older NIPA conventions, the profits that Coca-Cola earns in foreign countries were part of GNP, even though they have very little to do with domestic economic activity. Suppose that Coca-Cola were to receive the exclusive franchise to sell cola drinks in China. That would be great news for Coca-Cola employees and stockholders, but it would have virtually no bearing on US economic activity. Yet it is included in GNP.

DaimlerChrysler is almost a perfect example in the other direction, since Daimler-Benz bought Chrysler. However, even before that happened, Daimler-Benz decided to manufacture cars in Alabama; the operation was successful and increased their profits. Those profits do have a close relationship with US economic activity; but they were not included in GNP because Daimler-Benz is a foreign corporation. Furthermore, when Daimler-Benz bought Chrysler in 1998, that transaction had no impact on GDP (except for investment banker fees). Yet GNP declined because of this purchase, since Chrysler profits were now part of a foreign corporation. Large multinational mergers emphasize the importance of using GDP instead of GNP.

These anomalies are reversed in GDP. The foreign earnings of Coca-Cola are not included, whereas the domestic earnings of Daimler-Benz are. The earnings of the Chrysler division of Daimler-Benz remain part of GDP.

Virtually all economists agree that GDP is a better measure of aggregate economic activity than GNP, which is why most other industrialized countries, especially those with relatively large foreign sectors, switched to using GDP long before the US. However, because GDP does not include all corporate profits of US firms, an adjustment must be made when moving from GDP to NI. That adjustment comprises most of net factor income.

2.5 Balancing items linking GDP, NI, PI, and DI

The difference between GNP and net national product (NNP) is equal to depreciation allowances, called **capital consumption allowances** by the BEA. Since depreciation is a bookkeeping rather than a cash item, a few economists used to claim that NNP is a better measure of the current state of the economy. Yet NNP is seldom mentioned, since gross investment is much more important than net investment on the product side of the accounts. For that matter, the BEA does not even consider the concept of net domestic product.

The difference between NNP and NI consists of several small items (including the statistical discrepancy) and one large item, which is indirect business taxes. As noted above, the most common examples are real estate taxes, sales taxes, and

Table 2.3   Links between GDP and NI (2001 values)

Category	Value*
Gross domestic product	10,082
Less: net factor income from abroad	−22
Equals: gross national product	10,104
Less: depreciation	1,329
Equals: net national product	8,775
Less: indirect business taxes	775
Less: other small balancing items**	−5
Less: statistical discrepancy	−117
Equals: national income	8,122

* All figures are in billions of current dollars
** Business transfer payments less subsidies of government enterprises
Source: BEA website, www.bea.gov

"sin taxes" on gasoline, alcohol, and tobacco. The term "indirect business taxes" may sound misleading: they are primarily paid by consumers, and there is nothing indirect about them when the check for your restaurant meal very clearly contains an additional item of $14.63 for sales tax.

In economic terms, "indirect" means these taxes are levied on the amount sold of goods and services instead of on income. Outside the NIPA nomenclature, they are usually referred to as excise taxes. "Business" refers to the fact that the tax is included in the price of the product or service purchased by the end user, and hence is akin to a factor payment. That definition may be questionable for real estate taxes, although the tax is supposed to reflect the market value of the property. The key fact to remember is these taxes are based on some measure of the value for goods and services being taxed, not on income. The links between GDP and NI are listed in table 2.3.

Links Between GDP and Disposable Income

As noted above, national income represents payments to all factors of production, both labor and capital. Personal income represents all sources of income received by individuals, whether earned or not. The three major differences between NI and PI are as follows. First, transfer payments are included in PI but not NI. Second, the only part of corporate profits included in PI is dividend payments. Third, interest payments by governments and individuals are included in PI but not NI.

Two other areas of possible confusion should be mentioned here. First, retirement income received by individuals from their private sector pension plans is not included in PI or NI. Instead, income is recorded when the payments are originally made, and as the interest accumulates. Second, all capital gains are excluded from both PI and NI. As a result, PI is substantially understated during periods when the

Table 2.4   Links between NI, PI, DI, and SP (2001 values)

Category	Value*
National income	8,122
Less: corporate profits (adjusted for IVA and CCA)	732
Less: net interest income	650
Less: contributions for social insurance	726
Plus: personal interest income	1,091
Plus: personal dividend income	409
Plus: government transfer payments to individuals	1,137
Plus: other minor items[a]	33
Equals: personal income	8,685
Less: personal income taxes	1,292
Equals: disposable personal income	7,393
Less: consumption	6,987
Less: interest payments by individuals	205
Less: transfers to foreigners	31
Equals: personal saving	170

[a] Business transfer payments to persons minus wage accruals less disbursements
* All figures in billions of current dollars
Source: BEA website, www.bea.gov

stock market is rising rapidly, which also leads to an understatement of personal saving.

The linkages between NI and PI reflect the fact that NI represents income earned by all factors of production, whereas PI represents all income received by individuals, whether earned or not. Table 2.4 also shows the links between PI, disposable income (DI), and personal saving (SP).

NI is usually about four-fifths of GDP, while PI is invariably larger than NI because transfer payments are greater than corporate profits.

Because of the nature of the double-entry system for the national accounts, several components of income are included in personal income but not national income. The main category is government transfer payments, which consist primarily of social security and healthcare, but also include unemployment benefits and what are commonly known as "welfare" payments, such as aid to families with dependent children. Government retirement benefits are also included in transfer payments when they are received by individuals.

Contributions to private sector pension plans are included in PI when the original payments are made and as interest accumulates, but not when the funds are paid out. Suppose you (or your employer) makes a contribution of $5,000 per year to your pension plan. That $5,000 would represent an entry in PI each year. Also suppose the interest income on your investment was $500 the first year, $1,000 the second year, and so on. Those imputed interest payments would also be part of

PI. However, note that if your money is invested in the stock market instead of the bond markets, there is no imputed interest because capital gains are not part of PI.

Now suppose that at age 65, you retire, and start drawing payments of $100,000 per year. That is *not* considered part of PI, because there is no offsetting activity on the income side of the accounts. To look at it another way, suppose someone accumulated $1 million in their retirement account and then started to draw down the principal. That would not be counted as part of personal income either.

To the extent that your invested money continues to earn interest, it will be included in the imputed interest part of PI. But that has no direct relationship to the amount of money you are receiving as pension payments. Monetary and imputed interest earned are included in both NI and PI. However, interest payments on government securities, and interest payments on personal loans, are included in PI but excluded from NI. Both of these represent payments of income without any generation of income in the NIPA.

The main items included in national income but excluded from personal income are corporate profits less dividends and social security "contributions." Most people think of these payments as taxes, since they are not voluntary, but NIPA lists them as contributions; that is a distinction without a difference. Both employer and employee contributions for social insurance are subtracted from NI in determining PI.

Capital gains and losses are not included in any measure of income, whether personal or corporate. It is not surprising that capital gains and losses are excluded from NI, since there is no item corresponding to a change in production or demand on the product side of the accounts when the prices of capital assets change. The same logic holds for capital gains on housing or any other type of asset. Similarly, capital losses are not subtracted from the NIPA definition of income.

On the other hand, if you own a stock whose price rises from $50 to $100 per share, at which point you sell it, your income for that year has risen. The IRS think so too. But the NIPA economists do not. One can readily understand why capital gains and losses are not included in national income, but realized capital gains by individuals should be included in personal income. Because they are not, some of the lack of correlation between short-term changes in disposable income and consumption simply reflects the exclusion of realized capital gains.

Disposable income represents current income that consumers can spend, and is equal to personal income minus personal income taxes; it is the measure of income economists most often use when determining consumer behavior. One might assume personal saving is equal to disposable income less consumption. However, the NIPA also subtract interest paid by consumers, and transfer payments made by consumers to foreigners, such as contributions to the Jewish National Fund, or funds sent back to relatives in the "old country," when calculating personal saving.

Personal income can also be calculated directly from the components of national income that are earned by individuals, plus those components of income that are received but not part of factor production. The general schematic for PI is summarized in table 2.5.

Table 2.5 Components of personal income (2000 values)

Category	Value*
Total personal income	8,319
Wages and salaries	4,951
Other labor income	570
Proprietors' income	728
Farm	19
Nonfarm	709
Rental income	138
Personal dividend income	409
Personal interest income	1,091
Transfer payments	1,170
Old age, survivors, health and disability ("social security")	664
Unemployment benefits	32
Veterans' benefits	27
Other[a]	448
Less: personal contributions for social insurance	372

[a] Mainly government retirement benefits and welfare payments, including Medicaid

* All figures are in billions of current dollars

Source: BEA website, www.bea.gov

MANAGER'S BRIEFCASE: UNDERSTANDING PERSONAL SAVING

The personal saving rate, as reported by the BEA, dropped almost steadily during the 1990s from a peak of 8.7% in 1992 to only 2.3% in 2001; in some quarters, it was hardly above zero. Many managers, when hearing this figure, assume that it does not include the amounts set aside by individuals and their employers toward retirement plans, but that is incorrect. These deductions and contributions *are* included in the BEA measure of personal saving. How, then, could the personal saving rate be so low?

In fact there are several reasons for this apparent anomaly, but most of them are related to the understatement of personal income. That could occur for several reasons. During the 1990s, the sharp rise in the stock market generated realized capital gains that were much larger than usual, and presumably some of that additional income was spent. That boosted consumption but not personal income. However, when the stock market crumbled in 2000–2002, the personal saving rate did not rise at all except for the impact of the tax cut, so that could not have been the only reason.

As long as interest rates are declining, many people refinance their homes. That reduces their mortgage payments, hence freeing up more money to be spent on goods and services. Also, to the extent that people withdraw money based on the increased equity in their homes, that really is dissaving, and to a certain extent offsets the increase in saving stemming from contributions to pension plans. Indeed, home equity loans rose an average of

continued

MANAGER'S BRIEFCASE (*continued*)

24% in both 2000 and 2001 and then advanced at an astounding 44% annual rate during the first seven months of 2002.

A third distinct possibility is that income is understated because of the underground economy, which is extremely difficult to measure accurately. However, even if that impact were significant, it probably did not cause the major decline in the personal saving rate during the 1990s.

Because personal saving is a residual, it is subject to wider error – and larger percentage revisions – than most of the other numbers in the NIPA. Thus it must be interpreted with even more caution than the other data. Nonetheless, to the extent that the personal saving rate declines, there is a shift in the economy toward more consumption and less investment, ceteris paribus. For a while, during the 1990s, the gap was filled by an increase in government saving and net foreign saving. However, when the Federal government moved back into deficit and net foreign saving declined along with the weaker dollar, the investment gap became more visible. Thus to that extent it is important to recognize that a very low reported personal saving rate, whatever its empirical flaws, means either (a) the investment gap must be offset by higher saving elsewhere in the economy, or (b) investment will decline as a proportion of GDP, which will generally reduce the average long-term growth rate.

2.6   Value added by stages of production: an example

One of the key concepts necessary to understand the NIPA bookkeeping system is the **value added** at each stage of production. The total value added at each stage of production must be equal to factor payments at that stage of production. This insures that total aggregate demand is equal to total aggregate income, validating the double-entry bookkeeping framework on which the NIPA figures are built.

A simplified example of value added is shown for the production of an automobile, starting from the initial stages of production of raw materials to the finished product. This case assumes the car is produced and sold domestically, although it would undoubtedly have some imported components. If that were the case, the total value added – the total contribution to GDP – would be reduced by the amount paid for those imported components.

The importance of the concept of value added can be summarized as follows. To measure the total amount produced and the total income earned in any economy, we only want to count everything once. Excluding intermediate goods removes double counting. Also, the double-entry system of bookkeeping should insure that total income and total production are the same. This identity can also be checked by calculating the value added at each stage of production. The methodology could break down only if some items (such as the use of new technological services) were not counted at all, in which case income would grow faster than product. Even in this case, though, the lack of balance between demand and production would indicate that something is amiss. Finally, we note that the double-entry method of bookkeeping works only for current dollar amounts – nominal values. When constant prices are used, additional complications can arise.

Table 2.6

Aggregate Demand		Aggregate Income	
Stage I. Production of Basic Materials			
Iron and steel	500	Rent and royalties	300
Plastics and chemicals	1,000	Labor costs	700
Semiconductor chips	500	Interest and depreciation	600
Total value added	2,000	Profits	400
Stage II. Manufacturing Parts			
Cost from previous stage	2,000	Labor costs	600
Tires, battery, etc.	500	Rent	200
Electronics	1,000	Interest	400
Margin at this stage	1,500	Depreciation	800
Total price of parts	5,000	Profits	1,000
Stage III. Assembling the Motor Vehicle			
Cost of parts	5,000		
Value added	10,000	Wages and salaries	2,000
		Healthcare and other benefits	1,200
		Rent	400
		Interest	600
		Depreciation	1,500
		Marketing costs	2,000*
		Profits	2,300
Stage IV. Selling to Final Consumer			
Manufacturer's price	15,000		
Value added	1,000	Transportation costs	400*
		Distribution costs	400*
		Profits	200
Wholesale price	16,000		
Retail margin	2,000	Labor costs (commissions)	500
		Rent	300
		Advertising	1,000*
		Dealer profit margin	200
9% sales tax	1,620	Indirect business tax	1,620
Retail price	19,620	Total value added	19,620

* These are then split further into wages and salaries, rent, interest, depreciation, and profits. All profits are before deduction of income tax

2.7 Inclusions and exclusions in the NIPA data

So far, the description of the components of GDP and NI has been fairly straightforward, with the possible exception of corporate profits. However, in several cases, the treatment of components of purchases and income are unexpected. We now turn to several key examples where definitions are not as obvious.

Transfer of Assets

Transfers of assets are not included in either GDP or NI. Individuals often talk about "investing" in the stock market. In terms of the NIPA figures, no investment has taken place; the only entry in GDP is the brokerage commission, which is part of consumption. If someone buys 100 shares of Microsoft, no additional goods or services have been created when that transaction occurs. The stock certificate – or electronic computer record – is merely transferred from one person to another. Even buying a new stock in an initial public offering is not investment in the NIPA sense. Except for the brokerage commission, GDP does not change until the company issuing the new stock spends the money on new equipment or construction, in which case it is counted as investment.

Similarly, if someone buys a house – even a new one – the transaction is merely a transfer of assets. Construction activity is included in the NIPA figures as the house is being built, not when it is sold. The only parts of this transaction included in NIPA at the time of purchase are the brokerage commission, the cost of title insurance, and any transfer taxes, since these represent taxes or income to various factors of production.

The same logic applies when buying any other existing asset, such as a painting, coins, or stamps. When someone buys a used car, only the dealer margin and any applicable sales taxes are part of GDP. Only when a newly created asset is sold – such as a "collectible" from the Franklin Mint or similar institution – is the entire transaction part of GDP.

Barter and Similar Items

Only items bought and sold in the marketplace are included, not implicit items such as mowing one's own lawn. Payment to a baby-sitter outside the immediate family is theoretically part of GDP (although often it is not recorded); if older children sit for the younger ones, it isn't. Payments to maids or cleaning services are part of GDP; work done by the spousal partner who stays home and cleans the house is not. Technically, the value of bartered goods and services should also be included in taxable income, although few if any taxpayers follow that procedure, so these items rarely if ever are recorded in GDP.

CASE STUDY 2.4   TREATMENT OF MORTGAGE PAYMENTS

For many families, their biggest monthly cost is the mortgage payment, so it would seem to be a very important part of consumption. However, that raises several

continued

CASE STUDY 2.4 (*continued*)

methodological issues in the NIPA. For one thing, some proportion of the mortgage payment represents the reduction of principal; since no new good or service is being created, and no factor payments flow to anyone, that would not be part of GDP. By the same token, if someone pays off their mortgage entirely, GDP should not decline just because the mortgage payments stop, since that certainly does not mean GDP has decreased. Similarly, if someone takes out a second mortgage, that should not boost GDP.

Because of these reasons, mortgage payments are treated quite differently than other consumer purchases in the NIPA. Instead of recording the amount actually paid each month, government statisticians estimate how much the homeowner would receive each month if the house were rented to someone else. That is the amount entered in "consumption of housing services," and is independent of the size of the mortgage, the current interest rate being charged, or whether it is a new, old, or nonexistent mortgage.

This is not a trivial point, and one we will revisit when examining the determinants of consumption. Consider the case of someone with a variable rate mortgage, and the rate rises from (say) 6% to 8%. The mortgage payment will rise accordingly, leaving less money to spend on other goods and services. As a result, there will be an ex ante decline in aggregate demand even though aggregate income has not changed.[4]

Now suppose the mortgage rate falls from 8% to 6%, and the homeowner refinances at the lower rate. He now has more money to spend on other goods and services, so in a significant sense, real income has risen. However, no such entry appears in the NIPA. As a result, when interest rates fall, the reported personal saving rate has declined. That is another reason why the BEA measure of personal saving dropped so much during the 1990s, when many homeowners refinanced their mortgages at lower rates.

Foreign Expenditures

If someone flies to Europe on American Airlines for personal (as opposed to business) reasons, that is consumption. If the same passenger chooses British Airways, that is still consumption, but there is an equal and offsetting item in imports, so GDP doesn't change, except for any commission paid to the travel agent. Any money spent in Europe by this traveler is an import. If a British national travels from London to New York on American Airlines, that is considered a US export. Any item purchased by foreigners in the US, including hotel and restaurant bills, is an export; the item doesn't have to be shipped to a foreign country.

Now suppose someone travels to Europe for business purposes. That is neither consumption nor investment, at least in the NIPA sense. However, if a foreign airline is used, that item is considered an import, which reduces GDP, ceteris paribus. Similarly, any purchases for business reasons while in Europe are considered imports even if they are intermediate goods, such as business dinners or entertainment. Thus if an American travels to London on British Airways for a vacation, US GDP is unchanged; if the trip is for business purposes, GDP declines.

Different Types of Government Expenditures

Only about one-third of total expenditures by the Federal government are purchases of goods and services: the main components are defense weaponry, salaries of military and civilian personnel, operating expenses, and construction. The other two-thirds of expenditures are transfer payments, which are payments made to individuals without receiving a specific good or service in return. The major categories of transfer payments are social security benefits, retirement benefits for government employees, and Medicare and Medicaid payments. Interest payments made by the government are also treated as transfer payments.

Starting in December 1995, the NIPA economists divided government purchases into consumption and investment components, which had never been done before in the US, although the practice was already utilized by most other industrialized countries. This split emphasizes the economic difference between government purchases for, say, salaries of Congressional staffers, and building roads or schools. That decision required adding an extra line to the income side of the NIPA for depreciation of government assets; previously, depreciation allowances had applied only to privately held assets. Because NIPA figures for government expenditures now include depreciation, they are significantly larger than the government budget figures, and are no longer directly comparable.

The Underground Economy

The BEA undertakes a thorough and painstaking process to measure GDP, NI, and PI. Yet these numbers will not be accurate if some people do not report part or all of their income. The proportion of transactions that is not reported is generally known as the **underground economy**.

Most unreported income falls into three categories. First, the BEA estimates that only about 50% of net unincorporated business income is reported; people either underreport gross income or overreport deductions. Second, income is not reported in the informal or barter economy. Third, individuals engaged in sales of illegal activities (drugs, prostitution, loansharking, etc.) report little or none of their actual income.

In general, consumption is more likely to be reported than income. If a drug dealer reports virtually no income but buys a $60,000 car, the latter will show up in the consumption figures.[5] As a result, it is quite possible that over time, *reported* consumption will grow faster than reported income even though *actual* consumption is growing at the same rate as actual income. Some economists think the reported decline in the personal saving rate during the 1990s was partly due to this phenomenon.

Obviously no one really knows how large the underground economy is. Most estimates place the total value at about 5% of GDP in the US, which would be about $500 billion; a few estimates are as high as 10%. For Italy, the figure has been estimated as high as 40%.[6]

In terms of NIPA, the existence of the underground economy will affect the balance between the income and product sides of the accounts only to the extent that the relative proportion of unreported income changes, thereby affecting the personal saving rate. Of course, if overall GDP is underreported, productivity and the standard of living are higher than government figures show. The BEA economists use IRS figures to estimate how much income is understated on tax returns, and expand the figures by that proportion. But no one pretends they get it all. To the extent that people do not pay all the taxes they owe, reported national income will always be understated.

2.8   Circular flow between aggregate demand and production

On an ex post basis, C + I + F + G is equal to GDP by definition. However, on an ex ante basis, there is no particular reason why the amount one group of economic agents (mainly consumers) plans to purchase should equal the amount that another set of economic agents (mainly firms) plans to produce.

Suppose personal income rises. In general, that will boost consumer spending. If consumer spending rises, then production will usually rise, hence creating more jobs and more income. There is a two-way relationship between consumption – the main component of aggregate demand – and personal income, which is the main component of aggregate income. However, under certain circumstances, an increase in personal income might not boost consumption. A rise in income might be accompanied by higher interest rates or a restriction in consumer credit. Other times, a rise in consumption might not boost production because the increase in sales could be offset by reduced inventory stocks, or more goods might be purchased from foreign producers.

Similarly, a rise in production often leads to an increase in fixed investment, but that link could be severed by more stringent monetary conditions. A rise in fixed investment often boosts production, but it might be offset by lower inventory investment or a rise in imports.

These examples indicate that the circular flow between demand and income is not always matched on an ex ante basis, although by definition they must be equal on an ex post basis. When ex ante demand and ex post production are not equal, the equilibrating factor often turns out to be interest rates. However, changes in inventory investment, production schedules, or foreign trade may also play an important role.

By definition, aggregate demand must equal aggregate income on an ex post basis. Nonetheless, sometimes aggregate demand and income move in opposite directions on an ex ante basis, as indicated above. In these cases, how are the two sides of the NIPA equated?

There are several basic mechanisms. First, interest rates may adjust. If consumption declines while income rises, for example, interest rates would fall, hence offsetting the initial decline in consumption. Also, the interest income component of income would fall.

Second, even if domestic product and income do not change by the same amount, the adjustment might occur in foreign product and income. A decline in consumption might be met by a similar drop in imports, in which case total GDP would not fall. If aggregate demand does fall on an ex ante basis, hence reducing interest rates, foreign investors might be less likely to invest in US assets, which would also offset the decline in domestic demand.

Third, firms may adjust their production schedules. In line with the above example, a decline in consumption would initially be met by an unplanned rise in inventory investment, so that total aggregate demand would not decline.

Fourth, after a while, the unplanned increase in inventory investment would cause a reduction in production, employment, and hence in income. Thus eventually the drop in consumption would be matched by a drop in income. A corollary of this theory is sometimes called the *paradox of thrift*: if consumers plan to save more, they may actually end up saving less, because the drop in consumption translates into a decline in income and hence a decline in saving. Of course this paradox does not automatically occur, and it is more likely that interest rates will adjust. However, even if interest rates do not serve as the equilibrating mechanism, aggregate demand and income must always be equal on an ex post basis by definition. As shown in the appendix, this is equivalent to the statement that saving and investment must always be equal on an ex post basis, even if they change in different directions on an ex ante basis.

KEY TERMS AND CONCEPTS

Capital Consumption Adjustment	National Income
Capital Consumption Allowances (Depreciation)	National Income and Product Accounts (NIPA)
Capital Spending	Net Exports
Consumption	Net Factor Income
Corporate Profits	Net Interest Income

Depreciation
Disposable Income
Double-Entry Bookkeeping System
Final Goods and Services
Government Purchases of Goods and Services
Gross Domestic Product
Indirect Business Taxes
Intermediate Goods and Services
Inventory Investment
Inventory Valuation Adjustment
Investment

Personal Income
Personal Outlays
Personal Saving
Proprietors' Income
Rental Income
Residential Construction
Supplements to Wages and Salaries
Transfer Payments
Underground Economy
Value Added
Wages and Salaries

SUMMARY

- The *national income and product accounts* (NIPA) represent a double-entry bookkeeping system for the overall economy. Every good or service purchased by a final user must be balanced by equal entries of payments to factors of production, plus depreciation and indirect business taxes.
- *Gross domestic product* (GDP) is the total amount of goods and services purchased for final use, plus inventory investment. It consists of purchases by consumers (consumption, C), capital spending (producers' durable equipment plus nonresidential construction), residential construction, inventory investment (I), net exports (F), and government purchases of goods and services (G). The GDP identity is written as $GDP \equiv C + I + F + G$.
- There is no corresponding term for gross national income. *National income* (NI) is the total amount of income paid to the factors of production. It consists of wages and salaries, supplements to wages and salaries, unincorporated business income, corporate profits, net interest income, and rental income.
- The difference between GDP and GNP (gross national product) reflects the differential treatment of corporate profits. GDP includes all profits earned in the US, whether

by domestic or foreign companies. GNP includes all profits of US corporations, whether earned in this country or abroad.
- The difference between GNP and NI consists primarily of depreciation, indirect business taxes, and government subsidies; there are also a few smaller items. Any remaining difference is shown in the statistical discrepancy. This number used to be a very small proportion of GDP, although in recent years it has exceeded −$100 billion.
- NI is the total amount of income earned by all factors of production; *personal income* (PI) is the total amount of income received by individuals. The only component of corporate profits included in PI is dividends. PI also includes all transfer payments to individuals, including consumer and government interest payments. NI includes social security taxes, but PI does not.
- *Disposable income* (DI) equals PI minus personal income taxes. *Personal saving* (SP) equals DI minus personal outlays (POUT), which are equal to consumption plus interest on consumer loans plus personal transfer payments to foreigners.
- Constant-dollar inventory investment equals the change in the amount of physical stock held by businesses from one period to the

next. It is included in GDP even though it is not part of final sales, because these items will eventually become part of final sales.

- With the exception of inventory investment, only final goods and services are included in GDP. Any purchase or factor payment must have a corresponding entry on the other side of the NIPA; otherwise it is not part of GDP or NI.
- GDP excludes all purchases of intermediate goods and services, which are used to produce final goods and services. In particular, items purchased by businesses for use in the productive process are not considered part of GDP unless they are capital goods. Thus the same item that is included in final demand if purchased by a consumer may not be included in GDP if purchased by a business.
- The value added at each stage of production equals the sum of factor payments at that stage of production. The sum of value added at all stages of production equals GDP.

- Transfers of assets are not included in GDP; only the commissions paid on these transfers are included. Thus purchases of stocks, bonds, other financial assets, and real estate are not part of GDP. Also, sources of income that do not represent production are not part of NI. That includes capital gains on both financial assets and real estate. All capital gains are excluded from GDP and NI whether realized or not.
- Rent and mortgage payments per se are not considered part of consumption; instead, consumption of housing services is measured as the amount homeowners would receive if they rented their house. Thus a change in mortgage rates that changes the amount of the monthly mortgage payment does not change disposable income, but is likely to change consumption and hence personal saving. For this reason, much of the shift in the personal saving rate in recent years reflects changes in capital gains and monthly mortgage payments.

QUESTIONS AND PROBLEMS

1. Classify the following as consumption, fixed business investment, residential construction, inventory investment, exports, imports, government purchases, intermediate goods, or none of the above.
    - (A) Student purchases PC to do problem set.
    - (B) Professor purchases PC workstation for class use.
    - (C) Student takes trip to Mexico for vacation.
    - (D) Professor takes trip to Mexico for consulting.
    - (E) Investor purchases 100 shares of Microsoft.
    - (F) Employee contributes to retirement plan.
    - (G) Student has lunch at McDonald's.
    - (H) Dean hosts reception at La Francais.
    - (I) Student pays tuition to Northwestern University.
    - (J) Student pays tuition to University of Illinois.
    - (K) Driver buys auto policy for $1,000; later that day has $10,000 accident.
    - (L) Japanese investor buys Van Gogh painting.

(M) GM buys tires to put on new cars.

(N) Same as above, but it buys them on December 20th and doesn't put them on the cars until January 15th.

(O) Consumer purchases used car for $5,000; the dealer bought it for $4,000.

(P) Caterpillar Corporation builds new factory.

(Q) Homeowner gets dishwasher repaired.

(R) Homeowner buys new dishwasher.

(S) Landlord replaces old dishwasher.

(T) Neighbor cuts lawn in return for baby-sitting.

(U) IRS demands $1,000 payment from neighbor for not reporting barter income: $500 is tax, $100 is interest, and $400 is penalty.

(V) Anti-smoking lawyer receives $1 billion to show smoking is bad for you.

(W) Lawyer purchases old Kennedy mansion in Palm Beach for $7 million.

(X) Lawyer tears house down, builds $20 million replacement.

(Y) Lawyer receives $2 million tax bill from Palm Beach County.

(Z) Lawyer pays another lawyer $100,000 to sue Palm Beach County.

2. (A) What are the principal differences between government purchases of goods and services and transfer payments?

   (B) What are the most common kinds of transfer payments at the Federal level? At the state and local level?

   (C) Besides purchases and transfer payments, what other kinds of expenditures are included in total government spending?

3. Assume the government was paying 500,000 people an average of $10,000 per year for unemployment benefits.

   (A) Under the new regime to end welfare, all these people are hired by the government to perform various tasks, such as serving lunch in the Congressional dining rooms. What happens to GDP, wages and salaries, personal income, personal saving, and national saving?

   (B) Under an alternative scheme to end welfare, all these people are required to find jobs in the private sector, and all are successful. What happens to GDP, wages and salaries, personal income, personal saving, and national saving? Assume these people are paid their marginal product, so profits do not change.

4. The Advanced Silicon Devices semiconductor factory costs $20 million to build and is depreciated (on a straight line basis, to make this simple) over 20 years. Also it borrows the money to build the factory at 8% interest. The factory has a capacity of 400,000 chips per year that sell for $30 apiece. Labor costs are $1.5 million, and raw material costs are $0.5 million. Ongoing research and development costs are $3 million.

   The factory sells all its chips to the Itty Bitty Machine company, which manufactures 40,000 computers a year that sell (wholesale) for $800 each. That factory costs $35 million to build, with the same rate of interest and depreciation as the semiconductor factory. Besides paying for the chips, the costs are $4 million for labor, $2 million for other parts (half of which are imported), and $2.5 million for ongoing R&D. The computer company sells its entire stock to Computers R Us, which then sells them to individuals at an average retail price of $1,200 plus 5% sales tax. The store has labor costs of $6 million, advertising costs of $4 million, and rent of $1 million.

(A) Calculate the value added at each stage of production.

(B) Calculate total GDP by components.

(C) Calculate total gross national income for each factor payment.

5. Last year, assume that McDonald's had a profit of $1.2 billion, of which $0.8 billion was earned in foreign countries. Toyota had a profit of $2 billion (converted from yen), of which $0.6 billion was earned in the US. If US GDP was $10,200 billion, calculate GNP based on the above data.

6. Why are interest payments by the government considered part of personal income but not part of national income?

7. Joe buys a Buick. To keep it simple, ignore the sales tax. In all cases the cash price of the new car is $25,000. Show how components of consumption and investment are affected if Joe:

(A) Pays cash.

(B) Pays cash but has a $10,000 trade-in.

(C) Pays over time, 48 monthly payments of $625.

(D) Leases the car, 36 monthly payments of $400.

(E) His corporation, Shifty Tax Consultants Inc., buys the car.

(F) Buys car personally but uses it 50% for business.

(G) Rents car from Hertz at a cost of $1,200 per month (which includes all insurance and maintenance).

Now redo (A)–(G) under the assumption Joe buys a Toyota produced in Japan. Transportation costs are $1,000 and gross dealer margin is $2,000. Show how consumption, investment, and net exports are affected in each case.

8. What are some of the major types of transactions included in the underground economy but not in GDP or NI?

9. (A) Peggy buys a house for $200,000, with a monthly mortgage payment of $2,000. The current interest rate is 8%. A year later, the interest rate drops to 7% and her monthly payment falls to $1,800. What happens to GDP, NI, PI, C, and SP?

(B) Peggy decides to remodel the house at a cost of $50,000, and gets a second mortgage, which boosts her monthly payment to $2,300. What happens to GDP, NI, PI, C, I, and SP?

(C) The municipal taxing authority decides to boost her real estate taxes from $4,000 to $5,000 based on the increased value of house. What happens to GDP, NI, PI, C, and SP?

Appendix: key macroeconomic identities

Aggregate Demand

$$C + I + F + G = GDP. \tag{2.1}$$

C = consumption, I = investment, F = net exports, G = government purchases.

National Income

$$NI = W + TSOCE + OLI + YP + IN + R + Z. \tag{2.2}$$

NI = national income, W = wages and salaries, TSOCE = employer contributions to social security, OLI = other labor income, YP = proprietors' income, IN = net interest income, R = rental income, Z = corporate profits. Note that TSOCE + OLI = supplements (S).

Links Between GDP, NI, PI, and DI

$$NI = GDP + NFI - D - TB - TRBP - TRBF + GSUB. \tag{2.3}$$

NFI = net factor income, D = depreciation, TB = indirect business taxes, TRBP = business transfer payments to persons, TRBF = business transfer payments to foreigners, GSUB = government subsidies. The statistical discrepancy is omitted here.

$$PI = NI - Z - TSOC + INC + ING + DV + TRGP + TRBP. \tag{2.4}$$

Z = corporate profits, TSOC = social security taxes, INC = interest paid by consumers, ING = interest paid by government, DV = dividends, TRGP = transfer payments paid by government to persons, TRBP = transfer payments paid by business to persons. Also

$$PI = W + OLI + YP + IN + INC + ING + R + DV + TRGP + TRBP - TSOCP. \tag{2.5}$$

$$DI = PI - TP, \text{ therefore} \tag{2.6}$$

$$DI = GDP + NFI - D - TB - TRBP - TRBF + GSUB - Z - TSOC$$
$$+ INC + ING + DV + TRGP + TRBP - TP. \tag{2.7}$$

This equation is formulated by substituting (2.3) for NI in (2.4).
PI = personal income, DI = disposable income, TSOCP = social security taxes paid by individuals.

Saving and Investment

$$SP = DI - C - INC - TRPF \tag{2.8}$$

$$SC = Z - TC - DV + D \tag{2.9}$$

$$SF = -F - NFI + TRF, \tag{2.10}$$

where $TRF = TRGF + TRPF + TRBF$ (total transfers to foreigners).

$$SG = TP + TC + TB + TSOC - G - TRGP - TRGF - ING - GSUB. \tag{2.11}$$

$$
\begin{aligned}
S ={}& SP + SC + SF + SG \\
={}& GDP + NFI - D - TB - TRBF + GSUB - Z - TSOC \\
&+ INC + ING + DV + TRGP - TP - C - INC - TRPF \\
&+ Z - TC - DV + D - F - NFI \\
&+ TRGF + TRPF + TRBF + TP + TC \\
&+ TB + TSOC - G - TRGP - TRGF - ING - GSUB.
\end{aligned}
$$

Rearranging these terms:

$$
\begin{aligned}
S ={}& (GDP - C - F - G) \\
&+ (TP - TP + TC - TC + TB - TB + TSOC - TSOC) \\
&+ (INC + ING + DV - INC - ING - DV) \\
&+ (TRGP - TRGP + TRBF - TRBF + TRPF - TRPF \\
&+ TRGF - TRGF) + (Z + D - Z - D) \\
&+ (GSUB - GSUB + NFI - NFI). \tag{2.12}
\end{aligned}
$$

The first term is identically equal to I (investment). All other terms cancel out. We have thus shown arithmetically that $S = I$. The economic relevance of this will become clear in chapter 5.

Notes

1. When the figures were originally released, they showed a gain from 2.3% to 5.7%, indicating an increase of 3.4%, compared to the revised estimates issued in July 2002 that showed only a 2.2% gain. Those revisions showed that growth was slower in 2000, and the recession more severe in 2001, than previously reported. Problems caused by incorrect data are discussed in more detail in the last chapter of this book.

2. This distinction, recently implemented by the BEA, has exacerbated the distortions in the GDP data. Many economists think it is unrealistic to consider a blank CD ROM, or one with economic data, as an intermediate good and hence not part of GDP, but the same CD that also contains a program as part of investment.
3. The numbers on the vertical axes of figure 2.3 sum to less than unity because unincorporated business income and indirect business taxes are omitted and are shown separately in figure 2.4.
4. In chapter 7 we will show how aggregate demand and income remain in balance on an ex post basis through the equilibrating mechanism of saving = investment.
5. Car dealers are supposed to report any purchase over $10,000 in cash, but many of them fail to observe this requirement.
6. In 1982, IRS Commissioner Roscoe Egger estimated that the total amount of unpaid income taxes in 1981 was $97 billion, and claimed that figure had increased steadily as a proportion of PI over the past decade. At 2002 levels of PI, that would imply an unpaid tax gap of more than $336 billion. For further information and related references, see Michael K. Evans, *The Truth About Supply-Side Economics* (New York: Harper & Row, 1983).

chapter three

Key data concepts: inflation, unemployment, and labor costs

Introduction

When the Bureau of Economic Analysis (BEA) releases the figures for GDP, the level and change in current dollar GDP are usually ignored. Instead, economists and financial analysts are primarily interested in the change in real growth and inflation, since those describe and measure the well-being of the economy. Furthermore, the consumer price index and producer price index are more important measures of inflation than the implicit or chained GDP deflator.

The other economic report that generally receives the most attention is *Employment and Earnings*, which provides the latest monthly figures for employment, unemployment, and wage rates. Since one of the goals of any society is to try and provide jobs for all who want to work, the unemployment rate is of great political as well as economic importance.

Employment, wage rates, and inflation provide quite a bit of information about the state of the economy, but further data are needed to generate measures of labor costs. While they do not receive as much publicity, data on employment costs and productivity can provide additional valuable information for managers.

Yet there are several different measures of inflation, unemployment, and labor costs, and none of them is perfect. Here we discuss the various advantages and shortfalls of each major alternative, and indicate which ones should be preferred.

The chapter concludes with a few brief comments about economic data generally. The indexes of leading and coincident indicators can be used to summarize where the economy is heading, and where it is currently. Because virtually all government data are seasonally adjusted, this topic is covered briefly. Finally, managers are warned that while the preliminary data issued by government agencies are avidly followed, those numbers are often subject to substantial revision.

3.1 Measuring inflation: three different types of indexes

The latest figures for GDP not only make the headlines in the business section, but are often featured on the front page. However, the articles seldom if ever mention how much current dollar GDP has changed. Instead, emphasis is placed on the change in "real," or inflation-adjusted GDP, and on the rate of inflation. The change in real GDP is supposed to measure the change in the volume of goods and services produced, excluding any changes in prices.

The distinction is quite important. A report that current dollar GDP rose 6% last year tells us very little about the state of the economy. Perhaps real GDP rose 4% and inflation rose 2% – a very satisfactory performance. Or maybe real GDP rose 2% and inflation rose 4% – much less satisfactory. It could even mean that real GDP *fell* 2% and inflation rose 8%, in which case the economy is in the midst of a recession. Without further information it is not possible to tell how well the economy is doing.

Theoretically the distinction between real growth and inflation should reflect a straightforward separation of the change in volume and the change in the price of any good or service. In the case of homogeneous commodities, this creates few if any data problems: a ton of steel, a quart of milk, or a gallon of gasoline are virtually the same items from one year to the next. The problems magnify when dealing with goods where quality has improved, such as motor vehicles or TV sets, or where rapid changes in technology occur, as in computers.

The BEA reports data for GDP and its components in nominal and real terms. The nominal figures are, by definition, in current dollars. The real figures, which used to be labeled constant dollars, are now called "chained" dollars. According to the BEA, the price of computers has fallen an average of about 15% per year. That is not an unreasonable estimate, but that trend would lead to distortions in the NIPA data if it were to continue indefinitely. Thus, in the figures based on the 1992 benchmark – which were first released in late 1995 – the BEA introduced new methodology to reduce this distorting effect. The details are discussed below; at this point we note that the older nomenclature of "current" and "constant" dollars has been replaced by "current" and "chained" (also known as "real") dollars.

Data for real or chained quantities of goods and services are not collected directly. Instead, government economists in the Bureau of the Census or the BEA (both part of the Commerce Department) collect the data for current dollar amounts. Economists in the Bureau of Labor Statistics (BLS) collect data on prices. The real dollar figures are then calculated as current dollars divided by the relevant price index. If the nominal amount of purchases rose but the prices of those items did not, it is assumed the quantity must have risen, whether that actually represents more items or just better ones.

For example, a $1,000 suit is considered equal to five $200 suits. Thus if someone buys a $200 suit one year and a $1,000 suit the next year – and if the price of both suits has remained unchanged – the NIPA figures record that his purchases of clothing have risen fivefold.

In determining whether the figures for real growth are reported accurately, the principal issue is how prices and the rate of inflation are measured, since real GDP is defined as the current dollar value of purchases divided by the relevant price index. This is where the ambiguity starts, because there are three different types of price indexes used by government statisticians for various purposes.

1. **Fixed-weight price indexes**. The weight of each good or service is determined in the base period, and does not change until the sample is revised. That is the most common kind of index, and is the method used to calculate the **consumer price index** (CPI) and the **producer price index** (PPI). The CPI measures prices paid by consumers at the retail level. The PPI measures prices paid by producers, and is reported for three different levels of production: finished, intermediate, and crude goods. Technically these are known as *Laspeyres indexes*.
2. **Implicit price deflators**. The weight of each good and service is equal to the quantities in the current period, so it changes each time the index is calculated. This is the method used to calculate the implicit deflators for GDP and its various components. Technically these are known as *Paasche indexes*.

For many years these were the two major types of price indexes used. Many years ago, Irving Fisher proposed the concept of an "ideal" price index, which combines these two indexes, but it was seldom used. Recently, however, the rapid decline in the prices of computers and related goods has distorted the inflation rate calculated by the implicit deflators, so the third alternative of a chained price index has been added. Theoretically, it is very close to an ideal price index.

Implicit price deflators provide an accurate representation of the true rate of inflation as long as all important components of the price index are stable or rising. However, they provide distorted estimates of inflation if some prices are falling rapidly. That is because the weight of the good with the falling price continues to increase over time unless some other offsetting adjustment is made, or unless the entire set of NIPA data is rebenchmarked to a more recent year.

Suppose that a typical consumer spends $4,500 per year on food and $500 per year on computers, and the price of food rises 3% per year while the price of computers falls 15% per year. Using the fixed-weight deflator, the CPI would rise 1.2% per year. Using the implicit deflator, the calculation gets more complicated, since the weights change every year. In the second year, the constant-dollar quantity of food purchased is $4,369 ($4,500/1.03), whereas the constant-dollar quantity of computers has risen to $588 (500/0.85). Hence the weights have shifted from 9:1 to 7.4:1. After 10 years, the weights would be 1.65:1, which means the weight for computers would be 60% of the weight for food even though consumers are still spending nine times as much on food. By then, the implicit deflator would reportedly be falling 3.8% per year instead of rising 1.2% per year. Since this is an untenable result, an alternative price deflator was introduced in conjunction with the 1992 benchmark of the NIPA data.

3. **Chained price indexes**. These are a combination of (1) and (2) above. The weights are recalculated every period, but are linked – or chained – to

the previous period, so it is akin to resetting the clock each period. In the above example, the weight for computers would be reset to 0.1 every year. This method is similar to, although not identical with, Fisher's ideal price index. This would seem to solve the problems of both the overstatement of inflation by fixed-weight indexes and the understatement of inflation by current-weight indexes, but it has one drawback. When used for real GDP, the sum of the individual components does not equal the total. This difference is small at first, but becomes substantial if the index is not frequently rebased.

The major characteristics of these price indexes are as follows:

1. Fixed-weight indexes (CPI, PPI, etc.)
   - No change in weights; same market basket
   - Fails to take into account shift to less expensive products
   - Generally overstates the actual rate of inflation
   - Calculated with base period weights.
2. Implicit deflators (previously used for GDP deflator)
   - Includes changes in market basket weights
   - Will overstate inflation if quality improvements are not taken into account, but will understate inflation if some of the price components are declining rapidly
   - Calculated with current period weights.
3. Chained deflators (now used for GDP deflator)
   - Assuming no new or improved products, will neither overstate nor understate inflation
   - The sum of the components of constant dollar GDP do not add to the total
   - Calculated with current period weights, but the weights are reset every year.

3.2   Factors causing the inflation rate to be overstated

No price index is perfect. The errors that lead the calculated rate of inflation to overstate the true rate can be grouped into three major categories: changing weights, improvements in quality of existing products, and the introduction of new products.

When the price of product A rises and the price of product B falls, some consumers will switch from product A to B. As a result, a true price index will rise more slowly than a fixed-weight index, such as the CPI. For this reason, any fixed-weight price index overstates the true rate of inflation, ceteris paribus. That source of bias is absent from implicit deflators and chained price indexes.

When product quality improves, all three types of price indexes will overstate the true rate of inflation unless a specific adjustment is used to measure the increase in quality. If improvements in quality are substantial, the reported rate of inflation is generally overstated no matter which method is used for calculating inflation.

The bias from the introduction of new products depends on the length of lag from the time the product first appears to the time it is included in the market basket of purchased goods and services. Generally, many years elapse before new products or services are included in the calculation of the price level, so a substantial price decline has already occurred, but has never been measured. In such cases, all indexes would overstate inflation.

In the CPI, all three sources of error point in the same direction, so for many years that measure of inflation was overstated. However, starting in 1994, the BLS made several adjustments to reduce this overstatement. For the implicit deflator, the change in weights may cause an understatement of inflation, so no unequivocal statement about the direction of bias can be made. The chained price index should have no bias from changing weights, but to the degree that it underestimates the improvement in quality, or does not include new products on a timely basis, it could also overstate the actual rate of inflation.

Effect of a Fixed-Weight Market basket

We now consider in more detail why the CPI overstates inflation. The market basket argument is the simplest. The CPI, which is the index most frequently mentioned when people talk about "inflation," is a fixed-weight index. Yet when the price of a given item rises, consumers will generally tend to buy less of that item and more of a cheaper substitute. The usual cliché is apples and oranges; when the price of apples rises, consumers buy more oranges. If the price index assumes the weights are unchanged, it will overstate the actual inflation rate.

However, it isn't only apples and oranges, or lettuce and tomatoes, or beef and pork. Over time, consumers have shifted their shopping patterns to discount outlets from full-service department stores, restaurants, gasoline stations, and other retail establishments, and they use more generic and fewer brand-name drugs. As these shifts occur, a fixed-weight index overstates the true rate of inflation.

From a theoretical viewpoint, the systematic bias in any fixed-weight index could be eliminated by gathering data on quantities sold each year. As a practical matter, though, that is quite difficult. The BLS spends a great deal of time and money collecting data for 207 different classifications in each of 44 cities. Even that attempt, as thorough as it is, covers only a very small proportion of the total purchases of any given item. Collecting data on quantities requires a much more intensive data-gathering effort. As a result, before 1999, thorough revisions of the items in the CPI occurred only about once every 10 years.

Some of the differences can be estimated with fairly small-sample methods. Prices are less expensive at large discount outlets (Wal-Mart, Home Depot, etc.) than at department or hardware stores. Sales data can provide a relatively accurate estimate of the magnitude of the switch to discount stores. Prices of generic drugs are less expensive than the same name-brand drugs, and the proportion of generic sales can be closely estimated. However, the rapid proliferation of goods and services (such as books and airline travel) sold over the internet probably means the rate of inflation could continue to be overstated even if the BLS uses current samples and methodology to measure the CPI.

Measuring Quality Changes

The other two changes are even more difficult to fix. The second source of error, which is caused by the change in quality, can be illustrated as follows. In 1938, a new Buick with the usual optional equipment cost about $800. In 2002, a new Buick with the usual optional equipment cost about $23,000. Over the same period, the overall CPI has risen 12.5 times, so if car prices had simply kept pace with the CPI, a new Buick today would cost $10,000. On that basis, car prices have risen much faster than overall inflation.

Yet there have obviously been some quality changes. Given a choice between buying a "new" 1938 Buick today for $10,000 and a 2002 Buick for $23,000, virtually everyone would choose the 2002 car because of these quality improvements. The same argument holds for virtually any kitchen or household appliance, or any type of home electronic equipment.

Durable goods are not the only sector where quality has improved; that has also occurred for many services. You wouldn't want the doctor to operate on you based on what the medical profession knew in 1938, even if he charged 1938 prices. Nor would you want your lawyer to defend you based on 1938 case law, even at 1938 prices. In fact, there wouldn't be much point in studying economics from a brand new 1938 textbook even if it cost only $5.00.

The BLS does make some quality adjustment in their measures of inflation, and private sector economists have suggested further changes. But in the end it boils down to a value judgment. No price index will ever be able to handle this issue perfectly. Besides, as the BLS correctly points out, some services such as airline transportation have declined in quality, yet no adjustments are made in that direction.

New Products and Services

The introduction of new products and services, which is the third major source of error, also represents a significant source of overstating inflation. Cellular phones were added to the CPI only in 1998. Previously, there were similar lags for VCRs, CD players, color TVs, and before that, black-and-white TVs and LP record players.

When monochrome TV sets were introduced at $500 per set in the late 1940s, very few sales occurred for the first few years. Ten years later, when the average price had fallen below $200 per set, almost every household unit had purchased at least one. Yet for most people, the price did not fall more than 60%, because hardly any TV sets had been purchased at the higher price. Again, there is no perfect way to handle this issue.

Drawbacks to Implicit Deflators

Measures of inflation known as implicit deflators use current weights. The most widely used is the implicit GDP deflator, but implicit deflators are published for most individual components of GDP. The implicit GDP deflator is simply defined as current dollar GDP divided by constant dollar GDP. As a result, the weights are always the most recent period, so any market basket substitution is automatically included in this measure of inflation.

That might sound like a useful way to eliminate substitution bias, but in certain circumstances it can generate misleading results. For example, if consumers shift enough of their purchases from goods and services with relatively high price indexes to those with relatively low price indexes, the implicit price deflator could decline even if the price of every good and service has increased.[1]

The other problem occurs when the price of a particular good or service is declining rapidly, which is particularly true for computers. We have already shown how this distorts the overall measure of inflation when the price of computers is declining some 15% per year because of the improvement in technology.

The Chained Index: The Latest Compromise

It was precisely this kind of distortion that caused the BEA to introduce a third measure of inflation at the end of 1995, known as a chained index. The chained index calculates the rate of inflation using last year's weights; the current rate of inflation is "chained" or "linked" to data of the previous year. Essentially this means the weights are fixed in any given year, but then recalculated each year. That solves the problem of rapidly rising weights for items where prices have been declining sharply, such as computers. It also solves the problem of shifting weights to lower-priced goods and services.

The major drawback to the chained index is that the components of constant-dollar GDP no longer sum to total GDP. As the BEA puts it, "As with most improvements, there is a cost to the new chain-type indexes . . . the chained (1992) dollars are not strictly additive, especially for periods far away from the base period [when] . . . contributions to GDP growth computed from the chained-dollar components can differ significantly from those produced by the chain-type indexes." In simpler English, the farther we get from 1992, the larger the residual between total GDP and the sum of all the components becomes.

The Boskin Commission Report on Inflation

These differences in various measures of inflation are not trivial. The Boskin Commission (formerly known as the CPI Commission) estimated that the CPI overstated the actual increase in the cost of living by an average of 1.1% per year. According to their results, the principal sources of this error on an annual average basis can be disaggregated as follows.[2] Upper-level substitution bias is (for example) substituting apples for oranges, while lower-level substitution is substituting Granny Smith for Macintosh apples. The estimated average bias per year (%) from each major source is:

Upper-level substitution bias	0.15
Lower-level substitution bias	0.25
Outlet substitution bias	0.10
New products/quality changes	0.60
Total estimated bias	1.10

Recent Improvements by the BLS

Stung by this criticism, the BLS implemented many changes. As of 2002, the BLS reports that these changes have reduced the inflation rate by 0.8% per year relative to what would have been reported using the old methodology. In

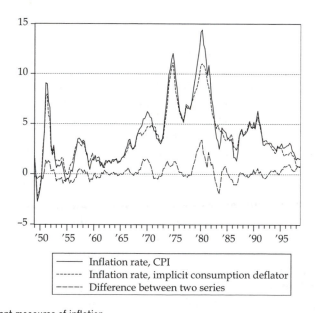

Figure 3.1 Different measures of inflation

Sources: CPI, Bureau of Labor Statistics website, www.bls.gov/cpi/home.htm; implicit deflator, BEA website, table 7.1, www.bea.gov

particular, the BLS has introduced several quality indexes for motor vehicles, TV sets, and other durables; now uses a chain-weighted average in some stages of the analysis; and includes many new products on a more timely basis. It is also using computer-assisted data collections, information from scanners, and telephone-based point-of-purchase surveys to revise and update their weights more frequently. Due in part to the findings of the Boskin Commission, virtually all of the previous upward bias in the CPI has now been eliminated. Historically, the difference between inflation as measured by the CPI, which overstates the actual rate of inflation, and the implicit consumption deflator, which probably understates it, is shown in figure 3.1.

CASE STUDY 3.1   FIXED-WEIGHT, IMPLICIT, AND CHAINED PRICE INDEXES

To illustrate how these three indexes yield different measures of inflation, we provide two examples: one during an era of high inflation, and one during an era of little or no inflation. The three items in this case study represent (a) a commodity whose quality does not change very much and whose price changes about the same amount as the overall rate of inflation, (b) a high-tech item whose price falls sharply relative to overall inflation, and (c) a service whose price rises faster than overall inflation.

In the first case, when inflation is rising rapidly, all three measures give approximately the same answer. In the second case, when inflation is not rising very much, the estimates diverge significantly. Among other things, that indicates how unrealistic it is to talk about "zero inflation" when the definition depends so much on how inflation is measured. By comparison, when prices are rising 10% a year, the method of measuring inflation is not as important.

These examples each have the same three items in the market basket: apples, computers, and medical care. Initially, the respective weights are 0.4, 0.2, and 0.4. In the high-inflation example, the price of apples rises 15% per year, computer prices are flat, and the price of medical care rises 20% per year. In the low-inflation example, the price of apples rises 3% per year, the price of computers falls 10% per year, and the price of medical care rises 7% per year.

The formulas for calculating the three types of price indexes are as follows:

$$\text{CPI (fixed weight)} = \frac{w_{11}}{p_{11}} \times p_{1t} + \frac{w_{21}}{p_{21}} \times p_{2t} + \cdots + \frac{w_{n1}}{p_{n1}} \times p_{nt}$$

where w are the weights of the respective commodities (they sum to unity), and p are the prices of the respective commodities. In the subscripts, the first number

continued

CASE STUDY 3.1 (*continued*)

(n) represents the 1st, 2nd, etc. commodity, and the second number (t) represents the year. Thus, for example, p_{21} would be the price of the second commodity (computers) in the first (base) year, and p_{2t} would be the price of computers in the year for which the CPI is being calculated.

In the other formulas we use the symbol q to represent the quantities of the goods or services purchased.

$$\text{IPC (implicit deflator)} = \frac{q_{1t} \times p_{1t} + q_{2t} \times p_{2t} + \cdots + q_{nt} \times p_{nt}}{q_{1t} \times p_{11} + q_{2t} \times p_{21} + \cdots + q_{nt} \times p_{n1}}.$$

$$\text{CPC (chained price index)} = \frac{q_{1t} \times p_{1t} + q_{2t} \times p_{2t} + \cdots + q_{nt} \times p_{nt}}{q_{1t} \times p_{1,t-1} + q_{2t} \times p_{2,t-1} + \cdots + q_{nt} \times p_{n,t-1}}.$$

We now turn to some numerical examples to see how these indexes differ during periods of high and low inflation.

Case #1: High inflation

	Year 1	Year 2	Year 3
Apples	2,000 @ $1	1,800 @ $1.15	1,600 @ $1.30
Computers	1 @ $1,000	1.25 @ $1,000	1.5 @ $1,000
Medical care	20 @ $100	20 @ $120	20 @ $140

$$\text{CPI, year 2} = 0.4 \times \frac{1.15}{1.00} + 0.2 \times \frac{1,000}{1,000} + 0.4 \times \frac{120}{100} = 1.14.$$

$$\text{CPI, year 3} = 0.4 \times \frac{1.30}{1.00} + 0.2 \times \frac{1,000}{1,000} + 0.4 \times \frac{140}{100} = 1.28.$$

The rate of inflation in the second year is 14%; the rate of inflation in the third year is 12.3%.

$$\text{IPC, year 2} = \frac{1,800 \times 1.15 + 1.25 \times 1,000 + 20 \times 120}{1,800 \times 1.00 + 1.25 \times 1,000 + 20 \times 100} = \frac{5,720}{5,050} = 1.133.$$

$$\text{IPC, year 3} = \frac{1,600 \times 1.30 + 1.5 \times 1,000 + 20 \times 140}{1,600 \times 1.00 + 1.5 \times 1,000 + 20 \times 100} = \frac{6,380}{5,100} = 1.251.$$

The rate of inflation as measured by the IPC is 13.3% in the second year and 10.4% in the third year. Note in particular that the difference between the inflation rate as measured by the CPI and the IPC is 1.9% in the third year, substantially more than 0.7% in the second year. Generally, this difference grows over time.

continued

CASE STUDY 3.1 (*continued*)

The rate of inflation for the CPC, the chain-weighted average, is the same as the IPC in the second year, because the previous year is also the base year. For the third year we have:

$$\text{CPC, year 3 over year 2} = \frac{1{,}600 \times 1.30 + 1.5 \times 1{,}000 + 20 \times 140}{1{,}600 \times 1.15 + 1.5 \times 1{,}000 + 20 \times 120}$$

$$= \frac{6{,}380}{5{,}740} = 1.111.$$

Thus in the third year, the rate of inflation as measured by the CPI is 12.3%, by the IPC is 10.4%, and by the CPC is 11.1%. The CPC is probably the best measure of inflation; by any measure, the inflation rate is uncomfortably high during these years.

We now turn to the low-inflation scenario, where the relevant data are as follows:

Case #2: Low inflation

	Year 1	Year 2	Year 3
Apples	2,000 @ $1	1,800 @ $1.03	1,600 @ $1.06
Computers	1 @ $1,000	1.25 @ $900	1.5 @ $800
Medical care	20 @ $100	20 @ $107	20 @ $114

Using the above formulas and performing the indicated arithmetic, we find that:

Inflation rate	Year 2	Year 3
CPI	2.0	1.6
IPC	1.4	−0.1
CPC	1.4	0.7

In this case, we don't know whether the price level is rising or falling in year 3, although the chain-weighted average inflation rate of 0.7% is once again the best measure. Note that if computer prices continued to decline at 10% or more per year, the IPC would decline by ever-increasing amounts in future years. That is one of the main reasons why the BEA switched from using implicit deflators to chain-weighted deflators in 1995.

3.3   Could the inflation rate be understated?

From the above comments, it might seem obvious that the CPI overstates the actual rate of inflation. Before 1994, that was clearly the case. However, the BLS has now implemented most of the recommendations of the Boskin Commission. In an effort not to overstate the actual rate of inflation, it is possible that government statisticians have put several changes in place that now have the net effect of *understating* the rate of inflation.

Inflation is likely to be overstated when shifts in the market basket of goods and services are not correctly recorded, when quality improvements are understated or ignored, or when new products and services are not introduced into the price index in a timely fashion. These are all relevant factors, and since 1994 all of them have been addressed by the BLS. Following the same logic, inflation might be understated if consumers increase the proportion of their income spent on more expensive goods and services, if quality deteriorates instead of improves, and if the BLS fails to measure the price increases that are actually occurring. Also, the CPI could exclude or underweight the price of items that are rising more rapidly than the average rate of inflation. In recent years, the major culprit in this category has been medical care costs.

The weights of each of the individual components of the CPI are designed to equal the relative importance of each category of goods and services in the average market basket. In most cases, that is indeed the case. However, the one glaring exception to that rule is medical care. In 2000, the NIPA data show that medical care represented 17.5% of total consumption. Yet the weight of this category in the CPI is only 5.8%, or about one-third of the actual proportion. The discrepancy arises because most healthcare services are covered by insurance. Yet directly or indirectly, the consumer pays the bill.

If medical care costs rose at the same rate as other prices, this discrepancy would not be serious. Yet medical care costs are rising much faster than the rest of the CPI. Furthermore, and even more serious, the BLS understates the actual increase in medical care costs. Finally, the BLS methodology has been revised to capture the shift from higher-priced name-brand prescriptions to lower-priced generic drugs, but does not measure the shift when someone loses their health insurance and must pay much higher prices for the same prescriptions.

In 2001, according to the BLS, medical care costs rose 4.7%, while expenditures on medical care rose 6.5%. After adjusting for more intensive use of medical care and the general aging of the population, those numbers seem consistent. At the beginning of 2002, though, many large medical insurers announced price increases ranging from 12% to 20%, yet that increase was not reflected in the BLS statistics.

Suppose someone shifts from a branded prescription that costs $70 per month to its generic equivalent that costs $20 per month. That is a decrease in the CPI, and is correctly measured by the BLS. Now suppose, however, that no generic equivalent of that drug is yet available. The patient has been paying a $10 per month co-payment through health insurance, which is then canceled, which means he must now pay $70 per month for the same drug. That is a substantial increase in the CPI, but that shift is *not* measured by the BLS.

Taking all these factors into consideration, the reported contribution of medical care costs to the overall CPI was inflation during 2001 was 0.058 times 4.7%, or 0.27%. However, the actual amount spent on medical care was 17.5%

of consumption. Hence medical care costs actually contributed about 0.82% to the inflation rate in 2001, which means the official figure published by the BLS understated inflation by more than 0.5%, ceteris paribus.

The other area in which reported inflation is understated is housing costs. In the short run, the price of a house does not provide the best measure of housing costs, since it implies that someone who just bought a house would have much higher costs than someone who has lived in an identical house for many years. Just because the title changes hands on a given house should not boost the CPI. Because of this issue, the BLS attempts to measure how much the house would rent for if in fact it were rented out to the occupants instead of owned by them. That measure is not without its flaws, but need not be biased either up or down.

While these two series do not necessarily agree in the short run, over the long run, the rate of increase in the CPI for owner-occupied housing should be roughly equivalent to the rate of increase in housing prices. However, over the 1992–2001 decade, the median sales price of existing homes rose 4.2% per year, compared to a 3.2% increase in the shelter component of the CPI. Since that component accounts for 30% of the total CPI, that error would understate the actual rate of inflation by 0.3% per year.

Taking these two factors into consideration, the current inflation rate could be understated by as much as 0.8% per year. Even if some of the criticisms of the Boskin Commission that have not been fixed by the BLS remain valid, the current understatement of inflation is probably at least 0.5% per year. This understatement occurs in services; the CPI for goods is now adjusted properly for continuing quality improvement and the introduction of new goods.

MANAGER'S BRIEFCASE: INTERPRETING AND USING THE INFLATION DATA

As a manager, you want to track how fast your prices and costs are rising relative to the national average. In particular, you do not want to be paying more for materials and supplies if your competitors are paying less. Also, you want to be alert to changing trends in inflation. By the time these trends are reflected in the CPI, it is often too late to take appropriate action.

Although the CPI is by far the most widely quoted index of inflation, it actually provides very little information for managing your business. About 30% of the CPI consists of shelter and rental housing costs, based on a survey that is widely believed to be inaccurate. As noted above, the increases in medical care costs are far understated compared to the increases your company has actually faced in recent years for employee medical care benefits.

Moreover, the monthly changes in the CPI do not provide very much information. These changes are heavily influenced by changes in prices of motor vehicles due to sales promotions, and changes in cigarette prices. They are also dominated by changes in food and energy prices. For this reason, most economists look at what is known as the *core inflation rate* – the CPI excluding changes in food and energy prices. The concept of the core rate would be improved by excluding cigarette prices, but the BLS has not yet made this adjustment. Over the long run, this series contains the same biases discussed above, but monthly changes in the core rate provide a better approximation to increases in the cost of living paid by consumers, albeit with the caveats given in the previous section.

continued

MANAGER'S BRIEFCASE (*continued*)

Yet the PPI provides more valid information about price and cost trends for managers; data are found at www.bls.gov/ppi/home.htm. Here again, when examining monthly or quarterly changes, most economists look at the core PPI, which excludes food and energy prices. However, monthly changes in that series are also dominated by fluctuations in the prices of motor vehicles and cigarettes.

The BLS prepares estimates of inflation for three stages of production for the PPI: finished goods, intermediate goods, and crude goods and materials. For purposes of identifying emerging trends in inflation, the most useful measure is the *core PPI for intermediate goods*. That is the best single indicator of price pressures on manufactured products, and is free from the distortions of monthly changes due to promotions, or the steady downward trend in computer prices. Also, because cigarette prices are not an intermediate good, those changes do not distort the monthly changes in this index.

The BLS also publishes price data for thousands of individual commodities. Most of these series are not included in the published monthly reports but are available on the BLS website. These can be quite useful, but contain two major drawbacks. First, most of them are not seasonally adjusted, so you have to be careful in determining whether a reported change represents a movement in the underlying price, or simply a normal seasonal pattern. Second, the BLS data usually represent list rather than transactions prices. During periods of economic slack, many firms will hold the list price at its previous levels but offer hidden discounts in terms of delivery charges, finance charges, partial shipments of large lots, and other givebacks. Hence the fact that the list price remains stable during a period of recession does not imply that you, as a manager, should not be receiving a more favorable price.

3.4   Different measures of unemployment

There are several different theoretical measures of unemployment, which can be described as seasonal, frictional, cyclical, and structural unemployment. The BLS also publishes six different rates of unemployment, although only one of them receives much publicity. We first discuss these various measures of unemployment, then turn to the concept and measurement of the full employment rate of unemployment.

- **Seasonal unemployment** includes those workers who are routinely laid off at the same time every year. Examples of seasonal unemployment include schoolteachers who don't work in the summer, construction employees who don't work in the winter, retail sales clerks who are laid off after Christmas, and so on. Most of the unemployment data are seasonally adjusted, and this type of unemployment is generally ignored by economists.
- **Frictional unemployment** occurs when people are between jobs, but expect to find new employment shortly. Even during the peak years of World War II, when there was a severe labor shortage, the unemployment rate averaged 1.7%.
- **Cyclical unemployment** occurs when employees are fired because of a recession, but are likely to regain their jobs when business improves again. While some government programs are directed at reducing structural unemployment, most broad-based monetary and fiscal policies are aimed at reducing cyclical unemployment.

- **Structural unemployment** applies to those people whose skills are no longer needed in the job market. For example, 55-year-old former steelworkers were not able to find similar employment after the number of employees in that industry fell by two-thirds during the 1980s. In other cases, people do not have the required intelligence or training to learn new skills, or they choose to live in areas of the country where there are few job opportunities. These people whose skills do not match current job vacancies are considered part of structural unemployment.

Since it would be extremely difficult, and also quite contentious, for the BLS to prepare empirical estimates for each of these four categories, it approaches the task in such a way that provides empirical estimates for six different classifications of unemployment, as follows:

- Long-term unemployed, 15 weeks or more. If someone can't find a job in 15 weeks, the presumption is that a prolonged bout of unemployment is more than frictional.
- Job losers and those who completed temporary jobs. This *excludes* people who quit their jobs, those who never had a job before, and those who dropped out of the labor force. Getting fired is a more serious social issue than becoming unemployed because you walked off your last job.
- Those who say they are looking for work but have been unable to find employment. This is the most common unemployment rate, and also the one usually quoted when people talk about "the" unemployment rate; it is often called the "official" rate.
- The official rate plus "discouraged workers" who have dropped out the labor force because they couldn't find a job, but would take one if it were available.
- The official rate plus discouraged workers plus "marginal workers," who are not looking for work because they cannot afford a baby-sitter, no jobs are available in their neighborhood, or they cannot afford the bus fare to the suburbs – but would work if some job were available without these hurdles.
- All of the above, plus employees working part time for economic reasons.

The official unemployment rate is higher than the long-term unemployment rate and the unemployment rate for job losers, but is well below the rates that include people who are not looking for work but would do so if conditions were more favorable. As the economy returned to full employment during the 1990s, the latter three rates become relatively less important.

The official unemployment rate – the one reported in the headlines when the *Employment and Earnings* reports are released – is disaggregated by the BLS into four categories: job losers, job leavers, new entrants to the labor force, and reentrants, as shown in figure 3.2. The unemployment rate for job leavers, new entrants, and reentrants does not change very much. Most of the change in the official unemployment rate occurs in the rate for job losers.

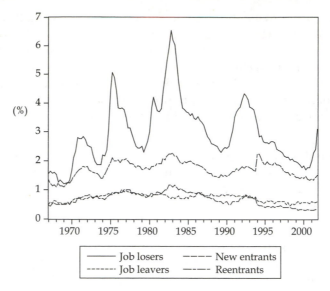

Figure 3.2   Percent unemployed by economic function
Source: BLS website, www.bls.gov/cps/home.htm (cps stands for current population survey)

The Duration of Unemployment

From both a theoretical and practical viewpoint, it is important to measure not only the number of people out of work, but the median time it takes them to find a new job. If, for example, the unemployment rate was 10% but it took people only a few days to find another job, the unemployment situation would be far less serious than if it took them an average of six months to find another job.

For this reason, economists also look at the median duration of unemployment, as measured in weeks. For many years, this series was closely correlated with the overall unemployment rate. However, since 1991 there has been a marked dichotomy, as shown in figure 3.3. While the unemployment rate in 2000 declined to the lowest levels since 1969, the median duration of unemployment remained fairly high. That could be one of the reasons why inflation did not accelerate at full employment: workers realized it would take them several weeks to find a new job, so they were less likely to risk leaving their current job in search of higher wages.

3.5   Collecting the employment and unemployment data

Employment – and unemployment – might seem to be relatively easy concepts to measure: just count the number of people who are employed, and those who are not employed but are looking for work. However, that raises questions about what "looking for work" means. Does that mean potential employees will accept any type of job, or only the type of job they previously held? It should matter

Figure 3.3   Unemployment rate compared to median weeks of unemployment
Source: BLS website, www.bls.gov

whether people are working part time because they want to, or because they can't find a full-time job. There is also the issue of how to count former rocket scientists laid off because of Defense Department cutbacks who are now driving taxicabs, or white-collar executives laid off by IBM or GE who now hang out their own shingles but actually have very little business.

From a statistical viewpoint, the BLS uses two different survey methods to collect employment data. One is called the payroll survey, and is based on reports from businesses. That method measures employment, but not unemployment. The other is called the household survey, and is based on data collected from 60,000 individual households each month. Members of the household are asked if they are employed; and, if not, whether they are seeking work. If that is the case, people are also asked how long they have been unemployed and why they left their previous job.

The household surveys are the sole source of the unemployment numbers. However, data for employment are collected from both the payroll and household surveys, and often yield different information about how much employment has changed over the past month or year. People who work two jobs are counted once in the household but twice in the payroll survey. Thus in a period when an increasing proportion of the labor force has two jobs, the payroll survey would show a more rapid increase in jobs than the household survey. Even so, the payroll data for employment are considered to be much more reliable than the household data for employment, which are usually ignored. When the *Employment and Earnings* report is released each month, both the change in employment measured by the payroll survey and the unemployment rate make the headlines, but the change in employment measured by the household survey usually isn't even mentioned.

The BLS "Fudge Factor"

In addition to this conceptual problem, the BLS also finds it necessary to make ad hoc adjustments each month to the payroll employment figures it reports. During the late 1990s, the actual number of people employed, as calculated from a more thorough survey taken each March, averaged more than half a million more than the number of employed reported on a monthly basis.

The BLS is well aware of the fact that its survey will never be able to include all the new start-up ventures on a timely basis. Thus after the change in payroll employment figures have been collected and calculated, the BLS adds a "fudge factor" to take into account all the workers they missed. This factor is not trivial; it is often around 150,000 per month, compared to an average monthly increase in employment of 150,000 to 200,000. For the first eight months of 2002, the adjustment factors were (in thousands) −184, 51, 97, 176, 221, 203, 44, and 114. Note in particular how much this series jumps around from month to month, and keep that in mind before placing too much emphasis on a change of +50 or −50 thousand in the monthly payroll employment figures. This figure is not well advertised, although it's not a secret; it is also available on the BLS website. The address is similar to the other BLS websites; this one is www.bls.gov/ces/home.htm. Go to the "benchmark" section and scroll down to the last item, which is called "bias adjustment and net birth/death model."

We are not suggesting that using an adjustment factor is a mistake. Indeed, in the early 1990s, the benchmark survey taken each March revealed that the BLS adjustment for the previous year, even though quite substantial, had been too small. Thus if the BLS had not used any adjustment factor in recent years, the employment figures would have understated the actual gain by a far greater amount. Our point is that the monthly employment figures, which are presented and analyzed in great detail, are nothing more than educated guesses. Also, during times of recession, employment may be falling more quickly than the estimates, since they are apt to include a fudge factor based on the previous full-employment situation.

Initial Unemployment Claims

Every Thursday (except in some weeks with holidays), the BLS publishes the number of initial unemployment claims, along with the number of people currently receiving unemployment insurance payments. That does not cover the entire labor force: on average, only about one-third to a half of those who are unemployed actually receive benefits. In particular, those who have not been previously employed are not eligible for benefits. The data for initial claims are not found on the BLS website; instead, they are at www.dol.gov. Scroll down the opening page to "latest numbers" and click on "unemployment initial claims."

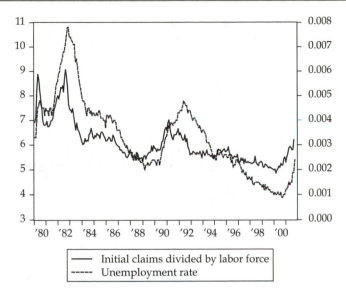

Figure 3.4   Changes in initial claims generally lead changes in the unemployment rate by several months
Sources: DOL website, www.dol.gov; BLS website, www.bls.gov

The key figure in the initial claims report is the number of people who have newly filed for unemployment during the past week. This is widely regarded as a valid leading indicator, and provides useful information about whether labor markets are improving or deteriorating. Because the weekly numbers are erratic, most economists focus on the four-week moving average of initial claims. Figure 3.4

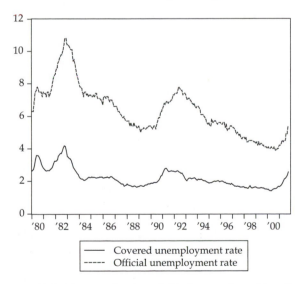

Figure 3.5   Only about one-third of the unemployed are eligible for unemployment benefits
Sources: DOL website, www.dol.gov; BLS website, www.bls.gov

shows how the monthly average of initial unemployment claims generally leads changes in the unemployment rate by several months, especially at turning points. For this reason, a quick perusal of the Thursday data provide managers with a useful snapshot of emerging labor market conditions. Figure 3.5 shows the comparison between the covered unemployment rate and the total unemployment rate.

MANAGER'S BRIEFCASE: HOW TO INTERPRET THE EMPLOYMENT AND UNEMPLOYMENT DATA

The *Employment and Earnings* report, which is generally issued by the BLS on the first Friday of each month, is considered the most important monthly economic indicator. Although two different measures of employment are given – the household and payroll survey – short-term changes in the household data are usually ignored. The unemployment rate is also considered an important political indicator, but it generally lags behind the changes in payroll employment by a month or two.

While the "headline" number gives the total change in employment, the change in private sector employment is more relevant. Seasonally adjusted government employment moves up or down depending on factors such as when school vacations start and stop, which has nothing to do with how rapidly the economy is growing. Because of the quality of the data, the change in manufacturing employment is usually considered the most reliable short-term indicator.

One well-worn rule of thumb in labor markets data states that the length of the workweek is a leading indicator, employment is a coincident indicator, and the unemployment rate is a lagging indicator. Hence it might be thought that hours worked per week would provide some advance indication of where the economy is heading. To a certain extent that is true for the manufacturing workweek, especially the series for overtime hours in durable goods. However, the data for hours worked in the nonmanufacturing sector are too erratic to be meaningful on a short-term basis.

A little-followed but nonetheless useful measure of employment is the diffusion index, found near the end of the report. That measures the percentage of industries reporting an increase in employment. Thus, for example, if employment declined sharply because of a major strike but most industries continued to post employment gains, that would present a stronger picture for the economy than if almost all industries showed a slight decline in employment. Diffusion indexes are calculated for the total economy and for the manufacturing sector.

Most of the additional measures of the unemployment rate do not provide much independent information about the current state of the economy. The average duration of unemployment serves as a measure of the strength or weakness of labor markets, and can have an important impact on the longer term rate of inflation. On a month to month basis, though, the number jumps around in an erratic fashion. Similarly, the percentage of job leavers relative to job losers does not provide much further elucidation about labor markets beyond the information provided by the overall unemployment and employment statistics.

A look at the Thursday figures on initial unemployment claims, with particular emphasis on the four-week moving average of claims, will generally provide useful information about where labor markets are headed in the

continued

near future, and whether the unemployment rate is likely to rise or fall over the next few months. By comparison, the unemployment rate itself is a lagging indicator, and in spite of its important political ramifications does not usually tell managers very much about where the economy will be heading.

CASE STUDY 3.2   DIFFERENCES IN PAYROLL AND HOUSEHOLD MEASURES OF EMPLOYMENT

Figure 3.6 shows the four-quarter percentage changes in employment as measured by the payroll and household surveys. The differences fall into the following categories:

1. Payroll employment always rises more during booms, and falls more during recessions, than household employment. That reflects the fact that people are more likely to have two jobs during boom periods. It also probably reflects the fact that more undocumented aliens are likely to come into the US and take jobs during boom periods; in general, those would be missed by the household survey.
2. During the Korean and Vietnam Wars, payroll employment rose much more sharply than during other boom periods. That indicates a greater proportion of the workforce took second jobs during those periods.
3. In the last two recessions, the difference between the two series has narrowed – but during the 1990s, payroll employment grew much faster than household employment. Hence these extra jobs were not part-time jobs that disappeared during the recessions. For that reason it seems likely that they were filled by foreign workers, who may have entered the country illegally or may have entered legally but maintained their residence in a foreign country, most probably Mexico. Since these workers are not counted in the household survey, that suggests the actual rise in unemployment during the past two recessions was greater than indicated by the official statistics.

The conclusions that managers should draw from these different measures of employment are (a) during booms, job creation is overstated because many people take two jobs, and (b) during recessions, the actual rise in unemployment is understated, because many foreign workers are not counted in the ranks of the unemployed.

continued

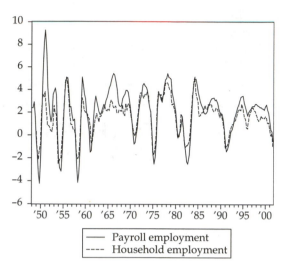

Figure 3.6   Four-quarter percentage changes in employment as measured by the payroll and household survey methods
Source: BLS website, www.bls.gov

3.6   The concept of full employment

Full employment is an elusive concept. The common-sense definition is that the economy is at full employment when anyone who wants to work can find a job. Technically, many countries define full employment as occurring when the number of job vacancies equals the number of people seeking jobs. However, this definition is not used in the US because data on job vacancies are not collected, although they are available for most other industrialized nations.

Full employment is obviously not zero unemployment. There will always be some people who are between jobs, who have just entered the labor force and have not yet found employment, or who are reentering the labor force. These types of unemployment are usually considered frictional unemployment, which is usually thought to be about 2%.

One of the principal dilemmas in defining full employment can be illustrated by the following example. Suppose someone used to receive a $100,000 salary as a middle manager, but because of downsizing, his skills are no longer required. The only available opportunities are earning $25,000 as a real estate or used car salesman or becoming a self-employed consultant. If the former employee refuses to take these jobs – which are available – is he unemployed? According to the BLS definition, yes. At least initially, the former manager would reject these relatively low-paying opportunities in hopes of obtaining a comparable position to his previous job. However, if the search remains fruitless for a year or more, that individual would probably either accept a low-paying job or drop out of the labor force. In either case he would no longer be counted as unemployed.

The situation was different in the Great Depression, when the unemployment rate remained above 15% for an entire decade; many unemployed people found there were no jobs available at any wage. When the economy is near full employment, however, some jobs are usually available, even if the pay is lower than desired and job conditions are not deemed optimal. In general, we will interpret the phrase "anyone who wants a job can eventually find one" to mean that after a while, unemployed people will either accept a suboptimal job or quit looking for work altogether.

Full Employment: Not a Fixed Rate

Even given this definition, full employment for the overall economy does not necessarily mean that full employment exists in all industries, all regions, or all demographic classifications. In July 1999, the overall unemployment rate for the US economy was 4.3%, which is full employment – if not overfull employment – by virtually anyone's definition. Yet the unemployment rate ranged from 2.3% in the financial services industry to 8.9% in agriculture, from 2.4% in South Dakota to 6.5% in West Virginia, and from 2.3% for married men, spouse present, to 30.8% for black male teenagers. Hence full employment may exist in one industry but not another, one region of the country but not another, one age cohort but not another, or one race but not another. Full employment is not an either/or situation.

Differences in measurement also occur across borders. In the US, someone who enters the labor force for the first time and is looking for work is considered unemployed. In Japan, however, people are not counted as unemployed unless they have previously been gainfully employed. Hence the published unemployment rate in Japan will always be lower than in the US for the same actual rate of unemployment because new entrants – who generally have a much higher unemployment rate – are not counted.

There will always be a "shortage" of 1,500 yard running backs or 20-game-winning pitchers, and, unless educational standards change dramatically, there will always be a surplus of people with insufficient skills to hold a steady job. When demand shifts, unemployed auto or steel workers may end up as waiters or taking orders for TVs at Wal-Mart. Middle and even senior managers whose jobs are terminated may have to become salesmen or hang out their own shingle. In non-recession years, there will invariably be a shortage of trained workers in rapidly growing industries, and a surplus of workers in shrinking industries.

We have listed some of the reasons why economists differ on which rate of unemployment represents full employment. However, even if there were general agreement with the statement that full employment exists when the number of people looking for work equals the number of job vacancies, that still would not imply that the full-employment rate of unemployment (full-N rate) has remained unchanged over time.

Determinants of the Full-Employment Unemployment Rate

In the late 1990s, many economists agreed that the full-N rate in the US economy was near 4%. However, in the 1980s and early 1990s, most of these same economists agreed it had risen to 6%. By 2000, they agreed it had fallen to 4% again. How are these numbers chosen? Why have they fluctuated between 4% and 6% over the past 50 years? And why did the full-N rate fall so much during the 1990s?

The three major factors that determine the full-N rate, as opposed to the actual unemployment rate, are demographic factors, the underlying growth rate of productivity, and government programs that encourage or discourage people to look for work. Thus the full-N rate in the US fell from 6% to 4% during the 1990s because the proportion of young workers in the labor force declined, the long-term underlying growth rate of the economy improved, and the 1996 decision to "end welfare as we know it" encouraged more people to look for work.

This situation can be compared to the labor market in continental western Europe, where the unemployment rate in the late 1990s was above 10%. Yet there is no great clamor for jobs among the unemployed in Europe. They receive adequate unemployment and welfare benefits. Because of sluggish growth, few new jobs are created each year, but apparently almost everyone who wants a job has one. Is 10% then the full-N rate for Europe?

Some economists would argue that must be true, for otherwise the unemployed would eventually find jobs. Temporary unemployment may last for a year or two while a search takes place, but eventually all those who want to work will presumably find jobs, even if at lower wages than their previous employment. However, it is more likely that people do not have jobs because inappropriate government policies have reduced the growth rate to the point where the economy can no longer provide the requisite number of jobs consistent with full employment. The fact that these people are reduced to living off the dole does not imply they would rather not be working.

Why does this matter? Because, as we will see later, if the unemployed really would prefer to work, then government policies that boost the growth rate need not be inflationary. On the other hand, if the unemployed are not willing to work, then policies that boost the growth rate would be inflationary, and hence ultimately self-defeating. To a certain extent, that decision will be influenced by the relative attractiveness of unemployment benefits.

The risk of boosting inflation by offering more jobs has been far overstated, and need not occur if credible monetary and fiscal policies are established and maintained, financial markets are transparent, and new technological advances are encouraged. Unemployment benefits are designed as a safety net for those temporarily out of work, not as a way of life. Thus countries where unemployment rates remain near the double-digit range for an extended period of time suffer from suboptimal macroeconomic policies and interference with labor markets.

Even if the government actively pursues full-employment policies, though, the full-N rate is not a static number. During wartime, young men (and today, young

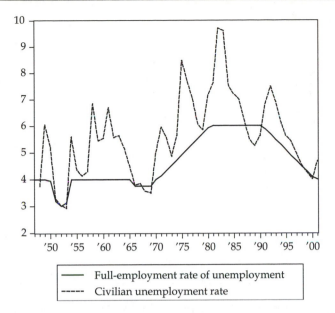

Figure 3.7   The full-N rate of unemployment does not fluctuate as much as the actual rate, but it does not remain fixed either

Sources: Author's calculations; BLS website, www.bls.gov

women) who would ordinarily enter the civilian labor force join the armed forces instead. Since the unemployment rate for younger workers is larger than for the rest of the labor force, an increase in the proportion of people serving in the armed forces reduces the full-N unemployment rate. In some circumstances, these people are killed or permanently injured in battle, causing an acute labor shortage after the war, which reduces the full-N rate for many years. That is what happened in Europe in the 1950s and 1960s. Conversely, a big jump in the percentage of high school and college graduates entering the labor force for the first time causes the full-N rate to rise for a while, since it usually takes longer for first-time employees to find a job.

Figure 3.7 shows the comparison of the actual and full-N unemployment rates for the US since 1948. Note in particular that the full-N rate dipped during the Korean and Vietnam Wars, rose sharply during the 1970s, and then declined again in the 1990s.

Figure 3.8 shows the relationship between the full-N rate and the proportion of new entrants in the labor force (shown here as 20–30 year olds). The correlation is not particularly strong because other factors influence the full-N rate. However, it does show that when the proportion of young people in the labor force rose in the 1970s, the full-N rate also rose; when that proportion declined in the late 1980s and 1990s, it fell.

Figure 3.9 shows the average three-year growth rate of the US economy compared to the full-N rate. When the economy slowed down in the 1970s, the full-N rate rose, and when the growth rate recovered in the 1990s, it fell.

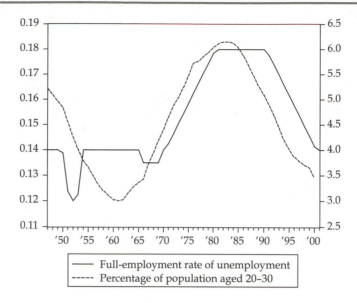

Figure 3.8 The full-N unemployment rate is positively correlated with the proportion of the population aged 20–30
Source: Population data, BLS website, www.bls.gov

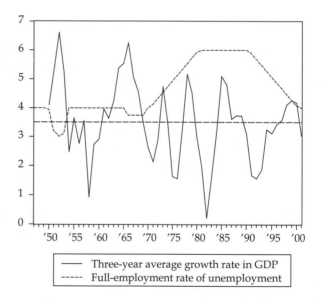

Figure 3.9 When the economy grows faster than average for an extended period of time, the full-N rate drops; when growth is below average, it rises

Suppose the economy has recently emerged from a recession and is now growing rapidly. When demand increases faster than the long-term underlying growth rate (which has been $3\frac{1}{2}$% for the US economy since 1947), the actual unemployment rate falls. If this situation persists long enough, eventually the unemployment rate will drop to the full-N rate. However, as we have seen, that rate is not a fixed number. If the economy has grown very rapidly in the meantime, the unemployment rate may decline to a very low level before the full-N rate is reached because the increase in capital stock and technology has created many new jobs. Yet if the economy has remained sluggish, and there are few job opportunities, the full-N rate could occur at a much higher level of unemployment.

3.7   Unit labor costs

Unit labor costs (ULC) are defined as total compensation paid to employees divided by **productivity**, which in turn is defined as output per employee-hour. Most managers would agree that bigger wage gains must be tied to bigger productivity gains. By the same token, large increases in compensation are appropriate to retain valued employees if their productivity has risen substantially.

None of this comes as any surprise. However, in practice, the measurement of productivity – and unit labor costs – at the macroeconomic level has proven to be an elusive quarry. There are severe problems due to changing mix. Furthermore, in some cases, such as financial services, government statisticians are not able to measure productivity properly. For example, if a bank installs an ATM machine, thus freeing bank personnel to undertake tasks other than dispensing bills of various denominations to their customers, it should be clear that productivity has risen; however, as measured by government statisticians, it has fallen.[3] For this reason, productivity figures are also published excluding the financial service sector.

Thus while most managers know precisely what their labor costs are, it is not straightforward to measure them for the entire economy. In fact, the BLS publishes three different measures of labor compensation per hour. The first measure is average hourly earnings for production workers. That is the most straightforward but suffers from several defects. First, it does not adjust for overtime hours or interindustry mix. Thus, for example, if relatively highly paid auto workers went on strike, average hourly earnings would decline even if no one received a pay cut. Second, it applies only to production workers, not white-collar workers or management. Third, it does not include fringe benefits. Fourth, it does not include bonuses, profit-sharing, or payments of stock options.

As a result, the BLS also publishes two other series for labor compensation. One is the *employment cost index* (ECI), which should reflect all but the last of these factors, and the other, which is the most comprehensive, is simply known as compensation per hour. It is this figure that is combined with estimates of productivity growth to generate the data for unit labor costs. While the overall trends of these three series are similar, the quarterly and annual differences can be quite substantial, as shown in figure 3.10.

All three series are on the BLS website. The first is at www.bls.gov/lpc/home.htm, the second is at www.bls.gov/ces/home.htm, and the third is at www.bls.gov/eci/home.htm.

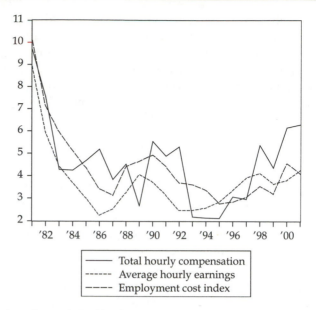

Figure 3.10 Percentage changes in total hourly compensation, average hourly earnings for production workers, and employment cost index for all private sector employees
Source: BLS website, www.bls.gov

From the viewpoint of economic policy and forecasting, the key variable ought to be ULC rather than total hourly compensation costs. If workers receive unusually large gains that are nonetheless matched by corresponding gains in productivity, inflation will not rise, and the economy can continue to expand and prosper. On the other hand, if wage gains outstrip the increase in productivity, either inflation will rise or profits will decline. For this reason one might naturally assume that the ULC figures are followed very closely. Yet they are almost completely ignored in the business press and by economists generally. Considering the very substantial gains to be made by following the economy closely and understanding what lies ahead, there must be a good reason why. Nonetheless, these data do contain some valuable information – otherwise we would not discuss them here at all.

In terms of timing, the productivity release – which contains the ULC data – is published well after the underlying information on output and wages has been released, so in that sense it does not capture the hearts and minds of financial analysts. However, the lack of interest is caused by a more fundamental reason: short-term measures of productivity are very erratic. For example, the reported figures state that productivity rose at an annual rate of 7.8% in 1999.4, did not increase at all in 2000.1, rose 6.7% in 2000.2, and then increased only 1.6% in 2000.3. Essentially what happened during this period was that real GDP, as reported by the BEA, fluctuated wildly, while employee-hours did not change very much. In economic terms, short-term fluctuations in output were not matched by similarly wide swings in employee-hours. That is indeed a sensible way to manage a company, but as a result the reported short-run fluctuations in productivity are almost meaningless. Some of this problem can be finessed by using four-quarter averages, but many of the underlying problems remain.

What, if anything, can be salvaged from these numbers? Over the long run, for reasons discussed in detail in chapter 10, productivity growth in the US economy has averaged between $1\frac{1}{2}$% and 2% per year. It is possible that during periods of unusually strong growth, a high rate of capital formation, and rapidly developing new technologies, productivity growth might rise to as much as 3% per year, although even those figures are often tainted – or later revised down. It is important to note that if recent gains in labor costs are well above the 3% maximum increase in productivity growth that could reasonably be expected, something is amiss: either inflation is about to take off, or profits are about to plummet. We first look at the 2000 experience in case study 3.3, and then turn to a more general discussion of how managers should use these wage and productivity data.

CASE STUDY 3.3   RISING LABOR COMPENSATION COSTS IN 2000

Figure 3.11 shows the four-quarter percentage changes in the rate of inflation as measured by the CPI and total compensation per hour for the nonfarm business sector. As will be shown in chapter 8, these series usually move together. However, a major divergence occurred from 1997 through 2000. When these data are combined with the information shown in figure 3.10, it becomes apparent that base wage rates for productivity workers did not accelerate very much; almost all of the gains in labor compensation reflected increases in bonuses, profit-sharing, stock options, and other forms of compensation generally granted to management and other white-collar workers.

To be more specific, during the late 1990s, the core rate of inflation did not accelerate at all: it averaged only 2.3% in 1999 and 2000, compared to 2.4% the previous three years. Furthermore, there was no acceleration in average hourly earnings: they rose an average of 3.7% per year in 1999 and 2000, unchanged from their average during the previous three years. To some economists, that all seemed in line: there was no acceleration in either prices or wages. Yet at the very same time, profit growth had come to a halt. After increasing at better than a 12% annual rate from 1992 through 1997, corporate profits posted only slightly better than a 1% annual increase from 1998 through 2000 before plunging a record amount in 2001.

There are several possible reasons for this surge in labor compensation in the late 1990s. Undoubtedly, a decline in the unemployment rate to 4% made it more difficult to attract qualified employees without offering greater incentives. Then too, most of the increase in manufacturing sector jobs occurred in the high-tech

continued

CASE STUDY 3.3 (*continued*)

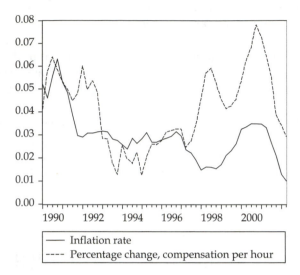

Figure 3.11 Four-quarter percentage changes in the CPI and compensation per hour in the nonfarm business sector
Source: BLS website, www.bls.gov

sector, where employees were attracted by signing bonuses, profit-sharing, and stock options, rather than higher hourly wages. The figures for compensation in many of the service industries were also boosted by these same factors.

Businesses defended these moves on the grounds that when the economy did slow down, they would not be saddled with high fixed labor costs. That sounds like a very sensible argument, yet when the mild recession finally did arrive, the percentage decline in corporate profits was the largest since the Great Depression of the 1930s. Hence corporate planning to keep compensation gains in line with productivity gains failed. That strongly suggests that business managers, especially in the high-tech sector, failed to see the recession developing. Yet a simple look at the chart in figure 3.11 should have convinced some managers that these gains could not continue indefinitely, and some slowdown in the economy was imminent. That discovery presumably would have precluded some of the larger signing bonuses and profit-sharing arrangements that were still being offered in late 2000.

A similar lesson could have been drawn from these data by any competent financial analyst. At the same time, while most economists were applauding the lack of any acceleration in average hourly earnings, more emphasis should have been placed on the figures for total compensation. Since these rose at an unsustainable 8.1% annual rate during the latter three quarters of 2000, at the same time that prices were hardly budging, it should have been clear that profits were
continued

CASE STUDY 3.3 (*continued*)

in for a tremendous shellacking – and stock prices would follow suit. Yet the huge decline in profits and stock prices which occurred in 2001 caught most analysts by surprise. Closer attention to published government data would have resulted in better performance for most financial managers.

MANAGER'S BRIEFCASE: USING THE DATA FOR WAGE AND UNIT LABOR COSTS

From the viewpoint of managers, these different series for labor costs are best used for different purposes. For determining production worker wages for the manufacturing sector, the monthly data on average hourly earnings by two-digit (SIC Code) industry are the most appropriate. For other purposes, though, total hourly compensation provides a more accurate indicator of how much labor is being compensated. Note in particular that the unusually large rise in this series in 2000 corresponded with a sharp drop in corporate profits in the latter half of that year.

Sharp-eyed managers really ought to look askance at an industry to which they sell their product or service if employee compensation is rising twice as fast as the national average. Of course the job is to get the sale, but will those companies be able to pay if their cash flow situation is seriously compromised by overpaying their workers? Even more to the point, does this huge increase in compensation point to a situation in the fairly near future where lower or negative profits will reduce the orders from this industry, which would flash a very strong caution light over the plans for expansion? The economic health of your customers may be just as important as the economic health of your own business.

In determining wage increases for your employees, it is useful to know how much their cost of living has actually increased over the past year, as opposed to what is shown in government reports. Of course, wage gains by workers in other firms and industries are also important, although it usually does not pay to get into a bidding war – as all too many "dot.bust" companies belatedly learned.

Determination of fringe benefits has become an increasingly important part of compensation in recent years. For this reason, it is useful to have a benchmark to compare increases in healthcare costs with those of your competitors. After all, if your healthcare costs were really rising at 5%, and all healthcare insurers insist on quoting increases of 15% per year, it would pay to self-insure. However, it is more likely that your costs are rising at 15% at the same time the government statistics say they are increasing at 5%. To the extent that fringe benefit costs are important, the data for these costs contained in the employment cost index are much more reliable than the CPI data.

In the last analysis, no set of government data releases, no matter how accurate, will automatically make the right decisions for you. Yet it is suboptimal to work in an information vacuum. The figures for average hourly earnings will provide reasonable estimates of how much production worker wage rates are changing in all major industries. The figures for employee costs will provide an accurate assessment of how fast fringe benefit costs are rising. The data for total compensation should alert you to be careful about basing capital expansion plans on sales to industries whose costs are running far ahead of gains in prices or productivity. All these different measures of wage costs can help improve managerial performance.

3.8   Summarizing the economic data: indexes of leading and coincident indicators

Although changes in the economy are important to virtually all business managers, most do not have the time to focus on the economic data in detail. Thus it would be useful to have a shorthand summary of where the economy is at any given time, and where it is likely to be heading in the near future. That is the purpose of the indexes of leading and coincident indicators. A set of lagging indicators is also calculated and published, but these are not generally followed and are not included in the current discussion.

For many years, these indexes were prepared by the Commerce Department, but in 1995, this function was sold to the Conference Board, which continues to issue them on a monthly basis. They are available at www.conference-board.org.[4] The leading indicators receive the most press because they allegedly indicate when the economy is heading into a turning point. For many managers, though, the index of coincident indicators is also useful.

The leading indicators allegedly signal when an upper or lower turning point is about to occur. The list of indicators has changed over time, and hardly any of the components currently in the index were in the original version. This index will be discussed in more detail in chapter 15. Here we confine our comments to the usefulness of this indicator for business managers.

In general, the index of leading indicators never misses a turning point, but gives many false signals. Furthermore, the lag is quite variable: an upturn in the index in any given month might mean the economy will start to improve next month, or it might start to improve six months from now. Thus managers should use this index in conjunction with other economic data. However, they did signal the 2001 recession well ahead of time when many economists and financial analysts were apparently convinced the boom could continue "forever."

The current version of the index of leading indicators contains the following ten components: length of the workweek, initial unemployment claims, new orders for consumer goods, new orders for capital goods, delivery times (vendor performance), building permits, S&P 500 stock price index, real money supply, the yield spread between the 10-year Treasury note yield and the Federal funds rate, and index of consumer expectations. The stock market is the best known of these indicators, but actually has one of the worst track records. The best track record, as we will see, is the yield spread, but the overall index has a better track record at predicting turning points than any single component. This index is discussed in more detail in chapter 15.

The index of coincident indicators consists of four components: total payroll employment, real personal income excluding transfer payments, the index of industrial production, and business sales in constant dollars. It does not receive as much publicity, but provides a useful shorthand method of tracking where the economy is now. In this author's opinion, the index of coincident indicators provided a more accurate guide to the true state of the economy during the 2001 recession than the preliminary GDP data.

In particular, the index of coincident indicators earned peaked in December 2000 and continued to decline throughout 2001, not turning up until January 2002. The US economy was indeed in recession throughout the year. However, the GDP statistics showed a different picture. According to the preliminary data issued throughout 2001, real GDP rose in the first two quarters of the year, and was about to rise in the third quarter before 9/11 temporarily brought the economy to a halt for a few weeks; it then reportedly rose 1.7% in the fourth quarter.

Every July, the BEA issues a comprehensive revision of the NIPA data over the past three years, and, lo and behold, the revised data showed a recession after all. Instead of rising 1.3% in the first quarter, the BEA now decided that it had fallen 0.6%. And instead of rising 0.3% in the second quarter, the BEA decided it had actually fallen 1.6%. These revisions are much larger than the average change, although they are within the range published by the BEA. It is just that when the revision is, say from 6% to 4%, it does not receive nearly as much attention.

Managers, financial analysts, and for that matter macroeconomists ought to have better things to do than complain about the poor quality of the preliminary NIPA data issued by the BEA. The reason for discussing this anomaly is to alert managers to the fact that it is well worth while spending a few minutes checking the index of coincident indicators when they are published every month, and when these data disagree with the preliminary GDP estimates, it is likely that the coincident indicators will provide a more accurate snapshot of what is really happening in the economy.

3.9 Methods and flaws of seasonally adjusted data

Virtually all government economic data, except prices of financial assets, are reported on a seasonally adjusted basis. In fact it would be counterproductive not to adjust the data to reflect these patterns. After all, certain seasonal patterns occur year after year. Some are associated with the weather: people use more heating oil in the winter and air conditioning in the summer. Retail store sales always soar in December. Many manufacturing plants shut down in July or August. Most schools are not in session in the summer, so many students and teachers find summer employment. Few new houses are started in the northern US in January and February.

Since a great deal of emphasis is placed in the change in key economic variables over the previous month or quarter, it makes sense to use statistical methods to extract the repetitive seasonal patterns that occur every year. The resulting seasonally adjusted data provides a much clearer picture of recent changes in economic activity. However, problems arise when seasonal patterns sometimes shift. As a result, the application of past seasonal patterns can provide a distorted picture of where the economy is heading.

While statistical programs used by the government are designed to take this into account, it often takes several years before the shift can be detected. When seasonal adjustment factors change sharply, the resulting "seasonally adjusted" data are likely to provide misleading information. Also, a shift in seasonal patterns cannot continue indefinitely; when seasonal patterns do stabilize, the statistical programs often assume it has continued for several more years. Thus the shift is missed in both directions.

In brief, there are two major methods of seasonal adjustment. The first simply assumes that past patterns will be repeated this year. If, for example, March sales have been 5% above the trend in previous years, it is assumed they will also be 5% above trend this year. The second takes account of previous changes in the seasonal pattern. If over the past five years, March sales have been 5%, 6%, 7%, 8%, and 9% higher than the trend, this method of seasonal adjustment would then assume they would be 10% higher this year. Most government data that are seasonally adjusted incorporate variable factors.

If the seasonal factors are stable, or if they change slowly over time, the method works fairly well. However, there are many cases where that does not occur. For example, when the overall inflation rate used to be higher, many firms, especially in the service sector, raised their prices at the beginning of the year. After a while that pattern was built into the seasonal factors. The rate of inflation then moderated, so the price increases instituted by these firms at the beginning of the year were much smaller. Hence for a while, every January brought "good news" about inflation when the "seasonally adjusted" rate fell sharply. Eventually the BLS fixed this problem.

Over the past few years, Christmas sales have become less concentrated in December. As a result, seasonally adjusted retail stores have incorporated "disappointing" sales for that month in 1995, 1996, 1997, and 1998. However, more consumers now choose to wait until after Christmas markdowns are taken, so sales were reported as unusually strong in January 1996, 1997, 1998, and 1999. We assume Census will eventually fix this problem too.

Financial markets and policy analysis are often based on changes in one or two months of data. Fortunately, the Federal Open Market Committee under Paul Volcker and Alan Greenspan has learned not to jump too quickly. However, the risk still remains that policy might be incorrectly driven by erroneous data – or that the policymakers would base their decisions on inaccurate preliminary estimates of key data series.

No method of seasonal adjustment is without its flaws. For that reason, many managers prefer to compare their sales, costs, profits, and other key variables to year-earlier levels. Nonetheless, since virtually all of the data issued by the government are seasonally adjusted, large changes in seasonally adjusted data that occur when non-seasonally adjusted data do not change very much should be viewed with suspicion.

3.10   Preliminary and revised data

Approximately one month after the end of each quarter, the BEA announces its "advance" estimates of real GDP and inflation. These figures are greeted with great anticipation, and can influence policy decisions. However, these advance estimates consist largely of estimated data. At the time the advance estimates are released, the BEA figures are based on fairly firm data for the first month of each quarter, preliminary data for the second month, and mostly guesses for the third month. As a rough order of magnitude, only about 50% of the data that are used to generate the advance estimates of GDP are actually known.

The BEA acknowledges that these numbers are guesses, and even circulates the estimates of missing data they use to calculate GDP and its components. The alternative, which would be waiting another month or two, would simply encourage private sector forecasters to fill in the blanks. No criticism of the BEA is implied because they use estimates for some of the components of GDP.[5]

Nonetheless, users of these data should be aware these estimates change significantly. According to the BEA, the average error for the percentage change in real GDP between the advance and final estimate is 1.4%. For example, if the advance estimate shows an increase of 3.0% in real GDP, there is a 1 in 3 chance that the final number will be less than 1.6% or more than 4.4%. Managers should keep that in mind when the BEA initially announces that the recession has ended because real GDP rose 0.5% last quarter.

The GDP numbers are a compendium of data collected from other sources: retail sales, inventory stocks, foreign trade data, manufacturers' shipments, construction put in place, and so on. The advance estimates for retail sales are based on a small sample that is only about 10% of the full sample, and hence are subject to larger revisions than most other data. Also, more than 50% of the data used in the initial estimate of industrial production is based on guesswork.

In one well-documented case, the advance estimate of retail sales for May 1995 rose only 0.2%; revised data showed an increase of 0.9%. That caused Alan Blinder, then Vice-Chairman of the Federal Reserve Board, to state that he would not have voted to reduce the Federal funds rate in July 1995 if he had known retail sales were that strong. In this particular case, inflation did not rise, so the Fed ultimately turned out to have made the right decision. Nonetheless, serious errors in advance and preliminary data can lead to policy errors.

There are many other similar examples. In another important case, revised data showed that the 1990–91 recession was about twice as severe as the preliminary data suggested; knowledge of that point probably would have led to earlier Fed easing and a more robust recovery instead of the near-stagnation that occurred for the rest of that year. A similar error by the BEA occurred in underreporting the severity of the 2001 recession, although in that case the Fed eased more rapidly.

The NIPA data are usually rebenchmarked every five years, based on the comprehensive economic censuses taken at that interval. These are not the same as the decennial population censuses, but contain complete enumeration of all firms in manufacturing, agriculture, and services. These data represent the most comprehensive benchmarks for US economic data. Such revisions usually do not alter the quarterly changes very much, but affect the underlying trends.

The change in methodology that introduced the chained deflators in 1995 resulted in a substantial downward revision of previous growth rates. Real growth in 1993 was reduced from 3.1% to 2.2%; growth in 1994 was lowered from 4.0% to 3.5%, and the increase in real GDP for the first half of 1995 was diminished from an annual rate of 1.5% to 0.5%. Hence this one-time change in methodology sliced almost 1% off the growth rate for this $2\frac{1}{2}$ year period. Admittedly, these were one-time changes due to a major switch in methodology that probably will not be repeated for many years. Nonetheless, the profile of how fast the economy was growing was seriously altered by this change in methodology. In October 1999, these growth rates were boosted back to 2.4%, 4.0%, and 1.1%. Further changes are expected in the future.

The main thrust of these comments for managers is that the preliminary government data must generally be greeted with some skepticism, since they are often revised substantially. That certainly does not mean the reports should be ignored, however. If your sales figures are moving in a direction that does not agree with preliminary government data, that might mean your company is gaining or losing market share – or it might mean the data will be revised. Particularly for retail sales and industrial production, it is best to wait at least one additional month before taking any definitive action based on preliminary government data. To track the economy on a monthly or quarterly basis, managers are well advised to focus on the index of coincident indicators rather than the preliminary GDP data.

KEY TERMS AND CONCEPTS

Chained Price Indexes
Coincident Indicators
Consumer Price Index (CPI)
Cyclical Unemployment
Fixed-Weight Price Indexes
Frictional Unemployment
Full Employment
Implicit Price Deflators

Leading Indicators
Producer Price Index (PPI)
Productivity
Seasonal Unemployment
Structural Unemployment
Unit Labor Costs

SUMMARY

- The key numbers describing the overall economy are the growth rate in real GDP and the rise in the price level, not the current dollar level of GDP.

- The government publishes three different types of price indexes: fixed-weight, implicit deflators, and chained price indexes. The fixed-weight index invariably overstates the true rate of inflation, while the implicit deflator understates it if some products have rapidly decreasing prices. The chained price index provides the closest approximation to the true rate of inflation, but has the drawback that the chained-dollar components of GDP do not sum to total real GDP.

- All price indexes may be overstated if they fail to take into account the timely introduction of new products, and the improvement in quality of existing products.

- The Boskin Commission estimated that through 1995, the consumer price index (CPI) overstated the true rate of inflation by an average of 1.1% per year. The Bureau of Labor Statistics (BLS) has implemented most of the Commission recommended changes. Currently, the CPI probably understates the true rate of inflation by 0.5% to 1.0% per year.

- There are four theoretical types of unemployment: seasonal, frictional, cyclical, and structural. Even at full employment, there will always be some seasonal and frictional unemployment in a dynamic capitalist society. Seasonal unemployment is erased by adjusting the data and is not reported.

- The BLS publishes six different measures of unemployment. The "official" rate, which is the one most widely quoted, consists of four categories: job losers, job leavers, new entrants, and reentrants.

- Full employment is not zero unemployment. It is often defined as the rate when the number of people looking for work equals the number of job vacancies, or the rate at which everyone who wants to work can find a job.

- The full-employment rate is not a fixed number, but varies considerably with changes in demographic factors, government policies, and the long-run growth rate. In the US, the full-employment rate of unemployment rose from less than 4% in the early post-WWII period to almost 6% by 1980, and then declined to 4% by the late 1990s.

- The BLS publishes three different estimates of labor costs. The most comprehensive measure, which includes fringe benefits and various types of bonuses, rose much more rapidly in 2000 than indicated by the more common measures of labor costs and inflation.

- Virtually all government data are seasonally adjusted. In some cases, the seasonal patterns will shift over time, so that these data will provide erroneous information about recent changes in underlying data.

- The advance and preliminary data published by various government agencies are subject to substantial revision, and the initial estimates are sometimes far off the mark. That is particularly true for retail sales, industrial production, and real GDP; errors for employment, unemployment, and inflation are usually much smaller.

QUESTIONS AND PROBLEMS

1. Calculate the various measures of inflation for the following data. Assume all price indexes are 100 in Year 1.

Year	1	2	3
College tuition	40 @ $20,000	40 @ $25,000	40 @ $30,000
Apples	300,000 @ $1.25	250,000 @ $1.65	280,000 @ $1.50
Computers	600 @ $1,200	750 @ $1,000	1,000 @ $800

(A) What factors cause the change in the CPI to overstate the actual rise in the cost of living?

(B) What are the differences between the CPI and the implicit deflator for GDP? Which do you think is a better measure of inflation?

(C) What is a chained price deflator? What are the benefits and drawbacks to this measure of inflation?

(D) Calculate the CPI, implicit consumption deflator, and chained price consumption deflator in years (2) and (3) with these data.

(E) What do you think the "actual" rate of inflation was in years (2) and (3)? Explain your answer.

2. (A) How is full employment defined, and why does the full-employment rate of unemployment keep changing?

(B) In December 1998, the BLS reported the following unemployment rates:

1. Unemployed over 15 weeks   1.1%
2. Job losers   2.0%
3. "Official" unemployment rate   4.3%
4. Plus discouraged workers   4.5%
5. Plus marginal workers   5.2%
6. Plus part-time workers   7.5%

Which do you think is the best measure of actual unemployment? Explain your choice.

(C) In 1990, most economists thought the full-employment rate of unemployment was about 6%, but in 2000 they thought it was about 4%. Were they wrong in 1990, or was this change based on economic factors? If so, what factors caused them to change their opinion?

3. Classify the following job losses as seasonal, frictional, cyclical, or structural unemployment – or no change in the unemployment rate at all.

(A) No work for bricklayers in Illinois in February.

(B) GM lays off 50,000 workers after Fed restricts credit.

(C) GM closes plant in Flint, MI; builds new assembly plant in Mexico.

(D) IBM shuts down economic research department.

(E) North Dakota wheat farmers abandon farms after Asian recession reduces worldwide price of wheat.

(F) NBA basketball players locked out by owners.

(G) Firm relocates headquarters from New York to Dallas. Half of staff decides not to accept relocation.

(H) Unnamed fast food chain goes bankrupt after E-coli bacteria poison customers.

(I) High interest rates cut housing starts by 50%, reducing construction employment by 650,000.

(J) Recent June graduates have difficulty finding employment.

4. In 1955, the last year when social security payments included only old-age payment (before disability), payments totaled $4.9 billion. For 2001, the figure was $433 billion (excluding Medicare, which was another $218 billion). During the intervening period, the CPI rose at an average annual rate of 4.2%, and the number of people over 65 rose an average of 2.0% per year. What would social security have been in 2001 if the program had not expanded after 1955 (i.e., if the only increases were due to inflation and population)? Now suppose the CPI had been overstated by 1.1% per year. What would social security payments have been in 2001 if the actual rate of inflation had been used?

5. What are the major causes of error in the preliminary NIPA data, and what could be done to reduce these errors?

6. If economists generally agree that fixed-weight price indexes overstate the actual rate of inflation, why is the CPI still the most popular and widely quoted measure of inflation?

7. What major factor causes the implicit price deflator and the chained price deflator to diverge over time? Under what circumstances would we expect to find very little difference in these two measures of prices?

8. As a manager, one of your responsibilities is to monitor recent changes in inflation. However, the recent statistics appear to be quite confusing. The CPI rose only 0.1%, but the PPI for finished goods increased 0.8%. A further examination of the core rates shows a gain of 0.2% in the CPI and 0.5% in the PPI.

    (A) What further information would be required to determine the underlying rate of inflation?

    (B) Suppose the core rate for the intermediate rate rose 0.1%. How would that affect your answer?

    (C) What other components of the CPI and PPI would you examine closely to try and narrow the discrepancy?

9. In August 2002, preliminary data showed that payroll employment rose 39,000, household employment rose 429,000, and the unemployment rate fell from 5.9% to 5.7%.

    (A) Based on these data, what conclusion would you reach about the current employment situation?

    (B) How would your answer change if you also noted that (a) the unemployment rate for men 20 years and over was unchanged, and (b) the number of initial unemployment claims rose from 386,000 to 398,000?

    (C) How would your answer change if you also noted that the biggest declines in the unemployment rate occurred in (a) teenagers, and (b) experienced wage and salary workers?

    (D) Based on this welter of confusing information – which is not unusual – what conclusions can be drawn about basing business plans on the latest monthly employment and unemployment data?

Notes

1. For a detailed discussion of these issues, see "BEA's Chain Indexes, Time Series, and Measures of Long-Term Economic Growth" in the May 1997 issue of the *Survey of Current Business*.
2. Michael Boskin et al., *Journal of Economic Perspectives*, Winter, 1998.
3. While this seems counterintuitive, the reasoning is as follows. "Output" in the financial service sector is defined as wages plus profits. Productivity is output per employee-hour. Thus if ATM machines replace tellers, wages, and hence "output," have fallen.
4. Because the Conference Board is a private organization, they have no obligation, as does the government, to supply these data free of charge. The reports can be purchased at $500 per year, including historical data. The latest monthly report, however, is always available on their website free of charge.
5. In the late 1970s and early 1980s, the BEA used to prepare a "flash estimate" of GDP based on information available until the last week of any given quarter. Because of the high degree of estimation, this figure was designed only for internal use, but it was widely "leaked" and eventually was issued on a public basis. However, the procedure was flawed enough that it was soon discontinued. At the time it was claimed that private sector economists would fill the void, but that did not happen, and today no one prepares a flash estimate.

part II

Aggregate demand and joint determination of output and interest rates

The most important measures of macroeconomic activity – the level of employment and unemployment, the rate of productivity growth and the standard of living, the rate of inflation, interest rates, equity market prices, and the value of the currency – are determined by the balance between aggregate demand and aggregate supply. The economies of many developing nations are constrained by aggregate supply – the amount that can be produced. Most people in those countries are saddled with a low standard of living because production methods are inefficient, capital is scarce, and employees have not been trained in modern methods. In advanced industrialized societies, though, it is far more often the case that aggregate supply is large enough that everyone who wants to work could be employed, but aggregate demand is weak. The amount that consumers, businesses, governments, and foreign economic agents want to purchase is less than the amount that can be produced with the available supply of labor and capital and the existing degree of technology.

When the imbalance is severe, severe depressions occur, and the institutions of democratic capitalism flounder, as was the case in the 1930s. In the late twentieth and early twenty-first centuries, the imbalances have been much less severe; yet recessions are a recurring factor even in the economies of North America, western Europe, and the advanced economies of East Asia. Most of these countries would be able to sustain a growth rate of at least 3% indefinitely, yet from 1992 through 2002, real growth in Germany averaged only 1.3%, and in Japan averaged only 1.1%. Although the US economy performed far better over this period, it entered a recession in early 2001, and suffered rising unemployment through 2002 even though the growth rate was positive.

Before the Great Depression of the 1930s, most macroeconomists focused on the conditions that maximized aggregate supply; it was generally assumed that demand would follow in its footsteps. During the 1930s, though, the US was unable to find policies that would reduce the unemployment rate below 14%; not until the massive military buildup of World War II did the economy return to full employment.

Since World War II, government policies have been more successful at keeping the economy moving ahead. If consumer spending is faltering, or if capital spending declines, it is generally agreed that tax rates should be cut, interest rates should be reduced, the availability of credit should be enhanced, and the Federal government should spend more to take up some of the slack left by the decline in private sector demand. Sometimes a reduction in the value of the dollar is used to stimulate net exports.

Obviously these methods are not completely successful; if they were, neither the US nor any other industrialized economy would suffer recurring recessions. The tradeoff is clear enough: policy measures that stimulate the economy in the short run are likely to lead to higher inflation and lower productivity in the long run, hence retarding the growth in the standard of living. If the government spends more, but in doing so reduces the incentive for capital spending, the economy will eventually be worse off. Thus a complete answer to how the macro economy functions clearly depends on an explanation of inflation and productivity – in other words, the factors that help determine aggregate supply.

In explaining how the economy works, however, it is necessary to proceed one step at a time. The first logical step is to explore the factors that determine the components of aggregate demand. As shown in chapter 4, consumption depends primarily on real disposable income and the cost and availability of credit. Chapter 5 describes the relationship between investment and national income and the cost and availability of both debt market and equity market capital. The determinants of net exports are also briefly discussed in this chapter; they include the level of domestic income and interest rates, which are an important determinant of the value of the currency.

Because interest rates play such an important role in determining all the key components of aggregate demand, the basic determinants of interest rates are examined in chapter 6, which also includes a brief introduction to the key elements of monetary policy. Chapter 7 then shows how the relationship between aggregate demand and interest rates can be combined into a single diagram, known as the IS/LM diagram, that jointly determines output and real interest rates. Since this diagram assumes a constant price level, it only serves as a stepping stone to an explanation of the interaction between aggregate demand, aggregate supply, interest rates, and inflation. However, it is useful in explaining some of the reasons why stimulative fiscal and monetary policy might not boost the level of aggregate demand, even during periods when the rate of inflation remains low and stable.

chapter four

The consumption function

Introduction

Consumer spending depends on three principal factors. The first is the average or expected income of consumers. The second is the cost and availability of credit. The third reflects the choice between spending and saving: spend more now and less later, or spend less now and more later. That factor is primarily related to the expected rate of return on assets.

Predicting short-term changes in consumer spending is difficult, both for economists and for managers. The 1990 recession started in July of that year, and income growth, stock prices, and consumer sentiment all declined sharply. As a result, total real consumption fell 0.2% over the next five quarters. The 2001 recession started in March of that year, and, again, income growth, stock prices, and consumer sentiment all declined sharply. Yet over the next year, consumption *rose* more than 3%.

Quarterly fluctuations in consumption are quite erratic. Changes in disposable income explain less than a quarter of these fluctuations, and changes in monetary variables – the yield spread, change in the money supply, change in stock prices, and change in consumer credit – explain only another quarter. Thus, on a quarterly basis, over half of the fluctuations in consumer spending are due to exogenous or random factors. This poses a major problem to managers of companies that produce consumer goods, and cannot be explained by the use of traditional economic or attitudinal variables.[1]

As the time horizon lengthens, changes in consumption become more highly correlated with the set of economic variables that includes income, the cost and availability of credit, and asset prices. For example, when the time period is lengthened to one year, about three-quarters of the fluctuations can be explained by these factors, as random events become less important. For a three-year period, about 95% of the changes in consumption can be explained by these variables. Managers must be careful not to overreact to short-term shifts in their own company sales that are likely to be reversed in the next month or quarter, but should be able to develop longer-term plans for consumer behavior.

This chapter blends the explanation of short-term and long-term changes in consumer spending into an overall theory of consumer behavior at the macroeconomic level. All of the factors listed above affect short-term fluctuations in consumption; in the long run, income and demographic factors emerge as the most important determinants. Changes in the cost and availability of credit, on the other hand, are more likely to impact short-term fluctuations in spending decisions.[2]

The determinants of consumption are reviewed in greater detail in section 4.1; in the remainder of the chapter, each factor is considered separately. Section 4.2 discusses the relationship between short-term fluctuations in consumption and income and introduces the concept of the *marginal propensity to consume*. Section 4.3 discusses the relationship between long-term levels of consumption and income, and introduces the concept of the *permanent income hypothesis*. The question of whether the impact of changes in tax rates on consumer spending depend on whether the tax changes are temporary or permanent is analyzed in section 4.4.

Several factors dominate short-term changes in consumer spending. Even if consumers would prefer to base their spending patterns on long-term average or expected income, many of them are subject to short-term liquidity constraints, which are discussed in section 4.5; this section also analyzes the impact of changes in the cost of credit. Section 4.6 shows how a decline in interest rates leads to refinancing of home mortgages and an increase in housing prices, which permits some homeowners to cash out the additional equity; these factors also boost consumption. Section 4.7 discusses the relationship between the expected rate of return on assets and the proportion of income that is saved. Section 4.8 shows that an increase in the ratio of debt to income does not necessarily depress consumer spending.

Turning to the longer-run determinants of consumption, section 4.9 discusses the changes in the consumption/income ratio at different ages in the life cycle, and introduces the concept of the *life cycle hypothesis*. The role of changes in net worth – both equities and homes – is then considered in section 4.10. Because disposable income excludes realized capital gains, and the gains in income that stem from refinancing a home or drawing down increased equity, the concept of *spendable income* and its impact on consumption is also introduced. The role of consumers' attitudes is presented in section 4.11. The effect of all these factors on consumer spending is summarized in section 4.12. The chapter concludes with an appendix that traces the historical development of the consumption function.

4.1   Principal determinants of consumption

What macroeconomic factors determine how much of the goods or services produced by your company will be purchased by consumers?

At the microeconomic level, price, quality, service, and distribution channels are all important. We assume these are already well under control. Yet even if the products or services you provide are properly designed, positioned, priced, and distributed, consumers may still fail to buy the expected amount because of macroeconomic conditions. The key factors affecting consumption are:

- Recent average disposable income (DI)
- Expected average DI
- Changes in income tax rates
- Cost and availability of credit
- Demographic factors and age distribution of consumers
- Expected rate of return on assets: debt, equity, and real estate
- Changes in spendable income not included in DI caused by fluctuations in asset prices
- Exogenous shifts in consumer attitudes not related to any of the above variables.

The recent level of disposable income is the single most important factor affecting consumer spending at both the macro and micro level, although even that is not an unerring indicator. Most of the time, when income is rising faster than usual, consumption will rise faster than usual; during years of sluggish growth or actual declines in income, consumer spending will also be sluggish or decline. In general, someone with disposable income of $100,000 per year spends about twice as much as someone with disposable income of $50,000. In any given year, employees who receive a big raise will generally boost their consumption by more than people who receive a small raise or none at all; and those suffering pay cuts or losing their jobs will diminish their consumption, although not by as much as income has fallen. A tax cut will boost consumption, and a tax increase will reduce consumption, although the impact will be larger if the tax change is permanent rather than temporary.

In the long run, the relationship between consumption and disposable income is almost proportional. In the short run, however, the relationship between changes in consumption this period and changes in income is not highly correlated, as shown later in figure 4.1. The reasons for this lack of correlation between consumption and income are discussed later in this chapter. The empirical evidence shows that:

- In the long run, the ratio of consumption to income is almost constant, although the reported ratio has risen in recent years because of deficiencies in measuring disposable income.
- In the short run, changes in consumption are not closely correlated with changes in income for several reasons. Consumption is based on average or expected (rather than current) income; this is often known as the permanent income hypothesis. Attitudes may frequently shift. Also, the cost and availability of credit are likely to influence consumer spending decisions in the short run. In

particular, a decline in income might not reduce consumption if it is accompanied by lower cost or increased availability of credit.

- Except for recessions, short-run changes in income are generally accompanied by smaller changes in consumption. That is particularly true if the changes in income are unexpected. During recessions, though, changes in income are usually accompanied by proportionately larger changes in consumption, reflecting decreased expectations.

- Changes in realized capital gains are not included in disposable income, although they affect consumption. A reduction in mortgage rates that results in refinancing will increase the amount of income available to spend on other goods and services. Similarly, an appreciation in the price of a house may induce some families to refinance with a larger mortgage and spend the extra cash; since 1990, that has been an increasingly important source of income for consumer spending. These factors are all significant, but none of them is included in measured disposable income, which is the major reason the reported personal saving rate declined so much during the 1990s.

- Many consumers face a short-term borrowing constraint whenever planned consumption exceeds actual income, since the average consumer holds relatively few liquid assets. Hence when the availability of credit diminishes, consumption is likely to decline much more than indicated by income, attitudes, or the cost of credit.

For all these reasons, short-term changes in consumption and income are not very highly correlated. This can lead to unexpected fluctuations in retail sales, affecting manufacturers and retailers alike. It can also make successful fiscal policy planning difficult.

Before the 1930s, economic theory generally did not include a separate consumption function; emphasis was placed on the equivalence between saving and investment. When the consumption function was first introduced, it was claimed that consumer spending was primarily tied to current income, and that the saving rate rose as income increased. The historical development of the modern consumption function, in which the principal arguments are "permanent" income, monetary conditions, and life cycle variables, is presented in the appendix. The modern consumption function is based on the following concepts:

1. Consumers base their spending patterns on their permanent or long-term expected income, rather than income in this quarter or year.
2. Consumers will change their spending patterns more if a change in income is perceived to be permanent rather than temporary.
3. Consumers are likely to spend a higher proportion of their income if they are optimistic about the future. That is most likely to happen when the unemployment rate is low, the inflation rate is low and stable, and the stock market is booming.
4. At any given level of income, consumers will base their spending plans in part on expected future changes in consumption and income. For example, many

parents save in order to send their children to college. They will dissave during those college years, save for retirement, then dissave again once they have retired. New college graduates often spend more than their current income to furnish a house or apartment, since they expect their income to rise rapidly over the next few years. This does not mean consumers can forecast the future better than anyone else, but they can make intelligent choices about what is likely to happen over their life cycle.

5. Financial variables are important in determining the timing of consumption in the short run. While changes in the cost of credit – interest rates – do affect consumption, the main linkage occurs because most consumers are subject to a borrowing restraint. Thus even if it would make sense for consumers to spend more now because their income will probably increase sharply in the near future, they might not be able to borrow the money right now.

6. Changes in stock prices affect consumption in opposite ways. To a certain extent, an increase in the stock of wealth might mean consumers spend more of their current income. Also, a rise in stock prices creates capital gains, some of which could be spent. Conversely, if consumers expect rapid gains in the stock market, they might decide to save more now in order to be able to spend more later – and if the stock market is expected to fall, they might decide to spend more now.

7. Since 1980, the reported personal saving rate has been closely correlated with interest rates. That is mainly because a lower interest rate boosts the value of the stock market, increases the value of one's home, permits refinancing mortgages at lower interest rates, and is generally accompanied by easier credit terms.

4.2   Short-term links between consumption and disposable income: the marginal propensity to consume

Ever since Milton Friedman's pathbreaking work on consumer spending in 1957[3] (see the appendix), it has generally been recognized that consumers base their spending pattern on their long-term average income, rather than income received in any given time period. To take an extreme case, suppose employees are paid once a month; obviously they do not spend their entire paycheck that day. Furthermore, if consumers receive a one-time bonus or windfall payment that they do not think will be repeated, they generally do not spend a very large proportion of that increase right away. Conversely, if someone is laid off and has no current income, that certainly does not mean their consumption falls to zero.

From an empirical viewpoint, and in terms of trying to determine how changes in income will affect the demand for your products, one of the key issues is the time horizon consumers take into account when determining their spending patterns. To provide some information on this subject, consider the following three comparisons between percentage changes in consumption and disposable income; all figures are in chained (real) dollars.

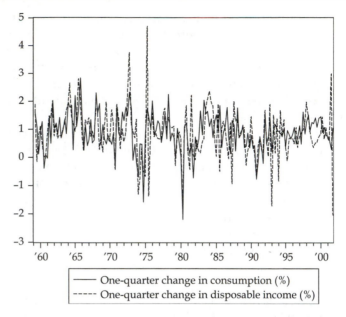

Figure 4.1 Over a one-quarter span, changes in income explain only about 20% of the variance of changes in consumption

Figure 4.1 shows the relationship on a quarterly basis. Because consumers base their spending patterns on average or expected income, there is very little correlation between changes in consumption in any given quarter and changes in disposable income in the same quarter. The **marginal propensity to consume** (MPC), which is defined as the marginal change in consumption for a unit change in disposable income, is only about one-third in the first quarter – and only about 20% of the changes in consumption are explained by the changes in income.

Figure 4.2 shows what happens when the time period is lengthened to one year. About half of the variance is explained, and the MPC rises to two-thirds. When the time horizon is extended to three years (figure 4.3), about three-quarters of the variance is explained, and the MPC rises to 0.87. These graphs make it clear that consumption is a function of average income over several quarters, not just current income.

Thus consumers generally take into account their average income over the past three years when making spending decisions. However, they also project what is likely to happen in the future. If the economy is at full employment and the inflation rate is low and stable, they are more likely to be optimistic about what lies ahead than if the economy is in a recession. They are also likely to be more optimistic if the stock market is rising than if it is falling, although the relationship there is not as clear-cut, because an expected increase in the stock market may cause them to save a larger proportion of their income. All these data can be found on the Bureau of Economic Analysis (BEA) website (www.bea.gov).

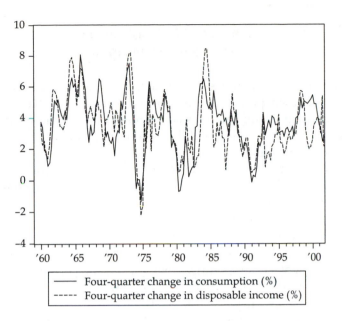

Figure 4.2 Over a four-quarter span, changes in income explain about 50% of the variance of changes in consumption

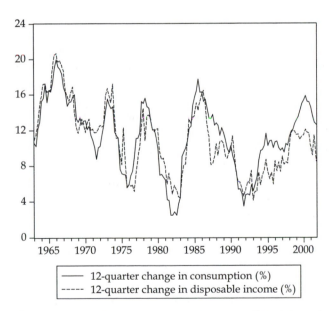

Figure 4.3 Over a 12-quarter span, changes in income explain about 75% of the variance of changes in consumption

4.3   Long-term links between consumption and income: the permanent income hypothesis

The **permanent income hypothesis** (PIH) states that the amount consumers spend is proportional to their permanent income, no matter what that level of income might be. According to this theory, a consuming unit with an income of $20,000 would spend the same proportion of that income as some unit with an income of $200,000 – or even $2 million.

At first this might seem to run counter to common sense: consumer studies by the Bureau of Labor Statistics (BLS) show that people whose income falls below the median generally spend at least 100% of their after-tax income, whereas people in the upper income brackets save a substantial proportion of their after-tax income. The principal argument of the PIH is that many of those people in the lower income brackets have suffered a temporary decline in their income; usually it is much higher. People might be temporarily unemployed, or perhaps they are retired. Similarly, many people in the upper income brackets are enjoying a temporary increase in their income; usually it is much lower. Perhaps they have sold their company, or their stock options have suddenly become very valuable, or they have received a big bonus.

The importance of the PIH now becomes clearer. Suppose a consuming unit ordinarily has an income of $50,000 per year; it drops to $30,000 for one year, but is expected to recover the following year. Its consumption will decline, but only by a small fraction of the decline in income. The consuming unit will reduce its stock of assets, or possibly borrow in anticipation of a return to normal income. If it turns out that income is permanently reduced to $30,000, however, consumer spending will gradually be reduced in line with that lower level of income. That switch may very well involve moving to a less expensive house or making other permanent life-style changes.

Now suppose a consuming unit that ordinarily has an income of $50,000 per year receives a $50,000 bonus. Consumption will increase somewhat, but if income is expected to return to $50,000 in subsequent years, it would be foolish to make life-style decisions such as moving to a more expensive house. The members of the consuming unit might be more likely to take an expensive vacation, purchase a new motor vehicle, or eat out at fancy restaurants more frequently, but would not be likely to place the children in an expensive private school or join an exclusive country club based on a one-year gain in income.

The same general logic can be applied to cyclical fluctuations in the economy. In a year when the economy grows rapidly, bonuses are larger than usual, and overtime payments are frequent, consumption will invariably rise, but not as much as income increases. Furthermore, the rise in consumption will generally be greater if the increase in income is also accompanied by an increase in asset prices. However, the overall answer is more complicated than that because the pattern of consumption also depends on what happens to monetary conditions: the gain is likely to be greater if inflation and interest rates remain at low levels than if they increase rapidly.

Furthermore, the argument is not symmetrical, for the PIH states that during recessions, consumption would fall less than income, resulting in a decline in the personal saving rate. Yet it generally increases during recessions. That occurs because many people are forced to cut back on their spending because of liquidity constraints even if they fully expect their income to recover quickly. This point is discussed in section 4.5. Before turning to this important issue, though, we focus on what has become an increasingly contentious issue in recent years, namely the question of whether tax cuts do indeed stimulate consumption and economic activity.

4.4   Consumer spending and changes in tax rates

As noted above, consumers will change their spending patterns less when the change in income is temporary, or unexpected, than when it is permanent, or expected. Most of the time this is a difficult proposition to test empirically because there is no way of determining whether these changes were expected or not. There is, however, one important case when we know in advance whether the changes are permanent or temporary, which is when the Federal personal income tax rate schedule changes. There have been eight significant changes in personal income tax rates since the end of World War II, which are summarized in table 4.1. The figures in the table show the change in the personal saving rate and average tax rate (total Federal personal income taxes divided by personal income) for the first four quarters after the tax cut was originally implemented.

This table should be interpreted as follows. When the personal tax rate decreases by 1 percentage point (e.g., from 11.0 to 10.0% of disposable income), disposable income increases by roughly 1%. If all of that money were spent, the saving rate would not change at all, and the MPC would be 1. If none of that money were spent, the saving rate would increase by 1%, so the change in column (2) would be equal and opposite in sign to the change in column (1). If 30% of the tax cut was saved and 70% was spent, then the saving rate would rise by 0.3%, and the MPC would be 0.70. Since some of the tax cut would be spent and some would be saved, the two columns should always have opposite signs. If they have the same sign, that means that if taxes were cut, consumption rose by more than the amount of the tax cut; or if taxes were increased, consumption fell by more than the amount of the tax increase.

The hypothesis that permanent tax changes have a bigger impact on consumption than temporary tax changes means the MPC would be less than 0.5 for temporary changes and more than 0.5 for permanent changes. That occurs five out of seven times, with the latest (Bush) tax cut being part temporary and part permanent. But we would also expect that the MPC would fall in the range from 0 to 1, and that does not happen in two of the cases.

Table 4.1   Major changes in personal income taxes after World War II

1948	Married couples allowed to split their income for tax purposes
1951	Higher tax rates to pay for the Korean War and increased defense spending
1964–5	Permanent 20% reduction in tax rates
1968	Temporary 10% tax surcharge to pay for the Vietnam War
1970	Termination of 10% tax surcharge
1975	One-time rebate to help end the recession
1981–3	Permanent 25% reduction in tax rates
2002	Phased-in permanent income tax cut; some funds distributed in 2001

Date	Change in personal income tax rate (%)	Change in saving rate (%)	Type	MPC*	Comment
1948.2	−3.3	+0.7	P	0.79	
1950.4	+3.1	+1.4	T	<0	Credit controls
1964.1	−1.6	+0.4	P	0.75	
1968.3	+2.8	−2.0	T	0.29	
1970.3	−1.8	+0.9	T	0.50	
1975.2	−1.9	+0.6	T	0.68	Monetary easing
1982.3	−2.1	−1.1	P	>1	Monetary easing
2002[a]	−3.7	+2.1	P	0.43	

* Calculated as the change in the personal saving rate with the opposite sign
[a] The permanent tax cut went into effect at the beginning of 2002, but some tax reduction checks were mailed in the summer of 2001 in an attempt to bolster the economy. These figures show the difference in the tax and saving rates between 2001.2 and 2002.2.

That does not mean that the distinction between temporary and permanent tax cuts is not important and significant. It does, however, emphasize the degree to which monetary factors also influence short-term changes in consumer spending. During the Korean War, consumers were required to put at least 20% down and pay off the remaining balance on a new car within 30 months; that substantially reduced sales. In 1975, and again in 1983, consumption was boosted substantially by a massive easing by the Fed, brought about by recession and a sharp decline in the rate of inflation. Monetary factors are clearly important, and are considered later in this chapter.

Before turning to the links between consumer spending and monetary policy, though, we offer an additional comment about fiscal policy. Trying to determine how consumer spending, and the economy in general, will react to a change in personal income tax changes is very much a hit-or-miss proposition without knowing how the tax cut will affect other components and sectors of the economy.

The answer will, we believe, become apparent by the end of this book after a discussion of the determinants of productivity, the interaction of monetary and fiscal policy, the inflow and outflow of foreign capital, the determinants of stock prices, and the role of consumer and business sentiment on aggregate demand. In a nutshell, however, the answer can be outlined here as follows. If a tax cut is accompanied by an improvement in consumer and business attitudes, a rise in stock prices, an inflow in foreign capital, and restrained government spending, consumer spending will probably rise by almost the full amount of the tax cut. Conversely, if it is accompanied by a deterioration in attitudes, declining stock prices, an outflow of foreign capital, and an acceleration in government spending, there will be little or no increase in consumer spending. Essentially, consumers and investors alike have to be convinced that the tax cut is "good" for the economy in the sense that it will increase their expected income in the future. If the deficit widens by more than the tax cut, that will usually cast a negative pall on financial markets and encourage an outflow of foreign capital, hence reducing stock prices.

Therefore, the concept of permanent, or expected, income is important not only in terms of whether the tax cut is expected to be temporary or permanent, but also whether consumers perceive that a tax cut will boost their expected income in the future. If consumers believe that will be the case, the MPC will be closer to unity. If they do not think so, it will be closer to zero.

CASE STUDY 4.1   COMPARISON OF THREE MAJOR PERSONAL INCOME TAX CUTS

In 1964–5, personal and corporate income tax rates were cut an average of 20%; this is known as the Kennedy-Johnson tax cut because the initial plans were formulated by John F. Kennedy but the actual tax cut was not passed until after his assassination. In 1982 and 1983, the Reagan Administration cut income tax rates 10% each year; there had also been a previous 5% cut in late 1981, but that was largely offset by an increase in social security taxes that year. In 2001, the George W. Bush Administration passed a tax cut that would eventually amount to about a 20% reduction in rates, but it was (a) phased in over several years, and (b) speeded up by sending tax refund checks to most taxpayers during the summer of 2001. That complicates the analysis because taxes went down in 2001.3, up in 2001.4, and back down again starting in 2002. Also, questions were raised about whether some of the later year cuts would be rescinded, which was not the case for the earlier tax cuts; that may also have had some impact on expectations.

In addition to the impact on consumption, relevant questions include the extent to which the tax cuts affected (a) overall real growth, (b) the budget position, (c) interest rates, and (d) the stock market. We include the latter variable as the best available measure of whether consumers, business executives, and investors thought the tax cut would benefit the economy. The comparisons shown are the data

continued

CASE STUDY 4.1 (*continued*)

for the four quarters before the first phase of the tax cut, and then the three succeeding four-quarter periods; these periods are referred to as "years" in table 4.2.

After the Kennedy-Johnson tax cut, the growth rate, which was already above average, rose even more until the increased expenditures associated with the Vietnam War caused monetary tightening and a slowdown. Yet the 6.9% average growth rate during the first two years of the tax cut is still a post-Korean War record. Growth rebounded very sharply after the Reagan tax cut, although part of that was due to the monetary easing after inflation declined. By comparison, the early stages of the recovery after the Bush tax cut were very weak.

Both the Reagan and Bush tax cuts increased the deficit ratio by 2.4% of GDP the first year. By comparison, the Kennedy-Johnson tax cut was followed by a budget surplus for two reasons. First, the economy was already growing rapidly. Second and more important, Lyndon Johnson kept government spending flat his first year in office.

Table 4.2 Economic performance after three major income tax cuts

First quarter of the tax cut	1964.2	1982.3	2001.3
Change in real GDP			
Year before	6.3	−1.2	−0.1
1st year	5.3	3.1	2.1
2nd year	8.5	7.9	2.5E
3rd year	2.8	3.3	
Budget ratio, NIPA basis (surplus or deficit as percentage of GDP)			
Year before	0.8	−2.6	2.1
1st year	0.3	−5.0	−1.3
2nd year	0.4	−4.5	−3.0E
3rd year	0.0	−4.3	
10-year Treasury note yield			
Year before	4.1	14.3	5.5
1st year	4.2	11.2	4.9
2nd year	4.4	12.1	4.0E
3rd year	4.9	11.8	
Change in S&P 500 stock price index (quarterly basis)			
Year before	18.3	−14.1	−14.8
1st year	11.6	42.6	−10.8
2nd year	5.8	−4.3	−15.7E
3rd year	−4.9	18.6	

CASE STUDY 4.1 (*continued*)

There is scant evidence that the tax cuts boosted interest rates. Interest rates remained constant in the first case. They fell under Ronald Reagan, but that was because the rate of inflation dropped even more. They fell under George W. Bush because of the weak economy. These data do not show any signs of crowding out in the sense of raising interest rates.

On balance, the stock market was neutral about the Kennedy-Johnson tax cut; the decline in the third year reflected negative reactions to the increased Vietnam War spending, not the tax cut per se. The market rebounded sharply after the Reagan tax cut; although much of that was probably due to lower interest rates, the tax cut obviously did not diminish investor enthusiasm. By comparison, investors were apparently unenthusiastic about the Bush tax cut.

At the time of writing, the long-term implications of the Bush tax cut have not yet occurred. It is likely, however, that the return to deficit financing discouraged investors and was one of the reasons for the stock market selloff. From the viewpoint of stimulating the economy, real growth probably would have been more robust if the tax cut had been accompanied by less growth in government spending. For purposes of comparison we note that total Federal spending rose an average of 3.3% per year during the Clinton Administration, while that figure ballooned to 7.7% per year during the first two fiscal years of the Bush Administration.[4]

4.5 Importance of cost and availability of credit in the consumption function

We now turn to the relationship between financial variables and consumption. There is virtually no question that consumer spending is negatively related with interest rates. This is an important linkage both theoretically and empirically. However, this linkage is based on several different facets, which can be summarized as follows. Each of these points will then be discussed in turn.

1. Where time payments are important and the amount of interest represents a substantial proportion of the total purchase price, lower interest rates reduce the monthly payment.
2. In general, lower interest rates increase the availability of credit.
3. A decline in interest rates permits many homeowners to refinance their mortgages at lower rates, resulting in more spendable income for other goods and services.
4. A decline in interest rates generally boosts housing prices, boosting the equity in homes and permitting homeowners to cash out that equity and spend it. As in (3) those gains are not recorded in disposable income.

5. A decline in interest rates boosts capital spending, which increases output, employment, and personal income, which also raises consumption. In this case, the consumption/income ratio would not necessarily change, but consumer spending itself would rise.

6. It has sometimes been argued that when interest rates rise, consumers save more now because they will then have more money to spend later, and when interest rates fall, consumers spend more and save less. The decision between spending and saving is an important one that does influence patterns of consumer spending. However, the current nominal rate of interest is an extremely poor measure of that decision; instead, the appropriate measure is the *expected* rate of return on all assets, including equity as well as debt instruments.

Thus, for example, an increase in the stock market might result in consumers saving more and spending less, ceteris paribus. While an increase in the stock market increases wealth, that does not necessarily boost consumption. In particular, suppose the stock market has been rising rapidly and consumers expect that trend to continue. In that case, they might decide to invest a larger proportion of their income in equities, hence spending less out of current income. Conversely, a severe and prolonged stock market slump might convince them to spend more and save less, since their stock market investments are likely to shrivel further in the future.

Studies that expanded on the work by Hall and Flavin, listed in notes 1 and 2, developed the concept of "excess sensitivity," estimating that 20% to 50% of all US consumers face binding borrowing constraints at some time during the business cycle. Based on permanent income, these consuming units would like to spend the amount commensurate with their income, but they cannot borrow enough because of restrictions imposed by lending institutions. Consequently, spending decisions are delayed until the credit restrictions have been lifted.[5]

The concept of the yield spread will be discussed in more detail in chapter 6. Here we note that when the Fed tightens, the level of short-term rates usually rises above their long-term counterparts; that is known as an inverted yield curve.[6] When that happens, banks are likely to buy more Treasury securities and make fewer loans to the private sector, especially consumers and small businesses. Thus when interest rates rise, not only do some consumers curtail their borrowing because loans are more expensive, but bankers and other lenders are more reluctant to make private sector loans. In this case, the availability of credit is more important than the cost, but since the availability diminishes as interest rates rise, this factor is consistent with a positive correlation between the saving rate and interest rates. Note, however, that this measure of credit availability means that consumer spending is likely to decline more when short-term rates rise above long-term rates than when rates rise equally across the yield spectrum.

Economists – and business managers – can usually tell that credit is restricted when the yield curve becomes inverted. It might seem that another measure of restricted credit would be the change in consumer credit outstanding. However, that is essentially an after-the-fact phenomenon; consumer credit turns out to be a lagging indicator. When credit is restricted by exogenous factors, such as the direct imposition of credit controls or severe constraints on lending by banks imposed by the Fed, consumer credit outstanding declines with a lag.

Credit Restrictions and Motor Vehicle Sales

Restrictions on credit availability primarily affect purchases of housing, which has some impact on household appliances, and purchases of motor vehicles. Since the latter case is important for explaining short-term fluctuations in economic activity generally, we examine it next in greater detail.

The cost of time payments is important for purchasing motor vehicles. For example, suppose someone purchased a new car for $20,000 and paid it off over four years. If the interest rate was 6%, the average monthly payment would be about $486. If the interest rate was 20%, the average monthly payment would be about $660, some 36% higher. Thus changes in interest rates have a significant impact on both the timing and the number of motor vehicle purchases.

However, even this apparently straightforward case has some exceptions. If the interest rate rises from, say, 6% to 12%, the monthly payment will obviously increase. On the other hand, suppose that increase reflects a rise in the underlying rate of inflation from 4% to 10% – and that high inflation rate is expected to continue. In that case, the price of new cars would also rise over the next few years, so an individual or business leasing a new car would be able to obtain a more favorable monthly payment because the residual value in (say) three years would be higher. In many cases that would offset the rise in interest rates. If the interest rate stayed at 12% but the rate of inflation fell back to 4%, then new car sales would be severely depressed. However, if the rate of inflation was expected to drop that much, interest rates would almost certainly decline as well.

CASE STUDY 4.2 ZERO-INTEREST RATE FINANCING FOR NEW MOTOR VEHICLES

In October 2001, the major automobile manufacturers advertised zero-interest rate financing to boost motor vehicle sales in the aftermath of the terrorist attacks of September 11th. The experiment was a resounding success – sales of new cars and light trucks rose from a seasonally adjusted annual rate of 16.1 million in the third quarter to a record 21.1 million in October. Sales then declined to 17.8 million in November, and 16.5 million in December, when the incentives were somewhat reduced although not entirely eliminated.

In spite of the blaring headlines announcing "zero-interest rate financing," the truth is more prosaic. According to the Federal Reserve Board, the average interest rate on new car loans in October dropped to 2.74% from an average of 6.0% in the

continued

CASE STUDY 4.2 (*continued*)

previous quarter. Also, according to Fed statistics, the average amount financed per new car was $24,443, with an average maturity of 53.7 months. On that basis, the average monthly payment fell by about $9 per month, or about 2% of the total purchase price. Assuming that the Fed data are correct, it is interesting to note that the incentives provided by the auto companies were considerably less than implied in the advertisements.

Taken at face value, these figures would suggest that a net reduction of approximately 2% in the price boosted sales by $\frac{5}{16}$, or more than 31% in October, implying a price elasticity of more than −15. Obviously that does not make any sense; the vast majority of increased purchases reflected timing adjustments rather than the decision to trade the car in more frequently or purchase more cars per household. Consumers reacted to what they perceived to be a "bargain."

There are two other ways to look at this elasticity. First, we note that the 5.0 million annual rate increase in October would be equivalent to an actual increase of 417,000 cars sold if October were a normal month, but since sales are usually heavier in that month, the actual increase was about 500,000 cars. One possibility is to assume that the extra 500,000 cars sold all represented permanent increases, in which case the implied elasticity is approximately −1.5. The other is to assume that most of the changes were temporary. That effect can be calculated by comparing sales in 2002 with those in 2001, and assuming that any shortfall in 2002 was borrowed from October 2001. Since there was no shortfall in 2002, we can assume the gains were permanent. That does not mean the average number of cars per person rose, but it does mean that people traded in their cars more frequently.

Because dealers had an unusually large number of 2001 model cars and trucks left over because of the recession and the drop in sales after the terrorist attacks, some attention-grabbing method was needed to move those extra vehicles.[7] Also, the "Big Three" have contracts with the UAW, which essentially stipulate that production workers will receive almost all of their full salaries whether they are working or not, so the marginal cost of producing an extra vehicle is much smaller than would be calculated from the cost of labor and materials. Hence relative to the alternatives, the de facto 2% price reduction did not cost the automobile industry very much. It was a very clever merchandising approach, and presumably boosted sales far more than would have been the case had the auto industry merely announced an actual 2% price reduction.

4.6 Consumption, housing prices, and mortgage rates

Until the late 1970s, most homeowners obtained a standard 30-year mortgage at an interest rate that was usually close to 6%. They made the same monthly payment – except for real estate taxes and insurance – until the house was sold. Refinancing only occurred for those homeowners who were in financial difficulty.

When mortgage rates moved up to the double-digit range, the entire concept of home financing changed; the concept of a variable rate mortgage started in 1980. For a 30-year mortgage and high interest rates, the monthly payment for principal and interest is almost proportional to the interest rate. Thus a rise in the mortgage rate from 8% to 12% increases the monthly payment by almost 50%. Consequently, when mortgage rates rose as high as 15% in the early 1980s, the majority of homeowners would have failed to qualify for a mortgage, based on the then current rule of thumb that the monthly payment should not exceed 28% of their income.

To bypass this roadblock, the concept of a variable rate, or adjustable rate mortgage (ARM) was implemented. Normally, short-term rates are significantly less than long-term rates, so the monthly payment based on a one-year interest rate would be much less than the payment based on a 30-year bond yield. Also, when interest rates declined, homeowners could refinance at a much lower rate.[8]

The implementation of variable rate mortgages has two impacts on the housing market and consumer spending generally. First, it permits more families to qualify for mortgages. Second, when rates decline, consumers benefit from smaller monthly mortgage payments, and hence spend more on other goods and services. Many consumers now take advantage of refinancing their mortgages at lower rates even if they do not have a variable rate mortgage. Of course, that works in both directions; if one has a variable rate mortgage and rates rise, that leaves less money to spend on other goods and services. As it turns out, though, consumers appear to be better at forecasting interest rate troughs than highly paid professional financial economists.[9]

There is also an important asymmetry between rising and falling interest rates. To see this, first consider a decline in interest rates from 10% to 8%. Assuming the homeowner has a relatively recent mortgage, his or her monthly payment declines by almost 20%, leaving more money to spend on other goods and services. Hence consumption rises for the same level of reported income, which is the same thing as saying the reported personal saving rate declines. Presumably the homeowner can refinance whenever rates decline enough to make the switch worth while, considering the cost of the loan transaction. Since that fee is often about 1% of the mortgage, it pays to switch if homeowners remain at their current residence for one year or more.

Now suppose interest rates rise from 8% to 10%. The dynamics are different because there is a lag of up to one year before the higher payments kick in. For a while, mortgage payments stay the same, so spending may not diminish until the year is up and the monthly mortgage payment would rise 25%, which would generally lead to cutbacks in other spending. For those fortunate enough to lock in long-term mortgage commitments when rates troughed, there is no penalty when they rise again. However, not all consumers have this sense of perfect timing; and in addition, if they move, a new mortgage must ordinarily be obtained at the going market rate. Nonetheless, even those whose mortgage payments will rise have almost a year before spending cutbacks are necessary, whereas when rates fall, consumption can rise much sooner.

In general, a decline in mortgage rates will permit more people to own their homes, hence increasing the demand for housing and boosting housing prices, ceteris paribus. Hence the value of existing homes will also rise. In some cases, homeowners will refinance their mortgage at 80% or 90% of the higher value, and use the additional funds for purchases of other goods and services. That was one of the major factors boosting consumer spending during the 1990s.

So far we have shown that when interest rates decline, consumption is likely to increase because (a) monthly time payments on motor vehicles will decline, (b) credit availability will improve, (c) mortgage rates will decline and many homeowners will refinance, and (d) housing prices are more likely to rise, permitting homeowners to cash out more equity. When interest rates rise, the reverse factors will occur, although often with a slightly longer lag.

4.7 Other links between consumer spending, the rate of interest, and the rate of return

The role of the rate of interest in determining consumer spending has been much debated. It is sometimes claimed that as interest rates rise, consumers save more because of the higher rate of return. Yet both time-series and cross-section data (see the appendix for further discussion of these concepts) show that there is very little correlation between interest rates and the personal saving rate.

The theoretical concept can be explained as follows. Suppose the rate of interest was 2%. If consumers set aside part of their income to be saved, the gains in future years would be very modest because of the low rate of interest, and it would hardly be worth waiting. However, suppose the rate of interest was 12%: then income set aside would increase very rapidly, and slightly less consumption now would result in a substantially higher level of consumption later. According to this argument the higher the interest rate, the higher the **personal saving rate**.

There are several serious flaws with this argument as presented. First, *why* would interest rates be 12% instead of 2%? There are several possibilities, but the main one is that investors think inflation will be high in the future, so the high interest rate reflects the expected erosion of their capital due to rising prices. The key is not the nominal interest rate at all, but the *real* interest rate, which is the nominal rate minus the expected rate of inflation.

Economists used to claim the positive correlation between personal saving and interest rates occurred because if real rates were unusually high, individuals could increase their consumption significantly in future years by saving more now. But that immediately raises the question of why real rates would be so high "now." Presumably it is because lenders and investors expect inflation to be high in the future. In that case, most of the gain in interest income from saving now would be offset by rising prices in the future. Indeed, if prices are expected to rise rapidly, many consumers will assume it is better to buy now. Hence the fact that real interest rates are high in any given year does not necessarily encourage higher saving if it serves as a signal that consumers expect inflation rates to remain high in the future. The key is not the actual real rate of interest, but the expected real rate.

The clearest empirical test of this hypothesis can be seen in the early 1980s, when the 30-year Treasury bond yield was 14% and the rate of inflation was only 4%. The spread between nominal interest rates and the rate of inflation had never before been as high as 10% in the US, and will probably never rise to that level again. Because the tax laws had just changed to encourage tax-deferred individual retirement accounts, such a situation represented a tremendous opportunity for individuals to set aside money for retirement. A one-time investment of $10,000 in Treasury bonds at those rates in 1982 would be worth over $500,000 when the bonds matured in 2012 – or $175,000 in real terms if inflation remained at its then current level of 4%. Since the actual rate of inflation fell even further, the amount would have been over $200,000 in real terms.

Yet most investors did not take advantage of this record high real rate of interest – even though the 1981 tax law contained an important expansion of tax-deferred saving plans such as IRAs, 401(k), and Keogh plans. Indeed, the personal saving rate actually declined in the early 1980s. Apparently investors did not believe that inflation would stay at or below 4%; if they had, nominal rates would have been sharply lower. Major financial institutions that ran advertisements at the time pointing out precisely this arithmetic were criticized by financial writers who said that the ads were misleading the gullible. Clearly, many investors thought inflation would soon return to double-digit rates. Of course they were wrong, but that was precisely the reason that the Treasury bond rate rose to 14%. If people really believed inflation would remain at 4% or less, the Treasury bond rate probably would have been only about half that high.

There are other reasons why the nominal rate of interest is not correlated with the personal saving rate. Interest rates generally decline to their cyclical lows during recessions. However, for many people, recessions raise the concern about the future; attitudes decline, and people try to set aside more for the proverbial "rainy day." Indeed, the personal saving rate usually rises during recessions even as interest rates are falling. In this situation, expectations about the future override the rate of return on saving.

Most consumers put their long-run saving into the stock market, not into bank accounts or bonds. Hence the relevant rate for determining the decision of what proportion to save depends on the expected rate of return on equities, not debt.

Many consumers will save a higher proportion of their income if they think the rate of return on assets – mainly equities – will be higher than usual in the future. However, the nominal rate of interest is a very poor measure of the expected rate of return on assets; most of the time, these two variables are negatively correlated.

Thus it is important for managers to realize that a higher rate of interest does not necessarily mean that the consumption/income ratio will fall, and a lower rate of interest does not mean that the consumption/income ratio will rise. From 1993 to 2000, the Federal funds rate rose from 3% to $6\frac{1}{2}$%. Yet over the same period, the personal saving rate fell from 7.1% to 2.6%. When the Federal funds rate then declined to $1\frac{1}{4}$% by the end of 2002, the personal saving rate rose back to 3.8%.

These comments may seem to fly in the face of the common-sense logic that business improves when interest rates fall, and declines when they rise. In presenting the economic outlook to business groups, this author is invariably reminded that interest rates are one of the most important variables influencing their sales. Indeed, business is usually better when interest rates are low than when they are high. However, the economy is more complicated than that. Think about it for a moment: during recessions, interest rates are usually at their cyclical lows, yet the economy is weak. Interest rates fell to 3% in 1992, and to $1\frac{1}{4}$% in 2002, yet the economy remained sluggish for several more quarters. For that matter, short-term interest rates in Japan fell to zero in the late 1980s, yet that economy remained mired in recession.

The reasons why low interest rates do not necessarily stimulate the economy cannot be encapsulated in one paragraph; the explanation hinges on many links to be explored in future chapters. Nonetheless, a few hints can be supplied at this juncture. First, capital spending will not rise when interest rates decline if substantial excess capacity exists and business expectations and profit margins are depressed. If capital spending is falling, employment and real personal income usually decline, hence reducing consumption. Second, lower interest rates are sometimes accompanied by credit restrictions, as occurred in mid-1980 and from 1990 through 1993. Third, low interest rates might not stimulate consumption if they are accompanied by widespread bankruptcies and a decline in housing prices. Conversely, if rising interest rates are accompanied by a capital spending boom, an adequate supply of credit, rising housing prices, and bullish expectations, they need not reduce the ratio of consumer spending to income.

All these are important factors, and should not be dismissed. However, in most cases, a rise in the rate of interest does *not* cause consumers to decide to save a larger proportion of their income now so they will have more to spend later. Indeed, the application of this hypothesis led many economists to underestimate the strength of the business cycle expansions in the late 1970s, the late 1980s, and the late 1990s: they expected consumer spending to decline just because interest rates had risen. There is no need to make that same mistake in the future.

4.8   Credit availability and the stock of debt

We have discussed several ways in which the cost and availability of credit affect consumer spending and saving, but have not yet specifically mentioned changes in the amount of consumer installment debt outstanding. It is often claimed that the ratio of consumption to income will be higher if (a) the debt/income ratio is lower and (b) the wealth/income ratio is higher.

At first glance, the arguments have a common-sense ring to them. Suppose someone has a salary of $100,000 a year, virtually no assets, and a mountain of debt. One might suppose such an individual would save a substantial proportion of that $100,000 in order to pay back some of this debt, and accumulate some assets for the proverbial rainy day. However, that is certainly not the case for many consumers, including but not limited to recently graduated MBAs.

Now suppose someone has a salary of $100,000 a year, $1 million in assets, and virtually no debt. Since such individuals do not have to worry about loans coming due or putting aside a little for the future, some might claim they are more likely to spend all their income. However, that is usually *not* the case. To see the other side of the picture, suppose you are in the banking business and you have to make a choice between issuing a credit card to (a) someone who never borrows and hence has no debt, and (b) someone with a very high debt/income ratio. Who would you choose?

Many people with no debt have chosen that life style precisely because they do not want to borrow, while those with large debts are often spendthrifts. Cross-section studies reveal – not too surprisingly – that the ratio of consumption to income is *positively* correlated with the ratio of debt to income, not negatively correlated.

To take this one step further, many credit card companies have found that customers who just declared personal bankruptcy are very profitable. Apparently such people like to spend, and they are not permitted to declare bankruptcy again for seven years. Hence they are likely to run up big bills again on their new credit cards. Also, because their credit record is poor, lenders can charge them hefty fees.

We can think of consumers being divided into two groups – spenders and savers. The spenders are invariably in debt. As soon as they have enough money for a down payment, or as soon as their credit card limits increase, they purchase more consumer goods. As a result, they have a high consumption/income ratio and a high debt/income ratio. Savers, on the other hand, virtually never borrow to purchase consumer goods, and prefer to save their money for retirement or bequests. As a result, they have a low consumption/income ratio and a low debt/income ratio.

Some people who are consistently in debt may eventually find the crushing burden of bills so great they will have to cut back on spending – or be forced to declare bankruptcy, after which their lines of credit will be reduced. Yet as long as the economy remains strong, such consumers can continue to borrow more, especially with the widespread acceptance of home equity mortgages starting in the 1980s.

Many spenders simply roll over their existing debt by taking out ever-increasing mortgages on their homes. That is not difficult to accomplish in a strong economy with rising housing prices. In a fairly typical example, assume someone has an income of $100,000 per year and a house that is worth $300,000. Its value appreciates an average of 5% per year, or $15,000. If this increased equity is regularly converted into a higher mortgage or a home equity loan and spent, an individual can spend more than his income every year. While that wipes out the saving that would otherwise accumulate, this is a not uncommon tactic for many homeowners.

Figure 4.4 shows the ratio of consumer debt (technically, installment credit outstanding) to personal income in the post-WWII period. In the years immediately

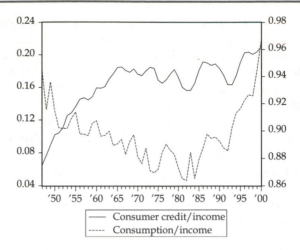

Figure 4.4   There is very little correlation between the ratio of consumer credit outstanding to disposable income and the ratio of consumption to disposable income, although both ratios rose in the 1990s
Sources: BEA website (www.bea.gov) except for consumer credit; Fed website at www.federalreserve.gov

following World War II, some rise in the debt/income ratio was almost inevitable because many consumers had no debt. They had saved much more than usual during the war, when income was higher than anticipated and many consumer durables were not available. Purchases of durables were also restricted during the Korean War. After the end of the Korean War, though, a big increase in the stock of consumer durables, coupled with the baby boom, rapidly rising income, and the switch to suburban living – hence more cars – resulted in a strong increase in the debt/income ratio for more than a decade. At the same time, the consumption/income ratio was little changed, although it did exhibit a slight downward trend.

After 1965, the upward trend in the debt/income ratio leveled off; it declined in the late 1970s and early 1980s because of rising interest rates. Once interest rates declined, the debt/income ratio rose sharply, but it then dipped again in the early 1990s, reflecting the crackdown on risky bank loans following the collapse of the savings and loan industry in 1989. This is a prime example of how restrictions on credit availability affect consumer spending. Once those restrictions were removed, the debt/income ratio returned to its previous highs. Thus on balance, the debt/income ratio has continued to climb since 1982. Yet the consumption/income ratio has also risen on balance over that period. Clearly, there is no negative correlation between these two series.

An increase in the consumer debt/income ratio does not necessarily curtail consumer spending. As long as the economy remains strong, many consumers keep rolling over their debt and remain current with lending agencies based on their current earned income. While there has been a significant increase in the proportion of consumer bankruptcies in the past decade, much of this gain can be traced to a change in the laws in 1987 that made it easier for individuals to file for bankruptcy. There is neither a theoretical nor empirical argument that a rise in the debt/income ratio curtails consumption.

4.9   The role of demographic factors and the life cycle hypothesis

We now turn to some of the long-run determinants of consumption, as embodied in the **life cycle hypothesis** (LCH). Essentially the LCH states that people distribute their consumption over their life cycle in order to maximize utility during their lifetime. That means dissaving when they are just starting out, saving during peak earning years, and then dissaving again during their retirement years. It is assumed that the more wealth people have accumulated during their working years, the more they will be able to spend during the period of retirement.[10]

The pattern of saving by age classifications is shown in table 4.3, where it is clear that this pattern does exist. The data are taken from the 2000 BLS survey of consumer expenditures. Note also that the average personal saving rate is calculated as 8.4%, compared to the BEA estimate of 2.8% (revised up from 1.0%). This shows another reason why we think the BEA methodology for measuring the personal saving rate is flawed, and do not focus on their estimates of the saving rate in this chapter.

This table clearly shows that younger people dissave, people in their working years save, and those in retirement dissave. It probably does not come as much of a surprise to find that people in college and retirement dissave, while they save during their working careers. Nonetheless, there is an important macroeconomic conclusion to be drawn from this. As the aging of the population continues, we would ordinarily expect the personal saving rate to decline, based on this pattern of results.

The fact that people save for their old age, however, does not necessarily mean that a rise in the real value of owner-occupied homes or in equities held directly

Table 4.3   Saving rate by age cohort

Age cohort	After-tax income	Total spending	Saving rate (%)
Total	41,532	38,045	8.4
Under 25	18,813	22,543	−19.8
25–34	42,665	38,945	8.7
35–44	52,626	45,149	14.2
45–54	54,149	46,160	14.8
55–64	44,109	39,340	10.8
65–74	27,553	30,782	−11.7
75 and over	19,759	21,908	−10.9

Sources: BLS website (www.bea.gov) and author's calculations

or indirectly by individuals will boost their wealth now, and hence raise their consumption in retirement. Instead, it is more likely that these increases will boost their consumption and income now, but *not* their wealth. The reason for this apparent paradox is discussed next.

4.10   The relationship between consumption and household net worth

We now consider the relationship between consumption and household net worth, often referred to as wealth. This is more complicated because a rise in stock prices generates both an increase in wealth and, in the case of realized capital gains, an increase in income (it may also affect consumer attitudes). However, an increase in the *income* generated from wealth is not at all the same as an increase in wealth, as shown next.

Consider $1 million invested two different ways: (1) in Treasury securities, which pay 6%, and (2) in the stock market, which historically has returned an average of 12% per year in dividends and capital gains. The individual who invests in Treasury securities is likely to spend that 6% per year. On the other hand, the person who invests in the stock market is more likely to be interested in capital gains, and not spend the unrealized gains that accrue each year. Over time, his or her wealth will grow much more rapidly. Thus the consumer with both a higher level of wealth and a bigger percentage increase in wealth has a lower level of consumption.

Now suppose the rate of interest rises to 8%. In that case, income from wealth rises, and consumption generally rises as well. But the increase in the rate of interest means bond prices have fallen, so wealth has actually decreased. Indeed, to the extent that such an investor also owns stocks, their value would also diminish. In this case, income and wealth have changed in *opposite* directions.

As instructive as this example may be, though, most consumers do not own a large portfolio of bonds that generates the majority of their income. For most consumers, their net worth is equal to the equity in their home plus their stock market investments, which for most people are their pension and retirement funds.

Suppose the value of your house goes up, and your equity increases as you pay down the mortgage. In your old age, you can afford to live more comfortably; or perhaps you will choose to leave a bigger estate. Alternatively, though, you may decide to draw down the increased value of the equity and spend it now. Thus if current income and consumption rises, wealth does not: if wealth rises, consumption does not. Essentially you can't have your cake and eat it too. Either the accumulated equity in your house rises because you do not spend it, or the value of the equity does not rise because you do spend it.

A similar argument could be made for a rising stock market. In most cases, the increase in the value of your portfolio will boost your wealth and raise consumption in your old age. However, some may choose to cash in their portfolio early, either by actually selling stocks they own, or borrowing against their pension plan benefits to boost current consumption.

As a result of these considerations, we reach the following conclusion. If asset prices rise, that is likely to boost current consumption, but that is an *income* effect, not a wealth effect. If wealth continues to rise, current consumption will remain the same, and only future consumption will increase.

Another important reason why consumption is not closely correlated with wealth is related to our earlier point about the expected rate of return. If stock prices are expected to rise rapidly, consumers are likely to save more and spend less. If they are expected to fall in the future, consumers are more likely to spend instead of save. That is the main reason why consumer spending held up so well during the 2000–2002 plunge in the stock market; many consumers decided it made more sense to spend the money instead of investing it in a declining market.

Here again, this analysis might appear to fly in the face of common sense. Isn't it true that the stock market collapse from 2000 to 2002 first caused the recession, and then retarded the recovery?

To a large extent that is true – but not because consumption was hurt. Instead, the massive stock market decline caused capital spending to decline 10%, and *that* is what caused the recession. In addition, net exports declined sharply because of the overvalued dollar. By comparison, real consumer spending continued to rise at a 3% rate during and shortly after the recession. Previously there had been no recession – except for 1949, when consumers were still buying durables they could not purchase during and shortly after World War II – when real consumption rose even as much as 2%.

To restate that point, consumer spending rose *more* during the 2001 recession than during any other post-WWII downturn, even though the stock market declined more than in any other recession. That fact casts grave doubt on the significance of the wealth effect.

We should also note that major declines in the stock market in the spring of 1962 and the autumn of 1987 did not slow down consumer spending or the economy at all, and in both cases the expansion continued for several more years. Hence a complete treatment of this issue must also explain the lack of any impact in those years.

During the 1990s, the consumption/income ratio did rise sharply at the same time that the ratio of stock prices to GDP rose sharply. However, that correlation does not imply causality. The consumption/income ratio could have risen for one of several other reasons. First, declining mortgage rates resulted in more refinancing of mortgages at lower rates, boosting **spendable income**. Second, in the same vein, the rapid rise in housing prices unlocked increased equity, which could then be cashed out and spent. Third, lower nominal interest rates boosted purchases of consumer durables. Fourth, rising expectations meant that consumers increased their expectations for the long-term growth rate of their own incomes, and hence spent more.

Finally, there is the behavior of the net worth/income ratio itself during the 1990s. What do you think happened to median household net worth during the 1990s? Your initial answer is likely to be that it increased sharply, considering the stock market boom and soaring house prices. However, that is not correct. Median household net worth hardly increased at all, according to government statistics,[11] for two reasons. First, the average consumer is not very heavily invested in the stock market. Second, and more important, many consumers took advantage of rising house prices to refinance their mortgage and pull out more cash.

As a result, the increase in median household net worth rose even less than the rate of inflation, and far less than the growth in income during the 1990s. The ratio of net worth to income *declined* significantly during the boom period – yet consumer spending went up more than would be anticipated from the rise in income. In general, people who converted the increased equity in their house to cash – i.e., those who decreased their net worth – were more likely to boost their consumption. Thus we find a negative correlation between wealth and consumption, to go along with the positive correlation between debt and consumption, for any given level of disposable income described in the previous section.

Previous economists who have analyzed the "wealth effect" have estimated that the marginal coefficient is between 0.05 and 0.08, which means a 1% change in wealth would reduce consumption by 0.05% to 0.08%. If that were the case, a 50% change in wealth would reduce consumption by 2.5% to 4.0%, which means the personal saving rate would rise that much, ceteris paribus.

The ceteris paribus conditions are seldom as well organized as we would like; in particular, the 2000–2002 stock market plunge was accompanied by a substantial tax cut. Nonetheless, we look at the seven major stock market corrections in the post-WWII period, which are summarized in table 4.4.

According to the wealth hypothesis, a 10% (say) decline in the stock market would reduce the consumption/income ratio by 0.5% to 0.8%, hence raising the saving rate by the same amount. The actual marginal coefficients are given in column (2) of table 4.4. None of the coefficients is nearly as large as would be predicted by the theory except for years of tax cuts, and two of the seven cases do not even have the expected sign. In fact, two of the three sizable increases in the personal saving rate were probably due to tax cuts, not declines in the stock market. The only other large increase in the personal saving rate occurred in 1987, and in that case the overall real growth actually accelerated following the stock market plunge, due to strength in capital spending and exports. Real GDP, which had risen 3.1% for the four quarters ending in 1987.3, actually rose faster in the fourth quarter – the period when most of the decline in stock prices occurred – and increased 4.4% over the next four quarters.

In this author's opinion, the personal saving rate does not rise when the stock market plunges because would-be investors perceive that the future rate of return on stocks would be lower, so they decided to save less and spend more. In that respect, the decision about whether to spend or save does depend on the expected future rate of return. That is still an important determinant of consumption. It is

Table 4.4   Changes in the personal saving rate during major stock market declines

	(1) % decline in S&P 500*	(2) Change in personal saving rate**	(3) Expected rise in saving rate***	Comment
1962	−23	−0.2	1.2–1.8	
1969–70	−28	1.4	1.4–2.2	Tax cut
1973–4	−43	0.5	2.2–3.4	
1981–2	−19	−0.2	1.0–1.6	
1987	−27	1.1	1.4–2.2	Growth rate rose
1990	−15	0.4	0.8–1.3	
2000–02	−45	1.0	2.3–3.6	Tax cut

* based on monthly average data
** difference between saving rate the quarter before the market started to decline and the quarter when the decline ended
*** equal to the % decline in S&P 500 times 0.05 to 0.08
Sources: Standard & Poor's; BEA website, www.bea.gov

just that the current nominal rate of interest is a very poor tool for measuring that rate.

MANAGER'S BRIEFCASE: INTERPRETING THE RETAIL SALES DATA

Several private sector institutions issue weekly reports on retail sales, based on data from the major chains. However, these figures generally do not provide much guidance about how much consumers are spending. Indeed, the Bureau of the Census (part of the Department of Commerce) used to issue its own report on weekly department store sales, but discontinued the practice when the numbers turned out to be erratic.

On or about the 10th of every month, Census publishes the advance estimate of total retail sales. Only about 20% of those sales are department or discount stores; the figures also include sales at car dealers, gasoline stations, grocery stores, restaurants, drug stores, and many other types of establishments. For purposes of tracking discretionary consumer spending, the most useful category is usually considered to be "GAF" sales, which includes general merchandise (department and discount), clothing, furniture, electronics and appliance stores, and a few smaller categories; however, this number is available only with a one-month lag. The retail sales figures serve as the base for the national income and product accounts (NIPA) data for consumption of goods, with two exceptions: motor vehicle sales are not included (instead, the NIPA figures are based on the number of cars and trucks sold); retail sales at hardware and building supply stores have no counterpart in the NIPA consumption figures.

continued

MANAGER'S BRIEFCASE (*continued*)

The retail sales number is subject to wide revisions; in particular, the advance estimate covers only about 10% of total sales. The figures are often substantially revised the following month, especially for some of the smaller categories. Hence the advance estimates should be used with caution. Nonetheless, the figures are widely followed and do occasionally move financial markets. Suppose Census announces that retail sales rose 1.2%, but sales of your consumer-goods company rose only 0.2%. Does that mean you are losing market share? It might mean just that, but before panicking, check out several other factors, including the following.

1. Was the increase caused by a temporary surge in motor vehicle sales, possibly due to rebates or low interest rates? This distinction is important enough that Census also publishes the percentage change of all retail sales excluding motor vehicles, and in fact that is the figure most closely followed by economists and financial analysts.
2. Sometimes the gain in retail sales is due to a sharp spike in gasoline or food prices. The retail sales reports do not provide data for current and constant dollars, although those are provided on the Census website with some lag. However, except for wars or embargoes, the levels of gasoline consumption or food purchases do not really change very much from one month to the next, so a big spike – or a big decline – is probably due to shifts in prices, and hence has no correlation with the volume of retail sales.
3. The "Wal-Mart effect." During 2001 and 2002, many economists started to notice that the gain in total retail sales as reported by Census seemed to be substantially larger than the gain in sales reported by major department store chains. We call this the Wal-Mart effect. Essentially what happened is as follows. During the recession and its aftermath, many consumers shifted their shopping patterns from smaller, relatively expensive stores to Wal-Mart and other major discounters. These big chains report their sales promptly and accurately. However, many of the smaller stores do not; in particular, if a store is about to go out of business, presumably the last thing the owners have on their mind is filling out another government form. As a result, the gains at Wal-Mart are fully reported, but the losses at other stores are not. As a result, the Census figures have an upward bias. That also means the NIPA figures for consumption, and hence for real GDP, have an upward bias, and the growth rate is overstated. Starting in 2003, the same general effect continued but growth in Wal-Mart sales slowed down somewhat as consumers moved to even lower-price chains.

Eventually, when the comprehensive business censuses are taken, these discrepancies will be discovered and reversed. However, the current reports for retail sales tend to overstate the actual gain. As a manager, you should be aware of this discrepancy when attempting to compare your own sales with the national totals.

MANAGER'S BRIEFCASE: HOW IMPORTANT ARE E-SALES?

In 1998, Census began to measure E-sales for four major sectors: manufacturing, wholesale trade, retail trade, and services. As of mid-2002, no attempt had yet been made to collect E-sales data for agriculture, mining, transportation, communications, utilities, or the public sector.

Census assumes that all E-sales in manufacturing and wholesale trade are B-to-B, while all sales in retail trade and services are B-to-C. That is a somewhat arbitrary decision, since some E-sales in the service industries, such as airline tickets and brokerage transactions, are obviously made by businesses, but that discrepancy does not affect our overall analysis.

continued

MANAGER'S BRIEFCASE (*continued*)

These figures are available only with a substantial lag, and subject to major revisions. In 2000, Census estimated that E-sales were $777 billion in manufacturing, $213 billion in wholesale trade, $37 billion in services, and $29 billion in retail trade. Census also prepares more recent quarterly estimates for retail sales, but not the other sectors. These figures are current as of October 2002 but will probably be revised substantially by the time you are reading this.

E-sales in services and retail trade are growing at about 20% per year; E-sales for manufacturing and wholesale trade are probably growing at about 10% per year in a normal year, less during recessions. These are impressive figures but are way below the 50% figures issued by some blue-sky forecasters.

It is believed that the major impact of B-to-B E-sales has been to reduce prices to manufacturers and wholesalers, who then pass the savings on to consumers. The evidence on this score is fairly impressive. E-sales started around 1996. For the previous five years, the core PPI for intermediate goods rose an average of 2.3% per year. Since then, the average gain has been a minuscule 0.1% per year. When economic history is written, it will probably show that the emergence of E-sales was one of the factors holding inflation steady during the great boom of the late 1990s.

The advantages of E-sales for consumers, as of late 2002, are less apparent. Airline tickets and books can be purchased somewhat less expensively, although discount tickets and bookstores were spreading even before the internet. Brokerage fees had already dropped sharply. In other words, these were areas where expensive, redundant middlemen were being phased out whether or not E-sales became prevalent. To date, most other attempts to sell other goods and services to consumers have not reduced prices to users and have not returned profits to investors. While the jury is still out, it seems reasonable to conclude that whereas B-to-B sales have had a substantial impact in reducing prices, the macroeconomic impact of B-to-C sales has been negligible.

4.11 The effect of changes in consumer confidence

The final factor that determines short-run fluctuations in consumer spending is the degree of consumer confidence about the future. In some years consumers "buy out the store," while in other years merchandise languishes on the shelf. Of course, the amount that income grew during the past year has some impact, but as we have shown above, the short-term correlation between consumption and income is fairly low. As already noted, changes in income and monetary conditions only explain half of the quarterly fluctuations in consumption. What other factors determine whether consumers are in a "buying mood" or not?

The answer is often found by turning to one of the various indexes of consumer confidence published on a regular basis. The two most closely followed indexes are those prepared by the Conference Board, which is released once a month, and the University of Michigan, which is released twice a month. *ABC/Money Magazine* offers a weekly index but it is not widely followed. There is not much difference between the other two indexes; we use the Conference Board index because the University of Michigan restricts circulation of their numbers; apparently they are afraid of losing most of their clients if they were to release their numbers publicly with no lag.

To start, we can divide factors that affect confidence into economic and noneconomic factors. The economic factors are tied closely to the quantity and quality of jobs. The inflation rate is also important during years of rapidly rising inflation, and the stock market has recently become more important. Noneconomic factors include events such as wars, energy shocks, terrorist bombings, and elections. While the terrorist attacks of 9/11 clearly depressed consumer spending briefly, that is hardly a predictable variable.

The next step is to relate the index of consumer confidence to the unemployment rate, the inflation rate, and changes in stock prices. However, the "quality" of jobs is also important. Suppose, to take an extreme example, the unemployment rate had risen to 10%, and in order to return to full employment, the government decreed that all employees would be forced to take a 10% pay cut, with the extra money used to hire the unemployed. It is quite doubtful that such a move would improve consumer confidence, even though unemployment would drop sharply.

Admittedly this is an extreme example, but during the early 1990s, a major move was taken toward what was called "downsizing" by employees and "right-sizing" by employers. The net result was that a proliferation of lower paying jobs replaced many higher paying jobs. This effect can be measured by dividing the total amount of wages and salaries by total employment; obtaining what is generally known as the implicit wage rate. This figure differs from average hourly earnings because it also measures the amount of downsizing.

The correlation of the Conference Board index of consumer confidence – as a function of the level of the unemployment rate, the change in unemployment over the past two years, the change in the implicit wage rate over the past two years, the

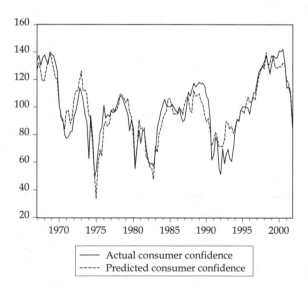

Figure 4.5 Determinants of consumer confidence: consumer confidence as a function of the level and change in the unemployment rate, the rate of inflation, change in stock prices, and change in the implicit wage rate

inflation rate over the past year, and the change in the S&P 500 stock price index over the past two quarters – is shown in figure 4.5. The underlying results show that a 1 percentage point change in the unemployment rate changes the confidence index by about 20% in the short run and 10% in the long run. A 1% change in the inflation rate changes the index by about 4%, while a 1% change in the stock market changes it by about 0.4%. Finally, a 1 percentage point change in the implicit wage rate – e.g., an increase in wages of 3% instead of 4% – changes the index by about 8%. Clearly the unemployment rate is the most important variable; the implicit wage rate is next, followed by inflation. Changes in the stock market are the *least* important variable.[12]

MANAGER'S BRIEFCASE: UTILIZING THE INDEXES OF CONSUMER CONFIDENCE

Many managers who do not have time to scrutinize the economic data closely but nonetheless are concerned about where the economy is heading follow the various indexes of consumer confidence. What can they tell you about the economy in general, and discretionary consumer spending in particular?

Consumers don't make decisions about their expectations in a vacuum. If the economy is booming, jobs are plentiful, interest rates are low, and stock prices are climbing, they will invariably be optimistic. Conversely, if all the reverse factors are true, they will be pessimistic.

Nonetheless these indicators can provide useful information about the strength of the upcoming recovery. Refer back to figure 4.5, and note that after the severe 1975 and 1982 recessions, the index of consumer confidence rebounded strongly. Now note that after the mild 1991 recession, the rebound was much more sluggish. The same is true of the 2001 recession. Most economists expected that real growth and consumer spending would also rebound vigorously after those recessions, but it did not occur. One can, in retrospect, point to the credit squeeze in the early 1990s and the disastrous stock market in the early 2000s, but based on the consensus forecasts of the time, the negative impact of these variables was not readily apparent. In such cases, the relatively small rebound in consumer confidence would have served as a valuable indicator that sales would remain sluggish until other components of the economy picked up the slack.

4.12   Review

In this chapter, we have shown that several different factors affect short-term fluctuations and long-term trends in consumer spending. In the long run, consumer purchases are based on what individuals expect their average income to be; that is generally known as the permanent income hypothesis. Also, consumers spend a higher proportion of their income when they are young or old, and a lower proportion during their peak earning years; that is generally known as the life cycle hypothesis. However, if these were the only determinants of consumption, short-run fluctuations in consumer spending would be smaller than the corresponding changes in income, since consumers would smooth their purchases over an extended time horizon. However, they are actually somewhat larger. That can be attributed to two major factors: changes in the cost and availability of credit, and changes in consumer attitudes.

The cost of credit – the interest rate – is an important determinant of consumption not only because time payments rise at a higher rate of interest, but because higher interest rates boost mortgage payments, reduce the amount of home equity that can be withdrawn for current consumption, and reduce the willingness of financial institutions to lend money to consumers. In addition, credit controls and restrictions, whenever they are enacted, have a very significant short-term effect on consumer purchases. The various indexes of consumer confidence and attitudes are usually tied to changes in the rate of inflation, the unemployment rate, and the real wage rate, including overtime and bonus payments. In addition, exogenous events such as 9/11 and energy crises can play an important short-term role.

The role of the stock market on consumer spending is ambiguous. It is often thought that when the stock market rises, consumers spend more because they are wealthier. However, that is not always the case. If the expected rate of return on equities rises, consumers might decide to save more now so they would have more to spend later; conversely, when the market declines, they might decide to spend more now. That was the main reason consumer spending kept rising during and shortly after the 2001 recession in spite of weak economic conditions.

KEY TERMS AND CONCEPTS

Life Cycle Hypothesis (LCH)
Marginal Propensity to Consume
Permanent Income Hypothesis (PIH)
Personal Saving Rate
Spendable Income
Time-Series Cross-Section Paradox

SUMMARY

- Consumer spending depends on three principal factors. The first is the average or expected income of consumers. The second is the cost and availability of credit. The third reflects the choice between spending and saving: spend more now and less later, or spend less now and more later. That factor is primarily related to the expected rate of return on assets.

- The *permanent income hypothesis* (PIH) states that consumption is a function of permanent or expected income, rather than only current income. Hence if the change in income is expected to be temporary, most of that change will be reflected in saving, whereas if the change in income is expected to be permanent, most of the change will be reflected in consumption.

- The *marginal propensity to consume* (MPC) measures the change in consumption per unit change in income. In the short run, the MPC will be higher if the change in income is expected to be permanent rather than temporary. In the long run, the MPC equals the average propensity to consume, i.e., the consumption/income ratio. The MPC is also affected by any changes that might occur in monetary conditions.

- A decline in the nominal rate of interest will boost purchases of consumer durables bought over time because it reduces the monthly payment. That is also the case for home purchase, which affects purchases of household appliances. Purchases of consumer durables are also significantly affected by the availability of credit, which can be measured by the yield spread between long-term and short-term interest rates.

- A decline in the nominal rate of interest permits many homeowners to refinance their mortgages at lower rates, hence boosting the amount of income available for purchasing other goods and services. Additionally, lower interest rates usually boost home prices, which permits homeowners to unlock the additional equity and spend it.

- A high real rate of interest will not raise the saving rate if consumers believe the only reason interest rates are high is that inflation is likely to rise sharply in the future.

- There is no positive correlation between the consumption/income ratio and the debt/income ratio. Some consumers continue to amass debts that far exceed their income, while others are inherently thrifty and prefer to save much of their income. Consumers are also more likely to accumulate debt early in their life cycle. Thus a rise in the debt/income ratio does not cause slower growth in consumer spending.

- Changes in stock market prices have an income effect on consumer spending but not a wealth effect. While an increase in stock prices boosts consumer net worth, most of those gains are in pension plans that cannot generally be spent in the near future. Even more to the point, an increase in the expected rate of return on stocks, which often occurs when the market is rising, may convince some consumers to save more now so they will have more money to spend later. Most of the observed correlation between consumption and stock prices occurs because an increase in stock prices boosts capital spending, which in turn raises output, employment, and personal income.

- Most of the decline in the reported personal saving rate during the 1990s occurred because the BEA incorrectly measured spendable income by excluding realized capital gains and increased home equity.

- The various indexes of consumer attitudes can serve as a useful shorthand for determining the strength or weakness of consumer spending, but most of the fluctuations in consumer attitudes are related to economic variables already considered above. The truly exogenous component of changes in consumer attitudes is not highly correlated with changes in consumer spending.

QUESTIONS AND PROBLEMS

1. According to both PIH and LCH, consumption depends on some measure of average or expected income rather than current income.

    (A) Explain why this would be the case most of the time.

    (B) In what circumstances would you expect it *not* to be the case?

    (C) Both of these theories predict that the personal saving rate declines in recessions. Yet it actually increases. What accounts for this discrepancy?

    (D) Both theories also rely on wealth as a determinant of consumption. Explain the situations under which a change in wealth would affect consumption, and the situations when it would not.

2. According to the PIH, the ratio of permanent consumption to permanent income is uncorrelated with the level of income. Thus someone earning $5,000,000 per year would save the same percentage of their income as someone earning $50,000 per year. Yet we find that for any given year, the saving rate has a strong positive correlation with the level of income. How can these facts be reconciled?

3. In early 1975, the government distributed $8 billion in one-time tax rebates to try to move the economy out of its most severe post-WWII recession. What impact do you think this had on consumption and saving? In mid-2001, a rebate of about $45 billion, representing the same proportion of disposable income, was distributed. Would you expect that rebate to have a relatively larger or smaller impact on consumption than in 1975? Why would that be the case?

4. In mid-1968, the government imposed a 10% income tax surcharge on personal and corporate income to pay for the costs of the Vietnam War. It was widely believed that the surcharge was temporary, and in fact it was removed in mid-1970. Based on the permanent income hypothesis, what would you expect to happen to the personal saving rate in late 1968, 1969, the first half of 1970, and the last half of 1970?

5. From mid-1996 to mid-1999, the personal saving rate fell from 5% to 3%. What were the principal factors that caused this decline?

6. The Kennedy-Johnson tax cut reduced personal income tax rates by 20% during 1964 and 1965; the personal saving rate was virtually unchanged from 1963.4 to 1965.4. The Reagan tax cut reduced personal income tax rates by 25% in 1982 and 1983; the personal saving rate fell sharply over that period. Why did the saving rate fall after the Reagan tax cut but not after the Kennedy-Johnson tax cut?

7. In 2001.3, the Bush Administration directed the Treasury to send checks of $300 to $600 to most taxpayers as an "advance" payment on the 2002 tax reduction, in order to pull the economy out of recession. The next quarter, in which there were no tax refunds, purchases of motor vehicles and parts (cars) rose $48 billion, stimulated by "zero-interest" financing, while other consumption rose $45 billion (all figures SAAR in billions of chained 1996 dollars). In 2002.1, when the permanent tax cut went into effect, car sales fell $34 billion while other consumption rose $84 billion. In 2002.2, car sales were flat while other consumption rose $33 billion. How do these observations square with the permanent income hypothesis? What can you say about the relative impact of monetary and fiscal policy on consumer spending?

8. During the 1990s, the age cohort that grew the most rapidly was the 45–54 cohort, which has the highest saving rate. Yet during that same period, the personal saving rate as reported by the BEA declined sharply. What factors accounted for this divergence?

9. Suppose that the Federal funds rate rose from 3% to 6% during the year. What would you expect to happen to the rate of growth in real consumption, and in the consumption/income ratio, under the following circumstances?

   (A) The corporate bond rate rose from 6% to 9%.
   (B) The corporate bond rate remained unchanged at 6%.
   (C) The stock market declined 20%.
   (D) The stock market was unchanged.
   (E) The unemployment rate rose from 5% to 6%.
   (F) The unemployment rate was unchanged.

10. Suppose the government decided to levy the current 15.3% social security tax on all levels of wages and salaries, not just the first $80,000, and used all the money collected to pay for prescription drug benefits for the poor and the aged. What do you think would happen to:

    (A) Total consumption?
    (B) Purchases of consumer durables?
    (C) The price of pharmaceutical company stocks?
    (D) The price of drug store stocks?
    (E) The overall stock market?
       How would your answers to (C) to (E) change if, as part of the legislation, drug prices were now set by the government?

11. According to legislation as of late 2002, the death tax (estate tax) is supposed to be fully phased out by the year 2010, but then reinstated at a maximum 55% rate in 2011. In terms of the LCH, how would these changes affect current consumption plans of those 65 and older?

Appendix: historical development of the consumption function

The standard theory of the consumption function states that spending by an individual consumer unit is related to its expected income, the cost and availability of credit, and the stock of wealth held by that consumer. In addition, people generally spend more than 100% of their income at certain stages of their life cycle, notably when they are in college or just starting to work and after they retire, and save a substantial proportion of their income during most of their working years.

The difference between actual and expected income is critical in understanding the pattern of consumer spending. Most consumer units have a reasonably firm expectation of the amount of income they will receive in the following year.

Of course, that expectation is not always correct. If income is decreased because of cyclical weakness and increased layoffs, but wage-earners believe they will soon be reemployed, consumption declines by less than the drop in income. If, on the other hand, wage-earners view the loss of job as a permanent development (such as the termination of relatively highly paid jobs in steel mills or coal mines), consumption might drop by the full amount of the decline in income.

Given this straightforward concept, it logically follows that in many cases, the income of consumers at the upper end of the income scale in any given year is well above their long-term expected income level, whereas the income of consumers at the lower end of the income scale in any given year is well below their long-term expected level. As a result, we would expect to find that the personal saving rate for those with very low incomes is negative, and the personal saving rate for those with very high incomes is quite large. That is precisely what the data show.

It was once thought such data meant that people with permanently low incomes dissaved, while those with permanently high incomes saved a large proportion of their income. However, that turns out not to be the case. People with low incomes in any given year dissave because their current income is well below their permanent income, not because their permanent income is low. In fact, most poor people could not dissave permanently because they cannot borrow very much and do not have very many assets. Most people who dissave are children, students, the elderly, or those who are temporarily unemployed.

Perhaps this seems fairly obvious, but that was not always the case. Following Keynes, most economists once thought the personal saving rate rose as income increased. That was one of the major points stressed in his *General Theory*. That assumption led to two untenable conclusions. One was that total GDP could be increased by transferring income from the "rich" to the "poor." The other was that an increase in income was accompanied by an increase in saving that would not be invested, so the only way the economy could remain at full employment was to increase the proportion of government spending to GDP.

Presumably economists know better now. Yet for the past decade, Japanese economists have been recommending ever-increasing public works projects, but the economy remains mired in recession. Some of the rhetoric directed against the Bush tax cut of 2001 claimed that it would eliminate the surplus and "rob" the Social Security "lockbox," but others claimed that giving the "rich" a tax cut would not stimulate the economy because they would not spend it. Old-style Keynesians also missed the distinction between the effect of temporary and permanent tax cuts. Hence vestiges of the old, outmoded theory are still found in public policy debates. For this reason, this appendix offers a brief review of the historical development of the consumption function.

Before the Great Depression, most economists were not concerned with the concept of an aggregate consumption function. They thought consumers would either spend their income or save it, in which case it would be invested. Thus the critical determinant of economic activity was how the interest rate balanced the scales between saving and investment, which in turn determined the long-run growth rate of the economy. A few economists, known as the "underconsumptionists," claimed that declines in economic activity occurred because consumers did not spend enough, but they were generally considered to be cranks.

All this changed when the worldwide economy fell into depression in the 1930s. Out of that maelstrom, Keynes developed his theory that as income rose, consumption also rose, but at a slower rate. Thus, he said, as income increased over time, the percentage gap between income and consumption would also widen. If that increased saving was not translated into investment, the economy would falter. Only the government, said Keynes, could pick up the slack. As a result, government spending would have to rise as a proportion of GDP in order to pull the economy out of perpetual stagnation.

Except for the part about consumption being related to income, this simple Keynesian theory is wrong on all accounts, bearing as it does a great resemblance to the claims of the discredited underconsumptionists. For if this hypothesis were true:

- Consumption would not rise as fast as income over time, and the personal saving rate would increase over time. Yet the saving rate shows no upward trend, and may have declined over the past two decades even when it is measured correctly.
- Consumption would be a function only of income, with financial variables playing an unimportant or negligible role in decisions to spend or save. Yet most short-term fluctuations in consumption are related to monetary factors.
- The saving rate would decline in recessions. Yet it invariably rises.
- Rich people would save a larger proportion of their income than poor people, because the saving rate rises as income rises. Yet in the long run, studies show that both rich and poor people save the same proportion of their average income.

The Time-Series Cross-Section Paradox

Figure 4.6 shows that consumption has been very highly correlated with income for the past 50 years; the key finding is there is no sign of a widening gap. Figure 4.7 shows that the gap between consumption and income varies cyclically over time. Figure 4.8 shows that the saving rate has not only been constant over long periods of time, but has declined on balance since 1980, although we have already explained why that decline is overstated. Figure 4.9 shows that the saving rate generally rises rather than declines in recessions; the only exception occurred in 1982, when interest rates fell by a record amount.

At first, the data shown in figure 4.10 would seem to support the hypothesis that rich people save a larger proportion of their income than poor people. Yet that statement is inconsistent with the long-run constancy of the saving rate. Real per capita disposable income has risen fourfold since 1929, yet the saving rate has stayed about the same.

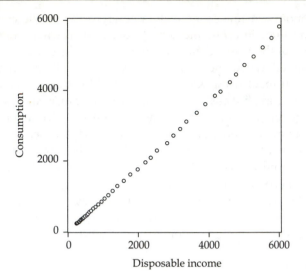

Figure 4.6 Scatter diagram, consumption and disposable income, 1947–98

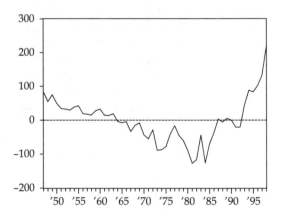

Figure 4.7 Residuals from simple consumption function (correlated only with disposable income)

This is known as the **time-series cross-section paradox**: on the one hand, saving does not rise as income increases over time, while on the other hand, saving appears to rise as individual income increases. Time-series data refers to data over many years, such as from 1947 through 1998. Cross-section data refers to a snapshot of different entities taken at the same time, such as the spending and saving patterns of all consumers in July, 1989.

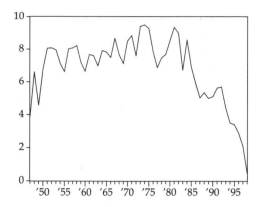

Figure 4.8   Personal saving as a percentage of disposable income

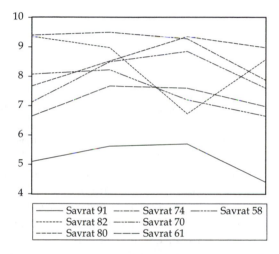

Savrat 91	Savrat 74	Savrat 58
Savrat 82	Savrat 70	
Savrat 80	Savrat 61	

Figure 4.9   Figures are the personal saving rate for the year before the recession started, the year of recession, and the next 2 years; in all cases, the saving rate rose during the recession except for 1982, when interest rates fell by a record amount

The Permanent Income Hypothesis

Even a brief reflection should reveal what is wrong with accepting the data in figure 4.10 at face value. It shows that the lowest income group has a saving rate of about −80%. Think about it for a minute. How could some people go through life spending almost twice as much as they earn? The only possibility would be that such individuals were very wealthy and were gradually depleting their assets, but in fact those with incomes of under $5,000 per year probably have very few assets.

The actual reason the saving rate is negative for low-income consumers is that most people in that income category don't usually earn less than $ 5,000 per year;

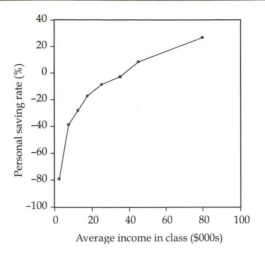

Figure 4.10   Personal saving rate by income class, 1989

they usually earn much more. In that year, reported income is well below the long-term average or expected income. These people may be students; or are taking a year off from work for vacation, because of illness, or because of temporary unemployment; or are retired. Clearly, individuals who earn an average of less than $5,000 per year over their entire lifetime and have no substantial assets cannot spend more than $10,000 every year. Most people who spend more than they earn in any given year are experiencing a year when their income is well below normal.

Thus one of the key modifications of the simple consumption function theory states that *consumption is based on expected or permanent income, not just income earned that year.* That concept is known as the **permanent income hypothesis** (PIH).

When the PIH was first introduced, it was subject to bitter criticism by the economics profession. The idea given in italics above was developed by Milton Friedman and, as has so often been the case, most economists initially disagreed with him. The greatest controversy focused on the top end of the income scale: it was generally thought that people in the top 1% of the income scale (above $350,000 at 2002 levels) save a larger proportion of their income than, say, people making $25,000 to $50,000 per year. And, it was argued, the constancy of the saving rate certainly is not true for someone making $5 or $10 million per year.

Friedman pointed out that just as most people in the lowest income classifications for any given year are earning far less than their average income, those in the very highest income classifications are earning far more than their average income. Perhaps they received a large bonus, cashed in stock options after 10 or 20 years of appreciation, sold their business, or received some other type of one-time payment that probably would not be repeated. They didn't spend anywhere near 95% of their income – but that was because their average income was well below what they received in that year.

What about people who regularly earn $1 million or more per year? How much they save depends on the individual person, but there are many stories of the rich who nonetheless ended up broke. When Donald Trump overextended himself and had to be monitored by his bankers, he complained bitterly because his "allowance" was cut to $450,000 per *month*. Sometime major league baseball player Jack Clark filed for bankruptcy because he could not pay all his debts from a salary of $3.8 million per year. These may be extreme examples, but there are many stories of sports and entertainment stars who end up impecunious in their later years. The cliché "from shirtsleeves to shirtsleeves in three generations" bears testimony to the patriarch who built up a fortune, only to see it frittered away by his progeny.

Although controversial when it was first released, the permanent income hypothesis is now accepted as a cornerstone of the modern consumption function. One of the most important empirical tests was to treat the value of one's house as a proxy for permanent income. The ratio of consumption/house value remains constant as income increases; there is no sign that those who live in expensive houses save a higher proportion of their permanent income. Other tests showed that the saving rate was invariant by professions: physicians, attorneys, and accountants did not save more of their income than blue-collar workers. These results are adjusted for volatility in income.

The principal concept of Friedman's theory of the consumption function is that consumers base their spending plans on some measure of expected or average income. Suppose, he said, someone got paid once a week. Does that mean they would eat a lot that day and nothing the rest of the week? Of course not. People base their spending plans on what they expect their average income will be. If their income is larger than usual in some week (or month, or year) they will save a larger proportion; if it is smaller than usual, they will save a smaller proportion.

This basic idea has evolved into the modern theory of the consumption function, which says consumers maximize their utility by taking into account all known information about their current income, its expected value in the future, the amount of assets they have, the rate of return on those assets, the amount they can borrow, and the rate at which they can borrow.

The PIH also states that if wealth rises, consumption rises for any given level of income. If interest rates rise, consumption declines. Monetary factors have always played an important role in the PIH; the issue is how to incorporate them empirically.

Other factors that may affect consumption, according to Friedman, are the volatility of actual income received, age of the consumer unit, and size of that unit. The change in consumption for any given change in income is likely to be smaller for someone with a highly volatile income – such as a farmer, independent business owner, or financial market trader – than for someone who receives steady wages or dividends. Friedman also found that large families spend a higher proportion of their income than smaller family units, although this factor is negligible at the macroeconomic level.

The key hypothesis of the PIH states that the ratio of permanent consumption to permanent income is independent of the level of income. Rich people do not save a larger proportion of their income than poor people.

From the viewpoint of *political* ramifications, the PIH stands as an effective rebuttal to Keynes. Most economists no longer think that as income increases, consumption does not rise as fast, so the government must fill the gap by spending more. Nor do they believe that aggregate consumption can be increased by taxing the rich more and giving it to the poor.[13]

Keynes said that a balanced budget generated by high spending and taxes was better for the economy than a balanced budget generated by low spending and taxes. In fact, Trygve Haavelmo, one of Keynes's followers, claimed that a $1 billion increase in both spending and taxes would boost real GDP by $1 billion. Friedman showed that was also incorrect, and today very few economists believe that statement.[14]

Some economists have claimed that Keynes, being an essential pragmatist and always interested in "what works," would certainly have modified his theories in view of the post-WWII full employment era; also, that these comments fail to take into account the important perspective of the time, when Keynes was trying to save capitalism from the twin evils of fascism and communism. Occasionally one reads a comment to the effect that "Keynes was not a Keynesian," meaning that he would have modified those views appropriately. Perhaps that would have been the case. However, to the extent that vestiges of the original Keynesian doctrine on the consumption function still enter the debate about the proper role of fiscal policy, a brief airing of these views seems appropriate here.

The Life Cycle Hypothesis

One popular extension of the PIH, developed by Franco Modigliani, is known as the **life cycle hypothesis** (LCH). The precise exposition has been changed over the years, but the general idea states that consumption depends on the total resources available to the consumer over his lifetime. That would include the present value of all current and expected future labor earnings, existing net worth (also known as wealth), the rate of return on capital, and the age of the consumer. Modigliani also places greater emphasis on expected income, as opposed to average past income, besides giving greater weight to the role of wealth relative to income.

According to the LCH, consumers plan their consumption over their lifetime. They dissave when first starting a family, gradually save more as retirement age approaches, and then dissave during retirement. As Modigliani says, "The cornerstone of the model is the notion that the purpose of saving is to enable the household to redistribute the resources it gets (and expects to get) over its life cycle in order to secure the most desirable pattern of consumption over life."

Today, almost all economists incorporate elements of the PIH and the LCH into their theories of the consumption function. Other recent developments have shown (a) the importance of the liquidity constraint when the monetary authorities decrease the amount of credit, and (b) the increasing important of confidence or sentiment variables. We have shown how both of these factors are empirically relevant.

Notes

1. The first economist to advance the theory that short-term fluctuations in consumption are random was Robert Hall, in his pathbreaking article, "Stochastic Implications of the Life Cycle-Permanent Income Hypothesis: Theory and Evidence," *Journal of Political Economy*, 86 (December 1978). Hall argues that the best forecast of a family's consumption next period is the amount of consumption this period.
2. This concept, known as excess sensitivity, was first developed by Hall's student, Marjorie Flavin. See her article "The Adjustment of Consumption to Changing Expectations About Future Income," *Journal of Political Economy*, 89 (October 1981).
3. Milton Friedman, *A Theory of the Consumption Function* (Princeton: Princeton University Press for NBER), 1957.
4. Bush Administration economists claim that the sluggish growth in 2002 reflected a massive decline in high-tech investment and a major decline in exports due to the overvalued dollar; if it were not for the tax cut, the recession would have continued and become much more serious. The unanswered question is whether the stock market would have rebounded if the Federal budget had not slipped back into a substantial deficit.
5. Two standard references are John Y. Campbell and N. Gregory Mankiw, "Consumption, Income and Interest Rates: Reinterpreting the Time Series Evidence," in O. Blanchard and S. Fischer, eds, NBER *Macroeconomics Annual* (Cambridge, MA: MIT Press, 1989), and Robert E. Hall and Frederic S. Mishkin, "The Sensitivity of Consumption to Transitory Income Estimates from Panel Data on Households," *Econometrica*, 1982.
6. Conversely, an inverted yield curve could occur because long-term rates fell sharply while short-term rates were unchanged.
7. As one GM executive remarked, "No new cars have ever been returned to the scrap heap."
8. As will be shown in chapter 6, the spread between long-term and short-term rates is likely to be unusually large when the Federal budget deficit is large, which was indeed the case in the early 1980s.
9. This point is discussed in detail in chapter 20.
10. The LCH was developed by Franco Modigliani, who has published many papers on the subject. The original formulation appeared in Modigliani and R. E. Brumberg, "Utility Analysis and the Consumption Function: An Interpretation of Cross-Section Data," in K. K. Kurihara, ed., *Post-Keynesian Economics* (Rutgers University Press, 1954). Modigliani's views were summarized in his Nobel laureate acceptance speech, published as "Life Cycle, Individual Thrift, and the Wealth of Nations," *American Economic Review*, 76, June 1986. A thorough discussion of this and other recent theories of consumption can be found in Angus Deaton, *Understanding Consumption* (New York, Oxford University Press, 1992).
11. These figures can be found in various issues of the *Federal Reserve Bulletin* and the *Statistical Abstract*, which can also be accessed from the Census website, www.census.gov.

12. The actual regression is as follows:

$$\text{CCIN} = 135.3 - \underset{(16.6)}{10.41}\text{UN} - \underset{(17.6)}{11.3}\Delta\text{UN} - \underset{(8.7)}{4.08}\text{INFL} + \underset{(5.5)}{0.53}\,\%\Delta\text{SP} + \underset{(9.3)}{8.58}\Delta\text{IWAGE}$$

where CCIN = Conference Board index of consumer confidence, UN = unemployment rate, INFL = inflation rate over the past four quarters, SP = S&P 500 stock price index and the change is over two quarters, and IWAGE = the implicit wage rate, where a polynomial distributed lag (PDL) is used over eight quarters. Also, an eight-quarter PDL is used for the change in the unemployment rate. Numbers in parentheses are *t*-ratios.

13. As Robert Bleiberg, former editor of *Barron's*, once said, he found it very difficult to believe that if he got mugged outside his New York apartment, that somehow increased total GDP.

14. With the passage of time, some economists doubt that Keynes ever made statements of this sort. However, his views in the *General Theory* are quite clear. "The fundamental psychological law, upon which we are entitled to depend with great confidence both a priori from our knowledge of human nature and from the detailed facts of experience, is that men are disposed, as a rule and on the average, to increase their consumption as their income increases, but not by as much as the increase in their income" (p. 96, Macmillan edition, 1960). "If our assumption is correct that the marginal propensity to consume falls off steadily as we approach full employment, it follows that it will be more and more troublesome to secure a further given increase of employment by further increasing investment" (p. 127). "If the Treasury were to fill old bottles with banknotes, bury them at suitable depths in disused coal mines which are then filled up to the surface with town rubbish, and leave it to private enterprise on well-tried principles of laissez-faire to dig up the notes again (the right to do so being obtained, of course, by tendering for leases of the note-bearing territory), there need be no more unemployment and, with the help of the repercussions [i.e., multipliers], the real income of the community, and its capital wealth also, would probably become a good deal greater than it actually is" (p. 129).

chapter five

Investment and saving

Introduction

Consumer spending represents about two-thirds of total GDP. And, in the long run, what consumers do or do not buy determines the course of the economy. Yet a theory of consumer spending alone would provide a very incomplete version of what determines economic activity. In the short run, most of the fluctuations in the economy occur in capital spending, housing, inventory investment, exports, and imports. In the long run, productivity growth depends more on capital formation than on consumer spending. Indeed, for a given level of GDP, the higher the proportion of total resources devoted to investment and saving, the faster the growth rate will be.

According to the fundamental aggregate identity introduced in section 2.2, $C + I + F + G = GDP$. Yet an increase in consumption does not always boost GDP. If consumers save less, that could reduce saving and fixed investment. Also, in the short run, the rise in consumption could be offset by a decline in inventory stocks. In some cases, the increased spending might boost the demand for imported goods, so total GDP would not change. In short, when consumption changes, we do not know what happens to total GDP until the changes in saving and investment are determined.

This chapter first discusses the logical equivalence of investment and saving. That is followed by a brief description of the principal determinants of fixed investment; further details are supplied in chapter 16. An initial description of exports, imports, and foreign saving is also presented. The role of government saving is briefly considered, and the linkages between saving and investment are then summarized.

5.1   The equivalence of investment and saving

The previous chapter discussed the determinants of consumer spending. By definition, the amount of income consumers receive that is not spent or paid in taxes is saved. But what happens to that saving?

In the case of an independent entrepreneur, it often goes directly into investment. However, that only accounts for a small proportion of total personal saving. In most cases, individuals save through financial intermediates: they deposit money in banks, or buy bonds or stocks (often through a mutual fund or their place of business) as part of their pension plan. Financial intermediaries then invest these funds.

In the long run, the growth rate of the economy is determined primarily by the proportion of GDP that is saved and invested, although other factors are also important. In the short run, cyclical fluctuations are due in large part to the imbalance between ex ante saving and investment; by definition, they must be equal ex post.

In some cases, the amount of money that businesses want to borrow to purchase capital goods could be precisely equal to the amount of money that individuals want to save. In that case, the economy would remain in equilibrium without any further adjustment. However, that rarely happens. Far more often, ex ante saving and investment are not the same, so some adjustment is required to attain ex post equilibrium.

Suppose businesses want to invest more than individuals want to save on an ex ante basis. There are several ways in which equilibrium could be reached. First, a rise in the interest rate could boost domestic saving and reduce investment. Second, more money could be attracted from abroad. Third, the government could increase its saving by cutting spending or raising taxes. Fourth, inventory investment could decrease because of the unexpected rise in sales. If none of these move the economy to equilibrium, and the economy is at full capacity, the delay in delivery of investment goods would cause ex post investment to fall below ex ante plans. In such a situation, which is likely to be inflationary, the central bank would presumably tighten credit conditions, which would also diminish investment.

This point should be emphasized. If ex ante investment exceeds ex ante private domestic saving, as usually happens during booms, either (a) the government deficit will decline (or the surplus will rise), (b) foreign saving will rise, which means the trade deficit will increase, or (c) interest rates will rise. If the Fed acts promptly, that increase will occur before inflation rises; otherwise inflation will rise first.

Now suppose ex ante saving exceeds ex ante investment, which is likely to occur in a recession. A decline in the interest rate could reduce saving relative to investment; less money could be attracted from abroad, the government could decrease its saving by boosting spending or cutting taxes, or inventory investment could decline. Nonetheless, the argument is not symmetrical. Whereas a rise in interest rates, restricted availability of capital goods, or monetary stringency are quite likely to reduce ex post investment, it is far less likely that lower interest rates, quick delivery of capital goods, or monetary accommodation would boost investment if business expectations have deteriorated. That is one of the main reasons that recessions occur.

Thus if ex ante private sector saving exceeds ex ante investment, either (a) the government surplus will shrink or the deficit will rise, (b) foreign saving will decline, which means the trade deficit will shrink, or (c) interest rates will fall. The Keynesian doctrine suggests that stimulatory fiscal policy – increasing the deficit – and stimulatory monetary policy – reducing interest rates and increasing the availability of credit – will be sufficient to bring recessions to an early end. Most of the time that is true, but the positive short-term stimulus of a bigger government deficit must be offset against the possibility that business confidence will be further eroded, hence causing a further decline in ex ante investment. In that case, the business cycle contraction could continue indefinitely. In particular, note that an attempt to raise taxes during a recession could have a severe negative impact on the economy, since such a move would decrease consumption without providing any offsetting stimulus to investment.

Because of the way the national income and product accounts (NIPA) are constructed, saving is identically equal to investment on an ex post basis. Hence if the economy slumps because of a reduction in planned investment, ex post saving must necessarily decline as well, even if individuals and businesses did not plan to save less. That might occur if output, employment, and income decline, thereby reducing consumer saving because income has declined. Also, government saving would decline as tax receipts drop and countercyclical transfer payments, such as unemployment benefits and welfare payments, rise. Finally, foreign saving would usually decline because imports would drop as domestic demand fell. The only reason that would not occur would be if the recession in the US spread around the world, hence reducing international demand for US exports.

Suppose, however, that stimulatory fiscal and monetary policy do not boost the growth rate very much. In such a situation, consumers might plan to save more, and businesses plan to invest less, because of reduced expectations. Assume the government is determined to keep the budget balanced, and hence does not reduce saving. Also assume that exports decline as much as imports, so foreign saving does not drop. In that case, how would equilibrium be reached?

The answer is that the recession would have to become so severe that consumers, businesses, and the government would all be forced to save less. Seen in this light, the sharp rise in the budget deficit is an important automatic stabilizer that keeps recessions from turning into depressions. The significant decline in imports during recessions also cushions the blow, since some of the drop in demand is shared around the globe. In addition, aggressive monetary easing reduces interest rates, reducing consumer saving and mitigating the decline in fixed investment. Most economists now realize these are important linkages that help stabilize the economy; without them, recessions would be more frequent and more severe.

5.2   Long-term determinants of capital spending

Consumers purchase goods and services because they derive utility, or pleasure, from these items. Most consumers are subject to a budget constraint, although for most people that can temporarily be bypassed by borrowing. Some consumers derive more pleasure from saving than others do but, in the aggregate, consumers save only a small proportion of their total income. When correctly adjusted for spendable income, the personal saving rate usually averages between 5% and 10% of disposable income.

The decision to invest by firms is made for quite different reasons. Firms will purchase plant and equipment if they think the rate of return earned on that investment will be higher than the rate of return that could be earned on alternative investments, such as in the bond market. In a world of perfect capital markets and perfect information, the amount of money firms have on hand is irrelevant; it is the expected future rate of return that is important. However, firms are subject to liquidity constraints just as consumers are.

As a result, capital spending decisions depend on the comparison of the expected future rate of return with the existing rate of return on existing assets. Even if firms have billions of dollars in cash and liquid assets, they will not invest in more plant and equipment unless the rate of return is expected to be larger than could be earned by investing in some other company or in government securities, or by repurchasing their own shares of stock.

Of course, businesses do not know what the future rate of return will be; they must make educated guesses about how much their sales and costs will grow in the future. This involves predicting both the increase in volume and the increase in prices. For example, if oil companies thought the price of oil would double over the next decade, they would boost capital spending sharply even if they did not expect the volume to rise at all.

When considering the interest rate that must be paid, firms also estimate the future rate of inflation to determine the amount of payback in real terms. For example, if the bond rate is currently 12% but the expected rate of inflation is 10%, firms will be much more eager to borrow than if the bond rate is 12% but the expected rate of inflation is only 4%. Hence in determining the cost of funds, firms look at the real rate of interest – the current rate of interest minus the expected future rate of inflation – rather than the nominal rate of interest. For many firms, the cost of equity capital is also important.

Firms must also consider the expected growth in the volume of sales relative to their existing capacity to produce these goods and services, which is usually measured by the current rate of capacity utilization: if excess capacity currently exists, the rate of return from additional investment will generally be less than if the firm is fully utilizing all existing plant and equipment. Finally, firms are more likely to replace equipment during periods of rapid technological advance than during periods when new machines offer only a slight competitive advantage.

Thus the long-term factors that determine the rate of capital spending under equilibrium conditions are the current nominal rate of interest, the expected rate of inflation for the overall economy, the expected rate of inflation for the particular goods or services it produces, the expected growth in the volume of sales, the current rate of capacity utilization, and the underlying growth rate of technology.

The formal theory of optimal capital accumulation, which incorporates these and other factors, is presented in the appendix to this chapter.

Yet in practice, an equation used to explain capital spending with the above variables generates very poor predictions. Several key factors are still missing. First, short-term timing decisions will depend on changes in the availability of credit. Second, expectational factors may cause projects to be advanced or postponed. The stock market plays an important role in both these decisions. Third, even if firms decide to order new capital goods immediately, there will be lags in deliveries that may depend on the stage of the business cycle. In some cases, such as jet aircraft or electrical generating equipment, the lag between orders and deliveries is several years. Fourth, changes in the tax laws affecting investment and corporate income may also influence investment decisions – or at least the timing of those decisions. Each of these factors is now considered.

5.3   The basic investment decision

The deployment of capital resources is one of the critical decisions senior business executives must make regardless of the line of business. Should a firm expand its existing line of business or not? Should it enter a different business, and, if so, should it build facilities itself or buy them from someone else? No intelligent decision can be made without considering the cost of capital.

In the broadest sense, a firm invests in plant and equipment because it expects to increase its profit. More specifically, it compares the cost of an additional capital good – including interest and depreciation, and adjusted for taxes – with the additional revenue that it expects to receive from the additional goods and services produced with that capital good.

Since the investment will be used for several years, the price of the investment itself is not the same as the annual cost. Of course, the price of the capital good is relevant. However, the key factor is the cost per time period, compared to the extra revenue produced in that time period. For purposes of exposition we assume the time unit is one year.

For example, suppose a machine costs $10,000,000, and can produce goods that generate an extra $1,500,000 per year in income after all variable costs have been paid. Is that a good investment?

With only the numbers given above, it is impossible to tell. More information is needed.

Suppose the interest rate is 7%.[1] Then interest costs will be $700,000 per year. We emphasize these costs will be incurred in an economic sense whether or not the firm actually borrows the money. For if it were to use its own funds, they could be invested elsewhere at 7%, thus bringing the firm an extra $700,000 per year if the investment was not undertaken. That is why the investment being considered must provide a higher rate of return than alternative opportunities.

The amount of depreciation must also be considered. The manager needs to know how long the capital good is expected to last. Suppose the machine purchased has a ten-year life, after which it becomes obsolete, either because it wears out or will be replaced by better technology. That means $1,000,000 per year must be set aside to replace the machine.[2]

Thus the increased revenues are $1,500,000 per year, but the increased cost of capital is $1,700,000, generating an annual loss of $200,000. The investment is not worth it – even though it brings in an extra $1.5 million each year on an EBITDA basis (earnings before interest, taxes, depreciation, and amortization). The money would be better spent on other projects, or invested through financial intermediaries at the market rate.

Now, however, suppose the interest rate drops to 3%, so annual interest costs fall from $700,000 to $300,000. That leaves a profit of $200,000 even after considering the cost of capital, so it is worth undertaking the investment.

Hence the more interest rates decline, the more investment projects will be undertaken. That is the basic idea underlying the inverse correlation between interest rates and capital spending. In fact the investment decision is much more complicated, because other factors affect the cost of capital. Nonetheless, the negative correlation between interest rates and capital spending is a valid one.

Some economists have tried to use the same approach to explain housing starts. When interest rates decline, housing starts rise both because builders can obtain credit more readily and at a lower cost, and because more consumers can qualify for a mortgage on a house of any given price. However, short-term fluctuations in housing are more closely tied to the availability of credit than its cost. Builders generally borrow the money for relatively short periods of time, so for them availability is more important than cost. While homeowners often have 30-year mortgages, rates are increasingly tied to short-term market rates. Furthermore, availability of credit is often the determining factor for whether a would-be homebuyer can obtain a mortgage. Thus the comments about the cost of capital apply primarily to capital spending rather than housing. We now examine this concept in more detail.

MANAGER'S BRIEFCASE: THE "HURDLE" RATE OF RETURN

Students often note that while the real interest rate is around 5%, companies usually require a projected 20% or 25% rate of return in order to undertake additional capital spending. How can these two figures be reconciled?

Three separate items must be considered. First, while capital spending decisions are actually based on the expected real rate of return – the nominal rate minus the expected rate of inflation – budgetary decisions are usually quoted in nominal terms. Second, the total rate of return must include setting aside capital for replacement purposes – the depreciation proportion. Third, the rate of return is calculated only after the payment of corporate income taxes. In some extreme situations, the benefit of the investment tax credit and accelerated depreciation allowances more than offset the burden of corporate taxes, but that rarely happens.

continued

MANAGER'S BRIEFCASE (*continued*)

During the 1990s, the Aaa corporate bond rate averaged about 8%, while the inflation rate was about 3%, so the real rate of interest was about 5%. However, depreciation allowances were about 7% of total capital stock on a straight-line basis, boosting the return on capital in nominal terms to about 15%. The marginal statutory corporate income tax rate was 35% at the Federal level, but that is partially offset by accelerated depreciation allowances, so the actual figure is closer to 25%. Hence the required rate of return would be equal to 15%/0.75, or 20%, right at the lower end of the usual range. If the nominal interest rate were 10% instead of 8% because of higher inflation, the hurdle rate calculated in this manner would be 22.7%, and if the nominal rate rose to 12%, the hurdle rate would increase to 25.3%. Hence there is no inconsistency between these measures of the rate of return and the cost of capital.

5.4   The cost of capital

While investment is negatively related to the expected real rate of interest, the rate of depreciation and the price of the capital good are also important factors in determining whether the investment will be made. In addition, tax laws regarding depreciation, the rate of investment tax credit, and the marginal corporate income tax rate also affect capital spending. It is useful to find some way to combine all these factors when specifying the investment function.

According to standard microeconomic theory, equilibrium in factor markets occurs when the marginal product of labor equals the real wage rate, and the marginal product of capital equals the real cost of capital. But what is the cost of capital?

It certainly is not the price of the capital good itself, since that lasts for several years. In the example given above, a firm purchased a machine for $10 million and the machine lasted for ten years. The sensible approach is to consider the annual cost of the machine over its economic lifetime.

For any given period of time (usually one year), the cost of capital – sometimes known as the rental cost of capital – equals the price of that capital good times the sum of the interest rate and the depreciation rate, adjusted for tax laws that affect the tax rate on business income. The real cost of capital is the rental cost divided by the average price of the product, which in the aggregate is the implicit GDP deflator.

As already noted, the relevant interest rate is the expected real rate of interest, which is the nominal rate minus the expected rate of inflation. Empirically, as discussed in greater detail in chapter 8, the long-run expected rate of inflation can be closely approximated by the average rate of inflation over the past five years. Hence in the figures and calculations that follow, the real rate of interest equals the nominal Aaa corporate bond yield minus the average rate of inflation over the past five years. Figure 5.1 shows the ratio of fixed business investment to GDP compared to a five-year weighted average of the cost of capital variable.[3]

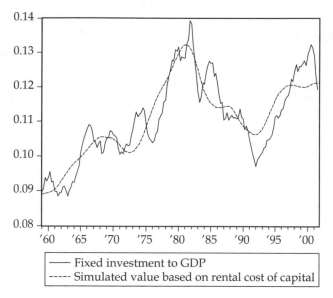

Figure 5.1 The ratio of fixed investment to GDP as compared to simulated values derived from a five-year distributed lag of the rental cost of capital

The various tax factors that influence fixed investment include the corporate income tax rate, the rate of investment tax credit, and the regulations affecting depreciation allowances, especially those that permit firms to write off plant and equipment more rapidly than the actual economic rate of depreciation. These are discussed in more detail in section 5.8.

The concept of the cost of capital can be formalized as follows. Let p_k equal the cost of the capital equipment, and p_{gdp} the price of the product. Both terms need to be included; otherwise the cost of capital would differ depending on whether p_k was measured in dollars, euros, yen, or some other currency. Besides, the cost of capital should reflect both the price of the capital good and the price at which the products can be sold.

Also, let r be the long-term real rate of interest, δ be the rate of depreciation, τ be the tax rate on income used to purchase capital goods, κ the rate of investment tax credit, and ζ the present value of the depreciation deduction. Then the cost of capital, rcc, can be written as:

$$\text{rcc} = (p_k/p_{gdp})(r + \delta)(1 - \tau\zeta - \kappa)/(1 - \tau).$$

If the price of the capital good rises relative to the price of the good produced, the rcc will rise, so fewer investment projects will be undertaken. If the rate of interest rises, investment will decline, and if the rate of taxation on corporate income rises, investment will also decline.

The cost of capital term developed above only includes debt capital; for many firms, the cost of equity capital is also important. However, that term is treated separately for several reasons. First, the tax treatment is different because interest costs are deductible, whereas dividends are not. Second, while the debt cost of capital is roughly similar for most firms, the cost of equity capital can vary widely, as some firms have P/E ratios of under ten while other firms have ratios over 100 – or, in the late 1990s, infinite ratios, since they had no earnings at all. Third, stock prices contain an important element of expectations. For all these reasons, the cost of equity capital is considered separately and is not directly included in the cost of capital term.

5.5   The availability of credit

Because most capital spending is undertaken by large firms, one might think that the availability of credit, as opposed to the cost of capital, would not have as large an effect on investment as is the case for consumption. However, it does have a major influence on the timing of investment patterns, particularly for relatively short-lived assets such as motor vehicles and high-tech equipment, which now account for almost half of all producer durable equipment.

   Yet if firms determine capital spending investments based on the expected future rate of return, why should the availability of credit be an important determinant of capital spending?

1. One major issue is that the corporation really does not know what lies ahead. If the firm spends money it already has, it will not face a crisis in repaying loans if business turns sour, while if it borrows the money, it may be difficult to repay loans on a timely basis if cash flow dries up. Under these circumstances, some firms might run the risk of violating loan covenants if they had borrowed heavily to finance capital spending.
2. The availability of credit also serves as an expectations variable. If credit is being tightened, the economy is probably heading into a slump, which would hurt sales for most firms even if they were not subject to credit restraints. In that sense, the yield spread between long- and short-term rates is one of the key variables in the index of leading indicators.
3. Borrowing money may push some firms into a higher risk category. Thus, even if market interest rates do not change, the interest rate paid by the firm might rise if it substantially increased the proportion of its borrowings to total capital. Such a shift could affect the rate the firm would have to pay on *all* its loans, not just the latest round of borrowed funds, so the marginal cost of borrowing more money could be very high.
4. Many smaller firms finance their capital spending through the equity market. When the stock market is booming, IPOs and secondary offerings are readily available; when the market is plunging, investment bankers will not bring these issues to market at all. In such cases, availability rather than cost is the principal criterion.

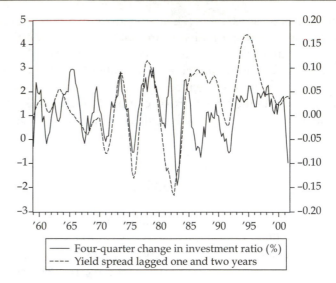

Figure 5.2 The four-quarter percentage changes in the ratio of capital spending to GDP in current dollars are correlated with the moving average of the yield spread between the Aaa corporate bond rate and Fed funds rate, lagged an average of one and two years

The same general arguments explain why cash flow is often an important determinant of capital spending even if firms have access to bank credit and capital markets. In a world of perfect information, these constraints would not be nearly as important. However, lenders have learned from bitter experience that a certified financial statement from a major accounting firm often conceals more information than it reveals. Decisions cannot be made about the appropriate risk factor based on published accounting data alone. As a result, many firms run the risk of being turned down for loans, even if their financial statements are actually in good shape, if their liquid assets appear to be a small percentage of their liabilities. Such firms would be more likely to invest available cash flow, as opposed to running the risk of having to pay a higher rate of interest or being rejected entirely by lending institutions or financial markets. The correlation between changes in the ratio of capital spending to GDP, and the lagged values of the yield spread, are shown in figure 5.2.

MANAGER'S BRIEFCASE: RAISING MONEY FROM BANKS OR CAPITAL MARKETS

Most firms, no matter how large, find that stockholder value is enhanced if they borrow money. For many years, E. I. du Pont was proud of the fact that they never borrowed any money. As the go-go years of the 1980s approached, it was pointed out to them that the lack of debt and leverage, and hence the relatively modest rate of return on total

continued

MANAGER'S BRIEFCASE (*continued*)

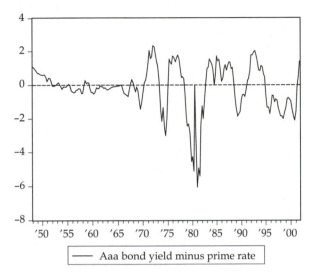

Figure 5.3   Yield spread between Aaa corporate bond rate and the prime rate

investment, made them a possible unwilling target for takeover. They quickly remedied the situation and borrowed for investments and acquisitions, including but not limited to purchase of the Continental Oil Company (Conoco), which was later sold and then merged with Phillips petroleum.

Because interest payments are deductible, the arithmetic of increasing stockholder return by borrowing money is obvious, no matter how large the company. Nonetheless, the fact that these loans must be paid back increases the risk of a cash flow crunch during periods of recession. Sometimes firms do borrow in the bond market when rates are low, raising money by floating 30-year (or even longer) bonds; of course, interest payments must be made, but by refinancing when the business is flush and interest rates are relatively low, the repayment of principal can be postponed indefinitely. When interest rates fell to unusually low levels in 1993, a few companies actually floated 100-year bonds.

While the company must make more information public with a bond offering than if it borrows from a bank, that cannot be the principal reason for large corporations, which offer information because of stock offerings anyhow. The principal determinant would appear to be the cost of borrowing from banks as opposed to borrowing in the bond market.

Figure 5.3 shows that some of the time, the Aaa bond yield is higher than the prime rate; other times it is lower. Over the 50-year period, there is virtually no difference between the average of the two rates. So cost alone would not appear to be a compelling factor either.

Nonetheless, one could reasonably argue that this graph is misleading, or at a minimum not the whole story. Many large companies desire lines of credit, for which they pay perhaps $\frac{1}{4}$%, allowing them to withdraw the money in times of unforeseen liquidity shortfalls without having the expense of managing a bond issue and paying interest for many years. In addition, many large corporations require that banks provide them with a large variety of services in return for "compensating balances," so that the true cost of borrowing to the corporation is far less than would be indicated by the prime rate itself. For these reasons, then, many large well-managed corporations

continued

MANAGER'S BRIEFCASE (*continued*)
continue to rely on bank financing. When the yield curve then becomes inverted, they may find their ability to borrow is either curtailed or becomes much more expensive. That is why the yield curve is an important determinant of capital spending even for large corporations.

5.6   The role of expectations

Because no firm can predict the future very accurately, all capital spending decisions are based on imperfect expectations. The role of the economist is to try to quantify the factors that determine these expectations.

Assume the firm has gathered the relevant information on the current rate of capacity utilization, the change in technology since the last similar investment, the cost of debt and equity capital, the current tax laws, internal cash flow, and the availability of funds in financial markets. Based on this information, it has calculated the expected rate of return for each projected investment. Should the firm go ahead with the project, or wait a while?

Several decades ago, many organizations, including the Commerce Department, McGraw-Hill, and what was then called the National Industrial Conference Board, prepared annual surveys predicting how much capital spending would change in the following year. These surveys were based on capital appropriations of large corporations. Since these firms represented a high proportion of total capital spending, it was initially thought these surveys would be quite accurate. However, the errors were so large that the exercise was finally downgraded or abandoned completely. In spite of the fact that large firms carefully prepare capital budgets every year, it is clear that they also change their plans in midstream.

Perhaps the most obvious case arises when the economy plunges into recession; even if various investment projects have been considered profitable based on existing data, many of them will be postponed because of the ongoing decline in sales. The expected rate of capacity utilization will fall, and existing plant and equipment will be adequate. For most firms, changes in the index of capacity utilization, stock prices, and corporate cash flow serve as the most important indicators that determine whether investment decisions should be postponed.

Since data on appropriations and anticipations for capital spending are no longer published on a regular basis, it is not possible to use recent data to determine which variables are most likely to affect changes in expectations. The key variable is probably the change in the volume of sales, which for manufacturing firms can be measured by changes in the rate of capacity utilization; if sales plunge, investment plans will be postponed even if the long-term outlook is still favorable. In addition, firms often modify existing plans for capital spending based on short-term changes in cash flow and stock prices. Even large firms with adequate access to capital markets usually trim capital budgets when cash flow targets are not met. Hence,

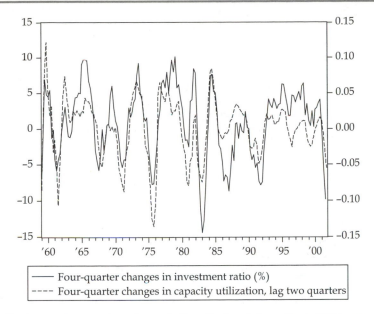

Figure 5.4   The four-quarter percentage changes in the ratio of capital spending to GDP in current dollars are correlated with the four-quarter changes in the index of capacity utilization, lagged two quarters

on an empirical basis, changes in capacity utilization, cash flow, and stock prices over the past few years are also important determinants of capital spending.

The correlation between the four-quarter percentage changes in the ratio of capital spending to GDP and the four-quarter changes in the rate of capacity utilization, lagged two quarters, is shown in figure 5.4. This lag is short, representing modifications of plans; the rate of capacity utilization also affects the equilibrium demand for capital stock with a longer lag. Similar lags occur for cash flow and stock prices as modifications variables, but the correlations are not as strong.

5.7   Lags in the investment function

When most consumers want to buy a particular good – even a durable good that is expected to last several years – they get in their car, go to the mall or dealership, and buy the item that day – or they check for the best bargains on the internet. However, except for consumer-type goods such as personal computers or motor vehicles, most capital goods cannot be delivered the day they are ordered. In addition, most capital budgeting undergoes a much more rigorous process than the average consumer purchasing decision.

In determining how investment affects the economy, several lags must be considered. The first is the appropriations lag: the time between changes in economic conditions and the time that the capital good is ordered. The second is the delivery lag, which varies widely depending on the type of equipment or plant. The third,

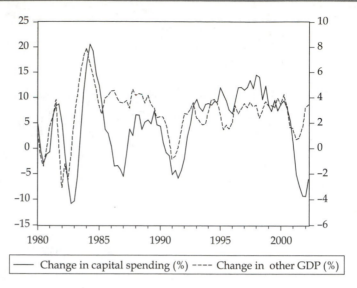

Figure 5.5   Four-quarter percentage change in real capital spending and real GDP excluding capital spending

which is really a corollary of the delivery lag, is what we call the asymmetry lag: the decision to cancel can be made much more quickly than the decision to purchase. That means, other things being equal, that capital spending has a longer lag on the upside than it does on the downside.

The empirical magnitude of these lags is illustrated in figure 5.5, which compares the percentage change in capital spending with the percentage change in the sum of all other components of GDP; both series are in real dollars. Three factors can be noted. First, the lags are not very long on the downside. Second, they are longer on the upside: in recent recessions, the rest of the economy usually turns up almost a year before capital spending started to improve. Because the 1980 recession was caused primarily by the imposition of credit controls, which primarily affected short-lived assets, the lags were not as long in that brief recession. Third, fluctuations in capital spending are much greater than the remaining components of GDP. The dip in capital spending in 1986, which is not mirrored in the rest of GDP, reflects the cancellation of the investment tax credit in that year.

5.8   The effect of changes in tax policy on capital spending decisions

The corporate income tax code changes virtually every year, but most of these changes represent minor tinkering with existing regulations, or attempt to adjust those regulations to mean what Congress and IRS thought they meant in the first place. Our comments consider only the major changes, which can be grouped into three categories: changes in the marginal statutory corporate income tax rate, adding or removing the investment tax credit, and adjusting depreciation schedules. The major changes in these categories can be summarized as follows:

1951–3: Certain wartime facilities can be written off over five years instead of the life of the capital good (known as accelerated amortization allowances, or AAA). An excess profits tax was also imposed during the war.

1954: AAA is terminated along with the end of the Korean War, but several other changes are made to the tax code, including a limited deduction of dividends against corporate income; some depreciation allowances are liberalized.

1962: Investment tax credit (ITC) introduced at a rate of 7%. The amount of the ITC, which is equal to the rate of credit times the amount of the qualified capital equipment purchased (it does not apply to structures), can be deducted directly from the income tax owed by a corporation.

1964–5: Terms of the ITC become more generous although the rate stays at 7%. The marginal statutory corporate income tax rate is lowered from 52% to 48% in two steps, and depreciation allowances are further liberalized, permitting quicker writeoff times.

Sept. 1966–Mar. 1967: ITC and accelerated depreciation temporarily suspended.

Mid-1968 to mid-1970: 10% corporate income tax surcharge.

Apr. 1969–Aug. 1971: ITC and accelerated depreciation temporarily suspended.

1975: Rate of ITC increased to 10%.

1981: Further liberalization of depreciation allowances, especially for structures, and several other corporate income tax breaks; income tax rate is cut from 48% to 46%.

1982: Some of the 1981 advantages are terminated, but accelerated depreciation allowances remain on the books.

1986: Most corporate tax advantages are terminated, including the end of the ITC and accelerated depreciation. The top marginal corporate income tax rate is lowered from 46% to 34% in two steps.

1993: Corporate tax rises from 34% to 35%; other changes raise the effective tax rate slightly.

Economists are divided in their opinion about the impact of these tax changes on purchases of capital equipment, other than to change the timing (e.g., firms rushed to place orders shortly before the ITC was canceled). Figure 5.6 shows the relationship between the rate of investment tax credit and the ratio of purchases of producers' durable equipment to GDP for the four major categories: industrial, high-tech, transportation, and other, which is largely resource-based equipment such as energy and agriculture.

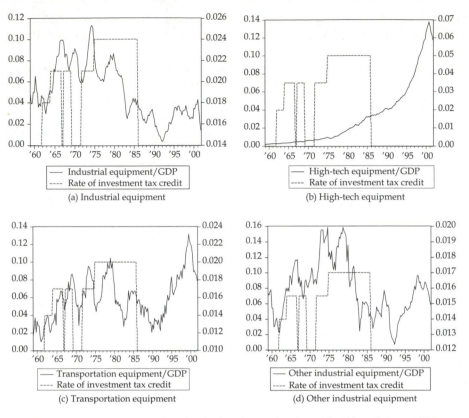

Figure 5.6   Rate of investment tax credit and ratio of purchases of producers' durable equipment to GDP

CASE STUDY 5.1   DID THE INVESTMENT TAX CREDIT BOOST PURCHASES OF CAPITAL GOODS?

One of the hotly debated issues in both economic and political circles is whether the investment tax credit actually boosted purchases of capital goods (it did not apply to structures). Figure 5.6 compares the ratio of the four major types of capital goods purchases with the rate of investment tax credit. In all cases, the graphs show investment as a proportion of GDP.

We have already noted in figure 5.5 that capital spending fell sharply in 1986 because the ITC was canceled. Yet that decline does not seem as obvious in these sectoral graphs. Except for high-tech spending, which appears to follow almost a

continued

CASE STUDY 5.1 (*continued*)

steady upward trend until 2000, there is a dip in 1986 and 1987; as it turns out, figure 5.8 shows that high-tech spending also grew at a slower rate during those two years. The major point of these graphs is to illustrate that while changes in the ITC do have a significant *short-run* impact on capital spending, over the long run, factors other than the rate of ITC are more important. In particular, high real interest rates diminished capital spending in the early 1980s, and a booming stock market boosted capital spending in the late 1990s, although industrial equipment did not share in this general boom because of low profit margins in manufacturing and low rates of capacity utilization.

It turns out that the impact of any change in the tax laws designed to stimulate investment cannot be considered in isolation. In particular, tax breaks will reduce tax receipts, which will raise interest rates and reduce stock prices, ceteris paribus. Hence the advantage from lower tax rates is partially offset by less favorable conditions in capital markets. Admittedly this is a highly politically charged issue, and the answer cannot be found in a few simple equations. The work we have done, however, suggests that an environment of rapid growth, low and stable inflation, a balanced budget, and a strong and stable dollar will stimulate capital spending more than tax advantages undertaken during a period of less favorable overall economic conditions. Thus while it is true that the marginal coefficients of changes in the tax laws are significant, they must be considered within the overall framework of the economy.

MANAGER'S BRIEFCASE: SUMMARIZING THE FACTORS THAT DETERMINE CAPITAL SPENDING

We have discussed a large number of variables that affect capital spending. As a manager, you might be asked to make two different types of decisions. First, what capital spending projects do you recommend for your company? Second, if you sell goods or services to firms that produce capital goods – including the information processing sector – what variables should you monitor?

To answer these questions, we divide these relevant variables into the following three categories (these are in addition to any changes in the tax laws that affect your individual situation):

1. Long-term factors that determine investment plans in equilibrium, assuming the current trend rate of growth is expected to continue, and flows of credit are adequate. The key variable is the expected rate of return, which depends on the current rate of interest, the expected rate of inflation, expected change in volume and prices of the goods and services your company produces, the improvement in technology since the last time a similar investment was made, and the current and expected rate of capacity utilization.

continued

MANAGER'S BRIEFCASE (*continued*)

2. Short-term cyclical factors tied to the cost and availability of credit. The conditions for obtaining a loan are an important variable in this category, which also includes the amount of cash flow firms have and the recent performance of the stock market.

3. Short-term cyclical factors tied to changes in expectations. If sales start to decline, cash flow diminishes, or the stock market heads down, many firms will postpone their decisions to purchase plant and equipment until their sales, and the overall economy, have started to improve again. The stock market also has a major impact on business confidence and expectations, and hence is included in both categories (2) and (3).

Figure 5.7 shows how well the combination of these variables tracks the ratio of capital spending to GDP in the sample period. Note in particular that this function fails to capture the full decline in spending in the 2001 recession, for reasons that are discussed in case study 5.2.

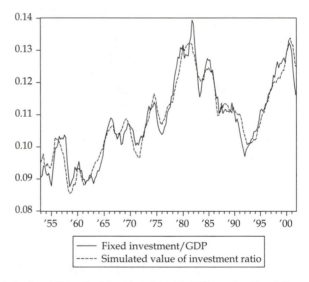

Figure 5.7 Simulated value of the ratio of fixed investment to GDP as a function of the cost of capital, ratio of loans to GDP, value of the dollar, relative price of oil, productivity trend, budget ratio, index of capacity utilization, changes in stock prices, and changes in corporate cash flow

CASE STUDY 5.2 THE PLUNGE IN CAPITAL SPENDING IN THE 2001 RECESSION

In most post-WWII recessions, the downturn in economic activity was preceded by a sharp rise in inflation and interest rates and a tightening of monetary policy.

continued

CASE STUDY 5.2 (*continued*)

Purchases of consumer durables and housing declined first, followed by other consumption and inventory investment, while capital spending lagged the cycle.

However, this pattern did not occur in the 2001 recession. Inflation did not rise, and while the Fed tightened slightly, it was not enough to cause a downturn. Consumer spending and housing held up fairly well, and in the early stages of the recession – before 9/11 – most of the decline in real GDP occurred in capital spending. For the first time, capital spending caused the downturn instead of lagging it.

Based on the data shown in figure 5.6, the ratio of high-tech spending to GDP appears to have risen almost steadily for the past 40 years, with the first downturn occurring in 2001. However, figure 5.8 shows that the percentage decline in high-tech investment in 2001, while larger than other recessions, was hardly unique. The major difference is that high-tech spending used to represent about 1% of GDP, but that figure had risen to about 6% of GDP. Note that these ratios are shown in current dollars; in constant dollars, the distorting influence of the computer deflator would make high-tech investment seem even more important. Figure 5.8 also shows that high-tech spending has a much shorter lag relative to the reference business cycle than other components of capital spending.

The sharp decline in high-tech investment in 2001 was caused primarily by over-capacity and was amplified by the plunge in high-tech stock prices. Note that the previously largest drop in high-tech investment in 1975 also followed an unusually

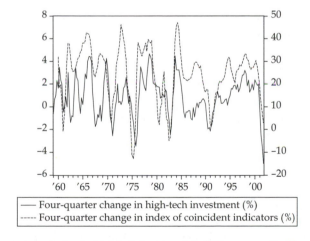

— Four-quarter change in high-tech investment (%)
----- Four-quarter change in index of coincident indicators (%)

Figure 5.8   The percentage decline in high-tech investment in 2001 was greater than other recessions. In addition, it had a much more significant impact on the economy because it had become a much larger proportion of total GDP

continued

CASE STUDY 5.2 (*continued*)

large decline in stock prices (about 50% over the previous two years). Hence once the Nasdaq index retreated from its unsustainable peaks, high-tech spending could logically be expected to follow.

That does not explain why the Nasdaq index rose to unprecedented heights, only to give back all of the gains that occurred during the bubble, falling 75% from its March 2000 peak to its October 2002 trough. That question is not so easy to answer, and the discussion is deferred to chapter 17 on financial business cycles. At this point, however, our conclusions can be summarized by saying that the combination of belief in the "new technology," the lack of any increase in inflation at full employment, and failure by the Fed to tighten on a timely basis apparently encouraged investors to bid up stocks beyond reasonable levels, so eventually the bubble burst of its own weight.

CASE STUDY 5.3   THE GREAT CONSTRUCTION BOOM OF THE EARLY 1980S

One would expect nonresidential construction to be more sensitive to interest rates than purchases of producers' durable equipment, since those projects generally have a much longer average life. Interest costs represent a much higher proportion of the total amount paid for a building with a 30-year mortgage than for a computer with a useful life of no more than three years.

Thus it may be surprising to find that the ratio of nonresidential construction to GDP peaked during the early 1980s at precisely the same time both the nominal and real rate of interest were at all-time peaks. This would seem to contradict the importance of the real rate of interest as a determinant of aggregate demand in general and capital spending in particular.

As shown in figure 5.9, the boom occurred primarily in two sectors: construction in the mining industry, which is primarily oil and natural gas, and construction of commercial buildings. The ratio of mining construction to GDP more than doubled in the late 1970s and early 1980s after the price benchmark of crude oil rose from $13 to $35/bbl – and many speculators believed it would rise to $100/bbl over the next two decades. As it gradually became obvious that such forecasts were way off the mark, energy construction fell back to previous levels, and the brief increases in oil prices back above $30/bbl in 1990 and again in 2000 and 2002 had virtually no impact on that sector of investment. This example does, however, show the importance of the relative price component of the cost of capital.

continued

CASE STUDY 5.3 (*continued*)

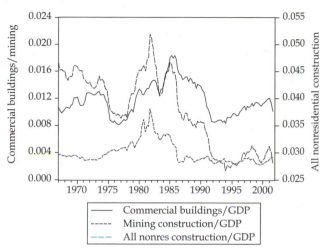

Figure 5.9   Construction in commercial buildings, mining, and total nonresidential construction as a proportion of GDP

The boom in commercial construction, notably office buildings and shopping centers, occurred in the early 1980s because of an unusually favorable tax treatment in the form of rapid writeoffs of such buildings. Without going into all the details, tax shelters proliferated like mushrooms, designed to reduce the tax burden of high-income individuals without giving any thought to whether the buildings, when completed, would ever be profitable. As can be seen from figure 5.9, this ratio declined sharply as soon as the tax laws were changed again in 1986.

The point of this case study is not to lampoon entrepreneurs who thought a price of $100/bbl for oil was viable, or to rail against those who distorted the intent of the tax code. We simply point out that the terms in the rental cost of capital for relative prices, expectations of future prices, and changes in the tax laws, as well as the rate of interest, are important determinants of capital spending. Indeed, when compared with case study 5.1, it seems that these factors, including depreciation allowances, had more of an impact on capital spending than changes in the rate of the investment tax credit.

MANAGER'S BRIEFCASE: NEW ORDERS AND CAPITAL SPENDING

One of the most reliable leading indicators ought to be new orders for capital goods. After all, most capital goods are not purchased without first placing an order. After eliminating leased automobiles, and low-cost personal

continued

MANAGER'S BRIEFCASE (*continued*)

computers and the related computer software, capital goods new orders should lead purchases of producers' durable equipment by several months. The most relevant figure is new orders for nondefense capital goods. Orders for aircraft and defense help boost the economy too, but (a) these tend to come in large lumps, so monthly or even quarterly swings can be distorted by one large order, and (b) the lag time for this equipment is generally much longer than other capital goods, so the mean lag time would be much longer than the median lag time, hence reducing the usefulness of this indicator for determining what lies ahead in the near future. This series is available on the Bureau of the Census website (www.census.gov).

The results are unexpected in the sense that there is virtually no lead time. Most of the time, including but not limited to the latest recession, orders and shipments appear to turn up and down at about the same time. Also bear in mind that the monthly new orders data are very erratic, so it takes three months to determine a change in direction. By that time, shipments have also switched. In real life, new orders are a coincident rather than a leading indicator.

In addition, an odd quirk popped up in the numbers in 2002. Following the widespread accounting scandals, many firms decided maybe it was not such a good idea to stuff the order books at the end of each quarter with deals that might or might not close the following quarter. As a result, there was less padding of the books in the last month of each quarter, so the "seasonally adjusted" series declined sharply in March, June, and September. Eventually, we assume that the seasonal factors will adjust to this anomaly, so by the time you are reading this, the published data may not contain that glitch. Our point in mentioning it is that patterns in reporting orders are likely to change further in the future, and managers should not jump to unwarranted conclusions based on one large change in the monthly new orders data.

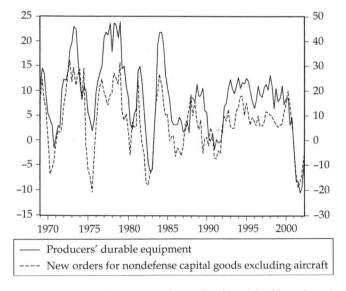

Figure 5.10   Four-quarter percentage changes in purchases of producers' durable equipment and new orders for nondefense capital goods excluding aircraft and parts, both in current $

5.9   Determinants of exports and imports

The role of foreign trade on the economy is widely misunderstood by the "man in the street." Virtually everyone agrees that a rise in consumer spending raises the growth rate now, and a rise in capital spending raises the growth rate both now and in the future. However, it is often claimed that a rise in imports reduces the level of GDP; so if only imports could be curtailed, it is sometimes suggested, real GDP, output, employment, and income would increase. When plants are shut down, those in the community often bewail the loss of jobs as if there were no offsetting factors. That simply is not the case.

To put matters in perspective, consider the contrasting cases of the US and Japanese economies in the 1990s. The US had a steadily increasing trade deficit, accompanied by a decade of almost unparalleled prosperity. The Japanese had a huge trade surplus, yet their economy remained mired in recession for almost an entire decade. Obviously the Japanese trade surplus did not help that economy.

But isn't it true that if a consumer buys an American car, that boosts employment in Detroit, whereas if he or she buys a Japanese car, that boosts employment in Nagoya?[4]

If you are a lobbyist for the auto – or steel, or textile – industry, that is precisely what you tell your easily persuaded Congressman. However, the underlying economics are not that simple.

When someone buys a Toyota produced in Japan, $20,000 (say) goes back to Japan. The Japanese don't spend dollars any more than we spend yen in this country. Those funds can easily be converted to yen on the foreign exchange markets, but that simply means someone else holds the dollars. As long as the surplus of dollars does not reduce the value of the greenback, and as long as the world is on a de facto dollar standard, the dollars come back to this country. *The money from the trade deficit is reinvested in the US economy.*

Don't try this if you are Botswana, or Sri Lanka, or Macedonia, because few if any investors want to hold their funds in pulas, rupees, or denars. They want to hold dollars. As a result, the US economy can prosper with an ever-increasing trade deficit, whereas that is not the case for other countries.

What advantages do US consumers gain by buying foreign products?

1. In many cases, foreign products are less expensive, so consumers have more money to spend on domestic products.
2. Even if the products are identically priced, the spur of foreign competition boosts productivity growth and increases quality of US products. (Think of the improved quality of cars and trucks produced in the US when Detroit had to catch up with the Europeans and Japanese.)
3. At times of full employment and capacity, increased imports can serve as a "safety valve" to keep domestic inflation from rising.

4. The money that flows into the country can be loaned to businesses, used to purchase stocks, or invested in capital plant and equipment.
5. Finally, an increase in US imports boosts the exports of other countries, raising their GDP and permitting them to buy more US goods and services.

Admittedly this argument can be carried to ridiculous extremes. For instance, if imports are so good for the economy, why not wipe out all manufacturing and import everything? Quite simply, that doesn't make any sense, and no rational economist pretends that it does.

To obtain the maximum benefits from international trade, the value of the dollar should be near its equilibrium value, known as purchasing power parity. That means the average cost of producing a market basket of goods in the US equals the average cost of production in the rest of the world. If the dollar is under-valued, productivity growth will be reduced and inflation will increase. If the dollar is overvalued, the manufacturing sector is likely to shrink – the hollowed-out economy – and the loss of jobs will depress real growth.

MANAGER'S BRIEFCASE: REACTING TO TARIFF INCREASES

This is a difficult point for many managers to grasp. You work for a company that produces a reliable product at a fair price. Some other company opens a firm in Latin America or Asia and produces the same good at half the price, so you lose sales and eventually your company goes bankrupt. How can that benefit the US economy?

That is what happened to many firms in the steel industry in the early 1980s, when employment fell by more than half, and to the apparel industry after the North American Free Trade Agreement (NAFTA) was signed in 1994, when its employment also fell by half.

Those who have recently lost their jobs may not be amenable to rational arguments. But look at it from the viewpoint of the consumers. They are able to buy goods at lower prices. That means they have more money to spend on other goods and services. They might spend, for example, less on clothing and more on medical care. Or to turn this example around, if they have to spend more on medical care, they may have no choice other than to spend less on clothing.

What about the workers in Brazil, Pakistan, or Thailand, who receive a higher wage — even though it is much lower than their American counterparts — than they would earn otherwise? Some of it is spent on goods and services produced domestically, but some of it is used to purchase goods produced in other countries. Still, in all, if the US has a gigantic trade deficit, at least some other countries must have sizable trade surpluses, which is indeed the case. However, those funds are reinvested in the US, hence creating more jobs in new industries — some of which may be in the service sector.

When the value of the dollar rises, total employment need not decline. Table 5.1 shows the major job gainers and losers in the manufacturing sector from 1995 through 2000, when there was a modest net loss of 55,000 jobs in man-ufacturing in spite of a 32% increase in the trade-weighted average of the dollar. By comparison, when the economy headed into recession, manufacturing employment plummeted even when the value of the dollar declined.

In 2001 and 2002, by comparison, manufacturing employment fell 1.7 million — with declines recorded in virtually all two-digit (SIC Code) industries — even though the dollar fell sharply in 2002. Obviously the recession was much more damaging to manufacturing employment than the overvalued dollar.

continued

MANAGER'S BRIEFCASE (*continued*)

Table 5.1   Gainers and losers in manufacturing employment, 1995–2000

Biggest losers		Biggest gainers	
Apparel	303	Fabricated metals	100
Textiles	185	Electrical machinery	94
Leather	34	Wood products	62
		Transportation equipment	59
		Industrial machinery	53
		Furniture	49
		Stone, clay, and glass	39
		Rubber and plastics	31

All figures are in thousands

When tariffs of up to 30% were imposed on steel imports in early 2002, orders and profits in the steel industry rebounded immediately – but steel industry employment remained at 188,000. Furthermore, employment in the principal metal-using industries declined some 45,000 over the next six months. Maybe that would have happened anyhow, but the economy did grow better than 3% during that same period, so one would have ordinarily expected stability if not some modest increase in durable goods manufacturing employment.

If you are a manager of a firm that will directly benefit from higher tariffs, of course you will favor such a change. But that is not really the issue here. Except for industries that are directly affected, sales are likely to be hurt rather than helped by higher tariffs. Higher steel prices caused an increasing proportion of metal-using firms to move their operations to offshore locations, hence further weakening employment and real growth. Managers should carefully consider how their own businesses might be hurt because of the higher prices and possible shortages caused by the imposition of tariffs in other industries.

As a general rule, imports depend on US income and production and the value of the dollar, while exports depend on foreign income and production and the value of the dollar. However, several other factors are also important.

1. When domestic aggregate demand rises, imports rise more than proportionately. As the economy approaches full capacity and domestic prices rise, capacity constraints on imported goods are usually less severe and import prices rise less, so more imports are substituted for domestic goods. Many imports are discretionary items – especially consumer durables and semi-durables – so imports of cars, TV sets, computers, and clothing represent a much larger proportion of total consumption than imports of food. Except for foreign travel, hardly any services are imported. Similarly, when the economy heads into recession, the decline in imports is proportionately greater than in total GDP, which tends to cushion the downturn. The proportionately greater swings in imports are shown in figure 5.11; note that the percentage changes on the right-hand axis are much greater than on the left-hand axis.

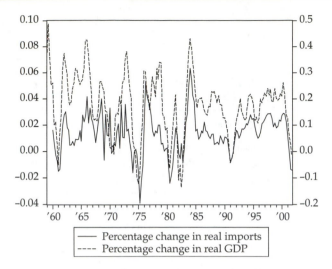

Figure 5.11 Four-quarter percentage change in imports compared to four-quarter percentage change in GDP, both in real (chained) dollars

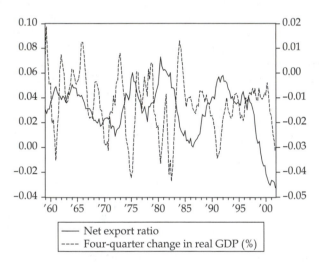

Figure 5.12 The net export ratio is negatively correlated with the change in GDP even though the fundamental aggregate demand identity would indicate a positive correlation

2. By definition, GDP = C + I + G + F. Thus on a ceteris paribus basis, a rise in the net export ratio, F, would boost GDP, and a decline in F would reduce GDP. Yet as shown in figure 5.12, until the most recent recession, changes in F and GDP were *negatively* correlated. When the economy is in the midst of a boom, the net export ratio generally declines; it rises during recessions. That fact alone should call into question the conventional wisdom that a rise in imports reduces GDP, while a decline in imports boosts GDP.

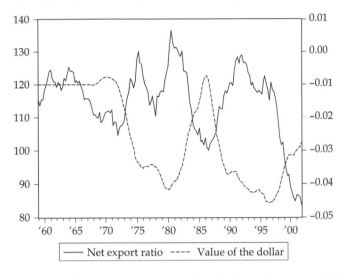

Figure 5.13   Ratio of net exports to GDP, both in constant $, divided by moving average of the trade-weighted average of the $, lagged two to eight quarters

3. Net exports – exports minus imports – are negatively correlated with the value of the dollar. However, the price elasticity is greater for exports than imports. Because the world is on a de facto dollar standard, the prices of imports tend to change more in line with the prices of domestic production. Thus when the dollar strengthens, importers raise prices in terms of their own currencies, and when the dollar weakens, they reduce prices in their own currencies. The negative relationship of the overall trade balance with the value of the dollar can be seen in figure 5.13. The negative correlation between changes in exports and changes in the value of the dollar is shown in figure 5.14. There is some positive correlation between changes in imports and changes in the dollar, but that relationship is weaker and is not shown separately.
4. The change in exports lags changes in US economic activity by almost a year. A decline in US economic activity reduces US imports, which are exports of other countries. Hence their GDP and income decline, and after the usual adjustment lag, they buy fewer goods from the US. That is another linkage that occurs because the world is on a de facto dollar standard. In particular, legislation to reduce our imports would not boost real GDP for very long, since exports would decline the following year. This relationship is shown in figure 5.15.
5. As already shown in figure 5.13, there has been a substantial decline in the net export ratio – exports minus imports divided by GDP, all in chained dollars – over the past decade. The net export ratio was near zero until the early 1980s, when it dropped sharply because of the overvalued dollar. It then returned to zero in the early 1990s, but since then has declined sharply even though the dollar has not returned to its peaks of the mid-1980s. Figure 5.16 shows that almost all of the recent slump has occurred in consumer goods; net exports of

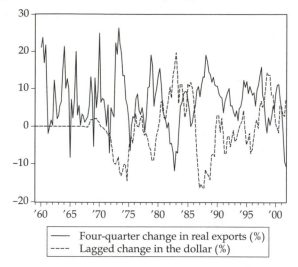

Figure 5.14   A 1% change in the value of the dollar changes exports by about $\frac{2}{3}$% in the opposite direction

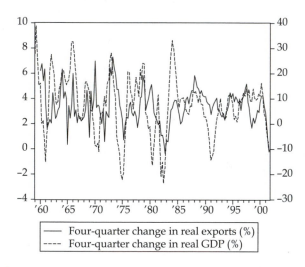

Figure 5.15   Except for the most recent recession, the change in exports tends to lag the change in GDP by almost a year

all other goods are close to zero, as they were in the mid-1980s, but did not actually turn negative.

There are two main reasons why net exports of consumer goods – mainly autos, other durables, and clothing – have slumped so much in recent years. First, the decline has been particularly steep since 1994, the year that the North American Free Trade Agreement went into effect. Second, growth in southeast Asia plunged

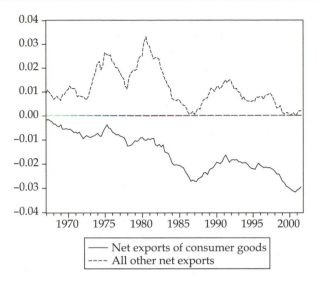

Figure 5.16 Most of the decline in net exports in the past decade has occurred in consumer goods (figures are net exports/GDP)

in 1997 and never recovered to its earlier pace. The fact that the dollar became overvalued in 2001 exacerbated the situation, but was not the root cause. Even so, in line with our earlier comments, the US economy prospered as long as the dollar was near equilibrium; the drop in net exports only began to contribute to the recession when the dollar became overvalued.

We said that both exports and imports depend on the value of the dollar, but have not yet explained what causes the value of the currency to fluctuate. That subject is addressed in part IV; there is no one simple answer. It was once thought that the exchange rate for any currency depended on (a) the size of the trade surplus or deficit, and (b) the value of relative interest rates and stock prices, since a high rate of interest or a booming stock market would attract more foreign capital, hence boosting the value of the currency. However, in 2001 the US trade deficit worsened, the Fed cut short-term interest rates 11 times, and the stock market plunged – yet the value of the dollar soared. Most investors apparently thought that the dollar, in spite of whatever problems were occurring in the US economy, still represented the best currency in which to invest their funds. Hence the value of the dollar depends even more on expectations than do other financial market prices.

The determinants of net exports also depend in part on the time frame that is being considered. Short-term changes are correlated with changes in the growth rate of the US economy and its major trading partners. Medium-term changes reflect changes in the value of the currency, usually with a lag of one to two years. Long-term changes are tied to political and socioeconomic factors, notably the fact that the US has a more open-door policy toward imports than most other nations.

One standard rule of thumb economists followed for many years said that net exports declined during booms and rose during recessions. The logic seemed straightforward enough: when US income declined, purchases of both domestic and imported goods fell, whereas exports depended on foreign income. However, another shibboleth fell by the wayside during the 2001 recession. While imports declined sharply, falling 7.5% in real terms, exports plunged even more, falling 11.6%. As a result, net exports declined $17 billion during that year.

The explanation is fairly obvious once we have the facts. Real growth dropped from 4.4% to 1.4% in Canada, from 6.9% to 0.1% in Mexico, from 4.5% to 1.3% in Brazil, from 2.4% to −0.8% in Japan, from 8.8% to 1.7% in South Korea, and from 3.4% to 1.6% in Euroland. Yet that simply moves the question to the next step. Why did the worldwide economy slow down so much? Can all this be tied to the US recession?

Basically, yes. There were no exogenous shocks in the rest of the world, no substantive increases in inflation or interest rates, and no attempt to institute fiscal contraction. The decline in European GDP was fairly modest, but the situation was more serious in the western hemisphere, and even worse in East Asia, where the high-tech collapse hurt emerging nations the most. The situation was exacerbated by the fact that real imports represented 17% of real GDP in 2000, almost double the ratio during the previous US recession.

As noted above, the US has the luxury of importing more than it exports. Most countries do not. When their exports to the US decline, they have little choice other than to reduce their imports from the US. Thus it seems likely that exports and imports will both decline during future US recessions.

The situation was also worsened during 2001 because the value of the dollar increased to the point where, by the end of the year, it was 20% above its equilibrium value. That was probably another reason why net exports fell during the recession instead of rising, as had previously been the case.

Because of the free-trade orientation of the US, the ratio of net exports to GDP will probably continue to decline in the years ahead. We discuss the implications of that development in part IV. Here we can say that while such an event would hurt other countries, it doesn't matter to the US as long as the dollar remains near its equilibrium value. Since its value actually rose during the recent slump in exports, that does not appear to be a major issue. As long as the world remains on a de facto dollar standard, further declines in the US net export ratio will not harm the economy as long as the extra dollars earned from these imports flow back into the US, hence increasing total national saving. Assuming the economy is not weakened by other forces, that boosts investment as well.

The historical simulation of the net export ratio as a function of the value of the dollar, the change in industrial production, the change in high-tech investment, and relative oil prices, is shown in figure 5.17. In essence, the latter two variables are proxies for growth in the rest of the world that is not directly related to worldwide cycles of industrial production. This approach actually

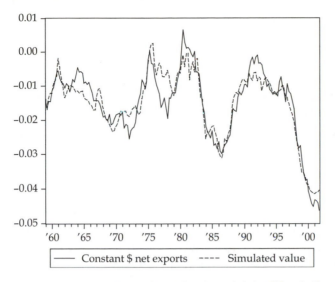

Figure 5.17   Net export ratio as a function of value of the dollar, change in industrial production, ratio of high-tech investment to GDP, and relative oil prices

explains exports somewhat better than inserting some "worldwide" average of industrial production, probably because the figures for many foreign countries are suspect.

MANAGER'S BRIEFCASE: HOW TO USE THE TRADE DATA

The Bureau of the Census publishes a fairly detailed report on exports and imports every month, although it occurs with an average lag of five weeks. While the report contains 18 tables, the major categories are (a) trade balance, exports, and imports by one-digit categories; (b) the same figures for about 100 detailed categories; and (c) the same figures for individual countries. However, categories (b) and (c) are not seasonally adjusted and very little historical data is given, so it is sometimes difficult to use these reports unless you collect data from several different releases. In general, monthly changes in the trade data have very little impact on either domestic or international financial markets, mainly because the monthly fluctuations are usually due to exogenous disturbances and do not provide very much information about underlying trends.

A better place to look for international trade is on the internet. Commerce has a website that can be accessed at www.stat-usa.gov, which provides access to over 100 of the key economic series. It is available by subscription only, at a cost of $175 per year. In most cases the results are available free elsewhere on the web, so if you simply want the latest releases, and are not a financial trader who needs them immediately, you might not subscribe. In addition, though, there is a wealth of international data collected under the aegis of GLOBUS (global business opportunities) and NTDB (national trade data bank), which has a subscription fee of $300 per year, and contains an almost limitless amount of trade data. Exports and imports are available at the one-digit, two-digit, six-digit,

continued

MANAGER'S BRIEFCASE (*continued*)

or ten-digit classifications, which total over 21,000 series, going back monthly for several years. Also, there are numerous articles about individual countries: over 100 countries are included, although of course there are fewer articles for Azerbaijan than for China. Also, this service contains daily listings of trade opportunities for US firms around the world. For most managers involved in international trade, this source of data can be extremely valuable, and certainly more relevant than the monthly foreign trade reports on net exports.

5.10   The role of government saving

Most economists agree the budget should be balanced when the economy is at full-employment equilibrium, in surplus when the economy is at overfull employment or inflation is rising, and in deficit when the economy is in recession.

Recent political discussions about the budget have become obfuscated with rhetoric about "robbing the social security lockbox" and other meaningless statements. These issues are discussed in more detail in part VI; our attention here is focused on how the Federal government budget, measured on a NIPA basis – i.e., excluding asset purchases and sales – fluctuates over the business cycle. We ignore the artificial distinction between the "social security" and the "other" surplus or deficit because, on an economic basis, money is fungible.

Figure 5.18 shows that the ratio of the Federal budget surplus or deficit to GDP always rises in booms and declines in recessions. That pattern occurs for several reasons. First, the personal income tax schedule is progressive, so as personal income rises, taxes rise at a faster rate. Second, the stock market rises during booms and declines during recessions, so capital gains taxes fluctuate accordingly.

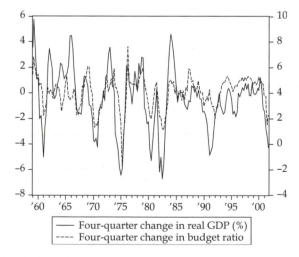

Figure 5.18   The Federal budget ratio always declines in recessions and rises in booms

Third, the ratio of corporate profits to GDP rises during booms and falls during recessions, and corporate income is generally taxed at a higher rate than personal income. Fourth, during recessions, unemployment benefits and welfare payments rise sharply, whereas they decline relative to trend values during booms.

In addition, taxes are usually cut during recessions; that has happened during four of the last five full-length downturns (the brief 1980 downturn was over before any Congressional action could be taken). However, our comments about the cyclical pattern of the government budget position are based entirely on automatic changes, and would occur even if Congress did not cut taxes during recessions.

Even without the Bush tax cuts and the additional government expenditures necessitated in the aftermath of 9/11, most of the Federal budget surplus would have disappeared in FY 2002 because of the recession. If the government had attempted to keep the budget in surplus, the accompanying tax increases clearly would have prolonged and deepened the recession.

5.11   Recap: why investment always equals saving on an ex post basis

We can now offer a more complete economic explanation of why investment always equals saving on an ex post basis. In this case, assume there is some improvement in both consumer and business optimism, so the economy is rising at above-average rates. As a result, ex ante investment rises, but ex ante personal saving declines. Hence there must be a substantial increase in the remaining components of saving: business, foreign, and government. While a rise in interest rates might conceivably boost consumer saving, the personal saving rate declined almost steadily during the 1990s whether interest rates were rising or falling, so we focus primarily on the changes in other types of national saving.

The ratio of profits to GDP rises in booms and declines during recessions. Since dividends change slowly relative to profits, a booming economy boosts corporate saving. Imports generally rise faster than exports during a boom, so net exports decline, and with the world on a de facto dollar standard, those additional dollars return to the US and boost foreign saving. Finally, as shown in the previous section, government saving rises during a boom. These sources of increased saving support the rise in planned investment even if the personal saving rate does not change.

Suppose, however, these mechanisms did not kick into place. In particular, suppose the government decided not to increase its saving during a boom: either it boosted expenditures or cut tax rates. That would create a situation known as "crowding out." The demand for funds by the government during a boom period would boost interest rates, hence reducing actual investment below its planned level.

When ex ante investment declines, equilibrium is often maintained by a reduction in government saving. If the government tries to balance the budget during a recession, the downturn will become even worse until the government is eventually forced to run a deficit. When ex ante investment rises, equilibrium can be maintained by an increase in government saving. If the government does not trim its expenditures, interest rates will rise, and ex post investment will decline instead of increasing.

Thus the ex post equilibrium between investment and saving is much more than an accounting identity. Behind the scenes, so to speak, we see the vital role of the government sector as a balancing agent. In addition, the decline in net exports during a boom helps to maintain equilibrium; interference with that mechanism would also throw the economy out of kilter. The worst economic declines have occurred when an attempt was made to interfere with the normal changes in foreign and government saving.

KEY TERMS AND CONCEPTS

Cost of Capital
Foreign Saving
Investment Tax Credit

SUMMARY

- By definition, investment must always equal saving on an ex post basis. However, planned saving and investment may be quite different. If planned investment rises or falls, that change must be matched by an equal change in saving; otherwise the change in investment will not occur.
- The principal long-run determinants of capital spending are the cost of capital, the rate of capacity utilization, expected changes in volume and prices of the product or service produced, and the change in technology since the last similar capital good was purchased.
- The cost of capital is equal to the real rate of interest plus the rate of depreciation, multiplied by the price of the capital good relative to the price of the product, and adjusted for tax laws that affect corporate income and capital spending. The real rate of interest is the nominal rate minus the expected rate of inflation.

- Firms will not undertake capital spending projects unless the expected rate of return is greater than the cost of capital. Even if the project would generate a positive rate of return, it would not be undertaken unless that return is greater than could be earned by investing the money in other companies, or buying back the company stock.
- Because of the imperfections of capital markets and incomplete knowledge, the availability of credit is also an important determinant of capital spending.
- Even after capital budgets have been determined, they are likely to be modified because of unexpected changes in economic conditions, notably in the rate of capacity utilization, cash flow, or stock prices. Hence capital budgeting plans made last year are an unreliable guide to capital spending this year.
- Investment typically lags the rest of the economy in the upturn by several quarters, but the

lag is much shorter in the downturn, because the decision to cancel an order generally takes less time to make than the decision to place an order. Also, delivery lags for many types of capital goods can be substantial.

- Changes in the rate of investment tax credit, the marginal statutory tax rate, and depreciation schedules also affect capital spending. Empirically, changes in depreciation schedules appear to have had the biggest impact on US capital spending over the past 50 years. The impact of the investment tax credit has also affected short-term changes in purchases of capital goods.

- While the identity for aggregate demand states that a rise in imports reduces GDP, ceteris paribus, there are several beneficial impacts to an increase in imports as long as the dollar remains near its equilibrium value. An increase in imports generally reduces inflation and boosts productivity growth. It also increases net foreign saving, which can boost investment as long as the economy is growing at normal rates and is not in a recession.

- Imports are a function of domestic economic activity and the value of the dollar. Exports are a function of foreign economic activity and the value of the dollar. Changes in the dollar generally have a larger impact on exports than imports, because the world is on a de facto dollar standard, so importers adjust their prices to US levels when the value of the currency changes.

- Government saving rises in booms and declines in recessions because the personal income tax rate schedule is progressive, capital gains rise in booms, and the ratio of corporate profits to GDP also increases in booms. During recessions, when tax revenues slump, government expenditures rise faster than usual because of increased unemployment and welfare benefits.

- When ex ante investment rises, much of the gain in saving is provided by increases in foreign and government saving; when it declines, much of the reduction in saving is also provided by declines in foreign and government saving. Attempts to interfere with this mechanism – such as trying to balance the budget during recessions – would invariably make downturns lengthier and more severe.

QUESTIONS AND PROBLEMS

1. The ratio of capital spending to GDP rose sharply during the latter 1970s, even though bond yields rose sharply during that period. It then increased even further during the early 1980s, when bond rates peaked. When bond rates declined during the latter half of the 1980s, the ratio of capital spending also fell. Explain how each of the following factors contributed to these changes.
   (A) The nominal rate of interest.
   (B) The real rate of interest.
   (C) Changes in depreciation schedules.
   (D) The rate of capacity utilization.
   (E) The relative price of capital goods.

2. What were the principal factors that caused the ratio of the purchase of producers' durable equipment to GDP to rise so much during the 1990s? Why was this pattern suddenly reversed in 2001?

3. Assume Congress is considering reinstating a 10% investment tax credit in order to stimulate the economy. The bill would apply to purchases of all new capital equipment, so it would increase the budget deficit by $100 billion per year on a static basis (i.e., before considering any feedback attempts). Explain why you would advocate or oppose this bill as a lobbyist for (a) General Motors, (b) Disney, (c) Exxon Mobil, (d) Georgia Pacific, (e) Citigroup, (f) Toyota, (g) Merck, (h) Capital One (subprime consumer loans), (i) Toll Brothers Builders.

4. Boeing is the major beneficiary of the US Export-Import Bank, which provides subsidies for exports. Proponents of the bill say it is necessary to meet hidden subsidies offered by Airbus, and creates thousands of jobs in the US. Opponents say the cost of the subsidy per additional job is far higher than the value of those jobs.

   (A) Assume initially that the cost of the subsidy equals the value of the jobs (e.g., if 30,000 jobs are saved at an average cost of $50,000 per year, the subsidy equals $1.5 billion per year). If that were indeed the case, do you think the subsidy is good public policy? (Hint: consider the impact on productivity and quality as well as changes in the number of employed.)

   (B) How would your answer change if the cost of the subsidy were twice the value of jobs saved? Half the value of jobs saved?

   (C) Would your answers be any different if McDonnell Douglas were still in business as a competitor?

5. During the 1990s, capital spending grew faster than consumption. As a result of this, total capacity also grew faster than usual, so the rate of capacity utilization fell from 1994 to 2000 in spite of a booming economy. Why did firms continue to boost their capital spending even as the rate of capacity utilization declined? (Hint: did this occur in all major sectors of investment?)

6. Also during the 1990s, the ratio of capital spending to GDP rose, while the personal saving rate declined almost to zero. The profit ratio did not rise very much; hence almost the entire increase in saving came from the foreign and government saving. This implies that if the trade deficit had not expanded, and if the Federal budget position had not shifted from deficit to surplus, there would have been no investment boom.

   (A) Explain why you agree or disagree with this last sentence.

   (B) If the government budget had remained in deficit, what do you think would have happened to the personal saving rate? (Hint: what would have happened to interest rates?)

   (C) Suppose the P/E ratio of the stock market had remained constant during the 1990s instead of increasing, which means stock prices would have risen at the same rate as GDP. In that case, what do you think would have happened to investment, personal saving, foreign saving, and government saving?

7. During 1983, 1984, and 1985, the dollar was overvalued and kept rising. During that period, real imports rose $160 billion and real exports rose only $27 billion, while real GDP rose an average of 5.1% per year. During the next four years, the dollar declined and returned to equilibrium. Real imports rose $118 billion while real exports rose $188 billion, but the growth rate moderated, rising at an average of 3.6%.

   (A) In order to explain the difference in growth rates of the economy during these two periods, what other information would you need?

   (B) The turnaround in the dollar occurred when the Fed made a publicly announced decision to reduce the real rate of interest. However, that would ordinarily stimulate domestic demand, yet the figures above indicate that it grew at a slower rate. Why did the economy grow more slowly when the dollar was declining and interest rates were low than when the dollar was rising and interest rates were high?

   (C) To what degree was the slower growth in investment during the 1986–9 period directly related to the decline in foreign saving? What other components of saving declined?

8. From 2000 to 2002, the sharp decline in capital spending was almost completely matched by the sharp decline in government saving.

   (A) How do you think the overall economy would have responded? However, suppose government saving had not declined.

   (B) How would ex post investment and saving have been balanced under those conditions?

   (C) What do you think would have happened to foreign saving? Would the change have occurred mainly in exports or imports?

Appendix: the theory of optimal capital accumulation

In equilibrium, the value of the marginal product of capital, which is the value of the output produced by using one extra unit of capital, is equal to the rental cost of capital, which is the cost of using one extra unit of capital.[5]

In the standard Cobb-Douglas function, which states that $Y = AL^\alpha K^{1-\alpha}$, the value of the marginal product of capital is equal to $p_w(Y/K)$, where p_w is the product price. Y is output of the firm (in constant prices), K is the capital stock of the firm, and L is labor input. A is a scale factor, and α is the proportion of output that is produced by labor. On a macroeconomic basis, Y is total real GDP. If

$$Y = AL^\alpha K^{1-\alpha}, \tag{5.1}$$

then by differentiating we obtain

$$\Delta Y / \Delta K = A'L^{\alpha} K^{-\alpha} = A'(Y/K) \tag{5.2}$$

where A' is a new constant term.

This equation shows that if the firm is operating on the constant part of its cost curve, the marginal product of capital is equal to the average product of capital (Y/K). In equilibrium the marginal product of capital must also be equal to the marginal cost of capital.

At first it might seem that the marginal cost of capital would be the total number of additional units produced divided by the total cost of the capital good. However, that calculation would be incorrect for two reasons. First, it fails to specify how long the capital good will last. Second, it would exclude the time value of money. If a firm buys a machine today that is expected to last for 10 years, the total cost should be divided by 10 to obtain the annual cost, and should then be adjusted to include the cost of borrowed funds; or alternatively, the amount that could have been earned on the money if it had been invested elsewhere.

Thus for any given time period, the cost of the machine is not its purchase price, but that price multiplied by the sum of the rate of depreciation and a weighted average of the cost of debt and equity capital. Since stock and bond prices often move together, we will simplify the exposition and represent this weighted average cost by the interest rate. The formula then becomes more complicated when corporate income taxes are taken into account.

The cost of using one extra unit of capital depends on the price of the capital good, p_k, the interest rate at which the funds are borrowed, denoted by r, and the rate of depreciation, denoted by δ. It doesn't matter whether the investment is internally or externally financed, since the funds could otherwise be invested at the market rate of interest r. Many firms will use both equity and debt financing; it is assumed here that the cost of equity capital is proportional to the cost of debt capital.

The interest rate is the real rate of interest, because the important factor is the real value of the money when the loan is repaid. Hence the expected inflation rate is subtracted from the nominal interest rate. We also need to consider whether the value of the capital asset will appreciate in price, as might be the case for a commercial building. Most capital assets are worth very little at the end of their useful life (such as a computer), but some assets appreciate in value, in which case the depreciation term should be modified by the average annual gain. Also, we need to consider both the price of the capital good and the price of the product to convert the marginal physical product terms to the value of the marginal product.

In the case of no taxes, and assuming the weighted average cost of debt and equity capital can be represented by the interest rate, then the cost of capital (rcc) is given as:

$$\mathrm{rcc} = p_k(r + \delta) \tag{5.3a}$$

if there is no capital appreciation, and

$$\text{rcc} = p_k(r + \delta - \Delta p_k/p_k) \tag{5.3b}$$

if the price of the asset appreciates over its lifetime. Since that is only the case for certain types of assets, we will drop that term here.

As noted above:

$r =$ the real rate of interest, adjusted by the expected rate of inflation,

$\delta =$ the rate of depreciation, and

$p_k =$ price of the capital asset.

If there are no income taxes and no capital gains, then in equilibrium, the value of the marginal product of capital is equal to the value of the cost of capital, or

$$p_w Y/K = p_k(r + \delta), \tag{5.4}$$

which can be rewritten as:

$$K = Y(p_w/p_k)/(r + \delta). \tag{5.5}$$

Remember that Y and K are equilibrium values.

We next consider how the cost of capital is affected when changes in tax rates are considered, omitting the change in the capital gains tax rate. The imposition of a corporate income tax will raise the cost of capital in almost all cases. The only exception would occur if all capital goods could be depreciated in the year they were purchased, in which case the rate of corporate income tax would not affect the investment decision.[6] Since that rarely happens, the cost of capital will increase as the corporate income tax rate rises. However, to a certain extent that will be tempered by the rate at which firms are permitted to write off their capital goods; the faster the rate of depreciation, the smaller the negative impact of the corporate income tax rate on investment.

Unlike depreciation allowances, the investment tax credit reduces taxes dollar for dollar. Suppose a firm purchased a capital good for $10 million, which it could depreciate at a rate of $1 million per year. Also assume there was a 10% investment tax credit. The $1 million annual depreciation would be subtracted from pretax income, so if the corporate income tax rate were 35%, taxes would be reduced by $0.35 million. However, the investment tax credit would reduce taxes by the full $1 million. Hence its impact on the cost of capital does not have to be multiplied by the corporate income tax rate.

Given these considerations, we can modify the rcc term to take into account the corporate income tax rate, rate of investment tax credit, and depreciation rates as follows:

$$\text{rcc} = p_k(r + \delta)(1 - \tau\zeta - \kappa)/(1 - \tau), \tag{5.6}$$

so that

$$K = Y(p_w/p_k)/[(r + \delta)(1 - \tau\zeta - \kappa)/(1 - \tau)] \qquad (5.7)$$

where τ is the marginal statutory tax rate, κ is the rate of investment tax credit (ITC), and ζ is the present value of the depreciation deduction. (Money that can be deducted from taxes sooner is worth more than money that is deducted later.)

If there were no corporate income tax, the rate at which capital goods were depreciated would depend on the accounting method used. On an economic basis, the depreciation rate ought to be equal to the rate of economic obsolescence. In the "one horse shay" assumption, where the capital good remains fully useful up until the day it becomes useless, all depreciation might be taken only at the end of the useful life. Since that would boost profits in the near term but severely depress them at some future date, most firms use an accounting depreciation schedule that approximates the economic depreciation.

However, the situation changes significantly once the corporate income tax rate is introduced. Because of the time value of money, it is always better to pay any given amount of tax later rather than sooner. Hence firms would prefer to take rapid depreciation writeoffs, which would reduce their book profits in the first few years after purchasing the capital good, because the discounted value of taxes would be worth less several years in the future.

Thus, accelerated depreciation regulations partially offset the cost of the corporate income tax. In the extreme case where the firm could expense all of its capital purchases – i.e., write them off entirely in the year when they were purchased – the rate of corporate income tax would have no effect on the cost of capital. If goods could be completely written off in the year of purchase, the decision to invest would then be independent of the corporate income tax rate.

Now consider the extreme case when interest rates are zero. In that case, the firm could borrow the money but would never have to pay it back. Also, the time value of money would have no discount rate, so earnings received later would not be any less valuable than earnings received now. In that case, the earnings received from the capital good would be worth just as much 10 years from now as they would be currently, so there would be no advantage of rapid depreciation rates.

Of course, neither of these extremes is likely to exist. However, these polar cases do reveal that as tax benefits increase, the effect of the corporate income tax on the cost of capital becomes smaller; and as the interest rate declines, the effect of the corporate income tax also becomes smaller. That means the tax benefits are more valuable at higher corporate tax rates and higher levels of real interest rates.

Consider the case where $\kappa = 0$. In equation (5.7) above, it should be clear that when $\zeta = 1$, which means all capital goods could be depreciated immediately, then the term $(1 - \tau\zeta - \kappa)/(1 - \tau)$ becomes unity. Thus if firms were permitted to expense all capital purchases – writing them off in the year they were purchased – a higher corporate tax rate would not diminish investment.

Now suppose that there is no accelerated depreciation and capital goods must be written off over their entire useful life. The ζ factor will vary depending on interest rates and the length of life, but an average value would be about 0.6. In that case, if there were no ITC, the tax term would be $(1 - 0.6\tau)/(1 - \tau)$. If τ were $\frac{1}{2}$, then this term would be 1.4, which means in this case that a corporate income tax rate of 50% would boost the cost of capital by 40%.

Before the tax cuts of the early 1960s, approximate values were $\tau = 0.5$, $\zeta = 0.8$, and $\kappa = 0$, so the fraction $(1 - \tau\zeta - \kappa)/(1 - \tau) = 1.2$. In that era, corporate income tax rates boosted the cost of capital by about 20%. The value of ζ was high mainly because interest rates were low.

In the 1960s and 1970s, approximate values were $\tau = 0.5$, $\zeta = 0.7$, and $\kappa = 0.1$, so the fraction $(1 - \tau\zeta - \kappa)/(1 - \tau) = 1.1$. The negative impact of higher interest rates was offset by more rapid depreciation and the introduction of the investment tax credit, so corporate income tax rates boosted the cost of capital by only about 10%.

When additional tax breaks were introduced in 1981, the net effect of these advantages more than offset the cost of the corporate income tax rate, with the result that some capital-intensive firms were actually paying a corporate income tax rate of less than zero. That provided some firms with valuable tax losses that could be carried forward for many years.

After most of the tax preferences were terminated in 1986, the values shifted to $\tau = \frac{1}{3}$, $\zeta = 0.6$, and $\kappa = 0$, so the term $(1 - \tau\zeta - \kappa)/(1 - \tau) = 1.2$. Hence, after 1986, corporate income taxes boosted the cost of capital by about 20%.

In recent years, the real rate of interest has averaged about 5%, depreciation is about 15% per year (although it varies widely depending on the type of investment), so the tax rate factor has averaged about 1.2. Since p_k is an index number, we can set it equal to unity without any loss of generality, although if the p_w/p_k ratio varies over time, that would also affect the cost of capital. If relative prices do not change, that would put the cost of capital at about 24%, or essentially the same as the commonly stated "hurdle rate" of 25%.

Note that the depreciation factor is much larger than the real rate of interest or the tax factor. An 18% annual rate of depreciation, assuming a geometric rate of decline, which is closely approximated by double declining balance, implies about a 15-year life for the average capital expenditure; lives for equipment are usually shorter, and for structures are usually longer. If straight-line depreciation were used, the annual factor would be only 6.67% per year.

The theory of profit maximization says that the optimal stock of capital is positively related to the level of output, negatively related to the cost of capital, and positively related to the ratio of the product price to the capital goods price. That latter term is important only in two cases. One is for computers, where the price of the capital good declines while the price of the product (i.e., what computers are used to produce) rises. Since computers are almost ubiquitous, in this case the price of the "product" is simply the overall GDP deflator.

The other case where capital and product prices do not always move together occurs in the oil industry. During the early 1980s, many investors expected that energy prices would continue to rise very rapidly, which increased the demand for capital spending in the oil industry above the amount that would be given by this formula. In this case, the relative price term – with current prices of oil being a proxy variable for expected future increases – is also relevant.

So far we have generated an equation for the optimal capital stock, but this equation must now be transformed into an investment function. The stock adjustment principle states that the *actual* change in capital stock this period is proportional to some fraction of the change between the *desired* capital stock this period (K^*) and the actual stock last period.

There are several reasons why capital stock does not adjust fully in one period. The two most important are (a) firms will react cautiously to a change in output and costs, not knowing if they are permanent or temporary, and (b) even if all the desired new capital goods were ordered immediately, they could not be delivered simultaneously.

Replacement investment – the difference between gross and net investment – is proportional to the capital stock. We can thus write:

$$K - K_{-1} = \lambda(K^* - K_{-1}) \tag{5.8}$$

or

$$I_n = \lambda(K^* - K_{-1}). \tag{5.9}$$

Since replacement investment (I_r) is proportional to existing capital stock, then

$$I_g = \lambda(K^* - K_{-1}) + \delta K_{-1} \tag{5.10}$$

where I_n and I_g are net and gross investment respectively and $K^* = p_w/p_k$ (Y^e/rcc) where $\text{rcc} = (r + \delta)(1 - \tau\zeta - \kappa)/(1 - \tau)$.

There are several empirical problems in estimating this function. First, although we have included the cost of capital, the equation does not include any variables that reflect the transmission of monetary policy in ways other than the rate of interest, such as the availability of credit and fluctuations in stock prices.

Second, the importance of the rate of capacity utilization depends on the phase of the business cycle. If firms have excess capacity, they are unlikely to expand even if sales are growing rapidly and the cost of capital is relatively low.

Third, the investment function is asymmetrical; firms are much more likely to cancel orders on bad economic news than they are to expand orders on good economic news.

Fourth, Y^e represents expected sales, but these have not yet been defined. Firms do not merely take an average of sales over previous years; even though they cannot really forecast the future, investment decisions are often based on whether business executives believe the overall climate is favorable for business expansion.

Fifth, different types of investment have different lag structures, depending on how long the capital good is expected to last, and also how long it takes to be delivered or constructed. The firm may decide to increase its capital spending "today" but not take delivery of the goods for several years (for example, jet aircraft or utility power plants).

Sixth, for international firms, excessive fluctuations in the value of the currency will reduce investment.

The profile of capital spending has changed significantly over the past 50 years. Computers now account for a major share of total capital spending. Purchases of transportation equipment are an increasing share of total capital spending because more cars are leased and the rental car business has grown; hence some purchases of motor vehicles that used to be considered "consumption" are now part of "investment." Finally, because the computer deflator falls about 15% per year, the constant-dollar figures for computers take a much larger share of total producers' durable equipment in constant than in current dollars.

The investment function we have developed to this point is of the form:

$$I_g = \lambda(p_w/p_k \cdot Y^e/\text{rcc} - K_{-1}) + \delta K_{-1}, \tag{5.11}$$

or

$$I_g/Y^e = \lambda(p_w/p_k \cdot 1/\text{rcc}) - (\lambda - \delta)K_{-1}/Y^e \tag{5.12}$$

where Y^e is an estimate of the expected level of sales. For most firms, Y^e is a trend-adjusted weighted average of past sales. We have already indicated that the yield spread and changes in stock market prices should be added to this function.

The rcc term is less important for capital goods with shorter lives – computers and motor vehicles – than for those with longer lives, except for the ITC, which comes right off the tax bill and affects purchases of short-lived investments. The timing of purchasing capital goods with short lives is also affected by credit availability, much as is the case for consumer durables, because smaller firms buy a significant proportion of total sales of computers and motor vehicles.

The K_{-1}/Y^e term enters with a negative sign, assuming that λ is greater than δ. We could thus take the inverse of this term, or $[Y/K]_{-1}$, which would then enter the equation with a positive sign. That term approximates the rate of capacity utilization, which is actual output divided by maximum output; that term is lagged one period, assuming Y^e is proportional to Y_{-1}.

Notice that the term $(\lambda - \delta)$ could have an ambiguous sign. For capital spending, λ is probably about 0.3 to 0.4, while δ is less than 0.2. However, in a situation where goods are replaced more frequently – such as high-tech equipment or motor vehicles – the sign on the last term might be close to zero, in which case the stock adjustment principle would not apply.

By dividing gross investment by Y^e and substituting Cp, the rate of capacity utilization, for the term K_{-1}/Y^e, the investment function can be linearized as follows:

$$I_g/Y^e = f(p_w/p_k, \text{rcc}, \text{Cp}), \tag{5.13}$$

with appropriate lags. That is the investment function in equilibrium, omitting issues of short-term availability of credit or changes in expectations. Those additional variables are then added for empirical estimation.

Notes

1. This is assumed to be the real rate of interest, with zero inflation. The expected rate of inflation is generally positive, in which case the nominal rate would be somewhat higher, but that would be offset by the increase in nominal receipts in later years. The concept is the same whether inflation is zero or positive.
2. Because of inflation, more will have to be set aside, but that is supposed to be offset by accelerated depreciation allowances.
3. The actual term is a 20-quarter polynomial distributed lag, starting with a four-quarter lag, and constrained to zero at both ends of the distribution.
4. Even this question is no longer easily answered if someone buys a BMW produced in Spartanburg, South Carolina.
5. The approach in this section was first developed by Dale Jorgenson, who has written many articles on the subject. Two early references are his ''Capital Theory and Investment Behavior,'' *American Economic Review*, 53 (May 1963), and Robert W. Hall and Dale Jorgenson, ''Tax Policy and Investment Behavior,'' *American Economic Review*, 57 (June 1967).
6. The analogy can be made with consumer spending. The rate of personal income tax would be almost irrelevant if you could write off all your expenditures as they occurred.

chapter six

Determination of interest rates and introduction to monetary policy

Introduction

Interest rates are the equilibrating force between investment and saving, and between aggregate demand and supply. With current institutional arrangements, the availability of credit is also an important factor in determining the timing of many purchases of consumer and capital goods.

In the short run, fluctuations in monetary variables affect both the real growth rate and the rate of inflation. In the long run, they affect only the rate of inflation. In the long run, no country can boost its growth rate simply by expanding the supply of credit or holding interest rates at artificially low levels. During periods of severe recession or outright depression, even reducing the rate of interest all the way to zero will not necessarily return the economy to prosperity. In particular, the severe stock market decline and the 2001 recession were not preceded by an increase in bond yields, significant tightening by the Federal Reserve Bank, or credit restrictions; instead, that downturn was due primarily to the emergence of excess capacity, which in turn was caused by a below-equilibrium cost of equity capital. That also happened to Japan a decade earlier. Thus monetary policy per se cannot always control the business cycle.

In the absence of a central bank, the level of interest rates would be related to the demand and supply of loanable funds, the expected rate of inflation, and the amount of borrowing by the private and public sectors. In equilibrium, the central bank is likely to set short-term interest rates at the level indicated by these market conditions; but at other times, it will often choose a different level. For example, it will supply additional liquidity to the economy and reduce interest rates during times of financial crisis; it will reduce short-term interest rates below their equilibrium levels during times of recession; and it will raise short-term interest rates above their equilibrium levels when inflation is accelerating.

We thus need to distinguish between changes in monetary *conditions* that reflect underlying changes in the economy, and changes in monetary *policy* that are not tied to those changes. For example, suppose the inflation rate rose by 1%. A 1% increase in the short-term rate of interest would represent no change in policy, even though nominal interest rates have risen; a 3% change would represent a tightening of policy, while no change at all would represent an easing of policy. Changes in monetary conditions usually have a much smaller impact on aggregate demand if they are not accompanied by changes in monetary policy.

Recessions are often preceded by higher interest rates and restricted credit availability. That is, of course, not the same thing as saying that changes in monetary policy cause recessions. If the economy starts to overheat, interest rates would rise and the growth in real monetary and credit aggregates would decline even if there were no central bank. Indeed, it was precisely the severe changes in these variables that led to the formation of the Federal Reserve Bank, which was supposed to reduce sudden and severe changes in both monetary conditions and the real growth rate. In some cases, monetary policy was responsible for recessions not because the Fed tightened too much or too soon, but because it failed to react in a timely fashion, hence permitting inflation to accelerate and requiring a much more severe reaction later.

Monetary policy also affects the economy through the availability as well as the cost of credit. The yield spread between long- and short-term rates is an important measure of the availability of credit. When the yield spread is inverted – when short-term interest rates are higher than long-term rates – the US economy has always headed into recession the following year, because an inverted yield curve curtails the availability of credit to the private sector.

Since the yield spread between different maturities of interest rates is a key determinant of economic activity, it is necessary to dispense with the concept of "the" interest rate, and determine what causes the yield spread to fluctuate over the business cycle. That means analyzing the determinants of short-term and long-term interest rates separately. One of the major factors is the difference between the expected rate of inflation in the short run and the long run. Hence the concept of the expected rate of inflation is a major determinant of both interest rates and economic activity.

Understanding monetary policy is a critical component of understanding macroeconomics, since it is an important determinant of both real growth and inflation in the short run, and of inflation in the long run. Having said that, however, one should not think that monetary policy is omnipotent. It is not the major cause of recessions, and it is not always able to return the economy to prosperity if other elements of government policy have damaged the economy.

Many years ago, when the debate about the importance of monetary policy was at its zenith, someone observed that macroeconomists could be divided into three camps: money does not matter, money matters, money is all that matters. For the most part, both fringe camps have faded away, and most economists now accept the fact that monetary policy is important, but other factors also influence economic growth. Claims that "The Federal Reserve Chairman is the second most important man in Washington" are grossly exaggerated. In particular, the dazzling performance of the US economy during the late 1990s was due more to the return of the budget surplus – i.e., fiscal policy – than to monetary policy per se. In the same vein, Federal Reserve Chairman Alan Greenspan was apparently powerless to prevent the 2000–2002 nosedive in the stock market and the accompanying recession.

The material in this chapter first describes the key interest rates and briefly describes how monetary policy works today. The determinants of long- and short-term rates are examined next, followed by a discussion of the methods by which changes in monetary conditions and policies affect the components of aggregate demand. Having examined these links, we then explain why monetary policy cannot always achieve the desired results.

6.1   Definitions of key interest rates and yield spreads

The **Federal funds rate** is the rate at which banks lend each other money on an overnight basis. It is also the rate the Federal Reserve System (Fed) changes when it wants to implement monetary policy through a shift in interest rates.

The **discount rate** is the rate at which commercial banks borrow from the Fed. It is no longer very important, because the Fed discourages such borrowing for all but emergency uses. The Fed used to change the discount rate to implement monetary policy, but now changes the Federal funds rate for that purpose. Changes in the discount rate are usually taken to keep it in line with the funds rate, not to signal a tighter or easier monetary policy. Under an amendment to the Fed's Regulation A on January 9, 2003, the discount rate was discontinued and replaced by the "primary credit" rate, which was initially set 1% above the Federal funds rate.

The **prime rate** is the loan rate that banks allegedly charge their "best" customers; all other loan rates are then supposed to be scaled up from prime. Before 1974 there was no fixed relationship between the prime and other market rates; it depended on loan demand. However, when banks were discouraged from raising the prime rate during the period of wage and price controls in 1973, they gradually switched to a "formula" that set the prime rate $1\frac{1}{2}$ percentage points above the Federal funds rate. In 1992, Alan Greenspan encouraged the banking system to raise this spread to 3 percentage points to improve bank liquidity, and it has remained at that level since then.

Other short-term commercial rates, such as the rates paid on large **certificates of deposit** (CDs), and **commercial paper**, which represent unsecured borrowing by major banks or corporations, are very closely tied to the Federal funds rate.

The Treasury issues a variety of securities to fund the national debt. These are divided into **bills**, which have a maturity of one year or less, **notes**, which have a maturity of one to ten years, and **bonds**, which have a maturity of over ten years. Notes and bonds are sometimes collectively known as coupons, because owners of these securities used to mail in their coupons to receive regular semiannual interest payments. Now this is all done electronically, but in the old days such investors used to be known as "coupon clippers." By comparison, bills are sold on a discount basis and are redeemed at par without any coupon clipping. Currently, the longest dated Treasury security is a 30-year bond; this maturity was not issued before 1977. In 2001, the Treasury announced plans to phase out the 30-year bond.

Throughout this chapter, and indeed throughout the book, it is important to distinguish between the **nominal rate of interest**, which is the actual rate quoted in the financial press and in business transactions, and the **real rate of interest**, which is the nominal rate minus the expected rate of inflation and is used in the determination of capital spending. Also, while there is an entire spectrum of maturities, it is often useful to distinguish between "short-term" and "long-term" interest rates as follows.

As a general rule, the price of any asset invested at the short-term rate of interest is fixed in value. The value of your bank balance – or the company bank balance – will be unchanged regardless of how much interest rates fluctuate. Treasury bills are purchased on a discount basis, which means the bill is discounted at the current rate of interest so that it is worth its face value on the day of redemption. Although Treasury bills are actively traded, and their prices do fluctuate slightly, most investors hold these bills until maturity. Similar comments apply to short-term commercial paper and certificates of deposit.

By contrast, the price of a bond can fluctuate substantially, even if it is a US government bond with zero risk of default; any other dollar-denominated bond carries a higher rate of interest to account for possible default risk. If the bond were issued in perpetuity – as is the case for British consols – the price of the bond would simply be equal to the coupon value divided by the interest rate. For example, a bond with an annual coupon of $60[1] and a yield of 6% would have a price of $1,000. If the bond yield then rose to 8% the following year, the price of the bond issued in perpetuity would fall to $750. If the bond had a 30-year maturity, the price would drop to approximately $818, and so on.

Several factors might cause the bond yield to rise; at this point, assume the increase occurred because of a 2% rise in the expected rate of inflation, which would leave the real rate of interest unchanged. However, investors might expect that increase to occur right away, or over the next several years. Their expectations might also be influenced by whether the Fed expects the same increase in inflation and adjusts the Federal funds rate accordingly, or does not change the funds rate. Depending on differing expectations about the short- and long-term rates of inflation, and based on what action the Fed takes, the yield spread between long- and short-term rates can change substantially. Those changes have an important impact on the level of aggregate demand over and above the effect from changes in interest rates.

CASE STUDY 6.1   DETERMINANTS OF THE TREASURY YIELD SPREAD UNDER ALTERNATIVE CIRCUMSTANCES

The Treasury **yield spread** measures how interest rates on Treasury securities vary by length of maturity. Under ordinary circumstances, the yield spread is positively

continued

CASE STUDY 6.1 (*continued*)

sloped; the longer the time to maturity, the higher the interest rate, because investors demand an increasing premium for holding longer-dated securities to compensate them for the market risk that prices will drop in the years before maturity. The yield spread is closely followed as an indicator of monetary policy and a precursor of economic activity.

An increase in short-term rates above long-term rates with the same risk factor is known as an inverted yield spread. Every time that has happened in the past 30 years, the US economy has headed into recession the following year. This relationship is no fluke; differences in the yield spread often contain important information about inflationary expectations and economic activity in the future.

The Treasury yield curve diagram is published daily in the *Wall Street Journal* and other financial publications. Figure 6.1 shows some examples of normal and inverted yield curves.

In August 1981, debt market traders thought the Federal funds rate was well above its equilibrium value, inflation would soon decline, the economy would head into recession, and the Fed would ease. In fact, that is precisely what happened.

In October 1993, traders thought inflation was about to increase and the Fed would tighten. The Fed did indeed tighten, but inflation remained steady – possibly because of that timely action. In any case, the higher rates were validated.

In January 2001, traders thought the economy was weakening, although they did not foresee an actual recession. They thought the Fed would ease in the short run, but would then have to tighten again later. The economy was actually somewhat weaker than anticipated, and Fed easing was substantially greater than anticipated at the time.

In October 2001, traders realized the economy was in a recession; since they did not know when it would end, the yield curve was flat at the short end. However, investors expected the Fed to tighten once the recession did end. They were quite wrong; the Fed eased further in 2002.

The yield spreads between the 10-year Treasury note and 3-month Treasury bill, and between the Aaa corporate bond yield and the Federal funds rate, are shown in figure 6.2. The 10-year yield is used because the 30-year bond was not issued before 1977, and new issues were discontinued in 2001. This diagram also shows that the yield spread turned negative slightly before each recession since 1969.

Corporate bond yields are rated by several private sector agencies based on the perceived degree of creditworthiness. These rates are scaled up from the Treasury bond rate. Aaa corporate bond rates, the highest private sector rating, are usually about $\frac{3}{4}$% above the Treasury bond rate, although the rate widened significantly in 2000 and 2001. Rates on high-yield corporate bonds, or "junk bonds," are usually

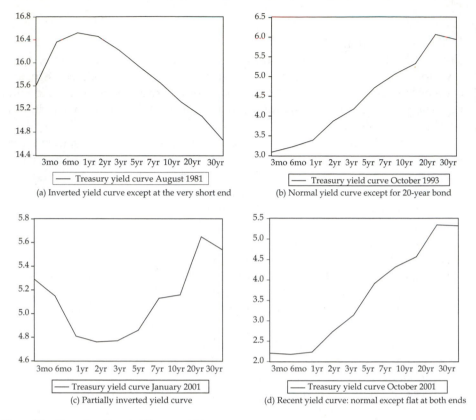

Figure 6.1 Normal and inverted Treasury yield curves

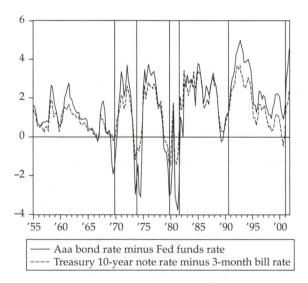

Figure 6.2 Yield spread for Treasury and high-grade private sector interest rates (the vertical lines are the quarters in which recessions began; note that the yield spread has previously turned negative in each case)

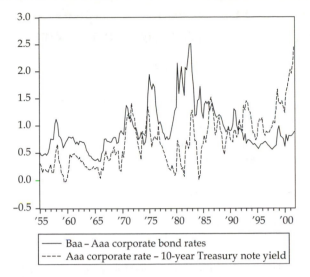

Figure 6.3   Interest rate spreads for the Aaa corporate bond rate relative to the 10-year Treasury note yield and the Baa corporate bond rate

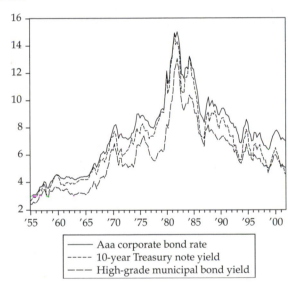

Figure 6.4   Comparison of Treasury, corporate, and municipal bond yields

3% to 8% above the Treasury bond rate. The spreads between the Treasury note yield, the Aaa corporate bond, and the Baa corporate bond are shown in figure 6.3.

The interest on municipal debt securities is generally tax-exempt, so rates are substantially lower than for Treasury or corporate securities. The rate on high-grade municipal bonds is generally about 75% of the Aaa corporate bond rate. Thus an individual in the 40% tax bracket who desired interest income would presumably prefer municipal to corporate bonds. The spreads between yields on these different types of bonds are shown in figure 6.4.

MANAGER'S BRIEFCASE: INTERPRETING THE YIELD SPREAD

Suppose that the yield spread, as measured by the 10-year Treasury note yield minus the Federal funds rate, has just turned negative. How should you react?

If your firm typically is affected by business cycle recessions, you generally have two to three quarters to get ready for a recession. The lag time is somewhat variable, so if the 7th or 8th month passes and the economy has not yet turned down, that doesn't mean there will not be any recession. Sometimes the lag can be as long as five quarters.

To serve as a valid signal of recession, though, the yield curve should invert from the top rather than the bottom. In other words, the inversion should occur because short-term rates rose, not because long-term rates fell. In mid-1998, the yield curve briefly turned negative because of concerns about financial market stability, not because of Fed tightening; indeed, the Fed eased during this period. Subsequently the economy continued to grow at above-average rates in 1999.

Suppose the product or service your firm provides is not affected by cyclical variations, such as healthcare. An inverted yield curve means the cost of borrowing will soon decline sharply, so it is advisable to postpone any borrowing if possible, especially in the bond market; the timing of variable-rate loans from banks that are tied to the prime rate is not as important. Also, an inverted yield spread is always followed by a decline in the stock market, which suggests any proposed equity financing ought to be undertaken sooner rather than later. Managers of pension plans would be well advised to shift some of their assets from stocks to bonds for a while.

6.2   The role of monetary policy

It is often said that the principal role of monetary policy is to keep the rate of inflation low and stable. An even more important goal, however, is to provide adequate credit for the needs of industry and commerce and insure that the economy does not falter because of insufficient liquidity. During times such as the 1987 stock market crash, or the feared meltdown of major financial institutions after the collapse of Long-Term Capital Management in 1998, the first responsibility of the Federal Reserve System – or any other central bank – is to insure that the financial sector remains intact. In 1929, failure of the Federal Reserve Bank to rescue the banking system was one of the major causes of the Great Depression.

In the absence of financial sector emergencies, any central bank should indeed concentrate its efforts on controlling the inflation rate. However, one should never forget that it also has the responsibility to insure the economy does not choke to death from a lack of liquidity.

Most of the time, shifts in monetary policy have a significant impact on changes in the real growth rate and the rate of inflation. These links are usually stronger than the short-term fluctuations caused by changes in fiscal policy. Monetary policy can override fiscal policy, and sometimes does. Fiscal policy could conceivably offset monetary policy, but because of the lags in Congressional approval, that rarely happens.

On various occasions in the post-WWII economy, it appears that monetary policy has been ineffective because the government, for one reason or another, has directed that it not be used. In particular, monetary policy was unable to fight inflation right after World War II because President Truman directed the Fed to support the long bond at its original issue price, thus prohibiting interest rates from rising to reduce inflation. During the period of wage and price controls in 1972 and 1973, President Nixon directed the Fed to hold short-term interest rates below equilibrium levels. In 1979, Fed Chairman G. William Miller decided to increase the growth in the money supply to boost the economy enough to insure President Carter's reelection in 1980; instead, inflation accelerated, and he was soon replaced by Paul Volcker. In all three cases, when prudent monetary policy was overruled to boost real growth, the result was higher inflation.

The primary role of monetary policy is thus to assure adequate liquidity for the needs of industry and commerce while keeping the rate of inflation at a low, sustainable level. Some say inflation ought to be zero, but since there is an asymmetry between a small positive rate of inflation and a small negative rate, a slightly positive rate of inflation generally enhances overall economic performance. Fed Chairman Paul Volcker once said that inflation should be low enough that it does not influence economic decisions,[2] and this view has been generally accepted in financial markets. This statement means inflation should be low enough that consumers do not choose to purchase certain goods (such as a car) now rather than later, businesses do not choose one kind of investment over another because prices are expected to rise, and investors allocate their capital to try to achieve the maximum real rate of return instead of investing in an asset only because its price is expected to rise.

Assuming this is a worthwhile and reasonable goal, how should it be implemented? In the past, many monetary economists, notably Milton Friedman, have suggested this goal can best be achieved by having the money supply grow at a constant rate, rather than permitting discretionary changes in policy. For when discretion is introduced, Friedman claims, policy analysts misread the situation or – even worse – are swayed by political considerations, and end up making things worse rather than better. However, now that the banking sector has been deregulated, and the central bank cannot control changes in the money supply, the Friedman hypothesis no longer applies. Today, very few monetary economists still believe a simple rule of this sort is still appropriate for all contingencies.

Following a dogmatic rule for targeting money supply or interest rates would not allow any flexibility when the economy is bombarded by exogenous shocks. Immediately following the 1987 stock market crash, for example, it was essential for the Fed to provide enough liquidity to forestall a market meltdown; many thought that was its finest hour. It was also important for the Fed to ease in mid-1982, when a severe recession was bedeviling the US economy, and the Mexican economy was about to collapse. Fed easing was also appropriate in 1991 and 1992, when the economy showed little ability to rebound from the 1990 recession. On the other hand, Fed tightening was appropriate in 1994, when inflationary pressures threatened to choke off the emerging recovery, even though the broad-based indicators of inflation had not yet risen. Hence in the era of banking deregulation, there have been numerous instances where departure from a rigid rule has benefited both the US and world economies.

If the economy were always in equilibrium, the task of monetary policy would be quite simple: just leave well enough alone. However, the economy has been and presumably will continue to be affected by exogenous shocks: energy embargoes, wars, strikes, fluctuations in the value of the currency, stock market meltdowns, and international crises. Also, if the government decides to increase the full-employment deficit, the Fed must make an unpleasant choice: either boost interest rates, or eventually allow inflation to rise. Thus an "automatic pilot" method of monetary policy works only if the budget remains balanced at full employment and the economy is never subject to shocks.

Once a recession is underway and inflation is declining, monetary policy can often be used to end the recession quickly and help the economy grow faster than its equilibrium rate – otherwise the unemployment rate will remain too high indefinitely. However, once the economy has returned to full employment, monetary policy should be used to reduce the rate of growth to its long-term sustainable level. A one-size-fits-all rule for monetary policy does not work.

Central bankers invariably state that their only role is to keep inflation low and stable, not to influence the real growth rate. That is what they are supposed to say, yet it is not really true. Monetary policy should also be used to increase the growth rate when the unemployment rate is too high, and reduce it when the economy is in danger of overheating. The rest of this chapter will discuss the best ways to attain those goals.

6.3   The Federal Reserve System

When the Federal Reserve System was founded in 1913, many members of Congress outside the Northeast were concerned about domination by New York bankers and Washington politicians. Hence they sought to insure a measure of independence for other regions of the country by forming 12 Federal Reserve Banks, each of which would make its own decision on interest rates and credit policy. In fact the system does not work that way; all the important decisions about monetary policy are made in Washington and executed in New York. Nonetheless, the original structure has remained in place with few changes.

The Federal Open Market Committee (FOMC) consists of the seven members of the Board of Governors and five of the presidents of the regional Federal Reserve Banks. Of these 12 presidents, five are designated as voting members at any given time. This group of five always includes the President of the New York Fed, either the Cleveland or Chicago Fed president, and three of the remaining nine regional bank presidents, who serve on a rotating basis.

The FOMC meets in Washington, DC approximately once every six weeks, mainly to determine the level of the funds rate, although other business is also discussed. Sometimes the Chairman, after telephone consultation with the other FOMC members, changes the funds rate between these regularly scheduled meetings. About two weeks before each FOMC meeting, the Fed releases a document known as the *Beige Book*, which contains a summary of economic conditions in each of the 12 Federal Reserve districts. The Beige Book is used as the focus of discussion about whether to change the funds rate, and is supposed to provide more information about the data that FOMC members will be discussing.

The decisions of the FOMC used to be shrouded in secrecy. However, since 1994, at the end of each meeting, the FOMC has issued a brief communiqué, stating either that it has decided to change the Federal funds rate by the amount indicated, or has decided to leave the funds rate unchanged. If the funds rate is left unchanged, the release will say something like, "The FOMC adjourned at 1:40 PM today. There is no further report." – at which point all investors and traders know the FOMC voted to keep the funds rate unchanged.

Starting in 1999, the Fed communiqués have included additional information about whether monetary policy had a tightening bias, was neutral, or had an easing bias. A tightening bias means that while rates were not changed, they would probably be raised in the near future if growth remained strong or inflation increased. A neutral bias means the FOMC does not plan to change rates unless some unexpected development occurs in the economy. Previously, this information was available only with a six-week delay.

Before 1994, traders could only guess whether the FOMC had voted to change the rate. That generated a great deal of confusion about what the Fed "really" did, causing an entire industry to spring up to interpret the Fed's moves. With the FOMC issuing these communiqués, the method of changing the funds rate is still the same, but the mystery of what did or did not happen has disappeared.

Of course, FOMC members do not sit around the room plucking alternative interest rates out of the air. They carefully consider all the available economic evidence: inflation, real growth, the change in employment and unemployment, foreign developments, and so on. They also try to estimate how inflationary expectations are likely to change in the future. In the late 1990s, the FOMC members in general, and Greenspan in particular, have evaluated recent changes in the bond market. If bond yields have recently declined, that suggests inflationary expectations are steady or falling, and easing might be appropriate. If yields have recently risen, that suggests no further easing, or perhaps tightening, would be more appropriate. Paul Volcker, Chairman of the Fed from 1979 to 1987, did not focus on the bond markets, and in the future FOMC members may also place less emphasis on bond yields. From 1994 through 2002, though, recent changes in bond yields have been one of the key factors determining how much the Federal funds rate will change in the near term.

Before deregulation of the banking sector in 1982, the Fed was able to exercise much closer control over the money supply, primarily through open market operations – the purchase and sales of Treasury securities to the banking system. However, that discipline could be enforced only when the maximum interest rate banks could pay on deposits was regulated, and a certain proportion of all deposits had to be kept as non-interest bearing reserves at the Fed. Today, for most classes of deposits, banks can offer the market rate of interest, and many types of deposits are not subject to reserve requirements. Hence open market operations, while they still occur on a regular basis, no longer have much influence on interest rates or monetary policy.

However, the Fed can still influence the terms under which credit is made available to consumers and businesses. In 1980, Paul Volcker imposed consumer credit controls for three months, which plunged the economy into recession. They were so effective that authority for such controls has since lapsed.[3] In the early 1990s, following the collapse of the savings and loan industry, banks were directed to follow much stricter guidelines for issuing loans, which also retarded the recovery that started in 1991. In the future, it is likely that credit guidelines issued by the Fed will continue to have a significant influence on the level of overall economic activity.

6.4   Determination of the Federal funds rate

As a general rule, the Fed tries to set the funds rate at a level that will keep the inflation rate low and stable and encourage equilibrium growth in the economy; during times of financial crisis, it is likely to deviate from these norms. That is a very broad mandate, and it is important to realize that different Federal Reserve Chairmen interpret this mandate differently. The Federal funds rate did not officially exist before early 1955; before then, the Fed used other tools to implement

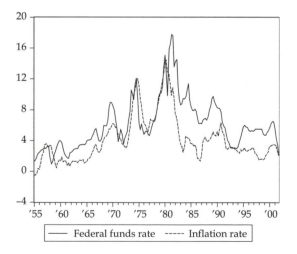

Figure 6.5   Federal funds rate and inflation rate

monetary policy. Figure 6.5 shows the relationship between the Fed funds rate and the rate of inflation, measured here as the percentage change in the consumer price index (CPI) over the past four quarters. Obviously the two lines do not move together very closely, so other factors clearly influence the Fed funds rate.

CASE STUDY 6.2   DIFFERENCES IN THE FEDERAL FUNDS RATE UNDER DIFFERENT CHAIRMEN

Table 6.1 shows that the behavior of the Federal funds rate relative to its two major economic determinants – inflation and unemployment – varies greatly depending on who was Fed Chairman at the time. It is not possible to issue any sweeping generalizations about what factors determine the funds rate. The average real Federal funds rate – the nominal rate minus the percentage change in the CPI over the past year – averaged 0.0% under both Burns and Miller, jumped to an average of 4.5% under Volcker, then retreated about halfway under Greenspan.

Table 6.1   Varying behavior of Fed funds rate under different Chairmen

Chairman	Dates in office	Average real Fed funds rate	Change in real funds rate for 1% change in unemployment rate
William McC. Martin, Jr.[a]	4/1/55–1/31/70	1.5	−0.4
Arthur F. Burns	2/1/70–1/31/78	0.0	−1.3
G. William Miller	3/8/78–8/6/79	0.0	*
Paul A. Volcker	8/6/79–8/11/87	4.5	*
Alan Greenspan	8/11/87[b] –	2.3	−1.8

[a] period when Fed funds rate existed; Martin's term started 4/2/51
[b] data are through the middle of 2002
* coefficient was positive

The last column in this table shows the average percentage change in the real Federal funds rate for a 1% change in the unemployment rate, calculated as a simple regression. During Volcker's term, there was no negative correlation between the unemployment rate and the real Fed funds rate. Miller's term was so brief that no meaningful regression results can be calculated. Figure 6.6 shows the relationship between the real Federal funds rate and the unemployment rate under the various Fed Chairmen listed in table 6.1.

continued

CASE STUDY 6.2 (*continued*)

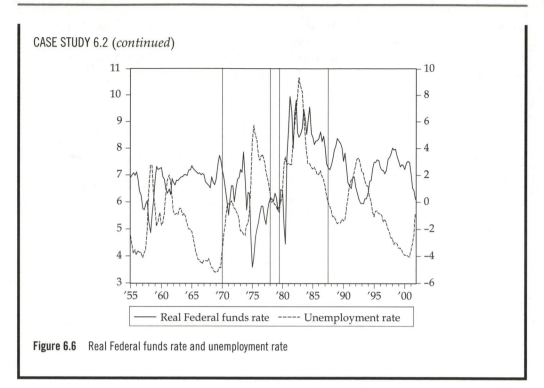

Figure 6.6 Real Federal funds rate and unemployment rate

Virtually all economists now agree that holding the real funds rate at an average of 0.0% during the 1970s was a mistake, since it led to an unacceptably high rate of inflation when the economy returned to full employment. In the future, it is likely that during periods of equilibrium growth, the real Federal funds rate will be approximately equal to the growth rate of productivity plus the growth rate of the labor force, both as measured by the Bureau of Labor Statistics (BLS). When inflationary expectations start to rise, or when the economy reaches full employment, the real funds rate should increase – which means the nominal rate would rise more than the expected rise in the rate of inflation – and when unemployment starts to rise, the real funds rate will usually decrease. From time to time, the funds rate will be altered because of domestic or international financial crises.

Historically, the Fed has kept short-term rates above or below equilibrium for extended periods of time; the major periods are as follows.

- Shortly after World War II, the Treasury directed the Fed to hold the long-term bond rate below 3%, even though the rate of inflation was as high as 18%. The Fed purchased enough long-term bonds to keep their price at par.
- In mid-1968, the Fed boosted money supply growth and reduced interest rates as a quid pro quo with the government for raising tax rates, even though the economy was already at full employment and inflation was starting to spiral out of control.

- After Nixon imposed a wage/price freeze in August 1971, the Fed was ordered to keep short-term interest rates low even though the increase in demand stemming from the Nixon program was highly inflationary. The Fed temporarily lost its independence.
- In the late 1970s, the Federal funds rate was consistently held below the rate of inflation for several years, under both Republican and Democratic administrations.
- In 1993, the Fed reduced the real funds rate to zero (i.e., the nominal rate was 3%, and so was the inflation rate) to offset the contractionary influences of reduced credit availability in the aftermath of the savings and loan industry scandals. In this case, Greenspan was also trying to rebuild bank liquidity, following widespread bank defaults after the real estate market collapsed in the late 1980s.
- During 2002, the Fed reduced the funds rate to $1\frac{1}{4}$% over the year even though the core inflation rate was 1.9% and real growth averaged 2.9%. In this case, the Fed was concerned about the strength of the recovery, and the sharp decline in the stock market throughout most of that year.
- The Fed can also keep rates above equilibrium levels for extended periods of time. In 1983–4, the funds rate averaged 9.6% even though the inflation rate fell to 4%, as Volcker was determined to wring inflationary expectations out of the economy. Even after these expectations had declined, the funds rate averaged 7.7% over the 1986–90 period, while the inflation rate averaged only 4%.

In a perfect world, a beneficent and omniscient Fed would always keep the funds rate near its equilibrium position, hence reducing the likelihood of endogenous business cycles. However, it is also possible that future Fed Chairmen will inadvertently make mistakes. If that does happen, we can learn from lessons of the past by examining how the economy reacted during previous times when the Fed funds rate was far away from its equilibrium value. That record is summarized in figure 6.7.

Whenever the Fed funds rate was kept below its equilibrium value for an extended period of time, the growth rate for nominal GDP was above average. If the economy had just recently emerged from a recession, real GDP rose faster; if the economy was close to full employment, inflation rose faster. Whenever the Fed funds rate was kept above its equilibrium value for an extended period of time, the growth rate for nominal GDP was below average. At first, real growth declined; in the longer run, the rate of inflation did not accelerate when the economy approached full employment. This finding goes far to explain why the rate of inflation exhibited an upward trend in the 1960s and 1970s, a downward trend in the 1980s and early 1990s, and then remained stable when the economy returned to full employment in the late 1990s.

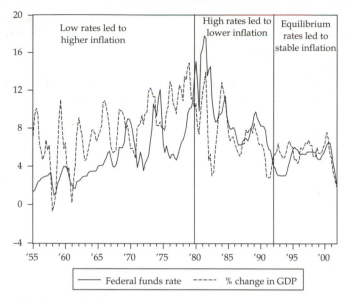

Figure 6.7   Federal funds rate and percentage change in nominal GDP

CASE STUDY 6.3   THE TAYLOR RULE

It is sometimes claimed that the behavior of the Federal funds rate under Alan Greenspan can be described by a so-called Taylor Rule, which says the behavior of the Fed funds rate is closely correlated with the rate of inflation and the rate of unemployment. The original Taylor Rule used the percentage deviation of real GDP from its trend value, but the empirical relationship is improved by adding the unemployment rate. Taylor estimated such a function from 1987.3 through 1997.3 and found that it fit the available data very well.

The Taylor Rule is often quoted as saying that a 1% change in the core inflation rate changes the funds rate by 1%, and a 1% change in the growth rate also changes the funds rate by 1%. In fact, during the Greenspan regime the Fed has reacted somewhat more vigorously to changes in inflation. Empirically, it has been the case that a 1% change in the inflation rate changes the funds rate by about $1\frac{1}{2}$%, although the 1:1 relationship with the growth rate remains intact. The actual regression is:

$$FF = 7.27 + 1.54 \times \text{core CPI} - 1.78 \times \text{UN} + 0.18 \text{ IPM} \quad \text{Adj R-Sq} = 0.927$$
$$(22.6) \qquad\qquad (17.0) \qquad (9.2) \qquad \text{D/W} = 0.60$$

continued

CASE STUDY 6.3 (*continued*)

where

   FF   = Federal funds rate

   CPI = percentage change in core rate of inflation over past six quarters (a distributed lag is used)

   UN = current rate of unemployment

   IPM = percentage change in the index of industrial production for manufacturing over the past four quarters

The simulated values from this equation, composed with the central Federal funds rate, are shown in figure 6.8. The original Taylor Rule used the deviation of actual real GDP from its trend value.[4] However, the recent GDP data have become increasingly erratic and hence are no longer used by the Fed; it is a simple matter to add the percentage change in real GDP to the above regression and verify that it is not significant. Over the long run, a 1% change in real GDP changes the unemployment rate by 0.4% and changes industrial production by 2%, so converting the coefficients in the above equation to a GDP basis, the implicit coefficient would be $1.78 \times 0.4 + 0.18 \times 2$, or 1.07, not significantly different from 1.0.

Over the long run, a 1% change in inflation changes the funds rate by 1%. Since 1987, though, the coefficient has been 1.5%, indicating that the Greenspan Fed is more sensitive to inflation, and moves ahead of expectations, which has worked out well. The earlier mistake by previous Fed Chairmen probably was to boost the funds rate only by the amount of inflation instead of anticipating further gains, which often led to inflationary cycles.

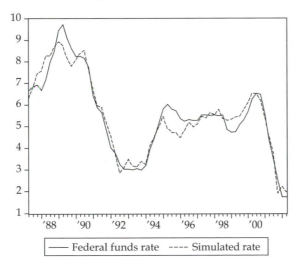

Figure 6.8   Federal funds rate as a function of the unemployment rate, core rate of inflation over the past year, and percentage change in manufacturing industrial production over the past year

MANAGER'S BRIEFCASE: TRACKING THE FED

Suppose you have the responsibility of determining when to borrow money for your company, either through the banking system or in capital markets. The timing depends on how much the Federal funds rate will change in the near term. Which indicators should you track? Or, to put the same question in different words, which indicators does the Fed track?

On Saturday, January 19, 2002, a front page *Washington Post* story quoted Greenspan saying in essence that his earlier pessimistic comments had been misinterpreted, the recession was over, and the Fed would not cut the funds rate any more. The futures markets, which had previously assigned a better than 50 : 50 chance for a further Fed rate cut at the upcoming January 30 FOMC meeting, immediately revised their estimates to show less than a 10% chance. And sure enough, the Fed left the funds rate at $1\frac{3}{4}$%. The question raised here is: what indicators caused Greenspan to decide the recession had ended?

After the tragic events of 9/11, the index of leading indicators had recovered much more sharply than most economists had expected, rising 0.9% in November, 1.1% in December, and 0.4% in January. The key movers in that index were the improvement in the stock market, the decline in initial unemployment claims, and the pickup in new orders. The various indexes of consumer expectations also rebounded rapidly.

There is an old saying on Wall Street that "Dr. Copper is a better forecaster than 95% of PhD economists." Copper prices, which had been falling steadily during most of 2001, turned around in late November and headed higher. We point this out in particular because the PPI, which is the index most people look at to gauge future price movements, fell sharply in December, but apparently that didn't distract Greenspan.

Weekly unemployment claims is a key leading indicator. After peaking shortly after 9/11, they declined in November, December, and January. In fact, when the January *Employment and Earnings* data were released on February 1, they showed a decline in the overall unemployment rate, which made Greenspan's decision look good in retrospect.

Bond and stock prices had also risen significantly from their post-9/11 lows, and although their pattern had been erratic in recent weeks, both indicators suggested that the economy was strengthening.

New orders for nondefense capital goods, after plunging in September, had also recovered during the next two months (January data were not yet available). Also, the index of consumer expectations, which had understandably plunged from 93.7 in August to 70.7 in October, rebounded strongly to 92.4 in December and 96.9 in January.

In the future, these variables – initial unemployment claims, stock prices, capital goods new orders, consumer expectations, and copper prices – are likely to indicate what action the Fed will take in the near future. In this respect, it is also useful to note which variables were excluded: Greenspan paid little or no attention to the continuing declines in employment, industrial production, shipments of capital goods, or the trade deficit. Not too surprisingly, he focused on leading rather than coincident indicators.

One place you do *not* want to look, by the way, is the futures markets. Early in 2002, the values of futures markets indicated that the funds rate would rise to 4% by the end of that year. In fact it fell from $1\frac{3}{4}$% to $1\frac{1}{4}$%. That forecast was based on an unrealistically optimistic recovery, as monetary economists failed to realize that the upturn would probably be sluggish, similar to the pattern in 1991 and 1992, rather than robust, as in 1975 or 1983.[5]

6.5   Effect of Federal Reserve policy on the availability of credit

Before the deregulation of the banking sector in 1982, the Fed could control the amount of money that banks had available for making loans. Most deposits were subject to ceiling rates set by the Fed; if short-term interest rates were boosted above that ceiling rate, money would be withdrawn from the banking system, hence curtailing the funds that banks had available to lend. Also, if the Fed sold Treasury securities and boosted interest rates, the banking system would alter its portfolio of assets to hold more Treasuries and fewer loans. Finally, the Fed could boost required reserve ratios, which meant the banking system would have less money to loan because it was required to keep more money in non-interest-bearing reserves at the Fed.

Since banking deregulation, banks can decide what interest rate to pay on deposits, so funds do not necessarily leave the banking system when short-term rates rise. Many types of deposits do not have required reserve ratios, and even where these ratios still apply, they have not been changed for several decades. Hence the old measures of Fed control are no longer relevant.

Nonetheless, the Fed can still have a major impact on the amount of loans granted by persuading banks to tighten the standards for granting loans. After many scandals were uncovered in the savings and loan industry in the late 1980s, bankers sharply curtailed the amount of loans granted; in some cases, officers and directors were concerned that stockholder suits could force them to resign or even go to prison if loans were made under false pretenses. As a result, loan demand dropped much more sharply than would have been indicated by the relatively mild recession, as shown in figure 6.9. Consumer credit also dropped sharply in the early 1990s, although by a smaller proportion than loans.

6.6   Determinants of long-term interest rates

Theoretically, long-term rates are a weighted average of expected short-term rates for any given risk category.[6] Yet that statement, while unexceptional, does not tell us very much. After all, what determines interest rate expectations? More to the point, what determines fluctuations in the yield spread? In particular, why do long-term rates sometimes fail to respond when short-term rates change?

The general answer is that investors perceive that the change in short-term rates is temporary. For example, suppose the economy heads into recession and the central bank eases substantially. Long-term rates may not drop very much if at all because investors expect that short-term rates will rise again as soon as the recovery gets underway. Or suppose the central bank tightens in order to reduce inflationary expectations. Investors may expect the central bank will be successful, in which case long-term rates do not rise very much.

Of course, sometimes these expectations are wrong. One notable example occurred in 2001 and 2002. The Fed cut the funds rate from $6\frac{1}{2}\%$ to $1\frac{3}{4}\%$ in 11 steps during 2001, but the 10-year Treasury note rate remained

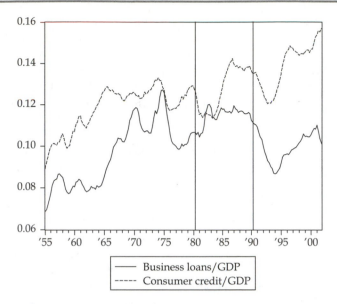

Figure 6.9 Business loans and consumer credit outstanding as a proportion of GDP: the first vertical line represents the credit controls of 1980; the second, the cutback in loans following the savings & loan scandals in 1990

around 5%. Through the first half of 2002, only when the stock market plunged again and the economy faltered a second time did investors perceive that the Fed would not tighten for quite a while, so the 10-year note rate finally declined to $3\frac{1}{2}$%. Note, however, that it took a year and a half for investors to react, even though markets sometime digest financial news in about five seconds.

Actually this pattern is not as unusual as it might initially seem. In most post-WWII recessions, the yield spread narrowed after the recovery was well underway because the bond yield declined. During the first year of recovery, it is often the case that inflation stabilizes or even declines, so bond yields are reacting to that reduction. One might think that after the same pattern had occurred several times, bond traders would begin to get the picture and realize that bond yields usually fall in the first full year of recovery. Maybe that will indeed be the case in the future, but it did not occur in 2002.

A simple regression equation in which the 10-year Treasury note yield is related to current and lagged values of the 3-month Treasury bill rate and the rate of inflation (CPI) explains about 95% of the variance. Figure 6.10 shows both the actual and simulated values, which may appear to agree closely, and the residuals, which show how this simplistic formula sometimes errs by as much as 2 percentage points. Based on the lower portion of this graph, it seems clear that such a simplistic formula cannot usefully be used to generate accurate short-term forecasts of bond yields.

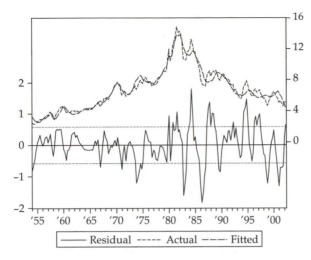

Figure 6.10   Actual and simulated values of the 10-year Treasury note rate (simulated values are based on a 20-quarter distributed lag of the 3-month Treasury bill rate and the core rate of inflation)

Trying to predict short-term fluctuations in the yield spread is not a very satisfying experience, any more than trying to predict short-term fluctuations in the stock market. In the longer run, the following factors are likely to influence long-term rates.

1. The nominal bond yield changes proportionately with the expected rate of inflation. That is likely to occur whether or not the central bank adjusts the short-term rate proportionately to these changes. While markets are sometimes acutely sensitive to even minute suggestions that the rate of inflation is about to change, the empirical evidence suggests that bond market investors rely on the average rate of inflation over the past five years to determine the current bond yield.[7]
2. A change in the real growth rate changes the real bond yield only inasmuch as investors think that change will affect the long-term growth rate. For example, a decline in the rate of growth from +4% to −2% as the economy heads into recession, and then an improvement back to +4% may not change the bond yield at all. Indeed, it is often the case that bond yields decline during the first year of recovery because, most of the time, the core rate of inflation reaches its trough level early in the recovery.
3. For a given level of real growth, bond yields are negatively correlated with the ratio of the government budget ratio (e.g., a bigger surplus will reduce interest rates), and are positively correlated with the ratio of capital spending to GDP. During a recession, when the deficit rises and capital spending declines, changes

in these ratios are likely to offset each other and have little net effect on the bond yield.

6.7 The difference between changes in monetary conditions and monetary policy

One of the principal mistakes that economists – and forecasters – often make is failing to distinguish between changes in monetary conditions and changes in monetary policy. A change in monetary conditions without a change in policy would occur if there were a change in the underlying rates of real growth or infla- tion. Under the set of monetary rules that have been in place at least since 1987, a 1% change in the core rate of inflation would change interest rates by $1\frac{1}{2}$%, and a 1% change in the growth rate would change interest rates by 1%.

It would be incorrect to state that a change in monetary conditions that is not accompanied by a change in policy has no impact on the economy. Suppose, for example, the rate of inflation rose by 5%, and interest rates also rose 5%. Some individuals and businesses would have more difficulty repaying loans at that rate, which would reduce consumption and investment respectively. Nonetheless, the negative impact on aggregate demand would be far less than if interest rates rose 5% when the rate of inflation did not change – or if interest rates rose 10% when inflation rose 5%.

Now suppose a recession occurs, and the growth rate declines from 4% to −1%. As a result, the Fed reduces the funds rate from (say) 7% to 2%. Everyone will agree that "The Fed has eased" which is indeed the case. Nonetheless, there has been no change in monetary policy in the sense that the decline in the funds rate simply reflects the decline in real GDP and the corresponding reduction in the demand for loanable funds. If the Fed were not to ease at all, or were to reduce the funds rate by substantially less than the decline in the growth rate, that would represent a change in monetary policy. As a result, while there will be some improvement in the growth rate because of lower interest rates, the recovery will often be sluggish unless other exogenous factors – notably fiscal policy – are used to boost real growth.

True changes in monetary policy occur when the real rate of interest moves in a manner that is not congruent with the underlying growth rate. Such changes occurred, for example, when the Volcker Fed boosted the Federal funds rate by 10 percentage points in the latter half of 1980. On a less dramatic scale, changes in monetary policy occurred when the Greenspan Fed eased following the 1987 stock market crash, and the 1998 contretemps following the collapse of Long-Term Capital Management and the Russian ruble. In all these cases, the changes in real GDP were greater than would have been expected had monetary policy not changed. By comparison, although the Fed cut the funds rate by $4\frac{3}{4}$% during 2001, that was in line with the drop in the growth rate and real growth remained sluggish for several quarters.

Bond yields are an important determinant of economic activity, but they are only one of several factors. To determine how changes in bond yields affect economic activity, it is also necessary to look at what is happening to short-term rates, the rate of inflation, the yield spread, and the availability of credit. These latter two points are discussed in the next two sections.

MANAGER'S BRIEFCASE: INTERPRETING CHANGES IN THE BOND YIELD

We know that interest rates are negatively correlated with aggregate demand. But when the bond yield rises, does that mean the economy will necessarily slow down the following year?

In the first place, it is the real rate of interest, rather than the nominal rate, which causes aggregate demand to grow more slowly or actually decline. Thus an increase in the bond yield that is matched by higher inflation will have very little negative impact on the overall economy.

The bond yield will rise if the ratio of capital spending to GDP rises, ceteris paribus, and it will rise if the budget deficit ratio rises, ceteris paribus. If investment rises, or if fiscal policy is expansionary, the resulting rise in the bond yield may partially mitigate this increase in demand, but in many cases will not completely offset it. Thus it is quite possible that real growth will remain strong even with a rising bond yield.

During the 1970s, rising bond yields often occurred simultaneously with rapid growth, but that was primarily because the rate of inflation was also increasing and real bond yields were falling, or were already at unusually low levels. However, in 1987, both the real and nominal Aaa bond yield rose approximately 2 percentage points, yet the real growth rate advanced from 3.4% in both 1986 and 1987 to 4.2% in 1998. In this case, real growth was stimulated by the rise in the stock market in the first half of the year and then, when it quickly collapsed, by the Fed injecting liquidity into the economy in October of that year.

6.8 Factors causing the yield spread to fluctuate

We said earlier that the long-term bond yield was a weighted average of expected future short-term rates plus a risk factor ρ. That can be written as:

Bond yield $= \alpha$ (current short-term rate) $+ (1 - \alpha)$ expected short-term rate $+ \rho$

where the expected short-term rate is a function of expected rate of inflation, real growth, the budget ratio, and the capital spending ratio.

Now suppose that one of the factors affecting the expected short-term rate changes. If the actual short-term rate changes by the same amount, so will the bond yield, in which case the yield spread will remain unchanged. If the actual and expected short-term rates do *not* change by the same amount, then the yield spread will change. Usually, the short-term rate does not change as much as the bond yield when the budget ratio changes, so that is one of the key determinants of the yield spread.

Another key factor is whether the current short-term rate is above or below its equilibrium value. That difference from equilibrium is negatively correlated with the yield spread. For example, suppose the Fed has failed to boost the funds rate even though inflation has started to increase; the yield spread will widen because the short-term rate is too low, as investors will expect Fed tightening shortly. Conversely, suppose monetary policy has been very tight, and inflation then starts to fall. The yield spread will narrow because investors expect the Fed will soon ease. As a result, we find that the lagged value of the *real* funds rate – the nominal rate minus the change in the CPI over the past year – is negatively correlated with the current value of the yield spread.

The yield spread is also negatively correlated with the inflation rate. Suppose the rate of inflation rises; usually, the Fed will tighten promptly. Because the bond yield is based on the expected future rate of inflation, and investors perceive that Fed tightening will eventually reduce the rate of inflation, bond yields rise less than short-term rates, which means the yield spread narrows. In the same vein, a decline in the rate of inflation is likely to be followed by a bigger drop in the funds rate than in the bond yield, so the yield spread widens.

Essentially the same argument applies for changes in the unemployment rate. When the economy goes into recession, the Fed eases, and the yield spread widens; when the unemployment declines, the yield spread narrows.

The relationship of the yield spread and these variables is shown in figure 6.11. The most important variables in this relationship are those that measure expected inflation: the change in the CPI over the past year, the current budget surplus or deficit ratio, and the lagged real Fed funds rate, indicating whether recent monetary policy has been tight or easy. The change in the unemployment rate, and the ratio of fixed investment to GDP, are also important, but not quite as significant.

This relationship strongly suggests that bond market investors are not easily fooled when the funds rate diverges from equilibrium. When inflationary pressures are stronger than indicated by the current level of the funds rate, the yield spread widens. When those pressures are weaker than indicated by the current level of the funds rate – often because the Fed has just tightened significantly – the yield spread narrows and sometimes turns negative. However, it is important to remember the importance of the lagged real funds rate; if monetary policy has been easy and the Fed tightens, the yield spread generally will not change very much until Fed policy is seen to have moved into the range of tightness. This point is revisited in section 6.11 on the "conundrum."

If that is the case, why doesn't the Fed just keep the funds rate at its equilibrium value, based on recent economic conditions? After all, members of the FOMC certainly have at least as much knowledge of current economic conditions as bond traders and investors.

If the economy is growing at its equilibrium rate, the unemployment rate is stable and close to its full-employment level, and the rate of inflation is low and

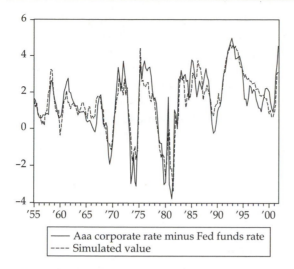

Figure 6.11   Yield spread as a function of the rate of inflation, change in the unemployment rate, the real Fed funds rate, the budget ratio, and ratio of fixed investment to GDP

stable, there is little reason for interest rates to change. However, this optimal situation obviously does not hold all the time. Because of changes in fiscal policy and exogenous shocks, equilibrium rates cannot always be maintained. To see this, consider the following alternative scenarios where monetary policymakers must implement a conscious decision to move the funds rate temporarily away from equilibrium.

1. The economy is near full employment and full capacity, and inflation starts to accelerate. The Fed must act to reverse the growth in inflationary expectations. Most of the time, that is not possible unless it boosts short-term interest rates above their equilibrium value, which leads to an inverted yield curve and a recession. While that used to be a fairly standard description of what caused business cycle expansions to come to an end, increased credibility of Federal Reserve policies since 1982 has reduced the likelihood of higher inflation in the later stages of business cycles.
2. An exogenous shock boosts prices. The major example for the US economy in the past 30 years has been energy shocks, but other major exogenous changes in prices could have the same impact. In this case, the Fed will have little choice other than to tighten, which will probably cause at least a brief recession. It must achieve a balancing act between averting a serious economic meltdown and setting the stage for higher inflation in the next business cycle. In 1974–5, Fed Chairman Arthur Burns eased too much and validated the next round of inflation; in 1980–81, Paul Volcker kept real interest rates very high even after the recession started, prolonging the recession for an additional six months but eliminating inflationary expectations in future business cycles.

3. The economy heads into recession and inflation declines. The Fed comes under intense political pressure to implement massive easing. This is no idle threat, since failure to do so could compromise the ability of the Fed to act independently in the future. However, since inflationary pressures generally diminish during recessions, the issue is not whether to institute aggressive easing, but when to stop so equilibrium targets are not overshot.

4. If the budget deficit remains substantial even at full employment – as opposed to a large deficit during a recession – inflationary pressures are likely to intensify if the Fed accommodates that additional funding. If it does not, higher interest rates, and a slower rate of growth, are likely to occur. The job of the monetary authorities is clearly easier if the budget is in balance at full employment.

5. From time to time, a domestic or international financial crisis may force the Fed to flood the system with liquidity. That decision is clearly preferable to a meltdown of major financial institutions. However, that liquidity is likely to translate into excessive growth, pushing the economy beyond its full-employment limits. Hence the Fed must be ready to tighten with alacrity, otherwise the economy may overheat and a recession will eventually develop. Under Greenspan, the Fed acted promptly to forestall liquidity crises but sometimes failed to reverse course soon enough.

6. An exogenous shock *reduces* prices, especially one that boosts productivity. That might appear to be even better than steady growth; what could be wrong with a scenario in which inflation declines and employment and output rise even faster? As it turns out, there may be a serious problem if this faster growth creates unrealistically optimistic expectations, leading to speculative bubbles in financial markets, and an eventual crash. In situations of this sort, the Fed would be well advised to offset some of the additional growth now in order to maintain robust growth later.

That last point is a fairly accurate description of what happened to the US economy during the late 1990s. In 1997 and 1998, the annual increase in the CPI, which had been averaging about 3%, dropped to 1.6% because of the stronger dollar, lower energy prices, and the "new technology" that boosted the growth rate in productivity. By itself, this situation might not have led to any untoward circumstances, but in the summer of 1998, the combination of the devaluation of the Russian ruble and the collapse of Long-Term Capital Management generated a financial crisis that threatened many major New York City financial institutions. As a result, the Fed temporarily reduced the funds rate by 1% and supplied additional liquidity to the banking system. The combination of these events, coupled with boundless optimism, generated a stock market bubble that caused the Nasdaq composite to triple over the next year and a half. Once the bubble burst, the Nasdaq gave back all its gains, and the resulting decline in high-tech investment was a major contributor to the mild 2001 recession. While it is difficult to fault the Fed for reacting promptly and decisively to the financial crisis of 1998, it does seem likely in retrospect that the injection of liquidity, when combined with the benign price shock, did create an unsustainable boom that should have been throttled by more vigorous tightening in 1999 and 2000.

This entire episode touches on one of the basic factors that determine business cycles, which are discussed in greater detail in chapter 15. Over the past few decades, government economists have learned how to manage monetary and fiscal policy much more successfully, with the result that recessions are less frequent and less severe. Obviously that development is to be applauded. However, the great success of these methods plants the seed for an eventual turndown if it encourages speculators to assume there will never be another setback in the economy. Under these circumstances, they leverage to the hilt, so that even a mild shock that the economy could ordinarily handle without undue interruption leads to a recession. For this reason, mild business cycles are likely to occur in the future even under optimal monetary and fiscal policies.

Thus in the future, the central bank will presumably be required to take steps every so often to move the Federal funds rate at least temporarily away from its equilibrium value. Such moves will also affect bond yields and equity prices. In the final sections of this chapter, we first turn to a discussion of the ways in which monetary policy is transmitted, discuss the importance of the inverted yield spread as a predictive tool, and finally explain the "conundrum" of why the Fed cannot always hit its target even if it has all the facts and is fully in control of the situation.

6.9   Transmission of monetary policy

There are several different channels for the transmission of monetary policy to changes in the rate of inflation and real GDP; we identify the four most important ones. (For purposes of exposition we discuss the effect of monetary tightening. Note that in the diagrammatic treatment given below, "M" represents a change in monetary policy, not a change in the money supply per se.)

1. The cost of debt capital rises (interest rates increase)
2. The availability of debt capital diminishes (bank loans decline)
3. The cost of equity capital rises (stock prices fall)
4. The availability of equity capital diminishes (IPOs become much more difficult to bring to market and bank loans based on balance sheets are diminished).

Frederic Mishkin, former director of research at the Federal Reserve Bank of New York, lists eight different methods of transmission of monetary policy.[8] Since the effects are not precisely symmetrical, and generally are more forceful when policy is contractionary, we follow his approach and consider a tightening of policy, as measured by a decline in the money supply or a rise in the real Federal funds rate. These are short-term transmissions; in the long run, countervailing factors come into play. The methods of transmission catalogued by Mishkin can be grouped under the four headings listed above: higher cost of debt capital, reduced availability of bank loans, negative impact of lower stock prices on equity capital, and negative impact of lower stock prices on bank loans. They can also be expressed as follows:

Higher cost of debt capital
(key link is rise in interest rates)

$$M \Downarrow \Rightarrow r \Uparrow \Rightarrow I \Downarrow \Rightarrow Y \Downarrow$$
$$M \Downarrow \Rightarrow r \Uparrow \Rightarrow \$ \Uparrow \Rightarrow F \Downarrow \Rightarrow Y \Downarrow$$

Reduced availability of bank loans
(key link is decline in loans)

$$M \Downarrow \Rightarrow r \Uparrow \Rightarrow \text{Cash flow} \Downarrow \Rightarrow \text{Loans} \Downarrow \Rightarrow I \Downarrow \Rightarrow Y \Downarrow$$
$$M \Downarrow \Rightarrow \text{DEP} \Downarrow \Rightarrow \text{Loans} \Downarrow \Rightarrow I, C \Downarrow \Rightarrow Y \Downarrow$$

Negative impact of lower stock prices on equity capital
(key link is decline in stock price)

$$M \Downarrow \Rightarrow \text{SP} \Downarrow \Rightarrow \text{Cost of equity capital} \Uparrow \Rightarrow I \Downarrow \Rightarrow Y \Downarrow$$
$$M \Downarrow \Rightarrow \text{SP} \Downarrow \Rightarrow \text{Wealth} \Downarrow \Rightarrow C \Downarrow \Rightarrow Y \Downarrow (*)$$

Negative impact of lower stock prices on bank loans
(key link is decline in loans)

$$M \Downarrow \Rightarrow \text{SP} \Downarrow \Rightarrow \text{Perceived risk} \Uparrow \Rightarrow \text{Loans} \Downarrow \Rightarrow I \Downarrow \Rightarrow Y \Downarrow$$
$$M \Downarrow \Rightarrow \text{SP} \Downarrow \Rightarrow \text{Financial assets} \Downarrow \Rightarrow \text{Loans} \Downarrow \Rightarrow I \Downarrow \Rightarrow Y \Downarrow$$

---

* Generally dismissed as too small to be relevant (Meltzer)

Here:

M	=	monetary policy
r	=	real rate of interest
I	=	fixed investment
Y	=	real GDP
$	=	value of the dollar
F	=	net exports
C	=	consumption
DEP	=	deposits
SP	=	stock prices

These may appear to be quite similar, but there are some important differences: these are discussed next.

Channels through a rise in interest rates
1. Higher interest rates reduce fixed investment because fewer projects are profitable when the cost of capital rises.
2. Higher interest rates boost the value of the dollar, hence reducing net exports.

Channels through a drop in deposits and loans
1. Higher interest rates increase the risk of loan default, so firms are more likely to buy Treasury securities and grant fewer loans. This is also known as credit rationing, and is the main reason why the growth rate declines following an inverted yield curve.
2. Higher interest rates cause depositors to withdraw funds from checking accounts and invest them in assets earning higher rates of interest, hence reducing capital available for loans.

Channels through a drop in equity prices, raising the cost of equity capital
1. A rise in the cost of equity capital reduces capital spending.
2. A drop in equity prices reduces consumer wealth and spending.

Channels through a drop in equity prices on bank loans
1. A drop in equity prices reduces the balance sheet value of firms, making it more difficult to raise either debt or equity capital.
2. A drop in equity prices increases defaults and bankruptcies.

To a certain extent, all of these linkages are empirically valid. However, since the changes in the cost and availability of debt capital are somewhat more important, we concentrate on those effects.

The *cost* of credit and the *availability* of credit have some correlation: when the cost of credit rises, the availability often diminishes. However, the correlation is not particularly strong. That is why a rise in real interest rates sometimes has little negative impact on aggregate demand, whereas if credit availability is restrained, aggregate demand may decline sharply even when real rates are quite low.

The importance of credit availability has two parts. First, when interest rates rise, banks are more likely to buy more Treasury securities and grant fewer private sector loans. Second, when interest rates rise, both the income statement and balance sheet of corporations are likely to deteriorate, hence increasing the risk of default.

To illustrate the first reason, consider the following example. Suppose the Treasury bill rate is 3% and the Treasury bond rate is 6%. If the bank wants to loan money on a short-term basis, it will probably lend at the prime rate, which is now fixed at 3% above the Federal funds rate. If it wants to loan money on a long-term basis, such as a fixed-rate mortgage, it will probably lend at a rate that is 1% to 2% above the Treasury bond rate.[9] The bank thus chooses between investing in Treasury bills or Fed funds at 3% with no risk, making short-term loans at 6% and higher with some default risk but no market risk, buying Treasury bonds at 6% with no default risk but some market risk (if rates rises), or making long-term loans at

7% or 8%, and higher, with both default risk and market risk. The bank will allocate its portfolio based on its perception of these risks.

Now suppose the Fed tightens to the point where the yield curve is inverted. Assume that the Treasury bill and Fed funds rates are now 9% and the Treasury bond rate is 8%, as occurred in 1989. In that case, the bank faces the following menu of choices: 9% with no risk, 12% with default risk, 8% with market risk, and 9% to 10% or higher with market and default risk. No matter what values the bank assigns to these two risk factors, it is clear that 9% with no risk is much better than 9% with market and default risk. As a result, the bank is more likely to buy more Treasury bills and grant fewer loans.

In addition, borrowers are more likely to default when the interest rate on their loan is 12% instead of 9%. Hence the banks may perceive that market risk rises when interest rates rise. When the prime rate rose to $21\frac{1}{2}$%, as it did in early 1981, relatively few firms could afford to borrow profitably. That is another reason why banks are likely to reduce the amount of loans they make when interest rates rise: the higher interest charges borrowers must pay, the lower their net income, and hence the higher the risk of default.

A rise in interest rates will also reduce stock prices, ceteris paribus. Higher interest rates will boost carrying costs and hence reduce net income, while lower stock prices will cause the balance sheet to deteriorate. With lower stock values, many firms will find it much more difficult to raise capital in equity markets, so they will not be able to repay their indebtedness through an initial or secondary public offering. Also, to the extent that the stock prices of high-tech firms have collapsed, they may not be able to entice top talent to work for the company if the likelihood of substantial stock price gains appears minimal.

For all of these reasons, an inverted yield curve causes bank borrowing to decline. Rates are relatively high, and banks will make fewer loans because the risk-adjusted yield is higher from short-term Treasury securities. Consequently, bank loans are reduced, and the economy heads into a recession the following year.

6.10 The importance of the yield spread as a predictive tool

We now return to figure 6.2, which shows that since 1969, the US economy has always plunged into recession about a year after the yield curve turns negative.

The results do indeed seem impressive. The yield spread turned negative in 1969, 1973–4, 1979, 1981, 1989, and 2000; recessions occurred in 1970, 1974–5, 1980, 1982, 1990, and 2001 (the graph shows real growth was positive in 1990 on an annual basis, but the recession started in July 1990, and real growth fell more than 2% during the second half of the year). This is a remarkable finding given the fact that economists have never been able to predict a recession a year ahead of time; yet all they had to do was to look at the yield spread. No other information would have been necessary.

Furthermore, this is not some goofy hypothesis like the Super Bowl Theory,[10] but is based on reasonable economic theory. When the yield spread is inverted, bank lending diminishes, and purchases of houses, consumer durables, producer durables with relatively short lives, and nonresidential construction all decline. That is precisely what happens during recessions.

While it is not very easy to predict interest rates, and even more difficult to predict the yield spread, this rule of thumb requires no prediction at all. A negative yield spread *this* year, means a recession *next* year. There is no need to predict a downturn until the yield spread actually turns negative. Yet in spite of that, the economic forecasting profession was unable to predict any of these downturns.

Is this really the magic bullet all forecasters have been seeking to predict recessions? And if that is indeed the case, why has the economic forecasting profession been unable to predict *any* of these recessions in advance?

These questions will be deferred until part VI of this book, when the pitfalls of forecasting are discussed. At this juncture we merely note that forecasters did not realize the importance of the yield spread until the late 1980s. They then predicted the 1990 recession too soon; when it did not occur "on schedule," most forecasters then scratched their recession forecasts, only to find that the downturn actually started a couple of quarters later. In 2000, forecasters were not sure how to proceed, since the negative yield spread was caused more by a drop in long-term rates rather than a rise in short-term rates. As a result, virtually no one predicted that recession either. Nonetheless, the downturn began in March 2001, although there is some doubt whether the slowdown would have been certified as a recession if not for 9/11.

A large positive yield spread indicates boom times ahead, but the size of that spread is not correlated with the percentage rise in real GDP. That depends on other factors, including the amount that interest rates have declined, fiscal policy, trade policy, and exogenous events such as world growth or the change in oil prices. It could also depend on the growth rate in technology, changes in demographics, or a pent-up demand for durables if they had not been available in the previous cycle (because of wars or rationing).

To summarize, the yield spread has been inverted six times in the past 35 years (counting two or more consecutive years of decline as one recession). In all cases, a recession has occurred the following year. Furthermore, there has never been a recession during this period that was not preceded by an inverted yield curve.

Forecasting the economy is obviously more complicated than this. On the other hand, the yield spread serves as a useful rule of thumb that should keep economists from predicting recessions when there is no evidence of any such development, or missing downturns when they are about to occur.

When is the yield spread most likely to become inverted? Until 2000, it occurred when the rate of inflation rose, and the Fed tightened to the point where financial market traders then expected the rate of inflation to decline again, so bond yields fell. Perhaps that suggests the Fed should not have tightened so much in the first place. Yet if the Fed followed that strategy, inflationary expectations would

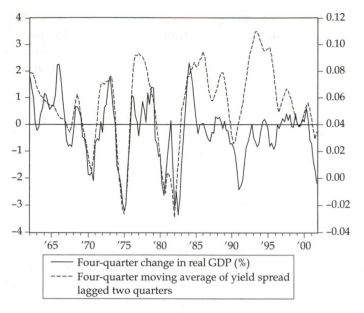

Figure 6.12   The inverted yield curve correctly signaled all of the recessions since 1969, but underestimated the decline of the two most recent recessions

continue to rise on the grounds that the monetary authorities were not really serious about fighting inflation.

Sometimes that puts the Fed in a no-win situation. If it tightens too much, a recession will occur; but if it doesn't tighten enough, inflation will continue to rise, so eventually the Fed will have to push interest rates to the level that a recession will occur. Either way, the economy plunges into a downturn. This situation, often known as the "conundrum," is discussed in the next section.

MANAGER'S BRIEFCASE: WILL LOW INTEREST RATES BOOST YOUR BUSINESS?

The obvious answer might seem to be: it all depends on whether your business is sensitive to interest rates. Obviously changes in purchases of motor vehicles, homes, and capital goods are more closely related to fluctuations in interest rates than are purchases of food, medical care, or educational services.

As usual, the answer is not quite that simple, because low interest rates often mean that aggregate demand is very weak, and interest rates have fallen to bridge the gap between a bigger drop in ex ante investment than in ex ante saving. Interest rates might be low because the demand for loanable funds is low. It is also possible that interest rates are low because the inflation rate is low, and that real interest rates are not much below average.

continued

MANAGER'S BRIEFCASE (*continued*)

Predicting interest rates is notoriously difficult, as we have already pointed out, but assume you "knew" that short-term rates were going to decline 5% over the next year, although you didn't know why. For purposes of this discussion, also assume that sales of your product are sensitive to changes in interest rates. Would it be time to gear up the production facilities and start planning for expansion?

Probably not, because the decline in interest rates would probably signal a recession, in which case the decline in income and confidence might overwhelm the increase in sales stemming from lower interest rates. Hence once again our point is that it is changes in monetary *policy*, rather than changes in monetary *conditions*, that determine how interest rates will affect your sales. If the Fed cuts the funds rate because of declining growth or lower inflation, it will probably have only a small impact on sales. If, on the other hand, the Fed cuts rates in the absence of these developments because of an explicit directive to get the economy moving again, it probably will boost sales. That might happen, for example, if the Fed reduces rates to stave off what it perceives as financial meltdown, even though real growth is still robust. By the same token, if inflation rises but the Fed decides not to boost interest rates for a while, that will help your sales for a while – although eventually the Fed will have to take corrective action.

6.11   Why targeting interest rates doesn't always work: the conundrum

It cannot be a simple matter for the Fed to set the funds rate equal to the inflation rate plus the growth rate, and then sit back and watch the economy perform optimally for many years – or that is just what it would do. However, we know that exogenous shocks periodically move the economy away from equilibrium. When that happens, the economy sometimes responds more sluggishly to changes in monetary policy than usual, so the Fed overshoots its target. Sometimes the data are inaccurate or misleading, so that the Fed does not know what the recent growth rate is. That happened in late 1990, when initial data indicated a 2% decline in real GDP, but revised data showed the actual rate of reduction was 4%. It also happened in 2001, when preliminary data said the economy was still expanding, while revised data issued in July 2002 said GDP declined 1.1% during the first half of the previous year. This time, however, the Fed realized the GDP figures were inaccurate and reacted as if there really were a recession underway. In the past the Fed has set rates too low for political reasons, although not since 1979.

Yet as relevant as all these reasons may be, they are not the main reason why the Fed cannot always target rates. Once the economy and interest rates have moved away from equilibrium values, changes in inflationary expectations in response to Fed policy keep shifting the equilibrium rate. This is known as the **conundrum**.

The conundrum states that when the Federal funds rate is below equilibrium, inflationary expectations are usually rising, so the funds rate remains too low even after the Fed begins to tighten. However, as soon as the Fed boosts the funds rate to its equilibrium value, inflationary expectations diminish – so the funds rate is suddenly too high, and the Fed should ease again. Yet if it does so too quickly, inflationary pressures will rise again.

When inflation rises, expectations of future inflation also change. Unless the Fed can demonstrate convincingly that the rise in inflation was due to an exogenous event and was not caused by overly accommodating policy, investors will expect the Fed to waffle the next time inflation rises. As a result, the Fed may have to overshoot its targets in order to convince economic agents that it is willing and able to stop inflation. Eventually, expectations will adjust to this reality, but it often takes at least one complete business cycle to convince the skeptics.

The long lag time between changes in monetary policy and changes in real growth and inflation must also be taken into consideration when the monetary authorities are deciding whether or not to tighten. If the Fed accommodates higher inflation in the current cycle, that will not only lead to a recession in the near future, but will make its job more difficult during future business cycles. Paul Volcker realized this when the Fed continued to tighten even though real GDP declined in late 1981 and early 1982. The initial result was painful, but the US economy has undergone only two minor cycles in the past 20 years, and its economic performance has become the envy of the rest of the world.

The best way for the Fed to proceed is not to let inflation get out of hand in the first place. That means acting vigorously to tighten if signs of higher inflation are apparent even if it has not yet reached the retail level. That is what the Fed did in 1994. On the other hand, when truly exogenous events boost the inflation rate, a recession is likely to follow whether the Fed acts vigorously or not. The difference is that if the Fed tightens right away, the recession will be painful but the inflation rate will then return to normal, whereas if it tries to finesse the situation, the inflation rate will keep rising, the recession will be prolonged, and the inflation rate will remain high. Most economists now agree it is better to "bite the bullet" the first time around instead of suffering through several inflation-induced recessions.

KEY TERMS AND CONCEPTS

Discount Rate
Federal Funds Rate
Monetary Conundrum
Nominal and Real Rate of Interest
Prime Rate

Term Structure of Interest Rates
Transmission of Monetary Policy
Treasury Bills, Notes, and Bonds
Yield Spread

SUMMARY

- Changes in monetary policy are the primary determinant of fluctuations in output and inflation in the short run. In the long run, monetary policy determines the rate of inflation, but has no impact on the real growth rate. Monetary policy is set by the central bank, which in the US is the Federal Reserve Bank (Fed).

- The principal roles of monetary policy are (a) to insure adequate supplies of liquidity for the needs of industry and commerce, and (b) to keep the rate of inflation low and stable.

- The inflation rate need not be set at zero for optimal economic performance, but should be kept low enough that it does not influence economic decisions.

- When the economy is in equilibrium, this rule can be implemented by setting the Federal funds rate equal to the recent rate of inflation, plus an adjustment based on how far the unemployment rate is from full employment.

- However, when exogenous shocks occur, no simple rule can be followed. In the case of a negative shock (a rise in commodity prices), the Fed must choose between higher inflation or higher unemployment; it cannot keep the economy at full employment with low inflation.

- Today, monetary policy is determined by the Federal Open Market Committee (FOMC), which sets the value of the Federal funds rate. The Fed can no longer control growth in the money supply, and the authority for credit controls has lapsed.

- Nominal short-term interest rates are set by the Fed; real short-term rates are equal to the nominal short-term rate minus the near-term expected rate of inflation, which is closely correlated with the actual rate of inflation over the past year. However, real long-term interest rates are determined by financial markets, and are based on expectations of future inflation.

- The difference between recent and expected rates of inflation may cause fluctuations in the yield spread between long- and short-term rates. If inflation were expected to rise in the near future, the yield spread would be unusually large. If inflation were expected to fall in the near future, the yield spread would be unusually small or even negative.

- Sometimes the monetary authorities appear to be taking the right steps, but the economy does not respond appropriately. Often that is because inflationary expectations have not yet adjusted. For example, continued easing in monetary policy might not stimulate real growth if economic agents think it will lead to higher inflation, causing them to bid up interest rates proportionally.

- In a similar vein, even if monetary tightening caused a sharp decline in the inflation rate, bond yields might remain high if investors expected that inflation would soon rise again. Not until monetary credibility had been established would the economy benefit from the decline in inflation.

- The level of long-term interest rates depends on (a) a weighed average of current and future short-term rates, and (b) the demand for and supply of borrowed funds.

- Inflationary expectations are based in part on the size of the expected Federal surplus or deficit ratio and how it is financed, and in part on recent changes in monetary policy. For example, boosting short-term rates well above the rate of inflation would diminish inflationary expectations even if the actual rate of inflation was still rising.

- In equilibrium, the short-term rate of interest equals the recent inflation rate plus the underlying rate of productivity growth plus the labor force.

- Fed policy can keep short-term interest rates far away from equilibrium for an extended period of time. It tends to keep rates below equilibrium during periods when the economy is sluggish, inflation is low, and unemployment is high, while it tends to keep rates above equilibrium if the unemployment rate is low and inflation is expected to accelerate. Before 1980, Fed policy was often influenced by political considerations, but not since then.

- Most of the time, the Fed eases as soon as it is clear a recession has started. However, it continued to tighten for a while in the 1973–4 and 1981–2 recessions because of renewed fears of inflation, hence extending both those recessions by about six months.

- The Fed tightens during periods of full employment if the rate of inflation rises, but if inflation does not accelerate, short-term rates are likely to remain unchanged.

- Since current short-term interest rates are a function of the inflation rate over the past year, the difference between long- and short-term rates is a function of the difference between the expected and current rate of inflation. That in turn is based on whether Fed policy has recently been easy or tight, and the size of the Federal budget ratio.

- Under normal circumstances, the longer the length of maturity, the higher the interest rate. Thus most of the time, long-term interest rates are higher than short-term rates. That is known as a normal yield spread. An inverted yield spread means short-term rates are higher than long-term rates. That occurs when investors expect inflation to drop significantly in the near future, which happens when the Fed has recently tightened so much that the funds rate is now well above equilibrium, as measured by the recent inflation rate plus the underlying growth rate of the economy.

- When the yield spread is inverted, lending institutions switch a greater percentage of their asset portfolio into riskless short-term government securities, hence reducing the amount of funds available for private sector loans.

- Whenever the yield spread has turned negative, the US economy has plunged into recession the following year. Furthermore, since the mid-1960s, when monetary policy began to be used as a countercyclical tool, there has never been a recession year that was not preceded by a negative yield spread. Hence a negative, or inverted, yield spread has been a perfect predictor of recessions since 1969.

- Changing interest rates is an important method of transmitting monetary policy, but it is not the only one. In addition to changing the cost of debt capital, monetary policy can also be transmitted by changing the availability of debt capital, and the cost and availability of equity capital. Thus changes in bank loans, stock prices, and venture capital are all significant avenues of transmitting monetary policy.

- Targeting interest rates does not always work because of the conundrum, which reflects inflationary expectations. When the Fed funds rate is below equilibrium, inflationary expectations may remain high even as the Fed tightens. However, as soon as the Fed funds rate rises to its equilibrium level based on those high expectations, they are reduced, so the funds rate is now too high. As a result, monetary policy may have to proceed through several iterations before interest rates return to equilibrium.

QUESTIONS AND PROBLEMS

1. From 1982 through 1985, the Federal funds rate averaged almost 10% even though the inflation rate for that period was 3.8%. Why do you think the Fed kept it so high?

2. Explain how a decline in the stock market reduces the availability of credit.
3. What is likely to happen to inflationary expectations – rise, fall, or unchanged – under the following circumstances?
   (A) Tax cut.
   (B) Higher oil prices.
   (C) Drop in the unemployment rate.
   (D) Dollar strengthens.
   (E) Crop failure.
   (F) Boost in the minimum wage.
   (G) Advance in technology.
   (H) Boom in capital spending.
   (I) Boom in consumer spending, drop in saving rate.
4. In 1993 the funds rate fell to 3% while the rate of inflation was also 3%. Bond yields also fell sharply that year. Since the funds rate was well below its equilibrium value, why didn't inflationary expectations push bond yields higher?
5. What causes an inverted yield spread, and why has it always been followed by a recession the next year?
6. What are the major factors that determine the size of the yield spread?
7. In October 1987, the US stock market crashed, with the Dow Jones Industrial Average falling 508 points, or 22%, in a single day. Yet the economy continued to prosper, with real GDP rising faster in the four quarters following the stock market crash than the previous four quarters. Why did the decline in stock prices fail to slow the pace of economic activity? (Hint: what steps did the Fed take to offset the collapse in stock prices?)
8. What would you expect to happen to the yield spread under the following circumstances?
   (A) An energy shock doubles the price of crude oil.
   (B) A major tax cut.
   (C) A war.
   (D) Credit restrictions.
   (E) Consumer spending boom.
   (F) Unemployment declines to full-N level.
   (G) Value of the dollar appreciates.
9. In the late 1970s interest rates soared but the economy remained healthy. Why did higher interest rates fail to slow down the economy in 1977–8, but cause recessions in 1980 and 1981?
10. In 1979, Fed Chairman G. William Miller boosted the growth in the money supply in order to keep the economy from falling into recession and cause Jimmy Carter to have to run for reelection in a recession year. However, the economy did indeed plunge into recession in 1980. What was Miller's principal mistake?

11. Why would the Fed choose to keep the funds rate away from equilibrium for extended periods of time? In view of the performance of the economy after this occurred, explain why you would or would not expect the Fed to repeat that performance in the future.

Notes

1. For purposes of this discussion we ignore the fact that most bonds have quarterly or semi-annual payments.
2. See, for example, Paul Volcker and Toyoo Gyohten, *Changing Fortunes: The World's Money and the Threat to American Leadership* (New York: Random House, 1992). Volcker writes, "In a speech in San Francisco in December of 1983, I defined 'reasonable price stability' as a situation in which ordinary people do not feel they have to take expectations of price increases into account in making their investment plans or running their lives" (p. 176).
3. This statement is not meant to be ironical. Congress decided that the use of credit controls was "overkill" and the Fed should not have that much power over consumer spending decisions, so the authority was not renewed.
4. Several different versions of the Taylor Rule exist. One standard source is John B. Taylor, "The Inflation/Output Variability Tradeoff Revisited" in *Goods, Guidelines, and Constraints Facing Monetary Policymakers* (Federal Reserve Bank of Boston, 1994). In updating this rule, some economists have used the GDP deflator instead of the core CPI rate, and some have used the deviation of the unemployment rate from its full-employment level.
5. This is not just Monday-morning quarterbacking. At the beginning of 2002, this author pointed out in his weekly newsletter – as did others – that traders could buy December 2002 Eurodollar options and quadruple their money, based on the assumption that the Federal funds rate would not change during the year.
6. For a more complete discussion of the alternative theories explaining long-term interest rates, and the term structure of interest rates, as a function of short-term rates, see Burton G. Malkiel, "The Term Structure of Interest Rates: Theory, Empirical Evidence, and Applications" in Thomas M. Havrilesky and John R. Boorman, eds, *Current Issues in Monetary Theory and Policy*, 2nd edn (Arlington Heights, IL: Harlan Davidson, 1980).
7. This is not just a recent finding. Stephen Leuthold, in his *Myths of Inflation and Investing* (NTC Publishing Group, 1980), finds that the relationship between the current bond yield and the five-year average rate of inflation extends back into the nineteenth century.
8. See his *Money, Banking, and Financial Markets*, 6th edn (New York: Little Brown). For a similar treatment, also see Havrilesky and Boorman, *idem*, part II.
9. Many banks no longer hold mortgages; they just do the initial paperwork and then sell the mortgage to some organization that lumps thousands of mortgages together into a single security. However, banks are then major customers for these mortgage-backed securities.

10. The Super Bowl Theory says that if the Super Bowl is won by a team in the NFL – or an AFL "crossover" that used to be in the NFL – the stock market will go up that year, whereas if it is won by a "new" AFL team, the stock market will go down that year. It worked 23 years in a row; if the observations were truly random, the odds of that happening are 1 in 8,388,608. However, the string was broken in 1990, and since then it has worked only six times out of nine; the odds of that happening by chance are roughly 1 in 6.

chapter seven

Joint determination of income and interest rates: the IS/LM diagram

Introduction

In the previous three chapters, we have shown that (a) consumption is a function of income and interest rates, (b) fixed investment is a function of income and interest rates, (c) net exports are a function of income and the value of the dollar, which to a certain extent is a function of interest rates, and (d) interest rates are a function of the demand for money and credit, which are tied to income, monetary policy conditions, and the expected rate of inflation. To complete the picture, it is necessary to explain the rate of inflation and the value of the dollar, which are analyzed in more detail in parts III and IV.) The first essential building block is to explain the joint determination of income and interest rates, assuming no change in the expected rate of inflation and no change in the value of the dollar.

The approach used in this chapter is known as the IS/LM diagram, dating back to a famous article by Sir John Hicks entitled "Mr. Keynes and the Classics" in which he showed that the explanation of the economy expounded in Keynes's *General Theory of Employment, Interest, and Money*, published the previous year, was not a general theory at all but "a theory of depression." Hicks essentially argued that during times of depression, when interest rates were already at very low levels, further monetary easing probably would not stimulate the economy, but during normal times, monetary policy remained important. He thus reinstated the role of monetary policy, which had been a critical part of macroeconomic analysis used by mainstream economists – including Keynes – before the mid-1930s.

The basic structure advanced by Hicks can be briefly summarized as follows. On an ex post basis, investment must always be equal to saving. However, an increase (say) in interest rates boosts ex ante saving but reduces ex ante investment, yet they must be equal ex post. The combination of a rise in saving and a drop in investment reduces income, which would partially offset the initial rise in interest rates. More important, a decline in income would cause a bigger drop in saving than in investment. Hence when interest rates rise, both saving and investment would decline on an ex post basis. Saving would fall because the negative impact from a drop in income would outweigh the positive impact from a rise in interest rates. Hence an increase in interest rates will reduce income, and a decline in interest rates will – except during times of depression – raise income. Income and interest rates are thus jointly determined.

7.1   Review of the effect of changes in interest rates and income on saving and investment

First we summarize the impact of the change in interest rates and income on the major endogenous components of aggregate demand discussed in chapters 4 and 5. Government purchases are assumed to be exogenous, although in some cases, construction undertaken by state and local government declines when interest rates are unusually high. Also, since virtually all state and local governments are required to have balanced budgets, their purchases may expand when income rises, although they always have the option of reducing taxes or saving the surplus for a "rainy day." These impacts on government purchases are not very important, but to the extent they occur at all, they reinforce the patterns found for the other components: demand rises when interest rates decline, and domestic demand rises when income rises.

These key relationships between the components of aggregate demand and *interest rates* can be summarized as follows.

- All endogenous components of aggregate demand are negatively related to the real interest rate, which is the nominal rate minus the expected rate of inflation.
- The real interest rate represents the cost of credit to borrowers. However, even if economic agents do not need to borrow funds, the cost of credit is still a relevant consideration, because those funds could always be invested at the market rate instead of used for their own purchases.
- Real interest rates and capital spending move in opposite directions, ceteris paribus; when interest rates rise, fewer projects are profitable.
- A rise in interest rates reduces investment in residential construction, primarily because of the reduced availability of funds.
- A rise in interest rates boosts personal saving for several reasons, including the time value of money and the expected rate of return on saving, the cost of time payments, reduced availability of funds, variable-rate mortgage payments, and changes in capital gains. For the average consumer, though, the availability is more important than the cost.
- A rise in interest rates raises foreign saving.
- A small negative correlation exists between government construction and interest rates.

- A rise in real interest rates reduces the growth rate of the economy, and is often followed by a recession. A drop in real interest rates is one of the major factors causing recessions to end.
- The availability of credit is also an important determinant of aggregate demand. Since it is also inversely related to interest rates, this relationship may initially be subsumed under the cost of credit argument in the IS/LM diagram.

When interest rates change, ex ante investment and saving move in the *opposite* directions, ceteris paribus. Yet we know that saving and investment must always be equal on an ex post basis. The factor that links saving and investment is the change in income.

The links between aggregate demand and *income* can be summarized for a short-term increase in income (the argument is symmetrical for a decline in income):

- All four components of the aggregate saving rate – personal, corporate, foreign, and government saving – rise in the short run, ceteris paribus.
- The personal saving rate rises because consumption adjusts slowly to short-term changes in income, especially if they are unexpected.
- The corporate saving rate rises because profits increase as a proportion of GDP and dividends do not change very much.
- The net foreign saving rate rises because imports increase faster than exports, leading to a bigger trade deficit and hence a greater inflow of foreign capital.
- The government saving rate rises because taxes rise faster than income, and social welfare expenditures rise less rapidly in a booming economy.
- Because decisions to purchase capital goods are based on expected changes in income over the longer run, short-run changes in income, especially those that are unexpected, change investment less than proportionately. Also, if excess capacity exists, firms may not boost investment even if the economy is growing rapidly and credit conditions are favorable.
- Thus when income changes in the short run, total ex ante saving changes more than proportionately, while ex ante investment changes less than proportionately.

These links can be summarized in the following table.

	Effect of lower interest rate	Effect of higher income
Investment	rises substantially	rises slightly
Personal saving	falls	rises
Corporate saving	rises slightly	rises
Net foreign saving	falls	rises
Government saving	rises slightly	rises

7.2   Equilibrium in the goods market

Although aggregate demand is negatively correlated with the real rate of inter-est, and domestic demand is positively correlated with income, these statements, taken by themselves, do not explain why aggregate demand must always be equal to aggregate production, or why consumption (C) + investment (I) + net exports (F) + government purchases (G) must always equal GDP on an ex post basis.

To understand the economic relationship behind this identity, it is sometimes convenient to express it in the form that saving must always equal investment (S = I) on an ex post basis. We have already shown in the appendix to chapter 2 that the identities S = I and GDP = C + I + F + G are the same equation.

Admittedly, the algebraic equivalence does not always convince students. What are the economic linkages behind this equation?

Let's start with consumers. After paying taxes, they can either spend their income or save it. They could use their saving to purchase securities directly, but typically they utilize the services of a financial intermediary such as a bank, money market fund, or mutual fund, either directly or through a retirement account. Financial institutions then invest these funds in debt or equity securities, or provide loans. Eventually, these funds are used to purchase capital goods. That is the common-sense meaning of the equivalence between saving and investment.

Suppose, however, the bank cannot find any suitable investment opportunities. After all, it is not realistic to expect banks to find appropriate investment oppor-tunities all the time, especially during recessions. If that is the case, one of the following three events may occur:

1. Interest rates decline. As already shown, that would reduce saving and increase investment. Eventually, the change in interest rates would be large enough that saving would equal investment on an ex post basis.
2. Inventory investment temporarily fills the gap. Suppose consumers turn more pessimistic, reducing their spending and increasing their saving, but businesses do not want to invest more. For a while, production levels will remain the same, but sales will decline, which initially boosts inventory investment. Hence the increase in saving caused by more pessimistic consumer attitudes will initially be matched by a rise in inventory investment. However, that is only a short-term solution.
3. If consumption does not recover quickly, production will also decline, and employment and personal income will drop. In this case, while consumers *planned* to save more, the drop in income means they actually save *less*. This case is sometimes known as the "paradox of thrift," since a decision by consumers to boost their planned saving results in a decline in their actual saving.

While the paradox of thrift used to be a staple of many economic textbooks, its importance should not be overstated, since the personal saving rate has not fallen during recessions since the 1930s. Indeed, it is a relic from the days of the Great

Depression, when the personal saving rate was negative and investment was also very low. As we have seen, *in all post-WWII recessions, the personal saving rate rises while investment falls.* The "gap" is closed by some combination of a substantial drop in imports, which reduces foreign saving; a big increase in the government deficit, which reduces public sector saving; and a decline in corporate profits, which reduces corporate saving.

Consumers usually plan to save a higher proportion of their income when interest rates rise and credit availability declines. Conversely, when the Fed eases, the personal saving rate usually declines. Nonetheless, it is possible that an exogenous development – an oil shock, or an unpopular war – could depress both consumer and business sentiment, resulting in an ex ante rise in saving but an ex ante decline in investment. Under such circumstances, if interest rates do not serve as the equilibrating mechanism, ex post personal saving will eventually decline.

That is the economic logic underlying the identity that I = S on an ex post basis. We now use this identity to derive the IS curve.

7.3 Derivation of the IS curve

The **IS curve** represents all the points in the economy where I = S on an ex post basis. That is the same as saying C + I + F + G = GDP, so either identity represents all the equilibrium points in the goods market. Each different level of income represented along the I = S curve corresponds to a different level of interest rates. The lower the level of interest rates, the higher the level of I, S, and GDP.

When interest rates decline (a) fixed investment increases, (b) the personal saving rate declines, which means consumption rises, (c) net foreign saving falls, which means net exports rise, and (d) state and local government spending may rise slightly. Thus all four major components of aggregate demand rise when interest rates decline.

Since consumption, investment, and net exports depend on the level of income as well as the level of interest rates, the economy has not reached a new equilibrium point when interest rates change unless we also include the changes in investment and saving caused by the change in income and GDP.

To visualize this geometrically, first consider a diagram in which investment is negatively related to the real rate of interest, and saving is positively related to the real rate of interest. This is shown in figure 7.1a. Both curves are drawn under the assumption that GDP is at level Y_1, so the curves are labeled $I(Y_1)$ and $S(Y_1)$.

Now suppose an exogenous change in monetary policy reduces interest rates. Initially, we would expect investment to rise and saving to fall. That would create a gap between ex ante saving and investment, as shown in figure 7.1b. However, that gap must be closed on an ex post basis, which is accomplished as follows.

When interest rates fall, both investment and consumption rise; in addition, net exports rise, and government purchases may also rise. Hence GDP has increased. At the higher level of GDP, denoted as Y_2, both saving and investment have risen. As

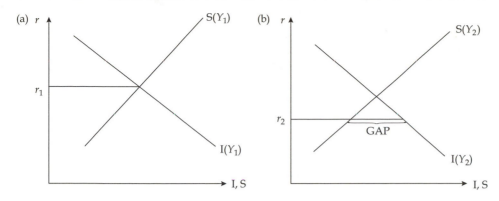

Figure 7.1

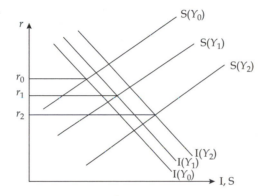

Figure 7.2

explained previously, saving rises more than investment. Hence the saving curve shifts further to the right than the investment curve. A new equilibrium point is reached, shown by the intersection of $I(Y_2)$ and $S(Y_2)$, as shown in figure 7.2. Similarly, if an exogenous shift in monetary policy had boosted interest rates, GDP would have fallen to level Y_0, in which case the I and S curves would have shifted to $I(Y_0)$ and $S(Y_0)$, as also shown in figure 7.2.

We can now create another diagram with the real rate of interest on the vertical axis and real GDP on the horizontal axis, instead of putting saving and investment on the horizontal axis. First plot the point (r_1, Y_1), which is the equilibrium condition before the monetary authorities changed interest rates. Point (r_2, Y_2) represents the new equilibrium condition at lower interest rates. Similarly, point (r_0, Y_0) represents the new equilibrium condition at higher interest rates. The line combining all such points for different levels of interest rates and income is known as the IS curve, which represents all the equilibrium points for the goods markets. It is shown in figure 7.3.

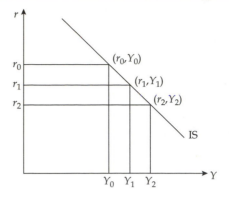

Figure 7.3

These linkages between saving and investment can also be explained with a simple algebraic model. The terms here are represented in first differences, so constant terms are not needed. The r term is the real interest rate; b is the marginal propensity to consume; f is the marginal propensity to invest; and h the marginal propensity to import.

$$C = bY - dr. \tag{7.1}$$

$$I = fY - gr. \tag{7.2}$$

$$F = -hY - kr. \tag{7.3}$$

G is exogenous (and doesn't change in this example). Combining these equations, we have:

$$C + I + F + G = Y = (b + f - h)Y + G - (d + g + k)r. \tag{7.4}$$

This can be written as:

$$Y[1 - (b + f - h)] = G - (d + g + k)r. \tag{7.5}$$

For simplicity, let m (for multiplier) $= 1/[1 - (b + f - h)]$. We then have:

$$Y = [G - (d + g + k)r]m. \tag{7.6}$$

That is the equilibrium condition under which ex ante changes in aggregate demand equal actual changes in production. It is the same IS curve shown in figure 7.3.

We next consider the approximate empirical magnitudes of these coefficients. Over a one-year period, consumers spend about $\frac{2}{3}$ of the change in disposable income (DI), but there are several intermediate links between DI and GDP, such as corporate profits, transfer payments, and taxes, so b is actually about $\frac{1}{3}$.

Recently, f is about $\frac{1}{6}$ and h is about $\frac{1}{8}$, so $m = 1/[1 - \frac{1}{3} - \frac{1}{6} + \frac{1}{8}] = \frac{8}{5}$, and:

$$Y = (8/5)G - (d + g + k)/(8/5)r. \tag{7.7}$$

That means if G rises and r does not change, Y will rise about 1.6 times the amount that G increases. This term is sometimes known as the **multiplier**. It is based on the assumption that interest rates do not change, the expected rate of inflation does not change, and the value of the dollar does not change. For that reason it is not a very useful concept, although it is a mainstay of many elementary economics texts.

It is more difficult to assign a single value to the interest rate parameters because their values depend on the phase of the business cycle and inflationary expectations. Some actual empirical estimates are given later. We can summarize these figures here by saying that if r changes by 1 percentage point – e.g., from 7% to 6% – then Y would change by about 1%, ceteris paribus. We have not yet discussed lags, but interest rates usually affect real output with an average lag of about one year, so a 1 percentage point change in interest rates this year usually changes real output by about 1% next year, ceteris paribus. Note that this is the real interest rate; a change in nominal rates that mirror the change in inflation would have a much smaller impact on the economy.

On an ex ante basis, the amount consumers, businesses, foreign investors, and the public sector plan to save could be quite different from the amount they plan to invest. Even if these amounts tend to equalize over the longer run, there is no a priori reason to expect them to be the same over shorter periods of time. Yet by definition, ex post saving and investment must always be equal.

Let us review how this works. Consider a situation where ex ante saving is greater than ex ante investment. For some reason, which might be reduced expectations about the future, consumers increase their saving. Unless they bury their extra money in the back yard, the additional saving is used either to buy securities directly, or deposited in a bank or other financial intermediary, which then decides how to invest the money.

Over the long run the logic is fairly straightforward. If the banks have excess funds that cannot be loaned to the private sector at the current interest rate, they will use these funds to buy Treasury securities, hence bidding up their price and causing interest rates to decline. Eventually, lower interest rates will boost investment. However, even if interest rates do decline, investment plans take a while to be formulated. What about the short run?

In an extreme case, suppose the bank can't find any borrowers for the money right away, so it doesn't loan the extra funds to anyone. Instead, it accumulates excess reserves that earn zero interest. It might seem that such "hoarding" would short-circuit the entire process. Yet even under this set of circumstances, saving must equal investment on an ex post basis.

Here is where inventory investment enters the picture. In the short run, if consumers decide to buy less and save more, they buy fewer goods than are being produced. In that case, the excess saving is matched by an equal rise in *inventory* investment.

That situation wouldn't last very long, because firms would soon reduce their production and employment. When that happens, profit margins shrink, so corporate saving declines. Tax receipts do not grow as rapidly, so government saving declines. Imports decrease, along with domestic demand, so foreign saving declines. Thus if lower interest rates and declining inventory investment do not bring saving and investment back into equilibrium, the decline in corporate, foreign, and government saving will serve as the equilibrating mechanism.

7.4   Slope of the IS curve under varying economic conditions

In the previous section, we assumed that all of the coefficients in equation (7.5) $(Y[1 - (b + f - h)] = G - (d + g + k)r)$ remained constant. That may or may not be the case. Some coefficients may vary depending on the phase of the business cycle, the rate of inflation, and the size of the gap between actual and full employment.

Let's look at the income terms first. During recessions, b (the marginal propensity to consume) tends to be higher than during booms. During recessions, more people are out of work, and many others feel "poorer" because their overtime hours or bonuses have been reduced. Thus when income is increased, consumers are likely to spend more of the extra income, catching up on items postponed during the recession. In the same vein, a tax increase would be disastrous because those who are already strapped would have to cut back drastically to meet the rise in taxes. Conversely, during a boom, a tax increase would not reduce consumer spending as much because income is still rising rapidly. As we will see later, that is why the effects of changes in tax rates during booms and recessions are quite different.

There is no consistent pattern to f (the marginal propensity to invest) over the course of the business cycle; as we have pointed out earlier, it is not as important. However, h (the marginal propensity to import) tends to be higher during booms; if the economy reaches a point of overfull employment, further increases in demand are often funneled into foreign goods, since domestic goods are not readily available.

Thus during recessions, b is relatively high and h is relatively low, so the multiplier is larger; during booms, the multiplier is smaller. For that reason, the IS curve is steeper at full employment than during periods of slack labor and capital resources.

7.5   Factors that shift the IS curve

The IS curve is drawn under the assumption that exogenous levels of spending are held constant. A shift in any exogenous component of aggregate demand will cause the entire IS curve to shift, as opposed to a movement along the curve.

Before listing these changes, we reemphasize that a change in the real rate of interest does *not* shift the IS curve, but represents a movement *along* the curve.

That is because the IS curve is drawn with r on the vertical axis. On the other hand, an exogenous shift in spending causes the IS curve to shift in or out.

A change in the IS curve will occur any time there is a change in fiscal policy – government spending programs or tax rates – or an exogenous change in expectations. An increase in either government purchases or programs that boost transfer payments will raise total spending, causing the IS curve to move out. The IS curve will also shift out if personal tax rates are reduced, hence boosting disposable income for the same level of (pretax) personal income. And the IS curve will again shift out if corporate income tax rates are reduced; in this case, investment is likely to increase because the cost of capital has declined.

Note, however, that while the IS curve will shift if there is a change in government programs, a decline in tax receipts caused by a recession would *not* cause the IS curve to shift out. That is not a tax rate cut; individuals are paying less taxes only because their income has declined. Similarly, an increase in transfer payments because more people are unemployed would not shift the IS curve out. Hence an increase in the budget deficit during a recession will not shift the IS curve out if none of the underlying tax rates or spending programs have changed.

Changes in the foreign sector represent another major cause of shifts in the IS curve. An increase in foreign GDP will boost net exports, shifting the IS curve out. Similarly, a reduction in the value of the dollar will initially boost net exports, although as we will show later, that may be inflationary and hence self-defeating. For stable domestic prices, though, a lower value of the currency will boost net exports and shift the IS curve out.

However, just as a change in the government deficit caused by economic conditions will not shift the IS curve, a change in net exports caused by a change in the growth rate will not shift the IS curve either. For example, if net exports rise during a recession because imports drop, that does not shift the IS curve out. Similarly, a rise in imports and the resulting decline in net exports because of a booming US economy does not shift the IS curve in.

Although most of the shifts in the IS curve are due to changes in government policy or foreign economic conditions, the curve may also shift because of exogenous changes in C and I. Suppose the cost of capital does not change, but an improvement in technology boosts the rate of return on capital. In that case, capital spending would rise even if output and interest rates did not change, shifting the IS curve out. A change in business optimism or pessimism would also cause the IS curve to shift.

An exogenous change in consumer spending could also shift the IS curve. However, changes in consumer "attitudes" that affect spending are often tied to economic conditions, notably the rate of inflation and unemployment, or reflect changes in monetary policy conditions. None of these conditions would cause the IS curve to shift. A shift in consumer spending caused by fluctuations in the stock market that were tied to changes in interest rates would not move the IS curve either. On the other hand, an exogenous shock to the stock market that was not related to interest rates or growth rates would shift the IS curve.

These results can be summarized as follows. In each case, we consider an increase in the exogenous shift; the table is symmetrical if these factors decline.

Increase in exogenous variable	IS curve shifts
Government purchases	Out
Tax rates	In
World income and production	Out
Value of currency	In
Rate of technological growth	Out
Business sentiment	Out
Change in expectations about profits	Out
Exogenous consumer sentiment not tied to economic factors	Out

7.6   The demand for money: liquidity preference and loanable funds

So far in this chapter, we have discussed equilibrium in the goods market under the assumption that interest rates and monetary policy are exogenous. The next step in the joint determination of income and interest rates is to develop a corresponding curve that contains all equilibrium positions in the assets market for varying levels of interest rates and income.

For any given level of the money supply – which in an era of banking deregulation means a given set of monetary regulations – the demand for money and credit will be positively related to income, and negatively related to interest rates. The "demand for money" means the preference for holding money relative to other assets, not the absolute demand for money per se.

To facilitate this discussion, consider two classes of financial assets – "money" and "bonds." In this simplified scheme, *money* has the following characteristics: it is used for transactions and serves as an immediate method of payment, and it pays a zero rate of interest. *Bonds* are not used directly as a method of payment, and pay a positive rate of interest.[1] In general, bonds cannot be converted into money immediately except at a substantial discount.

Bonds carry substantial market risk, even if they are Treasury securities and have no default risk. Economic agents do not put all their assets into bonds, even if the real rate of interest on bonds is quite high, because they will need some money to pay current bills, and might not be able to utilize those funds immediately except by selling bonds at a sizable discount.

To a minor extent, even if bond prices did not change, money is more convenient. Funds can be withdrawn from the bank immediately without calling a broker, waiting for delivery, and converting bonds to cash. However, this is a minor factor;

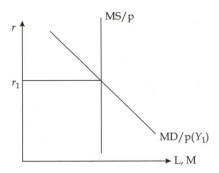

Figure 7.4

the main factor is that as a tradeoff for the higher return on bonds, the consumer could face substantial market risk.

The preference for holding money instead of bonds is generally known as **liquidity preference**, representing the "L" term in the LM curve. When interest rates are low, economic agents will hold a greater proportion of their assets in money; when they are high, they will hold a greater proportion in bonds.

If the expected real rate of interest remains unchanged, the demand for money is proportional to the price level. The extreme example of this phenomenon would be a currency reform. For example, in 1961, Charles de Gaulle decided that he didn't like to see the old French franc as an example of a devalued currency, so he simply decreed that 100 old francs = 1 new franc. Nothing changed at all, except the amount of money demanded and supplied also fell by a factor of 100.

In the more usual case, when the price level rises (say) 10% but there is no change in real income, the demand for money will also increase 10%. Economic agents are buying the same amount of goods and services using the same payment mechanisms, but since the average cost of goods and services has risen 10%, the amount of money required for these transactions has also risen by 10%. Note this holds only if real interest rates remain unchanged; if they are affected by the change in inflation, the demand for money would also change.

In the long run, the demand for broad-based measures of money has been proportional to growth in the overall economy. From 1959 through 2000, nominal GDP in the US has risen an average of 7.4% per year, while in terms of money supply, M2 has risen 7.0% per year and M3 has risen 7.9% per year. After banking deregulation in 1982, changes in the money supply have also been correlated with changes in business loan demand. Later we will use this factor in determining the slope of the LM curve during different phases of the business cycle.

This downward slope of the demand for money in real terms relative to the real interest rate is shown in figure 7.4. When interest rates rise, some economic agents will shift assets from money into bonds, since the latter pay a higher rate of interest rate. This curve is drawn under the assumption that income is held constant. Thus

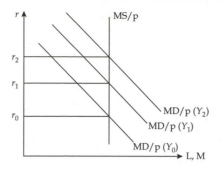

Figure 7.5

when income rises, the demand for money rises for any given level of interest rates. A rise in income represents a change in the ceteris paribus conditions, which causes the curve to shift out, as is shown in figure 7.5.

7.7 Equilibrium in the assets market: derivation of the LM curve

The combination of the downward-sloping MD/p curve shown above and the assumption of a vertical money supply curve MS/p – which means the supply of money is not affected by changes in interest rates – can be used to derive the LM function.

Earlier in this chapter we showed how an exogenous shift in interest rates caused the I and S curves to shift and reach a new level of equilibrium in the goods market. Now the logic is reversed: we assume there is an exogenous shift in income, and see how the MD/p and MS/p curves shift (if at all) to reach a new level of interest rates.

Suppose some exogenous stimulus moves the IS curve out and raises the level of Y. At a higher level of real income, economic agents will want to hold more money, so they will adjust their portfolios by holding fewer bonds and other non-monetary assets. Sales of these bonds will push their price down, thereby raising the interest rate.

The rise in income shifts the MD/p curve out. Since we are assuming a stable rate of inflation and no change in monetary policy, the MS/p curve does not shift. Thus on an ex ante basis, money demand exceeds money supply. The assets market can return to equilibrium only if interest rates rise. Hence the MD/p curve now intersects the MS/p curve at a higher level of interest rates. The new equilibrium point (Y_2, r_2) will be at a higher level of both income and interest rates than the old point (Y_1, r_1). Similarly, a decline in aggregate demand would shift the MD/p curve down, resulting in a new intersection point (Y_0, r_0), which represents lower income and interest rates. These shifts are shown in figure 7.5.

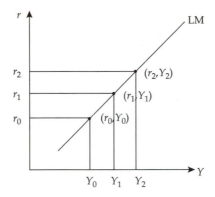

Figure 7.6

We can now think of all the possible shifts of the MD/p curve, and all the possible combinations of (Y_k, r_k) that would occur. All these points can be combined into an upward sloping line with interest rates on the vertical axis and income on the horizontal axis. That curve is known as the LM curve, and is shown in figure 7.6. It represents all the equilibrium points where MD/p = MS/p. This curve thus shows how economic agents would balance their assets between money and bonds at all levels of income, and hence represents equilibrium in the asset market.

So far only the MD/p curve has shifted. Now consider what happens to Y and r if the MS/p curve is shifted, i.e., the Fed decides to increase or decrease the availability of credit, as represented here by the money supply. When the Fed makes such a decision, it could literally print more money, but the usual course of action is for the Fed to buy Treasury securities from the banking sector. Alternatively, it could change the terms under which credit is available. If the Fed buys Treasury securities, two things happen. First, buying bonds raises their price and reduces their yield. Second, if deposits do not change, banks now have more funds available for loans to the private sector, since they are holding fewer Treasury securities. Both of these changes boost real GDP. Thus an outward shift in the MS/p curve also results in an outward shift in the LM curve, which raises real GDP and reduces real interest rates.

7.8   Slope of the LM curve under varying economic conditions

The shape of the LM curve is based on the parameter estimates for income and interest rates. The next issue is whether these parameters tend to stay constant, or whether they shift over the course of the business cycle.

Earlier we noted that, in an era of banking deregulation, the demand for money is closely related to the demand for loanable funds. During periods of recession, the demand for loans is relatively low, since investment is depressed because of greater uncertainty and excess capacity. Thus when income increases in the early

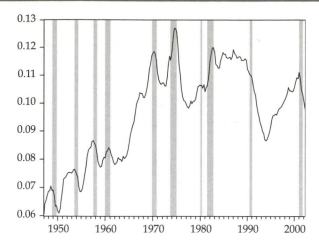

Figure 7.7 Ratio of business loans to GDP (shaded areas are recessions): this ratio usually declines in recessions and continues to fall in the early stages of business cycle recoveries

stages of recovery, the demand for loans, and hence the demand for money, does not shift very much. Conversely, when the economy is booming, an increase in income results in a much bigger increase in the demand for loans.

There are two principal reasons why the loan/GDP ratio usually declines in the early stages of recovery, as shown in figure 7.7. First, capital spending lags the business cycle, both because of uncertainty that the upturn has actually started and because of excess capacity. Second, inventory investment is usually low relative to sales in the early stages of recovery. Thus an increase in income during periods of excess capacity and low interest rates will not increase the demand for money as much. For any autonomous shift in income, the MD/p curve usually shifts more when income is high than when it is low. That causes the LM curve to be flatter during recessions and steeper during booms.

During the 1930s, rates on Treasury bills were actually negative for a while because large firms had nowhere else that they thought was safe to invest their money. Because of the weak economy, few investors purchased equities, and investors were concerned that banks might default. Hence they were willing to pay a slight premium for placing their money in risk-free Treasury bills. Then, banks had huge excess reserves amounting to almost 100% of required reserves; today, excess reserves are only about 2% of required reserves.

The same phenomenon occurred in Japan in late 1998, when short-term interest rates actually dipped below zero in late 1998, falling to a rate of −0.004%; the long-term Treasury bond rate fell to 0.62% around the same time. Investors were afraid of bank defaults, and hence were willing to pay a slight premium to hold their assets in Treasury securities. This development actually served as a wake-up call to the Japanese authorities that banking reform was necessary; short-term rates soon returned to positive levels, and the long-term government bond yield rebounded to 2%. Nonetheless, this episode shows once again that when the demand for funds is weak, even a move by the monetary authorities to reduce interest rates to zero may not stimulate economic activity.

In colloquial terms, it is sometimes said that the Fed can pull but it can't push on a string. That means when loanable funds are already being fully utilized, a tightening of monetary policy will have a marked impact on reducing economic activity; but when credit conditions are slack, monetary easing will have little or no impact on boosting economic activity because it will simply add to excess reserves.

In the case of Japan, the capital position of the banks had eroded so severely that many of them could no longer make loans that would be routine under normal circumstances, especially to foreign nationals. Indeed, the collapse of the southeast Asia economy worsened the position of virtually all Japanese banks. In this case, low interest rates failed to stimulate loans because of the inadequacy of capital reserves, and the likelihood of further default on foreign loans.

Such situations arise only after a period when real growth has been sluggish or negative for several years. The US doesn't have negative interest rates or huge free reserves any more, so the chance of a 1930s-style situation occurring again is minimal. In fact, US recessions generally end two to three quarters after the Fed starts to ease. However, holding the Federal funds rate almost a full percentage point below the core rate of inflation in 2002 still resulted in below-average growth for the year. While 3% growth is obviously better than zero or negative growth, that episode emphasizes how low interest rates do not always stimulate economic growth when the rate of capacity utilization is low and consumer and business sentiment is weak and declining.

Thus while easier monetary policy has quickly ended all post-WWII recessions, aggregate demand sometimes remains sluggish, and real growth in the early stages of the recovery remains below average rates; particularly the recoveries of 1971, 1991, and 2002. In those cases, the economy did not recover very quickly in spite of aggressive Fed easing. In particular, the 1991 recovery was hampered by the crackdown on questionable loans.

Thus the LM curve is generally flatter in recessions and steeper in booms for three reasons. First, when income rises during or shortly after a recession, the MD/p curve does not shift out very much. Second, when interest rates are low, the MD/p curve is flatter. Third, the MD/p curve would not shift very much when the economy is far away from full employment and full capacity if the banking system were holding substantial excess reserves.

To summarize this section, the LM curve is flatter in recessions when interest rates are low because the demand for loans is sluggish during recessions, and consumers do not want to hold as many bonds when interest rates are low. Additionally, the expansionary impact of monetary policy under these conditions could be offset if the banking system simply increased its excess reserves, hence short-circuiting the process.

7.9 The IS/LM diagram and introduction to monetary and fiscal policy

We now show how the intersection of the IS and LM curves jointly determines real output and interest rates, starting with the case where the economy is growing steadily but without bottlenecks. In these diagrams, the IS and LM curves are flatter during recessions and steeper during booms.

First consider a rise in the government deficit, caused either by increased expenditures or reduced taxes. That shifts the IS curve out, increasing GDP. However, the rise in GDP will be partially offset by the rise in interest rates; so the increase in real income will be less than if interest rates had remained steady. Typically, the increase is only about half as large.

Now consider an increase in the growth in the money supply, perhaps caused by a desire to stimulate economic activity. In this case, the LM curve shifts out, resulting in higher GDP and a lower real rate of interest. The change in GDP caused by a change in M appears to be substantially larger than for a similar dollar increase in G, because when M rises faster, aggregate demand benefits from both higher income and lower interest rates, whereas when G rises, the gain in income is partially offset by higher interest rates. However, remember that this assumption holds only if the expected rate of inflation is being held constant. Since a rise in either G or M might boost the inflation rate, it would be incorrect to draw any premature conclusions about the relative efficacy of these two types of policies. Furthermore, even if inflation did not rise immediately, an increase in the *expected* rate of inflation might boost interest rates immediately, hence offsetting the stimulatory impact of the increase in the Federal budget deficit.

Next, consider the joint impact of a change in fiscal and monetary policy. Once again, assume that G rises or T (taxation) declines, moving the IS curve out. The Fed then has three choices: it can hold the money supply constant, boost the money supply to keep real interest rates constant, or try to defuse a rise in expected inflation by reducing the money supply.

It should come as no surprise that tighter money will lead to a higher interest rate. However, the point to be emphasized here is that monetary policy can override fiscal policy if the central bank so chooses. Congress, or the President, may want to stimulate the economy by boosting spending or cutting taxes, but the monetary authorities can always offset such moves by selling the newly issued Treasury securities to the banks, hence reducing the amount of loans they can make to the private sector. This is another way of emphasizing that monetary policy, rather than fiscal policy, has a more important role in determining short-term fluctuations in the economy.

Figure 7.8 shows the three options facing the Fed when the IS curve shifts out, presumably because of a larger deficit. Assume the initial position is (r_0, Y_0).

- The Fed can *accommodate* the larger deficit by boosting the money supply enough so that the LM curve intersects the new IS curve at the old rate of interest.

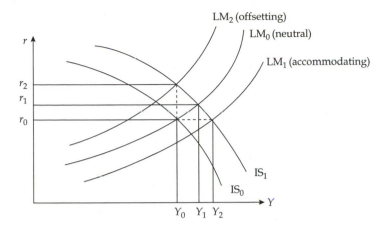

Figure 7.8

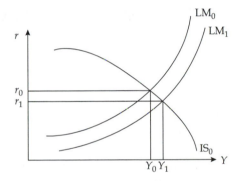

Figure 7.9

- The Fed can follow a *neutral* policy by holding the money supply constant, in which case the interest rate rises somewhat.
- The Fed can *tighten* to offset the allegedly inflationary impact from a bigger deficit; it might even tighten so much that output does not increase and only interest rates rise.

Figure 7.9 shows that if the LM curve shifts out, output will always rise unless there is a specific contractionary action taken in fiscal policy. Hence the combination of those two policy shifts – expansionary monetary and contractionary fiscal policy – might appear to leave output unchanged but reduce interest rates. That is what the President's economic advisors thought in 1968. However, when that combination was tried then, the result was higher inflation and a recession. The explanation for this apparently counterintuitive result is given in the next section.

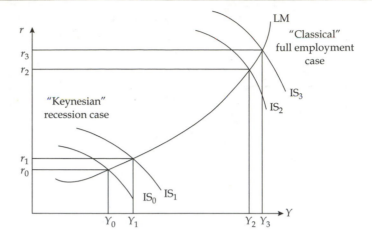

Figure 7.10

7.10 The IS/LM diagram in booms and recessions

We now consider the two polar cases of the IS/LM diagram: when the economy is in a recession and real interest rates are low, and when it is at full employment and real interest rates are high.

In the first case, the LM curve is almost horizontal and the economy already has excess liquidity, so a change in the money supply will have very little impact on interest rates, and hence on the economy. Banks would invest any increase in deposits in Treasury bills or similar assets at very low rates of interest, leaving long-term rates virtually unchanged. That is in part because investors view bonds as overpriced and do not want to buy more of them.

If an increase in the money supply has little or no impact on the real long-term interest rate, a rise in the IS curve will result in a relatively large increase in GDP. Similarly, a cutback in the IS curve will cause a relatively large decrease in real GDP – without much of a change in interest rates. This often occurs when the economy is far away from full capacity and interest rates are already low. In such cases, further monetary easing usually has only a small effect on boosting growth. This is shown in figure 7.10.

In the other polar case, the LM curve is almost vertical, and the economy is operating at full employment and full capacity. The major impact of an increase in the IS curve will be to raise interest rates, so real GDP hardly increases at all. Similarly, the major impact of a decrease in the IS curve will be to reduce interest rates, so real GDP hardly falls at all, even if government spending is reduced. That change is also shown in figure 7.10.

This diagram suggests that when the economy is in a recession, further doses of monetary expansion will have relatively little expansionary effect, or at a minimum, the effect will be delayed. Tax cuts or spending increases, on the other hand, are likely to boost the economy more quickly. By the same token, raising taxes during a recession is disastrous, and will make the recession far worse. Thus fiscal policy has a greater impact on the economy when it is far away from full employment.

When the economy is near full employment, the results are reversed. Fiscal policy has little impact on real growth; an expansionary policy would not boost the economy further, while a cutback in spending or an increase in taxes would not reduce growth very much. However, because loan demand is high, a tighter monetary policy would slow the economy down substantially, whereas a further dose of easy monetary policy would boost inflation. Thus monetary policy has a greater effect on the economy when it is near full employment.

We can now see why the experiment of 1968 failed. The tax increase had only a limited impact on reducing real growth, especially because it was known to be a temporary surcharge. Meanwhile, the concomitant switch to an easier monetary policy boosted inflation. Eventually the Fed had to reverse course and tighten, resulting in the first recession in almost a decade.

Keynes suggested that the only way to end the miseries of the 1930s was to increase government spending, so the recession case is sometimes known as the Keynesian case. In fact the massive expenditures during World War II proved he was right – for the special case of the Great Depression. The classical economists believed that the economy was either at or would soon return to full employment equilibrium, and the important factor governing growth was monetary policy, so the full-employment case is known as the Classical case.[2]

We have presented the Keynesian and Classical cases of the IS/LM diagram to show that fiscal policy is more important when the economy is far away from full employment and capacity, and monetary policy is more important when the economy is near these goals. That is not only a lesson from the 1930s; it also applies to the Japanese economy in the late 1990s.

This diagram can also be used to show how raising taxes or cutting government spending during a recession will prolong the downturn and could lead to a depression. Similarly, if interest rates remain high during a downturn, further doses of contractionary monetary policy can be devastating and could lead to a depression. The finding that monetary policy will not stimulate the economy after a recession holds if interest rates are already very low, banks have large excess reserves, and loan demand remains sluggish.

7.11   Factors that shift the IS and LM curves

The various economic factors that cause the IS and LM curves to shift are now summarized. The factors for both curves have been listed in a single table, rather than treating them separately, in order to emphasize that many economic factors cause *both* the IS and the LM curve to shift.

	IS curve	LM curve
Increase in fiscal stimulus (rise in government spending or tax cut)	shifts out	shifts in
Increase in value of the dollar	shifts in	shifts out
Increase in inflationary expectations	variable	shifts in
Drop in propensity for personal saving	shifts out	neutral*
Exogenous rise in stock market	shifts out	neutral*
Change in sentiment boosts investment	shifts out	neutral*
Change in tax rates that reduces the cost of capital	shifts out	prices – shifts out deficit – shifts in
Exogenous boost in productivity	shifts out	shifts out

* Movement along the LM curve, assuming no exogenous change in monetary policy

The factors moving the IS curve are fairly straightforward except for the change in inflationary expectations, which is listed as "variable." If inflation is expected to accelerate, some economic agents will purchase goods sooner rather than later because they will cost more later. Yet concerns about higher inflation may reduce consumer sentiment, hence boosting the saving rate; the various indexes of consumer confidence invariably decline when inflation increases. On balance, all three energy shocks have been followed by recessions, although that was due more to inward shifts of the LM curve rather than the IS curve.

The Fed, if it so desires, can always shift the LM curve by a change in policy. Hence the tabular results given above are based on no change in monetary policy. Under these circumstances, the LM curve shifts in if inflation rises or the deficit increases, shifts out if prices fall because of an exogenous boost in productivity or greater capital formation, and shifts out if foreign saving increases.

In particular, note that (a) an increase in the deficit shifts the IS curve out but shifts the LM curve in, and (b) a rise in the value of the dollar that increases inflows of foreign capital shifts the IS curve in but shifts the LM curve out. As a result, we cannot say with certainty what effect these changes have on real output. This approach shows, however, the old saws that a bigger budget deficit boosts output, and a stronger dollar reduces output, are generally not true, especially in the longer run. The answer hinges on what impact they have on inflationary expectations, which is covered in the following chapters.

7.12 A numerical example: solving for income and interest rates using the IS/LM model

We now present some empirical estimates. Assume real GDP is about $9,000 billion, and a change in monetary policy reduces real interest rates by 1 percentage point (e.g., from 5% to 4%). For the moment, assume this change is exogenous.

Change in interest rates		Change in GDP		Total change	
Fixed investment	30	Fixed investment	10	Investment	40
Personal saving	−20	Personal saving	15	Personal saving	−5
Corporate saving	0	Corporate saving	10	Corporate saving	10
Foreign saving	−10	Foreign saving	15	Foreign saving	5
Government saving	0	Government saving	30	Government saving	30
Total saving	−30	Total saving	70	Total saving	40

These numbers are not drawn at random but are taken from the equations given below. They are representative of 2000 magnitudes. Both investment and saving rise $40 billion when interest rates fell 1%, but by itself that does not tell us how much GDP rises. Also, the table shows that personal saving fell $5 billion, but does not say how much consumption and income rose. To determine the change in GDP requires an explicit consumption function. If that is added, these changes can then be calculated either by using the identity $I = S$, or the identity $C + I + F + G = GDP$. The arithmetic is the same in either case. However, since we are primarily interested in obtaining the values for GDP, we will use the latter identity.

The equations chosen here are based on actual empirical estimates based on the theories developed throughout this book. Here, we use greatly simplified versions of these equations; however, the income and interest rate elasticities are realistic. All equations are based on chained 1996 dollars and a 4% real rate of interest. These equations, although still oversimplified, are more robust than the simple algebraic equations discussed in the previous two sections. Also, they are in levels instead of first differences.

$$C = 2,379 + 0.68(Y - T - SC + TR) - 20r$$

$$I = 510 + 0.15Y - 30r$$

$$F = 708 - 0.115Y - 10r$$

$$G = 1,570, \quad TR = 1,100$$

$$T = -540 + 0.39Y$$

$$SC = 440 + 0.11Y$$

In these equations, G is total government purchases, T is total tax receipts, TR is transfer payments, and SC is corporate saving (including depreciation). This example does not treat personal, corporate, and business taxes separately.

Adding these together in the GDP identity and combining terms, we have:

$$4,413 + G + 0.375Y - 60r = Y,$$

or

$$0.625Y = 4,413 + G - 60r,$$

which can also be written as:

$$Y = 7,061 + 1.6G - 96r.$$

G is treated separately because it is a policy variable.

Of course we cannot solve this equation until we know r, but assume for the moment that the real interest rate is 4%. Since G = 1,570, then Y = 9,189 under these circumstances.

This equation can be used to determine what happens if G or T are changed. If G rises by $1 billion, for example, then Y rises by $1.6 billion. The coefficient of 1.6 is sometimes known as the "multiplier" because, under these circumstances, a $1 billion rise in government expenditures will raise Y by $1.6 billion. However, this turns out to be a meaningless concept unless we know how much interest rates, inflation, and productivity have changed.

Similarly, one can determine how much a cut in T would raise Y. The arithmetic is not the same, because a $1 billion drop in T only raises C by $0.68 billion, according to the coefficient in the C function. Thus the rise in Y due to a $1 billion cut in T is only 68% of $1.6 billion, or $1.088 billion.[3]

Yet if you think about it for a minute, the conclusion that a given increase in government purchases boosts real GDP more than an equal decrease in taxes doesn't make any sense for two reasons. First, if less money is spent from the tax cut than from the rise in government spending, then saving does not decline as much. Hence interest rates would not rise as much either, and the impact on private sector GDP would not be as negative.

Second and more important, a tax cut could result in a smaller gain in prices and a larger gain in productivity than a rise in government spending, especially if marginal rates were reduced. Hence interest rates would be likely to rise more if government spending were raised than if taxes were cut. Similarly, interest rates would be likely to fall more if government spending were cut than if taxes were raised.

Hence it would be a serious mistake to conclude that an increase in government spending will have a bigger impact in boosting GDP than a similar sized cut in taxes. In fact, the opposite is more likely to be true. That is why we cannot yet draw any conclusions about how fiscal and monetary policy affect the economy until, at a minimum, we include the LM equation. Even this answer will not be realistic if there is a change in inflation, productivity growth, or the value of the dollar.

The equilibrium condition for the assets market, which is MD = MS (= M), all in real terms, can be written as follows. All terms here are in constant prices, so we drop the explicit use of the price deflator. Once again the parameter estimates are based on actual empirical equations. Assume the money supply is $5,000 billion. If the M2 measure of the money supply is used, an empirical approximation can be estimated as $M = -127 + 0.57Y - 32r$. This can be rewritten as: $0.57Y = M + 32r + 127$.

We now have two equations in two unknowns, with G and M both exogenous. There are several ways to solve this two-equation system, but the simplest is to multiply the second equation by 96/32 (= 3) and then add them together; the r

terms will drop out. That yields:

$$1.71Y = 381 + 3.00M + 96r$$
$$Y = 7,061 + 1.60G - 96r$$

Adding these equations together yields:

$$2.71Y = 1.60G + 3.00M + 7,442$$

Since $G = 1,570$ and $M = 5,000$, we can solve this equation for Y and obtain $Y = 9,208$. Putting this value in the equation for M yields $r = 3.8\%$.

We showed above that a $1 billion increase in G would raise Y by $1.6 billion, assuming interest rates were constant. But they are not constant; a $1 billion increase in G also raises interest rates. After taking this into account, and realizing that higher interest rates would reduce private sector GDP, Y would rise only about $0.75 billion when G rises $1 billion, which means private sector GDP would shrink by $0.25 billion. Thus the rise in r when G rises reduces the impact of an increase in government purchases by more than half, from 1.6 to 0.75.

There is no analogous offsetting relationship when the money supply is expanded. Then, a $1 billion increase in M raises Y by $1.40 billion, because r is reduced by 3.125 basis points for each $1 billion rise in M, ceteris paribus. However, that is only because this approach assumes no changes in inflationary expectations.

We hasten to point out that these are not the final answers. Several other factors can change, including but not limited to the price level. Nonetheless, we have made some progress. Government spending is not a "free ride." By increasing spending, the government reduces private sector investment. While an increase in M might seem a better way to boost the economy, that is only because we have not yet taken into account the impact of changes in M on the expected rate of inflation. That is usually substantial, although it occurs with a significant lag.

Because of this lag, the economy is likely to get a temporary "pop" from faster money supply growth before inflation catches up. Yet even that will not happen if anticipated inflation rises ahead of actual inflation. Thus the question of how much changes in G and M affect Y cannot really be answered until we determine how actual and expected changes in the rate of inflation affect interest rates.

CASE STUDY 7.1   THE 1973–4 RECESSION, THE FIRST ENERGY SHOCK, AND THE IS/LM DIAGRAM

The 1973–4 recession was the longest and most severe recession of the post-WWII period. The situation was exacerbated by the removal of wage and price controls in May, 1974, which briefly sent inflation rates to record levels.

continued

CASE STUDY 7.1 (*continued*)

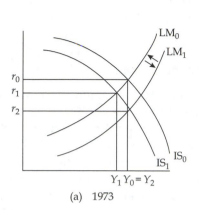 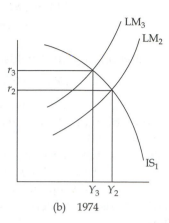

    (a) 1973   (b) 1974

Figure 7.11

The recession actually occurred in two parts. When the oil embargo and increase in oil prices initially occurred in October 1973, that negative shock reduced aggregate demand, and real GDP fell about 2% at annual rates that quarter (i.e., an actual decline of $\frac{1}{2}$%). In order to counter that, the Fed eased, and real GDP then rose about $\frac{1}{2}$% the next quarter. However, inflation then started to zoom, in part because of monetary easing and in part because wage and price controls ended. Subsequently, the Fed had to reverse its steps and tighten a second time, which brought about the second and more severe leg of the recession, when GDP fell 3%.

These shifts are shown in figure 7.11 using the IS/LM diagram. In part (a), the IS curve first shifted in because of the decline in demand due to the energy shock, reducing income and real interest rates. The Fed then eased, moving the LM curve out. During this period, nominal interest rates rose sharply, but not as fast as the rate of inflation, so real rates eased. As the inflationary spiral worsened, the Fed was forced to tighten again, as shown in part (b), which raised real interest rates and sent the economy back into recession.

CASE STUDY 7.2   THE 1983 RECOVERY

Many people were skeptical about whether the "Reagan recovery" would work. The budget deficit soared, real interest rates were at an all-time high, and the dollar was not only overvalued but was continuing to rise. Nonetheless, real GDP rose

continued

CASE STUDY 7.2 (*continued*)

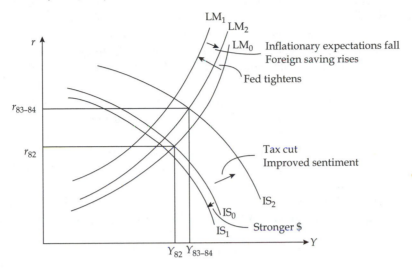

Figure 7.12

an average of 4.3% over the next seven years, and the unemployment rate declined from a peak of 10.7% to 5.3%.

In terms of the IS/LM diagram, the LM curve had shifted in because the Volcker Fed decided to sell bonds to pay for the Reagan deficit. However, that was partially offset by an outward shift out of the LM curve as foreign saving poured into the US economy; as a result, the M2 measure of the money supply rose at a very rapid average of 9.4% per year until the dollar started to decline. The IS curve shifted in because of the overvalued dollar, but that was more than offset by an outward shift in that curve because the Reagan tax cut boosted consumer spending. In addition, business expectations improved because of the pro-business attitude of the Reagan Administration and the no-nonsense approach of the Fed. These shifts, relative to the position of these curves during the 1982 recession, are shown in figure 7.12.

CASE STUDY 7.3   THE 2001 RECESSION AND 2002 RECOVERY

This was an unusual recession relative to the experience of the past 30 years in the sense that there was no increase in inflation and no Fed tightening; the Treasury yield curve turned negative but the corporate yield curve did not. Hence the

continued

CASE STUDY 7.3 (*continued*)

entire downturn was caused by an inward shift in the IS curve, which occurred in two separate phases. First, the collapse of the Nasdaq bubble reduced high-tech investment. Second, the drop in sentiment shortly after the 9/11 tragedy reduced consumer confidence and also caused further declines in capital spending and inventory investment. Throughout this period, the overvalued dollar reduced exports.

Discussion of this recession in the popular and business press has been polarized depending on one's political affiliation. Most Republicans claimed that the timely Bush tax cuts kept the recession short and mild. Most Democrats claimed that the tax cuts were wasted; that they materially contributed to the return of the budget deficit but real growth remained sluggish because of the decline in business confidence stemming in part from the deficit.

Taking the published GDP data at face value, real growth fell from almost 5% in the four quarters from 1999.3 through 2000.2 to slightly less than 1% in the latter half of 2000. It then was flat during 2001, and rose 3% in 2002. That figure was about 2% less than the average increase in real GDP during the first year of recovery, although the 2001 recession was much milder than usual; usually real GDP declines during the years in which recessions occur.

Why did the growth rate fall from 5% to 0%? The real government and corporate bond rates were virtually unchanged, so that was not the reason. Also, credit was not restricted. The major negative factors were (a) the stock market collapse, (b) substantial excess capacity, and (c) the overvalued dollar. All three of these factors represent an inward shift in the IS curve. The 9/11 attack also moved the IS curve in, although its impact on aggregate demand was short-lived. While it probably is not possible to assign precise parameters to each of these factors, it would not be unreasonable to assume that of the 5% drop in the real growth rate, about 2% was due to the initial decline in the stock market, 2% to excess capacity, and 1% to the overvalued dollar.

The Fed eased vigorously throughout 2001, but long-term rates hardly budged. Hence a 5% drop in short-term rates probably did not boost real growth more than $2\frac{1}{2}\%$. Thus the LM curve moved out only slightly, as shown in figure 7.13. Assuming the normal marginal propensity to consume, as discussed in chapter 4, the Bush tax cut probably boosted real growth by about $1\frac{1}{2}\%$. Offsetting these gains, the stock market continued to plunge during the first half of 2002, which probably reduced real growth by another 1%. Summing these factors yields the actual growth rate of 3% in 2002.

To a certain degree, this approach admittedly starts with the answer and works backward. However, the point in presenting these numbers is to note that if the stock market had rallied vigorously in the early stages of recovery, as indeed had been the case in every previous recovery, real growth probably would have

continued

CASE STUDY 7.3 (*continued*)

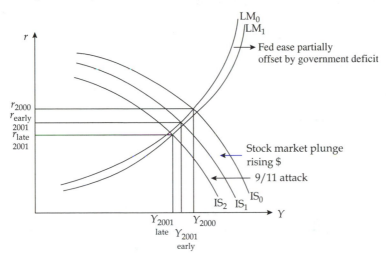

Figure 7.13

averaged 5% in 2002 instead of 3%. Seen in that light, stimulative monetary and fiscal policy had about the same impact as usual; it was the continued stock market decline in the early stages of recovery that was unprecedented.

One could perhaps argue that the Bush tax cut, and the return of the deficit, caused the stock market to decline. However, considering how rapidly the market rose in late 1982 and 1983, shortly after the larger Reagan tax cuts were passed, that appears to this author to be a highly unlikely answer. It is much more likely that the massive accounting scandals and frauds were the principal factor causing the stock market to nosedive from May to July of 2002. That development was a truly exogenous factor, and probably explains why the economy rebounded sluggishly. If that is indeed the case, the traditional IS/LM analysis and the usual stimulative effects of monetary and fiscal policy continue to hold, with the important caveat that exogenous shocks will continue to have unexpected impacts on the economy.

In the 2001 recession, almost all of the decline in the first phase occurred in capital spending, contrasting sharply with previous recessions, where the initial declines occurred in consumer durables and housing. In terms of I = S, the drop in investment was matched by a decline in government saving as the economy faltered, and a decline in business saving, as profits fell by the largest percentage in the entire post-WWII period. Hence this case study also shows that the IS/LM mechanism can still explain business cycle recessions even when the proximate cause is not monetary tightening.

KEY TERMS AND CONCEPTS

Classical and Keynesian Cases (of the IS/LM diagram)
IS Curve
Liquidity Preference
LM Curve
Multiplier

SUMMARY

- A rise in the interest rate will reduce investment and raise saving, ceteris paribus. Personal and foreign saving will rise the most; corporate and government saving will be little changed by an increase in interest rates, although they will usually decline slightly.
- A rise in interest rates will usually restrict the availability of credit, hence leading to a decline in aggregate demand and a rise in saving.
- A rise in income will boost both investment and saving, ceteris paribus. All four components of saving – personal, corporate, foreign, and government saving – increase when income rises.
- The identity $C + I + F + G = GDP$ is the same as the identity $I = S$. Both identities must hold on an ex post basis.
- On an ex ante basis, the sum of the components of aggregate demand may not be equal to production, and investment may not be equal to saving. In particular, a rise in interest rates would reduce I but would raise S, ceteris paribus.
- There are three ways in which an ex ante gap between I and S can be closed. First and most important, interest rates can serve as the equilibrating factor. Second, in the short run, inventory investment may move in the same direction as saving. Third, production can decline, which reduces Y and

hence S on an ex post basis, mainly through a decline in corporate, foreign, and government saving.
- Suppose the economy is initially in equilibrium, and the monetary authorities reduce the interest rate. Initially, I will rise while S will fall, hence leading to a disequilibrium situation. However, the reduction in the interest rate will boost aggregate demand, and hence Y. Since S is more highly correlated with Y, an increase in Y will boost S more than I, ceteris paribus. As a result, I will once again equal S on an ex post basis.
- The combination of all points where I = S on an ex post basis for different levels of income and interest rates is known as the IS curve.
- Both changes in interest rates and changes in income help to equilibrate I and S on an ex post basis whenever there is an exogenous shift in aggregate demand or monetary policy.
- Any exogenous shift in aggregate demand will cause the IS curve to shift. These include changes in government spending and tax rates, changes in foreign income and the value of the dollar, an increase in technology, and autonomous shifts in consumer and business sentiment.
- Changes in income and interest rates cannot be considered in isolation, because a change in income usually affects interest

rates, while a change in interest rates usually affects income. Thus when determining the course of the economy caused by a change in interest rates, we must take into account the effect of changes in income on investment and saving.

- If interest rates decline and income rises, investment would increase sharply. Personal saving and foreign saving would be almost unchanged, since the changes caused by lower interest rates would be largely offset by the changes caused by higher income. Hence the rise in saving would occur primarily in corporate and government saving. However, if government saving did not increase – if, for example, the decline in interest rates were accompanied by a tax cut – then total saving would not rise, and the initial decline in interest rates would be reversed.
- All major components of aggregate demand are negatively related to the real rate of interest, and all are positively related to income except for net exports, since imports rise faster than exports when income increases.
- The demand for money in real terms is positively related to income and negatively related to the real rate of interest.
- If monetary policy does not change, an increase in income will shift the real demand for money (MD/p) out and to the right, raising interest rates.
- The intersection of various positions of the MD/p curve with the real money supply (MS/p) is known as the LM curve. It represents all the equilibrium positions in the assets market, and shows a positive relationship between interest rates and real income.

- During recessions, the MD/p curve does not shift out very much when income rises because demand for loans is sluggish.
- When interest rates are high, a change in rates will result in a relatively small change in the demand for money. When they are low, a change in rates will result in a relatively large change in the demand for money. During recessions, excess reserves held by the banking system may increase.
- As a result of these three factors, the LM curve is flatter during periods of recession and low interest rates, and steeper during periods of boom and high interest rates.
- The combination of the IS and LM curves jointly determines real interest rates and real output. A policy of fiscal stimulus shifts the IS curve out, which would raise both output and interest rates if the LM curve does not shift.
- A policy of fiscal stimulus that increased the deficit could result in a tighter monetary policy, which might completely offset any rise in output. Conversely, a policy of fiscal contraction, such as a tax hike or cutback in spending, might result in little or no decline in output if the economy were already at full employment and capacity.
- An attempt to stimulate net exports by reducing the value of the dollar would shift the IS curve out in the short run, but would also shift the LM curve in, so that the result might turn out to be higher interest rates but no rise in output.
- When the economy is already at full employment, a combination of tighter fiscal policy (raising taxes) and easier monetary policy is likely to result in little change in output but an increase in the rate of inflation.

QUESTIONS AND PROBLEMS

1. Use the IS/LM diagram to show what would happen to real output and interest rates when the following policy changes are implemented. In this problem, assume that prices remain constant.

(A) The Fed hires a helicopter to fly around the country and drop an average of $100 for each person.

(B) The Treasury mails a $100 check to everyone in the country. Fed policy accommodates this decision.

(C) The Treasury mails a $100 check to everyone in the country. The Fed does not accommodate.

(D) Congress votes a $100 income tax reduction for everyone in the country (those who do not pay any income taxes receive a $100 credit).

2. Explain why a tax cut would have a greater stimulatory impact on the economy during a recession than during a boom.

3. In 1998, Japanese real GDP fell $2\frac{1}{2}$% in spite of a sharp decline in interest rates and massive increases in government spending. In terms of the IS/LM diagram, what factors must have shifted to offset the monetary and fiscal stimulus?

4. In the spring of 1980, the Federal funds rate fell from 17.6% to 9.0%, while real GDP declined at a 9.6% annual rate, the biggest one-quarter decline in history. Use the IS/LM diagram to show what factors caused this massive change. (Hint: that was the quarter the Fed imposed credit controls.)

5. Explain why the ratio of loans to GDP usually declines in the beginning stages of recovery.

6. Explain the circumstances under which a policy of fiscal expansion is accompanied by:

(A) A substantial rise in real GDP and little or no change in interest rates.

(B) A moderate rise in both real GDP and interest rates.

(C) A substantial rise in interest rates but no change in real GDP.

7. Under what circumstances is the Fed most likely to tighten when the budget deficit increases, and when would it be most likely to accommodate an increase in the budget deficit?

8. Explain why an increase in the value of the dollar is usually accompanied by faster growth in the money supply in an era of banking deregulation.

9. Show what happens to C, I, F, G, Sp, Sc, Sf, and Sg in each of the following cases. Remember that I is always equal to S on an ex post basis. Take these step by step.

(A) Government cuts personal income taxes by $100 billion;
Consumers spend all the money on Japanese cars;
Japanese invest excess dollars in Treasury securities.

(B) Government cuts income taxes by $100 billion;
Half goes to consumers, who buy domestic new cars;
Half goes to corporations, which build new motor vehicle plants.

(C) Government raises personal income taxes by $100 billion;
Consumers think the tax increase is temporary, so they don't cut spending;
Treasury uses extra money to reduce national debt.

(D) Government spends $100 billion on public works projects.

(E) Government hires helicopters to drop $100 billion over the country; Consumers spend one-third of the money and save two-thirds of it.

10. In the early 1980s, both US interest rates and the value of the dollar rose sharply, reducing the current account balance. In the late 1980s, US interest rates rose again, but the value of the dollar did not increase, and the current account balance did not decline. What factors caused these varying reactions?

11. Explain the major reasons why an increase in income raises saving more than investment on an ex ante basis.

12. Suppose the government cuts corporate income taxes, hence boosting I. However, S has declined because the deficit has increased. Explain how the economy returns to equilibrium where I = S on an ex post basis.

13. Because of a stock market crash, consumer and business optimism declines, so both consumption and investment drop. On a ceteris paribus basis, a drop in C is equal to an increase in Sp, so saving rises while investment falls. Explain how the economy returns to equilibrium where I = S on an ex post basis.

14. Suppose growth in Europe rises, boosting US exports. That would reduce Sf, ceteris paribus. Explain what happens to the other components of I and S, and show how the economy returns to equilibrium.

15. Explain which of these changes represent a move along the IS curve, and which represent a shift of the IS curve.
    (A) Stock market boom boosts consumption and investment.
    (B) Government cuts taxes by $50 billion.
    (C) Government passes $50 billion public works bill and pays for it with a $50 billion tax increase.
    (D) Fed boosts interest rate from 5% to 6%.
    (E) Tax receipts fall $30 billion as economy plunges into recession.
    (F) Value of the dollar rises 10%, cutting net exports by $40 billion.
    (G) Net exports rise $20 billion as Asian economy recovers.
    (H) Rise in interest rates diminishes housing starts.
    (I) Mortgage interest is no longer deductible, so housing starts decline.

16. Calculate the simple multiplier if the marginal propensity to consume is 0.4, investment rises $0.05 for every $1 billion increase in income, and net exports decline $0.08 for every $1 billion increase in income.

17. Explain which factors would cause the IS curve to be steeper, and which would cause it to be flatter. When is the IS curve more likely to be steep – during recessions or booms?

18. Assume real GDP is $9,000 billion, and disposable income is $6,000 billion. The government cuts personal income taxes by 1% of DI (i.e., $60 billion). As a result, interest rates rise by $\frac{2}{3}$%. Assume transfer payments are not changed. Using the equations given in section 7.12, determine how much real GDP changes, and how much I and each of the components of S changes.

Notes

1. Before banking deregulation, money paid a zero nominal rate of interest, which means it paid a negative real rate of interest. While currency and some checking deposits still pay no interest at all, most checking accounts now pay a rate of interest approximately equal to the inflation rate, so money generally pays a zero real rate of interest. In almost all cases, bonds pay a positive real rate of interest.
2. The "Keynesian" and "Classical" terms used here refer to earlier discussions of this curve. More recently, the dichotomy between "new Keynesians" and "new Classical" economists is based on how long proponents of these theories think it takes markets to clear; new Keynesians think it takes much longer than do new Classical economists. The descriptions used here do not refer to that classification.
3. This equation assumes that the change in T is not correlated with income; it is a one-time rebate or lump-sum payment. The arithmetic is more complicated if there is a change in the tax rate, although the general idea is the same.

part III

Aggregate supply: inflation, unemployment, and productivity

Part II of this text presented the basic elements required for the joint determination of real output and real interest rates using the components of aggregate demand. In deriving the IS/LM diagram, prices were held constant, yet the increase in inflation when demand outstrips supply is one of the key issues in macroeconomics. However, this element cannot be adequately discussed without a more complete explanation of aggregate supply.

Hence part III presents the determinants of the major elements of the supply side of the economy: inflation, wage rates, unemployment, and productivity. It starts with a detailed treatment of inflation, since the assumption that prices do not change is clearly unrealistic. Chapter 8 covers the determinants of inflation, which are based largely on expectations about how economic agents – both business and labor – think prices will change in the future. In the long run, inflation is primarily a monetary factor. In the short run, changes in the rate of inflation are tied to changes in unit labor costs, particularly wage rates. Inflation is also determined by institutional factors that influence wage rates, government regulations affecting domestic and international competitive practices, productivity growth, supply shocks, and changes in the value of the currency.

Chapter 9 explains several possible reasons why high unemployment often persists even in the long run. Chapter 10 introduces the production function, and reviews the basic determinants of long-term productivity growth. These chapters show that while monetary policy is the principal policy factor affecting short-term fluctuations in real growth, and is a key factor in determining the rate of inflation in both the short term and the long term, fiscal policy is the primary determinant of the long-run growth rate in productivity and hence real GDP.

chapter eight
Causes of and cures for inflation

Introduction

During the latter half of the 1990s, the rate of inflation in the US was lower than at any time since the early 1960s – even though the economy was booming. Furthermore, that was not just the case for the US; inflation was also well below its long-term average in most other industrialized nations. What changed?

In the long run, inflation is a monetary phenomenon. In the short run, in the absence of exogenous shocks, inflation is closely correlated with the change in unit labor costs, which are wage rates divided by productivity. However, wages and prices jointly depend on expectations about how the monetary authorities will react, so this merely bounces the question of what determines inflation in the short run back one more level. In addition to rapid gains in productivity, inflation was low in the late 1990s around the globe because the monetary authorities established credibility and convinced economic agents that even at full employment, they would not permit prices to rise very fast. Any attempt to raise prices would result in lost sales and profits for businesses, and lost job opportunities for employees. It is important to note that these expectations affect both wages and prices. In a properly functioning competitive economy, prices do not rise faster than labor costs in the absence of exogenous shocks.

If controlling inflation is that simple, why didn't central banks try the same tactic long ago? After all, given the choice, very few people would vote for high inflation.

We can safely assume no central bank sets out to encourage higher inflation. The problem usually starts when the government runs a big deficit, and its attempts to sell bonds to domestic investors are unsuccessful. Foreign investors do not want to buy these bonds unless they are denominated in dollars or other stable currencies, but most countries do not have a large supply of foreign exchange. As a result, the government basically sells the bonds back to itself, which is known as monetizing the debt and akin to printing money. Not until the profligate spending patterns are reversed can inflation be brought under control.

Yet a large deficit does not necessarily mean inflation will rise. One of the biggest mistakes made by many economists in the early 1980s was to predict that the rate of inflation would rise because of the Reagan deficits. Instead, it fell from 13% to 4% in a year and a half, and after stabilizing at that level eventually declined even further. In the case of the US, there were plenty of investors – both domestic and foreign – willing to buy Treasury securities at high interest rates, and there was a Fed Chairman who was determined that inflation would decline on his watch.

Several other important developments occurred at the same time. First, the value of the dollar rose substantially in the early 1980s. Second, the Reagan Administration moved to a more pro-business stance and enhanced competition, although some of the groundwork for deregulation was laid in the Carter Administration. Third, regulations that had encouraged labor to demand outsize wage increases were changed, and the Reagan Administration took a much harder line against Federal government employees who illegally went on strike.

Inflationary expectations can be kept under control if the government is willing to encourage a credible monetary policy, strong currency, balanced budget at full employment, vigorous domestic and international competition, and removal of artificial barriers that interfere with equilibrium prices in both labor and product markets. That list of goals is not easy to accomplish. It also helps if there are no exogenous disturbances such as energy shocks, which sent inflation higher in 1973–4 and 1979–80 in almost all countries in the world.

In the short run, the inflation rate is closely correlated with changes in unit labor costs, whose main component is wage rates. Thus in the short run, the theory of prices is the theory of wages. They too depend on expectations that are related to credible monetary, fiscal, and trade policies, as well as institutional factors that affect the labor market directly. Short-run movements in inflation are also negatively correlated with productivity growth.

To address these various issues, this chapter is organized as follows. *First*, in the long term, we show that inflation is a monetary phenomenon. *Second*, in the short term, we show that the inflation rate follows changes in unit labor costs, but is not closely related to the level of capacity utilization. *Third*, the role of expectations in determining the rate of inflation is discussed, with an explanation of how different facets of monetary policy can affect inflation. *Fourth*, since inflation follows unit labor costs in the short run, the determinants of wage rates and productivity are examined, including the tradeoff between wage rates and unemployment. *Fifth*, the impact of supply shocks on the rate of inflation is examined for both the short and long run. *Sixth*, the effect of the lagged responses of wages and prices on the inflation rate is analyzed. *Seventh*, we explain how hyperinflations can quickly end as soon as inflationary expectations change significantly. *Eighth*, the issue of why inflation and unemployment both declined in the US economy during the latter half of the 1990s is examined.

8.1 In the long run, inflation is a monetary phenomenon

Figure 8.1 shows a scatter diagram between the average rate of inflation over the period from 1967 through 1994 and the average percentage change in the broad money supply for the same period for 22 countries. The correlation is unmistakable: mature countries with relatively low growth rates for the money supply have low inflation; emerging nations with rapid growth in the money supply have rapid inflation; and many Latin American countries with triple-digit growth in the money supply have hyperinflation.[1]

The vertical axis is the average annual percentage change in the CPI from 1969 through 1994; the horizontal axis is the percentage change in the money supply for the same years. The sample is truncated at 1994 because many of these countries have had sharply lower rates of inflation after that date.

During times of genuine shortages, the inflation rate will often surge as consumers bid up the prices of scarce commodities. However, that is an exceptional case. It is much more common to find that countries with double or even triple-digit inflation have massive unemployment and low rates of capacity utilization. In those cases, how does money supply determine the rate of inflation in the long run?

To answer that question, consider how an inflationary spiral starts when an economy is not at full employment and is not ravaged by exogenous shortages (such as famine). In virtually all cases, either the government runs a large deficit that must be financed by issuing more credit, or the value of the currency declines, hence raising the price of imported goods and services. While the increase in government

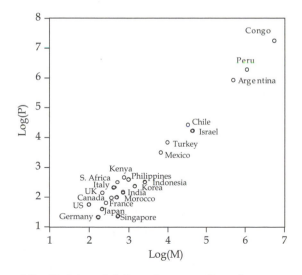

Figure 8.1 Long-term relationship between inflation and money supply growth
Source: International Monetary Fund statistics

spending could stem from a huge increase in public works or defense spending, it is much more likely to be caused by big increases in wages for government employees or pension benefits. The increase in these wages and benefits spurs other workers to demand equally large raises, and firms grant them because they expect to be able to pass along the higher costs through higher prices because of the rapid growth in money and credit. In the case of a sharp rise in the price of imported goods and services, the logic is even more straightforward. The spiral continues until a monetary or political crisis causes a sharp break in past procedures and returns inflation to normal levels.

In the past, many governments apparently believed that high inflation was more politically acceptable to the voters than the alternatives of balanced budgets and tight money. Gradually, that belief has disappeared to the point where hardly any countries still remain in the throes of inflationary spirals. Because higher inflation was a direct product of government policies, it could quickly be stopped by a reversal of those policies, and today few policymakers still believe that their country will somehow be better off under high and rising rates of inflation. Hence while the mechanisms of hyperinflation are now well understood, they have little to do with economic conditions in the industrialized world in the early twenty-first century.

8.2   In the short run, inflation is determined by unit labor costs: the price markup equation

Figure 8.1 showed a strong correlation between long-term changes in the money supply and the rate of inflation for a wide variety of countries. However, this relationship is much weaker in the short run. Figure 8.2 shows the relationship between annual changes in the inflation rate and the percentage changes in the M2 measure of the money supply lagged two years for the US economy from 1950 through 2001; the correlation is even weaker for other lags. Figure 8.3 shows the same relationship using a time-series graph. Note that except for the years of energy crises, there is very little correlation between the inflation rate and changes in the money supply lagged two years, which is the preferred lag claimed by monetarists. Unless one believes that a big increase in the money supply caused the energy crises two years later, there is no short-run correlation at all. In particular, above-average rates of growth in M2 in the late 1990s were accompanied by no increase at all in the rate of core inflation – even though the economy had returned to full employment. That does not mean monetary conditions are not an important determinant of inflation. It means that expectations are not well measured by lagged changes in the money supply – especially since banking deregulation has sharply reduced the influence the Fed has on determining money supply growth.

What does determine inflation in the short run? We start by assuming that firms seek to maximize the rate of return on equity. Admittedly there are some crooks who willfully misstate earnings, temporarily boosting the stock price, and permitting top executives to rob the rest of the shareholders. As revolting as these episodes may

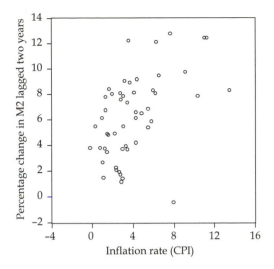

Figure 8.2   Short-term relationship between inflation and money supply growth
Sources: CPI data, Bureau of Labor Statistics website, www.bls.gov; money supply data, www.federalreserve.org

Figure 8.3   Inflation rate and changes in M2
*Years of energy shock

be, they have very little impact on the overall price level, and recently occurred during a period when the inflation rate was unusually low relative to previous experience, particularly for a booming economy at full employment. These isolated instances play no role in determining the overall price level.

Firms realize that if they set prices at a level that generates an above-average rate of return, that will encourage other existing firms – either domestic or foreign – to expand their operations, or will entice new firms to enter the industry. Eventually,

Figure 8.4   The rate of inflation is closely correlated with percentage changes in unit labor costs (the spike in inflation in 1980 represents a sharp increase in mortgage rates, which are no longer included in the CPI)
Source: BLS website, www.bls.gov

overcapacity will result and the above-average rate of return will disappear. That would not be the case if firms operated illegally to restrain trade, or if government regulations prohibited new entries into the industry (for example, through licensing). Except for those cases, though, firms will seek to generate a normal rate of return by marking up prices over variable costs, with the markup factor related to the capital intensity of the operation.

Some will argue that this one-size-fits-all theory is inappropriate. If a firm finds it is losing sales because foreign competitors (who face a lower cost structure) have cut their prices, it has little choice other than to follow suit. In other cases, a recession may cause a sharp drop in sales, causing other domestic firms to cut prices and slash profit margins in order to remain in business. In other cases, such as the high-tech industry, variable labor costs may represent a tiny proportion of total costs and have very little impact on the pricing decision.

We do not dispute these real-life examples. Yet the fact of the matter remains, as shown in figure 8.4, that the rate of inflation is indeed closely correlated with percentage changes in unit labor costs. Figure 8.5 shows *no* correlation between the rate of inflation and the rate of capacity utilization. How can these apparently contradictory facts be reconciled?

At the macroeconomic level, the argument can be constructed as follows. Suppose a firm finds it necessary to reduce prices in order to maintain market share. Profit margins plummet. As a result, executives of that corporation are almost certain to require some offsetting reductions in cost – otherwise they will not remain in business very long. In some cases, costs will be reduced by cutting

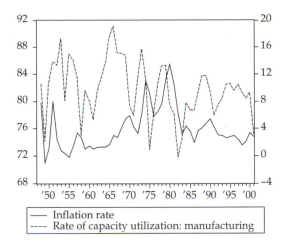

Figure 8.5   There is no correlation between the rate of inflation and the rate of capacity utilization
Sources: BLS website, www.bls.gov; Fed website, www.federalreserve.org

discretionary expenditures and postponing capital purchases. Most of the time, however, labor costs will be reduced even if base wage rates are not cut. That could be accomplished, for example, by trimming staff, reducing overtime, reducing the proportion of the fringe benefit package paid by the company, or skipping bonuses for the year. The net result is that both prices and unit labor costs decline but, at the aggregate level, the spread between prices and unit labor costs does not change. The decline in profit margins stems from spreading the same capital costs, which are fixed, over a smaller revenue base.

It has been noted that business airline fares, for example, drop sharply during recessions even though labor costs cannot change very much. However, at a macroeconomic level, lower fares mean lower costs to most businesses, which would boost their profit margin, ceteris paribus. In this case, lower profits for one industry are partially offset by lower costs, and hence higher profits, elsewhere. The same general argument can be made for the price of most intermediate goods and materials that are endogenously determined.

Empirically, then, we can show that in the short run, measured inflation and unit labor costs move together closely – even if some individual firms do not mark up prices by a constant proportion over variable costs, and even if the measured rate of inflation is not an accurate indicator of how fast prices really are rising. Thus, except for exogenous shocks, inflation starts to rise because wage gains accelerate or productivity gains decline, and firms pass along higher labor costs to consumers.

As noted above, figure 8.4 shows that, in the US, changes in the inflation rate are closely correlated with changes in unit labor costs on an annual basis, whereas figure 8.5 shows *no correlation* between inflation and the rate of capacity utilization.[2] The spread between prices and unit labor costs does *not* increase when the economy is near full capacity.

Since the aggregate markup factor – the difference between prices and unit labor costs – does *not* increase as the economy approaches full employment and full capacity, the explanation of short-term changes in inflation is largely an explanation of wage rates and productivity, adjusted for supply shocks. This chapter discusses the overall determinants of wage rates; chapter 9 examines the various imperfections in labor markets that often keep wage rates and the unemployment rate well above equilibrium.

When Samuel Gompers, the first head of the American Federation of Labor (AFL), was asked what his workers wanted, he said, "more." Businesses gave the same answer, sometimes in more refined terms, sometimes not. Cornelius Vanderbilt, the owner of the New York Central Railroad, is probably best known for his remark that "the public be damned." J. P. Morgan also said that he owed the public nothing.

No value judgments are implied here, other than what once seemed to be the obvious comment that both labor and business are supposed to observe the laws of the land. "Ghost workers" who are paid without ever showing up for work, and business executives who rob the shareholders by treating the company treasury as their own private piggy bank, have always been illegal, and not just in 2002. Nonetheless, a labor leader who did not try to maximize the benefits of his workers would soon be replaced. A business executive who did not try to maximize stockholder return would also soon be replaced. Our point is that human nature has not really changed over the past century, or for that matter, over the past 100 centuries. Inflation is not higher in certain decades because people are "greedier" at those times. Human nature does not change during so-called "decades of greed." The question is whether labor thinks it can get higher wages without losing jobs, and business thinks it can get higher prices without losing sales.

The increase in wage rates is primarily determined by inflationary expectations, which depend on the credibility of monetary policy, the size of the deficit, and the way it is financed – but these are not the only factors. Other variables determining wage rates include the amount of international competition, the value of the currency, the degree of domestic competition, regulations that apply to labor policy, the average and marginal tax rates paid by labor, and the ratio of the minimum to the average wage rate.

Occasionally, changes in the growth rate of fringe benefits can be a significant factor affecting inflation. The slower growth in fringe benefits starting in 1995 was probably one of the factors that helped reduce inflation during the latter half of the decade. Large increases in healthcare costs paid by employers had been a major factor boosting the overall inflation rate; from 1947 through 1993, fringe benefits rose almost 5% per year faster than wage rates. They rose at about the same rate in 1994; then for the rest of that decade, they rose about 1% per year *less* than wages and salaries. That reflects both lower healthcare costs and smaller contributions to pension benefits made possible by a rapidly rising stock market. Also, the generally rising social security tax rate from 1954 through 1991 helped to boost the inflation rate; when the rate leveled off, employee compensation costs also rose less rapidly.

The other component of unit labor costs is productivity. If bigger wage gains are offset by concomitant increases in productivity, unit labor costs do not rise. Conversely, even modest wage gains can be inflationary if productivity growth is sluggish or nonexistent.

To summarize this section, even though individual firms may find that their pricing decisions deviate from a straight markup over variable costs, this general rule holds very closely for the overall economy, both in booms and recessions. At the macroeconomic level, variable costs consist primarily of unit labor costs and exogenous changes in energy and food prices.

MANAGER'S BRIEFCASE: WHY IT WAS SO DIFFICULT TO RAISE PRICES IN THE LATE 1990S

It might seem like good business practice for a firm to try to raise its prices when business is strong. However, historically that has seldom been the case, and it certainly was not true during the 1990s. From a microeconomic viewpoint, the issues are twofold. If a company raises its prices without a concomitant increase in costs, that would be an open invitation for competitors to expand and increase their market share. Even if the price increase is justified by higher costs, consumers will eventually turn away from that product and choose a less expensive substitute. That is true even if the firms in question have monopoly power. OPEC thought it could raise oil prices with impunity, but when it pushed them to $35/bbl, world demand declined and substitute sources of energy became more common. In recent years, nominal benchmark crude oil prices have averaged six to eight times their level in 1972, the year before the first energy crisis, but over the same period, the overall CPI has risen $4\frac{1}{2}$ times, offsetting most of those gains in real terms.

From a macroeconomic viewpoint, an increase in the rate of inflation invariably sets into action forces that offset the initial short-term advantages to businesses. First, labor demands higher wage rates. Second, the value of the currency will often decrease, raising the prices of imported parts and materials. Third, the monetary authorities will usually act to reduce the rate of inflation by raising the cost and reducing the availability of credit. Fourth, in the long run, higher inflation reduces productivity growth, which means real income and the standard of living rise less rapidly, so consumers cannot afford as many goods and services, and demand for the product will decline.

For many years, the prices of steel and nonferrous metals and of motor vehicles were considered bellwethers for the overall rate of inflation. Figure 8.6 shows the four-quarter changes in metals prices; in particular, note the huge increase that occurred when wage and price controls ended in May 1974 (as discussed next in case study 8.1). Other major events that sent prices higher were the Korean War, devaluation of the dollar, and the energy crises. Also note, however, that nonferrous metals prices generally dropped very sharply after those big gains; the higher prices generally reduced demand the following year. Thus if firms granted big wage increases based on these price hikes, their profits would have fallen in future years. Also, those big gains induced foreign competitors to increase their shipments to the US.

Figure 8.7 graphs the fluctuations in prices of new motor vehicles against the unemployment rate. First, note there is no negative correlation between these two series; the major gains in prices reflected many of the same exogenous factors that boosted metals prices. Even more to the point, however, note that a sharp increase in auto

continued

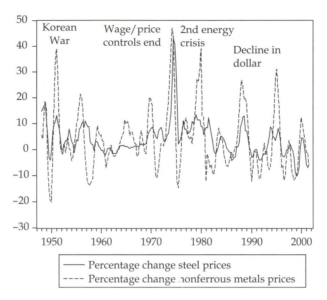

Figure 8.6   Fluctuations in metals prices
Source: BLS website, www.bls.gov

Figure 8.7   Fluctuations in auto prices and the unemployment rate
Source: BLS website, www.bls.gov

MANAGER'S BRIEFCASE (*continued*)

prices was generally followed by an increase in the unemployment rate. When inflation in general – and auto prices in particular – rose rapidly, demand diminished, boosting unemployment the following year.

The evidence presented in these two graphs suggests that big increases in steel, nonferrous metals, and motor vehicle prices were generally followed by recessions, as both private sector purchasers and the monetary authorities reacted to these higher prices. But even if your company produces goods and services that are not important enough, in a macroeconomic sense, to register on the Washington political Richter scale, it has become increasingly difficult to raise prices and keep them at those higher levels.

Part of the reason reflects the increasing globalization of the US economy; there are very few goods that cannot be made cheaper elsewhere around the globe. Even if that is not the case immediately, an increase in prices is likely to represent an open invitation to other firms to expand operations overseas. NAFTA and other trade agreements signed in the 1990s and early 2000s have extended the reach of global competition.

Additionally, both individual and business customers are much more price sensitive now than in the past. Some of the major airlines thought they could raise the price of business class airfares indefinitely; when the recession came, several of them went bankrupt.[3] Restaurants that routinely raised prices each year soon found themselves shuttered. The downward pressure on prices does not apply only to goods.

Over the past three decades, the firms that have grown the most rapidly have been the well-managed discount retail firms. Wal-Mart is the primary example, but many other chains have prospered by offering consumers lower prices. Furthermore, some of their biggest gains occurred during the rapid growth in incomes and stock prices in the late 1990s. Even when times were flush, an increasing proportion of consumers voted for lower prices.

It is unrealistic to predict that higher rates of inflation will "never" return. However, given the increasing pressure from international operations and the greater tendency of shoppers to prefer lower prices, most firms will continue to emphasize cost-cutting rather than higher prices as the better method of boosting profit margins.

CASE STUDY 8.1   WHAT CAUSED DOUBLE-DIGIT INFLATION IN THE 1970S?

Richard Nixon often claimed he lost the 1960 election because the economy headed into recession in April of that year, the result of an attempt by the Eisenhower Administration to curb inflation. Whether that was really true or not, it clearly influenced his subsequent political decisions. The recovery from the 1970 recession had been unexpectedly anemic; the unemployment rate had risen to 6% and seemed stuck at that level. Polls showed him losing the 1972 election to Edmund Muskie. Thus in the summer of 1971, when the economy still seemed stalled, Nixon decided to take direct action. On August 15, 1971, he surprised the nation and the world by announcing a new economic plan that provided stimulus to the economy through tax cuts and a devaluation of the dollar – but to make sure that his plans

continued

CASE STUDY 8.1 (*continued*)

were not thwarted by Fed tightening due to higher inflation, he also announced a wage and price freeze for 90 days, to be followed by controls. That way, Nixon calculated, the economy would move into high gear in the months before election, yet inflation would remain low and stable. For a while, it seemed that the plan worked brilliantly: the unemployment rate fell to 5% in 1972, real GDP reportedly rose at a 7% annual rate – and he beat George McGovern in a landslide.

Nonetheless, in retrospect it was the worst mistake Nixon ever made. Viewed from a distance, many people think he was forced out of office by "Watergate," but double-digit inflation and a severe recession certainly helped grease the skids. After the election was over, and the economy went to Phase III of the wage and price controls, which were downgraded to "guidelines," inflation started to skyrocket. The coup de grace was administered by the first energy crisis, but even before that happened, the inflation rate had moved up from 3% to 8%. What went wrong?

Almost everything. By demanding that the Fed keep interest rates low and boosting growth in the monetary and credit aggregates, Nixon lit the fuse for higher inflation as soon as the controls were removed. The government ran a full-employment deficit, and the dollar was devalued approximately 20%. Even worse, under the wage and price guidelines, firms were allowed to raise prices if they could show that their costs had increased, but not otherwise. As a result, firms whose costs had risen were rewarded, whereas those who had reduced their costs were penalized. Naturally that cut the legs out from under productivity growth.[4]

The energy embargo, and the subsequent quadrupling of benchmark crude oil prices, were bad enough, but the situation was exacerbated by the decision of the Fed to ease shortly after energy prices skyrocketed to forestall a recession, rather than tightening to offset further inflation. The dam finally broke when wage and price controls formally ended on May 1, 1974. The wholesale price index (as the PPI was called then) rose a record amount in May, inflation zoomed to 13%, and the economy plunged into the most severe recession of the post-WWII period.

8.3   Monetary policy and the role of expectations

The empirical data presented for both the US and other countries indicate that in the long run, inflation can be held at a low, stable rate by controlling the growth in monetary and credit aggregates. However, the short-run correlation between money supply growth and inflation in the US is not robust, especially after 1982, when banking deregulation took effect. After that period, there is no correlation between the inflation rate and changes in money supply, or loans or consumer credit outstanding. Thus controlling inflation does not mean simply setting money supply or credit growth at some preassigned target and leaving it alone. Some of these issues are discussed in this section. Monetary policy is still important, but it is no longer adequately measured by looking at the money supply.

Firms will not raise prices unless they believe those increases can be validated in the marketplace. Employees are more likely to push for bigger wage increases if they believe these increases will not reduce the demand for their labor. Both these statements hold whether or not there is any central bank. After all, surges in inflation occurred in the US long before the Federal Reserve Bank was established, and long before unions were an established force. However, those bouts of inflation were short-lived; when the exogenous shock that caused prices to increase disappeared, prices usually returned to their previous level. From 1800 to 1940, the CPI actually *fell* an average of 0.1% per year.

During and after World War II, the situation changed dramatically. From 1940 through 1967, the inflation rate in the US averaged 3.3%; from 1968 through 1982, it averaged 7.3%. However, from 1983 through 1992 it declined to 3.4%, and from 1993 through 2001, the average fell to 2.5%. Human nature did not change; expectations did.

Expectations about whether the attempt to increase wages and prices will be successful depend largely on how economic agents expect the monetary authorities to react. If they accommodate these initial increases in a misguided attempt to keep real growth rising at above-average rates, inflation will almost certainly rise. Conversely, if they are able to convince business and labor that any attempts to raise prices and wages will be unsuccessful, inflation will not rise. In that respect, expectations about how the central bank will act are critical in determining whether inflation will rise as the economy approaches full employment and full capacity.

Yet even though central bankers invariably claim their only responsibility is to keep inflation low and stable, sustained bouts of high unemployment may generate sufficient political pressure to erode their independence. The monetary authorities may be forced to choose between higher inflation and higher unemployment, and they may cave in. Once credibility has been established, this unpleasant choice will arise far less frequently. However, because of the formidable hurdles in establishing credibility, some central banks never attain that goal.

Credible monetary policy can keep inflation low and stable regardless of what else is happening in the economy. However, it may take several years to establish that credibility; in the meantime, political events may make it virtually impossible to assert that authority. Hence, at least in the past, high inflation has remained endemic in some countries even though the unemployment rate is also relatively high and no malign supply-side shocks are present.

Monetary policy is also an important determinant of *wage rates*, since wages also depend on how much workers and businesses think inflation will rise in the future. If workers think inflation is about to accelerate, they will demand bigger wage increases. If businesses think these higher wage rates can be passed along to final users in the form of higher prices, they are more likely to acquiesce to these inflationary wage demands. Workers are no better off if prices rise at the same rate as wage rates; indeed, to the extent that the economy has a progressive tax system that is not indexed, they are worse off, since as inflation rises a larger proportion of their income goes to pay taxes.

Seen in this light, it is in the best interests of both workers and businesses to keep the rate of inflation low. Workers will find their paychecks are not eroded by higher taxes, while businesses will see their real income is not diminished by a decline in real sales caused by higher prices. The economy functions better when both business and labor expect monetary policy to keep the inflation rate low and steady.

Credible monetary policy exists when the rate of inflation is low enough that it does not influence economic decisions. Whether that rate is 0%, 1%, or 2% is not really important; the key idea is that economic agents should not make their decisions based on a significantly positive rate of inflation.

The Fed establishes monetary credibility by word and by deed. However, simple ''jawboning,'' unless backed up by explicit action when required, is the proverbial paper tiger. The Fed must stand prepared to raise the cost and reduce the availability of credit when higher inflation threatens, whether this is accomplished through raising interest rates, reducing the growth in the money supply, restricting credit availability, or other tools of monetary policy.

Starting in 1982, the Fed has recently been able to maintain credibility by setting the Federal funds rate during non-recession years at the recent rate of inflation plus the underlying long-term growth rate of the economy, and raising that rate whenever the threat of inflation increases. If the Fed were to ignore that threat in the future – even before it was actually translated into higher inflation – inflationary expectations would undoubtedly rise as soon as the economy approached full employment.

We have already stated that monetary policy, if applied forcefully enough, can always be used to reduce the inflation rate close to zero. However, in any transition period before credibility is established, the unemployment rate may rise substantially, placing a great deal of political pressure on the government. In an extreme case, the government might be overthrown; in a less dramatic situation, it might be voted out of office. In that case, credibility might never be attained, and monetary policy would be forced to accommodate higher inflation indefinitely. Even without a revolution, the central bank may lose much of its credibility if it repeatedly bows to political pressure. The most common political problems faced by the monetary authorities are:

- Large full-employment deficit
- Regulations that reduce productivity and competition
- An exchange rate that remains below its equilibrium level. But if the government holds the exchange rate steady for a while even though domestic costs are rising faster than those of foreign competitors, the currency will eventually be forced to devalue, generating an explosive increase in inflation.

Not all budget deficits are inflationary. When the Federal government deficit increases, the Treasury must sell securities to pay for the rise in expenditures or decline in tax receipts. However, these deficits can be financed in one of two ways. The central bank can buy the additional Treasury securities issued to finance the deficit, known as monetizing the deficit; sometimes this is referred to as "printing money" because the government is essentially selling the securities to itself. The other way is to borrow money from the private sector, including foreign investors, in which case the funds are used to purchase Treasury securities instead of goods and services. That method of financing the deficit is not inflationary.

During the early Reagan years, the ratio of the Federal budget deficit ratio to GDP rose to unusually high levels, but the inflation rate declined sharply and then stabilized. The Fed decided to buy a smaller proportion of the extra government securities, thus forcing private sector investors to purchase them. That decision resulted in unusually high real interest rates, which also boosted the value of the dollar. As a result, much of the extra government debt was purchased by foreign investors; Edmund Phelps has suggested that it was the Europeans rather than the Americans who paid the bill for the Reagan deficit. Inflation declined because the Fed did not buy these extra government securities, and the currency strengthened.[5]

The central bank must always act within the confines of political realities. It is easy enough to show that countries with independent central banks have lower inflation than those where central bankers are beholden to their political masters. Nonetheless, this begs the question: how did those independent central bankers manage to establish their autonomy? The answer must be that the political powers, realizing the advantages of low inflation as an essential ingredient for a healthy economy, permit the central bank to operate without interference.

The deficit financing of the Reagan era coincided with an unusually high growth rate in the money supply – but it was not inflationary. The massive inflow of foreign capital used to purchase these Treasury securities occurred at the same time the banking sector was deregulated. As that happened, money supply growth lost its role as the principal measure of monetary policy, and was replaced by the real Federal funds rate.

When the US deficit ballooned in the early 1980s, both domestic and foreign investors were eager to purchase Treasury securities at high real interest rates. Many countries are not so fortunate; if the deficit remains large and the Treasury cannot sell the required amount of securities to the private sector, these securities end up being purchased by the central bank. That is particularly true for smaller countries without well-developed capital markets.

Thus the reason some countries have consistently high inflation rates and others have low inflation rates turns out to be the combination of rapid money supply growth and a large deficit ratio. If the government did not generate a large deficit, the money supply would not grow as rapidly. Theoretically, the monetary authorities could implement an independent strategy, but politically that is often impossible. In addition to political pressures, the market may not exist for, say, Bolivian Treasury securities unless they are denominated in dollars, in which case they must be backed by scarce foreign reserves. These points will be analyzed in more detail in section 8.7, when hyperinflation is discussed.

8.4 Determinants of changes in unit labor costs

We have shown that in the short run, changes in inflation follow changes in unit labor costs closely. This section discusses (a) the principal determinants of nominal wage rates, (b) whether there is any inverse relationship between the change in real wage rates and inflation, sometimes known as the inflation-adjusted Phillips curve, and (c) the cyclical determinants of productivity. In the long run, the percentage increase in the real wage rate is equal to the growth rate in productivity; the discussion of the long-run determinants of productivity is deferred until chapter 10.

Determinants of Nominal Wage Rates

The vertical line in figure 8.8, corresponding to 1979, represents the first year of a two-decade slowdown in the real wage rate. Before 1979, wage rates rose an average of 5.4% per year, compared to a 3.5% annual gain in the consumer price index. From 1979 through 2001, wage rates rose an average of 3.9% per year, compared to a 4.5% annual gain in the CPI. Hence starting in 1979, the real wage rate rose $2\frac{1}{2}$% per year less than in the previous period. Furthermore, this lack of increase in the real wage continued throughout the 1990s even as the economy returned to overfull employment.

While wage rates do rise more rapidly in years of high inflation, workers are not entirely successful in their attempt to keep pace with the cost of living; the real wage usually drops substantially during years of high inflation. Also, figure 8.8

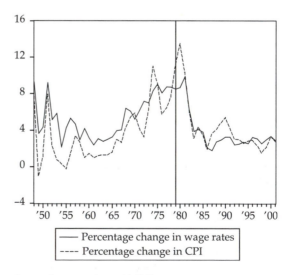

Figure 8.8 Percentage changes in wage rates and inflation
Source: BLS website, www.bls.gov

shows that wage gains hardly accelerated at all during the late 1980s, when the rate of inflation briefly rose substantially.

The next subsection examines the question of whether the real wage rate is inversely correlated with the unemployment rate; we first turn to the institutional factors that determine the nominal wage rate. The following items are the principal determinants of nominal wage rates, in addition to the lagged rate of inflation: the average and marginal tax rates paid by labor, government regulations on competitive structure, degree of foreign competition, the value of the currency, ratio of the minimum to average wage rate, relative strength of unions, and the composition of the total compensation package.

- *Average and marginal tax rates paid by labor.* If the tax system is not indexed relative to inflation, workers will be pushed into higher marginal tax brackets as their nominal wage rates rise, even if their real wage rates remain unchanged. Thus they pay a higher proportion of their income in taxes when inflation rises. Under such circumstances, workers will bargain for bigger wage increases, which boosts inflation even more.

  A tax system is indexed when the marginal rates are adjusted each year by the rate of inflation. Suppose, for example, that the marginal tax bracket jumped from 20% to 28% for incomes over $30,000. If the inflation rate were 5%, then under an indexed system, the maximum income taxed at a 28% marginal rate would rise from $30,000 to $31,500 the following year. If someone's nominal income increased at the same rate as inflation, they would remain in the same tax bracket. Only if real income rose would they move to the next higher tax bracket. The US instituted an indexed tax code starting in 1985. That is one of the reasons, although obviously not the only one, why inflation has remained low and stable during the 1990s.

- *Government regulations on competitive structure.* Deregulation and privatization of many key industries in the US also helped to keep inflation low and stable throughout the 1990s. To the extent that the government encourages vigorous competition, the job of the monetary authorities is made that much easier, and monetary policy is much more likely to remain credible. Other government directives that may also affect how much wage rates change include policies on unions and wage bargains as determined by the National Labor Relations Board (NLRB); policies on whether replacements for strikers can be hired on a permanent basis; the size of unemployment benefits; policies on paid and unpaid leave; notice that must be given to terminated workers; and government regulations affecting whether jobs can be transferred overseas.

- *Degree of foreign competition.* Government policies that boost free market competition and productivity will boost real growth and diminish the rate of inflation, ceteris paribus. Yet while many governments claim their policies encourage domestic competition, they often take a jaundiced view of foreign companies taking market share away from domestic producers.

Domestic firms may try to compete vigorously, but face a common cost structure. Consider, for example, the case of an oligopoly where production workers are represented by a single union (auto workers, steel workers, or mine workers). To the extent this industry is insulated from foreign competition, management may not contest inflationary wage increases very strongly, may fail to boost productivity, and may be indolent about introducing technological innovations. Vigorous foreign competition insures that domestic management will pay close attention to controlling costs and improving productivity.

- *Value of the currency.* One key measure of the strength of international competition is the value of the currency. If the currency frequently declines in value, firms will often have little to fear from foreign competitors, because the government will "bail them out" by devaluing the currency frequently. In addition, consumers will be forced to pay more for foreign goods, which will boost inflation. Most of the time, a weak currency is aided and abetted by excessive growth in the money supply or the decision to keep real interest rates below equilibrium.

  It is difficult for a country to maintain price stability if its currency is habitually declining in value. That has not been a severe problem for the US because other countries tend to price their goods to US markets. Nonetheless, it is significant; and is more important when the economy is near full employment. For many countries, the inflation rate is closely related to changes in the value of the currency. The monetary authorities can stabilize the currency by raising real interest rates, but since that would boost unemployment in the short run, it might not be politically feasible. If speculators are convinced devaluation is imminent, even sky-high interest rates often fail to keep the value of the currency from plunging.

- *Minimum wage.* The effect of the minimum wage on inflation is discussed in more detail in the next chapter. At this point we say any increase in the minimum wage that boosts wages above the marginal product of lowly paid employees is likely to cause higher inflation. The more workers are affected, the larger the impact on inflation, ceteris paribus. Conversely, an increase in the minimum wage that still leaves it at a relatively low level and affects very few workers will generally have a negligible impact on the overall rate of inflation, even if some industries are substantially impacted. That was the case for the increases in the minimum wage during the late 1990s.

- *Relative strength of unions.* At first glance, the relative strength of unions and the stance of the monetary authorities might seem to be unconnected. However, if government policies encourage unions to press for big wage increases, but the monetary authorities do not permit businesses to raise prices, the net result will be higher unemployment. Since that forces the central bank to make the unhappy choice between higher inflation and higher unemployment, it often takes the easy road and permits inflation to rise when unions are strong.

- *Composition of the total compensation package.* Suppose someone receives a total compensation package of $60,000 per year. They could receive the total amount in straight salary, or could receive a base salary of $40,000 and a bonus of $20,000.

If the firm does well, total compensation would be the same in either case. However, the bonus would be earned only if certain profit goals were met, so if sales were sluggish, the firm would not be saddled with excessive wage payments. The same argument applies to stock options, signing bonuses, and other forms of compensation that are not included in the base wage rate. If these supplementary forms of compensation rise at the same time that the base wage rate remains unchanged, inflation is less likely to rise.

All of these items have some impact, but what are the most important ones that reduced the average annual change in the real wage rate from 1.9% in the 1948–78 period to −0.6% in the 1979–2001 period? In this author's view, the following factors emerged as preeminent. *First*, it became much easier for manufacturers to shift operations to overseas locations. *Second*, the reestablishment of monetary credibility meant that higher prices could not be validated in the marketplace. *Third*, the shift in government policy, which was inaugurated with the firing of the air traffic controllers in 1981, made it quite clear to labor unions that the government would no longer acquiesce to inflationary wage contracts; instead, permanent jobs could be offered to strikebreakers. President Reagan broke the power of government unions when he terminated the PATCO walkout. He still gets a lot of credit – or blame – for what happened in the economy during the 1980s and 1990s, but that one decision is often underrated as the reason that high inflation came to an end.

The Relationship Between the Real Wage Rate and Unemployment

A more contentious issue among economists is whether the real wage rate rises during periods of declining or low unemployment. This inverse relationship, often known as the **Phillips curve**, is discussed in the appendix to this chapter. The theoretical argument used to support this tradeoff is that when the unemployment rate is above full employment (full N), workers can be hired from the ranks of the unemployed, and paid the going wage. When the unemployment rate is below full N, additional workers can be hired only by paying them more than the going wage, which causes wage rates to accelerate and boosts inflation. According to this argument, the real wage rises in booms and falls in recessions.

Figure 8.9 shows the relationship between annual changes in the real wage rate and the level of the unemployment rate. At first it might appear that the real wage rate does drop during periods of recession, but although that occurred in 1954, 1958, 1970, 1974, and 1980, it did not happen in 1949, 1961, 1982, 1991, or 2001. Furthermore, in three of those five years when it did occur – 1970, 1974, and 1980 – the drop in the real wage was due to a substantial increase in the inflation rate either in the current or previous year. Hence the apparent inverse relationship actually shows that when inflation accelerates, the gains in wage rates are likely to lag behind the increase in the CPI. That is a valid and important relationship, but has nothing to do with the inverse correlation between wage rates and unemployment.

Figure 8.9   Changes in the real wage rate and the unemployment rate (vertical lines are years of recession)
Source: BLS website, www.bls.gov

What about 1954 and 1958? As it turns out, those declines are due to anomalies in the data rather than the underlying economy. Before 1964, data for total private sector wage rates are not available, so the series shown is only manufacturing sector wages. During recessions, the biggest declines generally occur in the highly paid durable goods industries, notably autos and steel. Thus the average wage rate would have declined even if none of the individual industry wage rates fell. Other data for total compensation, which also include fringe benefits, show no such decline in either 1954 or 1958. Hence the dips shown for those years represent a change in the mix, not an actual decline in the real wage.[6]

Thus during periods of stable inflation, there is no tradeoff between the real wage rate and the unemployment rate. The so-called Phillips curve is a statistical illusion.

The same conclusion is reached by glancing at a scatter diagram between annual percentage changes in the real wage rate and the inverse of the unemployment rate. The results for private sector wages and the unemployment rate are shown in figure 8.10. That graph also shows there is no correlation between these two variables.

Cyclical Patterns of Productivity

Until the business cycle expansion that ended in 2001, productivity had always declined once the US economy reached full employment for the following reasons:

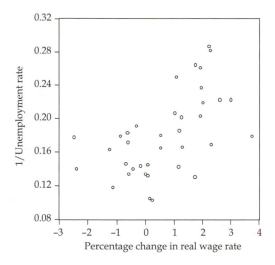

Figure 8.10 Relationship between annual changes in the real wage rate and the inverse of the unemployment rate

- The remaining available employees lack basic skills in the marketplace, are untrained, uneducated, or are unfamiliar with the work ethic (bottom of the barrel effect).
- Current workers increase their overtime hours. This not only boosts costs (because of time-and-a-half or double time) but also reduces productivity and efficiency, because tired workers tend to make more mistakes.
- Machinery requires a certain amount of down time for routine maintenance. If this is bypassed, the error rate may also increase. Also, firms may use less efficient and outmoded machinery that would ordinarily be replaced by more modern equipment.
- When times are good and the orders keep coming in, managers often slacken off and stop looking for ways to cut costs. This can lead to higher costs and higher prices rather than higher productivity (fat and sloppy).
- Even if management keeps its eye on the ball, when business first turns down, it would be counterproductive to lay off or fire valuable workers, so these people are kept on for a while even though there is not as much for them to do.

Until the late 1990s, that looked like a fairly formidable list. However, it too has been consigned to the dustbin, as the growth rate in productivity actually accelerated during the latter half of the 1990s, rising from a modest 1.0% per year in the 1993–5 period to 2.5% per year in the 1996–2000 period.

Future generations of economists may be able to discern, with perfect hindsight, whether the unprecedented rise in productivity growth during the late 1990s was the harbinger of a sea change in economic behavior, or a one-time phenomenon that was not repeated. High-tech stock prices – and high-tech capital spending – grew at record rates near the end of the decade, and another stock market boom of those proportions is not expected for many decades. Also, at the end of the boom, the index of capacity utilization calculated by the Federal Reserve Board was actually lower than it had been at the end of the previous recession, whereas in all previous booms, that rate had climbed sharply. Clearly there was a massive increase in the capital/labor ratio during the 1990s, fueled by the unprecedented high-tech stock market boom.

The available data also show that in the late 1990s (a) the length of the work-week and overtime hours did not rise, (b) a stronger dollar sharply boosted the trade deficit and intensified foreign competition, and (c) profit margins actually fell during the last three years of the recovery. As a result of these factors, business executives maintained their vigilance on cost reduction. Also, because of the unusually large increase in capital spending, outmoded machinery was not rushed into service when demand increased. Hence the previous reasons for a decline in productivity near the peak of business cycle activity were invalidated. The two major differences were probably the high-tech boom and the strengthening dollar. A credible monetary policy also helped, although that had not kept inflation from rising somewhat in the late 1980s.

The determinants of unit labor costs, and the relationship to inflation, can thus be summarized as follows:

1. Nominal wage rates are determined by the rate of inflation and institutional factors. However, it takes wages several years to adjust fully to significant changes in the inflation rate. Although an inverse relationship between the unemployment rate and the change in the real wage rate is often alleged, we find no supporting empirical evidence except in years of wartime when market forces are short-circuited.
2. If real wage rates do rise, businesses face the following choices: try to pass along those cost increases in the form of higher prices, offset those gains by faster growth in productivity, offset those gains by hiring fewer workers, or accept lower profit margins.
3. The decision on whether or not to pass along these cost increases depends primarily on the credibility of monetary policy, the value of the currency, and degree of domestic and foreign competition.
4. If businesses attempt to boost prices but the Fed tightens, prices will not rise very much, but growth in output and employment will diminish moderately. If businesses attempt to boost prices and the Fed does not initially intervene, nominal wages will rise further, and an inflationary wage/price spiral will develop, eventually leading to a more serious recession.
5. Attempts to boost productivity growth through an increase in the ratio of capital spending to GDP are much more likely to succeed if the budget is in surplus and equity market prices are rising rapidly, hence reducing the cost of debt and equity capital. If the full-employment budget remains in deficit, productivity

growth probably would not improve as much in the later stages of the business cycle expansion.

8.5   Malign and benign supply shocks

The term **supply shock** refers to any unexpected exogenous event that impacts prices, as opposed to endogenous changes in wages and prices that result from a high level of economic activity or overly accommodative monetary policy. Supply shocks can move prices in either direction; the unusually rapid growth in productivity during the late 1990s can be considered a benign supply shock, as was the increase in the value of the dollar from 1997 through 2001. A big increase in the minimum wage or a government-mandated decline in productivity would qualify as a negative, or malign, supply shock. However, the term usually refers either to changes in the cost of raw materials that are big enough to have a noticeable impact on prices at the macro level, or to major changes in the value of the currency. The most important cases have been the energy shocks, which are discussed in case study 8.2.

Other supply shocks include (a) major swings in food prices, (b) major changes in the value of the currency, and (c) major changes in the productivity growth rate. As shown in figure 8.11, food prices had a substantial impact on the overall inflation rate in the 1950s, somewhat less in the 1960s and 1970s, and since then, hardly any impact at all. Food prices have become a less important part of the CPI, and price fluctuations have also been far smaller than earlier in the post-WWII period.

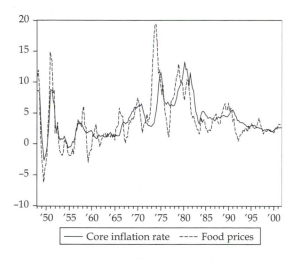

Figure 8.11   Four-quarter percentage change in the CPI core rate of inflation and the CPI for food prices
Source: BLS website, www.bls.gov

A substantial devaluation of the currency that pushes it below its equilibrium value will almost always boost inflation. The only time that the US dollar was formally devalued in the post-WWII period occurred shortly after the decision to abandon the international gold standard on August 15, 1971. After wage and price controls were lifted, inflation did indeed soar, but that was due to the first energy shock and inept monetary policy management as well as devaluation. Much larger swings in the value of the dollar in the 1980s had less impact on the overall price levels, partly because the world is on a de facto dollar standard. However, we include this factor in the list because in other countries it has been one of the major factors leading to inflationary spirals.

CASE STUDY 8.2   THE IMPACT OF ENERGY SHOCKS ON THE RATE OF INFLATION

There have been several major changes in energy prices since 1973. The first big increase occurred in 1973 and early 1974, when OPEC boosted the price of crude oil from $3 to $13/bbl. The second occurred in 1979 and 1980, when OPEC raised crude oil prices from $13 to $35/bbl. That increase set in motion a series of events that culminated in a decline in oil prices to $12/bbl in 1986. They then bounced back to $18/bbl in 1987 and remained near that level until mid-1990, when Iraq invaded Kuwait. That briefly pushed prices as high as $40/bbl, but as soon as Kuwait was liberated, prices returned to their previous levels. The drop in benchmark crude oil prices from $20 to $10/bbl in 1998 was considered by some to be a benign supply shock, but it was short-lived, as prices briefly soared above $30/bbl in 2000 before retreating to $20/bbl. They then moved up as high as $38/bbl in anticipation of another war with Iraq but quickly retreated after hostilities actually began.

As shown in figure 8.12, the *real* price of gasoline (i.e., divided by the CPI) was the same in 2001 as it was in 1947. Major swings in oil prices no longer have as large an impact on overall inflation as occurred in the 1970s and 1980s, as shown in figure 8.13, which compares changes in the core CPI with changes in the PPI for refined petroleum products.

Why did the sharp increases in energy prices in 1973–4 and 1979–80 have such a great impact on the core rate of inflation then, but much less impact in 1990 and 2000? Remember that we are comparing changes in energy prices to the *core rate* of inflation, which excludes both food and energy prices.

First, energy is a far smaller proportion of GDP now than it was earlier in the postwar period. Some liberal Congressmen and columnists like to pretend that

continued

CASE STUDY 8.2 (*continued*)

our recent energy problems are the direct results of more SUVs on the road, but figure 8.12 also shows that the amount of energy used per real dollar of GDP has fallen by half since 1973, when relative energy prices first rose.[7] Thus even if nothing else had changed, fluctuations in energy prices would have only half the impact on the core rate of inflation.

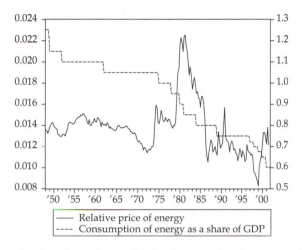

Figure 8.12 Relative price of gasoline to the overall CPI, and consumption of energy as a share of GDP
Sources: Energy prices, BLS website, www.bls.gov; consumption of energy, US Energy Information Administration, *Annual Energy Review*; GDP, BEA website, www.bea.gov

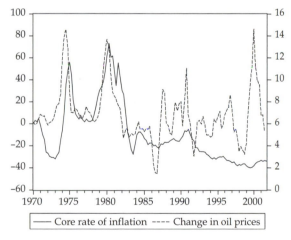

Figure 8.13 Four-quarter percentage change in the CPI core rate of inflation and the PPI for refined petroleum products

continued

CASE STUDY 8.2 (*continued*)

Second, consumer expectations have changed. At first, energy price increases were met by vigorous demands for higher wages to offset the rise in the cost of living. Now, it is realized that a spike in energy prices will probably be short-lived.

Third, businesses have become much more sophisticated in terms of hedging against future increases in energy prices. The initial energy shock in 1973 was a complete surprise to domestic users, but now transportation services and other firms plan ahead and buy oil futures when it falls to $10/bbl, and postpone purchases or sell short above $30/bbl. Hence some of the fluctuations in benchmark crude oil prices are not passed through to consumers.

Fourth, monetary policy now acts quite differently when energy prices rise than was initially the case. In 1973–4, the Fed eased monetary policy following the oil price hike in a misguided attempt to offset the contractionary impact of higher oil prices on consumers. At the time, economists claimed that the rise in oil prices was similar to a $40 billion "tax" on the consumer that would reduce aggregate demand, which should therefore be offset by an easier monetary policy. This argument failed to realize that domestic oil producers would spend their extra money on increased consumption and investment, while OPEC nations would import more from the US; both of these moves would boost real GDP. As a result of the Fed's mistake, the inflationary impact of higher oil prices lingered almost a decade. The Fed did not make the same mistake following oil shocks in 1980 or 1990, so the rate of inflation, after briefly rising, soon declined again. During the first energy shock, the Fed validated higher levels of inflation; it did not make that mistake again.

MANAGER'S BRIEFCASE: PLANNING AHEAD FOR FUTURE ENERGY SHOCKS

Given the unpredictable nature of Middle East politics and fluctuations in oil prices, how should managers plan ahead for the next major swing in oil prices?

Several separate elements of planning are involved. First, energy-intensive industries should stockpile energy supplies — either physically or through futures contracts — when prices are below average, and supplies should be reduced when prices are above average. Most firms now have sophisticated techniques for accomplishing this. Second, a substantial increase in energy prices is likely to reduce the growth rate of the economy in general, so cyclically sensitive products may be affected even if they are not directly tied to energy. Third, there may be some increase in the rate of inflation and interest rates, although there was hardly any impact when oil prices tripled in

continued

MANAGER'S BRIEFCASE (*continued*)

1999 and early 2000. Fourth, if the US goes to war, the initial impact on consumer sentiment and the stock market is likely to be negative – although if the war plans are announced in advance, the reaction upon the outbreak of hostilities may not be negative.

In 1973, the first energy crisis was one of the major factors causing a severe recession. In 1979, the second energy crisis was accompanied by a rise in inflation to 13.3%, an increase in the prime rate as high as $21\frac{1}{2}$%, and another severe recession. In 1990, a doubling of energy prices and a drop in consumer sentiment and stock prices were the major factors responsible for a moderate recession and a weak recovery. Yet in all these cases, exogenous developments occurred over and above the rise in energy prices: either there were actual shortages, or the economy was plunged into preparation for war.

What happened in 1999 and 2000, when oil prices rose sharply but there were no accompanying exogenous developments? Benchmark crude oil prices rose from $12/bbl in late 1998 to $32/bbl in late 2000; in the same time frame, natural gas prices rose from $2.50 to $10.00/mcf, although they quickly retreated to the $4–5/mcf range. The growth rate for real GDP over this period can best be described as erratic; it rose to 5.4% in the latter half of 1998, fell slightly to 4.3% in 1999 and 3.7% in the first half of 2000, and then plunged to 0.8% in the second half. However, most of that decline reflected a drop in capital spending because of the stock market slump rather than higher energy prices. In this author's opinion, the fluctuations in oil prices affected the growth rate by less than 1%.

In terms of planning ahead, when oil prices rise substantially, the effects on the core rate of inflation, and on the overall real growth rate, are likely to be subdued, whether the cause of higher oil prices is simply demand and supply, anticipation of a possible armed conflagration in the Middle East, or a surprise disruption of supplies due to a sneak attack or an embargo. Having said that, it obviously pays for energy-sensitive firms to buy ahead when prices are unusually low and reduce purchases when prices are unusually high.

8.6   Lags in determining wages and prices

Up to this point we have essentially presented a static analysis. The inflation rate rises when unit labor costs rise, malign supply shocks occur, overly accommodative monetary policy boosts inflationary expectations, or when productivity growth declines. When these factors move in the other direction, inflation declines. So far, very little has been said about the lag structure inherent in the determination of inflation. No definitive answers are available; even if the long-run factors that affect inflation can be positively identified, the length of lag is difficult to measure and remains variable. Several key points are now considered.

1. When inflation accelerates, the initial impetus usually stems from higher unit labor costs unless a supply shock occurs. Prices usually adjust quickly. If the monetary authorities do not act to defuse the rise in inflationary expectations, wages adjust to the increase in prices with a lag of about one year.
2. Inflationary expectations often take several years to adjust, so a change in monetary policy may not have the desired impact on inflation until it becomes credible.

3. Even if monetary policy is credible, a malign supply shock will initially boost the inflation rate if wages and prices are sticky.

We have shown throughout this chapter that if monetary policy remains credible, inflation is unlikely to rise significantly even when the economy reaches full employment, assuming no malign supply shock. However, a major supply shock that came as a surprise – i.e., if there was no advance opportunity to hedge against the price increase – would boost core inflation for a while even if optimal monetary policy were activated.

Assume another substantial supply shock boosts prices; in this case the shock is caused by some military action rather than the ebb and flow of energy prices that can be offset by hedging. Regardless of whether or not monetary policy has been credible, energy prices, and the prices of energy-intensive goods and services (such as transportation) will immediately rise. There will undoubtedly be a ripple effect throughout the economy. Because wages are based on lagged prices, wage gains are likely to accelerate the following year. Either that will boost inflation further, or it will raise the unemployment rate, because at a higher real wage less labor will be demanded.

Note that if prices and wages were to adjust immediately to monetary policy, inflation need not rise even in the case of a supply shock: higher oil prices (in this example) could be offset by lower prices of other goods and services. If the amount of money people had to spend remained the same, an increase in the amount spent for energy would result in a decline in spending for other goods and services. If prices and wages were completely flexible downward, they would decline enough that the quantity purchased of other goods and services would not change.

However, that is not what happens. Prices of other goods and services do not immediately decline; they are more likely to rise, especially if they are energy-intensive. As a result, demand declines and unemployment rises for a while. Thus even if Fed policy has been credible, workers will demand an increase in their paychecks equal to the rise in inflation caused by higher commodity prices. That means the inflation rate must start to decrease before employees are convinced the value of their paychecks will not erode further. Because of these lags, inflation will rise even in well-managed economies when malign supply shocks occur.

We emphasize that when a major supply shock does occur, the money does not vanish into thin air; it is redistributed from one group of people to another. Even if the group benefiting from this distribution is outside the US, the fact that the world is on a de facto dollar standard means that most of that money will either be spent on US exports of goods and services, or will be deposited in dollar-denominated financial instruments. As a result, the decline in aggregate demand from this supply shock is far overstated simply by looking at the figures for real consumption and disposable income. That was probably the major mistake made by both Federal Reserve and private sector economists in 1973. After that, the Fed recognized that because of sticky prices and wages, inflation is likely to increase over the next year or two even if demand has slackened, so more emphasis has been put on fighting inflation and less on worrying about whether the economy is about to head into recession. That is another reason why the ripple effects from energy shocks have become increasingly milder.

8.7   The beginnings and ends of hyperinflation

The importance of expectations in determining inflation can also be seen by examining the abrupt way in which hyperinflations come to a halt. Indeed, one of the lasting legacies of the incorrect Phillips curve analysis (see the appendix) was the hypothesis that just as it takes many years for inflationary spirals to develop, it takes several years for them to wind down. Thus, for example, when inflation reached a peak of 13.5% in 1980, economic forecasters generally believed the inflation rate could decline only about 1% per year. That turned out to be an extremely poor forecast. By 1982, inflation had dropped to 4% and, after a brief rise in the late 1980s, it fell below 3% during the 1990s.

The theory that inflation takes a long time to diminish should never have been admitted into evidence in the first place. Just as the conventional wisdom was claiming inflation would not decline very rapidly, Tom Sargent, one of the pioneers of the rational expectations theory, wrote a paper entitled "The Ends of Four Big Inflations."[8] Sargent analyzed the hyperinflations of Austria, Germany, Hungary, and Poland in the 1920s. While there have been several more hyperinflations in the post-WWII period, including Hungary (again), several Latin American countries, and Israel, the analysis is virtually the same in all cases. As Sargent shows, once fiscal and monetary policy were reformed, inflation stopped on a dime in all these countries. No gradual accommodation was required.

In all of these cases, hyperinflation was caused by several factors, which can be summarized as follows.

1. A massive government deficit.
2. Financing of that deficit by monetizing the deficit, which means the securities issued to pay for the government deficit were purchased by the central bank.
3. Enormous growth in the money supply.
4. Severe depreciation of the domestic currency.
5. A flight of foreign capital; domestic savings were also converted into foreign capital whenever possible.

Of the four cases analyzed by Sargent, the buildup of inflation rates to stratospheric levels was the most spectacular in Germany.[9] The wholesale price index (July 1914 = 100) had already risen to 1,440 in December 1920, 3,490 in December 1921, and 147,480 in December 1922. Yet the worst was still to come. By December 1923, the price level had risen by an astounding 85,543,802,500% to 126,160,000,000,000% (all figures are from Sargent). However, as soon as the fiscal and monetary authorities agreed to end the deficit, stopped printing money to finance that deficit, and stabilized the currency, inflation stopped immediately. There was no long lag until inflation rates returned to normal. Sargent describes the adjustment process as follows:

> The essential measures that ended hyperinflation...were first, the creation of an independent central bank that was legally committed to refuse the government's demand for additional unsecured credit and, second, a simultaneous alteration in the fiscal policy regime.... Once it became widely understood that the government would not rely on the central bank for its finances, the inflation terminated and the exchanges stabilized...it was not simply the increasing quantity of central bank notes that caused the hyperinflation, since in each case the note circulation continued to grow rapidly after the exchange rate and price level had been stabilized. Rather, it was the growth of fiat currency which was unbacked, or backed only by government bills, which there never was a prospect to retire through taxation.... Earlier attempts to stabilize the exchanges...failed precisely because they did not change the rules of the game under which fiscal policy had to be conducted.

The Sargent paper thus shows that the expectation about the future, as well as the growth in the money supply, is a critical factor in determining the rate of inflation. It also shows that the unemployment rate has nothing to do with hyperinflation, or in general, the overall rate of inflation. Inflation can be ended immediately, even if prices have been rising at millions or even billions of percent per year, if expectations about future government policy are changed.

As we have seen, the inflation rate increases at full employment when monetary policy is accommodative; it may also rise if malign supply shocks occur, the value of the currency declines, or productivity growth diminishes. Since in the past such changes have occurred in the majority of business cycles, there once was a natural tendency to say that inflation rises once the economy reaches full employment. However, as the US experience of 1995–2000 has taught us, that need not be the case.

The cases of hyperinflation show the linkage between growth in the money supply, large budget deficits, and higher inflation in its purest form. In all these cases where hyperinflation occurred, the overly rapid growth in the money supply was originally caused by a large government deficit that was funded by sales of securities to the central bank. When excessive money supply growth and deficits were brought to an end, the inflation rate returned to normal within a few months.

In recent years, many Latin American nations have discovered the "secret" to ending hyperinflation. Thus the inflation rate as measured by the CPI fell from 7,486% in 1990 to 7% in 1994 in Nicaragua; from 7,482% in 1990 to 11% in 1995 in Peru; from 3,076% in 1994 to 3% in 1999 in Brazil; and from 3,080% in 1989 to a near-invisible 0.2% in 1996 in Argentina. In all cases, the growth rate responded from the negative range – usually double-digit negative growth – to above-average increases.

CASE STUDY 8.3   200+ YEARS OF INFLATION

Figure 8.14 shows four different views of inflation from 1800 to the present; no data for the CPI are available before then, and no data for manufacturing wage rates are available before 1860. Figure 8.14(a) shows the levels of the CPI and wage rate over

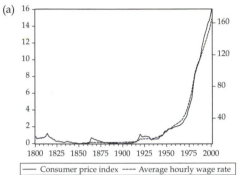

(a) CPI starting in 1800 and wage rate for production workers in manufacturing starting in 1860 (CPI is indexed to 1982-4 = 100; wage rates are dollars/hour

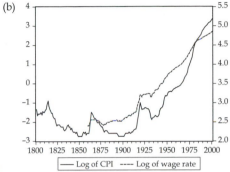

(b) Logarithms of CPI and wage rate (slope of the curves are the growth rates)

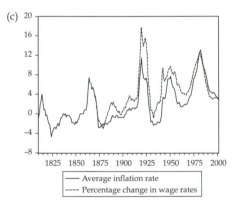

(c) Percentage changes in CPI and wage rates, ten-years averages

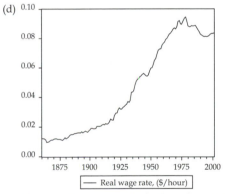

(d) The real wage rate climbed steady to 1973, but since then has tended to move lower

Figure 8.14   Four different views of inflation
Sources: Historical Statistics of the US through 1970; after that, BLS website, www.bls.gov

continued

CASE STUDY 8.3 (*continued*)

the past 200 years. The price level did not rise very much before World War II except for periods of wartime; in 1800, the level based on 1982–4 = 100 was about 17, and it had declined to 14 in 1940. Thus for the first 140 years, there was no increase in consumer prices; over the past 60+ years, the average increase has been 4.2%. Wage rates have risen even faster. In 1860, the average wage was about $0.10 per hour, compared with $15 per hour in 2001, for an average annual increase of 3.6%.

Since the data are dominated by recent observations, the more usual way to present data for long time series of this sort is by using logarithms, as shown in figure 8.14(b). That figure shows how wage rates rose substantially faster than prices for most of the period from 1860 through 1973, but then rose less rapidly.

Figure 8.14(c) shows the decade-long changes in inflation and wage rates; annual data would have been almost impossible to see for this many years. In particular, note that surges of inflation following each of the major wars were reversed in the next decade, except for the period after World War II. Also note that on a decade-long basis, the increase in inflation during the 1970s was quite a serious matter, and although it now seems to have been a false alarm, there was genuine concern that the US economy could be headed for permanently higher and escalating rates of inflation. That is why the determination of Paul Volcker to reverse that trend was so important.

Figure 8.14(d) shows the change in the real wage rate since 1860. From that date through 1973, the real wage rose almost steadily, climbing 7.5 times, or an average of 1.8% per year, very close to the long-range increase in productivity growth. Since then, it fell sharply through the rest of the 1970s and the 1980s, although it recovered slightly in the 1990s. The reasons for this are addressed in the next chapter, but to a certain extent reflect the fact that further rapid wage gains in the face of an increased determination to fight inflation would simply result in more jobs being transferred to foreign locations.

8.8 Summary of why inflation remained low in the 1990s – and what might occur in the future

We now summarize the reasons why the rate of inflation in the US declined during the late 1990s even though the unemployment rate also declined over the same period, and also offer some comments about what might transpire in the future.

Even when the unemployment rate falls below the full employment rate, inflation might not accelerate if the following conditions apply:

1. Businesses vigorously oppose wage increases in excess of productivity gains because they think the monetary authorities will not permit inflation to rise. Expectations play a major role in this decision. Businesses will fight wage increases more vigorously if they *expect* the Fed will not validate their cost increases in the form of higher prices.

2. Workers are less likely to push for large wage increases if they have good reason to believe their jobs will disappear permanently, especially to foreign locations. Also, government policy may tilt against labor in its policies and decisions. In particular, an important ruling during the Reagan Administration was that firms could hire permanent strikebreakers. Workers are also more likely to accept modest wage increases if they realize that a gain in nominal wages will not push them into a higher marginal tax bracket.

3. In industries where high labor turnover rates are common, wage increases that stabilize the workforce may increase productivity substantially and hence are not inflationary. In 1996, some long-distance trucking companies offered workers a 23% wage increase, but that was widely viewed as noninflationary because it reduced the turnover in truckdrivers and boosted productivity proportionately.

4. Increases in total compensation are more likely to be paid in the form of stock options, bonuses, and profit-sharing, so base wage rates do not rise. As a result, unit labor costs do not increase as much because the gains in compensation are directly related to higher profits or stock prices.

While supply shocks often have an impact on the inflation rate that is independent of wage rates, productivity, or the unemployment rate, one should not exaggerate their importance. The first and second energy shocks in 1973 and 1980 did indeed boost the inflation rate for virtually all countries in the world. They also reduced worldwide inflation when they fell in 1986. Since then, though, oil prices have generally been trendless, yet the overall worldwide rate of inflation has continued to decline. Figures are summarized in table 8.1 for the G-7 nations, which are the leading industrialized countries of the world.

The worldwide rate of inflation declined sharply from 1987 through 2000 even though oil prices had not exhibited a trend in either direction. Hence other factors must have diminished the inflation rate. In the 1992–7 period, only Germany posted a slightly higher inflation rate, and that was because inflationary pressures from a major political event – unification – caused politics to override what would have been the economically correct decisions by the Bundesbank. Part of the decline in inflation was clearly due to improved monetary policies. Some of it was also due to the "virtuous circle" of free trade, especially in Europe, where the European Monetary System and the preparation for a common currency encouraged more foreign competition.

The experience of the 1990s represents the first time in the US in the post-WWII period when inflation has *not* risen at full employment. This development has been due to several factors:

- Fed policy has not been perfect, but it has been credible. Instead of waiting until inflation accelerates and then trying to reverse it, the Fed now undertakes "preemptive" strikes by tightening before inflation rises at all.
- Fiscal policy has also played an important role, with the Federal budget deficit slashed from $290 in FY 1992 to a $236 billion surplus in FY 2000.

Table 8.1 Average rates of inflation (CPI)

	US	Canada	Japan	France	Germany	Italy	UK	Average
1982–6 (oil prices falling)	3.8	5.8	2.0	7.5	2.6	11.4	4.7	5.4
1987–91 (oil prices up, then down)	4.4	4.6	1.9	3.2	2.1	7.4	6.4	4.3
1992–7 (oil prices steady)	2.8	1.5	0.9	1.9	2.6	4.1	2.7	2.4
1998–2001 (oil prices down, up, down)	2.3	2.0	−0.1	1.6	1.8	2.2	2.3	1.7

Source: BLS website, www.bls.gov

- Productivity growth accelerated rather than declined from 1995 to 2000. This is due in part to the revolution in microcomputers and telecommunications, which makes more information available and keeps prices from rising because of insufficient knowledge of market prices. The stock market boom in high-tech stocks also contributed to a massive increase in capital spending.
- A credible monetary policy has encouraged businesses to seek more innovative solutions for cutting costs rather than raising prices, and remain "lean and mean" throughout the cycle, not permitting excess costs to build up that will have to be rescinded later.
- Outside the US, more disciplined fiscal policy is now fashionable, including large-scale privatization and balanced budgets in countries where inflation had previously run rampant.
- The "virtuous circle" has reduced inflation in key countries, causing other countries to keep inflation low so their goods are not priced out of world markets. That is particularly true in Europe, where the formation of a common currency means weaker countries can no longer use competitive devaluations to offset to higher domestic inflation.
- More jobs are leaving the US for countries where labor costs are only 10% of US levels, reducing import prices and stifling gains in wage rates.

Just as many generals make the mistake of fighting the last war, many economists make the mistake of predicting the last business cycle. Thus just because inflation did not rise in the late 1990s does not insure that will happen again during the next business cycle.

Yet having said that, the correlation between full employment and higher inflation has been far overstated. Since the end of World War II, there have been six times that the rate of inflation has accelerated, which we define as an increase in the core rate of at least 1% in any given year. The years of acceleration – when this occurred for more than one year, the first year is given – were 1946, 1951, 1956, 1966, 1973, and 1979. The first period followed the end of wage and price controls of World War II. The second was caused by a scramble for goods because of expected shortages at the beginning of the Korean War. The third followed the termination of price controls during the Korean War, which had been instituted after the aforementioned surge in inflation. The fourth was the expansion of the Vietnam War. The fifth and sixth were the first two energy crises, although to a certain extent the rise of inflation in the late 1970s also reflected the concern that the government would reimpose price controls, and firms that had not already raised their prices would be unable to do so.

It thus turns out that all the bursts of inflation in the post-WWII period in the US economy were due to wartime conditions, the surge in prices after controls were ended, or major energy shocks. Absent these shocks, inflation is likely to remain low and stable even at business cycle peaks.

MANAGER'S BRIEFCASE: PLANNING AHEAD FOR POSSIBLE CHANGES IN INFLATION

With inflation averaging only slightly more than 2% per year since 1995, concerns about rising inflation may appear to take a distant back seat to concerns about boosting sales and reducing costs. Nonetheless, some guidelines may be helpful in adjusting to "unexpected" developments in the future.

1. The inflation rate generally lags the change in real economic activity by about one year. That means the rate of inflation often peaks during the early stages of recession, and troughs during the early stages of recovery. We mention this because economists and politicians often used to talk about "rising unemployment and rising inflation" at the same time, as if that were a wholesale indictment of how the economic system works. However, any continuing increase in inflation during an economic downturn reflects the lagged impact of wage rates, and does not continue for much longer. Recessionary conditions will invariably be followed by lower inflation.

2. At least historically, inflation in the US has never risen significantly before the economy has returned to full employment. That does not mean, of course, that it must necessarily accelerate when full employment is reached, as we saw in the 1990s. However, this experience does suggest that concerns about rising inflation during periods of substantial unemployment should be put near the bottom of the list.

3. Along the same lines, wage increases should be kept in line with productivity gains during periods of substantial unemployment, because firms will not be able to pass along any increase in labor costs. If labor demands are unrealistic, an increasing proportion of firms have found that their only viable choice is to move to foreign locations.

4. Under certain circumstances, the Fed is likely to boost short-term interest rates even if inflation has not yet risen. That would probably happen when the Fed funds rate has previously been below equilibrium, defined as the average growth rate in nominal GDP, and is almost sure to happen if the funds rate has been below the core rate of inflation. As a result, the cost of financing may rise sharply even if inflation remains low and stable.

5. The biggest question is likely to be: what happens to the inflation rate when the economy does return to full employment? In this author's opinion, if the Fed has moved the funds rate to or above the growth rate in nominal GDP, the core inflation rate will not rise much if at all. If, however, the Fed has chosen to keep the funds rate below its equilibrium value, higher inflation is likely to occur.

KEY TERMS AND CONCEPTS

Core Inflation Rate

Hyperinflation

Phillips Curve

Productivity (output/employee-hour)

Supply Shocks

Unit Labor Costs

SUMMARY

- In the long run, inflation is a monetary phenomenon.
- In the short run, prices are marked up by a constant proportion over unit labor costs, adjusted for supply shocks. The markup factor is not correlated with the rate of capacity utilization.
- Wage rates depend on inflationary expectations, which are related to the credibility of monetary policy, the deficit ratio and how it is financed, government regulation, the degree of foreign competition, and the value of the currency.
- Other factors that influence wage rates include the level of average and marginal tax rates, the ratio of the minimum to the average wage, the relative strength of labor laws and unions, and the composition of the total compensation package.
- There is no negative correlation between inflation and unemployment. Bigger increases in the real wage rate need not boost inflation if (a) productivity growth rises, (b) benign supply shocks lower exogenous prices, or (c) a decline in inflationary expectations reduces the willingness of employers to grant wage increases that exceed productivity growth.
- Supply shocks can be either malign or benign. A malign shock will raise inflation temporarily if prices and wages are sticky, even if monetary policy is optimal. However, if the monetary authorities mistakenly accommodate the higher inflation stemming from a supply shock, the rise in inflation is likely to continue indefinitely.

- In the past, productivity growth in the US had always declined once the economy reached full employment, but because of credible monetary policy and stable inflationary expectations, and the unusually robust investment boom, that did not happen in the late 1990s.
- While the monetary authorities can always control inflation, their job is much simpler if other determinants of inflation are favorable. In particular, government interference in product and factor markets will boost inflation unless offset by the central bank. If monetary policy tightens, the result will be reduced output and higher inflation.
- To the extent that competition is enhanced by foreign markets, a commitment to free trade will reduce the inflation rate – providing that at the same time, the monetary authorities are committed to maintaining the value of the currency near its equilibrium value.
- During the latter half of the 1990s, the rate of inflation and the rate of unemployment declined simultaneously in the US. The principal reasons were credible monetary policy, stable inflationary expectations – which were due in part to the budget surplus – faster growth in productivity, a stronger dollar and more intense foreign competition and a massive increase in capital spending fueled by the unprecedented gains in high-tech stock prices.

- The abrupt halt to hyperinflations reinforces the importance of expectations in determining the rate of inflation. Once credible monetary and fiscal policy had been established, and expectations had changed, inflation returned to normal levels within a short period of time.

QUESTIONS AND PROBLEMS

1. Suppose you are CEO of a manufacturing company, and oil prices suddenly double, which boosts the inflation rate by 5%. While your principal job is to keep quarterly earnings rising, you are concerned that a recession might occur, and failing to maintain market share could be very costly in the longer run. Explain what steps you would take under the assumptions that:
   (A) Both wages and prices are flexible.
   (B) Prices can change quickly, but wages will respond only with a substantial lag.
   (C) Both prices and wages are sticky.
2. The inflation rate in Argentina fell from over 3,000% in 1989 to 25% in 1992 and virtually zero in 1998.
   (A) What do you think happened to the money supply growth over the same time?
   (B) What do you think happened to the real growth rate over the same time?
   (C) Explain how the Argentinean government was able to reduce inflation so quickly and keep it low.
   (D) In mid-1999, the Argentinean unemployment rate was about 15%. Explain why that figure had many foreign investors worried that high inflation would soon reoccur in Argentina. (After all, according to the Phillips curve, high unemployment means low inflation.)
3. From time to time, including but not limited to the 1971–3 experience in the US, wage and price controls have been imposed to reduce inflation. Yet when these controls were eventually lifted, the price index quickly rose to a level that was even higher than would have been the case without controls. Explain why that happened. (Hint: what happens to productivity?)
4. The annual data for the US economy in the 1960s are given below.

	1960	1961	1962	1963	1964	1965	1966	1967	1968	1969
Inflation	1.7	1.0	1.0	1.3	1.3	1.6	2.9	3.1	4.2	5.5
Unemployment	5.5	6.7	5.5	5.7	5.2	4.5	3.8	3.8	3.6	3.5

   (A) Show these data graphically.
   (B) From 1966 through 1969, the unemployment rate was virtually unchanged, yet the inflation rate rose almost 3%. Why did it rise that much?

(C) In 1974, the unemployment rate was 5.6%. What would have been the projected inflation rate using the Phillips curve based on these data alone? The actual inflation rate that year was 11.0%. What factors accounted for the additional inflation?

(D) The inflation rate fell from 12.5% in 1980 to 3.8% in 1982 (on a monthly average basis) even though the unemployment rate rose "only" 2.6% during those two years. What other factors caused the inflation rate to decline so quickly?

5. In 1998, the rate of inflation in the US economy fell from 2.3% to 1.6% at the same time that the unemployment rate fell from 4.9% to 4.5%. What were the principal factors that caused the inflation rate to decline in 1998?

6. During periods of hyperinflation, real growth invariably declines and the unemployment rate rises sharply. Explain the mechanism by which this occurs.

7. In 1980, the inflation rate in Italy was 21% and the unemployment rate was 4.4%. By 1998, the inflation rate in Italy had declined to 2% and the unemployment rate had risen to 12.3%.

(A) What were the principal factors that caused the inflation rate to fall so much?

(B) What were the principal factors that caused the unemployment rate to rise so much?

(C) Explain whether or not this is an example of the Phillips curve tradeoff at work.

8. During the early 1960s, wage and price "guidelines" were in place that were supposed to limit the gains in wages to the increase in productivity, hence holding prices almost constant. Since the CPI rose at an average rate of only 1.1% from 1961 through 1964, the program was considered a big success by Kennedy Administration economists.

(A) What were the real reasons inflation was so low in the early 1960s?

(B) The guidelines remained in place under Johnson, but the rate of inflation gradually rose to almost 6% (see problem 4). What factors rendered the guidelines ineffective?

9. Following the first energy shock in 1973, when oil prices rose $10/bbl, the rate of inflation averaged 8% for the next five years. Following the second energy shock in 1979, when oil prices rose more than $20/bbl, the rate of inflation averaged $6\frac{1}{2}$% per year for the following five years. Following the third energy shock in 1990, when oil prices rose $20/bbl, the rate of inflation averaged only 2.8% per year for the next five years. Explain why the rate of inflation reacted so differently to similar changes in oil prices.

10. In Europe, the UK is the only country where there has been a consistent tradeoff between inflation and unemployment. What factors caused this tradeoff to occur in Britain but not in Continental Europe?

Appendix: historical explanations of inflation: the rise and fall of the Phillips curve

Before World War II, inflation in major industrialized countries was perceived as being either a temporary problem, or one arising from exogenous shocks affecting the economy, such as a war or revolution. For example, inflation surged during the Napoleonic Wars in Europe, during the Revolutionary and Civil Wars in the US, and during World War I in both the US and Europe. However, these bursts of inflation were quickly reversed once the shock had passed; secular inflation was not considered a recurring problem for well-managed economies. Indeed, in spite of rapid increases in prices during wartime, the wholesale price index for the US was lower in 1940 than it had been in 1790. Also, the CPI fell by almost 50% between 1865 and 1900. Admittedly it had been temporarily boosted during the Civil War, but even from 1875 through 1900 it fell at an average of about 1% per year. The gold standard and cheap immigrant labor combined to reduce prices.

During the Great Depression of the 1930s, prices did rise somewhat, but most of the attention was understandably focused on the unacceptably high rate of unemployment, and inflation was almost ignored. In the aftermath of the double-digit inflation that occurred directly after World War II – when the inflation rate rose as high as 18% in 1946 – most economists quickly changed their emphasis, and standard economics texts of the time focused on the difference between "demand-pull" and "cost-push" inflation. Demand-pull inflation, it was said, occurred when the economy was at full employment and full capacity – "too many dollars chasing too few goods." Cost-push inflation, on the other hand, allegedly occurred when wage rates rose faster than productivity even during times of relatively high unemployment.

With the onset of what economists dubbed "stagflation" in the early 1970s – high and rising inflation simultaneously with high and rising unemployment – this artificial distinction collapsed. It was replaced in part by the introduction of rational expectations, and in part by a dichotomy between the short-run and long-run determinants of inflation.

In the short run, it was argued, inflation did tend to rise near full employment and full capacity, but in the long run, the growth rate of the economy had no impact on the rate of inflation, which was entirely a monetary phenomenon. That would explain, for example, why countries such as Germany and Japan had little inflation in the decades following World War II, while countries such as Brazil and Argentina regularly succumbed to triple-digit inflation. The inflation rate in Italy was habitually in the double-digit rate; but when it chose to join the European Union, it suddenly managed to put its monetary and fiscal policies in order, and its inflation rate quickly dropped to about 3%.

In the short run, changes in inflation are determined by changes in wage rates, productivity, and exogenous shocks, while in the long run, changes are determined by monetary policy. When the economy approaches full employment, real wage rates may rise at a somewhat faster level, but that need not boost the rate of inflation if those gains are matched by increases in productivity. That is essentially what happened in the US economy in the 1990s. Hence we can say that any short-run tradeoff between wage rates and inflation, besides being adjusted for changing expectations, also has to be adjusted for changes in productivity. Indeed, there is a strong negative correlation between the rate of inflation and productivity growth in both the short and long run.

The theories of inflation that started to circulate in the 1970s took a major step forward by assigning an important role to expectations. If labor and management think inflation will remain stable, they are more likely to limit wage hikes to productivity gains. On the other hand, if they believe higher prices can be validated in the marketplace, wages will rise much faster than productivity, and inflation will accelerate. That still means we have to identify empirically those situations where labor and management believe prices will be stable, and when they expect them to increase.

The monetary authorities are much more likely to succeed at controlling inflation if a variety of other factors – fiscal policy, trade policy, competitive structure, value of the currency, productivity growth, and technological innovation – cooperate in keeping inflation low. If these factors are not operating properly, the central bank can still reduce inflation, but usually at the cost of higher unemployment.

Brazil learned this lesson in early 1999. After virtually conquering inflation – it had fallen to a 2% rate in 1998 – the huge budget deficit, plus some ill-timed political maneuvers, caused a crisis of confidence and forced the Brazilian government to let the real float to its new equilibrium level, resulting in an initial devaluation of about 40%. The monetary authorities did their best to offset an inflationary spiral, temporarily raising short-term interest rates as high as 45%, but inflation still spiked up to 25% before declining again. After many years of price stability when the Argentine peso was tied to the dollar, prices rose very rapidly in that country when the peso was devalued by more than 50% in early 2002.

Regardless of the stance of monetary policy, the inflation rate and changes in unit labor costs invariably move together. That is true whether or not the economy is close to full employment, whether supply shocks are present or absent, and whether monetary policy is tight or easy. Prices and wages are jointly determined by labor and management. If monetary policy accommodates higher wages and prices, they are likely to rise as the economy approaches full employment and full capacity; if it does not, unit labor costs and prices will show little or no gain even under those circumstances. That is because in a free market economy, firms will produce up to the point where the real wage is equal to the marginal product of labor, so if labor costs rise, prices will rise proportionately. If labor costs do not rise, aggregate prices will not increase either.

In 1958, British economist A. W. Phillips published an article documenting the empirical tradeoff between changes in wage rate and unemployment for the US and the UK since 1891.[10] This tradeoff soon became known as the Phillips curve, even though the same empirical relationship had been noted by Irving Fisher in

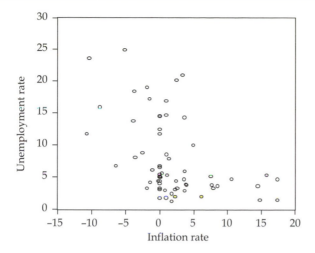

Figure 8.15   There is a slight nonlinear relationship between the unemployment rate and the inflation rate for the period from 1890 through 1955

1926. The spread of dates indicates that such a relationship had existed for many decades. The original Phillips curve article related changes in wage rates to the unemployment rate, but because prices are generally marked up over wages by some constant percentage, the argument quickly shifted to the tradeoff between inflation and unemployment.

Even at the time, there should have been some question about this relationship, because closer examination would have shown that virtually all of the statistical correlation was due to very high rates of inflation and very low rates of unemployment during and immediately following World War I and World War II. If these years are excluded, there is no significant correlation between these two variables, as shown in figure 8.15. Nonetheless, in the decade following the publication of that article, the US experience seemed to describe this relationship almost exactly, as shown in figure 8.16, which shows a strong nonlinear correlation between these two variables during the 1960s. As a result of these data, it was widely believed at the time that the tradeoff was about 1 : 1. A 1% increase in unemployment would reduce inflation by 1%; conversely, if policymakers were willing to boost the inflation rate by 1%, the unemployment rate would fall by 1%.

This correlation emboldened many economists to expand on this concept. In 1970, two future Nobel laureates, Paul Samuelson and Robert Solow, published an article in the *American Economic Review* indicating that the US government faced a "menu of choices" between the rate of inflation and the rate of unemployment. Samuelson also emphasized this tradeoff in some of his *Newsweek* columns of the time, thus (presumably) reaching a wider audience. Later, Samuelson downplayed the importance of his contributions, suggesting that his comments were little more than a recycling of information that had appeared in the "influential" 1969 Economic Report of the President.

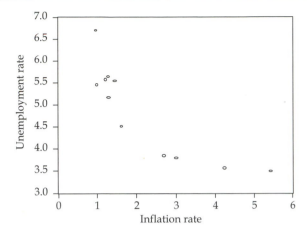

Figure 8.16 The unemployment–inflation relationship seems to fit almost perfectly for the period from 1959 through 1969

The point of these comments is not to criticize the contributions or forecasts of Samuelson, but he was arguably the most influential economist of his time, and his views carried substantial weight, especially in the policy debates in Washington. The vast majority of economists at the time really did believe that if inflation was too high, fiscal and monetary policy should be used to reduce that rate of inflation, albeit at the cost of slightly higher unemployment. Conversely, if the unemployment rate was too high, fiscal and monetary policy should be used to boost aggregate demand, albeit at the cost of slightly higher inflation. It was, economists claimed, the duty and responsibility of the government to determine the preferred point along the Phillips curve.

Not all economists agreed with Samuelson, and in any case the Phillips curve soon disintegrated. The credit goes to Milton Friedman for identifying this development *ahead of its actual demise*. In one of the most widely read and quoted articles in economics, Friedman stated, in his Presidential Address to the American Economic Association in 1967, that:

> Phillips' analysis of the relation between unemployment and wage change is deservedly celebrated as an important and original contribution. But, unfortunately, it contains a basic defect – the failure to distinguish between *nominal* wages and *real* wages.... Implicitly, Phillips wrote his article for a world in which everyone anticipated that nominal prices would be stable and in which anticipation remained unshaken and immutable whatever happened to actual prices and wages.... There is always a temporary trade-off between inflation and unemployment; there is no permanent trade-off.... A rising rate of inflation may reduce unemployment, a high rate will not.[11]

Friedman thus accurately predicted the demise of the Phillips curve. Edmund Phelps also reached the same conclusion at about the same time, although his

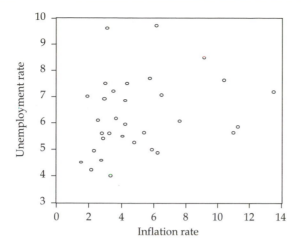

Figure 8.17   The unemployment–inflation relationship completely falls apart starting in 1970 (these data are for 1970 through 2001)

statements were more formal and mathematical and hence are not as widely quoted.[12]

The collapse of the Phillips curve starting in 1970 is shown in figure 8.17. During the next decade, the US suffered rising unemployment and rising inflation at the same time. The rate of inflation was just as likely to worsen when the unemployment rate was increasing as when it was falling. Suddenly, fine-tuning the economy no longer worked.

Economists now generally agree that the Phillips curve relationship – a negative relationship between inflation and unemployment – cannot exist if inflationary expectations are not stable. For if they are rising, workers will demand bigger wage increases to keep pace not only with the higher inflation that has already occurred, but also the higher inflation that is expected. In such circumstances, the monetary authorities will tighten and real growth will eventually diminish, hence diminishing the demand for labor. Even if *real* wage rates were to decline because of higher unemployment, *nominal* wage rates will continue to increase because workers are demanding bigger wage hikes.

When demand declines, firms find they cannot raise their prices as rapidly, but wage rates continue to accelerate for a while because they are based on expected gains in inflation. That means the real wage increases, and hence unemployment rises. Hence for a brief period, the economy suffers *rising inflation and rising unemployment at the same time.*

Even if the Fed initially tried to reduce unemployment by boosting money supply growth, unemployment would eventually rise just as much – or perhaps even more – than if it had initially tightened. As a result, there is no long-run relationship between the inflation rate and the unemployment rate. Instead, in the long run, the rate of inflation remains highly correlated with the growth in the money supply and other measures of monetary policy.

The Friedman-Phelps argument was particularly impressive because it accurately predicted the demise of the Phillips curve for the right reasons. Employees began to realize that expansionary fiscal and monetary policies were a scam in the sense that even if employment rose in the short run, higher inflation diminished the value of their paychecks. Thus workers started to bargain much more aggressively for higher wage rates. Their bargaining demands were then based on what they *expected* the rate of inflation to be in the future, not just what it had been in the past.

As inflation increased, and expectations of higher inflation became widespread, wage earners started demanding, and were able to obtain, large wage increases even when the unemployment rate remained high. As inflationary expectations rose, the entire Phillips curve shifted up. Overly easy monetary policy was a major contributor to this upward shift in inflationary expectations.

It turns out that the so-called Phillips curve tradeoff never existed for most other countries. In particular, the inflation rate in Germany during the 1960s was less than 3% at a time when the unemployment rate averaged less than 1%, and the inflation rate in Japan was 2% during the 1980s when the unemployment rate averaged only $2\frac{1}{2}$%. Furthermore, there is little or no evidence of a Phillips curve for Canada, France, the Netherlands, Belgium, or Sweden.[13] Thus even in the decade of the 1960s, when the Phillips curve received its widest acceptance, it applied to only two countries – the US and UK.

Economists who still supported the concept of the Phillips curve refashioned it after the broadside attack by the rational expectations economists, claiming that some negative relationship between inflation and the unemployment rate still exists if one also takes into account expected inflation and exogenous supply shocks, notably in energy prices. However, during the 1990s, the unemployment rate steadily declined and eventually dipped below 4% and inflationary expectations did not change, yet the inflation rate did not rise at all. That would seem to drive the final nail into the coffin of this relationship, but it did not. Which raises the question: if the Phillips curve really did collapse, why is it still such a popular staple of most macroeconomics textbooks?

During periods of low unemployment – including but not limited to the late 1990s – total compensation per worker – including overtime payments, bonuses, profit-sharing, and stock options – does rise at a faster rate. Conversely, during recessions, total compensation rises at a slower rate, and in many cases actually declines. This reflects the realities of labor markets, and in that sense, the *original* Phillips curve formulation, which related wage rates to unemployment, had some economic and statistical merit.

Yet if the rate of inflation follows unit labor costs closely, and wage rates are the major component of labor costs, why was there no rise in core inflation in the late 1990s, and no decline in core inflation in the early 2000s?

One should always be hesitant about generalizing based on what is essentially one observation, but it seems likely that two major changes occurred in the most recent business cycle. First, productivity growth accelerated near full employment instead of declining. Second, most of the gains in total compensation were tied to profitability, which in turn was tied to faster productivity growth. In some cases, of course, firms paid huge bonuses and employees received huge benefits from stock options based on fraudulent accounting techniques, but that one factor itself probably did not cause a significant change in the underlying relationship between wage rates and unemployment.

Why bother with this extended exposition of the Phillips curve if it is just a statistical artifact? The fact that this material has been relegated to the appendix suggests it is not of overriding importance. Nonetheless, there are a few lessons to be learned from this relationship, other than the ubiquitous one that economists, like everyone else, make mistakes.

First, it shows the extent to which misguided attempts to fine tune the economy – turning this knob to boost growth, that knob to reduce inflation – are counterproductive. As a result, those methods are not tried any more.

Second, it unintentionally highlights the extent to which interference with market mechanisms unintentionally *increases* the long-run rate of inflation. Let's review the period when the empirical Phillips curve appeared to be most accurate, which is the 1950s and 1960s. After World War II, prices skyrocketed because they had been artificially depressed by wage and price controls not only during the war but, more seriously, after hostilities had ended. In particular, the huge increase in farm prices in 1946 occurred because farmers withheld their produce from markets until price controls were belatedly lifted. During the Korean War, wage and price controls were in effect; when they ended, various distortions had been built into the economy for both wages and prices. These caused higher inflation during the 1956–7 period.

After two recessions in three years that had been preceded by tight monetary policies, the economic advisors of President Kennedy thought that inflation could be controlled by instituting wage/price "guidelines," which essentially stated that since productivity growth was about 3% per year, if wages rose 3% per year, prices would not rise at all. These guidelines also introduced various distortions that were not apparent until the economy hit full employment, when they disintegrated. We thus see in essence that attempts to control wages and prices are successful during periods when they aren't needed; when they are needed, they fall apart. In the long run, such schemes end up boosting inflation higher than would otherwise be the case.

In summary, higher inflation does not occur because too many people want to work. Nobel laureate Robert Mundell, the intellectual father of supply-side economics, stated this same conclusion more elegantly in 1971, when he wrote, "The economy of the unemployed . . . has a GNP potential of about twice the GNP of, say, Belgium . . . . It is absurd to argue that unemployment on such a scale or duration is socially necessary . . . . But if it were indeed true that employing, say, two-thirds or three-quarters of the unemployed would cause inflation – and I deny that any evidence for it has been advanced – it would be a shocking indictment of the system itself."[14]

There never was a tradeoff between unemployment and inflation – except during periods when market forces were not permitted to work, namely periods of war, and during times when wage and price guidelines were imposed and later forsaken. Thus unless these conditions reappear, if monetary policy continues to be aimed at fighting inflation and the budget remains close to balance at full employment, it is likely that in the absence of major supply shocks, inflation will remain at low, stable levels indefinitely.

Notes

1. The 22 countries are the G-7 nations – US, UK, Germany, France, Italy, Japan, and Canada – plus Turkey, Israel, India, Indonesia, Korea, Singapore, Philippines, Congo, South Africa, Kenya, Morocco, and Argentina, Chile, Mexico, and Peru. They were chosen to represent a wide variety of inflation rates, and taken from a list of countries with complete data for the 1969–94 period.
2. There may appear to be some correlation to the unaided eye; however, those years are offset by other years when the two series move in different directions. A simple correlation between these two series yields an adjusted R-square of only 0.01, and the t-statistic on the capacity utilization rate is -1.3, indicating a nonsignificant *negative* correlation between these two variables.
3. Some of the woes of the airlines were caused by the sharp cutback in travel after 9/11. In October 2002, airline executives said that of the $8 billion loss over the previous year, about half was due to exogenous developments beyond their control and about half was due to erroneous management decisions, including boosting business class fares too much.
4. Published productivity statistics for the period of wage and price controls and guidelines show above-average gains, but that almost certainly reflected the fact that firms overstated output and understated price increases in order to conform with the guidelines. For as soon as they were lifted, reported productivity fell by record amounts. This fact was first pointed out by Edward Wolff.
5. In part IV of the book we will see that an increase in investment and a decline in domestic saving tend to boost the value of the currency, ceteris paribus, hence attracting more foreign capital.
6. This may appear to be an arcane statistical result little suited to a general macro textbook. However, the issue of whether inflation will invariably rise as the economy approaches full employment remains a central and contentious issue in macroeconomics. To the extent that some earlier empirical studies produced flawed results based on a misinterpretation of these wage data, a brief comment seems appropriate.
7. A graph relating the volume of gasoline used by consumers to real GDP would show virtually the identical relationship and is not duplicated here.
8. In *Inflation: Causes and Effects*, edited by Robert E. Hall (NBER, 1982).
9. The post-WWII inflation in Hungary was even greater.
10. A. W. Phillips, "The Relationship between Unemployment and the Rate of Change of Money Wages in the United Kingdom, 1891–1957," *Economica*, vol. 25, 1958.

11. Milton Friedman, "The Role of Monetary Policy," *American Economic Review*, March 1968, pp. 8–11.

12. "Money Wage Dynamics and Labor Market Equilibrium," in Edmund Phelps, ed., *Microeconomic Foundations of Employment and Inflation Theory* (W. W. Norton, 1970), pp. 124–66.

13. For further information, see M. K. Evans, "International Comparisons of Phillips Curves" in *The Truth About Supply-Side Economics* (Harper & Row, 1981). The point here is that the lack of Phillips curves in other countries was already well documented long before the recent decline in inflation at full employment in the US during the late 1990s.

14. Robert A. Mundell, "The Dollar and the Policy Mix: 1971," *Essays in International Finance*, International Finance Section, Princeton University #85, May 1971.

chapter nine
Why high unemployment persists

Introduction

During the 1980s and the 1990s, most countries in the world learned how to conquer the problem of high inflation. The inflation rate declined to about 2% not only in the US, but in western Europe as well. The hyperinflation that plagued Latin America for most of the twentieth century also disappeared.

However, the US was virtually the only major country to solve the problem of high unemployment in the 1990s. The unemployment rate remained in double digits in much of Europe and Latin America, and rose steadily in Japan and southeast Asian countries. Hence, at least in the 1990s, the problem of high unemployment turned out to be more intractable than high inflation. Why did the unemployment rate rise – and remain so high?

To answer this question, start with the growth rate. Countries with rapid growth rates invariably have low unemployment, while countries with sluggish growth rates invariably have high unemployment. The analysis developed in part II might suggest the growth rate could be boosted by using stimulatory fiscal and monetary policies. However, attempts to boost the growth rate with these measures have failed in western Europe, Latin America, and Asia.

During the Great Depression of the 1930s, many countries suffered double-digit unemployment rates for the entire decade. At that time, the concept of stimulating the economy through large government budget deficits was not well understood. Yet during the 1990s, a wide variety of countries, including but not limited to France, Italy, Spain, Argentina, Finland, and India, had double-digit unemployment throughout the decade. In most cases, these countries had large deficits and a rapidly growing money supply.

Hence stimulatory fiscal and monetary policies are not always sufficient to boost aggregate demand and reduce unemployment. Indeed, the US returned to full employment in the 1990s by instituting contractionary fiscal measures: raising tax rates and reducing real per capita government spending. That in turn reduced interest rates and boosted expectations, raising the growth rate. In contrast, many other areas of the world are saddled with structural imbalances, especially too little capital formation, which retards the growth rate enough that even stimulatory fiscal and monetary policies cannot return those economies to full employment. Stimulatory government policies are likely to boost employment only if they raise investment, capital stock, and the standard of living, rather than simply boosting consumption.

In a free market society, firms hire labor until the wage rate equals the marginal product of labor, which means an increase in the real wage rate would reduce the demand for labor, ceteris paribus. Thus interference with market mechanisms that boost the real wage rate above its equilibrium value will also raise the rate of unemployment. Sometimes these labor market imperfections originate in the private sector, and sometimes in the public sector. However, the argument is not symmetrical: increases that boost the wage rate to its equilibrium level if it had previously been below equilibrium do not reduce employment.

The supply of labor may be artificially augmented if the government offers overly generous benefits for not working. That may encourage some people who have no intention of finding a job to apply for unemployment benefits. It may also entice other people to hold out for the "right" job instead of accepting alternative employment at a lower real wage rate or inferior working conditions. In addition, harsh penalties that employers must pay for firing workers will reduce the number of people that are hired in the first place.

To a certain extent, high unemployment exists because of all these factors: insufficient aggregate demand and capital formation, above-equilibrium real wage rates, and interference with the supply of labor. It is quite possible that the latter two factors would cause the unemployment rate to remain high for an extended period of time even if optimal fiscal and monetary policies were followed. However, even if labor markets are in equilibrium and the government does not distort the supply of labor, high unemployment will generally persist indefinitely if the growth rate of the economy, and the rate of increase in capital formation, remains too low. Most of the time, high unemployment starts because real GDP is not growing fast enough to create enough jobs for all who want to work. It then persists in situations where firms are reluctant to hire workers for a variety of reasons associated with labor market imperfections – as discussed in this chapter – so the expansionary impacts of stimulatory fiscal and monetary policy are blunted, and the unemployment rate remains high indefinitely. The combination of these two factors thus explains why high unemployment persists.

9.1 The basic labor market model

In equilibrium, the marginal product of labor is equal to the real wage rate. If firms are operating on the constant part of their cost curves, then the marginal product of labor is equal to the average product of labor. Symbolically, this can be written as $w/p = \alpha(Y/N)$, where w/p is the real wage rate, Y is real output (GDP), N is the

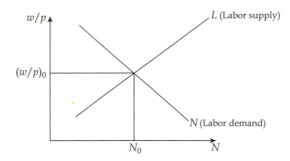

Figure 9.1   Labor market demand and supply

demand for labor, and α is the share of GDP received by labor. Graphically, this is represented as a downward sloping demand curve for labor, with w/p on the vertical axis, N on the horizontal axis, and Y an exogenous variable. An increase in Y will cause an outward shift in the demand for labor curve; a decrease in Y will cause an inward shift in the curve.

The labor supply curve is upward sloping relative to the real wage. The higher the real wage, the more people will want to work. However, the supply of labor is quite inelastic. To a large extent, the decision of whether to work is based on sociological and demographic factors, rather than the real wage offered. For example, the steady increase in the labor force participation rate for women in the US starting in 1964 occurred because of a change in the mores of society, not because the real wage suddenly rose. Additionally, the so-called "backward-bending" supply curve states that as real wages rise, some people would use their extra earnings to purchase more leisure, a superior good. Many people would not work as hard if they had an annual income of $1 million. The principal exogenous factor affecting the labor supply curve is government policy on unemployment benefits. The more generous the benefits, the further the labor supply curve will shift out.

The labor demand and supply curves are shown in figure 9.1. N represents labor demand, while L represents labor supply. In equilibrium these are equal at real wage $(w/p)_0$. Now suppose there is an exogenous decline in the demand for labor, which could be due to a change in fiscal or monetary policy, international disturbances, or a change in consumer or business sentiment. This change would cause the N curve to shift in from N_0 to N_1. The four changes that could occur are illustrated in figure 9.2.

1. The real wage could decline from $(w/p)_0$ to $(w/p)_1$, so labor markets would remain in equilibrium.
2. Stimulatory fiscal or monetary policy could be used to shift the demand for labor curve, N, back from N_1 to N_0, so the real wage would stay at (w/p_0).
3. The L curve could shift in from L_0 to L_3, resulting in a lower equilibrium wage rate at $(w/p)_3$ and a smaller labor force.

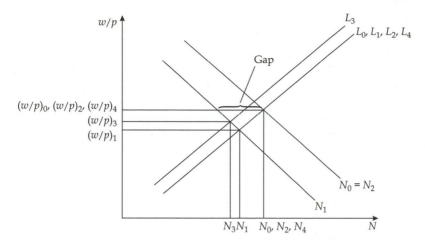

Figure 9.2   Changes in employment and the real wage rate when the demand and supply curves for labor shift

4. The real wage could stay at its previous level $(w/p)_0$, resulting in a gap between N_0 and N_1. That would boost the unemployment rate and represents a disequilibrium position in labor markets.

Before the Great Depression, economists generally assumed that any rise in unemployment was temporary and would soon be reversed. This fundamental assumption underlying the neoclassical labor market model is that both firms and employees quickly return to their respective demand and supply curves for labor, so any departure from equilibrium would be brief.

In the neoclassical labor market model, an outward shift in the N curve results in a higher demand for labor at each real wage rate. Initially, the demand for labor would exceed the supply at the old real wage, so the real wage would rise. At a higher real wage, more workers would be attracted into the labor force. As the real wage rose, the quantity demanded of workers would decline along the new, higher labor demand curve. Eventually a new equilibrium point would be reached at higher levels of employment and the real wage rate.

By the same reasoning, if the demand curve for labor shifted down, wages would be flexible downward, so the real wage would decline. That would raise the quantity demanded for labor, ceteris paribus, partially offsetting the decline caused by a lower demand for the product. At the same time, a lower real wage would reduce the supply of labor, so the labor market would return to equilibrium.

Even the classical economists realized that in the short run, a decline in the demand for labor would temporarily result in higher unemployment. After a while, though, it was argued that employees would accept a lower wage rate rather than remain unemployed indefinitely. If the cost of labor declined, the number of employees demanded would rise.

This argument became discredited during the Great Depression of the 1930s and has never really recovered. Even in the 1990s, many countries suffered double-digit unemployment rates for almost the entire decade. While it might take a year for labor markets to return to equilibrium, it cannot reasonably be argued that it takes markets an entire decade to adjust. A better hypothesis is required.

Part of the problem with the neoclassical argument is that the ceteris paribus assumption might not hold. A decline in the real wage rate causes a decline in real personal income, which reduces the purchasing power of consumers. In addition, investment might decline during periods of sluggish demand because of increased uncertainty and excess capacity. As a result, unemployment would continue to rise even as the real wage declined.

Some policymakers still think the straightforward cure is to institute stimulatory fiscal and monetary policy. However, we have ample evidence that doesn't always work. Japan reduced interest rates to zero in the late 1990s and implemented at least eight different fiscal stimulus programs, but the economy remained in recession. Most western European economies have substantial budget deficits and low real rates of interest at the same time that the unemployment rate is in the double-digit range. Note the title of this chapter is "Why high unemployment persists," not "The determinants of unemployment."

In summary, case (1) is the neoclassical solution, which seldom happens. Case (2) might appear to be the preferred solution in most cases, but European, Asian, and Latin American governments have all found that doesn't always work. Case (3) would be very unusual; most workers do not usually quit the labor force voluntarily. Case (4) occurs when various mechanisms preclude the real wage from declining; some of these are discussed in this chapter.

Before proceeding to these cases, though, it is useful to discuss the dynamics of labor markets in slightly more detail. Even the neoclassical economists realized that labor markets do not adjust immediately, although they claimed the period of adjustment was of relatively short duration.

Part II of the text described the economy in terms of comparative statics: a move from one equilibrium situation to another without paying much attention to the path of adjustment. This methodology assumed that (a) the path toward the new equilibrium, and the time it takes, are not particularly important, and (b) a new equilibrium is always reached. The underlying assumption is that goods and assets markets always clear quickly.

However, that assumption is seldom true for labor markets. The lags are much longer, since many wage contracts are adjusted only annually. Furthermore, and even more serious, there is no guarantee that a new equilibrium position will ever be reached. The unemployment rate may remain above full employment indefinitely. While goods and assets markets always clear, the same cannot always be said for labor markets.

Suppose that the demand for a particular good declines, so at the old price, firms are producing more than they can sell. First, firms will try to cut prices; as that reduces profits, some firms will shut outmoded plants or exit the business entirely.

Eventually the supply of the product will shrink to the point where it equals the decreased demand, and that market will return to equilibrium. However, labor markets do not work the same way. If the demand for labor is less than the supply, there is little or no "shrinkage" in the size of the labor force; instead, the excess workers become unemployed.

Neoclassical economists claimed that labor would continue to offer its services at a lower and lower wage until full employment is reached. That would be the case in a true barter economy. However, in an industrialized society, there is some wage rate below which it does not pay to work, since that wage would not cover the cost of basic necessities. Furthermore, as wage payments decline, so does aggregate demand: workers cannot buy anything if they are paid a zero wage. Thus if demand declined substantially and did not recover, excessive unemployment could continue for an extended period of time no matter what happens to wages and prices. Here again we see the importance of sufficient aggregate demand.

Assume the economy goes into a slump. Workers are handed pink slips with their final paycheck. Business executives are downsized out of their jobs. "No hiring" signs are posted on the doors of major businesses. Even in the late 1990s, when the US economy was at full employment, an average of almost 3 million people lost their jobs each year, although most of them quickly found other employment. In the meantime, the newly unemployed face several choices. They can look for another job, receive unemployment benefits or welfare payments, or drop out of the labor force entirely.

Initially, many employees will be undecided about the choice they should make. Some will look for the same type of work while receiving unemployment benefits. If their job search is unsuccessful, eventually it will become clear that no jobs are available at the desired levels of experience and wage rates. The next step is then to look for a lower paying job, become self-employed, remain unemployed at a lower level of benefits, or drop out of the labor force. However, those who were already on the bottom rungs of the wage schedule may find no lower paying alternatives.

Even during periods of full employment, major hotels in large cities found that whenever they ran help-wanted advertisements for menial jobs – bellhops, busboys, dishwashers, and so on – hundreds of applicants waited outside even in sub-zero weather for the few positions that were quickly filled. Clearly for this class of society, the unemployment rate remained high even during a period of overfull employment for the nation at large.

These people failed to find employment for a variety of reasons that are not in the neoclassical labor model. Some may not be able to afford transportation to areas where jobs are available. Some may lack the basic skills that should have been taught in school. Some may have criminal records. Some may not be chosen to work because they live in "bad neighborhoods" and are thus assumed to have deficient work ethics. Many of these points are discussed in greater detail in *When Work Disappears* by the noted Harvard University sociologist William Julius Wilson.

There are many reasons why the neoclassical labor model is incorrect and high unemployment may persist indefinitely. Often, these reasons reflect imperfections and distortions in labor markets. However, before turning to an examination of these factors, we first discuss the important link between unemployment and the overall growth rate.

9.2 Real growth and unemployment: Okun's Law

The rate of unemployment can remain well above full employment for extended periods of time. It is not necessary to refer back to the Great Depression to provide empirical evidence for this statement. Throughout the 1990s, double-digit unemployment rates persisted in France, Italy, and Spain, as well as many developing nations. For most of the decade, the unemployment rate remained in the double-digit range in Germany, the UK, and Canada. Even in the US, the unemployment rate rose to a peak of 10.8% in 1982, and did not decline to 6% – which was then considered full employment – until 1989.

While the unemployment rate can remain high over extended periods of time for a variety of factors, one reason is preeminent: *the growth rate of the economy is too low*. Of course the complete answer is more complicated than that, and as shown later, labor market imperfections often contribute to sluggish growth. Nonetheless, countries with rapid growth rates invariably have low rates of unemployment, while countries with sluggish growth rates invariably have high unemployment rates.

Is it possible to develop some useful rule of thumb that links changes in the growth rate with changes in the unemployment rate? This question was analyzed many years ago by Arthur Okun, and the resulting equation still bears his name.[1]

Empirically Okun found that, on average, if real GDP changes by 1%, the unemployment rate changes by about 0.4%. There are several reasons why this ratio is less than 1:1. First, an increase (say) in output will increase the length of the work-week. Second, to the extent that existing workers were partially underemployed, cyclical productivity will rise as well, so the percentage increase in the demand for employee-hours will be smaller than the percentage increase in output. Third, as more jobs become available, the labor force may rise at a more rapid rate. This relationship is graphed in figure 9.3. Statistically, for the past 50 years it has been:

$$\Delta UN = 1.4 - 0.40 \times \%\Delta GDP$$

where UN is the unemployment rate, and GDP is in real dollars.

This equation states that if real GDP is rising $3\frac{1}{2}$% per year, the unemployment rate would be constant, while a zero growth rate would boost unemployment by 1.4% per year. Thus $3\frac{1}{2}$% is seen as the long-term sustainable growth rate of the US economy that would keep the unemployment rate unchanged. That reflects about a $1\frac{1}{2}$% growth in the labor force and a 2% growth rate in productivity.

Furthermore, Okun's Law holds for virtually all countries that measure unemployment the same way as in the US (the principal exception is Japan); in particular,

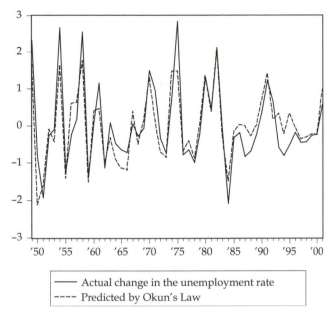

Figure 9.3   Changes in real GDP and the unemployment rate for the US economy

it holds for the industrialized countries of Europe, even though their unemployment rate is much higher. The French economy, for example, is different in many ways from the US economy. Government spending accounts for about 55% of GDP, compared to about one-third in the US, and labor contracts are much stickier, making it much more difficult to fire people. Nonetheless, estimating this equation for the French economy yields almost identical results:

$$\Delta UN = 1.2 - 0.4 \times \%\Delta GDP$$

Similar results can be obtained for most other European economies; the figures for Germany are distorted by unification in 1989, but if that event is treated separately, a very similar equation applies for the German economy as well. But what about Japan?

From 1992 through 2002, the growth rate in Japan averaged slightly less than 1%. According to Okun's Law, that would have boosted the unemployment rate by about 1% per year, hence raising it by 10%. However, the reported rate rose only from 2% to 5%. Doesn't Okun's Law apply to Japan – and if not, why not?

During that decade, total reported employment in Japan was virtually unchanged, which means output/employee, or productivity, dropped from about 3% to 1%. It is possible, but highly unlikely, that actual productivity growth dropped that sharply. It is much more likely that many people were kept on their jobs only for "show," and indeed it turns out that the Japanese government statisticians count someone as "employed" if they are at work as little as one hour per week.

Also during the same period, labor force growth fell from 1.2% per year to 0.5% per year. Perhaps some people retired earlier or simply gave up looking for work, but here again there is an alternative explanation. In Japan, people are not counted as "unemployed" until they have had a job and lost it; those who enter the labor force for the first time are not counted at all until they obtain their first job. Over the past decade, an estimated 3 million new high school and college graduates were excluded from the labor force statistics.

These comments suggest there is nothing wrong with Okun's Law, even when applied to Japan, but there are serious methodological issues with the way in which the Japanese measure their labor force and employment.

Thus when employment and unemployment – and real GDP – are measured correctly, there are virtually no exceptions to the general rule that a 1% decline in the growth rate below its equilibrium value will boost the unemployment rate by 0.3% to 0.4% per year. Having established this point, however, raises the next issue: since high unemployment rates are never politically popular, why don't governments routinely use stimulatory monetary and fiscal policy to boost the growth rate?

9.3 Why stimulatory monetary and fiscal policy might not reduce unemployment

Suppose aggregate demand is subjected to a negative shock, which initially reduces output and the real rate of interest. If the economy is now far away from full employment, where inflation is less of a threat, it would seem a simple matter to use expansionary monetary and fiscal policy to move the economy closer to full employment. The full-employment deficit could increase, and the central bank could ease policy by boosting the growth in monetary and credit aggregates and reducing real interest rates.

The initial exogenous shock that caused the Great Depression was the stock market crash. But that by itself was not the major source of economic woes that kept the economy in tatters until the US entered World War II. Long after the crash had occurred, an incredibly stupid set of blunders caused the government to *tighten* both monetary and fiscal policy. Credit was restricted as thousands of banks failed, and many depositors lost their life savings. A major tax increase was passed in 1932 in a vain attempt to balance the budget. Furthermore, US tariffs were boosted to an all-time high. Since Europe was essentially shut out of its principal overseas market, its economy also collapsed, which in turn reduced US exports. The attempts at competitive devaluations did not work because all major economies were declining, and the depression continued until World War II.

A major worldwide economic downturn has not arisen after World War II. However, double-digit unemployment rates persist in many countries. Central bankers and political leaders now know how to implement expansionary monetary and fiscal policies. However, in several cases, these polices have not worked well. Apparently it is not as easy to return to full employment as might be suggested by these "simple" rules.

Suppose the US economy fell into a serious recession, and the Federal government, in an attempt to boost the economy, mailed scrip to every man, woman, and child in the country entitling them to spend $1,000 at any retail outlets of their choice. Maybe a few people would throw these pieces of paper away, but we would venture to say very few. As a result, consumer spending would initially rise by approximately $300 billion, or about 3% of GDP. The stores would soon run out of merchandise, so they would order more goods, which would boost production at factories, putting more people back to work, and this pattern would continue for several more rounds. Soon the economy would be back to full employment.

This example may not sound very plausible, but in terms of its economic impact it is not much different – except in size – from the Bush Administration mailing most families a $600 check during the summer of 2001. Also, the economic impact is not much different from the Fed reducing the funds rate to 1% below the core rate of inflation and then encouraging lenders to flood the automated telephone lines, mailboxes, and internet with offers to refinance your house at interest rates as low as $2\frac{1}{2}$%. If you are wondering how successful those attempts were, note that home equity loans rose 37% in 2002.

Where would the Federal government get that extra $300 billion? It would, of course, issue more Treasury securities. The deficit has been 3% or more of GDP several times in the past 20 years, so this would not be an unprecedented level of deficit spending. And if the interest rate fell to 1%, the interest bill of the Federal government would increase by only $3 billion per year; it could always issue more securities to pay for the interest payments too. Unlike individuals, the Federal government never goes "broke."

Some economists would not recommend such a move, claiming that (a) eventually such a move would be inflationary, and (b) it would cause the value of the currency to decline, so that in the long run, the temporary gain in the standard of living would be reversed.

That is almost certainly the right answer for some small country with a weak currency, such as Paraguay, or Romania, or Sri Lanka, but it doesn't necessarily apply to the US, Germany, or Japan. In particular, Japan has managed to increase its Federal budget deficit to approximately 10% of their GDP (equivalent to a $1 trillion deficit in the US), yet none of the above happened. Inflation stayed very low, and while the value of the currency returned to its equilibrium value, which should have been a plus, the growth rate stayed near zero. Obviously, a more sophisticated explanation is needed.

Perhaps a huge increase in deficit spending would convince business executives that it was not worth while investing further in the home country, and funds might be better utilized investing in foreign countries. Also, consumers might spend most of that scrip on imports instead of domestically produced goods. Finally, consumers and businesses might decide to save and invest the additional money they received in foreign economies if they thought the domestic economy would remain weak for an extended period.

In addition to these demand-side factors, it is important to emphasize that the decision of whether to hire additional employees if demand picks up depends largely on whether labor market conditions encourage mobility, and whether workers can be hired at a wage that is equal to their marginal product. If that is not the case – if wages are set above marginal product, or if workers, once hired, can be fired only with great expense and difficulty – many will not be hired at all in the first place. As a result, the subsequent rounds of expansion that would otherwise stem from expansionary monetary and fiscal policy will be short-circuited, the economy will not recover very much, and the unemployment rate will remain well above its full-employment level indefinitely.

To summarize this section, assume that a given economy had been growing at equilibrium rates and was at full employment, but some exogenous shock occurs that reduces demand and causes a recession. The government tries expansionary monetary and fiscal policy, but labor market imperfections retard hiring, so the unemployment rate increases for a while. As expectations decline and optimism withers, more saving and investment is diverted to foreign economies, and further stimulus fails to achieve its desired result. In that sense labor market imperfections do indeed contribute to long-term unemployment. That is the principal message of this chapter.

9.4 Theories based on labor market imperfections: summary

Several different theories have been proposed to explain why labor markets do not return to full employment because of labor market imperfections. It is always possible that a strong union could drive wages in one industry well above their equilibrium level, hence reducing employment in that industry. However, if this were an isolated instance, it would not necessarily boost the overall unemployment rate in the longer run; employees would eventually find work in other industries, albeit at somewhat lower wages. The theories discussed in this section boost the overall rate of unemployment only if they are important enough to affect a significant proportion of total employment for an extended period of time.

Suppose that a given real wage rate, which had been in equilibrium, now increases. The firm is faced with more expensive labor. It can try to increase productivity, resulting in a decline in the demand for labor (each employee does more work, so fewer are needed), it can raise prices to offset his or her increased labor costs, or it can suffer a loss in profits. While the last case often occurs in the beginning states of recession, that is certainly not an explanation of why high unemployment exists for many years or decades.

In many cases, the response to higher wage rates is to raise prices, as shown in the previous chapter. But what happens then?

In general, an increase in the price of the product or service means the quantity demanded will decline. If airline mechanics receive a big raise and airline fares rise, fewer people will fly, or they will seek out discount fares more assiduously. If restaurant wait staff receive a big raise and the price of restaurant meals rises, fewer people will eat out, or they will skip dessert, and so on. However, higher prices per se are not the main reason employment declines; the interaction must be considered on a macroeconomic level.

In a closed economy (no foreign trade sector) with a monetary authority that accommodates on wage and price increases, the overall impact of higher nominal wage rates on unemployment will be minimal. Instead, inflation will rise, as the increase in wages is fully offset by the increase in prices. Of course, that means the real wage rate has not risen at all. Over the longer run, higher inflation leads to less domestic investment, so productivity growth suffers and the standard of living declines. Eventually this leads to a "crisis" and the formation of a new government that, at least for a while, pledges to keep the rate of inflation low.

In an open economy, higher inflation has several important negative consequences. First, firms price themselves out of world markets; although that is less important for the US than other countries, firms may move to different countries with lower inflation and lower wage rates. Second, the monetary authorities act vigorously to reduce inflation by restricting the growth in monetary and credit aggregates and raising interest rates. That raises the rate of unemployment. Third, higher inflation leads to lower productivity growth, which stunts the increase in the standard of living and eventually reduces the demand for employees.

It should be clear that excessive wage increases leading to tighter monetary policy or a decline in exports will boost the unemployment rate because of slower growth in the overall economy, and we return to this issue later. In the next five sections, though, we consider those cases where higher wage rates reduce employment directly instead of indirectly through higher inflation, and examine why those higher wage rates remain in force for extended periods of time. These cases can be grouped into several main categories.

1. Sticky nominal wages and prices. Prices don't change every minute – except in real-time financial and commodity markets or airline fares – or even every month. Wages are often set only once a year, and occasionally are renegotiated only once every three years, although when economic conditions change significantly, contracts can be reopened. Even following the mild 2001 recession, some employees found their compensation unilaterally negotiated downward. It was either that or being shown the door.

This is only a temporary reason, since it cannot explain why disequilibrium situations persist for more than a year. Some would claim that since most recessions do last about one year, there may be some value in this theory. However, it turns out that wages and prices are a lot less "sticky" than is apparent from casual observation, yet unemployment not only rises during recessions but generally continues to increase even after the economy starts to recover.

2. Sticky real wages imposed by employers. The efficiency wage boosts productivity and reduces turnover costs. These are sometimes known as quitting and shirking models.

According to these theories, workers are paid more than their marginal product because that increases loyalty and productivity. Hence fewer workers are hired than might otherwise be the case. Also, when times turn bad, real wages are not cut.

The concept of the efficiency wage has existed since the days of Henry Ford, so it is hardly a new theory. On the other hand, many economists think this creates a higher rate of unemployment than would be determined by the classical full-employment equilibrium.

3. Sticky real wages: insider/outsider models. Suppose the equilibrium wage rate for a certain skill is $20.00 per hour, but because of union restrictions, the actual wage is $25.00 per hour. In that case, many people who want jobs will not be able to attain them because the unions will not reduce their wage demands. Thus unions restrict the number of people who can join their group. This group of theories is often referred to as insider/outsider models. It also applies to public unions that are able to boost wages above equilibrium and saddle taxpayers with the bill – although eventually, many of them revolt by passing legislation limiting gains in taxes to the increase in inflation.

4. Sticky real wages: government restrictions. The minimum wage is one of the major examples in this category. Suppose the minimum wage was set at 50% of the average wage, and then indexed to inflation. While that still might appear to be a "low" wage to some people, it might be well above their marginal product. Thus it could raise unemployment for those at the low end of the wage scale.

Government restrictions that require hairdressers to apply for expensive licenses, restrict taxicab licenses, or add unnecessary costs to construction jobs, fall into this category.

5. The wedge between private and social costs. In all industrialized countries, the amount the employer pays in labor costs is greater than the amount the employee receives because of various social welfare costs. Social security taxes are a major example; in many cases, pension benefits and healthcare costs are also a substantial proportion of the total wage package paid by employers. If employees receive (say) $10.00 per hour but the employer must pay $17.00 per hour, that wedge will often push the total wage rate above its equilibrium level. Currently, this problem is more serious in Europe than in the US or Asia.

6. Barriers to firing and overly generous unemployment benefits. This category covers those cases where unemployment benefits are so generous that people refuse to accept jobs that pay their marginal product. Suppose the marginal product of low-skilled people is $5.00 per hour, but unemployment benefits, together with food stamps, subsidized rent, and free medical care amount to $10.00 per hour. Such people are better off remaining unemployed than working. This problem is also much more severe in Europe.

Each of these market imperfections is discussed in turn. There is a certain degree of merit in each one. Nonetheless, after completing this list, it turns out these reasons have their most noticeable effect when combined with sluggish aggregate demand. The combination of these two factors has kept unemployment in the double-digit range for over a decade in many countries in Latin America, Europe, and Asia.

9.5   Sticky prices and nominal wage rates

Suppose the demand for a given product declines because of a change in aggregate income or a switch in tastes. If the firm cuts its prices, it can usually regain some of those lost sales. Similarly, if the demand for labor falls, some workers can retain their jobs by agreeing to a lower wage rate. Hence some economists claim that "sticky" prices and wage rates hinder the move to new equilibrium levels because prices and wages do not decline in tandem with lower demand.[2]

In the post-WWII era, the rate of inflation in the US has always declined by the time recessions have ended. Because prices and wages do not adjust instantaneously, inflation may still increase for a while during the early stages of recession, but before the economy starts to recover, inflation has always started to fall. Thus most firms do indeed make some attempt to reduce prices soon after demand weakens.

Yet it was also shown in the previous chapter that the margins between prices and unit labor costs are not correlated with the phase of the business cycle; they do not rise in booms or fall in recessions. That would mean unit labor costs also rise less rapidly during recessions and the early stages of recovery, which is indeed the case. That could be caused by smaller gains in wage rates or bigger gains in productivity. Productivity growth generally increases during recessions; in addition, average hourly compensation costs rise less rapidly.

Thus total compensation to employees may decline significantly during recessions even if base rates are left unchanged because overtime payments, bonuses, and promotions are curtailed during recessions. Fringe benefits may be severely slashed, as indeed occurred during the 2001 slowdown, so total payments to white-collar workers decline even if the amounts shown on monthly paychecks do not change. In some cases, notably the severe 1981–2 recession but also in more modest slumps, wage contracts are reopened if it is clear that the alternative will entail substantial job losses. In sum, the average implicit wage rate – total wages and salaries divided by employment – often increases much less during recessions even though the published figures for average hourly earnings are not inversely correlated with the unemployment rate.

It is sometimes claimed that prices are sticky because of institutional constraints. Some firms change their prices only once a year, such as educational institutions, hospitals, and other nonprofit institutions. Sometimes, changing prices requires substantial cost outlays, such as the price of a daily newspaper. In the case of oligopolistic firms with a "kink" in their demand curve, it usually does not pay firms to change their prices unless industry-wide costs have changed, although that argument is less important when vigorous foreign competition exists. By looking at such items as financial service charges, magazine subscriptions, and utility bills, as well as such industrial products as cement, steel, glass, and paper, some economists have claimed these prices did not change more than once a year, and sometimes even less frequently.

Yet there is something wrong with almost every one of these examples. Financial service charges on, say, bounced checks may not change very often, but the rate of interest paid can change every day. The cover price of a magazine may not change very often, but discounts on yearly subscriptions change frequently. When fuel surcharges or discounts are considered, the net rate of utility bills changes almost every month.

The biggest flaw in the argument for sticky prices is that most of the prices examined in these studies were list rather than transactions prices. Also, when costs change, prices usually change with alacrity. Paper prices were mentioned as one of the categories that hardly ever change; yet in 1995, increases in paper prices were announced almost every month because demand outstripped capacity; then when additional capacity came on line, prices fell.

In terms of using list rather than transactions prices, a common example used to be steel prices; when business was good, the list price might stay the same but deliveries took longer, and there were extra charges for getting steel "soon." When business slumped, delivery was faster, firms offered extended terms at low or zero interest rates, and they offered to store the extra steel for users until they needed it at no charge. Today, with intense foreign competition, steel prices are no longer offered as an example of sticky prices anyhow – and when steel import tariffs were raised in February 2002, steel prices immediately zoomed by more than the amount of the increased tariff rate.

Not too many years ago, airline fares were also given as a prime example of sticky prices. How the world has changed: now airline fares can vary almost instantaneously. In this case, there was nothing wrong with the pricing mechanism – once the government let it operate without artificial restrictions.

Another case frequently cited is the price of restaurant meals, and the cost of reprinting menus (hence the entire argument is often referred to as "menu costs"). Yet here again the fault is in not measuring prices correctly. When business slumps, restaurants may offer "rebate" coupons, twofers, a free cocktail or dessert, or any number of other enticements to induce otherwise reluctant patrons to eat there. For example, the Prime Rib restaurant in Washington, DC, used to offer two free side dishes with lunch during recessions; one free side dish during periods of moderate growth; and no free side dishes during booms. Meanwhile, the menu price remained the same. There are many other similar examples.

In an era of price deregulation, the theory of sticky prices is becoming increasingly less important. Sticky prices are not the reason why recessions and high unemployment occur and certainly had nothing to do with the 2001 recession. In general, the theory of sticky prices has deteriorated into a simple statement that when costs and demand do not change, prices don't change either.

Some economists still claim that a better case can be made for sticky wage rates, since wage bargains generally are set for at least one year at a time, and in the case of various union contracts, as long as three years. Yet during and shortly after a recession, many valued employees will probably find that although their salaries will not be reduced, bonuses will be cut to the bone or entirely eliminated. Furthermore, travel costs must be slashed to the bone, entertainment allowances will be suspended, and they can buy their own coffee every morning. Thus during 2001, while average hourly earnings continued to advance at a steady 4%, the gain in the implicit wage rate fell from 8% to 3% as a result of cutbacks in fringe benefits and other cost-reducing measures.

The other argument used to support the sticky wage hypothesis as a source of high unemployment is the existence of substantial lags in bargaining. Many labor unions bargain for their members once every three years, and even workers not represented by unions usually do not have their wages or salaries reviewed more than once a year. If workers did not expect inflation to accelerate in the following year but it actually did rise, they would have to wait between one and three years before their wage rates were adjusted for higher inflation. That essentially extends the horizon for "misinformation" from one to three years.

Yet that theory also had to be revised in the early 1980s, when labor union contracts were renegotiated downward because firms were losing money, the unemployment rate rose to the double-digit range, and jobs were being permanently transferred overseas. Also, that development caused economists to check the historical data and find that the lag in wages behind prices was about the same before the 1930s, when there were hardly any unions.

Thus while the idea of sticky wages may have been intuitively appealing, it too has generally been dismissed. Indeed, business cycle recessions are much less frequent now than they were in the years before labor unions. To repeat what by now should be an obvious point: so-called sticky nominal wages and prices do not cause recessions and are not the cause of continuing high unemployment. Sticky real wages may boost unemployment, as discussed later in this chapter, but that is a different phenomenon and is not related to adjustment lags.

If that is the case, why do we mention nominal sticky wages at all? Primarily because this model represented an important first step in breaking the old paradigm about markets always clearing, and it introduced the important role of expectations into labor markets. Workers were once uninformed, but now that the weekly and monthly economic data are plastered all over the front pages and often lead the evening news on TV, someone would have to live on Mars to be unaware of what is happening in the economy these days.

Because changes in wage rates are often based on last year's changes in inflation, it turns out that during periods of supply shocks, the Fed is faced with an unpleasant short-term choice: higher inflation or higher unemployment. Nonetheless, the fact remains that the unemployment rate starts to rise only after output has declined.

In the short run, changes in the unemployment rate can be explained quite well by changes in output, and changes in real wages have virtually no influence. Since the argument for sticky prices and wages is strictly a short-term argument, persistent high unemployment rates must be explained by other phenomena, which are considered next.

9.6   Sticky real wage rates: efficiency wages

We next turn to the topic of *real* wage stickiness, which means that even after workers are fully aware of what happened to inflation and all short-term adjustments have been made, their real wage remains above their marginal product. That means workers are off the demand curve for labor, and employment is not determined by the production function or the marginal productivity conditions. Under that circumstance, a disequilibrium situation could persist indefinitely.

The efficiency wage hypothesis states that if employers pay their workers more than the equilibrium wage rate, in return they will get greater loyalty, higher productivity, less shirking on the job, and less quitting. The tradeoff is that boosting wage rates above equilibrium could result in a higher overall unemployment rate for extended periods of time.

The term *efficiency wage* was coined by George Akerlof and Janet Yellen.[3] The general idea is straightforward: firms will pay valuable workers "more than they are worth" in order to insure that they remain loyal employees and work efficiently. In the long run, that benefits both employer and employee. Edmund Phelps calls this the *incentive wage*, which means people will work harder and do less shirking, for if they are fired, they would probably end up taking a pay cut. As a result, these models are sometimes known as quitting and shirking models.[4]

In 1913, Henry Ford offered his workers $5.00 per day on the automobile assembly lines, which was more than twice the going wage. He did so not from altruism – a characteristic not generally associated with Henry Ford in any case – but because he wanted to get the best workers, and wanted them to be more productive and not quit so often. Ford also had another visionary idea, which was that if labor income rose to the point where workers could afford cars, his market would increase tremendously. Of course he was right about that too; but we confine these comments to efficiency wages.

The modern theory of the efficiency wage was not that employers realize paying their workers more will improve their efficiency and keep them on the job longer, which had been known for almost a century. Instead, it was the realization this could boost the unemployment rate significantly above full employment for an extended period of time without any countervailing economic forces moving labor markets back to full employment. In terms of the neoclassical labor market diagram, labor markets are not in equilibrium, because workers are being paid a wage that is above their marginal product. Thus fewer workers are hired, and the unemployment rate rises.

Furthermore, there is no recourse for the unemployed. Suppose someone applies for the job and offers to work for 20% less. The normal reaction of most employers will be "what's the catch?" Either such employees are no good and can't get a job anywhere else, they just want some experience and plan to leave in the near future, they plan to demand a big raise once they are settled in, or they really work for the competitor and are engaged in industrial espionage. If none of these cases apply, the employer would have a group of valued employees, who are worth just as much as the rest of the staff, continuing to earn 20% less, a situation that could not endure indefinitely. So the neoclassical postulate – if unemployment rises, employees offer to work for less – has been effectively broken by the concept of the efficiency wage.

One variant of this theory is turnover costs: it is often expensive to search for, hire, and train new employees. Another variant, the shirking model, says that many workers have a normal tendency to shirk when not being monitored.[5] However, if they are paid an "above market" wage, and the unemployment rate is above the full-employment rate, they will be less likely to goof off on the job, since if they do get caught and get fired, they will forfeit that wage premium.

With massive downsizing in the US during the early 1990s, the concept of the efficiency wage lost much of its importance. That was particularly true for long-time white-collar workers. The cost of pension contributions and healthcare benefits for older workers became so high relative to those costs for new employees that many career employees were encouraged to take early retirement. The efficiency wage, and the greater loyalty it engendered, were no longer relevant.[6]

The empirical evidence supports the claims by Akerlof and Yellen, and Phelps, about the efficiency wage: it does create higher unemployment. When the efficiency wage disappeared in the US economy in the 1990s, the unemployment rate fell and remained low for many years. As the efficiency wage premium disappeared, the real wage returned to the marginal product of labor, and employment rose enough to reinstate full employment.

When that happened, there were claims that workers would not work as diligently and would be more likely to quit their jobs, hence reducing productivity growth. However, that did not occur. For all its vaunted claim to "treat workers better," paying an efficiency wage did boost the unemployment rate somewhat. Eventually, most employers found the additional cost was greater than the presumed benefit.

Stripped of its frills, the efficiency wage argument can be summarized as follows. Suppose a company has a workforce of 1,000, each of whom produces 10 xygots per day. These workers are paid $20.00 per hour. By increasing their wage to $24.00 per hour, production rises to an average of 12.5 xygots per day. The company is better off. The workers are better off. But there are less of them, as employment drops to 800. The remaining 200 workers are unemployed – at least for a while, until they find lower paying jobs elsewhere.

Now suppose that foreign competition forces the firm to reduce wages, so it cuts them back to $20.00 per hour (in reality, this is done by offering wage increases that are less than the inflation rate). However, the workers retain their improved work habits, so their production rate remains at 12.5 xygots per day. The price of xygots drops, demand increases, and the firm rehires the 200 workers that were laid off. The net result is higher productivity, lower inflation, lower unemployment, and faster growth. But the efficiency wage premium has disappeared, and the real income of those workers has declined. With some obvious oversimplification, that happened in the US economy during the 1990s.

9.7   Sticky real wage rates: insider/outsider relationships

This concept of insider/outsider wage bargaining applies mainly to unions. The members of the union strike for, say, $25.00 per hour (including fringe benefits) even though they realize that without restricting the supply of labor, they would earn no more than $20.00 per hour. They are fully aware that firms in the industry will hire fewer workers at the higher wage – but they don't care. They are "insiders" and want theirs now, and are relatively unconcerned about "outsiders."[7]

Under John L. Lewis, coal miners went from among the most poorly paid to among the most highly paid of industrial workers (i.e., excluding craftsmen). As a result, employment in the bituminous coal mining industry dropped by two-thirds from 1948 to 1961. But the miners thought it was a difficult, dangerous job, and they wanted to be paid appropriately. Perhaps oil and natural gas would have replaced coal no matter what happened to the wages of mineworkers, but their wage demands probably contributed to the decline in coal mining employment.

A similar event occurred with the longshoremen unions. In this case it became clear that if wages kept rising, containerization would eventually put most of them out of work. The workers' response in that case was they wanted to make enough money now so their children could have a decent education and do something better with their lives. As a result, the number of unionized longshoremen dropped drastically. Also, steelworkers priced themselves out of the market; during the 1950s and 1960s, wages rose faster than productivity, and employment dropped by more than half from 1979 to 1985, as discussed in the following case study.

CASE STUDY 9.1   STEELWORKERS PRICE THEMSELVES OUT OF THE MARKET

Shortly after World War II, average hourly wages of steelworkers were about 14% above the average wage in manufacturing, and steel industry employment was almost 700,000, or about $4\frac{1}{2}$% of total manufacturing employment. During the 1950s, steel industry wages rose to about 25% more than the manufacturing average, resulting in a decline in both the relative and absolute number of steelworkers,

continued

CASE STUDY 9.1 (*continued*)

which fell to about 600,000. The relative wage then declined during the 1960s and steel industry employment rose somewhat. During the 1970s, though, wage rates rose much faster than the industry average, climbing to a peak of 36% above manufacturing wage rates in 1980. As a result, steel industry employment plunged from 600,000 to less than 300,000. Eventually, relative wage rates returned to

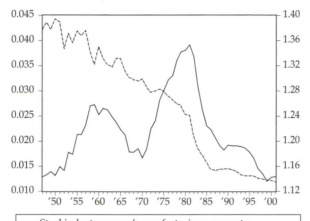

— Steel industry wage/manufacturing wage rate
---- Steel industry employment/manufacturing employment

(a) Relative steel industry wage rates and relative employment compared to total manufacturing

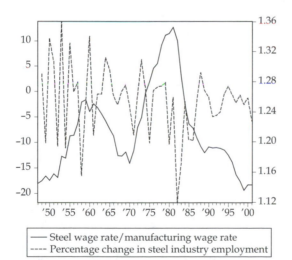

— Steel wage rate/manufacturing wage rate
---- Percentage change in steel industry employment

(b) Relative steel industry wages and percentage change in employment

Figure 9.4   Steel industry wage rates

continued

CASE STUDY 9.1 (*continued*)

previous levels, but by then it was too late for domestic steel to regain its previous importance, and employment continued to fall to 200,000 by the end of the 1990s. These developments are illustrated in figure 9.4.

It is clear from these diagrams that steelworkers priced themselves out of the market; the domestic steel industry itself also suffered because prices rose and it could not compete with imports. That is precisely the sort of microeconomic relationship one would expect.

However, the US economy gradually returned to full employment during the 1980s, and remained there for most of the 1990s, in spite of the sharp decline in steel industry employment. In this case, lower priced steel imports enabled consumers to buy more durable goods, and businesses to purchase more capital equipment, so the overall economy benefited from the rise in steel imports. This example illustrates how an increase in wage rates in an individual sector – even an important one – does not necessarily boost the overall unemployment rate.

The insider/outsider theory is still important where unions have the upper hand, as in France. However, in most countries, union power is on the wane. That has been the case in the US ever since Ronald Reagan fired the PATCO (air traffic control) workers in 1981. Phelps Dodge broke the back of the once-strong mining union in the late 1980s by hiring replacement workers. In 1996, the UAW threw in the towel in their multiyear strike against Caterpillar and admitted defeat.

German and Japanese employees have also found out, as did their counterparts in the US a decade earlier, that when domestic labor costs get too high, management is likely to transfer production facilities to lower-wage countries. It is not far from Germany to the Czech Republic, Poland, and Hungary. Japan now farms much of its manufacturing work out to Korea, Thailand, and other developing countries in southeast Asia.

Insider/outsider models are a valuable tool for understanding why wages are above equilibrium and unemployment remains high in those areas where unions are still strong. However, with the increased importance of international trade, private sector unionized workers who insist on above-market wages end up suffering more than non-unionized employees.

Unions are a political creation. If the government does not tilt toward unions, their ability to raise real wages in the marketplace will be very limited. Reagan destroyed the market power of unions in the US, while Thatcher did the same in the UK. In major industrialized countries where unions are still strong, notably France and Germany, political will has so far been lacking.

The concept of insider/outsider models does not apply where employers have the opportunity of transferring jobs to other countries that do not have similar restrictions. As a result, this phenomenon now occurs primarily either in service sectors where there is no foreign competition, or in the public sector. In the latter case, the issue is whether taxpayers want highly paid, highly motivated police officers, teachers, and other public sector positions, and whether it is worth paying above-market wages for these positions.

If voters decide that is indeed the case, then payment of above-market wages to public sector employees reduces the after-tax real income of private sector employees by raising their taxes. If the level of education and the quality of life improve, that may be a worthwhile tradeoff, but that belongs to the realm of normative rather than positive economics.

9.8   Barriers to market-clearing wages: the minimum wage

In recent years, the appropriate level of the minimum wage has been one of the most fractious issues in macroeconomics. Virtually all economists now agree that a full-employment balanced budget, moderate growth in government spending, and short-term interest rates equal to the inflation rate plus real growth rate represent appropriate fiscal and monetary policy. However, there is no consensus among economists about the optimal level of the minimum wage.

Yet if we strip the issue of its political connotations, the facts fall neatly into place. If an increase in the minimum wage boosts wage rates above equilibrium, it reduces employment. However, if the minimum wage was previously below equilibrium and an increase simply raises it to equilibrium, that move would not reduce employment. If the statutory minimum wage was so far below market conditions that an increase hardly affects any workers, an increase will have a similarly negligible impact on employment, but if it affects a large proportion of the workforce, an increase will have a larger impact. An increase in the minimum wage is also more likely to affect workers in the manufacturing sector, where jobs can be easily moved offshore, than in the service sector, where jobs cannot as easily be transferred out of the country.

Refer back to the labor market diagram in figure 9.1. Suppose the minimum wage represents an equilibrium wage rate, but the government raises that rate significantly. According to that diagram, either the real wage rate rises, in which case unemployment increases, or prices rise by the same proportion as wages, in which case unemployment is initially unaffected but inflation rises. That leads to higher interest rates, slower growth, and higher unemployment. The only other alternative would be that a rise in the minimum wage boosts aggregate demand and hence the demand for labor, but that rarely if ever happens. Seen on this basis, the minimum wage invariably boosts the rate of unemployment, and furthermore does so for the least advantaged members of society.

That might seem to be a logical result, but there are several well-regarded studies showing that an increase in the minimum wage has had virtually no impact on either inflation or unemployment. While there are several possible explanations,

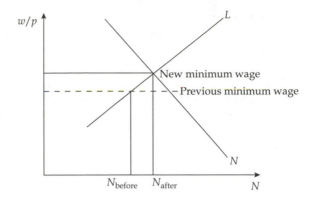

Figure 9.5

they all boil down to the same result: before the minimum wage rate was raised, it was below equilibrium.

If we admit that possibility, the entire argument changes. Figure 9.1, redrawn here as figure 9.5, shows a situation where the recent minimum wage is below equilibrium. Now suppose the government raises that wage to equilibrium. As shown in the diagram, the real wage rate rises *and* employment rises. The problem is solved.

However, that hardly disposes of the issue, since it raises another question – why was the minimum wage rate below equilibrium? According to the tenets of microeconomics, profit-maximizing businesses will hire workers until their real wage rate is equal to their marginal product, so hiring too few workers at a below-equilibrium wage rate would actually reduce profits.

The problem with the simplified micro theory is that it omits search costs. Some people might be willing to work at $5.00 per hour, but not $4.00 per hour. However, the availability of jobs at $5.00 per hour in suburban locations may not be known to inner-city youths. As a result, they do not apply for these jobs, nor does it pay employers to try and reach these potential employees because of the high cost of advertising and the relatively short time they are likely to remain on the job. However, if the minimum wage is now boosted to $5.00 per hour, inner-city youths would be more likely to apply for these jobs because they know the wage rate will be higher.

This may seem to be a far-fetched argument, but is precisely the result of a well-known study by Princeton professors Card and Krueger.[8] They found that an increase in the minimum wage in New Jersey in 1994 boosted employment at fast-food restaurants in that state, whereas there was no rise in employment at similar restaurants in Pennsylvania, where the minimum wage had not risen. Further-more, the minimum wage was raised in the US from $4.25 to $5.15 between October 1996 and 1997, and the unemployment rate continued to fall for minority group teenagers as well as the overall economy.

Hardly any economists think that continuing to boost the minimum wage indefinitely would improve the lot of the least fortunate. The impact of the minimum wage depends primarily on the level at which it is imposed. Suppose, for example, the government set the minimum wage at $20.00 per hour and prohibited firms from raising prices to compensate for the higher labor costs. That would boost the unemployment rate significantly. At the other extreme, suppose the minimum wage rose from $4.25 to $4.75 per hour but virtually everyone who was covered by that regulation was making at least $5.00 per hour anyhow. Then it would have virtually no effect.[9]

Thus one important factor that helps determine the economic impact of the minimum wage is its relationship to the average wage. Suppose the minimum wage had not been raised for several years, and thus had fallen well below the equilibrium wage. In that case, raising it back to equilibrium would not boost unemployment or inflation for two reasons. First, many low-paid employees would have already received wage increases. Second, since an increase in the minimum wage would affect very few workers, there would be virtually no "ripple" effect of boosting wage rates for those paid slightly more than the minimum wage. Conversely, if an increase in the minimum wage rate boosted it well above equilibrium, the negative impact on the economy would be substantial, both because of the reduced employment for those receiving the minimum wage and the ripple effect for the next several tiers of employees.

Thus the economic impact of raising the minimum wage rate depends on its level relative to the average wage rate. Figure 9.6 shows the percentage changes in the minimum wage rate on an annual basis for the post-WWII period. The minimum wage was first introduced in 1938 at $0.25 per hour, but since that was during the Great Depression, the results are not comparable. The minimum wage rose from $0.40 to $0.75 in 1950, and to $1.00 in 1956; since then, all increases in the minimum wage relative to the average wage rate (the minimum wage ratio) have been less than 10% per year.

Figure 9.7 shows the ratio of the minimum to the average wage rate. It peaked in 1950, with secondary peaks in 1956 and 1968. Since then the minimum wage has gradually failed to be an important force affecting wages or prices, as it has declined to about 40% of the average wage rate. Even the two-step increase in the minimum wage from $4.25 to $5.15 in 1996 and 1997 did not boost this ratio very much.

We next examine whether increases in the minimum wage ratio have any measurable impact on inflation or unemployment. Figure 9.8 shows this ratio relative to the change in the inflation rate. The big rise in the ratio in 1950 might have boosted inflation the following year, but that increase was probably caused by the beginning of the Korean War and the rush to stockpile scarce materials. The gains in 1956 and 1968 may also have boosted the inflation rate, but the evidence is not very strong.

Figure 9.9 shows the minimum wage ratio plotted against the unemployment rate. While theory suggests the overall unemployment rate might rise when the minimum wage ratio increases, the evidence does not support that conjecture. Thus

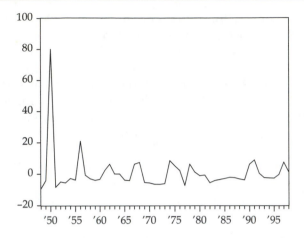

Figure 9.6 Since 1956, annual changes in the ratio of the minimum to the average wage rate have always been less than 10%

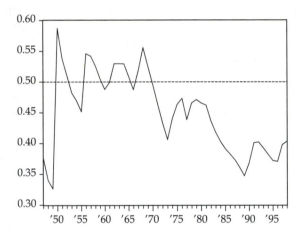

Figure 9.7 Since 1970, the ratio of the minimum to the average wage rate has remained below 0.50

we conclude that on a macroeconomic basis, an increase in the minimum wage ratio has no impact on the economy if it remains well below 50%; as it increases above 50%, inflation will probably rise slightly. Thus the effect on the unemployment rate is minimal in the service sector, where most employers are likely to raise prices rather than reduce employment. However, as is shown below, the effect is substantially greater in the manufacturing sector, where jobs are much more likely to move offshore.

Although an increase in the ratio of the minimum to the average wage rate has not been accompanied by an increase in the overall unemployment rate, it does not necessarily follow from that conclusion that an increase in the minimum

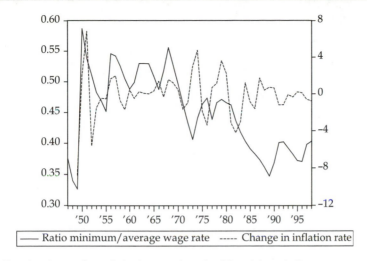

Figure 9.8   There is only a weak correlation between the ratio of the minimum to the average wage rate and the change in the inflation rate

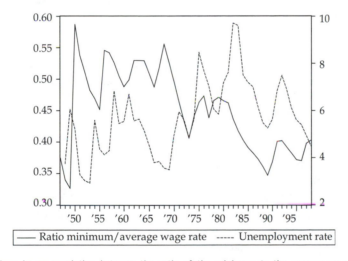

Figure 9.9   There is no correlation between the ratio of the minimum to the average wage rate and the unemployment rate

wage has no impact at all. Indeed, the results are different when we consider the sectoral results.

It is reasonable to surmise that teenagers are hurt the most by substantial gains in the minimum wage ratio, since they are most likely to be hired at relatively low wage rates. Figure 9.10 shows the correlation between the minimum wage ratio and the residual from a regression relating the teenage unemployment rate to the overall unemployment rate, phase of the business cycle, and a time trend. The big increases in the minimum wage ratio did not seem to have any impact on teenage

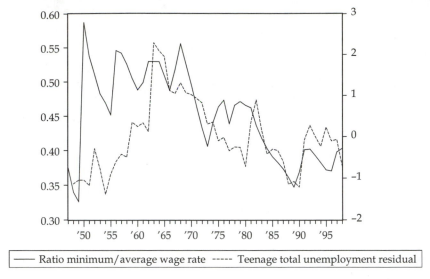

Figure 9.10 There is a significant correlation between the ratio of the minimum to the average wage and the residual between the teenage unemployment and total unemployment rates

unemployment rates in the 1950s, and the big increase in the early 1960s may have been due more to demographic factors than a relatively high minimum wage. Nonetheless, over the 50-year period, there is a significant relationship between these two variables.[10]

However, even that is not the end of the story, because an increase in the minimum wage has a different impact on manufacturing jobs, which can be easily shifted overseas, than on service jobs, which cannot, and has a bigger effect on low-wage manufacturing jobs than on high-wage jobs. If the minimum wage rises in the apparel industry, the factory may move to Korea or Indonesia. If the minimum wage rises in the fast food industry, customers will not travel abroad just to buy a hamburger and fries. The impact of an increase in the minimum wage on manufacturing jobs is examined in case study 9.2.

CASE STUDY 9.2   IMPACT OF A MINIMUM WAGE INCREASE ON LOW-PAID MANUFACTURING JOBS

To determine the impact of changes in the minimum wage by sector, we compare the percentage change in employment for the three years before the 1996 minimum wage increase, and the three years after. In particular, this case study

continued

CASE STUDY 9.2 (*continued*)

focuses on the difference between the percentage change in employment from 1993 through 1995, and from 1996 through 1998. The evidence is clear that manufacturing employment dropped, while employment in low-wage components of the service industry, such as restaurants and retail stores, rose faster. However, that is not a very rigorous test because the drop in manufacturing employment might have been due to the strengthening in the dollar and other exogenous factors. Hence a more sophisticated test is undertaken.

We have calculated the percentage change in employment for each of the 20 two-digit manufacturing industries for 1996–8 minus the change in 1993–5, and compared that difference with the average wage rate in each industry. If the rise in the minimum wage ratio is important, those industries with relatively low wage rates, such as apparel, would suffer a bigger drop in employment than those industries with relatively high wage rates, such as transportation equipment and petroleum refining.

The results are conclusive. In the apparel industry, which has the lowest wage rates in manufacturing, employment fell 0.7% in the three-year period 1993–5 but 18.4% in the 1996–8 period. By comparison, employment fell 2.2% in the transportation equipment industry from 1993 through 1995 but rose 5.2% from 1996 through 1998. Thus the hike in the minimum wage rate in 1996 and 1997 diminished employment in low-wage manufacturing industries.[11] The scatter diagram for all 20 manufacturing industries is given in figure 9.11.

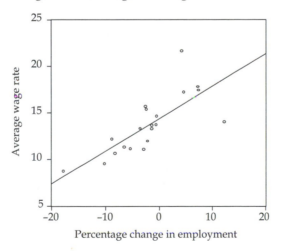

Figure 9.11   Industries with relatively high wage rates had faster growth in employment in 1996–8 relative to 1993–5 than industries with relatively low wage rates, which were adversely impacted by a higher minimum wage

The variety of data presented here offers an insight into why economists disagree so vigorously about the impact of an increase in the minimum wage ratio; the results are significantly different depending on which data are studied. The numbers given here will not settle the argument once and for all. Nonetheless, the following conclusions can be reached.

At the macroeconomic level
- When the minimum wage ratio is well below 50%, modest increases will have virtually no impact on either inflation or unemployment.
- When the minimum wage ratio is at or above 50%, further increases are likely to boost the inflation rate; that will eventually boost the overall unemployment rate if the rise in inflation boosts interest rates and reduces real growth. However, there is no immediate effect on unemployment.

At the sectoral level
- An increase in the minimum wage ratio above 50% boosts the teenage unemployment rate significantly relative to the overall unemployment rate.
- An increase in the minimum wage ratio is more likely to reduce employment in low-wage manufacturing industries than in similarly low-wage service sector industries.

To summarize this section, we have shown that theoretically, an increase in the minimum wage could have the following alternative effects.

1. Workers are fired and employment declines
2. Firms raise prices, so the real wage remains the same
3. The demand for the product or service increases, so employment does not decline
4. The minimum wage had been below equilibrium, so employment rises.

The actual effect will depend on the ratio of the minimum to the average wage, especially if it is below equilibrium, with different effects likely for manufacturing and services.

Some economists – and politicians – claim a higher minimum wage permits breadwinners to earn a living wage. For someone supporting a family with several children, the minimum wage is clearly inadequate. In such cases, though, a negative income tax or earned income credit is a more efficient way to boost annual earnings above the poverty level. Most employees earning the minimum wage are teenagers working part-time.

It is also claimed that paying workers a higher wage means they will be more productive, form better work habits, and remain on the job longer. However, that is just the old efficiency wage argument, which today sells at a substantial discount. Conversely, one could argue that since many minimum-wage jobs are entry-level positions, it is appropriate to attract more workers at a somewhat lower wage to permit first-time employees to establish valuable work experience, and then move on to more rewarding employment.

To the extent that employment is reduced by raising the minimum wage ratio, it is the poor and near-poor who will lose their jobs. No politician or economist is ever personally adversely affected by a rise in the minimum wage, and it may help the politicians get reelected.

When labor shortages occur, market forces will generally raise the de facto minimum wage, whether or not it is mandated by law. In regions or industries where labor shortages have not occurred, such as the apparel industry, raising the minimum wage will invariably reduce employment.

CASE STUDY 9.3   DOES DISCRIMINATION RAISE THE UNEMPLOYMENT RATE?

Figures 9.12 and 9.13 show the ratio of the unemployment rates for black and other workers to white workers, and female and male workers. The data do not start until 1954.

Since relatively few employers in the post-WWII period openly admitted that they ever practiced discrimination, we cannot pinpoint a particular year as the dividing line between discriminatory and non-discriminatory hiring practices. In general, however, anti-discrimination regulations started to become important in the mid-1960s, with much of the case law being written in the 1980s and early 1990s.

If some employers had previously declined to hire women or blacks (or other minorities), we might find one of two results. One, more minority workers could not find jobs, so their unemployment rate would be higher, ceteris paribus, and hence would decline in relative terms as anti-discrimination laws were enforced. Two, minorities would be able to find jobs, but at lower pay levels; in that case, the relative unemployment rates would not change, but the relative wage rates would increase over time.

While data for unemployment rates for blacks and women are available starting in 1954, weekly wages paid to men and women are not available until 1983; earlier data would have undoubtedly provided additional valuable evidence. Nonetheless, the results, as shown in figure 9.14, are fairly conclusive. The relative unemployment rates did not change, but the relative wage rates for women rose sharply from 1983 to the mid-1990s, at which point they leveled off.   *continued*

CASE STUDY 9.3 (*continued*)

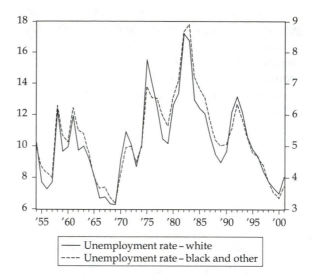

Figure 9.12   The unemployment rate for black and other minorities has remained consistently higher than for white workers, but there has been no trend change in the ratio

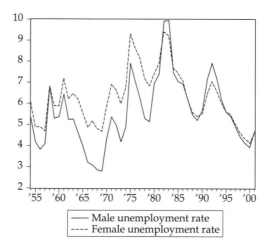

Figure 9.13   The female unemployment rate has declined relative to the male unemployment rate over the past 40 years

continued

CASE STUDY 9.3 (*continued*)

Figure 9.14   Ratio of weekly earnings of female workers relative to male workers

Removing discriminatory hiring practices for women employees did raise their relative wage, and also resulted in a lower unemployment rate for women relative to men. However, the same phenomena are not seen for black workers.

When coupled with the evidence from the minimum wage studies, the weight of the evidence suggests that raising wages of poorly paid workers, women, or blacks and other minorities does not increase the rate of unemployment, nor does it result in more people in these classes being "priced out of the market." The reason for this is that in many of these cases the wage rates previously offered were below equilibrium. If, on the other hand, the increases in wage rates had pushed them above equilibrium levels, the unemployment rate for those groups probably would have increased.

Since 1964, the number of women in the labor force has grown much faster than the number of men, although some of that gain is due to sociological as well as economic factors. Nonetheless, the conclusion is clear: when the economy is growing fast enough to provide jobs for all who want work, everyone benefits. A high unemployment rate is, first and foremost, the result of sluggish aggregate demand rather than imbalances in the wage rate. Raising the wages of women and minority groups did not increase the overall unemployment rate.

To summarize this section, the main reasons economists have been unable to agree on the impact of the minimum wage – besides their political differences – is completely different depending on the circumstances. At the *aggregate* level, the change will depend primarily on the ratio of the minimum to the average wage after the hike, and the phase of the business cycle. If that ratio is below 50%, it probably will not have much effect. If it is above 50%, it will probably boost inflation if the economy is booming, but will boost unemployment if the economy is already in a slump. At the *sectoral* level, the results are also quite variegated. In the manufacturing sector, an increase in the minimum wage is likely to cause firms to move operations to other countries, initially resulting in a substantial rise in unemployment in that industry. If the increase is in the retail or service sector, the result depends on whether the previous wage was below its equilibrium level; if it was, neither inflation nor unemployment will rise. If the increase is in the public sector – the so-called "living wage" now paid by an increasing number of state and municipal governments – the results will be higher taxes, which reduce the standard of living but are not usually included in the inflation statistics. For this reason, increases in the minimum wage must be considered on a case-by-case basis; general conclusions do not apply.

9.9   The wedge between private and social costs of labor

The previous section analyzed how a specific case of government intervention, namely the imposition of an above-equilibrium minimum wage, could reduce employment for low-wage workers over an extended period of time. However, the empirical results also indicated that in most cases, these workers were previously receiving below-equilibrium wage rates. Hence boosting the minimum wage, or instituting anti-discriminatory laws, are not a principal method by which government intervention reduces employment.

A more important case occurs when the government sector creates a sizable wedge between the wage that the employee receives and the cost of labor paid by the employer. Employers in every industrialized country must pay taxes for social security and unemployment insurance; most employers also offer pension and healthcare benefits. Many employers face substantial severance payments whenever employees are discharged without cause. In addition to these costs, many governments offer generous unemployment benefits that create an incentive not to work.

These problems are not inconsequential in any industrialized society, but are more serious for Europe. The data in table 9.1 are taken from the *World Economic Outlook* of May 1999, published by the International Monetary Fund.

The first column represents the initial amount of unemployment benefit relative to the average wage of a production worker. For the US these figures in 1999 were approximately $10,500 and $17,500 per year. The 60% ratio is not particularly out of line with other major countries and is substantially higher than the UK, Ireland, and Italy.

Table 9.1   Cost of unemployment benefits

Country	Initial benefit ratio	Minimum–maximum benefit duration (months)	Summary measure of benefit generosity
US	60	6–6	16
UK	36	12–12	51
France	70	27–54	55
Germany	61	6–32	54
Italy	42	6–6	19
Netherlands	69	6–54	69
Belgium	57	12–∞	59
Denmark	70	60–60	81
Finland	63	24–24	59
Ireland	49	15–15	37
Spain	73	4–24	49
Sweden	75	12–18	67
Switzerland	73	8.5–20	62

Source: International Monetary Fund

The second column shows the minimum and maximum number of months for which these benefits can be paid. In the US, the figure is the same: six months. However, that figure rises to 60 months for Denmark, and in the case of Belgium, there is no upper time limit.

The third column represents an index of benefit generosity calculated by the IMF; the figures are based on the ratio of unemployment benefits to income for two income levels, three duration categories, and three types of family situations. The benefit structure for the US is far less generous than in any European country, although Italy comes close.

Table 9.2 shows the average tax rate faced by a production worker with average earnings. In the US the figure is 35%, far lower than any European country. At 44%, the UK has the lowest tax rate in western Europe. The original Common Market countries have an average tax rate of 58%, while the remaining countries in western Europe for which data are available have an average tax rate of 56%. The cost of labor is raised, and the incentive to work is reduced, when over half of the average salary goes to the government.

Table 9.3 shows the maximum marginal effective tax rate – the tax rate from table 9.2 plus the effective rate of reduced benefits for those switching from unemployed to employed – and the range of earnings at which these top marginal tax rates apply, calculated as a percentage of average earnings of all production workers.

Table 9.2 Overall tax wedges

Country	Income tax	Payroll tax	Consumption tax	Overall tax wedge
US	18	7	10	35
UK	22	9	13	44
France	15	26	18	59
Germany	23	16	20	59
Italy	16	32	9	57
Netherlands	35	7	13	55
Belgium	19	26	16	61
Denmark	37	0	26	63
Finland	36	4	15	55
Ireland	21	11	23	55
Spain	10	24	13	47
Sweden	24	23	13	60

Table 9.3 Maximum marginal effective tax rate

Country	Maximum marginal tax rate	Applicable range of earnings (as percent of average earnings)
US	72	62–71
UK	97	46–65
	85	65–77
France	76	49–89
Germany	103	80–91
Netherlands	100	0–22
	91	22–58
	114	58–64
Denmark	102	2–47
Finland	100	0–64
Ireland	106	62–76
Sweden	91	0–100

Data not available for omitted countries

In many cases, these rates serve as a major disincentive to work. Even in the US, the maximum marginal tax rate is 72% for those workers earning 62% to 71% of the average production worker wage rate. In Germany, the Netherlands, Denmark, Finland, and Ireland, the marginal rate is 100% or higher: those returning to work are actually worse off. In Sweden, the marginal tax rate is 91% for *all* employees receiving less than the average annual wage.

Several additional factors not included in these IMF tables also serve to widen the wedge between wages received by employees and those paid by employers. Some European countries require that employers pay up to two years in severance pay for any employee fired for economic reasons (as opposed to firing with cause). Naturally, that makes firms wary of hiring additional workers unless they think they will need them for many years. In many cases, the least expensive alternative is not to hire them in the first place. Part-time employment would be the obvious solution but some countries, notably France, also prohibit that approach.

In almost all countries, the indigent and the unemployed receive a variety of benefits in addition to unemployment compensation, including food stamps, subsidized rent, reduced energy payments, free child care, and healthcare. If they return to work, most of these benefits are no longer available. Yet the alternative, which is to let poor people starve to death in the gutter, is hardly acceptable. In terms of the neoclassical labor market, the total package of unemployment benefits is equivalent to a "minimum wage" that is far above the equilibrium level, creating a gap between the demand and supply for labor.

Most free market economists argue that specific programs targeted to hire workers with low marginal products should be curtailed, and poorly paid workers should be given a subsidy, often referred to as a negative income tax, to bring their standard of living above the poverty level. However, the political barriers to implementing such a system remain formidable.

As noted above, these problems are much more severe in Europe than in the US. In the late 1990s, about 10% of the unemployed in the US were unable to find work for at least a year; in Europe, the figure is closer to 50%. In Japan, the reported unemployment rate has remained quite low in spite of a prolonged recession – although even there it rose from 2% to 6% – but that is due to different methods of measurement. Workers are counted as "employed" if they work as little as one hour per month, and those seeking jobs for the first time are not counted as unemployed at all. As a result, the reported unemployment rate is only about half of what it would be if calculated on the US basis.

In sum, overly generous severance and unemployment benefits can have a material impact on boosting the unemployment rates over long periods of time. Currently this problem seems most serious in Europe.

9.10 High unemployment rates and hysteresis

We are now in a position to offer a more complete explanation of why high unemployment persists as a result of the combination of sluggish demand and labor market imperfections. Two major strands of the theory that have been developed are known as hysteresis and structural slumps; both of them are considered next.

Suppose that for some reason, an economy grows slowly or actually declines for several years. Stimulatory fiscal and monetary policies are used to try and boost the growth rate. However, during this period, capital formation has been negligible, as many firms have relocated overseas. Also, some of the best talent has emigrated. Businesses have become discouraged and no longer want to invest in the country. As a result, an increase in the actual unemployment rate results, after a time, in an increase in the full-N unemployment rate. Because capital formation and technological development have lagged, job opportunities are scarce even when stimulatory policies are put into effect. Firms are also reluctant to hire employees because of high labor costs and large penalties for termination.

That is the concept behind what some economists call **hysteresis**, which comes from the Greek word that means "to be behind." Originally used in physics, the term has been adopted by some economists to suggest that the full-employment rate of unemployment "follows behind" the actual unemployment rate.[12]

Several reasons for the lack of skilled workers have been developed in this chapter. With an extended period of high unemployment, fewer skilled workers have been trained. Unions might not permit more people to work in the industries they control. Or perhaps firms do not want to hire workers because they do not believe the improvement in demand is permanent, and it is quite expensive to fire them again. In some cases, the unemployed do not really want to work because it means taking a de facto pay cut.

In one sense, the hysteresis theory is interesting because it failed. In particular, it was used to explain the high unemployment rates in Europe during the 1980s and 1990s, especially in the UK. However, the unemployment rate in that country fell from $10\frac{1}{2}$% to $5\frac{1}{2}$% during the 1990s, whereas the hysteresis theory would indicate that could not happen.

What did happen? For one thing, the devaluation of the pound to its equilibrium level spurred exports and aggregate demand. Just as important, labor market restrictions decreased. That was due not only to the more conservative policies of Margaret Thatcher, but even more importantly to the "new labor" policies of Tony Blair, who forced the old-line Labourites to face the new realities and understand that there would be very few jobs left in Britain if they continued their old policies of obstructionism. Thus the concept of hysteresis, even if it did not explain the sharp decline in the UK unemployment rate in the late 1990s, fits well into our overall discussion of high unemployment rates.

9.11 The structuralist school[13]

The structuralist hypothesis was developed by Edmund Phelps in his book entitled *Structural Slumps*.[14] As the name implies, this theory suggests there is some structural imbalance in the economy that not only boosts the unemployment rate to high levels but keeps it there. Because of inept or counterproductive government regulations, growth slows down enough that the deficit rises, keeping real interest rates at high levels and depressing aggregate demand. This decline is reversible only if the government takes steps to boost productivity, strengthen financial institutions and capital markets, privatize and deregulate, and reduce the size of the deficit.

First, consider what happens in the aftermath of a negative energy shock. Under the static analysis with stable prices, real interest rates and real output decline, as shown in figure 9.15(a). However, the energy shock has boosted the inflation rate at least temporarily, so nominal interest rates have risen. The central bank thus faces a dilemma. If it tightens, real output will decline further. However, if it does not tighten, inflation will rise, and that will eventually retard real growth as well. So whether it happens immediately or after a year or two, the LM curve eventually moves in, returning real interest rates to their previous level and reducing real output further, as shown in figure 9.15(b).

Particularly in Europe, social welfare payments, and hence government spending, had been rising rapidly before the first energy shock in 1973, but because the economy was also growing rapidly, the budget had remained in balance. However, when the IS curve shifted in, tax receipts grew at a slower rate, while social welfare payments grew at a faster rate because of the increase in unemployment. Also, in a misguided attempt to save jobs, labor market imperfections increased, exacerbating the employment situation. As a result, the government deficit ballooned. Because this is the result of more sluggish growth rather than a change in fiscal policy per se, the IS curve did not shift back out again.

Yet even though fiscal policies have not changed, the budget deficit has increased, and must be financed either through higher inflation or higher interest rates. Whichever route is taken, the net impact will be to reduce aggregate demand further. If inflation rises, goods will no longer be competitive in international markets, and capital spending will be skewed toward non-productive investments. If interest rates rise, the currency will become overvalued, so goods will no longer be competitive in international markets, and capital spending will fall because less projects will generate a positive rate of return. Hence the decline in net exports and capital spending shifts the IS curve in further, as shown in figure 9.15(c). Yet that will boost the deficit even further, resulting in yet another inward shift in the LM curve, as shown in figure 9.15(d). The economy enters into a vicious cycle where larger deficits lead to slower growth and higher unemployment, which in turn leads to still larger deficits.

Eventually the effects of the energy shock dissipate, and when combined with high unemployment and high real interest rates, inflation declines to very moderate levels. In that case, the central bank has more flexibility to reduce interest rates, boost growth in monetary and credit aggregates, and hopefully increase the growth rate and reduce the rate of unemployment. However, in most of Continental Europe, that did not happen.

Here is where the labor market imperfections become important. First, firms are reluctant to hire many new workers because they are so expensive; their rate of return will be far higher if they invest in other countries. Second, the penalties for

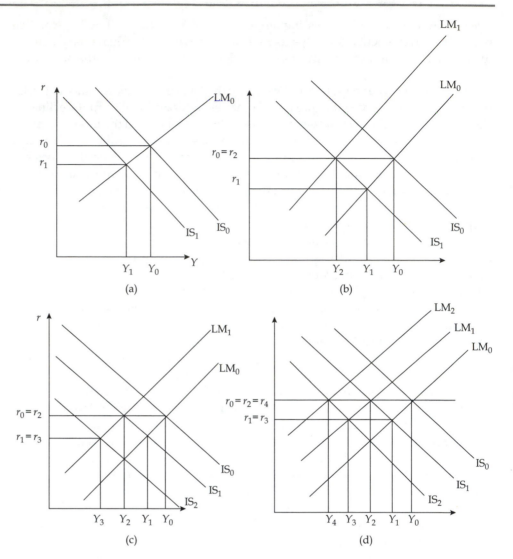

Figure 9.15 How structural slumps occur

hiring are severe if in fact these employers are fired in the future. Third, productivity growth remains sluggish because of the lack of capital spending, so many of the newest techniques are not introduced; labor continues to perform their jobs using outmoded skills. Fourth, because of overly generous benefits, many employees are better off not working at all.

What can be done to break this vicious circle?

- If the central bank reduces real interest rates without anything else changing, the currency will devalue, and the inflationary cycle starts all over again soon after real growth starts to accelerate. That is a most unpromising alternative.

- If the government tries to stimulate the economy by expanding the deficit even more, real interest rates will rise further to finance the deficit, hence offsetting the fiscal stimulus.
- If the government tries to increase productivity and reduce labor costs, slices the deficit, and makes the economy more competitive in world markets, or if it changes the laws to discourage unemployment and encourage employment, workers may riot in the streets, and the voters may elect a new government.

The last point contains the kernel of the issue: political hurdles are at the root of the problem. If the government were to encourage more free enterprise, reduce the fetters on new businesses, and entice firms to hire more people while reducing the generous benefits for the unemployed, labor market conditions would improve. Reforming the financial sector would attract more capital in both debt and equity markets, hence boosting new business formulation and raising productivity growth. Those new business opportunities would improve the overall growth rate, which would help reduce the deficit.

Hence the only way out of the trap is to reduce labor market restrictions and boost productivity, which will raise employment and government revenues. That will permit the central bank to reduce interest rates without creating inflationary problems or devaluing the currency. When productivity and the rate of return on investment improve, more capital will remain in the country.

It might seem that hardly anyone would oppose the move to faster productivity growth. However, this solution cannot be accomplished without some initial pain, reducing payments for workers who would be fired, and cutting benefits to those long-term unemployed who previously had no intention of finding jobs. In many countries, such moves are not politically feasible.

After World War II, many prominent forecasters predicted that the US economy would return to depression. Their argument was essentially that it took massive defense spending to pull the US economy out of the Great Depression, and as soon as that spending returned to normal levels, the economy would plunge back into depression. Today, a similar mistake is being made by those economists who have claimed that high unemployment cannot be reversed in Europe.

How could economists have been so misled in the 1940s? They failed to realize that balanced budgets at full employment, faster productivity growth, and reduced distortions in real wages had unleashed the economy from its shackles and permitted growth to flourish. Also, they completely failed to gauge how improved expectations following World War II victories would boost both consumer and business optimism. It was said at the time that pent-up consumer demand from wartime shortages bolstered the economy, but that lasted only a few years. Low real interest rates, properly functioning labor markets, appropriate fiscal policies, and higher growth in productivity all helped make US economic performance from 1947 through 1973 the envy of the rest of the world. When the government switched to deficit financing and high inflation, productivity slumped and the US lost its preeminent status. When credible monetary and fiscal policies reemerged in the 1990s, the US economy boomed again. Similarly, a reduction in the budget deficit, moves toward higher productivity, and removal of the worst distortions in the labor market could also recreate rapid growth in Europe in the twenty-first century if the respective governments are willing to take these steps.

Phelps brings fresh insights to the matter of high unemployment instead of sticking with outmoded and empirically invalid theories. He has said that much of the original intuition stems from Keynes, although he is also quick to point out that the structuralist school is not just another reworking of the *General Theory*. Nonetheless, some of these points were suggested by Keynes in the 1920s as well as the 1930s. In *The Economic Consequences of the Peace*, he used brilliant rhetoric to explain that by saddling Germany with punitive payments, that economy would never be able to recover and Britain would lose its chief export market, damaging its economy as well. In *The Economic Consequences of Mr. Churchill*, Keynes pointed out that if Britain set the value of the pound too high when it returned to the gold standard, it would not be competitive in world markets, and would have to keep interest rates too high to defend the beleaguered pound. Thus the British economy would be in perpetual recession.[15]

That is precisely what happened: while much of the rest of the world economy flourished in the 1920s, Britain did not. When the Great Depression reduced world growth around the globe, Britain became so demoralized that by 1938, it was unable to stand up to Hitler, and the rest, as they say, is history.

It should come as no surprise that incorrect government policies and labor market restrictions are at the root of high unemployment for extended periods of time. Furthermore, they are often intertwined and cannot be unraveled easily without tearing down existing political structures. Sluggish growth in productivity retards the move back to full employment, which can then occur only if the government reduces its intervention in product and factor markets and takes steps to boost productivity, which will then reduce real interest rates and permit the value of the currency to return to equilibrium levels.

These unfortunate developments need not be permanent. In preparation for the common Eurocurrency in 1999, most western European nations did indeed reduce their budget deficits, inflation, and interest rates. As a result, real growth improved markedly and the unemployment rate declined significantly for the first time in almost a decade. However, when the common currency actually went into effect, many of these same countries regressed on their commitment to keep reducing the deficit and providing incentives for investment, with the result that real growth failed to improve in the early years of Euroland.

It remains to be seen whether those improvements were permanent or temporary. If they can survive changes in the elected leadership, the European growth rate should return to robust levels, with a concomitant drop in the unemployment rate. This move will accelerate if the factors that led to above-equilibrium real wage rates are reversed.

KEY TERMS AND CONCEPTS

Efficiency Wage

Hysteresis

Insider/Outsider Models

Neoclassical Labor Model

Okun's Law

Sticky Nominal Wage Rates

Sticky Real Wage Rates

Structuralist School

Wedge Between Private and Social Labor Costs

SUMMARY

- In the neoclassical model, labor markets will quickly return to full-employment equilibrium, following a shift in the demand and supply for labor, because of adjustments in the real wage.
- However, we observe that unemployment often remains well above full-employment levels for years and even decades, so the relatively quick adjustment process underlying the neoclassical model does not exist in most countries.
- The principal reason why high unemployment persists is because real growth is too low. However, labor market imperfections can also keep the unemployment rate high for an extended period of time. The imperfections are caused by factors that can be grouped into the following three categories: above-equilibrium real wage rates, government incentives not to work, and structural imbalances that reduce the overall growth rate of the economy.
- The unemployment rate can remain high for extended periods of time if nonmarket forces keep the real wage above its equilibrium level. That could occur for several reasons: the existence of an efficiency wage, insider/outsider models, a minimum wage set above its equilibrium level, excessive government regulations, and a large wedge between the private and social costs of labor.

- On a macroeconomic basis, an increase in the ratio of the minimum to average wage rate does not boost inflation or unemployment if this ratio is well below 50%. If it is above 50%, further increases in the minimum wage are likely to boost inflation slightly.
- On a sectoral basis, increases in the ratio of the minimum to average wage rate are likely to boost teenage unemployment slightly, and will also result in declining employment in low-wage manufacturing industries where jobs may be easily shifted overseas.
- The unemployment rate may also remain well above full employment if generous unemployment benefits offer an incentive for some people not to work. Firms may not hire workers if severance benefits are set too high by government fiat.
- The concept of hysteresis states that when unemployment is high, it doesn't pay skilled workers to train for new jobs, so when growth improves, inflation rises instead of employment. However, that situation can be reversed by boosting productivity growth.
- The structuralist school hypothesis says that mismanaged fiscal and monetary policy keep real interest rates high and productivity growth low, leading to a widening budget deficit even if the full-employment budget is in balance. Until the deficit is reduced and incentives are provided for more rapid productivity growth, unemployment will remain high.

QUESTIONS AND PROBLEMS

1. From 1992 to 1997, the unemployment rate in the US declined from 7.5% to 4.9%, while at the same time it rose from 8% to over 12% in continental western Europe.
   (A) What factors caused the unemployment rates to diverge in these two regions?
   (B) In the UK, the unemployment rate rose sharply through 1993, peaking at 10.5%, but it then declined to 6.3%. What caused unemployment to decline in the UK at the same time it continued to rise across the Channel?
   (C) In 1998, the unemployment rate in France and Germany declined about 1%. What factors caused this turnaround?

2. The following article appeared on the front page of the *Wall Street Journal* on April 17, 1998:

   > The public, by 79% to 17%, favors raising the minimum hourly wage by $1 to $6.15. But Princeton economist Alan Krueger, whose research helped win a rise in 1996, is "less confident" another boost so soon "will have as benign consequences" on jobs as the last one seemed to have.

   (A) What research did Krueger use to "help win" a rise in the minimum wage in 1996? What did his results show?
   (B) What were the "benign consequences" of the previous minimum wage hike?
   (C) Assuming that Krueger is correct, why is he "less confident" that a further boost in the minimum wage would have no adverse effects?

3. From 1993 through 1995, compensation per hour in the US rose an average of 2.2% per year, down from 5.2% the previous three years. Much of this represented the disappearance of the efficiency wage. Partly as a result of this, the unemployment rate fell from 7.5% to 5.6% over that period, and then continued to decline to 4%. Using the standard labor market diagram, explain how these events were related.

4. Assume that a 1% change in the inflation rate causes a 1% increase in nominal interest rates, which in turn causes a 1% drop in real growth the following year. During the latter half of the 1990s, real growth averaged about 4%. Calculate how much inflation would have to increase for the following to happen, using Okun's Law.
   (A) A 1% increase in the unemployment rate.
   (B) A big enough change to cause a "typical" recession, where real GDP declines 2%.
   (C) Suppose real growth slows down to $2\frac{1}{2}$% because of a change in consumer and business sentiment. How much would the unemployment rate change each year?

5. From the end of World War II through the late 1980s, wage and price gains in the US always accelerated when the economy reached full employment. However, that did not happen in the 1990s. Part of the reason wage gains did not rise was credible monetary policy, part was the benign supply shock from a stronger dollar and lower oil prices, and part was the reduction in labor market imperfections. Explain how each of the following factors kept wage gains from accelerating.
   (A) Demise of the efficiency wage.
   (B) Reduced power of unions.
   (C) Less government regulations.
   (D) Clinton's plan to "end welfare as we know it."

6. The US unemployment rate rose from 5.8% in 1979, which was full employment then, to a peak of 10.7% in late 1982. It then returned to a full employment rate of 5.3% in 1989.
   (A) Based on Okun's Law, what do you think the average growth rate of the economy was from 1979 through 1982, and from 1983 through 1989?
   (B) In 1981, Reagan fired the PATCO workers because they illegally went on strike. What impact do you think that had on the real wage and employment gains for the rest of the decade?
   (C) Why did it take the US economy seven years to return to full employment?

7. Over the period from 1979 through 1989, manufacturing employment fell by 1.6 million, while in the previous decade it had risen 0.9 million, yet service sector employment rose 19.3 million, compared to 17.3 million in the previous decade. What factors caused the relative decline in manufacturing employment?

8. In September 1999, Senator Edward Kennedy released a report saying the minimum wage should be raised to $15.28 per hour. The reason for such a big increase, according to Kennedy, was that no one should have to spend more than 30% of their salary on housing, and the minimum price for acceptable housing in the Boston area for a family of four was about $800 per month.
   (A) What would happen to unemployment and inflation if the Kennedy plan were implemented?
   (B) Explain why or why not the cost of housing for a family of four is the appropriate criterion for determining the minimum wage.
   (C) What do you think would happen to Boston area rents and housing prices if in fact the minimum wage were set at $15.28 per hour?

9. In 1980, the inflation rate in the US was 12.5%. At that time, the consensus outlook claimed inflation could not decline by more than 1% per year. That turned out to be incorrect, as it fell to 3.8% in 1982 and remained near that level. Over the same period, the average gain in wage rates fell from 11% to 4%. What does this evidence say about the relevance of the claim that "sticky" wages and prices cause high unemployment?

10. Explain what impact an increase in the minimum wage from $5.15 to $7.00 per hour would have on:
   (A) The overall rate of inflation.
   (B) The unemployment rate for African-American male teenagers.
   (C) The price of hamburgers.
   (D) Employment of university professors and Senators.
   (E) Cost of college tuition.
   (F) Employment in the apparel industry.
   (G) Employment at Wal-Mart stores.
   (H) The price of new motor vehicles.
    (I) The price of used motor vehicles.
    (J) Employment of computer programmers.
   (K) The price of medical care services.

11. In mid-1999, the unemployment rate was 10.5% in Germany, 11.3% in France, and 12.1% in Italy. What steps should those governments take to bring the unemployment rate down to the 4.3% rate in the US and the UK without boosting the rate of inflation?

12. From 2000.3 through 2002.2, real growth slowed down substantially in the US economy, which was in a recession during most of 2001. Over that two-year period, real growth averaged 1.0%. According to Okun's Law, the unemployment rate should have risen 1% per year, for a total of 2%. In fact, the unemployment rate rose from 3.9% to 5.9% during that period, exactly what would have been expected. In that sense it was a "normal" recession. Yet repeated doses of fiscal and monetary stimulus failed to reduce the unemployment rate after the recovery got under way.
   (A) What measures of monetary stimulus were used?
   (B) What measures of fiscal stimulus were used?
   (C) Why did the economy fail to respond very much to these measures?
   (D) To what extent did institutional changes in the economy retard the recovery?
   (E) What parallels can be drawn between this situation and the decade-long slowdown in the Japanese economy that started in 1992?

13. As a business executive, you are asked to develop plans because of a newly passed 10% increase in the minimum wage for each of the next three years. What would you recommend if your company is in the following businesses?
   (A) Manufacturing auto parts.
   (B) Taxicab services.
   (C) Dry-cleaning plants.
   (D) High-priced restaurant chain (e.g., steak house).
   (E) Lumber mills.
   (F) Management consulting.

Notes

1. Okun developed this formula when he was a member of the Council of Economic Advisors under John F. Kennedy in 1962. A summary of Okun's views on this subject can be found in Arthur M. Okun, *Economics for Policymaking* (Cambridge, MA: MIT Press, 1983).

2. Many well-known economists have contributed to the theory of sticky wages. Keynes used it as one of the reasons that labor markets do not clear in his *General Theory of Employment, Interest and Money*. Milton Friedman discussed "worker misperception" models in his AEA presidential address (*American Economic Review*, March 1968). More recent contributions include John Taylor, "Aggregate Dynamics and Staggered Contracts," *Journal of Political Economy*, 1980; Julio Rotemberg, "Monopolistic Price Adjustments and Aggregate Output," *Review of Economic Studies*, 1982; and Laurence Ball, N. Gregory Mankiw, and David Romer, "The New Keynesian Economics and the Output–Inflation Tradeoff," *Brookings Papers on Economic Activity*, 1988.

3. George A. Akerlof and Janet L. Yellen, "A Near-Rational Model of the Business Cycle, with Wage and Price Inertia," *Quarterly Journal of Economics*, Supplement, 1985, and Akerlof and Yellen, eds, *Efficiency Wage Models of the Labor Market* (New York: Cambridge University Press, 1986).

4. Quitting and shirking models were first developed by Guillermo Calvo, "Quasi-Walrasian Theories of Unemployment," *American Economic Review*, May 1979, and Steven J. Salop, "A Model of the Natural Rate of Unemployment," *American Economic Review*, March 1979. Phelps's views on unemployment are summarized in his "A Review of Unemployment," *Journal of Economic Literature*, September 1992.

5. Often expressed as "Man does what is inspected, not expected."

6. A particularly noteworthy example occurred at IBM, where secretaries were paid up to $70,000 per year. When Louis Gerstner became CEO, he severely slashed those salaries, but hardly any of the secretaries left or, as far as is known, became less efficient.

7. This theory was developed by Assar Lindbeck and Dennis Snower in *The Insider–Outsider Theory of Employment and Unemployment* (Cambridge, MA: MIT Press, 1988).

8. David Card and Alan Krueger, *Myth and Measurement: The New Economics of the Minimum Wage* (Princeton: Princeton University Press, 1995). Also see Lawrence Katz and Alan Krueger, "The Effect of the Minimum Wage on the Fast-Food Industry," *Industrial and Labor Relations Review*, 1992. Katz was the first chief economist in the Department of Labor under Clinton, and was followed by Krueger.

9. When Clinton announced the minimum wage increase in October 1996, he said it would benefit "ten million people." However, the BLS said the actual number was only 780,000, representing only 0.6% of total employment.

10. In a more sophisticated multiple regression analysis relating the teenage unemployment rate to the overall unemployment rate, phase of the business cycle, a time trend, and the minimum wage ratio, this variable is highly significant with a t-ratio of 3.8.

11. This equation explains more than half the variance, and the t-ratio on the minimum wage term is 4.9.

12. This theory was developed by Olivier J. Blanchard and Lawrence H. Summers, "Beyond the Natural Rate Hypothesis," *American Economic Review*, May 1988.

13. This section can be ignored if the IS/LM diagram has been skipped.

14. Edmund Phelps, *Structural Slumps: The Modern Equilibrium Theory of Unemployment, Interest, and Assets* (Cambridge, MA: Harvard University Press, 1994).

15. Actually the fault was not Churchill's. He asked Keynes to explain his case to government leaders; Churchill favored a lower rate for the pound. However, Keynes was unable to convince the appropriate politicians, and Churchill was thus left with no choice; Keynes then criticized Churchill for his own inability to provide a convincing argument. For further details, see *Churchill* by Roy Jenkins (2001).

chapter ten

Aggregate supply, the production function, and the neoclassical growth model

Introduction

As a manager, maximizing the rate of return to stockholders involves several different operations: producing the right mix of products, effective marketing of those products, and optimal inventory controls. However, none of these will produce satisfactory profits unless the company also focuses its attention on increasing output per worker, which means boosting productivity. To a certain extent that is accomplished by increasing the amount of capital per worker, but it is also a function of what economists call "human capital" – the amount of education and training per worker. In recent decades, it has also meant working with the myriad of government regulations for both products and employees, and maximizing output per worker while observing these various requirements.

These might seem to be microeconomic rather than macroeconomic decisions, but in this increasingly internationalized world, managers should also be able to identify those foreign markets that will grow the most rapidly, which depends critically on the rate of productivity growth. Even on a domestic basis, managers should be able to identify those industries that are likely to grow faster or slower than the overall economy. This involves not only projections of overall demand, but an understanding of which industries are likely to expand domestically, and which are likely to be overcome by surging imports. All these decisions will be based in part on productivity growth by product, industry, and country. Hence an understanding of the macroeconomic factors that determine productivity can be quite useful for managers: in short, it enables them to identify "winners" and "losers."

The maximum amount of goods and services that any economy can produce is directly related to the level of productivity, the amount that each worker can produce. The higher the level of productivity, the higher the standard of living for any given economy; also, the more likely that an individual firm or industry will be able to expand more rapidly because it can reduce prices. The key factors that determine productivity at the macroeconomic level include the size and composition of the capital stock, the current level of available technology, the amount of education and training embedded in human capital, the strength and transparency of capital markets that permit capital to flow to its most efficient uses, and the degree to which international trade is encouraged. To the extent that government use of financial resources "crowds out" private sector investment, and other government factors impede progress through their impact on the functioning of private sector markets, productivity growth will be stunted.

The higher the ratio of saving and investment to GDP, the more rapidly productivity rises, ceteris paribus. However, high saving and investment ratios will boost productivity only if capital resources are allocated to their highest rate of return. Simply expanding plant and equipment for political purposes will not boost productivity in the long run. If bridges are built from nowhere to nowhere, impressively tall skyscrapers remain unoccupied, or if new plants are constructed to produce goods that can be sold only at a loss, long-term productivity growth will not be enhanced even if the ratio of investment and saving to GDP remains high.

Furthermore, as a country matures, productivity growth will diminish even if the saving and investment ratio remains high and no negative impacts occur because of government policies or troubled financial markets. This factor is generally known as convergence. After a while, an increasing proportion of total investment is used for replacement purposes rather than new plant and equipment. As a result, capital stock and productivity grow less rapidly. Even though countries with a higher ratio of investment and saving to GDP generally have a faster growth rate, the growth rate will diminish as a country matures *even if the investment ratio remains unchanged*. That is one of the main reasons why the growth rate of many emerging nations is very rapid at first, but then slows down as the countries become more mature.

10.1 Productivity growth and the standard of living

The principal goals of economic policy are to keep the economy at full employment, maintain an inflation rate that is low and stable, and create a high and rising standard of living. If the unemployment rate were 25%, the government could theoretically decree that everyone would work only three-quarters as many hours at the same hourly wage rate, with the remaining hours being redistributed to those who were currently unemployed. That would cut the unemployment rate to zero, ceteris paribus, but at the severe cost of reducing the standard of living of those previously employed by one-quarter.

This example may sound quite far-fetched for a free market economy, but it is a reasonable approximation of what happened in many Communist countries. The available work was spread out by finding a job for everyone, but at a very low level of productivity and an unacceptably low standard of living. As the old saying went, "We pretend to work – and they pretend to pay us." Yet it is not necessary to delve into the pathologies of Communism to find countries where full employment has been obtained at the cost of declining standards of living. A similar pattern occurred in many Latin American countries that had bloated government payrolls, huge deficits, and hyperinflation.

In capitalist societies where markets clear, the real wage of any employee is equal to the marginal product of labor – the additional output produced by adding the last unit of labor input to the production process. If the marginal product rises, real wages will increase; if it remains stagnant, real wages will also remain stagnant; and if it declines, real wages will fall. Thus over the long run, the level of productivity measures the standard of living. A sluggish growth rate in productivity will cause employees and consumers in that country to become poorer relative to other nations. Conversely, rapid growth can materially improve the well-being of a country fairly rapidly, as was the case for many southeast Asian nations before mid-1997.

Rapid growth in productivity ranks with full employment as one of the most important goals of any government. Indeed, low, stable inflation rates are important largely because they increase the likelihood of rapid productivity growth and full employment. Yet while economists agree that productivity growth is important, there is still no consensus about its determinants. Some of the elements are political, and others are not easily quantifiable. Much of the data are misleading, generating dubious empirical results. We will adjust for the most obvious data errors and concentrate on verifiable long-term economic trends.

CASE STUDY 10.1   THE NETHERLANDS IN THE SEVENTEENTH CENTURY[1]

What secret of success made the Netherlands the wealthiest country per capita in the world during the 1600s – and what factors caused its relative success to end?

We have chosen this example because, among other reasons, the Netherlands has virtually no natural resources, so it emphasizes the importance of other factors. Precise figures are not available for that century, but it is likely the Dutch saved a higher proportion of their income than neighboring countries – however, that was because they could afford it. What got them started in the first place? One obvious reason would seem to be their prowess as seafarers, but that description could also be applied to England, France, Spain, Portugal, and Italy, all of whom financed larger explorations to the New World and East Asia than the Dutch.

As is turns out, the reasons are sociological as much as economic. The system of canals meant the Dutch had to rely on each other; there was far less ruling of the country by isolated feudal lords. The Dutch were pioneers in offering political and religious freedom, and permitting a free press to flourish. The capitalist ethic was much in evidence, and that was also true for other northwestern European nations.

continued

CASE STUDY 10.1 (*continued*)

The Dutch had fought long and hard for their freedom from the Spanish, and used the opportunity to expand those fruits of freedom in the area of commerce and industry, and to encourage political and religious tolerance.

Their top rank did not last for long, however. Louis XIV wanted to divide up Belgium, with France taking the Southern part and the Netherlands taking the Northern part. However, the Dutch refused for humanitarian reasons, seeing no advantage in being conquerors. Inflamed, Louis XIV attacked the Netherlands. In the meantime, the British were very jealous of Dutch success, and were looking for an opportunity to defeat them on the high seas. The burden of having to fight both Britain and France at the same time proved too overwhelming for a small country, and it never really recovered from losing those wars. Indeed, France didn't recover from the Louis XIV wars either, although Britain, having chosen its battles more carefully and having a highly efficient system of raising money for those battles, continued to prosper. Also, by driving out the Huguenots, Louis XIV expelled precisely those people who had the ability to build superior ships, causing France to fall further behind in the battle for the supremacy of the seas.

This is not a very virtuous moral, but it repeated what had occurred in earlier times for what were essentially city-states: the collapse of civilization in Athens, and the rise and fall of Venice. In recent times, the riches of Kuwait were apparently too much for Saddam Hussein to ignore. No matter what the circumstances, human nature has not really changed very much over the centuries, and a country with the world's leading standard of living is likely to be viewed jealously by others. For a large country, a strong defense is an affordable luxury; small countries must rely on the good behavior of their larger neighbors in order for prosperity to continue.

The Importance of "Small" Changes in Productivity Growth

Why is the standard of living so much higher in the United States than in Mexico? Or Cuba? Or Russia? How did Germany and Japan manage to pull themselves up by their bootstraps so successfully after World War II, whereas Britain did not? Why is per capita income in South Korea ten times the level in North Korea? Why was the Netherlands the leading country in per capita real GDP in 1700, the United Kingdom in 1800, and the US in 1900? And why did the relative standard of living in Argentina and Brazil slip so much during the twentieth century?

For long-term performance, a 1% or 2% difference in the annual growth rate of productivity makes a tremendous difference. If per capita real output rises at 1% per year, growth will double every 72 years. At 2%, it will quadruple every 72 years, and at 3%, it will rise eightfold over that same 72-year period. In a country with 3% annual productivity growth, workers reaching retirement age will find their living standard to be eight times as high as someone in another country who started with the same living standard at birth but lived in a country where productivity remained stagnant.

Sometimes productivity growth can be even more rapid. The standard of living in South Korea has increased tenfold from 1960 to 2000, an increase of about 6% per year, although admittedly the country was very poor in 1960. Yet productivity actually declined in most communist countries after World War II – including North Korea – so that inhabitants of those countries were actually poorer in 2000 than in 1960.

A Quick Overview of the Causes of Productivity

An intelligent non-economist might assume that productivity rises fastest in countries where people work hard, a high proportion of income is saved and invested, the government helps rather than hinders capitalism, and financial markets function properly.

That's a pretty good start. Unlike some other areas of macroeconomics, the correct answer also turns out to be the obvious one. Yet that list is still incomplete, for we see that time and again, productivity growth slows down as countries become more mature even though employees continue to work hard, consumers and businesses save a high proportion of their income, and the government continues to encourage growth. This development can be explained formally with the use of growth models. More informally, we can say that once countries have caught up to the technology frontier, their growth rate is likely to diminish; this phenomenon is known as convergence. Yet even after taking convergence into effect, this broad-based explanation of varying productivity growth rates still leaves several critical pieces of the productivity puzzle unsolved, including the following:

- Why do some nations save and invest a higher proportion of their GDP?
- Why do people in some countries work harder than other countries?
- If growth is so important, why do some governments do such a good job of promoting it, while others do such a poor job?
- Under what form of government is real growth likely to be maximized?
- Why did productivity growth slow down so much after 1973 in virtually every industrialized country in the world – and why did it recover in the 1990s in the US but not in Europe or Japan?

After pondering these questions, it should become obvious that while working hard, saving and investing a high proportion of income, and promoting efficient markets is a good start to the answer, there is a lot more to the productivity puzzle. We will try to answer some of these questions in this chapter although, as it turns out, no one knows all the answers.

Table 10.1   Growth rates in per capita GDP (or GNP)

	1870–1913	1913–1938	1938–1950	1950–1960	1960–1973	1973–1985	1985–2001	1913–1973	1973–2001
United States	2.3	0.4	3.9	1.4	3.0	1.6	2.1	1.8	1.9
Canada	1.7	0.1	4.2	1.3	3.6	2.2	2.2	1.8	2.2
United Kingdom	1.2	0.7	1.0	1.9	2.6	1.3	2.1	1.4	1.8
Germany	1.6	1.1	−1.1	7.1	3.4	1.9	1.9	2.2	1.9
France	1.4	0.9	1.3	3.9	4.3	1.7	1.5	2.2	1.6
Italy	0.7	1.0	−0.2	4.5	4.5	2.3	1.9	2.1	2.1
Japan	2.2[a]	2.9	−4.2	7.7	8.1	2.5	2.5	3.4	2.5

[a] Starts 1879

Sources: 1950–present, OECD and BLS per capita GDP, converted to 1996 dollars; 1870–1950, output indexes are from Angus Maddison, *Economic Growth in the West*; population data are generally interpolated from decennial census data

Figure 10.1   Log of per capita GDP (1870–2001)

10.2   The long-term historical growth record

Table 10.1 shows the per capita growth rate for the seven major industrialized countries from 1870 through 2001. These figures are GDP (or GNP) per capita. The figures are also graphed, using annual data where possible, in figure 10.1. The "estimated" periods mean that GDP figures were generally not available during wartime. The data for the US and France are interpolated from decade benchmarks for the early years.

These numbers are not exactly the same as productivity, which is GDP divided by employee-hours. In the short run, the ratio of employee-hours to population can vary substantially. In the long run, though, these ratios remain almost constant; and given the difficulty of obtaining precise data on the length of the workweek for the nineteenth century, the measure of output divided by population will give essentially the same result for long-term trends.

Except for Japan, the average annual increase in real per capita GDP has been very close to 2% for almost an entire century. In very rough terms, this represents a contribution of about 1% per year from an increase in the capital stock, and 1% due to improvements in technology. A figure less than 2% generally indicates below-average growth in capital stock. The reason Japan grew faster – for a while – is discussed in case study 10.2.

The very long-term average rates for 1913 through 1973 and 1973 through 2001 are quite similar for most countries. Also, three countries have slightly higher productivity growth rates in the latter period, three countries have slightly lower rates, and one is unchanged. Perhaps the most striking finding is the lack of any evidence that productivity growth has slowed down in the past 30 years. Some economists once thought that as industrialized economies matured and the service sector became relatively more important, productivity growth would decline. That has not occurred.

However, there is a much bigger drop in the period immediately following 1973, with the drop ranging from 1.3% for the UK to a whopping 5.6% decline for Japan. At first glance it appears there must have been a major worldwide shift in the factors determining productivity after 1973; for a while, that shift was prominently identified with the first energy shock. More recent evidence suggests that was not the case; other reasons for this shift are identified later in this chapter. At this point, however, we note that the data in table 10.1 shows that productivity growth after 1973 returned to its long-term average. The unusual period was the earlier postwar years, as many countries rebuilt their capital stocks after World War II. Further details are given later in this chapter once we have filled in the framework for growth accounting.

CASE STUDY 10.2   JAPAN MOVES UP TO NUMBER 2 – BUT NOT NUMBER 1

In 1879 – the first year for which Japanese data are available – real per capita GDP in that country was approximately 24% of the US figure. That ratio increased slowly over the next 50 years, rising only to 33% in 1929. Considering that Japan was just emerging from a semi-feudal agrarian society where 65% of total output was generated by agriculture, that was a rather unimpressive performance.

continued

CASE STUDY 10.2 (*continued*)

Japan then made much greater strides during the 1930s, with real per capita GDP rising an average of 3.6% per year at the same time that per capita real GDP in the US fell 0.4% per year. As a result, per capita real GDP in Japan rose from 33% of US levels in 1929 to 48% in 1939. From a historical perspective, it is small wonder that so many nonaligned countries thought fascism offered a brighter future than capitalism at that time.

World War II destroyed those illusions; by 1947, per capita real GDP in Japan had sunk to 18% of US levels, well below the ratio even in 1879. However, recovery was swift, with an increase in the ratio of per capita Japanese/US GDP to 35% in 1960, 62% in 1970, 69% in 1980, and a peak of 81% in 1991. Japan was hard hit by the first energy crisis in 1974, and lost ground for a few years, but then recovered quickly. Since 1991, however, it has been all downhill for Japan, with real per capita GDP falling to 67% of the US level in 2001. Why was the post-WWII recovery in Japan so dramatic – and then why did it suddenly reverse course?

Much is made, and rightly so, of the celebrated Marshall plan to rescue western Europe after World War II, but it is less often noted that the US gave Japan a grant of $2 billion during the occupation period (1945 to 1951). For a country with total GDP of only about $23 billion at the time, that was a tremendous boost to the economy. Also, unlike the decisions to partition Germany, Korea, and Vietnam, the Truman Administration wisely refused Stalin's demand to partition Japan. There is no question that American aid, coupled with the imposition of an American-style constitution, pointed the Japanese economy in the right direction after World War II. After the aid associated with the occupation years was terminated, the Japanese economy was then boosted further by large US orders for goods needed for the Korean War. Also, by setting the yen at an artificially low level, the US gave Japanese foreign trade a major boost.

It is true that without an unusually high saving rate – during the 1960s, Japan saved and invested about twice as large a proportion of its GDP as did the US – a high level of education, and a continuing commitment to democracy, the Japanese economy would not have surged into the forefront of industrialized nations. However, there is also no question that the wise decisions made by the US during the period of occupation provided the initial impetus.

At the beginning of the 1990s, many economists assumed that real per capita GDP in Japan would exceed the US in another decade or two. If the average increase of 1.2% per year that occurred during the 1980s had continued, that goal would have been accomplished by 2008. However, there was virtually no growth in the Japanese economy during the decade of the 1990s in spite of a continuing high rate of saving and no fundamental change in the political or socioeconomic structure of the economy.

continued

CASE STUDY 10.2 (*continued*)

The convergence concept discussed later in this chapter would have indicated a slowdown in the growth rate of the Japanese economy from 10% to 5%, but not all the way down to less than 1%. Hence the diminishing contribution of capital in a mature economy cannot explain most of this stagnation.

Japan had undergone recessions in the past, notably following the first energy shock, but the economy quickly recovered. It also stumbled after the second energy shock in 1980, but once again quickly recovered. At first, the slowdown in 1992 looked like just another minor recession. But unlike previous times, the economy failed to snap back.

What was slowly revealed was a huge rotten underbelly of a financial sector. Many large industrial corporations had been propped up by an increasing injection of loans from the banking sector, and by floating equity issues selling at more than 100 times reported earnings, even though they were really losing money. Eventually this giant shell game had to come to an end. It no longer made sense for firms to expand further when they could not sell what they were already producing. As these losses became more obvious, the overvalued stock market slumped, with the Nikkei declining 75% from its 1989 peak to its trough in 2001.

The other major factor was the overvalued yen. One of the major sources of supercharged growth in Japan in the early postwar period was the rapid expansion of exports, aided and abetted by the undervalued yen. Eventually, however, labor costs rose rapidly, and the value of the yen kept climbing because of the huge trade surplus that regularly accumulated year after year. By 1995, according to the Bureau of Labor Statistics, manufacturing production costs in Japan were *twice* what they were in the US. Not only did this curtail the growth in Japanese exports, but firms also moved their manufacturing operations overseas, to Korea and other less expensive east Asian countries on the one hand, and to the US on the other.

Since so much of the Japanese demise is related to events in the foreign sector, a more detailed explanation will be postponed until part IV. Here we merely point out that the cessation of growth in per capita real GDP in Japan did not occur for any of the "typical" reasons, such as devoting a smaller proportion of GDP to saving and investment, massive government regulation that derailed progress, a less highly educated or motivated labor force, external wars, or internal dissension. Instead, the economy had expanded to the point where production outpaced demand, and the Japanese encouraged a massive cover-up of the financial sector to disguise this fact. Democratic institutions and organizations and the rule of law are necessary to keep productivity growth at high levels, but they are not sufficient; markets must clear, and financial organizations must be transparent. For that reason, it is important for managers to understand the national income statistics in order to assess accurately what is really happening in a given economy, and not fall victim

continued

CASE STUDY 10.2 (*continued*)

to the cover-up scheme. That is the main reason why we spend more time on the data than some might think is warranted.

If the Japanese had "bit the bullet" in the early 1990s and organized a thorough housecleaning of the financial sector early on, the recovery would have commenced much sooner. Instead, by delaying the inevitable, the recession dragged on for over a decade.

10.3   The aggregate production function and returns to scale

Unlike the rate of inflation, which has varied from slightly less than zero to several million percent per year in various countries over the past century, the growth rate of productivity may not seem to change very much. Nonetheless, as already shown, there is a tremendous long-run difference over the course of a century between a country with 1% productivity growth and one with 3% growth. Since that difference is sufficient to distinguish between winners and losers, it is worth while trying to explain differences of this magnitude. To accomplish that goal, a general framework has been developed into which the various factors can be placed. Just as the NIPA provided that framework for the national income accounts, **growth accounting** can be used to explain the determinants of productivity. That is best accomplished by considering the concept of the macroeconomic production function, with particular emphasis on the importance of capital formation.

In its most general form, a **production function** determines the maximum amount of output that can be produced with various different combinations of factor inputs. One can think of a production function for an individual firm; perhaps one that makes packaging machinery. The inputs to produce this machine include labor, raw materials, plant and equipment, entrepreneurship, and technology. Various factor proportions of these inputs can be used to produce one machine. If labor is relatively inexpensive, the firm is likely to use more labor per unit of machinery. If raw materials rise sharply in price, the firm may reduce the amount of materials per unit of output (that may not occur in machinery, but many newspapers made each page thinner and smaller when newsprint prices doubled). If a firm uses the latest technology, it requires less labor per unit of output. As the cost of integrated circuitry declines, firms use more chips. Finally, other factor inputs can be reduced if the firm uses "more" (which usually means better) entrepreneurship.

The same general concepts hold when we move to the aggregate level, with one exception: raw materials drop out, because their production is based on labor, capital, and entrepreneurship, and technology. One could argue that natural resource-based production, such as agriculture and mining, are based on land, but since that is almost always a fixed factor (with the possible exception of the Netherlands) it plays little or no role in explaining the productivity growth over time.

To determine the maximum potential output of the economy, the generalized production function can be written as:

$$Y = f(L, K, \gamma) \tag{10.1}$$

where Y is total real GDP, L is the size of the labor force, K is the capital stock, and γ is a technology trend.

If firms are maximizing profits, they will always be operating in the region of **diminishing marginal returns** for all factors of production. That means adding an additional unit of any given input (such as labor) will boost production, but by less than the average productivity of all workers. For example, if 100 workers were producing 1,000 machines, the 101st worker would produce less than 10 additional machines. If that were not the case – if the 101st worker could produce 11 machines – then his value to the company would be greater than all the other workers, and the firm would continue to hire additional workers until the additional output generated by the last worker started to diminish. Hence profit-maximizing firms that are operating on their production functions are always in the region of diminishing marginal returns.

However, the concept of returns to scale is a different issue. **Constant returns to scale** mean that if the firm boosts both L and K by 1%, then Y would rise by 1%, assuming that technology does not change. That may sound quite reasonable, but there are two major exceptions. The first one applies at both the micro and macro level. If the firm is relatively small, then adding both labor and capital may allow it to increase its size to the point where it is more efficient. That is why there are no small auto or aircraft manufacturers.

The second applies primarily to the macro level, especially in developing economies. As the manufacturing sector expands, more workers switch from agriculture to manufacturing. Since employees are more productive in the industrial sector, this switch causes total GDP to rise faster than indicated by the gain in labor and capital inputs alone. As a result, we find that many countries, especially emerging nations, are operating in the regions of **increasing returns to scale**: when factor inputs increase, output rises more than proportionately.

The way the production function is written, the technology trend γ seems to incorporate everything that boosts production except labor and capital stock. As the economy expands, the level of technology rises as countries adopt the most modern methods of production. That factor can also incorporate the level of entrepreneurship, the impact of government policies on production, better education and training for employees, and the use of more modern machinery even if the total amount of capital stock does not change. The major challenge of explaining the growth rate of productivity is to identify and quantify the principal factors that determine γ.

10.4   The Cobb-Douglas production function[2]

Many production functions have (a) diminishing marginal returns and (b) constant returns to scale. At this point we can add another condition, which is that the elasticity of substitution between labor and capital is unity. That means firms are operating at the point where in order to produce the same amount of output, a 1% decline (say) in the amount of labor will require a 1% increase in the amount of capital. That is a useful approximation at the macro level, although it does not apply to many industries and firms at the micro level.

Such a function can be written as:

$$Y = AL^\alpha K^{1-\alpha} e^{\gamma t} \qquad (10.2)$$

where A is a scale factor and e is the base for natural logarithms (2.718...).

This function can be closely approximated as:

$$\Delta Y/Y = \alpha(\Delta L/L) + (1 - \alpha)(\Delta K/K) + \gamma. \qquad (10.3)$$

That means a 1% rise in L will boost Y by α%; a 1% rise in K will boost Y by $(1 - \alpha)$%; and a 1% rise in γ will boost Y by 1%.

The next step is to determine the value of α. If the firm is maximizing profits, then the real wage of labor is equal to the marginal product of the last worker. If $(\Delta Y/Y)/(\Delta L/L) = \alpha$, and $\Delta Y/\Delta L$ is the marginal product of labor, and hence equal to w/p, then

$$\alpha = (w/p) \times (L/Y) = wL/pY, \qquad (10.4)$$

where wL is total wages and salaries, and pY is total production in current dollars, which must be equal to total factor income. Thus α equals labor's share of total income. For many decades, and in many industrialized nations, labor's share of total income has been about two-thirds. Thus capital's share is about one-third; this includes depreciation, net interest, and rental income as well as profits. Hence the above equation becomes:

$$Y = A L^{2/3} K^{1/3} e^{\gamma t}. \qquad (10.5)$$

The finding that returns to labor represent approximately two-thirds of GDP and returns to capital represent approximately one-third of GDP is often known as one of the "great ratios" of economics.[3] It has held for the US economy over at least the last century, and for most other industrialized economies as well. In the remainder of the chapter, this function will serve as the basic framework for analyzing the major factors that determine productivity growth.

10.5 Why growth differs among nations: the importance of saving and investment

In general, an economy can enhance its growth rate in one of two ways. It can increase the rate of growth of capital stock, or it can utilize existing resources

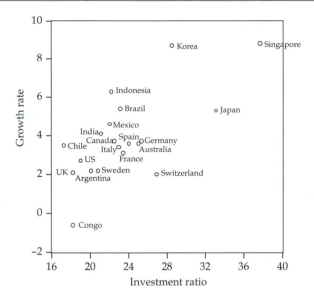

Figure 10.2   Relationship between investment ratio and growth rate

more efficiently. In order for capital stock to grow faster, a country must increase the ratio of its saving and investment to GDP. The funds could be generated either from domestic sources or foreign investors; the latter is particularly important for small, emerging economies. Whatever the source, an increase in capital stock per employee permits employees to be more productive, hence boosting the growth rate.

On the other hand, it would be a mistake to conclude that the investment ratio is the only determinant of the growth rate. Figure 10.2 is interesting both for what it shows and what it does not show. This figure graphs the relationship between the investment ratio and the growth rate for 20 countries, using 30-year averages. The actual figures are given in table 10.2.

While there is a significant correlation between the investment ratio and the growth rate, a regression equation using these data indicates that the investment ratio explains less than half of the variance in the growth rate. Some anomalies are obvious. For example, the growth rate for Korea and Singapore has been about the same, but the investment ratio in Singapore is almost ten percentage points higher than Korea.[4] Japan has generated a high growth rate – but lower than expected, given the very high investment ratio. Indonesia and Malaysia have generated very impressive growth rates with only moderate investment ratios. The country with the lowest investment ratio shown here, Chile, has posted an above-average growth rate; Switzerland, with an above-average investment ratio, has the lowest growth rate of any country shown here except Congo.

Table 10.2 Thirty-year average investment ratios and growth rates for selected countries

Country	Investment ratio	Growth rate
US	19.0	2.7
Canada	22.5	3.7
Japan	33.1	5.3
Australia	25.0	3.6
UK	18.2	2.1
France	23.4	3.1
Germany	25.3	3.7
Italy	23.0	3.4
Spain	24.0	3.6
Sweden	20.8	2.2
Switzerland	26.9	2.0
Argentina	20.1	2.2
Brazil	23.1	5.4
Chile	17.3	3.5
Mexico	22.0	4.6
India	21.1	4.1
Indonesia	22.2	6.3
Korea	28.5	8.7
Singapore	37.7	8.8
Congo	18.2	−0.6

10.6 Other factors affecting growth: the framework of growth accounting

The Cobb-Douglas function can be approximated by taking first differences and writing:

$$\Delta Y/Y = \tfrac{2}{3}(\Delta L/L) + \tfrac{1}{3}(\Delta K/K) + \gamma. \tag{10.6}$$

For example, if L rises $1\tfrac{1}{2}\%$ per year, K rises 3% per year, and technology rises at 1% per year, then Y would increase 3% per year. Also, productivity – measured as output per employee – would rise $1\tfrac{1}{2}\%$ per year. These magnitudes are close to what we observe in most industrialized democracies, although of course there are many differences among countries.

Each of the terms on the right-hand side of the equation can be disaggregated. Labor input is divided into quantity and quality, capital input is also divided into quantity and quality, and technology is disaggregated into increasing returns to scale, government regulations, other political and socioeconomic changes, and "pure" technological advances. After discussing the definitions of these terms, empirical estimates are supplied.

The quality of labor utilized can be measured by education and training. However, in countries where incentives are lacking, either because of excessively high marginal tax rates or totalitarian governments, workers may be properly educated and trained but still have a very low level of productivity because they are not encouraged to work very hard, or are penalized for suggesting improvements to the "master plan."

Even in democratic societies, though, levels of competition and incentives can vary dramatically. In an economy with little or no competition, coupled with strong oligopolies and unions, labor and management may reach an unspoken agreement not to "upset the applecart" by introducing too many innovations. For this reason, the amount of foreign trade is generally found to be one of the major factors that determines differential growth rates among countries.

Along the same lines, government regulation of key industries such as utilities, transportation, or communications, might reduce productivity growth in those sectors, and might also hamper other industries from attempting to initiate innovative solutions. For this reason, deregulation of these sectors in the 1980s and 1990s was one of the major reasons productivity growth accelerated in the US economy.

The quality of capital input can be measured by the average age of the capital, since more modern capital is usually more productive. Using the average age of the capital stock in the production function is often known as a "vintage" model, since the "vintage," or age, of the capital stock, is a key determinant of overall productivity growth.

Most major inventions that lead to mass production are generally considered changes in technology rather than increasing returns to scale per se. However, increasing returns can occur without new technology when workers move off the farms and into the manufacturing sector. Thus as countries switch from agrarian to industrialized economies, productivity may rise rapidly even if labor and capital inputs do not grow very much.

Changes in government regulations can also have a significant impact on productivity growth; some of the major changes can be summarized as follows. Wage and price controls diminish productivity growth because they penalize firms that have been the most efficient. The 55 miles per hour speed limit imposed in 1973 reduced productivity growth because it raised the amount of resources needed per unit of output in the transportation and distribution industries. Regulations that purify the air and water, and stricter occupational safety and health regulations, both reduce productivity to the extent that resources are diverted from productive capital spending to meeting the terms of government regulations; this may be offset to the extent that workers are healthier and safer. On the other hand, as already noted, deregulation of the transportation, communications, and financial services industries has increased productivity in those sectors.

Finally, productivity can be boosted by pure increases in technology: the invention of electric power, the internal combustion engine, radio and television, computers, transistors and semiconductors, miniaturization of computer power, and the proliferation of the internet are all key examples. However, it often turns out that major developments of this sort do not really start to boost productivity until two or three decades later. Many economists think we are just now beginning to reap the benefits of the microcomputer revolution that started in the 1970s.

10.7   Causes of growth in the US economy

Figure 10.3 shows the five-year percentage change in per capita real GDP for the US economy (the annual changes contain so many wiggles that the resulting series is very difficult to interpret). Per capita growth was unusually high in the years immediately following the end of the Civil War, as the country put itself back together again following that destructive war. The growth rate then gradually declined for almost the first half of the twentieth century. It recovered after World War II and continued to rise through 1973,[5] after which it declined for the next two decades. During the latter half of the 1990s, government data show that productivity growth improved to 2.5%.

The very long-run picture, then, shows that productivity growth in the US economy slowed from 3% to $1\frac{1}{2}$% from the Civil War through World War II, rose back to about $2\frac{1}{2}$% through 1960, accelerated to $3\frac{1}{2}$% during the 1960s, declined to $1\frac{1}{2}$% from 1970 through 1995, and then returned to $2\frac{1}{2}$% in the latter half of the 1990s and the early 2000s.

From the Civil War through the 1920s, productivity growth gradually diminished as the economy matured, as discussed in sections 10.9 and 10.10. Net capital formation was minimal during the 1930s because of the Great Depression; it then soared

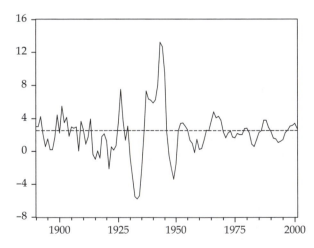

Figure 10.3   Five-year percentage change in per capita GDP for the US economy since 1890; this figure is about the same as productivity growth for longer periods of time

in the early years after the end of World War II. After that the pattern becomes more variegated. Productivity growth sagged in the 1950s, rose in the 1960s, sagged from 1970 through 1995, and rose again in the latter half of the 1990s. What factors caused these fluctuations?

Economists do not have all the answers to this question. In particular, the rebound in productivity growth from less than $1\frac{1}{2}$% for the 1973–95 period to $2\frac{1}{2}$% over the next several years came as a major surprise. Much of this can be attributed to the more rapid growth in capital stock, which is directly tied to the switch from a government deficit to surplus. The new technology spawned by the computer revolution had some impact – although its impact is often overstated. Also, some economists are suspicious about the recent growth rates and think they will be revised down because of the problems inherent in the rapidly declining computer deflator.

The general approach used here to explain productivity is to identify the separate contributions of capital formation and specific exogenous factors that affect it. The resulting "residual," which then is supposed to represent technological advance, should not change very much from one period to the next. Even this method is not entirely satisfactory, because there is a suspiciously large increase in the growth in technology from 1.5% to 1.8% during the 1960s and early 1970s; since those were also years of rapid growth in capital stock, it may be that newer capital stock is more productive. We have included a separate calculation for that factor but it may be understated.

Expanding the Cobb-Douglas production function to include the quality of labor and capital, increasing returns to scale, and other exogenous variables, the relevant statistics for each complete business cycle are presented in table 10.3. We have divided the last 12 years into two separate periods because of the sharp acceleration of productivity growth since 1995. In general these dates coincide with business cycle peaks in order to avoid the cyclical fluctuations that occur because of recessions.[6]

Because wage and price controls gave businesses an incentive to overstate output and understate prices, we estimate that real growth, and hence productivity, were overstated by about $\frac{1}{2}$% per year during the $2\frac{1}{2}$ years that this program was in effect, for a total of $1\frac{1}{4}$%. Hence the published figures for productivity growth are adjusted down by 0.3% per year during that four-year period, and up by 0.2% during the next six-year period.

Even with this adjustment, table 10.3 shows a sharp slowdown in productivity growth after 1973. However, that slowdown was not tied to changes in labor or capital inputs; total factor inputs actually rose from 2.1% to 2.4% in the next period. Instead, there was a sharp decline in productivity growth, which fell from 2.8% to 1.4% (after data adjustments). Most of that decline was caused by the combination of distortions caused by the wage and price controls, a massive increase in government regulations for occupational health and safety, and pollution abatement and control. Also, productivity growth was retarded by price regulations on energy and the reduced speed limit. The move toward deregulation that started in May 1975

Table 10.3 Causes of productivity growth, nonfarm private business sector, US economy

Category	'47–'53	'53–'59	'59–'69	'69–'73	'73–'79	'79–'89	'89–'95	'95–'01
Growth rate	**4.8**	**2.7**	**4.6**	**4.4**	**3.1**	**3.1**	**2.5**	**4.1**
Employee-hours	2.3	0.4	1.7	1.3	1.9	1.7	1.1	1.6
$\frac{2}{3}$* labor share	1.6	0.3	1.2	0.9	1.3	1.2	0.8	1.1
Quality of labor	0.0	0.0	0.0	−0.1	−0.1	−0.1	0.0	0.1
Total labor input	**1.6**	**0.3**	**1.2**	**0.8**	**1.2**	**1.1**	**0.8**	**1.2**
Capital stock	3.4	2.4	3.9	4.0	3.6	3.1	2.1	3.9
$\frac{1}{3}$* capital	1.1	0.8	1.3	1.3	1.2	1.0	0.7	1.3
Chg in age of cap stock	0.2	0.1	0.2	0.2	0.0	−0.1	−0.1	0.1
Total capital input	**1.3**	**0.9**	**1.5**	**1.5**	**1.2**	**0.9**	**0.6**	**1.4**
Total factor inputs	**2.9**	**1.2**	**2.7**	**2.3**	**2.4**	**2.0**	**1.4**	**2.6**
Residual	**1.9**	**1.5**	**1.9**	**2.1**	**0.7**	**1.1**	**1.1**	**1.5**
Incr ret to scale	0.3	0.2	0.1	0.0	0.0	0.0	0.0	0.0
Energy shock adjustment	0.0	0.0	0.0	0.0	−0.3	0.0	0.1	0.1
Regulation	0.1	0.0	0.0	0.0	−0.2	−0.1	−0.1	0.0
Dereg/privatization	0.0	0.0	0.0	0.0	0.0	0.1	0.1	0.2
Misstatement *	0.0	0.0	0.0	0.3	−0.2	0.0	0.0	0.0
Technology	**1.5**	**1.4**	**1.8**	**1.8**	**1.4**	**1.1**	**1.0**	**1.2**
Memo: Productivity *	2.5	2.3	2.9	2.8	1.4	1.4	1.4	2.5

* Productivity was overstated during the period of wage and price controls; these figures adjust for that misstatement

with the "big bang" in financial markets boosted productivity growth modestly, but had little immediate effect.

The figures in table 10.3 suggest that the rate of growth in technology has varied between 1.0% and 1.8% in the post-WWII period; however, the upper end of that range is probably overstated. It is more likely that the average annual increase in technology ranges between 1% and $1\frac{1}{2}$% per year. The decline in productivity growth after 1973, which also reflects changes in the quantity of capital, and the quality of both labor and capital, was much more definitive, and the recovery starting in 1995 much more striking.

In order to understand the fundamental determinants of productivity, it is useful to determine what caused the big drop in 1973. We have suggested that the misadventures of the Nixon Administration were partly responsible. However, productivity growth in other major industrialized nations also dropped sharply after 1973, and Nixon could not be blamed for their problems. For a while, that gave rise to the theory that the drop in productivity must have been caused by the energy shock; however, further energy shocks have not had the same impact, so that theory has also come to be generally disregarded. These two issues are addressed next.

10.8   The worldwide slowdown in productivity after 1973

Table 10.4 illustrates the slowdown in productivity after 1973. These results are similar to those presented in table 10.1 except that they measure GDP per employee instead of per person, and they include several more countries. Nonetheless, the drop after 1973 is roughly comparable to the data shown in table 10.1, and occurs for every country except Korea.

The figures in table 10.4 are based on BLS data for GDP per employed person for 14 major countries (data for Italy do not start until after 1980). These data are similar although not identical to the series used for the US economy; they differ in that (a) there is no adjustment for length of the workweek, and (b) total real GDP is used, without any subtractions of the government sector, rental value of owner-occupied dwellings, or the financial sector. However, if the relative importance of these sectors did not change after 1973, the comparison should be a valid one.

Both table 10.1 and table 10.4 show that a significant slowdown in productivity growth occurred after 1973 in all major world economies. That slowdown could signify one of two things. First, it could mean there was a permanent downward shift in productivity growth after 1973. Second, it could mean productivity growth was unusually rapid before 1973 and then returned to normal levels, in which case it is the immediate post-WWII period that is unusual, rather than more recent years.

The evidence overwhelmingly supports the latter hypothesis.[7] We have already shown that for the seven major industrialized nations, productivity growth for the long period from 1913 to 1973, which includes the periods of sluggish productivity

Table 10.4   Growth rates of GDP per employed person for major industrialized countries

	1960–1973	1973–1979	1979–1989	1989–1999
US	2.3	1.2	1.1	1.8
Canada	2.9*	0.8*	1.1	0.9
Japan	8.3	2.8	2.6	1.2
Korea	5.3*	5.2	5.1	4.2
Austria	5.0	2.5	1.9	1.8
Belgium	4.3	2.2	1.9	1.7
Denmark	3.0	1.3	1.3	2.1
France	4.9	2.4	2.1	1.3
Germany	4.1	2.6	1.4	1.9
Italy	4.5	2.3	1.8	1.6
Netherlands	4.3	1.7	0.8	1.5
Norway	3.8	2.8	2.0	1.8
Sweden	3.5	0.7	1.3	1.8
UK	2.7	1.2	1.8	1.3

* Data partially estimated

growth during the Great Depression and the two world wars, is about the same as productivity growth from 1973 to 2001. On a long-run basis, productivity growth in Japan has slowed down by just about the same amount as in North America and Europe, although the growth rate itself is slightly higher.

In a well-functioning, democratic, pro-capitalist, economy that is not rebuilding after a major war, the long-term growth in per capita output generally has ranged between $1\frac{1}{2}$% and $2\frac{1}{2}$% per year. Japan may seem to be an exception to this rule, but it had more ground to cover: when Admiral Perry steamed into Edo (Tokyo) in 1853, Japan was still a semiliterate feudal economy, far behind the rest of the western world. Not until the Meiji restoration ended serfdom in 1868 did the Japanese economy start to accelerate. It took Japan almost a century to catch up, but when it finally reached the technology frontier around 1990, its per capita growth also slowed down to $1\frac{1}{2}$%.

Table 10.4 does not include the so-called "growth tigers" – Hong Kong, Singapore, Korea, and Taiwan, followed more recently by Thailand, Indonesia, and Malaysia – which generated productivity growth of 6% to 8% per year until mid-1997. For a while, China was reportedly in that league, although its figures are tainted. These countries are examined in more detail in chapter 14. Also, although it is too early to tell, some of the newly capitalistic eastern European nations, especially Poland and Hungary, could end up posting strong growth rates for the next two or three decades if foreign investment were to increase substantially, although early results have been disappointing.

Productivity growth declined sharply after 1973 in virtually all industrialized countries of the world. Since the US was the only country to impose wage and price controls, this factor cannot be used to explain the slowdown in other countries. Also, productivity growth in emerging growth nations did *not* slow down after 1973. Hence the simple explanation that a big increase in the relative price of oil reduced productivity growth probably does not make much sense if it applies to one group of countries but not another. The slowdown in productivity growth after 1973 in industrialized countries was due in part to the gradual maturing of many of these countries, and the end of the "catch-up" phase after World War II.

Productivity growth for all industrialized countries did decline sharply after 1973; Korea was at a much earlier stage of development. The huge drop in Japanese productivity growth from 8.3% to 2.8% represents the end of their catch-up period, but the average decline for all countries excluding Japan and Korea was 2.0%, with the drop for individual countries ranging from 1.5% to 2.8%. Even though the data are not perfect, that big a change after 1973 cannot be ascribed to statistical gremlins alone.

The salient facts for solving the productivity slowdown puzzle are the following. First, the biggest declines in productivity growth after 1973 occurred in countries that previously had the biggest gains as they rebuilt their war-torn economies. Second, productivity growth for emerging nations that were still in their rapid expansion phase did not slow down at all, suggesting the energy crisis was not an important factor. Third, countries with more advanced social welfare policies slowed down the most. Fourth, productivity growth rebounded in later years for some countries, but not across the board. These latter two factors suggest that the dead hand of government intervention played a major role in reducing productivity growth around the globe as well as in the US, and only those countries that partially freed themselves from those shackles were able to boost their productivity growth rate again.

Nonetheless, even if all these factors are relevant, that still leaves unanswered the question of why such a sharp break occurred in 1973, as opposed to some other year. After all, Germany and Japan – and to a lesser extent, the Netherlands and Italy – had largely rebuilt their war-ravaged economies before that date.

The major remaining reason is found in the concept of "crowding out." Before 1973, when worldwide growth was quite rapid, most industrialized countries – including the US – expanded their social welfare systems rapidly. As long as the increased expenditures were supported by rapidly growing revenues, budgets remained balanced. However, the first energy shock materially reduced overall worldwide growth. As a result, government expenditures kept growing – in fact, they accelerated because of the recession – while revenues declined. Balanced budgets gave way to outsize deficits. The net impact was to crowd out private capital formation, which sharply reduced productivity growth. That is the answer to the question: "Why 1973 instead of some other year?" The slowdown in productivity growth coincided with the first energy shock because that led to ballooning government deficits in mature economies, not because the price of energy rose per se.

As already noted, some of the dropoff in US productivity growth after 1973 can be ascribed to special factors such as wage and price controls, the 55 mph speed limit, a raft of new government regulations, the spread of crime, deterioration of the educational system, and proliferation of abusive lawsuits. Most of these factors did not occur in other countries; yet the gradual spread of social welfare legislation occurred in Europe and Canada as well as the US.

To a certain extent, then, the productivity slowdown *started* with the energy crisis, but outlasted it. The surge in energy prices caused a worldwide slowdown in growth, especially for those countries with virtually no sources of domestic energy. At the same time, though, the growth in government spending accelerated because of the worldwide recession and hardships for poor people who had to pay sharply higher prices for energy. As a result, government deficit ratios increased in virtually all industrialized countries.

Besides reducing the investment and saving ratios, the combination of higher inflation and a bigger government sector reduced entrepreneurial spirit and led to fewer innovations. Along with the burst of inflation caused by the energy shocks, it became easier to boost prices than to find creative and innovative solutions to cutting costs. Since "everybody" was raising prices, firms could join the crowd without worrying about losing market share. The rate of inflation accelerated sharply in the late 1970s in almost all countries, not just the US.

The US reduced tax rates in the early 1980s and sparked a technological revolution, but that did not improve productivity growth until the 1990s, indicative of the long lag that sometimes occurs. Also, productivity growth was initially retarded by the unusually large budget deficits. During the 1980s, sluggish productivity in Europe also led to bigger budget deficits, more crowding out, less innovation, and a continuation of the vicious cycle.

A few countries broke out of this cycle. Ronald Reagan in the US and Margaret Thatcher in the UK recreated a more entrepreneurial spirit, although in the case of the US, crowding out continued until 1995. After many years, Sweden reined in its socialistic government. Yet many countries continued to encourage businesses not to hire, and employees not to work. As the size of the government sector continued to rise, productivity growth continued to shrink, although the move to a common currency in Europe initially helped to pull those countries out of their long-term slump.

We thus conclude that the first energy shock initially caused a major slowdown in productivity growth. After that, the accompanying inflation, larger budget deficit ratios, and decline in entrepreneurship and creativity caused productivity growth to remain sluggish even after relative energy prices had returned to pre-1973 levels. This sluggishness has often been called "Eurosclerosis" – as big government, business, and labor institutions mature, they become increasingly resistant to change, thus making it more difficult to break down established barriers and introduce more efficient methods of production and distribution.

All these reasons for the slowdown in productivity growth represent realistic possibilities. The only hypothesis we reject out of hand is the claim that somehow the growth in technology itself – new inventions and innovations – has died out. The microcomputer and telecommunications revolutions ought to put that idea to rest immediately. The argument that productivity growth is gradually slowing down because fewer new inventions are on the horizon is singularly inept, reminding

Table 10.5 Summary of factors affecting productivity growth after 1973

	US		Europe		Japan	
	1970s	1980–90s	1970s	1980–90s	1970s	1980–90s
Factors affecting capital stock growth						
Government sector	Larger	Smaller	Larger	Larger	–	Larger
Budget deficits	Larger	Smaller	Larger	–	–	Larger
Decline in investment ratio	No	No	No	Yes	No	Yes
Inflation rate	Up	Down	Up	Down	Up	Down
Convergence	Yes	–	Yes	Yes	Yes	Yes
Regulatory and tax policy						
More regulation	Yes	No	Yes	Yes	No	No
Dereg and privatization	Yes	Yes	No	No	No	No
Sclerosis	No	No	Yes	Yes	No	Yes
Venture capital/R&D	No	Yes	No	No	No	No

one of the oaf at the US Patent Office who wanted to shut down the office in 1899 because, as he declared, "Everything that can be invented already has been."

The comments in this section can be summarized as shown in table 10.5, which outlines the impact of the major factors affecting productivity growth for the US, Europe, and Japan in the 1970s, and the 1980s and 1990s.

CASE STUDY 10.3 HOW MUCH DID THE ENERGY CRISIS REDUCE PRODUCTIVITY GROWTH?

There is still no consensus about the impact of the energy crisis on productivity growth. An early viewpoint stated that when the price of energy rose, firms substituted more labor for energy, hence reducing productivity. A prime example of this occurred in the transportation services sector, where trucks and airlines reduced their average speed, hence resulting in more labor to deliver a given number of people or amount of goods.

Yet except for the imposition of the 55 mph speed limit in the US – which after a few years, was increasingly honored in the breach – these effects did not last very long. In the cases where energy conservation was important, new capital plant and equipment was purchased that was more energy efficient. Hence, if the cost of energy per se was the major impediment to productivity gains, the results would have quickly been reversed. Yet as shown in the above data, many countries have exhibited lower productivity growth ever since 1973 without any improvement.

The impact of the energy crisis on productivity, though, is important for two *indirect* reasons. First, higher energy prices initially boosted the rate of inflation, which distorts investment decisions and hence reduces productivity growth. When the rate of inflation rises substantially, investors are more likely to choose assets that will appreciate in value as inflation rises – or offer specific tax advantages – as opposed to those assets that would maximize the rate of return under stable prices. Since worldwide inflation did rise sharply from 1973 through 1981, that was a significant factor in reducing productivity growth during that period.

The second reason that the energy crisis reduced productivity was through its impact on the government sector. This reason has two strands: one is the straightforward crowding out relationship, in which a decline in government saving is matched by a decline in capital spending, and the other is the social welfare implications of higher energy prices. Any increase in the price of a basic commodity, whether it is food or energy, hurts the poor disproportionately. Poor people have great difficulty paying more expensive heating bills; some who must drive to work face sharply higher gasoline prices, while those who take public transportation also

continued

CASE STUDY 10.3 (*continued*)

face sharply higher prices if they are not subsidized. In addition, the 1973 energy crisis caused the first recessions in Japan and many European countries since the end of World War II. Additionally, the sharply higher price of energy brought the conservationists to the forefront, including the "Club of Rome" spokesmen who claimed the world would soon run out of all major natural resources. That led to a proliferation of regulations to conserve resources and improve the environment.

The combination of bigger government expenditures and deficits, and greater regulation, combined to reduce productivity growth in virtually all mature industrialized nations. Those countries, such as the US and UK, whose voters elected governments that reduced the scope of expanding government, posted larger productivity gains in the 1990s than other countries whose governments did not make this adjustment. In this regard, we emphasize that productivity growth in the US did not actually improve during the Reagan Administration; it was only when the Federal budget began to return to balance that productivity growth suddenly accelerated.

MANAGER'S BRIEFCASE: HOW FAST WILL US PRODUCTIVITY GROW IN THE FUTURE?

During the 1980s and early 1990s, most economists – and business executives – assumed that the long-term productivity growth rate was declining. By the end of that decade, however, thinking on the subject had done a 180-degree turn, with many of the same people claiming that we had entered a "new era" of rapid productivity growth. It would only be a matter of time before the "computer revolution" spawned a permanently higher growth rate. As Robert Solow famously remarked in the early 1990s, he saw computers everywhere except in the productivity statistics. Now they dominate the statistics as well.

Without trying to predict the annual growth rate of productivity for the next several years, it makes a great deal of difference in economic performance for the overall economy and individual businesses whether the sluggish 1.5% annual increase in productivity of the 1979–95 era will return, or the much more ebullient 2.5% gain of the 1996–2000 period will continue. Most of that additional 1% growth rate will be reflected in profits, so if profits are 10% of GDP, a 1% change in real growth that fell to the bottom line would result in a 10% annual difference in profit growth – enough to attract the attention of the most jaded business executive.

The material in this chapter has presented many different reasons for the change in productivity growth, but if we abstract from the information presented in table 10.3, by far the major factor boosting the productivity growth was higher capital spending, which helped both by increasing the amount of capital per worker and by introducing more modern equipment, notably in the area of technology. Will these trends continue?

One could argue we are not off to a very promising start, with real capital spending falling more than 5% per year in both 2001 and 2002; even if new technology is available, far fewer firms are adopting it. Some of the capital

continued

MANAGER'S BRIEFCASE (*continued*)

spending in the late 1990s resulted in excess capacity, and it will take several years before that disappears. Also, the investment boom coincided with, and was probably caused by, the return to a Federal budget surplus, which – at least in late 2002 – appeared unlikely for the next several years.

The long-term importance of the recent technological transformation – we hesitate to call it a revolution – cannot be ignored, but it should not be overstated. In this author's opinion, it is very unlikely that productivity growth can continue at an annual rate of 2.5% in the face of more sluggish capital spending and increasing budget deficits. Instead, it is more likely that revised data will eventually show productivity growth during the early 2000s moderating to the long-term average rate range of $1\frac{1}{2}$% to 2%. In one sense that might be considered good news, since it does indicate no long-term slowdown in the growth rate. However, a sustained acceleration, even with all the new computer applications, is an extremely doubtful proposition.

10.9 The neoclassical growth model and the slowdown of mature economies

Most of the theoretical and empirical work on growth rates stems from the seminal 1957 article by Nobel laureate Robert M. Solow,[8] although several other papers on the optimal growth rate, such as the Harrod-Domar model, preceded his work. Unlike other outstanding macroeconomists, such as Milton Friedman and Edmund Phelps, Solow's contributions have been concentrated in the area of growth economics.

The original Solow model assumed no growth in technology, so $\gamma = 0$. In that case, $Y = AL^{\alpha}K^{1-\alpha}$. Dividing through by L yields:

$$Y/L = A(K/L)^{1-\alpha}. \tag{10.7}$$

By definition, Y/L is productivity. The Solow model says productivity is proportional to the capital/labor ratio. The more capital per worker, the higher the level of productivity.

The change in capital stock is net investment (I_n). However, total investment also includes replacement investment, which is proportional to last year's capital stock. We can write:

$$I_g = I_n + \delta K_{-1}. \tag{10.8}$$

Suppose a country is just starting to develop, so K is very low. As a result, almost all investment will be new investment, which will boost the capital stock. Over time, though, K increases, so even if I_g remains a constant proportion of Y, I_n will fall, which means K will rise less rapidly.

This can be illustrated by a simple numerical example, where I/Y remains constant at 0.3. Without loss of generality, we can set L at unity, and can drop it from our calculations. Initially, assume $K = 75$ and $Y = 100$; D is depreciation.

Year	Y/L	K	I_g	I_n	D	$\%(Y/L)$
1	100	75	30	25	5	–
2	111.5	101.0	33.5	26.0	7.5	11.5
3	121.2	127.2	36.3	26.2	10.1	8.7
4	129.5	153.4	38.9	26.2	12.7	6.8
5	136.7	179.1	41.0	25.7	15.3	5.6
6	143.1	204.1	42.9	25.0	17.9	4.7
7	148.7	228.3	44.6	24.2	20.4	3.9

In this example, the percentage change in Y/L is one-third the percentage change in K. I_g is 0.3 times Y/L, D is 0.1 times K_{-1}, and I_n is the difference between I_g and D. Note that by the fifth year, I_n has already started to turn down even though Y/L and I_g are still rising. The growth in Y/L slows down each year even though I_g remains at 30% of Y/L.

If this pattern were to continue indefinitely, eventually D would account for all of I_g, in which case I_n would be zero. That means the capital stock would stop growing, and so would per capita GDP. Productivity growth would be zero.

Since productivity continues to rise even in mature economies, it is clear that this model is incomplete. The missing ingredient turns out to be the "growth" factor of γ. Nonetheless, it is worth stopping for a moment to reflect on the results to this point. Note in particular that:

• With no technological progress, eventually there would be no growth. Each country would reach a certain level of per capita GDP but would not progress further. This is often known as the **steady state**.
• Furthermore, with no technological progress, all countries would eventually reach the *same* steady state, except it would take countries with a lower investment ratio longer to reach that goal.
• Even with technological progress, countries that maintain their high ratio of saving and investment to GDP eventually post a slower growth rate because a greater proportion of total investment is used for replacement. That is evident in the recent slowdowns in Japan, Korea, and many southeast Asian nations.

10.10   Endogenous growth theory and convergence models

The main point of the Solow growth model is not that economies will eventually reach the steady state of no growth, but that a high rate of saving and investment does not necessarily lead to the same rate of rapid growth forever. Instead, as Solow points out, the driving force is not so much capital accumulation as it is *technology*. The inclusion of this factor in the production function is usually known as "endogenous growth theory."[9]

That is not a very surprising finding, but for many years after the seminal Solow work, most macroeconomists treated the growth in capital stock and technology as two unrelated factors, whereas in reality they are closely intertwined. One way to explain this is the concept of the "vintage" model, also developed by Solow, which says that the more modern the capital stock, the faster the growth rate in productivity. Thus an increase in *gross* investment can boost productivity even if net investment, and hence capital stock, does not rise at all.

Convergence Models

We now comment briefly on "convergence" models, which are based on the underlying logic of the Solow growth model. Recall that the original model assumed no growth in technology. If this assumption is relaxed, the theory then says that for a constant investment and saving ratio, productivity growth gradually slows down until it stabilizes at the rate of technological progress. The figures presented in this chapter suggest that describes real-world data much more closely.

Per capita GDP in emerging nations grows much faster than the rate of technological progress in the early stages of their development, but it then slows down to that rate when they become mature economies. Hence democratic countries with pro-capitalist governments should eventually all converge on the same rate of growth *regardless* of the level of their investment and saving ratio. Such models are, therefore, usually known as convergence models.

If the growth rate in a given country has been depressed by some combination of barriers – wars, totalitarian governments, or natural disasters – and these barriers are then removed, growth can progress at an extraordinarily rapid rate for a while until it catches up to where it would otherwise have been. This is a prime example of convergence.

Absolute convergence means that given enough time, even once-poor countries can catch up with the leaders and match them in per capita output. For a while this theory was quite popular, explaining as it did the post-WWII "miracles" of Germany and Japan. It was also used to explain the more rapid growth rate of the South and the West in the US, compared to the industrialized Northeast and Midwest.[10]

Economists also argued one of the reasons Germany and Japan recovered so impressively after World War II was that all the old institutions were destroyed and they had to start from scratch. Also, the American occupation helped: for example, the High Command made it illegal for the Germans to run a budget deficit. The thinking behind this was that Germany could never again build up a huge army with deficit spending. Yet what was originally meant as a restrictive measure turned out to have enormous benefits. Some would say it was too bad the same High Command wasn't in charge in the US in the 1970s and 1980s.

Nonetheless, this theory is incomplete. Germany and Japan were able to approach the per capita income levels of the US by 1973 in part because before World War II they were among the leading industrialized nations of the world.

Indeed, an underdeveloped nation could not have built up the fearful military capabilities that were so threatening during the war.

By comparison, countries such as India or Nigeria have made much less progress toward boosting real growth and per capita income; Nigeria has been a particular disappointment, given its oil wealth. The sharp divergence in growth rates in recent years between the Czechs and the Slovaks, or between the Hungarians and the Romanians, indicates that convergence alone cannot account for the differential in living standards.

Hence the theory has been modified to distinguish between *absolute convergence* and **conditional convergence**.[11] The latter term means that the standard of living for countries will converge only if the other determinants of productivity – such as the level of education, government policy variables, socioeconomic conditions, a useful legal system, a reasonably equitable tax system, and other noneconomic variables – are all the same.

Perhaps that seems obvious. Yet it does point out that two countries will converge to the same level of per capita GDP even with widely differing investment and saving ratios. It will just take the country with a lower investment ratio longer to reach an advanced standard of living.

These growth theories help explain how the standard of living in Japan, which used to be far below the US and western Europe, was able to catch up – followed by a decline in their growth rate to that of other major countries. This theory would also predict that the Asian tigers would eventually catch up with Japan and the US – although after the 1997–8 downturn, it will take longer than previously estimated. In those countries, even though the saving and investment ratios were quite high, banks were not allocating capital to its most productive uses but were lending it to personal friends and political cronies of the current regime. Eventually this situation led to a major downward revision in the growth potential for this region of the world. In particular, growth in these countries will be less likely to return to above-average levels until their financial sectors are dramatically reformed.

The economies of central and eastern Europe might eventually catch up with western Europe if they can provide stable, democratic, capitalistic forms of government for an extended period of time. Even if their domestic rate of saving is low, they could attract a great deal of foreign investment under those conditions. As of 2003, however, the prospects are not yet optimistic. Governments have swung back and forth between democracies and dictatorships, whether of the left or the right, hence reducing the attractiveness to foreign investors.

Growth model theories are useful because they show that even if none of the underlying conditions change, including but not limited to the saving and investment ratio, the per capita growth rate of an economy will eventually decline to the rate of technological progress as it matures. That is an important result. These theories also show that the living standards of countries that were temporarily hampered from saving and investing, perhaps by a war or a totalitarian government, can quickly "catch up" with the rest of the world if given the opportunity of a stable, democratic government.

Indeed, the correct application of these growth model theories would have shown that even though Japan had been growing much faster than the US, it would slow down once it reached that level. Perhaps this is obvious now, but that was not the case in the 1980s. Even sillier, some people took Khrushchev's claim that "we will bury you" (economically) seriously, when it should have been quite obvious that the growth rate in the Soviet Union was declining even as he spoke. More to the point, the Solow growth models should have warned economists that the super-heated 10% growth rates in southeast Asia could not continue indefinitely even if their banking systems had been functioning properly. Many useful nuggets can be gleaned from growth theory models, which can be used by informed economists to keep from making unrealistic predictions about growth rates.

Nonetheless, the standard of living in many democracies is *not* yet converging to that in the US, western Europe or Japan. In some cases this is due to a lack of saving and investment from both domestic and foreign sources. In other cases, governments do not really encourage capitalistic free markets; instead, most of the wealth is owned by the head of state and his family. Sustained rapid growth requires that governments permit free markets to operate in fact as well as in theory, especially in the financial sector. If that is not the case, even a high ratio of saving and investment to GDP will not produce continued above-average gains in productivity and the standard of living.

MANAGER'S BRIEFCASE: IDENTIFYING TROUBLE SPOTS AHEAD OF TIME

The Korean devaluation in 1997 and subsequent recession is not necessarily replicated in other countries that suddenly face a currency crisis and a recession, but there are enough elements of commonality that it can be used as a "textbook" example to alert managers to symptoms they can identify before the next foreign investment blows up in their faces. The key economic factors to monitor are:

- Current account balance
- Central government surplus or deficit
- Growth in monetary aggregates
- Balanced growth in domestic demand and exports.

Because the world is on a de facto dollar standard, and the US dollar appreciates in value even as the trade deficit increases to more than $400 billion per year, it is sometimes difficult to remember that most countries do not have the luxury of running a trade deficit. If their imports rise rapidly, this must be offset by rapid growth in exports, or the currency will eventually come under extreme pressure and be devalued, often by more than 40%.

In many cases, the situation develops precisely because the economy is growing rapidly, and consumers purchase more and more imports. These can be paid for only by boosting exports, which is sometimes undertaken by artificially boosting market share through tactics such as shipping goods that have not been ordered, disguised price-cutting, or offering unrealistic guarantees and warranties. When imports rise rapidly, and countries try to pay for these imports by boosting exports, make sure that these are solid orders instead of just wishful thinking.

continued

MANAGER'S BRIEFCASE (*continued*)

Sometimes, the government will buckle under to increasing pressure from the voters and decide to increase social welfare payments, hence leading to a substantial government deficit. In that case, it is likely that the deficit will be funded by "printing money," since most of these smaller developing countries do not have liquid debt markets. Hence rapid growth in the monetary and credit aggregates are almost a sure sign that the economy is not undergoing balanced growth.

While all these figures are tabulated and published by the International Monetary Fund, which is a useful repository for historical data, they are usually available only with a substantial lag. A better place to check is the current reports issued by the central banks of each country, many of which are available on the Web; others can be received by snail mail. There is usually plenty of time to react, even with the vagaries of the mail; for example, the current account deficit in Korea surged in 1996, well before the collapse of the won and the start of their recession in August 1997.

The other factor to monitor is the amount of foreign currency fleeing the country. The collapse of the Mexican peso in early 1995 was preceded by a massive drain of dollars and other hard-currency deposits from Mexican banks to US and European banks in late 1994. Those in the know got their money out ahead of time. This is an obvious variable to watch, and was not apparent in the case of Korea or the other Asian growth tigers; where it does occur, a devaluation of the currency is likely to follow in the near future.

10.11   Additional importance of saving and investment

In addition to increasing the size of the capital stock, a high investment ratio can boost real growth in several other ways, including the following.

- A high investment ratio means it is more likely that the latest technology will be utilized, because the capital stock is more modern.
- A high investment ratio permits countries to reap greater benefits from increasing returns to scale, especially nations that are emerging from an agrarian to an industrialized society.
- A high investment ratio increases the likelihood that countries will be able to compete in world markets, exposing them to the latest and best technology, which can then be used domestically as well.

As already noted, the standard Cobb-Douglas production function, on which Solow's work (and many others) is based, assumes constant returns to scale. In other words, if both labor and capital inputs are increased by 1%, output also rises by 1%. However, that is not true under conditions of increasing returns to scale. Doubling the size of productive facilities can result in a tripling of output when everything is now done more efficiently. Until very large plant sizes are reached, increasing returns to scale are the rule rather than the exception in most capital-intensive industries.

This factor is particularly important for small economies, where domestic consumption is not large enough to support fully efficient plants. Increasing returns to scale may also apply to the infrastructure and even the educational attainments of small countries; until the population reaches a critical mass, it would be too expensive to implement modern technology. Hence, a higher saving/investment ratio increases the likelihood the countries will be able to compete in world markets; exposure to foreign trade, which spurs innovation and productivity, also boosts the overall growth rate.

Thus when listing all the factors that determine productivity, the saving/investment ratio plays a critical role in determining the growth rate – but not only because the capital stock grows faster. In addition, technological progress is more likely, efficiencies from increasing returns to scale are more likely, and the ratio of foreign trade to GDP is also likely to be higher, hence boosting competitiveness, efficiency, and quality.

These factors work only if the government provides the proper incentives for saving to be directed to its most productive uses. In Thailand, for example, much of the money available for investment was "laundered" money from illegal activities, so it was converted into large, impressive – but unnecessary – office buildings that remained unoccupied. To a certain extent, a high rate of inflation can also cause investors to put their money into assets that are likely to appreciate over time, even if the real rate of return is negative. Thus we conclude that a high saving and investment ratio is a *necessary* factor for rapid growth, but may not be *sufficient* unless the underlying form of government also encourages productive investment. One necessary ingredient is to keep the inflation rate low and stable.

Saving may stem from either domestic or foreign sources. In many developing countries, much of the initial infusion of capital is supplied by overseas investors. However, this cannot continue indefinitely, or foreign interests will own most of the means of production in that country. Even if that were politically acceptable – which is seldom the case – the drain on the economy's resources as all those earnings flowed overseas would increase pressure to boost exports to pay back these debts. If export growth were then to decline because of negative worldwide conditions, the growth rate of such a country could quickly collapse. That is also part of the reason rapid growth in southeast Asia came to a stunning halt in late 1997.

After the initial development phase has occurred, rapid rates of real growth are usually based on high rates of domestic saving. The domestic economy also needs to provide enough opportunities for the richest members of that society to reinvest their money at home instead of sending it to New York, London, Zurich, or the Cayman Islands. Investors will only be persuaded to keep their money at home if government policies do not prohibit them from earning a competitive rate of return.

We now briefly revisit the identity between investment and saving. If a country does not have sufficient saving, either from domestic or international sources, the investment ratio will also have to decline, which will reduce the overall growth rate.

As already noted, investment funds can be generated by personal saving, corporate saving, government saving, or foreign saving. In developing economies, major swings in the personal saving rate are rare because most individuals do not save very much. Hence most of the changes in saving occur in the corporate, government, and foreign sectors.

During periods of recession in mature, industrialized countries, economists now agree that the central government should run deficits, rather than exacerbating the downturn by trying to balance the budget. That is because there is a liquid market for those government securities, and during recessions, when investment has declined because of reduced business sentiment, that drop should be offset by less saving in the government sector. Otherwise the recession will intensify.

In general, that doesn't apply to smaller, developing nations. An increase in the government deficit, which by definition reduces saving, must necessarily lead to a reduction in investment unless some other sector of saving increases. Rapidly emerging nations are generally not in the position of having too much capital stock and excess capacity. Hence a rise in the government deficit invariably translates into "crowding out" of private sector investment.

KEY TERMS AND CONCEPTS

Absolute Convergence
Cobb-Douglas Production Function
Conditional Convergence
Constant Returns to Scale
Diminishing Marginal Returns
Endogenous Growth Theory

Growth Accounting
Increasing Returns to Scale
Neoclassical Growth Model
Production Function
Productivity
Steady State Equilibrium

SUMMARY

- Productivity is defined as output per employee-hour; a closely aligned measure sometimes used is output per capita. The level of productivity is an appropriate measure of the standard of living.
- Even small differences of 1% per year in productivity growth can make a huge difference in the standard of living over long periods of time.
- For almost all industrialized countries, the long-term productivity growth rate has averaged between $1\frac{1}{2}$% and 3% per year.
- A production function is a relationship that determines maximum output for various different combinations of factor inputs. At the

macroeconomic level, output is a function of labor input, capital input, and technological progress.
- The Cobb-Douglas production function assumes diminishing marginal returns, constant returns to scale, and a unitary elasticity of substitution between labor and capital. That represents a close approximation to the macroeconomic data, although it does not necessarily hold for individual industries.
- The ratio of saving and investment to GDP is the single most important determinant of productivity, but it accounts for only about half of the variation in growth rates among countries.

- Other important factors that determine productivity growth include the quality of labor, average age of the capital stock, degree of technological progress, importance of increasing returns to scale, and fiscal and regulatory policies.
- After 1973, productivity growth fell sharply in all major industrialized countries. The energy shock may have been a temporary factor causing this decline, but higher inflation, a larger government sector and increased budget deficits, and decreased incentives to innovate were also major factors.
- The neoclassical growth model says that even if the saving and investment ratio does not decline, the growth rate will diminish as an economy matures because a larger proportion of investment is used for replacement instead of expansion.
- In the steady state economy, if there is no growth in technology, productivity will eventually stop rising no matter how large a proportion of GDP is used for saving and investment.
- However, the growth in technology is closely related to the investment ratio, so productivity will continue to rise as long as the capital stock continues to be modernized, even if it is no longer expanding.
- Countries with similar government, educational, and free market policies should eventually converge to the same standard of living even if their saving and investment ratios are different.
- A high saving and investment ratio boosts productivity growth not only because of rapid capital stock growth, but because it encourages the use of modern technology, creates increasing returns to scale for smaller countries, and increases the importance of foreign trade.

QUESTIONS AND PROBLEMS

1. From the early 1950s through 1973, the Japanese economy grew at an average annual rate of almost 10%. It then slowed down to 5% per year from 1973 through 1991, and 1% per year from 1992 through 1998.
   (A) What were the major factors causing growth to slow down after 1973?
   (B) To what extent were the same factors present in the post-1991 slowdown? What other factors caused the most recent slowdown?
   (C) After Japan emerges from its recession, what you would expect its long-term growth rate to be in the future?
2. Harvard historian James Landis has argued that most of the long-term differences in productivity growth among countries can be explained by their distance from the equator. Defend or reject this hypothesis.
3. Economic historians have determined that it took about 40 years from the harnessing of electricity for industrial power until it had a significant impact on productivity growth. The same argument is now being used about microcomputers and the internet, the claim being that the biggest gains in productivity from these new developments have yet to occur. Explain why you think that hypothesis is valid, or why not.

4. Explain why Hong Kong and Singapore have about the same growth rates even though the ratio of investment to GDP is twice as high in Singapore as in Hong Kong.

5. In 1998, Brazil had a per capita GDP of about $4,500, compared to per capita GDP of about $28,000 in the US.
   (A) If per capita growth were to average 2% per year indefinitely in the US and 5% per year in Brazil, how many years would it take Brazil to catch up with the US?
   (B) Using the assumptions of the Cobb-Douglas production function, how fast would capital stock have to grow for per capita GDP to rise 5% per year? How does that compare with capital stock growth of 3% per year in the US (assume technology advances 1% per year in both countries)?
   (C) In mature industrialized societies, the capital/output ratio is approximately 3.0. If the average depreciation rate is 0.04, what would be the current saving and investment ratio in the US? What would it be in Brazil if per capita GDP rose 5% per year?

6. The Netherlands has basically no natural resources, yet its per capita GDP was the highest in the world during the eighteenth century.
   (A) What factors accounted for its preeminence?
   (B) Why did it lose first place to Britain in the nineteenth century?
   (C) Why did Britain lose first place to the US in the twentieth century?

7. In the early 1990s, MIT economist Lester Thurow wrote that of the three major powers in the world economy in the twenty-first century, Europe would be the leader. However, its growth rate fell far behind the US in the 1990s. What were the major factors contributing to slower growth in Europe during that decade? To what extent do you think that slowdown will be reversed by the use of the euro in the early 2000s?

8. From the end of World War II to the dismantling of the Berlin Wall in 1989, per capita real GDP in West Germany rose from approximately $2,000 to $20,000, while per capita GDP in East Germany stayed around $2,000. If the investment/GDP ratio averaged about 25% during that period in West Germany, what do you think it was in East Germany? What factors other than capital stock contributed to the lack of growth in East Germany?

9. In the early 1980s, the US rate of inflation fell from 13% to 4%, government regulation decreased and deregulation increased, and the Reagan Administration passed significant tax incentives to boost saving and investment. Yet according to BLS statistics, productivity in the nonfarm business sector rose only 1.1% during the 1980s, compared to an average annual increase of 1.9% in the 1970s.
   (A) Explain how long lags in response to R&D expenditures might have caused the slowdown in productivity growth in the 1980s.
   (B) Most of the Reagan tax incentives for saving and investment were canceled in 1986. How did that affect productivity growth? (Hint: in answering,

remember that the incentives were not reinstated, yet productivity growth in the late 1990s was very rapid.)

(C) The dollar doubled in value from 1980 to 1985 and then returned to its previous level in 1988. What effect do you think that had on productivity growth?

(D) What other factors may have caused productivity growth to decline in the 1980s?

10. After the fall of the Berlin Wall, many foreigners decided to invest in the Czech Republic, Poland, and Hungary. Yet over the next decade their growth rates were only mediocre. What factors kept these countries from replicating the early successes of the Asian growth tigers?

Notes

1. This material is adapted from Simon Schama's *Embarrassment of Riches*.
2. Named after Charles W. Cobb and Paul H. Douglas. Douglas's presidential address to the AEA was entitled "Are There Laws of Production?" and appeared in the March 1948 issue of the *American Economic Review*. He later was elected as Senator Illinois.
3. This finding was stressed by Douglas, op. cit. An early attempt to measure the rate of technological change was attempted by Robert Solow, "Technical Change and the Aggregate Production Function," *Review of Economics and Statistics*, August 1957. Although this was a highly influential and pathbreaking work, his empirical results have been superseded by Denison, Kendrick, Jorgenson, and others (q.v.).
4. The contrast is even greater for Hong Kong and Singapore. See Alwyn Young, "A Tale of Two Cities: Factor Accumulation and Technical Change in Hong Kong and Singapore," *NBER Macroeconomics Annual*, 1992.
5. Output, and hence productivity growth, was overstated during the period of wage and price controls because firms did not want to admit to the government how much their prices has risen. Thus the official figures overstate productivity growth for the 1969–73 period and understate it for the 1973–9 period.
6. This approach follows the method of Denison, although our results are somewhat different. See his *Accounting for United States Economic Growth, 1929–1969* (Washington, DC: The Brookings Institution, 1974) and *Trends in American Economic Growth, 1929–1982* (Brookings, 1985). Using a somewhat similar method, Jorgenson et al. found a greater contribution for capital stock and a smaller contribution for technological progress. See Dale Jorgenson, Frank Gollop, and Barbara Fraumeni, *Productivity and U.S. Economic Growth* (Cambridge, MA: Harvard University Press, 1987). Denison found that capital stock accounted for only 0.6% of growth, while technology accounted for 1.0% per year; Jorgenson found 1.6% for capital and 0.8% for technology. Our findings show 1.4% for each of these factors, which are somewhat higher than either study because of the surge in growth in the late 1990s.

7. This point is suggested in Edward N. Wolff, "The Productivity Slowdown: The Culprit At Last," *American Economic Review*, December 1996.

8. Robert M. Solow, "A Contribution to the Theory of Economic Growth," *Quarterly Journal of Economics*, February 1957. Along with Milton Friedman's AEA presidential address, this is probably one of the two most widely quoted papers in macroeconomics. Solow's views are summarized in his *Growth Theory: An Exposition* (New York: Oxford University Press, 1988).

9. This term is usually credited to two articles: Robert E. Lucas, "On the Mechanics of Economic Development," *Journal of Monetary Economics*, July 1988, and Paul Romer, "Increasing Returns and Long-Term Growth," *Journal of Political Economy*, October 1986. Many other papers are included in Alwyn Young, ed., *Readings in Endogenous Growth* (Cambridge, MA: MIT Press, 1993). A more recent update, stressing the contributions of human capital and technological innovation, can be found in Gene Grossman and Elhanan Helpman, "Endogenous Innovation in the Theory of Growth," *Journal of Economic Perspectives*, Winter, 1994.

10. This point is emphasized by Mancur Olson, *The Rise and Decline of Nations* (New Haven: Yale University Press, 1982).

11. The case against absolute convergence is made by William J. Baumol, "Productivity Growth, Convergence, and Welfare: What the Long-Run Data Show," *American Economic Review*, December, 1986. The case for conditional convergence is made by N. Gregory Mankiw, David Romer, and David Weil, "A Contribution to the Empirics of Economic Growth," *Quarterly Journal of Economics*, May, 1982.

part IV
The international economy

Parts II and III of this book indicated how changes in monetary and fiscal policy affect the economy. For the most part, though, the discussion has been confined to the domestic sector. We now examine how the international sector affects real growth, inflation, and productivity, and also indicate what factors influence growth in countries other than the US.

At an elementary level, the identity $C + I + F + G = \text{GDP}$ implies that an increase in exports or a decrease in imports boosts total output, just as an increase in consumption or investment boosts total output. However, that identity disguises more than it reveals. Just as a change in consumption or investment that was stimulated by reducing interest rates or taxes might result in higher inflation or crowding out, the increase in GDP caused by a decline in the value of the currency that boosts net exports is often offset by higher inflation and lower foreign saving. Conversely, an increase in foreign saving that results from a larger trade deficit may stimulate domestic investment, resulting in no net loss to the economy.

It turns out that the primary impact of a change in net exports is not reflected in the GDP identity, but instead affects the supply side – through its impact on productivity, inflation, foreign saving, and investment. That is particularly true for the US economy, because the world economy is on a de facto dollar standard. Realistically, it does not make sense to suppose that the rest of the world can buy more goods and services from the US without an increase in US imports from its trading partners.

We have already seen that no country can boost its long-term growth rate by printing more money or running bigger deficits. Similarly, no country can boost its long-term growth rate by devaluing its currency. While a decline in the value of the currency initially raises exports and reduces imports, that effect invariably turns out to be short lived and never helps the economy in the long run. If it did, Bolivia and Brazil would be among the most prosperous economies in the world. On the other hand, an overvalued currency is not beneficial to real growth; it has hurt the UK economy in the past, and reduced growth in Germany and Japan during the 1990s. Any economy functions better when the value of its currency is near its equilibrium value.

Most countries are required to balance their external accounts over the longer run; if they do not, their supply of foreign exchange will diminish to the vanishing point, and they will be forced to devalue the currency and restrict imports. However, that is not true for the US. When the US runs a trade deficit, the extra dollars received by foreigners are either directly or indirectly redeposited back in the US. That is why the US was able to prosper during the 1990s with an ever-increasing trade deficit, even though other countries could not operate that way. Along the same lines, an increase in net foreign ownership of US assets does not hurt the performance of the economy in the long run as long as the dollar remains a key currency and the value of the dollar remains near equilibrium. Only if an increased trade deficit pushes the value of the dollar below equilibrium will economic performance be impaired.

Because the US economy has such a large impact on the rest of the world, changes in domestic economic activity will also affect its exports with a lag. If a small country reduces its imports from the US, the effect will hardly be felt domestically. Yet if the US reduces its imports from another country or region (say, Europe), that will probably reduce growth in Europe, so after a few quarters, US exports to Europe will diminish. That is known as the repercussion effect. Thus changes made in the US to try to increase its exports or diminish its imports will be partially offset the following year, unless those changes are also accompanied by global changes that boost worldwide growth (e.g., a sharp decline in oil prices). In particular, US exports usually fall sharply in the year after the country experiences a recession.

The supply-side impact of foreign trade is of major importance. An increase in imports will boost productivity and retard inflation, as firms are required to keep pace with the latest improvements in international technology and keep costs from rising. Thus a decline in the value of the dollar below its equilibrium value is likely to boost inflation for two reasons. First and more immediately obvious, imported goods cost more; however, that impact will be muted if foreign producers adjust their prices to reflect dollar terms. Second and arguably more important, productivity gains will slacken and firms will no longer focus as sharply on reducing costs.

Hence an increase in imports may not diminish real GDP at all, in spite of the fundamental national income accounting identity, if (a) it boosts domestic productivity and reduces domestic inflation, and (b) the excess dollars are reinvested in the US.

One should be wary of "too much of a good thing." After all, if a stronger dollar and higher imports caused unalloyed benefits, the argument could be carried to the absurd extreme that the US would be better off if it did not produce any goods and imported everything. No one believes that. Instead, the optimal foreign trade position is reached when the dollar remains near its equilibrium value. Economists generally stress that relative prices are important. Nowhere is that more important than for the relative price of money – interest rates – and for the relative price of the dollar – the exchange rate.

This point is sometimes difficult for managers to grasp. If the dollar is in equilibrium, but textiles, apparel, and steel can be produced much less expensively abroad, employees and owners of those industries are likely to claim it is grossly unfair when their jobs, and their equity, disappear. Obviously they are worse off. For the overall economy, though, the offsetting factors – less expensive products for consumers and other businesses, which enables them to purchase larger quantities of other goods and services – mean a net benefit occurs.

Conversely, it is difficult for any economy to function optimally if interest rates and exchange rates are not near their equilibrium levels. The value of the dollar should be set near its purchasing power parity, which means the average cost of producing a market basket of world-traded goods and services in the US is the same as the cost of producing that market basket of goods in a trade-weighted average of other countries. That does not mean the cost of production will be the same for each good and each industry; only that the weighted average cost is the same; in more colloquial terms, firms face a "level playing field."

The importance of net exports occurs more through their influence on supply-side factors, notably inflation and productivity, than through their impact on aggregate demand. If the dollar is undervalued, net exports may temporarily rise, but eventually productivity growth will suffer and inflation will rise. If the dollar is overvalued, manufacturing output will decline and unemployment will rise. These statements are also true for other countries, with the additional caveat that other countries do not have the luxury of running a sizable trade deficit indefinitely.

Our treatment of the international sector proceeds as follows. First, we establish definitions and describe the data for net exports, the current and capital account surplus or deficit, and the value of the dollar. That is followed by a brief explanation of the factors that determine exports and imports, and the importance of foreign trade on productivity and inflation as well as aggregate demand. Since the level of net exports depends critically on the value of the dollar, the determination of foreign exchange rates is discussed in detail in chapter 12. A more formal treatment of the role of net exports and the value of the dollar, using an extended IS/LM diagram, is presented in chapter 13; this material may be ignored without loss of continuity for those who skipped chapter 7. Finally, chapter 14 presents several case studies describing the factors that have affected major countries other than the US, with some suggestions about how to identify countries that will grow rapidly in the future.

chapter eleven

Basic determinants of exports and imports

11.1   The balance between current and capital accounts

For many years, financial and business columnists have railed against the "evils of the twin deficits" – the Federal budget deficit and the trade deficit. The vast majority of economists agree that a full-employment budget deficit has negative long-run effects on the economy because it raises interest rates and crowds out private investment. On the other hand, the "evil" of the trade deficit is more of a canard – especially for the US.

By definition, the **current account** surplus or deficit equals (a) the surplus or deficit on goods (often known as the trade surplus or deficit) plus (b) the surplus or deficit on services plus (c) net investment income plus (d) unilateral transfers abroad (which are almost always negative for the US; money sent back to the "old country," etc.). The **capital account** surplus or deficit for any country is equal to the net inflow of foreign capital into that country minus the outflow of domestic capital to foreign countries. By definition, it equals the current account with the opposite sign, except for the statistical discrepancy. Together, the current account and capital account represent the balance of payments data.

Table 11.1 provides figures for the US for 1993, 1997, and 2000; different years are presented to illustrate how many of these items change significantly from one year to the next.

Note how the huge increase in the trade deficit by 2000 was matched by an equally large increase in the inflow of foreign capital; this linkage is dis- cussed later in this chapter. The other enticing tidbit is the unusually large statistical discrepancy in 1997, which is very atypical. Apparently, the collapse of many southeast Asian economies that year resulted in a massive inflow of funds into the US that was not immediately recorded in the national income accounts.

As already noted, except for the statistical discrepancy, the current account deficit is identically equal to the capital account surplus. That means any excess dollars that are held by other countries are reinvested either directly or indirectly in dollar-denominated assets, unless foreigners decide to throw the dollars in the sea or bury them in the desert.

Table 11.1   Selected balance of payments data

Balance of payments category	1993	1997	2000
Net exports of goods	−132.5	−198.2	−452.2
Net exports of services	63.7	90.4	76.5
Net balance, goods and services	**−68.8**	**−107.8**	**−375.7**
Net investment income	23.9	8.8	−14.8
Unilateral transfers	−37.6	−40.8	−54.1
Balance on current account	**−82.5**	**−139.8**	**−444.7**
Change in US government assets (mainly holding of foreign currencies)	−1.9	−0.6	−0.5
Outflow of US private assets	−198.8	−486.7	−579.7
Less: change in foreign official assets (mainly purchases of dollars)	71.8	19.0	37.6
Less: inflow of foreign assets	210.3	740.3	986.6
Balance on capital account	**81.4**	**272.0**	**444.0**
Statistical discrepancy (current account minus capital account with the signs reversed)	1.1	−132.2	0.7

Source: Bureau of Economic Analysis website, www.bea.gov

The data in table 11.1 show a substantial increase in recent years for both invest-ment in the US by foreigners and in foreign countries by US entities. In the US, private sector flows dwarf the net flows of official assets. However, that is not the case for most other countries. In 2000, the total stock of foreign reserves held by the US was only about $50 billion, far less than many smaller countries and only about 3% of the world total.

Figure 11.1 illustrates the amount of foreign reserves held for the ten countries with the largest stock of reserves. Japan is far ahead of any other country, but note the large amount of reserves accumulated by Taiwan, Hong Kong, and Singapore, even though GDP in those countries is less than 5% of US GDP.

Figure 11.2 shows the recent current account balance for these same ten countries. Japan has the largest current account surplus, which is one of the main reasons for its massive holdings of foreign reserves. However, many smaller countries with moderate current account balances have large accumulations of foreign reserves. They believe these reserves reduce chances of speculation against their currencies.

By comparison, Brazil has a substantial trade deficit, even though it has substan-tial foreign reserves. For countries whose currencies are not widely traded, foreign reserves can be used to offset continuing trade deficits for a while, but eventually those reserves will dwindle to the vanishing point. When that happens, countries must attract more foreign capital, improve the competitive posture of their exports, reduce imports – or depreciate their currency significantly.

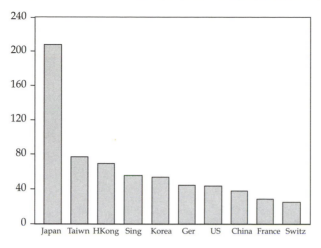

Figure 11.1   Total international reserves excluding gold, 1999 (ten countries with largest reserves) in billions of SDRs (1.37$/SDR in 1999)

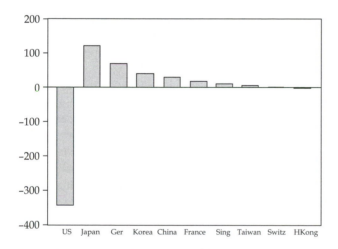

Figure 11.2   Current account, foreign trade balance, 1999 (US$ billions)

Figure 11.3 indicates that for many countries, the trade balance and the current account balance can be quite different. In particular, Germany has a large trade surplus but no current account surplus. That differential represents (a) a deficit in net exports of services; (b) a net outflow of investment income, which means other countries are earning more income from their German investments than Germans are earning on their investments in other countries; and (c) a large net outflow of unilateral transfers, representing "guest workers" sending remittances back to their native countries. The UK, by comparison, has a positive net balance on services and net interest income, and far fewer unilateral transfers abroad.

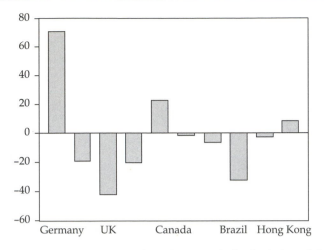

Figure 11.3 Trade and current account balances (for each country, the first bar is the trade balance, the second bar is the current account balance; all figures are for 1999 in billions of US dollars)

The current account balance is a more important economic determinant of the value of the currency than the trade balance, although most political discussion centers on the trade balance. However, as has been shown for Germany, a large trade surplus can be completely wiped out by other negative items in the current account balance.

The balance between the current and capital accounts is not always intuitively obvious. Let us illustrate this with an example. Suppose a Japanese auto manufacturer sells a car to the US but does not buy any American goods in return. The Japanese then hold (say) $20,000 in dollars. Those dollars cannot be spent in Japan. They can't be spent in China, or most other countries. That leaves the Japanese with three choices. They can simply hold on to these dollars and increase their stock of foreign exchange, invest them in dollar-denominated assets, or use foreign exchange markets to sell excess dollars to someone who is willing to buy them. If there is a substantial surplus of dollars, that would cause the dollar/yen ratio to decline.

Once upon a time, foreign businesses could demand payment in gold for their excess dollars. Because the gold standard was once an important mechanism for international payments, and it still helps to explain how payment mechanisms work today, it is discussed in greater detail in the next section. Yet ever since the US closed the international gold window on August 15, 1971, that option no longer exists, so we also examine the choices that are currently available.

The first alternative for the Japanese is simply to retain these dollars, thus increasing their stock of foreign exchange reserves. In that case, just as is the case for gold, the assets do not earn any interest. That would not seem to be the optimal choice; yet as shown above, Japan holds far more in foreign reserves than does the US.

Why would any country choose to hold such a large amount of foreign exchange reserves? Primarily because it strengthens and stabilizes the value of their own currency; the higher the ratio of foreign reserves to foreign debt, the smaller the chance that speculators would try to bet against the currency of a country with such massive reserves. Since a stable currency often leads to low inflation and more rapid growth, aggressive accumulation of foreign reserves is sometimes thought to boost real growth and the standard of living.

Smaller countries generally try to hold substantial foreign exchange reserves because of wide swings in their current account balance. For countries that rely on exports of a single agricultural or mineral commodity for most of their foreign exchange, a sudden drop in the world price of that commodity might lead to a shortfall of foreign exchange, which means the country could not buy needed imports unless it held substantial foreign reserves or borrowed the foreign currency from some international organization.

The excess dollars that countries do not hold in reserves are invested in dollar-denominated assets. For example, the funds can be used to purchase Treasury securities, corporate debt securities, equities, or deposited in bank accounts. They can also be used to purchase existing tangible assets, such as real estate, or invested in new capital equipment, such as a new automobile factory in the US. Whatever choice is selected, those excess dollars eventually return to the US.

The Japanese might not want to hold dollar-denominated assets, in which case they would sell their excess dollars to investors in other countries, using foreign exchange markets. If the supply of dollars exceeds the demand at the previous price, the value of the US dollar will decline until a new equilibrium value is reached.

Some countries that boost their exports to the US use the extra dollars to buy more goods and services from the US, boosting their imports proportionately. When the price of oil rose from $3 to $13/bbl in 1973–4, there was much hand-wringing about whether the US could afford to pay the massive bill for imported energy. In fact, OPEC nations used their newfound wealth to buy so many US goods and services that exports rose sharply and the US posted its biggest trade surplus ever in 1975 – although the recession that year also contributed to the surplus.

To demonstrate how the current account balance must always equal the capital account balance with the opposite sign on an ex post basis even when they are not equal on an ex ante basis, consider the following four cases:

1. *Current account deficit, net inflow of funds*. Foreign investors are eager to invest in the country with a trade deficit, so the accounts are in balance both ex ante and ex post. That is typically the case for the US.
2. *Current account surplus, net outflow of funds*. Investors in the home country are eager to invest abroad, so the accounts are in balance both ex ante and ex post.
3. *Current account deficit, net outflow of funds*. Foreign investors are not eager to invest in the country with a trade deficit. The difference must be made up by selling foreign exchange, which doesn't last very long. Often, the country is forced to get a loan and reduce its current account deficit, probably with an

austerity program that restricts imports. If that does not work, it will eventually have to devalue, hence reversing the current account deficit.

4. *Current account surplus, net inflow of funds.* The country accumulates foreign exchange, which leads to the buildup of massive international reserves. The currency strengthens until it is eventually overpriced and reduces the growth in exports. That is what happened to Japan in the late 1990s. Eventually, manufacturing operations move to other countries.

Later on we will explain how these various situations affect countries in different economic circumstances. First, though, it is useful to explain how balance of payments flows work under both fixed and flexible exchange rates. This section starts with a brief historical overview of the fixed exchange rate system even though it is no longer used, since many smaller countries have currencies that in essence are fixed relative to the dollar. Also, that mechanism can be used to illustrate some key points that apply to current foreign exchange markets.

11.2 Fixed and flexible exchange rates

From 1717 to 1914, most major countries were on the gold standard, which was suspended only during times of major wars, such as the Napoleonic Wars and (for the US) the Civil War. In fact, the value of one British pound was fixed at 0.139oz of gold by none other than Sir Isaac Newton.

The gold standard worked as follows. Suppose the United Kingdom, which was the center of international trade and finance until 1914, purchased more goods from abroad than it sold, so its current account balance was negative. Other countries could then require the Bank of England to make up the difference by shipping them gold bullion. The fact that the Bank of England stood ready to deliver gold meant most countries did not demand it.

For while gold was then considered an excellent store of value, its other uses are quite limited. In particular, it earns no interest; if prices are stable, it does not increase in value. As a result, as long as the UK currency and economy were thought to be sound, it would make much more sense for the other countries to invest those excess pounds in the UK and earn a positive rate of return, rather than have gold sitting in the counting house earning no interest. As a result, Britain never faced a gold drain except for periods of wartime, and the value of the pound remained stable.

Suppose an exporter in another country demanded to be paid in gold instead of British pounds. In order to remain on the gold standard, Britain would have to honor that commitment. If Britain started to run short of gold, it would face two choices. One would be to raise interest rates: a higher rate of interest would attract more capital, and the resulting reduction in economic growth would reduce the demand for imports, hence reducing the trade deficit. Alternatively, it could devalue the currency. Of course, if that happened very often, other countries would demand gold payment regularly, and Britain would soon cease to be a world center of finance.

Because the world supply of gold did not change very much, the price level in countries on the gold standard was stable except in times of war. That has caused some people to be nostalgic for the gold standard, since it coincided with a period of stable prices. What were the disadvantages?

For one thing, the gold standard led to recurring financial crises, partly because the supply of gold did not grow nearly as fast as the needs of international commerce. It also caused countries to raise interest rates and reduce domestic demand at a time when those steps would have otherwise been unwarranted. In general, the increase in the supply of gold simply did not keep up with the growing demands of international commerce. Also, raising interest rates to defend the value of the currency often led to economic downturns.

Once World War I began, the international gold standard became a sometime thing. European countries abandoned it shortly after war broke out, and while it was gradually reinstated after hostilities ceased, it broke down again in 1931.

In 1933, the US went off the domestic gold standard – which meant domestic economic agents could no longer demand to be paid in gold – and unilaterally devalued the dollar relative to gold, boosting the price of gold from $20.67 to $35.00/oz. While the international gold standard nominally remained in place, it limped along in tatters. During the 1930s, trade between most countries deteriorated to bilateral trade agreements: you buy our goods and we'll buy yours. Many countries tried competitive devaluations in an attempt to boost exports while reducing imports, which were known as "beggar thy neighbor" policies. Obviously such a system cannot work on a worldwide basis, and much of the industrialized world remained in depression throughout the 1930s. What remained of the gold standard was suspended after World War II began.

In 1944, in a meeting at Bretton Woods, New Hampshire, leading financiers, political leaders, and economists attempted to develop a mechanism for a "kinder, gentler" international gold standard to be implemented once the war ended. This new arrangement was to be implemented by the International Monetary Fund (IMF), which would serve as the world's banker.

Shortly after World War II, Britain was forced to devalue again, but outside of that one episode, the international gold standard worked fairly well through the 1960s. The mechanism was still the same: if exporters in a given country did not want to invest the excess currency in the economy of another country with a trade deficit, they could demand payment in gold.

The Bretton Woods agreement contained several clauses designed to make the gold standard more flexible, including a backup fund that could be used to offset unwarranted runs on individual currencies when countries suffered reverses not of their own making (such as a famine or other natural catastrophe). But such agreements were just temporary patches, and in the long run could not overcome the fundamental flaws in the system.

The remains of the gold standard unraveled when the Vietnam War boosted real growth, inflation, and imports in the US, and speculation increased that the US would soon run out of gold. Thus, on August 15, 1971, Nixon shut the gold window, and the international gold standard came to an end. After that date, anyone who had excess dollars could sell them to someone else, but only through the mechanism of foreign exchange markets; if the excess supply of dollars increased, its value would drop until a new equilibrium price was reached.

With the abandonment of the international gold standard, the value of all currencies "floated"; there was no fixed anchor. Values of the US dollar, the German Deutschmark, the British pound, and the Japanese yen all went their separate ways. Other, smaller currencies could also float, but for practical purposes, most of them either followed the dollar or, for European countries closely linked to Germany, the DM; in 1999 that was replaced by the € (euro) for international transactions, and in 2002 for all transactions. In the intervening years, there continued to be frequent devaluations of the French franc, the Belgian franc, the Italian lira, the Swedish krona, and the Spanish peseta. Only the Dutch guilder and the Swiss franc held their parity with the DM from 1971 through 1998.

World inflation for industrialized countries was low and stable during the period when the gold standard was in effect. However, in the 1990s, world inflation again became low and stable even with flexible exchange rates. The gold standard may have reinforced stable prices, but only at the high cost of frequent financial panics. We now know that inflation can be controlled without relying on this harsh method; consequently, hardly any knowledgeable economist now calls for a return to the gold standard.

CASE STUDY 11.1   NIXON CLOSES THE GOLD WINDOW ON AUGUST 15, 1971

After almost an entire decade of unparalleled prosperity, the US economy headed into recession in late 1969. Even worse, from the viewpoint of Nixon, the recovery that started in 1971 was unusually sluggish. In his view, drastic action was required to insure that the economy would be booming by election time in 1972. Every economist in the country knew how to stimulate the economy in the short run: cut taxes, increase government spending, boost money supply growth, and artificially suppress interest rates. Of course, that combination could be lethally inflationary in the longer run – but only after 1972.

There was one restraint left. If Nixon put his program into effect, there would undoubtedly be a run on the dollar. US foreign reserves had already fallen to

continued

CASE STUDY 11.1 (*continued*)

$12 billion, or about 8% of the world total, from $17 billion, or 27%, a decade earlier. The gold standard was the remaining check on fiscal and monetary profligacy – so Nixon chopped it off at the knees. He closed the international gold window, and for good measure added a temporary 10% surcharge on imports. On December 18, he devalued the dollar from $35 to $38/oz and removed the surcharge. Later, the US officially went off the gold standard, and the price of gold rose to $200/oz in 1974 and an all-time peak of over $800/oz in early 1980.

Nixon was trying to stimulate the economy; going off the gold standard was only a sideshow. He gambled that the inflationary impacts of the combination of a lower dollar, artificially depressed interest rates, rapid growth in the money supply, tax cuts, higher government spending, and the resulting substantial increase in the full-employment budget deficit could be postponed until after the election if wage and price controls were also kept in place through 1972. That turned out to be correct – with a vengeance.

Seldom has there ever been such a graphic example of short-term gain at the expense of long-term loss. Net exports improved in 1973, but only because of the agricultural shortages and huge increases in farm prices based on the Soviet grain purchases. The end result was the recession of 1974, the most severe in the post-WWII period. However, the decision to abandon the gold standard was not the principal villain. Instead, it was the attempt to suppress inflation during an election year with wage and price controls, while at the same time stimulating the economy beyond its capacity. The weaker dollar contributed to higher inflation, but was not the major cause.

11.3   US exports and imports: empirical review

Both exports and imports have grown rapidly over the post-WWII period as a percentage of GDP, as shown in figure 11.4. However, these strong common trends often mask how exports and imports change with respect to the value of the dollar. Hence figure 11.5 shows the relationship between the net export ratio – exports minus imports divided by GDP – and the value of the trade-weighted average of the dollar. While the correlation is far from perfect, a stronger dollar does cause the net export balance to decline, and a weaker dollar causes it to improve.

Figure 11.6 provides data for some of the major categories of international trade. The US has a slight surplus in high-tech equipment: computers, semiconductors, and telecommunications equipment. Its biggest sectoral trade deficits occur in motor vehicles, energy, and textiles and apparel (including shoes). The trade deficit in energy started with the sharp rise in oil prices in 1973. In addition to high-tech equipment, the two major categories where the US has a trade surplus are aircraft and major agricultural crops: wheat, corn, and soybeans. Figure 11.7 shows that the

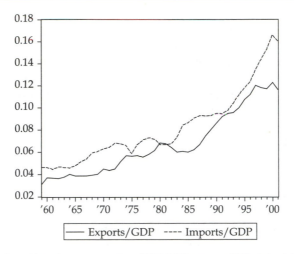

Figure 11.4 US exports and imports as a proportion of GDP (all figures are 1996 chained dollars)

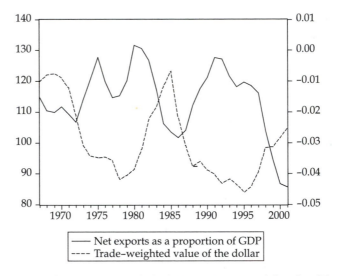

Figure 11.5 There is a significant negative correlation between net exports and the value of the dollar

large increase in the trade deficit in the late 1990s occurred primarily in consumer goods; capital goods maintained a slight surplus even in 2000.

Table 11.2 shows the 2001 figures for US exports and imports for major countries and regions of the world. Most of the trade deficit occurs with east Asia, a figure that widened in 1998 following the collapse of many southeast Asian currencies. By far the biggest imbalance occurs with China; not only is that the biggest deficit, but the ratio of imports to exports is more than 5:1. The US also had a substantial trade deficit with Canada and Mexico, although the deficit with the rest of Latin America

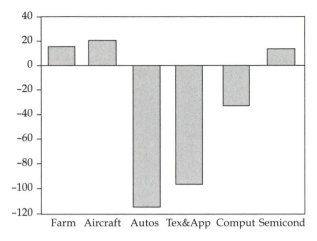

Figure 11.6   US net exports by major category, 2001 (farm is major crops; tex&app is textiles and apparel)

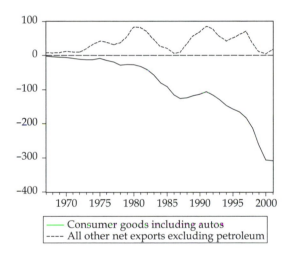

Figure 11.7   Net exports for consumer goods including autos have plunged over the past two decades, while other net exports have remained slightly positive

was much smaller. The deficit with Europe was substantial, but in the past the balance had been in surplus during years when the dollar was undervalued or European growth was stronger than in the US.

11.4   Income and price elasticities of US exports and imports

The analysis developed in this section assumes there are no significant barriers to trade. If a country devalues its currency but at the same time tightens restrictions

Table 11.2   US exports and imports with selected countries in 2001

	Exports	Imports	Balance
World	730.9	1142.3	−411.4
Western hemisphere	323.6	415.9	−92.3
Canada	163.7	217.0	−53.3
Mexico	101.5	131.4	−29.9
South/Central America	58.4	67.5	−9.1
Europe	182.0	253.6	−71.6
Western Europe	175.1	239.2	−64.1
Germany	30.1	59.1	−29.0
France	19.9	30.3	−10.4
Netherlands/Belgium	33.0	19.6	13.4
UK	40.8	41.4	−0.6
Eastern/Central Europe	6.9	14.4	−7.5
Asia	173.3	375.7	−202.4
Japan	57.6	126.6	−69.0
China	19.2	102.3	−83.1
Newly industrialized countries	72.1	93.2	−21.1
Other Pacific rim	24.4	53.6	−29.2
OPEC	20.1	59.8	−39.7
Other	31.9	37.3	−5.4

on imports, they might not rise at all. We also assume mobility of capital among countries, and flexible exchange rates.

Export and import functions for the US economy can be written as follows:

$$EX = f_1 + f_2 XW - f_3(p_{ex} \cdot \$/p_w) \tag{11.1}$$

$$IM = f_4 + f_5 Y - f_6(p_{im}/\$) \tag{11.2}$$

$$F = EX - IM \tag{11.3}$$

where XW is an index of world production, p_w is the average price level of traded goods produced abroad, and p_{ex} and p_{im} are the price levels for US exports and imports. Through the end of 1998, the "$\$$" term was the trade-weighted average of the dollar, an index compiled by the Federal Reserve Board and based on the values of the ten major world currencies: UK, France, Germany, Italy, Belgium, Netherlands, Switzerland, Sweden, Canada, and Japan. Starting on January 1, 1999, the euro replaced the French franc, German DM, Italian lira, Belgian franc, and Netherlands guilder in that index. The Fed now calculates six trade-weighted averages of the dollar instead of one. Here we use the broad-weighted average published by the Fed; specific indexes are discussed in chapter 12.

The terms in parentheses represent the relative costs of production. They could rise if (a) US production costs (p_{ex}) rise, (b) foreign production costs (p_w) fall, (c) the price of imports (p_{im}) falls, or (d) relative production costs remain constant but the value of the dollar rises. A rise in the cost of production, regardless of the particular reason, would reduce exports and boost imports, ceteris paribus.

The **income** and **price elasticities** vary considerably for different countries. For the US we find that:

- A 1% rise in domestic industrial production boosts imports by about 2%. The percentage change in imports is significantly larger than the percentage change in domestic demand.
- A 1% change in the relative value of import prices – the relative cost of production adjusted by changes in the value of the dollar – changes imports by about 0.4%, with a lag of about one year. That figure is relatively low because many foreign firms tend to adjust their prices in line with US prices, instead of following changes in the value of their currencies.
- A 1% rise in world industrial production excluding the US boosts exports by about $1\frac{1}{2}$% with a lag of one to two years.
- A 1% rise in US industrial production boosts US exports by about $\frac{1}{2}$% over the following two years.
- A 1% change in the relative value of export prices – the relative cost of production adjusted by changes in the value of the dollar – changes exports by about 0.7%. This coefficient is nonlinear; if the dollar rises far above its equilibrium level, exports would drop sharply and not recover until the dollar approached equilibrium again. Yet if the dollar is close to equilibrium, the same percentage changes in the currency have a much smaller impact on exports.

The estimates of the elasticities vary somewhat depending on the time period and precise specification of the equation chosen, but the important facts to note are that (a) the price elasticity of imports is lower than for exports, and (b) a change in US production will initially change imports in the same direction, but will also change exports with some lag.

The next six figures show the relationship between percentage changes in exports and imports and the relevant measures of income and prices. Both exports and imports have increased rapidly as a proportion of GDP over the past 25 years, representing the greater importance of international trade to the US. All these graphs show the correlations between percentage changes in all of these variables, thus removing the trend.

Figures 11.8 and 11.9 show that changes in constant-dollar imports are more closely correlated with changes in real GDP than with lagged changes in the value of the dollar. Figure 11.10 shows the relationship between changes in exports and changes in OECD industrial production excluding the US (Canada, western Europe and Japan). Figure 11.11 shows the correlation between changes in exports and the lagged value of the dollar; which was strong during the 1980s but has weakened during the 1990s. Also note the longer lag in 1986–7; exports did not rebound very

Figure 11.8   Imports and industrial production

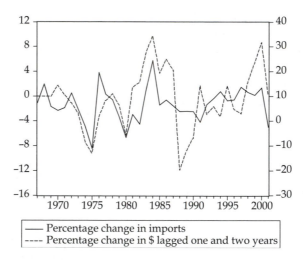

Figure 11.9   Imports and value of the dollar

much until the dollar had fallen far enough for US exports to become competitive again in world markets.

Figure 11.12 shows the percentage change in imports as a function of the percentage changes in industrial production and lagged values of the dollar. Figure 11.13 shows the percentage change in exports as a function of percentage changes in the current and lagged value of the dollar, OECD production, and lagged US production.

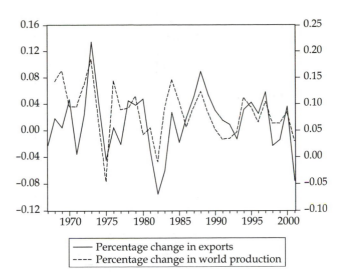

Figure 11.10 Exports and world production

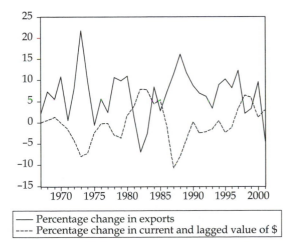

Figure 11.11 Exports and value of the dollar

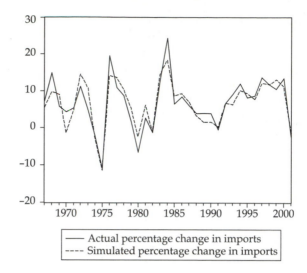

Figure 11.12   Import equation

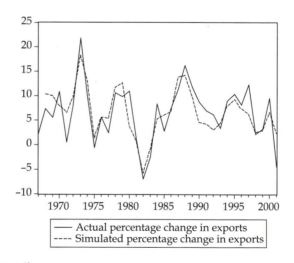

Figure 11.13   Export equation

MANAGER'S BRIEFCASE: PLANNING AHEAD FOR EXPORTS

Trying to estimate how much you will sell domestically next year based on upcoming economic conditions is never a simple matter for cyclical industries, especially during times of recession. It might reasonably be thought that trying to predict export sales, which go to many different countries and furthermore depend on the value of the dollar relative to foreign currencies, would be even more difficult. Nonetheless, based on the results given in the previous section, a few hints can be usefully employed.

On a global basis, the single most important fact to realize is that rapid growth in the US will ordinarily be followed by faster growth abroad the following year; whereas a US recession will generally be followed by slower growth abroad the following year. Claims that an increase in export business will help dampen domestic business cycles are generally just wishful thinking. Indeed, most of the evidence suggests the lag has been getting shorter; in 2001, total real GDP for the US economy was virtually unchanged on a quarterly average basis (i.e., 2000.4 to 2001.4), but real exports fell 11.4%. The stronger dollar was partly accountable for that decline, but most of it reflected slower growth on a worldwide basis. For example, growth in Euroland fell from 3.4% to 1.5%; in Mexico from 6.6% to −0.3%; in Japan from 2.4% to −0.4%; and in Taiwan from 5.9% to −1.9%. Note in particular that the sharp increase in the value of the dollar, which should have boosted exports in other countries, was swamped by the US recession.

If the dollar is overvalued by 20%, obviously that makes sales more difficult; the option is to cut prices substantially in an attempt to maintain market share. However, during periods when the dollar is rising rapidly, those gains can be offset by hedging. When the dollar is severely overvalued, it is likely that countervailing forces will soon return it to equilibrium, as discussed in the next chapter. Thus while an overvalued dollar does reduce exports, the more important variable in terms of corporate planning is the growth rate overseas, which in turn follows the US growth rate with a relatively short lag.

11.5   The repercussion effect

Because the US economy is the engine that drives world growth, its policy changes have a different effect on worldwide exports and imports than, say, a change in policy in the UK. Suppose US exports rise and imports decline. That temporarily helps the US economy but reduces growth abroad, since other countries now sell less to the US. The next year, US exports weaken because growth abroad has declined. When the US has a recession one year, the rest of the world economy slows down next year. That is known as the **repercussion effect**. To a lesser extent this also occurs for Germany and the European economy, and Japan and the southeast Asian economy. In particular, one reason the Japanese recession that started in 1992 lasted a full decade was that Japanese exports to the former "growth tigers" were depressed because those countries in turn could not afford to buy as many goods from Japan after their exports to Japan declined.

Hence an attempt to boost US growth by stimulating net exports would partially backfire the following year. The only exception would occur if some independent expansionary effect boosted real growth around the world at the same time that US exports rose. That happened in 1986, when the drop in oil prices and a coordinated

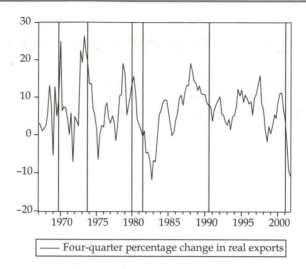

Figure 11.14 Evidence of the repercussion effect in the US economy (vertical lines indicate the onset of recession)

worldwide effort to reduce interest rates boosted worldwide real growth. As a result, the US net foreign balance improved not only because of the decline in the dollar, but because of faster growth abroad. Under normal circumstances, though, an improvement in the US trade balance reduces growth elsewhere in the world.

The repercussion effect does not apply to most other countries: an initial increase in the exports of Brazil, for example, will not reduce their export growth the following year, nor will a boost in their production boost their exports the following year. Yet even for smaller countries, attempts at unilaterally increasing net exports with another country seldom work, because they invite retaliation. That is particularly true for competitive devaluations. Thus even for smaller countries, an attempt to boost the growth rate by raising net exports – except to the US – usually has a much smaller impact on GDP than anticipated.

How important is the repercussion effect in the US empirically? Figure 11.14 shows the four-quarter percentage change in real exports and real GDP lagged one year. The evidence is significant although not conclusive. Usually, exports remain weak in the year or two after recessions: that happened in 1973, 1976, 1983, 1992, and 2002. In many cases, though, exports turned down *before* the recession started, which suggests that might have been one of the causes of the downturn. That is likely to occur when the inflation rate increases near the end of business cycle expansions, which means US firms are less competitive in world markets. However, this graph also suggests that from time to time, exogenous declines in major markets in the rest of the world depress exports enough that the US economy does indeed slow down. Although the world is on a de facto dollar standard, the US does not operate in isolation. Major declines that occur in the rest of the world – often because of sudden devaluations, such as in Mexico in 1995 or southeast Asia in 1997 – do have a noticeable impact on the overall US economy.

11.6   How serious is the burgeoning trade deficit?

So far in this chapter we have discussed the concepts of the current and capital account balances, fixed and flexible exchange rates, import and export equations, their income and price elasticities, and the repercussion effect. These tools are now used to explore the issue of how the trade deficit affects the US economy, and whether restrictions to free trade are beneficial to the overall economy. The latter problem received increased attention recently because of the sharp rise in the trade deficit ratio from 1.2% of GDP in 1991 to 4.3% in 2001.

The issues are basically as follows. An increase in the trade deficit reduces employment in some industries and increases employment in other industries. On the negative side, jobs are lost in some highly visible industries, including steel, textiles and apparel, and motor vehicles, and wages in those industries do not rise as rapidly. On the positive side, an increase in imports provides consumers with a better choice at lower prices, productivity and the standard of living rise faster, and the inflow of foreign saving boosts investment without raising interest rates. The loss in jobs, wages, and profits in some key manufacturing industries must be balanced against the gains in the rest of the economy.

The **theory of comparative advantage** states that if the value of the dollar is near equilibrium, some domestic industries will be able to produce goods at a lower cost than the world average, and will have an export surplus. Other industries will produce goods at a higher cost than the world average, and will have an export deficit. Under certain highly unrealistic assumptions (see the appendix), a corollary of this theory states that on average, countries have a zero current account balance. In such a situation, virtually everyone favors free trade.

Based on the data given above, it is clear that situation does not apply to the US economy, which has had a current account deficit every year since 1982 except for a minuscule surplus in 1991. Furthermore, the deficit ratio rose at unprecedented rates from 1995 through 2000. That is not necessarily bad for the economy, as can be seen by the robust growth rate of 4.1% over that period, a decline in the unemployment rate from 6% to 4%, and low, stable inflation even at full employment. Nonetheless, an increase of that magnitude in the current account and trade deficits, coupled with an overvalued dollar, raise some legitimate issues that need to be addressed.

Macroeconomic data indicate that when the dollar is overvalued (a) manufacturing employment decreases, (b) the real manufacturing wage decreases, (c) manufacturing profits decrease relative to total profits, and (d) the standard of living, as measured by the real wage rate, accelerates for those who do not work in the manufacturing sector. An overvalued dollar thus accelerates the shift from the manufacturing to the service sector. These relationships are shown in the next

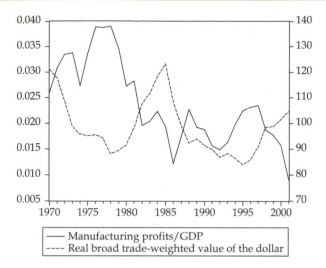

Figure 11.15   Manufacturing profit margins generally decline when the value of the dollar increases

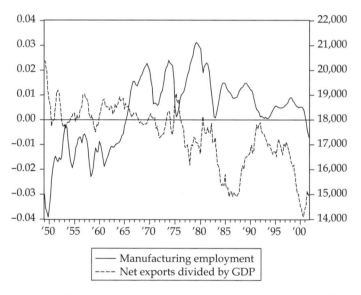

Figure 11.16   There is a slight negative correlation between manufacturing employment and the trade balance

four figures, some of which start in 1970 because the value of the dollar was fixed in terms of gold until mid-1971.

Figure 11.15 shows that, while the ratio of manufacturing profits to GDP has a long-term downward trend, that trend accelerates during periods when the dollar is overvalued. Figure 11.16 illustrates the negative correlation between the level of manufacturing employment and the ratio of net exports to GDP. Figure 11.17 is the

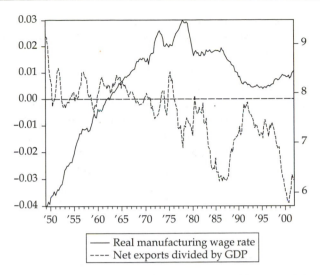

Figure 11.17   The real manufacturing wage rate declined after the trade balance turned negative

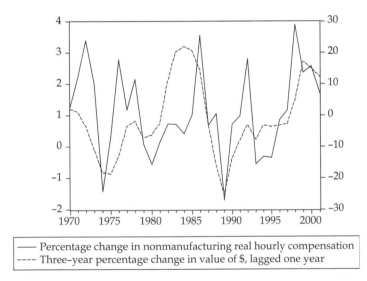

Figure 11.18   There is a significant correlation between real hourly compensation in the nonmanufacturing sector and the three-year percentage change in the broad trade-weighted average value of the dollar lagged one year

most striking relationship, showing how the value of the real wage in the manufacturing sector declined after 1973, when the net export balance turned negative.
Finally, figure 11.18 indicates a positive correlation between the percentage changes

in real hourly compensation in the nonmanufacturing sector and lagged percentage changes in the value of the dollar, which basically reflects the faster growth in productivity during those times.

The supply-side advantages of foreign trade are that it increases competition, boosts productivity growth, and reduces inflation. Or as an earlier generation put it, "tariffs are the mother of trusts." Hence barriers to trade reduce long-term growth. Nonetheless, the benefits of trade are greatest when the dollar (or any other currency) is near its equilibrium level. If the currency is substantially overvalued, the manufacturing sector will be penalized, employment and profits will fall, and eventually investment will shift to other countries. That is indeed what happened to Germany and Japan in the 1990s, and might have happened to the US in the 2000s if the dollar had remained overvalued for an extended period of time.

CASE STUDY 11.2   THE SHRINKING STEEL INDUSTRY

Few industries have been harder hit by rising imports – and have made greater demands at the political level – than the steel industry. Its persistence apparently paid off when, in March 2002, George W. Bush agreed to impose a tariff of up to 30% on steel imports. The steel industry claimed that was barely enough to offset the combination of a stronger dollar and "dumping" by steel companies around the world because of a glut of excess capacity. It also requested, but did not receive, money from the government to pay the retirement and healthcare benefits for those pensioners who had received generous benefits when the industry was profitable. Without jettisoning this cost, the industry claimed, it could not consolidate and hence become competitive against worldwide competition.

The positive impacts of such a move to employers and shareholders of the steel industry are obvious. But what about the negative impacts? Most economists pointed out that an increase in the cost of steel would (a) raise prices domestically, (b) make exports of goods that use steel even less competitive, and (c) would invite retaliatory tariffs or other barriers to trade from most countries that export steel. The steel industry might benefit, but most other exporting industries would suffer.

Figure 11.19 shows that the vast majority of the drop in steel industry employment and production relative to total manufacturing occurred before 1995, a year in which the dollar was approximately 10% undervalued. The recent overvaluation of the dollar had relatively little impact on steel production, which has remained almost a constant proportion of manufacturing production since then. Instead, the decline in the steel industry reflected the gradual switch away from heavy-metal to high-tech industries, an increase in

continued

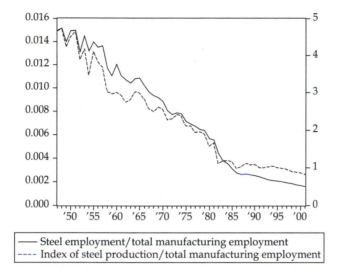

Steel employment/total manufacturing employment
---- Index of steel production/total manufacturing employment

Figure 11.19 Ratio of steel employment and production to total manufacturing employment and production (indexes of industrial production are 1982 = 100)

CASE STUDY 11.2 (*continued*)
the relative price of steel, and until 1982, an increase in the relative wage rates of steelworkers. Compared to these factors, increasing net imports of steel – which now account for about 25% of total production – have played a relatively minor role.

To help focus this argument, assume for a moment that a further increase in steel imports would leave GDP unchanged because of the beneficial aspects of higher productivity, lower inflation, and greater foreign saving. However, because of a worldwide glut of steel production, free trade would eventually cause *all* steel mills in the US to shut down, which would leave the US totally dependent on foreign steel, put 191,000 people out of work, and terminate pension and healthcare benefits for 110,000 retirees. Is that a good idea?

Advocates of free trade argue that reducing the price of steel will also reduce the cost of products that are intensive users of steel, such as motor vehicles, fabricated metal products, machinery, household appliances, and construction. Consumers and businesses will thus be able to buy more of these goods, and US exports of these industries will also remain competitive. Production and employment would increase in these industries, and the gains would be far greater than the loss of jobs in the steel industry.

Is this a reasonable claim? Assume that steel prices would be 30% cheaper if all steel were imported, and the prices of the products in steel-intensive industries

continued

CASE STUDY 11.2 (*continued*)

would decline an average of 5% except for construction, where the price reduction would be about 2%. Assuming a unitary price elasticity, that would boost demand for metal-using goods by 5%, and construction by 2%, hence boosting employment by approximately the same percentage. Since there are approximately 5 million jobs in each of these two major categories, total employment would rise by 350,000, about twice the loss of steel jobs. Furthermore, consumers would benefit from lower prices, so there would be additional multiplier effects.

The greatest risk of higher steel tariffs is that firms in the fabricated metals, industrial machinery, electrical machinery, and motor vehicles industries would find themselves at a severe competitive disadvantage by having to pay up to 30% more for steel than do their international competitors. That could result in a substantial loss of those 5 million jobs, either to foreign competition or as plants move offshore.

In markets with perfect labor mobility, displaced workers would find other jobs, but most of them are not young and would not be hired at wages approximating their previous paychecks. Some would end up in low-paid service occupations rather than highly paid jobs on the machinery assembly lines or on construction sites, and many would end up being permanently unemployed.

These are the arguments that invariably surface when one side is for "free" trade and the other is for "fair" trade, by which they usually mean tariff protection high enough so firms do not have to cut their prices and workers do not have to cut their wages. The political arguments will always be vigorous when such high stakes are at risk.

The steel industry poses a unique set of problems in the sense that steel demand has shrunk rapidly relative to total manufacturing production at the same time there has been a major increase in worldwide capacity. Unlike the textile and apparel industries, which primarily hire low-cost workers with minimal benefits, the steel industry has a very expensive legacy of retiree benefits to pay. One could argue with some justification that unlike textiles or apparel, steel is a basic material for the economy. Few economists would be comfortable with a scenario in which the US produced no steel. Yet because it is such an important raw material for a wide variety of other industries, raising its price puts many other jobs at risk.

One can reasonably argue that the steel industry should have consolidated 30 years ago, but it does little good to second-guess what should have happened in the past. There is no optimal solution for this problem; there are only "second best" scenarios. From the viewpoint of the overall economy, the worst idea is to raise the

continued

CASE STUDY 11.2 (*continued*)

price of steel to the point where other industrial jobs shift overseas. A much better idea would be to offer tax credits for firms that modernize, and provide some relief for pensioners who would lose their benefits under bankruptcy – although existing government programs would provide partial benefits. In the long run, the steel industry will survive in the US only if it is fully competitive with plants in other countries. Temporary relief from tariffs that raise the price of steel to all domestic users is a very poor solution.

MANAGER'S BRIEFCASE: REACTING TO TARIFF INCREASES ON MATERIALS

Case study 11.2 points out the negative macroeconomic impacts of higher tariffs on any key material used in production. However, that does not answer the following question: if your company is in manufacturing, and the price of one of your key inputs is raised by higher tariffs, what is the optimal solution? Any attempt to raise prices proportionately with the cost increase is likely to cause a substantial decline in market share to importers who do not face the same cost hike.

In the long run, the only viable solution may be to move the manufacturing operations to foreign locations. However, that is not costless either: the plant must be shut down, and severance pay must be offered to the workers. The key decision point is whether the tariff increase is likely to be temporary or permanent. It might be temporary because the government will remove the excess tariff when business conditions improve, or the increase might be challenged in court and overturned. If the tariff hike is expected to be temporary, the best course of action is to leave domestic production facilities in place.

If the tariff hike is expected to be permanent, the following issues need to be analyzed before switching operations to another country. First, to what extent will the increased tariff reduce foreign investment and lead to a weaker dollar? Second, will the increased tariff invite retaliatory measures around the globe and keep your goods out of foreign markets in the future? Third, was the tariff a reaction to recessionary conditions, and will domestic demand improve in the near future? Fourth, is it likely the government will also grant tariff relief – i.e., increases – to your business?

From 1995 through 2000, real growth averaged better than 4% in the US, yet there was a net loss of manufacturing jobs – even without tariff increases. Primarily, this reflected the stronger dollar, but lower labor costs abroad were another strong incentive to move. Thus if production labor costs are a large proportion of total costs, and sales of your product are sensitive to changes in the value of the dollar, a higher tariff on materials would generally hasten the decision to move operations to foreign countries. If highly skilled positions, communications infrastructure, and proximity to markets are important, a tariff increase on materials probably would not be enough to cause a location shift in production facilities. Between these two extremes, the four issues mentioned above should play a major role in determining whether to stay or move.

11.7 Recent progress toward free trade

One of the areas where a great deal of progress has been made in the post-WWII period has been the gradual reduction of tariffs. The General Agreement on Tariffs and Trade (GATT) has been a great success, in spite of occasional carping by its critics that GATT really stands for General Agreement to Talk and Talk. GATT is unusual in that it began as a trade agreement, not an organization. The following table shows the progress of the various rounds of negotiation since 1947.

Negotiating round	Dates	Number of participants	Tariff cut achieved (%)	Comments
Geneva	1947	23	–	
Annecy	1949	13	–	
Torquay	1951	38	73	
Geneva	1956	26	–	
Dillon	1960–1	26	–	
Kennedy	1964–7	62	35	Antidumping agreement signed
Tokyo	1973–9	99	33	Addressed nontariff as well as tariff barriers (optional) on government procurement, dumping, subsidies, standards, and customs valuation
Uruguay	1986–93	125	40	Addressed nontariff as well as tariff barriers

NAFTA, the North American Free Trade Agreement, is not included in this list. Although it has had an important impact on trade with Mexico – Canadian tariff barriers were lowered in previous agreements – it was really a bilateral trade agreement, rather than a multilateral agreement such as the various agreements listed above. The impact of NAFTA on the US and Mexican economy is considered in detail in chapter 14.

The principal accomplishments of the **Uruguay round** were as follows:

- Tariffs were eliminated completely in several sectors, including pharmaceuticals, steel, construction equipment, medical equipment, and paper.
- The agreement covered the agricultural sector for the first time, and includes nontariff as well as tariff barriers. For example, Japan and Korea could no longer refuse to permit rice imports.
- Trade barriers on textiles and clothing were to be phased out over the next ten years. This is particularly important because quotas are even worse than tariffs.

- Voluntary export restraints are now prohibited.
- The "domestic content" clause, which requires manufactured products to contain a certain percentage of parts produced domestically, will be phased out.
- The World Trade Organization (WTO) will serve as judiciary; previously, disagreements were subject to almost interminable hassling.
- GATS, the General Agreement on Trade and Services, will work to break down barriers, particularly in financial services, telecommunications, audiovisual and maritime transport services.

Current Status of International Trade Agreements

While GATT and GATS will work to reduce tariff barriers further, there are still several types of trade agreements that will be used to reduce nontariff barriers to trade in the future. These can be grouped into three major classifications.

1. Extension of so-called "most favored nation" (MFN) status
2. Reduction of nontariff barriers
3. Expansion of regional free trade agreements beyond tariffs on goods, focusing especially on intellectual property rights and investment flows.

Most Favored Nation Status

Any country that receives MFN status will enjoy the lowest tariff rates that the US offers to any country. In fact, most countries are currently MFN trade partners; the exceptions are those countries who are deemed to have dictatorships.

The major exclusion from MFN status occurred in 1974, when the passage of the Jackson-Vanik Act was designed to force the Soviet Union to permit more Jewish citizens to emigrate. MFN status was then withheld from any country that restricted emigration; a clause that has been widened to apply to countries with an assortment of various human rights violations. In order for such a country to be given MFN status an act of Congress is required, specifically exempting them from Jackson-Vanik. In recent years, the argument has essentially been reduced to a discussion of how to treat China. So far, China has always received MFN status in spite of grumbling by a considerable proportion of Congressional members.

Without passing judgment on whether Chinese human rights violations are serious enough to withdraw MFN status, the concept raises the whole issue of when politics and economics clash. In extreme cases, such as trading with the enemy during a declared war, the issue is not even debated. But short of all-out war, there are various shadings: the once and perhaps future Cold War, countries not currently at war who might become belligerents if they built or purchased atomic weapons, countries likely to engage in chemical or biological warfare, and countries that are exporting revolution, as well as those engaging in serious human rights violations.

Each case must be judged on its own merits. Human rights violations in China, while not trivial, are hardly of the magnitude of Nazi Germany or the Stalinist Soviet Union. Thus even though the US is firmly committed to worldwide free trade, there will be countries and circumstances where this precept will be overridden because of political considerations. At least we ought to be aware of such situations rather than blindly following those who chant the mantra of "free trade everywhere."

Reduction of Nontariff Barriers

Some countries still have high tariffs on US goods; for example, imports of motor vehicles from the US into Thailand, Malaysia, and Indonesia. However, most of the trade restrictions against the US take the form of nontariff barriers. These may be restrictions on goods, or outright bans on a variety of services, such as not permitting foreign nationals to compete at all in the areas of telecommunications, legal, or financial services. Also, many other nations take a cavalier attitude toward intellectual property rights, as witnessed by the "pirating" of many software programs, CDs, and other electronic sources of information.

A few examples of nontariff barriers will suffice to provide a flavor of the hundreds if not thousands of similar regulations US (and other) exports face around the world.

- When the French decide they want to reduce imports of a particular good, they reassign the import office to some unimportant inland city and claim the office is only open a few hours a week. That led some wag to propose relocating the US customs office to Boise, Idaho.
- The South Koreans wanted to reduce imports of expensive American cars, so they decided that anyone who bought such a car had his taxes audited to prove he could afford it. Naturally, most rich people declined that option.
- The Japanese would not permit imports of rice, claiming that the sensitive Japanese palates would not enjoy the taste and texture of American rice. Even sillier, they once claimed that American skis could not be used on the "unique" brand of Japanese snow.
- The Russians said they had nothing against American chickens except they did not meet the high sanitary standards of Russian production and hence could not be imported.

Of course, the US has a few zingers of its own. French cheese cannot be imported if it is made with unpasteurized milk. All cars must be tested for safety standards by crashing a few of them; for some fancy sports models with limited production, that is equivalent to crashing their entire year's profits. Some activists insist that clothing cannot be imported from certain countries that "mistreat" their workers by paying them a low wage. No country is completely blameless in this matter. On balance, though, the US has far fewer nontariff restrictions than most other countries.

Expansion of Regional Free Trade Agreements

As of 2002, the US government is currently involved in the following trade agreements:

- *FTAA*. The *Free Trade Area of the Americas* group seeks to achieve free trade in the western hemisphere by 2005. Working groups include: tariffs and nontariff barriers, custom procedures and rules of origin, investment, standards and technical barriers, sanitary and phytosanitary measures, antidumping and countervailing duties, problems of smaller economies, government procedures, intellectual property rights, services, and competition policy. Note that what is often considered the principal barrier to free trade, namely tariffs, represents only part of one of the 11 groups.
- *APEC*. The *Asia-Pacific Economic Cooperation* group, consisting of 18 Pacific nations, including China, seeks to bring free trade to the Pacific region within the next 25 years. APEC has already outlined trade liberalization in 135 specific areas, with explicit objectives, benchmarks, timeframes, and specific actions.
- The *Transatlantic Trade and Investment Initiative* is a partnership with the European Union to reduce trade barriers on services, investment, and intellectual property rights.

Such groups designed to expand the reach of free trade generally enjoy widespread bipartisan support, although NAFTA did receive some political flak. It seems likely that regardless of the political lineup in Washington, the push toward free trade will continue into the indefinite future.

It may seem that these agreements, because they often take many years to negotiate and have a slow-acting effect on world trade and growth, do not have a significant measurable impact on the real growth rate. However, that would be a mistaken impression; one of the reasons that the capitalist world economy has grown fairly rapidly since 1947, and without major recessions other than those induced by energy shocks, has indeed been the more open status of free trade. Case study 11.3 shows what happened in the past when tariffs have been raised to prohibitive levels.

In this author's view, and the view of most economists, economic performance in all countries is optimized when currencies are near their equilibrium value and trade barriers are minimized. Under these circumstances, the advantages of a rise in imports for the US economy can be summarized as follows.

- First, the excess dollars are reinvested in the US. If ex ante investment is greater than ex ante domestic saving, foreign saving fills the gap. Otherwise, investment plans would have to be cut back through rising interest rates, which would also depress stock market prices.

- Second, a decrease in imports would probably reduce quality and raise prices of domestic counterparts. Detroit might like it if there were fewer German or Japanese automobile imports, but consumers wouldn't.
- Third, the spur of imports generally leads to faster growth in productivity in domestic manufacturing, leading to less inflation and a higher growth rate.
- Fourth, the US economy is still the straw that stirs the drink. A reduction in US imports would mean a reduction in exports from other countries, and hence slower growth abroad. Eventually, US exports would also diminish. This is particularly true for US imports from smaller countries: for example, US exports to OPEC countries are directly dependent on how much oil money they have to spend. At least in the past, a rise in oil prices, which clearly raises US imports, has also boosted US exports because OPEC nations have spent much of their additional oil income on US goods and services.

Many other countries do not have the luxury of running large trade deficits for an extended period, because their currencies are not universally accepted. As a result, a decline in US imports from those countries would almost automatically translate into a decline in US exports to those countries. Yet as long as the world remains on a de facto dollar standard and the value of the dollar does not decline below equilibrium, excess dollars reinvested in the US will boost investment and productivity growth.

CASE STUDY 11.3   THE SMOOT-HAWLEY TARIFF

Figure 11.20 shows the average tariff rate for the US from 1820 to 2001. The tariff rate has been calculated two ways: on dutiable imports, which shows the actual average rates in the tariff schedule, and on total imports, including those goods that were not subject to any tariff, such as foodstuffs not available from domestic producers.

In 1930, the Smoot-Hawley tariff boosted dutiable tariff rates to the highest level ever, essentially shutting out foreign imports. As a result, US imports fell by two-thirds. However, also as a result of this record-high tariff, US exports fell by three-quarters, which meant Congress wiped out the US trade surplus, as well as providing a major cause of the worldwide depression. Trying to balance the trade account today would also hurt the world economy seriously, and would eventually damage US economic growth as well. These results are shown in figure 11.21.

The Smoot-Hawley tariff was particularly ill-timed for several reasons. First, the US had a trade surplus throughout the 1920s, so passing such a high tariff was akin to shooting itself in the foot, since other countries were bound to retaliate. Second,

continued

CASE STUDY 11.3 (*continued*)

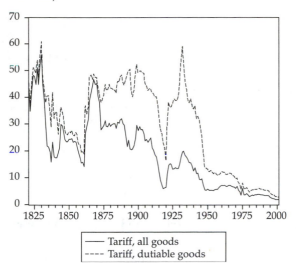

Figure 11.20   The Smoot-Hawley tariff was the highest for dutiable goods, but not for all imports

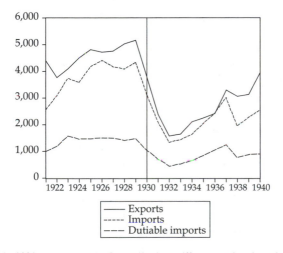

Figure 11.21   Passed in 1930, as soon as the Smoot-Hawley tariff was put into law, the US net export balance actually declined

although a moratorium on World War I debts had been passed, Europe still depended heavily on exports to the US to pay its back bills. Third, with the world still on the international gold standard, any substantial disruption in world trade caused by a tariff of that magnitude was almost bound to lead to massive bankruptcies in Europe, which is indeed what happened.

11.8   Arguments for and against a trade deficit

The traditional reasons why a trade deficit is thought to weaken an economy are discussed in this section. We will show these are generally not true, but since many of these are widespread fallacies, it is worth examining why they are wrong.

1. It is claimed that reducing net exports reduces real GDP and employment, and more people in the country are out of work when foreigners take their jobs away. Free trade is fine when the current account is balanced, it is sometimes argued, but not when it leads to a deficit year after year.

Note that this is *not* the same as saying that foreign trade reduces employment when the trade position is balanced; that is nonsense. However, one can conceivably make the case that a trade deficit costs jobs when it occurs year after year – at least when the excess currency is not reinvested in the home country.

2. It is also claimed that the extra dollars recycled back into the US because of the trade deficit result in greater foreign ownership of US assets. Thus over the longer run, the US will pay a greater proportion of its national income to foreign investors, hence reducing real GDP and the domestic standard of living.

The trouble with this oversimplified analysis is that it fails to consider what else happens in the economy after net exports initially decline. After all, the extra dollars received by foreigners do not disappear. How these excess dollars are invested determines whether a continuing current account deficit hurts the growth rate of any given economy.

For small economies with nontraded currencies, a decline in net exports will generally reduce GDP. However, in the US, the shortfall from the lower net exports is usually offset by a rise in total production and a greater level of investment without raising interest rates.

To the extent that US imports rise, exports of other countries increase, boosting their real growth. That eventually leads to a rise in US exports. In other words, both exports and imports rise under free trade; naysayers who see only the increase in imports fail to take the concomitant growth in exports into account.

US consumers buy more imports because they are less expensive. As a result, they have more money to spend on other goods and services. Thus while higher imports may put some firms out of business, they do not necessarily result in a lower level of total GDP and employment. Note this link works only if the dollar retains its value or moves higher; if a rise in imports is accompanied by a reduction in the value of the dollar, real GDP will eventually fall.

If the US runs a continued trade deficit and the dollar remains near its equilibrium value, the excess dollars recycled back into the country will either result in lower real interest rates, or an increase in investment as foreign firms build more plants in the US. Either way, capital spending will rise. The dollars do not simply float out to sea and vanish.

Thus an increase in the trade deficit would reduce real GDP only if there were (a) no repercussion effect, (b) a weaker dollar, leading to a rise in the prices of import goods and substitutes, (c) only a partial inflow of foreign capital, which would also be reflected in a weaker dollar, and (d) no improvement in productivity.

Many of these conditions do exist for small, developing economies, where excess currency is not recycled back into the country. Exports could also drop because the country becomes less competitive, or because the price of the principal commodity export declines. Imports might rise if the country liberalizes import conditions and there are no domestic substitutes. If the country is too small to have any measurable impact on world growth, there is no repercussion effect. If foreign investors do not choose to invest in that country, there is no net capital inflow, and because the imports don't compete with domestic products, there is no improvement in productivity.

So far we have said that an increase in the trade deficit does not hurt the US, while it does hurt other countries. That might suggest the rest of the world should run a continuing trade surplus with the US; that would boost growth both in the US and abroad. The bigger the US trade deficit, the faster worldwide growth.

Taken to its logical extreme, this argument makes no sense. The catch, so to speak, is that it works only as long as the dollar and other major currencies all remain near purchasing power parity. If currencies depart significantly from that level, the benefits of greater efficiency and higher productivity start to dissipate. Hence increasing US trade deficits boost worldwide real growth only if purchasing power parity equilibrium is maintained.

That also implies other major currencies should also remain near purchasing power parity. If they are significantly lower, higher inflation will retard growth in productivity and slow down the increase in the standard of living. If they are significantly higher, countries will find themselves priced out of world markets. During the 1990s, Germany and most other countries in continental western Europe suffered sluggish growth rates because their currencies were overvalued. Also in the 1990s, the growth rate in Japan averaged only about 1% because its trade surplus was so huge and the yen was so overvalued.

Devaluing the currency has been beneficial to countries in the case where its value was well above equilibrium; returning to equilibrium would then stimulate net exports without causing negative supply-side effects. However, most of the time, countries devalue their currency to offset higher inflation and lower productivity; these problems cannot be solved by devaluation. In 1998, the massive devaluations in southeast Asia led to a tremendous decline in the growth rate, not an improvement.

To understand the long-run supply-side benefits of international trade, it is necessary to jettison the false concept of "competition" in international trade. From the viewpoint of an individual firm or industry, the concept of competition seems natural enough. If consumers buy more Japanese cars, they buy fewer American cars; if foreign consumers buy more American wheat, they buy less foreign wheat. But as simple as it may sound, this explanation is incorrect because it fails to take into consideration what happens to the money that is spent on foreign instead of domestic goods.

Consider the shift that occurred many years ago in the textile industry, when most of the plants moved from New England to the South. Did that reduce employment in New England and raise it in the South? It definitely did for a while. But the relevant question ought to be whether consumers generally were better off because of this shift.

Consumers benefited because the price of textile goods declined. Since they spent less on clothing, they could spend more money on other goods and services, which offset the loss in real GDP stemming from higher imports. Also, new plants led to higher productivity. Because the workforce in New England was better educated, a new high-tech industry arose. So in the long run, everyone was better off, although the adjustment took many years.

There are several important lessons to be learned from this example. First, to the extent that goods are produced with less expensive labor, consumers are better off because the real purchasing power of their wages has increased. Second, the overall economy will operate more efficiently if more highly skilled and educated workers are making products and services with a higher value added. Third, since more modern plant and equipment is more efficient, productivity increases when new competitors enter the market.

We emphasize that not all workers, or all industries, are better off under free trade. Some workers will lose their jobs, and some businesses will close. But the gains from trade far outweigh these losses. Today, when cheap textiles and apparel flood the US market, firms that manufacture textiles, employees of those firms, and companies that supply textile machinery are indeed worse off. But the overall benefits of paying less for textiles and apparel far exceed those losses. For every $1 that would be saved in textile wages, consumers would end up paying $5 in higher prices. Eventually, if the US economy remains at full employment, textile workers get better jobs at better wages in industries that have expanded because consumers have more money to spend on other goods and services.

To summarize, the advantages of increased international trade are not found on the demand side; in the long run, faster export growth does not boost the overall growth rate because demand is rising faster. The benefits occur on the supply side: increased trade helps to reduce inflation and boost productivity growth, hence raising the growth in potential GDP. This is particularly true for smaller countries, which can benefit the most from increasing returns to scale.

In the presence of free markets and the absence of trade constraints, trade balances of individual countries will eventually tend toward zero. One of the major reasons the Japanese trade surplus is so high is that they restrict imports. But are they any better off for it?

We have already indicated that the recent evidence implies a resounding NO. While Japan used to be one of the world growth leaders, its real GDP rose less than 1% per year over the 1992–2002 period, new college graduates have great difficulty finding jobs, and the financial sector is in tatters. By comparison, real growth in the US has averaged about 4% over the same period, the unemployment rate fell from 7.5% to 4% although it rose during the recession, and stock prices rose at above-average rates, even after taking the 2001/2002 market plunge into account.

One final example: suppose Japan discovers a cure for cancer, and the US discovers a cure for heart attacks. Because of patents, these new medicines are not available from any other source. Japan refuses to buy any heart attack-curing medicine from the US because it does not want to increase its imports, while the US buys all the cancer-curing medicine that is needed. Which country is better off?

11.9 Foreign purchases of US assets: a non-event

We have shown that by definition, saving = investment; that is, of course, theoretically true for all countries. Hence on a worldwide basis, the global trade surplus or deficit must theoretically be zero.[1] The US's trade deficit is someone else's surplus. This is far different from the budget position, where a Federal deficit is not anyone's surplus.

Seen in this light, the terms trade "surplus" and "deficit" take on a somewhat different meaning. The US has a deficit on current account, but an equal and opposite surplus on capital account. Japan has a huge surplus on current account, but an equal and opposite deficit on capital account. As a result, Japanese money is invested in America; the US economy gets the benefit of that investment. In the mid-1980s, Europe ended up paying for a big part of the US budget deficit.

These global balances must be taken into account when assessing the statement that if the US continues to run a large current account deficit and a similarly large capital surplus, then over the long run, foreigners will own "too much" of America and the outflow of investment income will reduce the country's long-term growth rate.

Admittedly that would be a major problem for Bangladesh or Uruguay, but since the US is the cornerstone of the world economy, the same argument holds for outflows of investment income as for trade deficits. All excess dollars are indeed recycled back into the US economy. *Clearly, the result should not be any different for excess dollars received from one type of foreign trade activity than for another.*

To see the relationship between the trade deficit and the domestic economy, we can reconsider the identity $I = S = SP + SC + SF + SG$. SF, the capital account surplus, is equal to the current account deficit. This equation can be rearranged slightly to show that:

SF = (I − SP − SC) − SG, or

Current account deficit = Gap between private sector investment and saving

+ Public sector deficit.

If there is no gap between private sector investment and saving, the current account deficit is the same size as the government deficit. Under those circumstances, ending the government deficit would also eliminate the trade deficit.

However, in the 1990s, the government budget position returned to surplus at the same time that the trade deficit increased sharply. This fundamental identity thus shows there must have been an increasingly large gap between private sector investment and saving. Put simply, the US saved less and invested more, borrowing the difference from the rest of the world.

Some people think that is a bad idea. They argue that the US ought to do its own saving, so its "children" will not have to pay back foreigners in the long run. Otherwise, it is sometimes claimed, the US will end up paying interest income to foreign investors that will represent an uncomfortably large proportion of total GDP.

This argument claims that unlike the domestic deficit, which we "owe to ourselves," the foreign deficit is owed to people outside the country. To the extent that those outflows are not reinvested in dollars, this drain could eventually slow down US economic performance. But this is nonsense.

A few years ago, mass hysteria reigned in some quarters when the Japanese bought Rockefeller Center and Pebble Beach. Wags suggested the Statue of Liberty would be next on the block. Soon, it was suggested, the Japanese would own the entire country.

Of course such fears were totally misplaced. As it turned out, the Japanese vastly overpaid for these American icons and later sold them back at substantial losses. But even if that had not been the case, the net effect of this "buying binge" during the late 1980s and early 1990s raised foreign ownership of US assets from approximately 7% to 9%. If the Japanese had not bought such "trophy" properties, that slight increase probably would have gone unnoticed.

Furthermore, the Japanese are only the fourth largest foreign investor in the US, behind Britain, the Netherlands, and Germany. It seems that some Americans get more upset when the buyers are named Miazawa or Watanabe instead of Jones, Vanderhof, or Schmidt. When Daimler-Benz bought Chrysler and Deutsche Bank bought Bankers Trust in 1998, there was hardly a ripple about "foreigners" taking over prized US assets.

During periods of average growth, nominal GDP can be expected to rise about 6% per year, which would be about $600 billion at 2002 levels. Total private net worth is roughly three times GDP, which means it increases about $1,800 billion per year in an average year. Recently, the US current account deficit has averaged about $300 billion. Thus if this money were recycled back into dollar-denominated assets, about a sixth of newly created wealth would be in the hands of foreign investors. Admittedly this is higher than the 9% of all wealth currently owned by foreigners, which suggests that ratio could eventually double, based on these figures. Yet even that level is not enough to make any significant difference as long as the excess dollars earned from US investments continued to be recycled back into America.

Thus we find that in a large, open economy with a stable currency, a permanent trade deficit does not reduce the growth rate as long as the currency remains near its equilibrium value. That is true even if the deficit is caused by unfair trade practices of other countries. Only when the currency deviates from purchasing power parity can a trade deficit reduce the growth rate.

For small and medium sized countries, the major supply-side advantages occur because of economies of scale. Many countries that do not have rich natural resource endowments must pay for goods they cannot produce domestically, such as food-stuffs, minerals or energy. Thus free trade is even more important for smaller countries. However, economies of scale are only a minor issue for the US.

KEY TERMS AND CONCEPTS

Current and Capital Accounts
General Agreement on Tariffs and Trade (GATT)
North American Free Trade Agreement (NAFTA)
Price Elasticities of Imports and Exports

Repercussion Effect
Smoot-Hawley Tariff
Theory of Comparative Advantage
Uruguay Round

SUMMARY

- According to the fundamental aggregate demand identity, a rise in net exports – due either to higher exports or lower imports – should automatically boost GDP. However, a country certainly cannot boost its GDP in the long run by devaluing the currency and boosting net exports. Even in the short run, a rise in net exports may not raise real GDP; the gains could be offset by higher inflation, lower productivity, or an outflow of foreign capital.
- By definition, the capital account balance is equal to the current account balance with the opposite sign. That means an increase in net exports of goods and services is balanced by

a decline in foreign saving. That is one key reason why higher net exports may not boost overall GDP.
- When the world was on the international gold standard, exporters who did not want to be paid in the currency of that country could demand gold. However, that has not been the case since August 15, 1971. Now, if exporters do not want to accept the currency of the country to which they are exporting goods and services, they can sell that currency on the foreign exchange market and obtain another currency. For that reason, the value of most currencies is directly related to the size of the current account balance.

- However, because the world is on a de facto dollar standard, the value of the US dollar is not correlated with the current account balance. When the US has a trade deficit, the extra dollars are – directly or indirectly – reinvested in the US economy.
- As a result, the US economy does not necessarily grow at a slower rate when it has a big trade deficit – as long as the dollar remains near its equilibrium value. When the dollar is undervalued, inflation rises and productivity growth diminishes. When the dollar is overvalued, manufacturing production rises at a slower rate and, if the situation continues for an extended period of time, capital spending declines as firms relocate their plants in other countries.
- In most years, the US has a substantial trade surplus in major agricultural crops, aircraft, and high-tech machinery. It has a massive deficit in motor vehicles, textiles and apparel, shoes, and toys. When the trade deficit surged in the late 1990s, the deficit occurred in consumer goods including autos; all other net exports remained positive.
- The income elasticity of exports and imports is greater than one. The price elasticity of exports and imports is less than one. Thus an increase (say) in the value of the currency will invariably cause the volume of imports to rise and the volume of exports to fall, but may not result in the *value* of imports and exports changing in that direction.
- US exports depend on real GDP and production in the rest of the world, but they also depend on domestic GDP and production with a lag; this is known as the repercussion effect. An increase in the US growth rate would increase imports, which means exports of other countries would rise. They would grow faster, and hence they would import more the following year, which means US exports would rise. As a result, any attempt by the US to raise exports or decrease imports unilaterally would be largely offset in future years. Generally, the repercussion effect is not as important for other countries, although it is quite sizable for German foreign trade in Europe and Japanese foreign trade in east Asia.
- The Smoot-Hawley tariff, passed in June 1930, raised tariffs on dutiable goods to record rates. While that reduced US imports, it reduced US exports even more, and the US trade surplus disappeared. The decline in imports from Europe, and the corresponding reduction in exports to Europe, was one of the major causes of the Great Depression. After World War II, the US has worked together with virtually all its trading partners to reduce tariffs, and the benefits have been substantial. They have been reflected in rapid growth for most capitalist countries since the end of World War II, and virtually no worldwide recessions except for those caused by energy shocks.
- If the dollar remains near its equilibrium value, a trade deficit will not harm the US economy, but will improve real growth and raise the standard of living because of the beneficial supply-side effects on productivity. While some industries will not be able to compete, those losses will be more than offset by the gains that occur when consumers can buy other goods at lower prices. Furthermore, the spur of international competition usually improves the quality of goods. However, if the dollar becomes substantially overvalued, the slowdown in the manufacturing sector can retard the real growth rate and eventually lead to a slower rate of increase in productivity.
- A trade deficit is accompanied by an increase in foreign saving, which means a faster rate of capital spending and productivity growth without having to raise interest rates. The fact that foreigners own a slightly greater percentage of total US assets does not have any long-run negative ramifications; even if recent trends were to continue, foreign ownership of US assets would not exceed 20%. Foreign ownership of US assets is a non-event.

- The theory of comparative advantage explains why all countries benefit from international trade even if one country can produce every good more efficiently. The benefits of foreign trade are felt primarily on the supply side: productivity and quality are increased, and inflation is reduced by vigorous competition. Except for a relatively few cases where factor endowments are still important – agriculture, mining, and energy – patterns of foreign trade depend on the ability of firms in a particular industry and country to be more efficient than their counterparts. If firms start to coast and permit their relative efficiency to decline, they are likely to lose their export advantage fairly quickly.

QUESTIONS AND PROBLEMS

1. The Export-Import Bank helps Boeing by providing various subsides on aircraft sold to foreign countries. Boeing says it needs this help to offset subsidies given to Airbus Industrie by European governments, and would lose sales otherwise, hence reducing American jobs. Thus personal and corporate income tax payments would decline. How would you determine whether the American taxpayers are getting their money's worth?
2. Assume that US imports have an income elasticity of 1.3 and a price elasticity of −0.5, and US exports have an income elasticity of 1.2 and a price elasticity of −0.7. They also have a "repercussion elasticity" of 0.5, reflecting changes in GDP the previous year. To simplify matters, assume that both exports and imports are 10% of GDP. Determine what happens to the US trade balance this year and next when:
   (A) An easier monetary policy boosts the growth rate by 1%.
   (B) Export subsidies equal to 2% of total exports are granted.
   (C) The US reduces the average tariff rate from 4% to 2.5%.
   (D) US costs of production rise 2%, hence boosting export prices by that amount.
   (E) An inflow of foreign saving boosts the value of the dollar by 8%.
3. When energy shocks have occurred in the past and the price of imported oil has soared, both the US trade balance and the value of the dollar have increased, even though the US imports about half its oil. Explain why this occurs. (Hint: what happens to the foreign currency values of Europe and Japan, which import almost all their oil?)
4. Suppose the value of the Japanese yen rises 20%, but in order to maintain market share in the US, major Japanese companies decide not to raise the prices. As a result, their imports do not change, but profits of Japanese manufacturers decline, so they import less capital equipment from US machinery firms. Taking the effect on both consumers and producers into account, is the US better or worse off

based on the Japanese decision to hold import prices constant? Is Japan better or worse off?

5. In 1999 Brazil was forced to devalue the real by almost 50%, and in 2002 Argentina was forced to devalue the peso by almost 50%. According to the static model, that would boost net exports and raise GDP. However, both countries plunged into a deep recession. Explain why that happened.

6. The following graph shows a fairly high correlation between the ratio of capital spending to GDP and the inverted ratio of net exports to GDP over the post-WWII period in the US – i.e. the bigger the trade deficit, the higher the investment ratio. Explain the causal relationship between these two series. Would you expect this relationship to continue in the future?

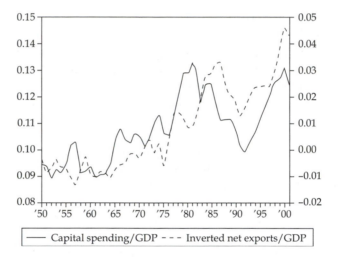

7. The dollar declined sharply in 1973–4 and 1977–8, and those declines were accompanied by sharply higher inflation. However, when the dollar declined even more sharply in 1986–8, the rate of inflation did not rise at all. What explains the different behavior of inflation in those two periods?

Appendix: the theory of comparative advantage and the modern theory of international trade

Long before there were economists, there was foreign trade. Originally the concept was based on the difference in natural resources; it made sense to import coffee, tea, sugar, spices, and other tropical foods to the temperate climates of northern Europe. The original Ricardian example showed the benefits of England importing wine from Portugal and exporting cloth.

In the industrial era, the concept of the benefits of foreign trade moved to encompass the principle of comparative advantage. Even if one country had an absolute advantage in producing all traded products because of its superior technology, the exchange rates between countries would adjust to the point where each country would have a comparative advantage in producing at least one good. Thus, for example, advanced countries would have a comparative advantage in producing machinery, computers, and transportation equipment, whereas developing countries would have a comparative advantage in producing clothing.

A simple example will suffice to illustrate the concept of comparative advantage. Suppose that it takes 50 employee-hours to produce a car and 10 employee-hours to produce a suit in the US, and it takes 300 employee-hours to produce a car and 20 employee-hours to produce a suit in Spain. Productivity in both industries is higher in the US. Suppose that the average hourly wage in the US is $30.00 for auto workers and $10.00 for textile workers, while in Spain the average hourly wage is 1,200 pesetas for auto workers and 400 pesetas for textile workers (before Spain started to use the euro as its currency). In this example, the labor costs are $1,500 and 360,000 pesetas for a car, and $100 and 8,000 pesetas for a suit. If the exchange rate were 150 pesetas/$, the dollar-equivalent cost in Spain would be $2,400 for the car and $53.33 for the suit. Thus production and consumption in both countries would be increased if Spain imported cars from the US and exported suits to the US, even though the US is more efficient in producing both commodities. By specializing in products where they are relatively most efficient, costs will decline, and consumers in both countries will benefit. At least that is the theory.

Perhaps it is not worth devoting even one page to such a concept, since it assumes among other things that the currencies are in equilibrium, both countries have full employment, the quality of the product is the same, labor and capital resources are mobile, there are no trade barriers, and the cost of materials is the same in both countries. However, recent reports from the Council of Economic Advisors precisely echo this sentiment. It is a theory often referenced by those who favor free trade. As managers, you should at least be familiar with the concept of comparative advantage.

The old theories explain only a small proportion of foreign trade. The US exports corn and wheat, and imports oil and coffee, because of different factor endowments. It does have a large trade surplus for computer software and a large trade deficit for clothing. However, this theory cannot explain, for example, why the US has a large trade surplus for airplanes and a large trade deficit for automobiles, since the technology and capital requirements for those two industries are quite similar.

That particular example is sometimes explained as a historical accident: after World War II, Germany and Japan were encouraged to build motor vehicles, but not aircraft, hence giving the US aircraft industry an insurmountable lead. Considering that Lockheed and McDonnell Douglas, two of the "big three" after World War II, are no longer in business as separate corporations building civilian aircraft, that can no longer be presented as a compelling argument. In recent years, Airbus Industrie has sold approximately the same number of new airplanes as Boeing. Japanese cars were originally of very poor quality, but through dedication to improvement became world-class competitors. After all, the US was once a net exporter of steel.

Firms become world leaders in exports because of creativity, innovation, rapid productivity growth, and relentless cost control. Free trade keeps dominant firms from falling asleep at the wheel. Even under these conditions, some labor-intensive industries will invariably find that emerging nations with low labor costs will have a comparative advantage when they import technologically modern machines for manufacturing. Hence employment in the textile and apparel industries in the US will probably continue to decline even if the dollar remains at its equilibrium value. High-tech jobs can be maintained only with constant innovation; without remaining at the frontiers of new technology, even those jobs will move to other countries. The modern theory of international trade simply states that for a currency that is near equilibrium, a given country will have a comparative advantage in those industries where productivity and technology have advanced the most rapidly, and will fall behind in other industries.

Note

1. In fact the IMF statistics always show the "world" has a trade surplus and a current account deficit. That strongly suggests that many lesser developed countries smuggle in goods from the leading industrial nations, and sneak money back out to major financial centers.

chapter twelve

International financial markets and foreign exchange policy

Introduction

Just as there is no one "interest rate," there is no one "exchange rate." There are hundreds of exchange rates for the dollar alone, and when all crossrates are taken into account, there are theoretically tens of thousands. When economists, business executives, and traders speak of the "value of the dollar," they are generally referring either to a trade-weighted average of the dollar, or the crossrate of the dollar relative to the other major currencies, such as the euro, pound sterling, or the yen. As was also the case for interest rates, trading is based on the nominal value of these exchange rates, but the economic impact is more important for the real rates. Various measures of exchange rates, together with some empirical background, are presented first in this chapter.

For those engaged in foreign trade, the key economic question is the relative cost of production for traded goods in the US compared with other countries. This relative cost can be tied to the concept of purchasing power parity, which is discussed next. The Bureau of Labor Statistics publishes relative labor cost figures for manufacturing production workers for all major countries; since many business managers find these figures useful, we present some detailed data for individual countries.

What determines foreign exchange rates? Even more than for interest rates or stock prices, expectations are the key variable. However, these expectations change much more slowly than is generally the case for bond or stock prices. As a result, foreign exchange rates often remain far away from equilibrium for many years or even decades, as compared to debt and equity markets, where dislocations from equilibrium prices are usually measured in months. The reasons for these extended periods of disequilibria are briefly discussed. The importance of the trade surplus or deficit is also considered; it turns out to be much less important for the US than for other countries.

In the past, many countries tried to "manage" their currencies, either by fixing their rates to one of the major currencies – often the dollar – or by instituting crawling bands or floating pegs. Without exception, these methods have failed. If the cost of production in a given country is significantly different from that cost in the US, the value of the currency must eventually diverge from the dollar. Attempts to manage the currency have caused many sudden devaluations that have at least temporarily led to serious recessions, notably Mexico in 1995, southeast Asia in 1997, Russia in 1998, Brazil in 1999, and Argentina in 2002. Some suggestions are provided that will help managers anticipate future devaluations that might occur.

The last section of this chapter discusses optimal trade and foreign exchange policy. For major world powers, floating exchange rates are clearly the best solution. However, for many smaller countries whose currencies may be whipsawed by speculators, an alternative approach is sometimes beneficial: the currency should be initially set at equilibrium relative to the dollar, and then changed often based on differentials in the relative rate of inflation. However, even that plan can only be recommended for the short run. Furthermore, this method does not work if the value is not initially set correctly. Brazil tried this method for several years, but because the currency was initially overvalued, and no serious attempt was made to reduce the budget deficit, a massive devaluation eventually occurred. With today's global markets, no one country can afford to defend its currency for very long if the underlying economic factors do not support that position.

12.1   The world dollar standard and major trends in other key currencies

In the short run, a change in the value of the dollar is usually accompanied by similar percentage changes in all major currencies. In the long run, though, the ratio of the dollar to many of these same currencies has exhibited a marked upward or downward trend. In particular, over the long run, the dollar has tended to rise relative to the currencies of those countries whose inflation rate is higher than in the US, and tended to fall relative to the currencies of those countries whose inflation rate has been lower than the US. Also in the long run, currencies of countries other than the US with current account surpluses have tended to be stronger than currencies of countries with current account deficits. However, the value of the dollar itself is not correlated with the level or change in the US current account balance.

Until the end of 1998, the four key currencies in the world were the US dollar, the Deutschmark, the pound sterling, and the yen. As of January 1, 1999, the 11 countries of the European Monetary System (EMS) introduced a new currency, known as the euro (€), which replaced those 11 currencies for international transactions immediately, and for domestic transactions starting in 2002. For the most part, the € moves similarly to the old DM. The expected economic impact of the

Table 12.1   Foreign exchange rates

Country	Monetary unit	2002 April	2002 March	2002 February	2001 April
*Australia	Dollar	0.5352	0.5256	0.5128	0.5016
Brazil	Real	2.3227	2.3450	2.4242	2.1934
Canada	Dollar	1.5815	1.5877	1.5964	1.5578
China, P. R.	Yuan	8.2772	8.2773	8.2767	8.2771
Denmark	Krone	8.4397	8.4795	8.5343	8.3657
*EMU members	Euro	0.8860	0.8766	0.8707	0.8925
Greece	Drachma	N/A	N/A	N/A	N/A
Hong Kong	Dollar	7.8000	7.7997	7.7996	7.7993
India	Rupee	48.94	48.77	48.72	46.79
Japan	Yen	130.77	131.06	133.64	123.77
Malaysia	Ringgit	3.8000	3.8000	3.8002	3.8000
Mexico	Peso	9.165	9.064	9.105	9.328
*New Zealand	Dollar	0.4428	0.4333	0.4187	0.4069
Norway	Krone	8.6102	8.8072	8.9492	9.0920
Singapore	Dollar	1.8285	1.8295	1.8312	1.8118
South Africa	Rand	11.0832	11.4863	11.4923	8.0783
South Korea	Won	1,318.09	1,322.90	1,320.55	1,327.76
Sri Lanka	Rupee	96.030	94.903	93.650	88.205
Sweden	Krona	10.3070	10.3324	10.5501	10.2035
Switzerland	Franc	1.6542	1.6743	1.6970	1.7131
Taiwan	Dollar	34.917	35.020	35.073	32.940
Thailand	Baht	43.442	43.415	43.854	45.494
*United Kingdom	Pound	1.4429	1.4230	1.4227	1.4348
Venezuela	Bolivar	871.38	922.66	898.51	710.39
Memo:					
United States	Dollar				
1) Broad	Jan 97 = 100	128.95	129.27	130.03	126.61
2) Major currency	Mar 73 = 100	107.03	107.76	108.82	105.16
3) OITP	Jan 97 = 100	138.86	138.49	138.64	136.22

The table shows the average rates of exchange in April 2002 together with comparable figures for other months. Averages are based on daily noon buying rates for cable transfers in New York City certified for customs purposes by the Federal Reserve Bank of New York. (Currency units per US dollar except as noted by*)

€ is discussed in chapter 14; at this point, we will show the historical relationships and data of the DM, even though it no longer exists.

At the end of 2001, the dollar was worth about 1.12 euros (€), 115 yen (¥), and 0.70 pound sterling (£). The dollar is quoted in many other currencies; the Federal Reserve Board, as well as many private sector banks, issues daily lists of these exchange rates. A typical release from the Fed – with monthly rather than daily data – is shown in table 12.1.

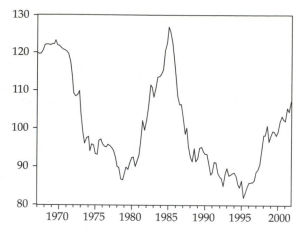

Figure 12.1   Real broad trade-weighted exchange value of the US dollar
Source: www.federalreserve.gov

Cash market quotes are available for virtually all crossrates: the value of one currency expressed in terms of another currency (e.g., €/¥). Active futures markets exist for the $ relative to the €, ¥, Swiss franc (SFr), Canadian dollar (C$), Australian dollar (A$), and the Mexican peso (MP), although the first three are the most important. The € is the only other currency with futures markets for crossrates: the €/¥, and the €/£. The DM had already replaced the £ as the principal European currency even before the formation of the €, a fact that annoys some of the British and led them to comment that the € is just a German scam.

To a large extent, all other currencies follow the lead of the dollar. As shown in figure 12.2, when the dollar appreciated sharply in the first half of the 1980s, all other currencies declined, although some declined a lot more than others (since these are typically measured in currency units per dollar, they are shown rising in the graph). When the dollar fell from 1985 to 1988, all other major currencies appreciated relative to the dollar. Similarly, most currencies declined relative to the dollar from 1995 through 2001.

Yet over the longer run, some currencies – such as the DM and the ¥ – have risen sharply relative to the dollar, while other currencies – such as the £ and the C$ – have fallen sharply relative to the dollar. These divergences are also shown in figure 12.2. Also, other crossrates vary substantially in the long run. Figure 12.3 shows that the DM rose substantially relative to the £ from 1967 to 1995, rising from £0.1 to £0.45. Since then it has declined somewhat. Yet while the DM also rose relative to the ¥ from 1967 through 1981, increasing from 90 to almost 140 ¥/DM, it has since declined, falling to a low of 65 ¥/DM in 1994 – and when linked to the €, as low as 50 in 2001.

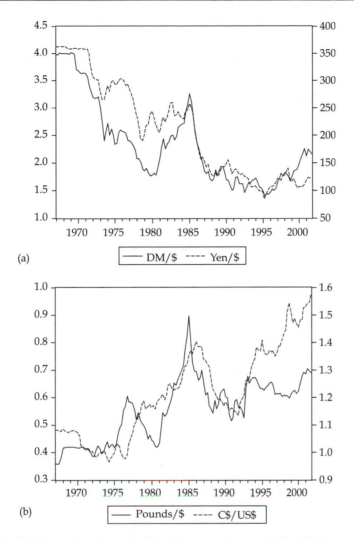

Figure 12.2   The US dollar's fall relative to the DM and the yen, and rise against the British pound and Canadian dollar, over the past 30 years

MANAGER'S BRIEFCASE: HEDGING FLUCTUATIONS IN FOREIGN CURRENCIES

The Federal Reserve data given in table 12.1 are all cash prices. However, there is a great deal of trading in futures contracts; a sample of the daily data given in the *Wall Street Journal* and other financial press pages for futures and options is shown in table 12.2. In addition, updated foreign exchange rates are posted

continued

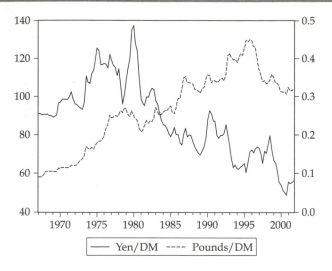

Figure 12.3   The DM relative to the pound and the yen

MANAGER'S BRIEFCASE (*continued*)

on the Web every day by the Fed at www.federalreserve.gov/releases/h10/update/. For the most part, corporations use futures prices to lock in a price at the expected time of delivery; the company hedges its foreign exchange risks in that manner. Of course, there are also many speculators, but for business managers, the main use of the futures markets is to reduce risk and hedge against currency fluctuations.

The simplest hedge occurs when a corporation has a contract to buy (or sell) goods to a foreign country denominated in that currency, but it does not want to speculate on whether that currency will rise or fall between the time of the initial order and actual payment for delivery. The firm can then buy enough futures contracts on that currency that the face amount of the contracts is equal to the delivery price; typically, futures contracts are purchased with 5% or less margin. If the price of (say) the € falls, the firm receives fewer dollars for its product, but that loss is offset by the gain on the futures contracts. On the other hand, if the price of the € rises, the firm receives more dollars for its product, but that gain is offset by the loss on the futures contracts. Hence the firm is indifferent to what happens in foreign exchange markets.

Of course there are more sophisticated strategies, many of which are touted as "riskless" by major financial institutions; obviously they are not. One common strategy is to use options, which differ fundamentally from futures because they are a wasting asset in the sense that if nothing changes, they expire worthless. That means an option writer can pocket the premium. The obvious risk is that the currency moves against the writer, which exposes him to unlimited risk unless the movement is hedged elsewhere. In this case, the hedge is the actual price of the product to be delivered. Thus if one were to write an option, and the price of the € remains unchanged, the option seller would profit by the amount of the premium. If the price of the € falls, the seller keeps the premium but takes some loss on the number of dollars received. If the price of the € rises, the seller loses the premium but receives more dollars for the product. The increased risk does not appear unless the price of the € falls by more than the amount of the options premium. If that situation appears to be likely, the treasurer of the corporation can then write another lower priced option to cover this risk, and so on. Alternatively, more sophisticated combinations of options can be written that limit total risk; generally the premiums on these are high enough that the writer, rather than the buyer, makes the profit.

continued

Table 12.2

Exchange Rates

The New York foreign exchange mid-range rates below apply to trading among banks in amounts of $1 million and more, as quoted at 4 p.m. Eastern time by Reuters and other sources. Retail transactions provide fewer units of foreign currency per dollar.

Country	U.S. $ EQUIVALENT Mon.	Fri.	CURRENCY PER U.S. $ Mon.	Fri.
Argentina (Peso)-y	.3636	.3617	2.7500	2.7650
Australia (Dollar)	.5280	.5304	1.8941	1.8855
Bahrain (Dinar)	2.6525	2.6525	.3770	.3770
Brazil (Real)	.4362	.4392	2.2925	2.2770
Britain (Pound)	1.4316	1.4335	.6905	.6976
1-month forward	1.4291	1.4310	.6997	.6988
3-months forward	1.4239	1.4258	.7023	.7014
6-months forward	1.4168	1.4188	.7058	.7048
Canada (Dollar)	.6271	.6291	1.5947	1.5896
1-month forward	.6269	.6289	1.5952	1.5901
3-months forward	.6264	.6284	1.5965	1.5913
6-months forward	.6254	.6276	1.5989	1.5933
Chile (Peso)	.001544	.001545	647.65	647.15
China (Renminbi)	.1208	.1208	8.2770	8.2770
Colombia (Peso)	.0004442	.0004422	2251.25	2261.50
Czech. Rep. (Koruna)				
Commercial rate	.02842	.02858	35.186	34.996
Denmark (Krone)	.1176	.1182	8.5004	8.4570
Ecuador (US Dollar)	1.0000	1.0000	1.0000	1.0000
Hong Kong (Dollar)	.1282	.1282	7.7996	7.7995
Hungary (Forint)	.003614	.003618	276.73	276.41
India (Rupee)	.02047	.02049	48.860	48.810
Indonesia (Rupiah)	.0001047	.0001047	9547	9550
Israel (Shekel)	.2096	.2103	4.7700	4.7550
Japan (Yen)	.007607	.007595	131.46	131.66
1-month forward	.007618	.007607	131.26	131.46
3-months forward	.007643	.007632	130.83	131.03
6-months forward	.007691	.007679	130.03	130.23
Jordan (Dinar)	1.4104	1.4104	.7090	.7090

Country	U.S. $ EQUIVALENT Mon.	Fri.	CURRENCY PER U.S. $ Mon.	Fri.
Kuwait (Dinar)	3.2595	3.2573	.3068	.3070
Lebanon (Pound)	.0006605	.0006605	1514.00	1514.00
Malaysia (Ringgit)-b	.2632	.2632	3.8000	3.8000
Malta (Lira)	2.1973	2.2041	.4551	.4537
Mexico (Peso)				
Floating rate	.1108	.1110	9.0290	9.0065
New Zealand (Dollar)	.4335	.4380	2.3068	2.2831
Norway (Krone)	.1146	.1149	8.7281	8.7043
Pakistan (Rupee)	.01665	.01665	60.075	60.075
Peru (new Sol)	.2905	.2902	3.4429	3.4455
Philippines (Peso)	.01960	.01958	51.025	51.075
Poland (Zloty)	.2438	.2449	4.1015	4.0838
Russia (Ruble)-a	.03203	.03204	31.220	31.210
Saudi Arabia (Riyal)	.2666	.2666	3.7509	3.7504
Singapore (Dollar)	.5450	.5448	1.8349	1.8355
Slovak Rep. (Koruna)	.02095	.02107	47.725	47.463
South Africa (Rand)	.0898	.0904	11.1400	11.0650
South Korea (Won)	.0007557	.0007544	1323.20	1325.50
Sweden (Krona)	.0964	.0974	10.3741	10.2685
Switzerland (Franc)	.5968	.6001	1.6757	1.6665
1-month forward	.5969	.6002	1.6752	1.6660
3-months forward	.5973	.6007	1.6741	1.6648
6-months forward	.5983	.6018	1.6713	1.6617
Taiwan (Dollar)	.02863	.02861	34.930	34.950
Thailand (Baht)	.02296	.02296	43.555	43.550
Turkey (Lira)	.00000076	.00000076	1316500	1310000
United Arab (Dirham)	.2723	.2723	3.6730	3.6729
Uruguay (Peso)				
Financial	.06173	.06431	16.200	15.550
Venezuela (Bolivar)	.001090	.001104	917.50	905.50
SDR	1.2520	1.2516	.7987	.7990
Euro	.8745	.8790	1.1435	1.1377

Currency

Japanese Yen (CME)
12,500,000 yen; cents per 100 yen

Price	May	Jun	Jly	May	Jun	Jly
7550	1.25	1.64	--	0.37	0.76	--
7600	0.92	1.33	--	0.54	0.95	--
7650	0.65	1.06	--	0.77	1.18	--
7700	0.45	0.84	1.30	1.07	1.46	--
7750	0.30	0.66	--	1.42	--	--
7800	0.20	0.51	--	1.82	2.12	--

Est vol 963 Fr 816 calls 1,916 puts
Op int Fri 34,184 calls 63,853 puts

Canadian Dollar (CME)
100,000 Can.$, cents per Can.$

Price	May	Jun	Jly	May	Jun	Jly
6150	--	--	--	0.06	0.20	--
6200	--	0.97	--	0.13	0.31	--
6250	0.45	0.67	--	0.29	0.51	--
6300	0.22	0.44	0.53	0.56	0.78	--
6350	0.10	0.27	--	--	1.11	--
6400	0.04	0.17	--	1.38	--	--

Est vol 339 Fr 136 calls 161 puts
Op int Fri 15,003 calls 4,352 puts

British Pound (CME)
62,500 pounds; cents per pound

Price	May	Jun	Jly	May	Jun	Jly
1400	--	3.02	--	0.20	0.54	--
1410	--	--	--	0.36	0.74	--
1420	1.14	1.60	--	0.66	1.12	--
1430	0.64	1.12	--	1.16	1.64	--
1440	0.34	0.76	0.90	1.86	2.28	--
1450	0.20	0.56	--	--	--	--

Est vol 177 Fr 139 calls 114 puts
Op int Fri 4,154 calls 5,916 puts

STRIKE	CALLS-SETTLE			PUTS-SETTLE		

Swiss Franc (CME)
125,000 francs; cents per franc

Price	May	Jun	Jly	May	Jun	Jly
5850	--	--	--	--	0.38	--
5900	0.98	1.25	--	0.26	0.53	--
5950	0.66	--	--	0.44	0.74	--
6000	0.47	0.75	--	0.72	1.05	--
6050	0.28	0.56	--	--	--	--
6100	0.17	0.41	0.64	1.45	1.68	--

Est vol 41 Fr 348 calls 31 puts
Op int Fri 3,405 calls 2,712 puts

Euro Fx (CME)
125,000 euros; cents per euro

Price	May	Jun	Jly	May	Jun	Jly
8600	--	1.79	--	0.28	0.64	--
8650	1.09	--	--	0.43	0.82	--
8700	0.79	1.20	--	0.63	1.04	--
8750	0.56	0.98	--	0.90	1.32	--
8800	0.37	0.61	--	1.21	1.61	--
8850	0.26	--	--	1.60	--	--

Est vol 1,683 Fr 1,849 calls 2,332 puts
Op int Fri 25,897 calls 17,366 puts

Currency Futures

Japanese Yen (CME)-12.5 million yen; $ per yen (.00)

June	.7616	.7655	.7615	.7638	.0010	.8776	.7449	68,685
Sept	.7676	.7695	.7663	.7683	.0009	.8620	.7495	739

Est vol 6,240; vol Fri 11,541; open int 70,172, –3,195.

Canadian Dollar (CME)-100,000 drs.; $ per Can $

June	.6290	.6290	.6257	.6266	–.0023	.6700	.6180	59,338
Sept	.6262	.6270	.6247	.6258	–.0024	.6590	.6175	4,042
Dec	.6250	.6263	.6242	.6252	–.0024	.6555	.6190	1,859
Mr03	.6255	.6255	.6250	.6246	–.0024	.6392	.6198	273

Est vol 6,913; vol Fri 8,672; open int 65,686, –140.

British Pound (CME)-62,500 pds.; $ per pound

June	1.4258	1.4298	1.4226	1.4248	–.0022	1.4550	1.3910	35,378
Sept	1.4202	1.4224	1.4156	1.4170	–.0022	1.4320	1.3990	880

Est vol 3,306; vol Fri 5,201; open int 36,261, –632.

Swiss Franc (CME)-125,000 francs; $ per franc

June	.6010	.6014	.5967	.5972	–.0039	.6220	.5813	31,047
Sept	.6014	.6017	.5984	.5982	–.0039	.6110	.5860	347

Est vol 4,253; vol Fri 6,973; open int 31,429, +1,010.

Australian Dollar (CME)-100,000 dirs.; $ per A$

June	.5271	.5278	.5231	.5249	–.0028	.5330	.4885	44,097

Est vol 1,071; vol Fri 3,258; open int 44,220, –501.

Mexican Peso (CME)-500,000 new Mex. peso, $ per MP

June	.10955	.10990	.10955	.10965	–.00017	.11010	.09730	41,381
Sept	--	--	--	.10808	–.00017	.10830	.09930	2,496

Est vol 2,130; vol Fri 3,005; open int 45,119, +440.

Euro FX (CME)-Euro 125,000; $ per Euro

June	.8767	.8769	.8710	.8716	–.0051	.9275	.8365	100,116
Sept	.8723	.8735	.8685	.8689	–.0052	.9235	.8375	1,226
Dec	.8735	.8735	.8676	.8669	–.0053	.9175	.8390	315

Est vol 10,749; vol Fri 12,819; open int 101,674, –2,839.

MANAGER'S BRIEFCASE (*continued*)

The plethora of lawsuits by major *Fortune* 500 companies against major financial institutions in recent years suggests that these options strategies often do not work out as advertised. For those corporations that do not wish to expose themselves to forex risk, the most sensible plan is to denominate contracts in dollars. For those that must face currency risk, the best strategy is to hedge that risk without further embellishments. Even more than bonds and stocks, foreign exchange trading is no place for amateurs.

12.2   Nominal and real exchange rates

So far we have assumed that the changes in the nominal and real exchange rates are the same. Suppose, however, the inflation rate was 5% in both Country A and Country B, but then it rises to 10% in Country B. As a first approximation, the cost of production in Country B would increase by 5% relative to Country A. Unless Country B devalues its currency by 5%, it would no longer be as competitive. By the same token, a 5% decline in the value of the currency in Country B would not mean its goods were cheaper; it would simply offset the rise in costs. In this case, the real exchange rate is a more accurate indicator of relative costs than the nominal exchange rate.

In the case of a hyperinflationary economy, such as used to occur regularly in Brazil, the currency would depreciate by a factor of 20 during years in which the inflation rate was 2,000%. In such cases, the nominal unit of currency (formerly the cruzeiro, more recently the real) had little meaning in international commerce, so virtually all transactions were denominated in dollars. Using the foreign exchange rate to measure competitive costs made no sense unless that rate was calculated in real terms.

However, we need not rely on such extreme examples. In years when the inflation rate in Italy averaged about 5% above the US rate, the value of the lira declined an average of about 5% per year relative to the dollar. These declines did not occur every year, but over a 20-year period, the gradual rise of the lira/$ ratio was roughly proportional to the relative decline in the US/Italian price ratio, as shown below.

The figures provided by the Federal Reserve, and the quotations in the *Wall Street Journal* and other financial pages, are always in nominal terms, just as is the case for interest rates. For economic analysis, though, the relevant figures are in real terms. When determining the impact of foreign exchange rates on net exports and overall economic behavior, the exchange rate should be adjusted for changes in the relative price ratio, just as rate of return on assets should also be measured in real terms – the nominal return minus the expected rate of inflation. That is the same convention used to develop the joint determination of output and interest rates in the domestic sector.

Note that we said the expected rate of inflation. Since investors do not know how to predict the rate of inflation, some qualified guesses are made, just as is the case for interest rate determination. When comparing international inflation rates, exogenous shocks (such as wars or energy prices) are likely to affect all countries similarly, so the important factor here is the *relative* price changes. Most of the time, expectations will be based on previous history, plus a forward look at any expected changes in monetary and fiscal policy.

Domestic and international expectations are not always the same. In the early 1980s, US investors apparently thought inflation would soon return to double-digit levels. Foreign investors, on the other hand, were sufficiently attracted by record high real interest rates that the value of the dollar doubled relative to many major currencies. It appears that expectations about US inflation were different for foreign and domestic investors.

CASE STUDY 12.1   DIFFERENT TRADE-WEIGHTED INDEXES OF THE VALUE OF THE DOLLAR

Currently, the Fed publishes six **trade-weighted averages of the dollar**; until late 1998, there was only one, which was the G-10 index. Three of these six indexes are calculated in nominal terms, and three in real terms. The "broad" index includes all of the currencies listed in table 12.1. The "major currency" is similar to the G-10 index except it substitutes the euro for the five currencies it replaces: the DM, French franc, Italian lira, Belgian franc, and the Netherlands guilder. The third average is listed as OITP, which stands for "other important trading partners" and is essentially the currencies shown in table 12.1 minus the major currencies; that is, (3) = (1) − (2) using the appropriate weights. The weights are based on recent US exports and imports with all of these countries. Figures 12.4(a) and (b) show the values of the broad and major currency indexes in nominal and real terms. The source for all these data is the Federal Reserve website listed above.

12.3   Measuring international labor costs

For business managers, one of the most important considerations for determining whether operations should be based in the US or abroad is the relative cost of manufacturing production workers. Other factors, such as transportation costs, size of the market, possible tariffs and quotas, barriers to entry, political stability, rule of law, and natural resource availability may also enter into this decision, but in general the most important determining factor is the cost of labor.

Labor costs have several dimensions. The most important, of course, is the wage rate. However, labor costs also include the level of productivity, mandated fringe benefits payable to the government, customary fringe benefits in the private sector, and hiring and firing policies. In most western European countries, for example, it is very difficult to discharge an employee, even for economic reasons, without a large severance payment. Also, for political reasons, it may be very difficult to shut down money-losing operations. The cost of fringe benefits in major European countries was discussed in chapter 9.

Of course, productivity is much lower in many developing countries. Yet that may be less important in the future if the US – or other major industrialized nations – install modern plant and equipment and train existing laborers to work

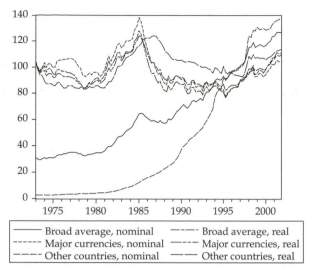

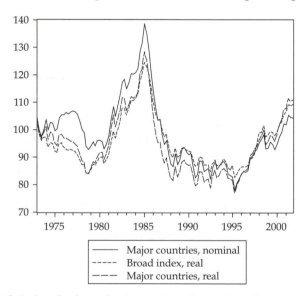

(a) Because of frequent devaluations, the broad market and total indexes in nominal terms do not provide a useful measure of foreign exchange rates

(b) Both the broad index and major country index are about the same in real terms, and either can be used as a useful measure of the trade-weighted average of the dollor

Figure 12.4 Broad and major currency indexes in nominal and real terms:

more efficiently. In other cases, countries may have restrictions on repatriating profits, US firms may be forced to pay higher wages than domestic firms, and prices of raw materials and other inputs may be artificially inflated. Obviously, all these factors must be carefully checked out before opening a plant. Nonetheless, relative wage rates often serve as a useful starting point.

In terms of calculating whether the dollar is overvalued or undervalued on a global basis, the best single measure is relative wage rates in OECD countries excluding Mexico and Korea, which are shown below in table 12.3. On this basis, the dollar was undervalued by 19% in 1995, but was overvalued by 7% in 2000. As this was written, the BLS had not yet prepared figures for 2001, but based on changes in the value of the dollar and wage rates in major countries, it appears the dollar was overvalued by about 20% near the end of 2001. That is certainly one of the reasons why the trade deficit rose in 2001 even though it usually declines during a US recession.

CASE STUDY 12.2   USING LABOR COSTS TO DETERMINE COUNTRY INVESTMENT OPPORTUNITIES

Given these figures, how does a business manager decide where to invest? Of course it depends to a certain extent on the type of business, the relative costs of transportation, the importance of highly educated and skilled labor, and the specific markets you want to reach. However, even with these caveats, labor costs appear to be much less expensive in Mexico and southeast Asia than in Europe.

The major country missing from this table is China, since figures are not published for that country by the BLS. However, based on our approximations calculated from total labor income divided by employment, the average wage in China in dollar terms appears to be between $1.00 and $1.50 per hour for manufacturing jobs. It is not necessary for our purposes to be more precise than that; even using the higher figure, wage rates there are only 10% of the US average.

Figure 12.5 shows US imports from four major regions: western Europe, Mexico, Asian NICs (newly industrialized countries), and China, all indexed for 1987 = 100. It is clear that imports from China have grown the most rapidly.

It does not necessarily follow that China is the best place to build a new plant; the restrictions placed on industry by the Chinese Communist Party often mean that foreign firms must buy domestic parts and materials at such a high price that it is not possible to generate a profit. Nonetheless, it is clear that the extremely low labor costs in China are one of the principal reasons for the very rapid growth in imports; and if one can skirt the bureaucratic restrictions, the cost basis will be very low.[1]

12.4   The concept of purchasing power parity

The previous section showed a comparison of wage rates for manufacturing employees for most major countries in the world. Admittedly, the comparison would be even more useful if similar tables were available for unit labor costs,

Table 12.3 Relative wage rates for manufacturing production workers (US = 100 each year)

Country or area	1992	1993	1994	1995	1996	1997	1998	1999	2000
North America									
United States	100	100	100	100	100	100	100	100	100
Canada	107	100	94	94	94	90	84	82	81
Mexico	14	15	15	9	9	10	10	11	12
Asia and Oceania									
Australia	81	76	84	89	95	91	80	82	71
Hong Kong SAR	24	26	27	28	29	30	29	29	28
Israel	57	53	55	61	64	66	65	62	65
Japan	102	116	127	139	119	107	98	109	111
Korea	32	34	38	42	46	43	31	37	41
New Zealand	48	48	52	58	61	59	49	48	41
Singapore	31	32	37	43	47	45	42	37	37
Sri Lanka	3	3	3	3	3	3	3	2	–
Taiwan	32	32	33	35	34	32	28	29	30
Europe									
Austria	126	122	128	147	140	120	120	114	98
Belgium	137	131	140	161	154	131	131	125	106
Denmark	126	116	120	140	136	121	122	120	103
Finland	124	101	113	140	132	117	117	112	98
France	109	102	105	116	113	99	98	94	83
Germany, former West	157	152	158	184	176	151	148	140	121
Germany	–	145	151	176	168	144	141	134	116
Greece	47	44	46	53	54	50	48	–	–
Ireland	83	73	75	80	80	76	73	71	63
Italy	120	96	94	94	100	96	92	87	74
Luxembourg	119	114	121	132	121	103	101	98	84
Netherlands	125	121	123	140	131	114	115	112	96
Norway	143	122	124	142	142	130	126	125	111
Portugal	32	27	27	31	32	29	30	28	24
Spain	84	70	68	75	76	67	65	63	55
Sweden	153	107	110	125	138	122	119	113	101
Switzerland	144	137	148	170	160	132	131	123	107
United Kingdom	89	75	76	80	80	84	88	86	80
Trade-weighted measures									
All 28 foreign economies	89	87	89	95	91	84	79	80	76
OECD	96	94	96	103	98	90	85	86	82
less Mexico, Korea	111	108	110	119	112	103	98	99	93
Europe	122	111	114	128	125	112	111	107	93
European Union	121	110	113	126	123	111	110	106	92
Asian NICs	30	31	34	37	39	37	32	33	34

Source: ftp://ftp.bls.gov/pub/special.requests/ForeignLabor/supptab.txt

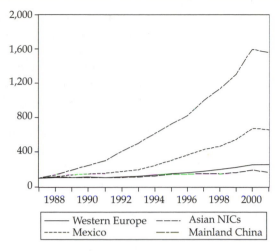

Figure 12.5   Index of US imports from major regions (1987 = 100)
Source: Bureau of Economic Analysis website, www.bea.gov

including productivity differentials. If they were, it would then be a relatively simple matter to construct indexes for the relative costs of production on a trade-weighted average basis. Under those circumstances, we could then measure **purchasing power parity** (PPP) accurately. PPP means the average cost of producing a market basket of tradable goods and services in any given country is equal to the trade-weighted average cost of producing that same market basket of goods and services in the rest of the world. Theoretically, that equivalence is obtained by permitting exchange rates to float freely until they are all in equilibrium. Under free trade and mobility of factor resources, world production is maximized when all countries are at PPP.

PPP is an old concept, developed by Swedish economist Gustav Cassel in 1917, who used it to calculate how much countries should have adjusted their currencies at the end of World War I based on the inflation rates that had occurred during wartime (countries on the gold standard before the war had very little inflation). The concept faded from view as countries returned to the gold standard, and recently has had only intermittent revivals even with flexible exchange rates, since it does not predict changes in currency values very well in the short run. On the other hand, the concept is not so outmoded as some international trade economists have claimed. In particular, it can be used to identify currencies that are currently overvalued or undervalued, and provide some hint of the next major move in those currencies.

PPP can be calculated two different ways. One way is to measure the CPI or the standard of living among various countries; in that case, the overall market basket of goods and services purchased by consumers would be included. However, for purposes of determining equilibrium values of exchange rates, it is best to use the concept of PPP as calculated for market baskets of *traded goods*, hence eliminating those goods and services that are not traded internationally. Such a concept would not include items such as hotel prices and taxicab fares, which (for example) are relatively much more expensive in Japan than in the US.[2]

Using this concept, we can theoretically develop an index that compares the cost of producing a market basket of tradable goods in any given country with the trade-weighted average cost of producing that market basket of goods in the rest of the world.

Suppose that exchange rates in each country adjusted to their PPP levels. In that situation, assuming complete mobility of all factor resources and no barriers to trade, all countries would receive the maximum benefit from international trade, because each country would specialize in the tradable goods and services in which it had a comparative advantage. As a result, all exchange rates would be in equilibrium. This condition is known as the "golden rule" of international trade, since if there are no restrictions to trade or mobility of factor resources, it would maximize world GDP. The logic behind this statement is based on the theory of comparative advantage, which was briefly discussed in the appendix of the previous chapter.

If all currencies were to move to PPP and there were no barriers to trade, eventually every country would have a balanced current account. However, that condition is only theoretical: the ¥ and the $ are both reasonably close to PPP but Japan has a huge trade surplus while the US has a huge trade deficit. Nonetheless, PPP does provide a useful method of predicting long-term trends in exchange rates, even though it does not predict short-term changes in exchange rates very accurately; nor does it indicate whether the current account balance will be in surplus or deficit.

Empirically, trade-weighted PPP ratios are difficult to compare because of differences in productivity of labor and quality of product. Wage costs can be readily determined – we have already shown the Bureau of Labor Statistics estimates for manufacturing wage rates in 29 major countries – but productivity data are much more difficult to assemble. Further problems exist because goods are not always the same in all countries: perhaps the quality levels of US and Japanese cars are no longer very different, but that is not true for Spanish cars. Market baskets also differ tremendously by countries: the Chinese eat far more cabbage and buy far fewer air conditioners than do Americans. Of course, cabbage is much cheaper in China than the US, while air conditioners are relatively more expensive.

Calculating the relative costs of production involves a great deal of painstaking research. Hence it is not surprising to find that shortcuts have arisen. One such attempt has been the collection of prices of a single world-traded commodity in various countries, with those prices to the dollar equivalent to determine which currencies are overvalued or undervalued.

The Big Mac Index of PPP

Over 15 years ago, the *Economist* magazine published its first "Big Mac" index. The magazine simply collected data on the price of Big Macs in local currencies, converted them to dollars, and then used that calculation to determine how much a given currency was over or undervalued, hence deriving a crude measure of PPP.

For a while, the Big Mac index attained a life of its own and received a fair amount of publicity, based in part on the conclusion of several academic studies that the Big Mac index did a better job of predicting changes in exchange rates over the next year than far more sophisticated econometric models of foreign exchange.

That's a nice story, but it isn't true. Comparison of the Big Mac indexes for 1996 and 1998 reveals no correlation between the amount that currencies were allegedly overvalued or undervalued in 1996 and the amount they changed over the next two years. During this period, the vast majority of these currencies declined about 20% relative to the value of the dollar, and the changes around that mean value were random. As it turns out, PPP doesn't predict currency values in the short run, whether it is measured using hamburger prices or some more sophisticated method. Making money in forex markets is not nearly as simple as pricing hamburgers at McDonald's.

Why Currencies Diverge from PPP

Setting the value of the dollar – and other major currencies – at their trade-based PPP levels maximizes world growth because it places all firms on the same level playing field. Of course that doesn't mean that all industries and all firms can compete equally; the point of international trade is that some countries are more efficient at producing goods and services than other countries. If the value of a currency is equal to its trade-weighted PPP level, some firms will find they cannot compete in world markets, but consumers of these goods will be able to purchase them at a lower price.

In spite of the clear long-run benefits of PPP, many currencies continue to diverge from that benchmark for extended periods of time. In some cases, the currency is managed, which means it is set above or below equilibrium by government intervention or exchange restrictions. However, this is less common than it used to be, yet there are still major gaps between actual and equilibrium values of many currencies. For some countries, PPP is not a relevant concept because their major exports are raw-materials based – food, energy, or minerals – and the countries manufacture very little, so there is almost no basis for comparison with industrialized countries. Such countries are also likely to have their currencies pegged to the dollar or the yen, with no independent market for their currencies. In that case, assuming the country accepts the concept of free trade in the first place, the value of the currency is determined by the current account balance. In such circumstances, PPP has little relationship with the value of the currency.

These arguments, while not without some merit, do not really explain why the dollar, the yen, and the Dmark have diverged from their PPP values for such extended periods. It would not be possible to "manage" these key currencies over a period of many years or even decades. In this case, the answer is found in the gap between ex ante investment and domestic saving. If investment is greater than saving, foreign capital is attracted and the value of the currency is likely to rise; if investment is less than saving, the value of the currency is likely to fall. Later we will examine the specific cases for Germany and Japan. For the US, however, the investment/saving gap is a major determinant of the value of the dollar. We now examine this relationship in greater detail.

12.5   Factors that determine foreign exchange rates

When discussing the determinants of prices and interest rates, we showed there was a very substantial difference between the short run and the long run. In the long run, the inflation rate is determined almost exclusively by monetary variables, but in the short run, unit labor costs and expectations are the key variables. In the long run, real interest rates are approximately equal to the growth rate of productivity, but in the short run, central bank policy and inflationary expectations are the principal determinants.

A similar dichotomy occurs for exchange rates. In the long run, exchange rates are determined by the relative rates of inflation, and are based on purchasing power parity. This long-run correlation is shown in figure 12.6 for the G-10 countries. These figures are based on average changes from 1970, the year before the US went off the gold standard, through 2000. Although the correlation is not perfect, there is

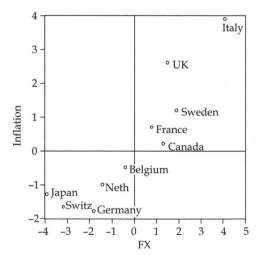

Figure 12.6   Change in value of currency per dollar and rate of inflation relative to US rate (annual % changes)
Source: compiled from data on the Federal Reserve website, www.federalreserve.gov

clearly a significant relationship between the relative rates of inflation and foreign exchange rates. The only major currency that does not fit closely is the Japanese yen, and that declined in value in 2001 and 2002 relative to most other currencies. In the long run, then, PPP is an adequate explanation of changes in foreign exchange rates – but it may take many years before equilibrium is reached.

In the short run, any correlation between the values of foreign exchange rates and PPP is usually quite weak. One reason is the tendency of many countries to try and "manage" their currencies. From time to time, even the US manipulated the value of the dollar, although it intervenes in foreign exchange markets much less often than other countries, and generally does so only to insure orderly markets, not to try to determine the value of the currency. The only major exception to this rule was the Plaza Accord, reached on September 22, 1985, when all of the G-7 countries agreed to reduce the value of the dollar.

In the remainder of this section we consider the economic factors that determine short-term fluctuations in foreign exchange rates, while realizing that rates may deviate from these values for substantial periods of time for political reasons as various central banks attempt to hold the value of their currencies constant. By the same token, though, the longer this practice continues, the more likely that the currency will face a major devaluation when the logjam finally breaks.

Even if we focus only on the equilibrium determinants of foreign exchange rates, it is still important to differentiate between the dollar and all other currencies, given that the world is on a de facto dollar standard. In the case of the dollar, the key determinant of the currency is the gap between ex ante investment and ex ante domestic saving. When ex ante investment is stronger than saving, foreign funds will tend to flow into the US economy, hence boosting the value of the dollar; when ex ante investment is weaker than saving, funds will tend to flow out, hence reducing the value of the dollar. The mechanics of these flows are discussed in more detail in the next chapter, where the Mundell-Fleming model is presented.

From the manager's viewpoint of explaining what determines foreign exchange rates, it may be well to state our objectives here. Nowhere in this book, or, to the best of our knowledge in any other book, will you find a set of formulas that accurately predicts how foreign exchange rates will change in the near future. That is not only because of the so-called efficient market hypothesis, but also because central banks are likely to intervene from time to time to create orderly markets, hence temporarily offsetting market forces that would move currencies in a specific direction. In the long run, as we have shown, purchasing power parity is important, and a country that tries to keep its currency pegged to the dollar even though its inflation rate is substantially higher than in the US will eventually have to devalue. The question is what determines foreign exchange rates in the "medium run," which we define here as a period from one to five years.

It is often thought that in this time frame, relative real interest rates are the key variable: as real rates rise in one country relative to another, the value of the currency will also rise. At least in recent years, that has simply not been the case. In 1994, real interest rates rose rapidly in the US while they were declining in most other major countries, yet the dollar fell. In 2001, the Fed reduced the funds rate 11 times, sending short-term rates down much more quickly than any other country, yet the dollar rose sharply. Some other factor must account for the major swings in the dollar over the past 20 years.

To determine this factor, we return again to the fundamental identity between saving and investment. Earlier we said that when ex ante investment is greater than ex ante saving, interest rates will rise, hence reducing investment and increasing saving. That is true for a closed economy. However, in an open economy, there is another option, which is that investment does not decline, but the gap is filled by an increase in foreign saving. As more foreign capital is attracted to a given country, the value of that currency will rise. Hence it is likely that an investment boom not matched by an equal increase in domestic saving will be funded by a substantial increase in foreign saving – without any increase in interest rates. That is essentially what happened in the US in the late 1990s. Similarly, when investment was relatively weak in the US in the late 1980s and early 1990s, the dollar declined sharply.

When an investment boom is due to new technology, increasing productivity, a rising stock market, and robust profit margins, it is easy to explain why foreign investment is attracted. Some of the other ramifications of this relationship may not be so obvious. Under certain circumstances, an *increase* in the Federal budget deficit could also boost the value of the dollar. That would occur if (a) the inflation rate did not increase when the deficit rose, and (b) total ex ante domestic saving fell while ex ante investment did not.

However, the linkage between the Federal budget surplus or deficit ratio and the value of the dollar is much more tenuous than was commonly assumed in the 1980s. In the first half of the 1980s, the deficit ballooned, while the dollar rose 42%; when the deficit diminished, the value of the dollar fell. Yet in the latter half of the 1990s, when the deficit disappeared and the budget balance shifted to a substantial surplus, the dollar rose 32%. One must be particularly careful to apply the ceteris paribus conditions here.

In the 1980s, much of the change in the deficit was due to changes in the tax laws that specifically affected investment, boosting it in the early 1980s and curtailing it in the late 1980s. Hence the rise in investment attracted foreign investors, while the decline in investment caused them to invest elsewhere. In the 1990s, by comparison, most of the change in the deficit was due to changes in economic conditions. The deficit from 1989 to 1992 rose when the economy – and investment – slumped; it then declined from 1993 through 2000 when the economy – and investment – boomed. In terms of the gap between ex ante investment and saving, the decline in saving caused by a bigger deficit during that earlier period was accompanied by lower investment, so foreign investment was not attracted. In the later period, an increase in saving caused by a smaller deficit was accompanied by higher investment, which did attract foreign investment.

It is often said that a rise in interest rates boosts the value of the currency, but *if a rise in interest rates reduces investment and increases saving, the dollar is more likely to fall*.

The key linkage is that *an increase in the gap between ex ante investment and saving boosts the dollar*. Relative interest rates play only a secondary role in determining its value.

Even for smaller countries, an increase in interest rates will not boost the value of the currency if it is obvious to speculators that such a step was taken in an attempt to keep the devaluation wolves away from the door. The UK boosted short-term interest rates to 15% in the summer of 1992, but that was not enough to keep the pound from being devalued. Similar attempts have been notably unsuccessful during recent decades.

Suppose, however, that a smaller country boosts real interest rates in an attempt to reduce inflation, and the currency is either floating or is not believed to be under attack from speculators. In that case, what is likely to happen to its value?

First, note that we said real interest rates. Suppose interest rates were 10% in the US and 5% in Germany. It might seem that money would flow to the US because of a higher rate of return. However, suppose the expected inflation rate in the US was 7%, whereas in Germany it was only 2%. In that case, the real rate of return would be equal in both countries. For if interest rates rise only by the amount that inflation has increased, that will not affect the value of the currency. Indeed, an increase in inflation is likely to diminish the value of the currency unless nominal rates rise more than the rate of inflation.

Even if real interest rates in a small country do rise, however, that will not necessarily boost the value of the currency. If higher interest rates reduce the growth rate and hence improve the trade balance by reducing imports, the value of the currency may rise for that reason. However, the decline in the growth rate may convince investors they do not want to invest in the assets of that country. It is important to remember that the positive impact of a higher real rate of return and an improved trade balance on the value of the currency are usually offset by slower growth and hence a lower rate of return on equities and on tangible assets.

As a result, it is difficult to issue any general rules about how currency values will change when real interest rates rise. On the positive side, the rate of return on fixed assets is higher. On the negative side, the rate of return on equities, and the rate of profit on tangible assets, is likely to be lower. In general, the value of the currency is likely to strengthen when the rate of inflation is low and productivity growth is high, and weaken when the rate of inflation is high and productivity growth is low. If both the rate of inflation and productivity growth are low, no firm conclusions can be drawn except to say that the currency will eventually return to its level dictated by purchasing power parity. Thus if it was previous overvalued when these conditions started, it will probably decline; and if was undervalued, it will probably rise. However, that shift will often take several years.

In general, the smaller the country, the more important the current account balance is in determining the value of the currency. In the US, the value of the dollar increased sharply in the late 1990s in spite of an unprecedented increase in the US trade deficit. Currencies of other industrialized countries, such as the UK, Germany, and Japan, depend largely on the expected rates of return on financial and real assets, but the current account balance does influence the value of those currencies.

The currency values of small countries with weak or nonexistent financial markets depend almost entirely on their current account balances.

In the medium run (one to five years), assuming that the central bank is not trying to manage the value of the currency, the following ceteris paribus conditions hold. The value of the currency will rise if:

- Ex ante investment exceeds ex ante domestic saving
- The rate of return of financial assets increases
- The rate of return on equities and tangible assets rises
- The rate of inflation declines
- The current account balance increases.

These conditions are symmetrical; the value of the currency will decline if the reverse conditions occur. The smaller the country, the more important the rate of inflation and current account balance become, and the less important the gap between investment and saving and the relative rates of return on assets.

Throughout this discussion we have emphasized that comparative rates of return are calculated in *real* terms; i.e., adjusted for the expected rate of inflation. Hence the following asset groups are all in *relative* terms. Thus, for example, to determine the value of the dollar, the appropriate interest rate is its performance in the US compared to the performance in other major countries. Keeping this in mind, these are the major factors that are likely to influence the values of exchange rates.

1. *Short-term riskless debt assets in real terms.* In practice, this is often estimated by taking the nominal difference in interest rates, treating the relative rate of inflation as a separate term.
2. *Expected changes in bond and stock prices.* A rise in bond and stock prices attracts foreign capital even if interest rates are low; conversely, a decline in bond and stock prices reduces foreign capital inflows even if interest rates are high.
3. *Rate of return on physical assets; plant and equipment.* That is usually measured by relative growth rates in the real sector. A useful proxy here is the change in the rate of industrial production, as well as corporate profits.
4. *Tax rates.* Lower marginal tax rates attract foreign capital. If the pretax rate of return is 15% in one country and 10% in another, but the top marginal tax rate – which is likely to apply to many investors – is 60% in the first country and 30% in the second country, capital will gravitate to the second country even though the pretax return is lower.
5. *Political stability.* It used to be said that "money moves to the right." Considering that the Clinton Administration in Washington attracted foreign investment, and the Labour government in London moved toward the center, that point may eventually fade in importance. Also, the election of the "Red/Green" coalition in Germany in 1998 had very little impact on the value of the Dmark, probably because Gerhard Schröder was not considered a doctrinaire socialist. However, any sign that a new government plans to implement expansionary policies

without giving due consideration to higher inflation would almost certainly face a massive withdrawal of funds by foreign investors.

6. *Expectations of how vigilant monetary policy will be in fighting inflation in the future.* These are based primarily on how central banks have acted in the past; in the case of a new appointee, investors will take their clue from the tenor of the current Administration. For example, when Jimmy Carter installed easy-money advocate G. William Miller at the Fed and sent Treasury Secretary Michael Blumenthal on the road to proclaim that a weak dollar was good for America, investors lost little time in switching their assets to other currencies.

Taking all these factors into consideration, we now present a more comprehensive discussion of the reasons for the major swings in the value of the dollar over the past 20 years in the following two case studies.

CASE STUDY 12.3   CAUSES OF THE "DOLLAR BUBBLE" IN THE 1980S AND STRENGTH IN THE 1990S

Table 12.4 shows the influence of the major factors that boosted the dollar 42% relative to the broad trade-weighted average of other currencies, and then caused it to decline to its previous value. The turning point, as mentioned below, was the Plaza Accord meeting of September 22, 1985; but the factors listed in the right-hand column carried the dollar back below its equilibrium value.

The dollar had clearly risen well above equilibrium values by 1984, yet it kept increasing nonetheless. Investors were attracted to the friendlier business climate, high real interest rates, and a booming stock market. They were also heartened by the decision of the Reagan Administration to strengthen the dollar, as directly opposed to the Carter dictum that a weak dollar was good for America. It is true that the large budget deficit boosted real interest rates, but while that deficit was severely criticized by many domestic economists, it did not seem to discourage foreign investors.

By 1985 it had become clear that the soaring value of the dollar was unjustly penalizing the US manufacturing sector, and threatened to drag the economy back into recession. Thus on the evening of September 22, 1985, the ministers of the G-7 nations – US, Canada, UK, France, Germany, Italy, and Japan – met at the Plaza Hotel in New York City and agreed that, starting the next day, all the central banks would engage in a coordinated effort to push the dollar back down toward equilibrium levels.

Of course, none of the economic variables changed between September 22 and 23 – only expectations. However, as time progressed, it became clear that several

continued

CASE STUDY 12.3 (*continued*)

Table 12.4   Principal factors affecting the dollar in the 1980s

Factor affecting dollar	1980–5	1986–8
Current real interest rate	Soared to record heights	Returned to normal
Capital gains/losses	Huge bond, stock market rally	Crash of 1987
Return on physical assets	Productivity started rising again along with rapid growth	Growth rate became more sluggish
Tax factors	Marginal rates on capital cut; 25% across-the-board tax cut	Most tax advantages for investment were terminated
Political factors	Return of Republicans; end of "Banana Republic" double-digit inflation under Carter	Reagan weakened by Iran-Contra scandal
Expectations	Inflation rate fell sharply; strong Chairman Volcker	Inflation started to rise again; initial concern about Greenspan

other economic variables were changing as well. Perhaps most important, in an attempt to reduce the budget deficit, Congress voted to terminate the investment tax credit and rescind most of the benefits of accelerated depreciation starting in 1986, which sharply reduced the ratio of fixed investment to GDP. The Fed also reduced short-term rates as part of the "package deal." On the political front, Reagan was weakened by international scandals and domestic disarray, and Paul Volcker stepped down from the Fed, to be replaced by the then-untested Alan Greenspan. As a result of these factors, the dollar not only returned to equilibrium, but continued to decline well below that level for the rest of the decade and into the early 1990s.

It is fair to say that few if any experienced currency traders thought the dollar would surge in the second half of the 1990s. At least in retrospect, the dollar bubble in the early 1980s could be ascribed to real interest rates as high as 10%, a rate which at least foreign investors thought represented an unprecedented opportunity. That boosted the broad-weighted average of the dollar by 42% from mid-1980 to mid-1985. However, that same measure of the dollar rose 32% from mid-1995 to late 2000 even though interest rates hardly budged at all. Hence the theories that the dollar had risen in the 1980s because of the huge budget deficit and unprecedented high levels of real interest rates did not apply this time. But what replaced them?

continued

CASE STUDY 12.3 (*continued*)

Table 12.5   Principal factors affecting the dollar in the 1990s

Factors affecting the dollar	1990–5 Plunged	1995–2000 Soared
Current real interest rate	Steady	Steady
Capital gains/losses	Normal	Record stock market rally
Return on physical assets	Sluggish growth	Technological boom
Tax factors	Marginal rates unchanged	Marginal rates unchanged
Political factors	Democrats control House	Republicans control Congress
Inflation	Stable	Stable at full employment
Expectations	Neutral	$ best safe haven

   As already indicated, the fundamental cause of dollar strength in the early 1980s and the late 1990s was the same: an increase in ex ante investment over ex ante saving. In both cases, the investment climate improved; in the early 1980s, that reflected the greater optimism under the Reagan Administration and the reduction in inflation; in the late 1990s, it represented the "new technology" and the resultant stock market boom. While there was a sizable budget deficit the first time the dollar soared above equilibrium, there was a sizable budget surplus the second time. Hence that fact by itself obviously does not influence the dollar. In the first case, total domestic national saving declined relative to investment because of the budget deficit; in the second case, total domestic national saving declined relative to investment because of the unusually large decline in the personal saving rate. The causes of the decline in saving were entirely different, yet the impact on the dollar was the same: the gap was filled by an influx of more foreign saving, which boosted the value of the dollar.

CASE STUDY 12.4   GEORGE SOROS, THE MAN WHO "BROKE THE BANK OF ENGLAND"

In the previous case study we showed that the dollar rose because of higher rates of return on assets and a shift toward greater optimism about the US; it then fell when the G-7 nations decided to mount a coordinated effort to reduce its value. In the case of the UK, by comparison, the Bank of England wanted to hold the £ steady with the $ and the DM, but it was unable to accomplish that goal; yet once the £ was devalued, it proved to be very beneficial to the economy. That was because

continued

CASE STUDY 12.4 (*continued*)

the £ was overvalued. The British had insisted on holding the £ at 2.95 DM, within the confines of what was called the European "snake." On September 16, 1992, however, the government was forced to let the £ float, resulting in an immediate 20% decline in its value.

Even though the £ had been devalued from $4.87 before World War I to $1.80 in 1976, some UK politicians still thought of London as one of the major world financial centers, perhaps second only to New York. As a result, even though the international gold standard had long since passed into oblivion, they tried to keep the £ linked to the dollar and the DM, even though the rate of inflation in the UK was higher than in Germany or the US. Consequently, growth in the UK had been subpar for much of the 1980s.

Figure 12.7 shows that the British had a tough time keeping up with either the Joneses or the Schmidts, as the £ fell sharply relative to both the dollar and the DM. Nonetheless, in the late 1980s and early 1990s, the UK held the £ at $1.80 even though that was clearly not its equilibrium value. Consequently, hedge funds run by George Soros bet against the £ so consistently that the Bank of England finally had to throw in the towel, dropping it to about $1.50 and handing Mr. Soros a gain of about $1.2 billion – not a bad hourly rate for that line of work.

The pride of a few Colonel Blimps may have been injured by this final abdication of the pound as a leading world currency, but the UK economy was far better off.

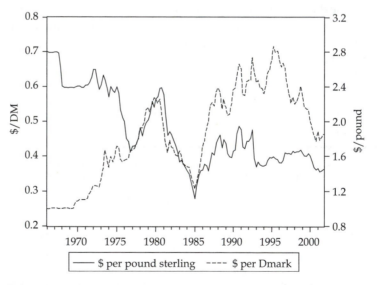

Figure 12.7   Trying to keep up with the Schmidts
Source: calculated from data on Federal Reserve website, www.federalreserve.gov

continued

CASE STUDY 12.4 (*continued*)

One reason for the improvement was that in an attempt to defend the £, the Bank of England had pushed short-term rates as high as 15% even though the rate of inflation was about 6%. Naturally that caused a severe slowdown.

When the £ was permitted to float freely, interest rates returned to normal levels. As a result, the growth rate rose to an average of 3.2% per year over the next five years, almost a full percentage point above the average growth rate of the previous decade. The unemployment rate, which had peaked at 10.5%, fell to 6%. Furthermore, the rate of inflation, which had been running around 6%, gradually fell to under 3%. This fact was grasped immediately by some journalists, including the economics editor of the *Times* of London, who wrote the following on that country's "Black Wednesday."

> Millions of Britons woke up this morning to read with horror about the devaluation of sterling, the utter collapse of the government's economic policy, the personal humiliation of the Prime Minister and Chancellor, and generally Britain's relegation to the third league of banana republics. But what will these dreadful events mean to the man in the street? Here are a few suggestions. By this time next year Britain will have the fastest growing economy in Europe and after Japan probably the strongest in the industrialized world. Interest rates will be down to 6 or 7 per cent and unemployment will be rapidly falling.[3]

When the US devalued in the 1970s, inflation surged, real growth fell, and the unemployment rate rose. When the UK devalued in the 1990s, inflation fell, real growth surged, and the unemployment rate declined. What lessons can be derived from these totally opposite results?

Actually it is the same lesson: any economy does better when its currency is near purchasing power parity. In the case of the US, the currency was already undervalued, so devaluation made a bad situation even worse. In the case of the UK, the currency was overvalued, so returning it to equilibrium benefited the entire economy.

MANAGER'S BRIEFCASE: ASSESSING THE 2002 DECLINE IN THE VALUE OF THE DOLLAR

At the beginning of 2000, the US dollar was roughly in equilibrium, as measured by PPP. Over the next year and a half, the trade-weighted average of the dollar relative to major foreign currencies then rose 20%. It slumped during the summer and after 9/11, but then quickly recovered to its previous peak early in 2002. It then fell 15% over the next two quarters before bottoming out in July and then rising about 5% during the next two months, after which it fell another 10%.

continued

MANAGER'S BRIEFCASE (*continued*)

While one is never sure about why any currency value changes, the likely causes were the US recession, the collapse of the stock market, the decline in short-term interest rates, the reduction in profit margins, and the belief that in the future, growth in the US economy would be far less than during the late 1990s. In terms of the investment/saving gap analysis discussed in this chapter, ex ante investment fell faster than ex ante saving in spite of the big increase in the Federal budget deficit.

However, the purpose of this particular section is not only to identify the causes of the decline in the dollar, but to pose the following questions to managers. It is the end of 2001, the value of the dollar is 20% above equilibrium, and your firm is getting clobbered in international markets and losing sales to imports. The choices are to (a) hope the dollar quickly declines, (b) start planning to shift operations overseas, or (c) reduce the size of the company. What do you recommend?

Before jumping to the "obvious" answer of (b), consider the following. Building plants overseas is not costless, and it is much more difficult to raise equity capital now than was the case in previous years. Closing down plants is likely to involve substantial severance payments and vicious arguments with the unions. Besides, if the dollar were to decline sharply, those overseas locations might turn out to be no bargain.

Obviously the complete answer depends on many more factors than are being discussed in this brief example. Nonetheless, there is an important point to be made. Unlike Germany and Japan, where the currency remained overvalued for many years, it is unlikely that the US dollar would remain substantially above equilibrium for an extended period of time. In both cases when the dollar rose substantially above equilibrium, namely 1985 and 2001, countervailing forces quickly moved to reduce its value. It is not in anyone's best interest – either the US or its principal trading partners – to have a permanently overvalued dollar, and with floating exchange rates, markets are not likely to support such a value for very long. In addition, a grossly overvalued dollar will reduce real growth in the manufacturing sector, hence bringing a turnaround in its value sooner rather than later.

The answer to the problem posed in this section, then, is to plan your company's future as if the dollar were going to remain near equilibrium in the long run. If, under those circumstances, it makes sense to move operations overseas, then that shift should be implemented. If, on the other hand, such a move is being contemplated only because the dollar is overvalued, it is better to maintain your facilities in the US.

12.6   Why foreign exchange markets overshoot equilibrium: the J-curve effect

Changes in the US current account balance do not have any measurable relationship to the value of the dollar, even under ceteris paribus conditions, because the world is on a de facto dollar standard. However, for most other countries, a rise in the current account balance will boost the value of the currency, while a decline will reduce the value of the currency. Most countries have a self-correcting mechanism in the sense that an increase in the value of the currency will reduce exports and boost imports, thereby keeping the currency from rising too far above equilibrium; similarly, a decline in the value of the currency will boost exports and reduce imports, hence keeping the currency from declining indefinitely.

However, that does not always occur: sometimes, currencies remain in a devaluation spiral that lasts for many years, while other times, currencies – notably the yen – continue to rise indefinitely in spite of an ever-increasing surplus.

Devaluation spirals usually reflect higher inflation in that country, and the problem disappears when real exchange rates are used. Even that does not cover all cases, though. For it can sometimes be the case that while the *real* current account balance falls, the *nominal* balance continues to rise. That is the case covered in this section.

The *current-price* (we refer to dollars, although the arithmetic holds for any currency) net export balance can be defined as.

$$\text{F\$} \equiv \text{EX} \times p_{ex} - \text{IM} \times p_{im}/\text{\$}. \tag{12.1}$$

This can be closely approximated by

$$\Delta(\text{F\$}) = \text{EX} \times \Delta p_{ex} + p_{ex} \times \Delta \text{EX} - \text{\$} \times p_{im} \times \Delta \text{IM} - \text{\$} \times \text{IM} \times \Delta p_{im}$$
$$+ \text{IM} \times p_{im} \times \Delta \text{\$} \tag{12.2}$$

where p_{ex} and p_{im} are the prices of exports and imports, and $ is the trade-weighted average of the dollar.

For ease of exposition, assume that after the $ changes, p_{im} remains unchanged, since it depends on foreign costs of production. Since p_{ex}, p_{im}, and $ are all indexes, they can be set equal to unity with no loss of generality. We will also assume that p_{ex} does not change when the $ changes, although a stronger dollar might reduce the cost of production by lowering the price of imports in dollar terms. Under these simplifying assumptions we have:

$$\Delta(\text{F\$}) = \Delta \text{EX} - \Delta \text{IM} + \text{IM} \times \Delta \text{\$}. \tag{12.3}$$

Assuming that EX and IM are approximately the same magnitude, we can divide through and obtain:

$$\Delta(\text{F\$})/\text{EX} = \%\Delta \text{EX} - \%\Delta \text{IM} + \%\Delta \text{\$}. \tag{12.4}$$

The percentage and actual change in the $ are the same in this example because the $ is set equal to unity.

Now suppose the $ rises by 1%. During the first year, EX will decline by about 0.3%, and IM will rise by about 0.4%. However, including the effect of the higher dollar, we find that the % change in F is *plus* 0.3% ($-0.3\% - 0.4\% + 1.0\%$). Thus, even though the value of the currency has appreciated, the current-dollar trade position has improved at the same time the constant-dollar position has weakened.

In this case, the currency may not move back toward equilibrium. The stronger the value of the currency, the more the current account improves – and the more the current account improves, the stronger the value of the currency. A disturbance from equilibrium, once set in motion, has no short-term mechanism that would return it to equilibrium.

It can be seen that the system will move back toward equilibrium only if the price elasticity of exports plus the price elasticity of imports is greater than unity. This is known as the **Marshall-Lerner condition**. The question is whether the price elasticities rise over time – and whether the relatively low elasticities for the US dollar also hold for other countries.

Empirically, the answer is "it all depends." However, we can be somewhat more specific. Many countries have a currency that rises or falls relative to the dollar for decades at a time; appreciation or depreciation does not seem to reverse these trends even when purchasing power parity is reached. That evidence would strongly suggest that even over the longer run, the sum of the price elasticities of exports and imports is less than unity.

In some cases, the value of the currency will not reverse direction until monetary and fiscal policy changes. Suppose that a currency is depreciating, but the trade deficit continues to worsen. Tighter monetary policy, or fiscal austerity, is then used to reduce real growth and imports, which in turn will reduce the trade deficit. By slowing down the economy, monetary and fiscal policy have accomplished what a depreciating currency could not do.

However, that is not the most common case. More often, the price elasticities of exports and imports rise as the time horizon increases. Recall from the previous chapter that the major impacts of changes in the dollar on US exports have occurred with at least a one-year lag. Indeed, whereas the one-year price elasticity of exports for the US is about -0.3%, the two-year elasticity is about -0.7%, which means the absolute value of the sum of the elasticities would then be greater than unity by the second year. Furthermore, even if the current account balance initially moves in the same direction as the currency, it might reverse direction if exports fell more sharply as the $ rises further; in other words, the relationship might be nonlinear. Similarly, imports might rise more rapidly as the $ moves further away from equilibrium.

This reversal – which occurs when the price elasticity of exports plus imports gradually rises above unity – is often known as the **J-curve effect**. For a while, the current account balances moves in the "wrong" direction; that is the left-hand side of the J. As the sum of the price elasticities approaches unity, the current account balance levels out, which is the bottom of the J. After that, the current account balance moves in the "right" direction, which is the opposite direction from the change in the currency; that is the right-hand side of the J.

If we plot the current account balance on the vertical axis, and time on the horizontal axis, the resulting function does resemble a J, as shown in figure 12.8. The slope of the right-hand side of the J is not vertical; the change in the current account balance is more gradual. The general shape, however, is close enough to the letter J to merit that description.

In addition, other variables, such as the rate of return, could influence the value of the currency. For example, if the dollar kept appreciating, interest rates might fall to a very low level, hence weakening net foreign investment because of a less attractive rate of return. If an overvalued currency choked off growth, that would reduce the rate of return on equities and physical assets, which would eventually reduce the value of the currency.

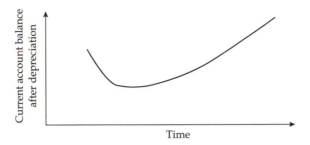

Figure 12.8   The J-curve effect on current account balance

However, there is an important offsetting reason why the change in the value of the currency might keep moving in the same direction as the current account balance indefinitely. In the arithmetical example above we assumed that p_{ex} was unchanged. Yet if the \$ were to rise 1%, the cost of production would probably fall because raw material costs are cheaper. If that happened, change in imports and exports would be less than otherwise expected from a 1% change in the value of the currency. That situation would be particularly important for countries that import most of their raw materials.

Because exports and imports usually do not react very much to changes in the value of the currency with a lag of less than a year, a short-term J-curve is commonly observed. However, after about a year, the combined price elasticities are usually greater than unity, and the current account balance moves in the opposite direction as the value of the currency. Only occasionally, as in the case of Japan, did the J-curve remain in effect for many years. That particular case is examined next.

CASE STUDY 12.5   THE JAPANESE YEN AND THE J-CURVE EFFECT

The J-curve effect is best illustrated with the Japanese yen. From 1985 through 1995, the Japanese yen rose sharply, not only relative to the dollar but also compared with virtually every other currency. Yet at the same time, the current account balance in yen also continued to rise. This seemed to be a clear disequilibrium situation; the more the yen rose, the bigger the trade surplus became.

However, as shown in figure 12.9, the volume of net exports was declining almost monotonically during the same period. When the value of the yen rose, the volume of exports fell relative to the volume of imports, but because those exports were priced higher in foreign currencies – and the volume of imports was priced lower in foreign currencies – the trade balance kept increasing. Clearly, the J-curve effect was at work, as the combined price elasticities of exports plus imports was less than unity.

continued

CASE STUDY 12.5 (*continued*)

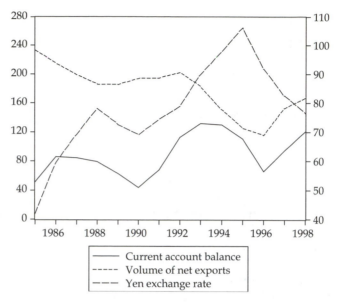

Figure 12.9 From 1985 to 1995, the yen and the current account balance in nominal terms both rose, while the trade balance in constant terms fell
Source: International Financial Statistics Yearbook

Finally, the yen became so overvalued that other events were set in motion. First, the Japanese economy headed into a decade-long recession. Second, investors began to believe that the US dollar was undervalued, and changes in the US economy now better represented an investment opportunity. Third, weakened expectations in Japan reduced capital spending, which also reduced the demand for foreign capital – although restrictions are much greater there than in the US. The combination of these factors caused the yen to decline. However, for the five-year period from 1990 through early 1995, the J-curve effect boosted the yen far above its equilibrium value.

Why did the J-curve effect persist so long in Japan? One reason was very low inflation in Japan, so the price of domestically produced raw materials generally declined. Even more important, the rising value of the yen meant import prices of raw materials and energy also kept declining. As a result, export prices rose far less than would have been expected from the value of the currency alone. Some of the decline stemmed from lower oil prices starting in 1986, which had a disproportionately large impact on Japan because it imports almost all of its energy requirements. However, lower oil prices alone would not have been sufficient to keep the J-curve effect alive through 1995. Japan was able to spend less on imports

continued

CASE STUDY 12.5 (*continued*)

generally, which boosted its current account balance even as the volume of imports rose faster than the volume of exports. Not until after the economy was driven into a severe and prolonged recession, and investment started to move overseas, did the value of the currency finally start to decline.

The Japanese yen rose from 240¥/$ in 1985 to a peak of 80¥/$ in 1995, an average annual appreciation rate of almost 12% per year; yet the rate of inflation in the US averaged 2.7% over that period, compared to an average rate of 1.4% in Japan. Hence changes in inflation rates accounted for only about one-tenth of the average annual appreciation of the yen. The average growth rate of Japanese industrial production was lower than in the US. Interest rates were also lower in Japan, even after taking into account the lower rate of inflation. The Japanese stock market did soar in the late 1980s but then collapsed in the early 1990s, falling 75% during that decade, compared to a tripling of the US stock market over the same period.

In effect there were many small J-curves; every time the yen appreciated, the Japanese trade balance rose for a while because of transactions undertaken at the previously lower yen. However, even that cannot explain most of the appreciation in the yen. Japan benefited by what might be called a "virtuous circle." When the value of the yen appreciated, the prices of imported raw materials, energy, and parts declined, offsetting much of the higher value of the yen. The fact that the Japanese inflation rate was an average of only 1.3% lower in the US does not really tell the story of the production cost of exports. With import prices (including oil) declining an average of 8% per year, many exporters could continue to produce profitably even with the much stronger yen. Not until it reached the overvalued level of 80¥/$ did profits of Japanese exporters disappear – at which point the yen finally did start to decline.

12.7 Other factors causing currency rates to diverge from equilibrium

We have identified several reasons why foreign exchange markets consistently overshoot equilibrium in both directions. To summarize, the main causes are:

- *Long lags.* Exports and imports do not respond quickly to changes in relative prices. This may extend the life of the J-curve, as happened for Japan.
- *Expectational effects.* Investors expect currencies to continue to keep moving in their previous direction, which influences capital flows and temporarily becomes a self-fulfilling prophecy.
- *Cost and price spirals.* If the value of a currency rises (say), prices of imported raw materials, energy, and parts decline, so some firms can remain competitive without raising their prices. Conversely, a declining currency will boost the price

of imports, hence wiping out much of the competitive advantage temporarily gained from a weaker currency.

- *Different rates of reaction.* When monetary policy changes, exchange rates can adjust immediately, while the variables they affect, namely relative prices and the trade balance, adjust much more slowly. Hence, even if foreign exchange rates do act as an equilibrating mechanism in free markets, they invariably overshoot equilibrium in both directions.

Part of the reason for the J-curve is that when the value of the currency changes, contracts that were originally signed at the old rate are valued at the new rate. However, that period generally lasts only a few months, whereas the left-hand side of the J-curve often continues for more than a year. Even after currency rates and relative prices have changed, it may take firms quite a bit of time to find alternative suppliers, especially where goods are customized.

Consider the case of auto parts. US dealers continued to order parts from Japanese manufacturers to service the existing stock of cars long after the value of the yen rose relative to the dollar. Indeed, it is often the case that imports from countries with strong currencies do not start to decline until firms in those countries decide to build new plants in the US. That is what happened for the Japanese and German motor vehicle manufacturers; it also applies to many other industries. In that case, the lag between changes in the currency and net exports could be several years.

We have already noted that if investors and speculators think the value of a given currency will continue to rise, capital flows into that country may generate a self-fulfilling prophecy. However, that is not the only role played by expectations.

Consider the case of a country that previously had recurring bouts of hyperinflation. A new government eliminates the deficit, reduces growth in the money supply, stops inflation, and stabilizes the currency. Because many investors have long memories, they may view such attempts with skepticism, assuming that because of the unpopularity of its austerity moves, the new government will soon be voted out of office or overthrown. Whether or not that assessment ultimately proves to be correct, investors may shun that currency, hence depressing its value, even though the economic criteria indicate that it should be strengthening.

Another possibility is that some currencies may decline by the taint of association. When the "growth tiger" currencies – the Thai baht, South Korean won, Malaysian ringgit, and Indonesian rupiah – collapsed in late 1997, speculation caused the value of the Philippine peso to plunge as well, even though the economy of the Philippines did not warrant that larger depreciation.

Different rates of reaction to changes in monetary policy may also cause international currency markets to diverge from equilibrium. If the central bank tightens monetary policy, exchange rates may react immediately. However, because of the long lags involved, the trade balance may not shift for the next year or two.

In equilibrium, the value of the currency depends both on financial factors – the expected rate of return and relative rate of inflation – and the current account balance. In the short run, though, changes in the value of the currency will primarily reflect the change in the rate of return, which usually causes the currency to over-shoot its target. Not until the trade balance has fully adjusted to the change in the currency will a new equilibrium be reached. Furthermore, if the value of the currency keeps changing, investors will be shooting at a moving target, and the return to equilibrium may be postponed for several years.

MANAGER'S BRIEFCASE: ANTICIPATING THE NEXT BIG SWING IN MAJOR CURRENCIES

This textbook is obviously not the place to offer precise currency forecasts. Nonetheless, some of the lessons provided in this chapter can be used to indicate what factors should be monitored to determine when the dollar – and other major currencies – are likely to post major moves.

Even if one were able to uncover the precise links between economic variables and exchange rates – which apparently no one has yet been able to do – those forecasts still might be inaccurate if the underlying economic projections were far off the mark. Nonetheless, astute business managers should be able to scope out the general direction of the economy over the next year or two without worrying about the erratic fluctuations and data quirks in the monthly and quarterly economic data.

As long as the US economy continues to grow at a rate that is below the long-term $3\frac{1}{2}\%$ annual average, the following conditions are likely to occur. Interest rates will be low, the Federal budget deficit will be substantial, the trade deficit will continue to increase slowly, and capital spending will rise at below-average rates. If our claim is correct that the gap between domestic investment and saving is the key variable determining the course of the dollar – and the trade deficit has no impact on its value – what can reasonably be expected?

Investment will be low. On the saving side, government and corporate saving will be low. Personal saving will either be average or low. Foreign saving will be rising, but not by very much. On balance, domestic ex ante saving and investment will be roughly equivalent, so the dollar won't change very much. In mid-2003 capital spending was showing signs of improvement, suggesting the sharp decline in the dollar since the beginning of 2002 was about to end.

Now suppose that after a while the growth rate rises above 4%, spurred by a capital spending boom. Personal, corporate, and government saving all rise, but not as much as the increase in investment. The gap is filled by attracting foreign investment, so the dollar appreciates.

The way we have told it so far, the dollar either remains stable or rises. Can't it ever fall?

Of course it *can* fall further, and probably would if Europe and Japan suddenly start to grow at rapid rates, hence attracting the lion's share of foreign investment. Funds would move back across the Atlantic and Pacific, causing the dollar to decline even more. The driving force would be a stronger € and a stronger ¥, which is why we focus on other major currencies instead of just the dollar. The key factor that would cause those currencies to appreciate is the same as in the US, namely stronger growth and the perceived higher rate of return for foreign capital.

12.8   Managed exchange rates: bands and crawling pegs

In early 1995, the Mexican peso suddenly devalued, losing more than half of its value relative to the dollar. This was followed by sudden and unexpected devaluations in Korea, Thailand, Indonesia, and Malaysia in 1997, Russia in 1998,

Brazil in 1999, and Argentina in 2002. In all of these cases, the currencies quickly became worth less than half their previous value in terms of dollars. Yet the underlying economic conditions did not suddenly deteriorate. Instead, these devaluations all followed failed attempts by central banks to keep the currency value fixed when the underlying economic factors, primarily the rate of inflation but also the current account balance and the outflow of foreign capital, indicated that some depreciation should have occurred. Why did all these countries persist in these actions even though each case ended in disaster?

Perhaps it is all too easy to criticize these countries after the fact. The central banks were trying to maintain a stable rate of exchange because they realized that if their currencies devalued, the standard of living would decline for consumers, investors would be far less likely to continue to put money in the country, and major financial institutions that had borrowed in dollars would be unable to repay the loans and hence would have to declare bankruptcy.

Also, while fluctuations in the value of the dollar do not have much of an impact on the US economy, that is often not the case for a smaller country, whose exporters and consumers could find them mercilessly whipsawed by voracious foreign exchange traders. The prime minister of Malaysia, Mohammed Mahathir, did indeed blame foreign speculators for the problems of that country after 1997, claiming in particular that George Soros was the chief wolf at the door.

Many smaller countries, then, find themselves between the proverbial rock and a hard place: fixed exchange rates lead to occasional massive and disruptive devaluations, yet flexible exchange rates lead to wild fluctuations in the value of the currency, causing economic and even political instability. Perhaps a middle way could be found.

The two principal methods that have been used in the past are known as **bands** – when used by the European monetary union, the various currencies were colloquially referred to as the "snake in the tunnel" – and **crawling pegs**. Each of these is now discussed briefly.

Using Bands to Defend Fixed Exchange Rates

At least in the short run, fixed exchange rates facilitate foreign trade, because economic agents in both countries know what the prices will be for upcoming transactions without the additional cost of hedging. However, this knowledge comes at a price. A major disadvantage of fixed exchange rates for central banks is they sometimes provide speculators with a "free ride."

Suppose a currency is generally thought to be overvalued, based on relative rates of return, the current account balance, and PPP. As a result, speculators sell it short. Either the central bank of that country will be successful in defending its currency, or it will be forced to devalue. In the first case, the speculators have lost very little, since the value of the currency remains unchanged; in the second case, they have gained a great deal. Speculators are essentially betting on a one-way street.

When a currency comes under fire, the only recourse of the central bank is to try to make it very expensive for speculators by boosting the short-term rate of interest to extremely high levels. It may also hope such a signal will attract other short-term investors to offset the sales of currency by speculators. However, the result is usually just the opposite: sky-high interest rates are generally a clear signal that the beleaguered currency is under great pressure, and such tactics seldom work. As a result, the currency is usually devalued a few days later.

Suppose investors thought they had "inside information" that the price of a certain stock was overvalued. They would sell the stock short on this news, which would probably reduce the value of the stock for a few days. At that point, one of two things would happen. Perhaps that information was right, in which case the other investors would also short the position, and the stock price would soon plunge a lot more. Or perhaps it was wrong, in which case the heavy hitters would step up to the plate and buy the stock at bargain prices, leaving the original speculators with substantial losses.

The same analogy can be applied to foreign exchange markets. Suppose a rumor starts that a currency is in trouble: perhaps the current account deficit is widening, foreign reserves are dwindling, or investment opportunities have deteriorated. Investors pull their money out of the country, and the value of the currency declines. If it is only a false rumor, other investors will buy on dips and return the currency to its previous level; if not, the currency will be devalued.

Yet countries operating under a fixed exchange rate do not want to be forced to defend their currency every time it dips. If most rumors are false, and the currency bounces back soon afterward, then central banks should not have to defend their currency every time there is a minuscule change in its value. For this reason, countries used to announce that their exchange rate was fixed within a fairly narrow band, say plus or minus $2\frac{1}{2}\%$. If the currency drifts by less than $2\frac{1}{2}\%$, it would stay within the band without requiring any intervention, but if it moved to the limits of that range, intervention would take place. The idea behind introducing these currency bands is the belief that most of the aberrations would indeed be temporary.

The EMS represented such an agreement among the major countries of western Europe. These countries wanted their currencies to remain in fixed ratios, so one country would not try to gain a temporary advantage by competitive devaluation. Thus currencies were allowed to move up or down by $2\frac{1}{2}\%$ without any intervention; when those limits were reached, each central bank was supposed to defend the currency by buying it back in foreign exchange markets.

Yet fixed exchange rates cannot long endure when inflation rates differ substantially. Thus, Italy was forced to devalue several times during the 1970s and the 1980s. The final straw occurred in September 1992, when high interest rates in Germany precipitated the foreign exchange crisis already described above. When the smoke had cleared, most other European countries had devalued relative to the DM, and Britain dropped out of the EMS completely and decided to float the £. The € will work only if the inflation rate in all 11 participating countries stays at approximately the same rate.

Currency bands based on fixed rates ultimately do not work for countries that have differential rates of inflation. Perhaps the central bank will be able to rescue its currency nine times out of ten, but eventually the strains become too great to cover up, and the currency must devalue. If it had been allowed to float, short-term fluctuations would have been greater, but there would have been no "big bang" that often disrupts growth for an extended period of time.

Using Crawling Pegs for Gradual Transition of Exchange Rates

We next consider the situation of a country that has an annual rate of inflation that is consistently higher than in the US; say 6% more. It is clear that the exchange rate of that country must decline relative to the dollar. On the other hand, the country does not want its currency to be freely convertible on foreign exchange markets because of insufficient liquidity and the likelihood of whipsawing by speculators.

The solution in this case is to institute a "crawling peg," which reduces the value of the currency by 6% per year, or $\frac{1}{2}$% every month. That would keep relative costs of production constant and avoid speculative dumping of the currency because of the expectation of a major devaluation. If the inflation differential widened to (say) 12% per year, the crawling peg could be readjusted to decline 1% each month. Brazil used such a system in the late 1990s. However, that did not keep the real from coming under speculative pressure because of the continuing budget deficit and the widespread belief that when the crawling peg was initiated, it was originally set too high. Eventually, the real was devalued by about 40%.

MANAGER'S BRIEFCASE: HOW TO SPOT THE NEXT MAJOR DEVALUATION AHEAD OF TIME

Unlike the previous manager's briefcase, this section analyzes the factors that will help anticipate devaluations of lesser currencies ahead of time. There are several different ways that a devaluation will affect your company, depending on your line of business and where your plants are located. If the currency of a country devalues sharply, that economy will probably go into a tailspin, and some major corporations will not be able to repay dollar-denominated loans. If they cannot borrow money to buy raw materials, production may temporarily grind to a halt. Even after the liquidity crisis has been cleared up with some help from the IMF, the standard of living of consumers will drop sharply, and they will not be able to buy as many imported goods. Thus if your company is selling goods and services to that country, your sales will drop sharply. On the other hand, if your company is buying raw materials, parts, or finished goods from that country, you will probably want to wait for a lower price. If your company has a manufacturing plant in that country and can obtain the needed raw materials and imports, export sales should zoom even though your domestic sales will be sharply curtailed. Thus depending on your particular

continued

MANAGER'S BRIEFCASE (*continued*)

corporate profile, devaluation may cut both ways – but in either case it is important. How can you tell when a major drop in the value of the currency is likely to occur?

Invariably, the proximate cause of these devaluations is that the countries in question run out of foreign exchange. However, this often happens with no advance warning. The question is which economic variables will provide an advance hint that a country has a high probability of devaluation.

The analysis usually starts with purchasing power parity: if the rate of inflation in that country is rising faster than in the US, or if the cost of production is higher than the US, the currency is at risk. The situation is likely to deteriorate quickly if the current account balance turns negative and the central bank fails to raise real interest rates quickly to maintain the value of the currency. The problems are often exacerbated by a large budget deficit, which means the central bank must hold interest rates artificially low in order to facilitate financing that deficit. That usually adds fuel to the inflationary fire, and the competitive situation of the country deteriorates further.

Thus the combination of (a) an increase in the inflation rate relative to the US, (b) a deterioration of the current account balance, and (c) an increase in the budget deficit, usually means devaluation in the near future. Even if only two of these three conditions are present, an upcoming devaluation is often likely for countries that are currently on a fixed exchange rate.

In some cases the country may not have done anything wrong: its exports may simply have plunged because of a decline in world commodity prices. This doesn't necessarily occur only in basic commodities, such as oil, coffee, or tin. The main reason for the collapse of the South Korean won in 1997 was a big drop in the price of semiconductors, which diminished their current-price exports substantially, even though the volume of exports continued to rise. In this case the situation was worsened by excessive overseas borrowing in dollar terms. However, it is often difficult to obtain this information ahead of time, so managers should focus on the three economic factors given above, for which data are readily available and are published with a short lag.[4]

12.9   Optimal trade and foreign exchange rate policy

We have already noted that any economy functions better when relative prices remain near their equilibrium value. That is particularly relevant for the two most important relative prices: interest rates and exchange rates.

Thus, from a policy viewpoint, it might seem there would be little or no disadvantage to setting the value of the exchange rate at purchasing power parity. However, as we have seen, exchange rates are governed by expectations, and hence may diverge from PPP for an extended period of time. In that case, what policy ought to be implemented?

Fixed exchange rates are almost never the correct answer. Large economies with key currencies should always allow exchange rates to float. Small economies, which do not have enough liquidity for that purpose, should peg their exchange rate to one of the key currencies, but it should always be a crawling peg in order to avoid the kind of crippling devaluations that hurt southeast Asia in the late 1990s.

That might seem to close the issue. The best policy, at least for large industrialized nations, is to reduce tariff barriers as much as possible and let the currency float freely. Nonetheless, this raises the following question. Suppose a country is doing everything right in the sense that it has a balanced budget, rapid growth, full employment, low inflation, no trade barriers, and the currency floats freely.

Under those circumstances, it would not be surprising if investors around the world decided they would prefer to invest their money in the assets of that country. As a result, so much money flows into that country that the currency soon becomes severely overvalued even though the country is following optimal policies. That is not a far-fetched scenario; with some oversimplification, that is what happened to Germany in the early 1980s, Japan in the early 1990s, and the US in the early 2000s. Sometimes the currency does not move back toward its equilibrium value even if correct policies continue to be pursued.

This may seem like a puzzling conclusion, but think about it for a moment. Suppose that one particular country demonstrated that it could grow faster, and generate a higher rate of return, than any other country. Also suppose this country welcomed free flows of foreign capital, had a well-defined system of law, and financial transparency for all its major institutions. Why wouldn't investors around the world want to put their money in that country?

The fact of the matter is that there is a correcting mechanism, but (a) it takes a long time to work and (b) it has unpleasant side effects. The correcting mechanism is slower growth. In fact that is what caused the US dollar to fall 15% in the first half of 2002.

Suppose money keeps flowing into a country, which boosts the value of the currency. Consumers benefit from cheaper import prices. Manufacturers, however, are penalized because even efficient firms can no longer compete. Eventually exports drop and, more important, firms decide to build new plants in other countries, so capital spending dries up. When that happens, the currency starts to decline again, because investors find they can no longer earn the highest rate of return in that country. Eventually, then, the currency returns to its equilibrium value as measured by purchasing power parity, but only at the cost of substantially slower growth.

The Dmark was severely overvalued in the early 1980s, and as a result, real growth in Germany averaged only 0.4% per year from 1980 through 1983. Eventually, faster growth in the US, the rise of the value of the dollar, and – later in the decade – the fall of the Berlin Wall boosted growth in Germany. But for a while, the overvalued currency led to virtually no growth. Very much the same thing happened in Japan, which went into recession in 1992 and except for a one-time increase in 1996, has remained in recession for an entire decade.

The overvalued dollar did not hurt the US so much in the 1980s, although it did reduce real growth to 3% for two years in 1985 and 1986. However, the vigorous decline in the dollar, coupled with much lower interest rates and a spectacular plunge in oil prices, saved the US economy from stagnation later in that decade. The overvalued dollar was one of the contributing factors to the 2001 recession, although it returned to equilibrium following the recession and the sharp decline in stock prices.

When determining optimal foreign economic policies, we should remember that the US is still by far the world's largest market, and the principal engine of growth for the world economy. Ever since World War II destroyed Europe, most of the major inventions and innovations over the past half-century – in entrepreneurship, management, financial sectors, telecommunications, microcomputers, etc. – have occurred in the US. Whatever the specific reasons, what is good for the US economy is good for the world economy, and what is good for the world economy is good for the US economy.

Keeping that in mind, US policy should be designed to maximize world, as well as domestic, growth. A policy that reduces US imports will inevitably reduce US exports a year or two later. If other countries insist on restrictive trade policies, that will eventually retard their own growth. There is no benefit in emulating those restrictive practices. Instead, US policy should incorporate the following:

1. Keep the value of the dollar near its trade-weighted purchasing power parity equivalent.
2. Balance the budget at full employment and maintain a credible monetary policy.
3. Reduce tax rates that will encourage saving and investment within the confines of (2).
4. Continue to push for free trade practices around the world.

If the US follows these four cardinal rules, it doesn't matter whether the country has a current account surplus or deficit. As long as the US economy is functioning properly, the excess dollars from a trade deficit will be recycled back into the country. Both the trade deficit and the deficit on net investment interest income are paper tigers, and will not affect the well-being of the US economy in either the short or the long run. The major risk is that the dollar remains overvalued for an extended period of time; yet even if that does occur, deviating from the last three rules given above will not improve the situation.

KEY TERMS AND CONCEPTS

Crawling Pegs and Bands
J-Curve Effect
Marshall-Lerner Condition
Purchasing Power Parity (PPP)
Trade-Weighted Average of the Dollar

SUMMARY

- The world is on a de facto dollar standard. That means when countries build up excess dollars because they export more to the US than they import from the US, those excess dollars are reinvested back in the US; they are no longer converted to gold.

- Purchasing power parity (PPP) occurs when the average cost of producing a market basket of tradable goods and services in any given country is equal to the trade-weighted average cost of producing that same market basket of goods and services in the rest of the world. That equivalence is obtained by permitting exchange rates to float freely until they are all in equilibrium. Under free trade and mobility of factor resources, world production is maximized when all countries are at PPP.

- In the long run, percentage changes in the value of the currency of one country relative to another country are approximately equal to the rate of inflation in that country relative to another country. That is equivalent to saying that in the long run, PPP provides a reasonably accurate estimate of movements in foreign exchange rates.

- However, it sometimes takes a decade or more for this equivalence to be reached. In the short and medium run, foreign exchange rates depend on the rate of return on financial and real assets, and the ex ante gap between investment and domestic saving. Also, for countries other than the US, the size of the current account balance is also an important factor affecting the value of the currency.

- Other factors that affect currency values in the short and medium run include short-term real interest rates, expected changes in bond and stock prices, rate of return on physical assets, tax rates on corporate income and capital formation, political stability, and expectations about future inflation.

- For the US economy, the gap between investment and domestic saving is the most important factor determining the exchange rate, the rate of return on assets is less important, and the value of the current account balance plays no role. As the countries examined become smaller and have less fully developed capital markets, the gap between investment and saving and the rate of return

on assets become less important, and the value of the current account balance becomes more important.

- The J-curve effect occurs if the value of the current account balance and the value of the currency move in the same direction for a while. It is most likely to occur when the sum of the price elasticities of exports and imports are less than unity, so that a rise, for example, in the value of the currency boosts the nominal current account balance even though it reduces the real current account balance.

- Currencies may also diverge from PPP equilibrium for an extended period of time because of expectations: if a currency is expected to rise, for example, more foreign capital will be attracted, which in turn will boost the value of the currency further. It often takes a major change in policy to break this cycle of rising or falling expectations.

- Many countries have tried to manage the values of their currencies over time with bands and crawling pegs. However, these experiments invariably end in massive devaluations, so floating exchange rates – coupled with occasional interference in foreign exchange markets to reduce disorderly conditions – will provide better long-term economic performance.

- US policymakers are best advised to keep the budget balanced at full employment and keep real interest rates at the growth rate of productivity, rather than trying to twist policy to manage the value of the dollar or reduce the trade deficit. Nonetheless, the risk remains that an excessive inflow of funds could boost the dollar to such a high level that the manufacturing sector would be penalized and the real growth rate would decline.

QUESTIONS AND PROBLEMS

1. Shortly before the UK devalued the pound sterling in 1968, Prime Minister Harold Wilson was heard to remark that the first time a Labour prime minister

devalued the pound, the party was out of power for 14 years, and the second time a Labour prime minister devalued the pound, the party was out of power for 13 years. If he were to devalue the pound a third time, he pontificated, "there would be no more Labour Party." Even allowing for the normal amount of vacuity in any such political proclamation, what did Wilson mean? Why was he wrong economically, and why was he wrong politically? (After being defeated by Ted Heath in 1970, Wilson returned as prime minister in 1974.)

2. Political vacuity is not confined to one side of the Atlantic. As already noted, Treasury Secretary Michael Blumenthal solemnly intoned in 1978 that "a good dollar is weak for America." It was not good for America, and it wasn't good for Jimmy Carter or the Democrats. Why was failing to devalue the pound the wrong strategy for the UK in 1968, while the decision to devalue the dollar the wrong strategy for the US in 1978?

3. Shortly after World War II, the US occupying forces set the value of the Dmark and the yen below equilibrium values in Germany and Japan. Over the next 25 years, those countries both staged an amazing recovery. Other factors were involved, but the undervalued currencies helped to stimulate their exports. Why was an undervalued currency good for Germany and Japan, but not for the US?

4. According to the BLS, wage rates in Mexico are only about 10% of those in the US. What factors would determine whether your firm should shut down its plants in the US and relocate to Mexico, or continue to produce in the US?

5. Since the pound sterling devalued in 1993, it has changed very little relative to the Dmark and its successor, the €. At the same time, the inflation rate in the UK, which used to be about 5% per year higher than Germany, has been about the same (2.5% compared with 2.0%). Yet it is often said that a stronger currency reduces the rate of inflation, while a weaker currency boosts it. Explain how the decision to float the £ in Britain also reduced the rate of inflation. (Hint: what happened to productivity?)

6. The C$ declined an average of more than 3% per year relative to the US$ during the 1990s, yet the inflation rate in Canada was almost 1% lower. Also, Canada has a positive trade balance, compared to the huge US trade deficit. Why has the C$ has been so weak? Do you expect it to turn around?

7. Why do you think the Japanese government permitted the ¥ to become so overvalued in the first half of the 1990s? Do you think they could have done anything about it? When the turnaround finally did occur, the ¥ fell 40% from 1995 to 1998 even though the dollar was rising only slightly relative to other major currencies. What caused this dramatic turnaround?

8. Historically, the value of the dollar has increased when the price of oil has risen, and declined when the price of oil has fallen. Explain why this has occurred,

taking into account the fact that the US imports about half its oil, whereas Europe and Japan import almost all of their oil.

9. Assume that the value of the currency of country J rises by 10% one year. Its price elasticity of imports is −0.6 and its price elasticity of exports is −0.7. Imports of raw materials and parts account for 30% of the total cost of imports. Trace the J-curve effect for this country, assuming no repercussion effect. If exports account for 20% of its GDP and imports account for 15%, and a 1% change in the current account balance changes the value of the currency by 2%, how much would the currency rise or fall in the following year?

10. The Brazilian real devalued by approximately 40% in 1999. Assume that Brazil's largest trading partner is Argentina. What effect would this eventually have on the Argentine peso even if that country had a balanced budget, a currency tied to the dollar and backed by gold, and no excessive growth in the money supply? Why did it take three years for the value of the Argentine peso to collapse?

11. Suppose the price elasticity of machinery exports in international markets is $\frac{2}{3}$, and the dollar is overvalued by 30%, so those exports drop 20%. Also assume that this reduces manufacturing employment by 500,000 workers, and all of them become unemployed. As an alternative, the US government decides to reinstate the investment tax credit of 10% for all machinery produced by domestic producers, and the cost of that tax credit is $20 billion per year. What effect would that tax credit have on the value of the dollar? (Hint: how would the investment/saving gap change?)

12. In recent years, labor costs in Korea have been rising about 10% faster than in the US. To what extent did this contribute to the devaluation of the won in 1997? If this trend continues, would you expect further devaluations in the won in future years? If so, what steps would your company take to offset those effects?

Notes

1. Developments in China in 2002, discussed in greater detail in chapter 14, suggest the Chinese have started to make more serious attempts to attract foreign investment.

2. The most comprehensive compilation of international data adjusted for PPP was undertaken by Alan Heston and Robert Summers. See their article, "The Penn World Table (Mark 5: An Expanded Set of International Comparisons, 1950–88)," *Quarterly Journal of Economics*, May 1991. More recent versions of these data can be found at www.nber.org/pub/pwt56. The BLS also has several related reports on its website.

3. For a useful summary of these events in non-technical language, and the source of this quote, see *Soros*, by Michael T. Kaufman (Knopf: 2002), chapter 20.

4. The BLS website provides links to international data for over 100 countries at www.bls.gov/bls/other.htm#international.

chapter thirteen

The Mundell-Fleming model: joint determination of output, interest rates, net exports, and the value of the currency

13.1 Links between domestic and international saving and investment

The key to understanding how changes in monetary, fiscal, and trade policy affect the exchange rate and the current account balance is to realize how these policies affect international as well as domestic saving and investment. To review briefly, previous discussion of the national income accounts has shown that saving must always equal investment on an ex post basis. If the four major components of saving are considered separately, this can be written as:

$$Sp + Sc + Sg + Sf = I \qquad (13.1)$$

where the terms on the left-hand side of the equation represent personal, corporate, government, and foreign saving respectively. This can be rewritten as:

$$Sp + Sc + Sg - I = -Sf. \qquad (13.2)$$

The term on the left-hand side of the equation represents the gap between domestic investment and saving.

Previously we showed that $-Sf = F$, the current account balance. Thus if the economy runs a current account surplus, foreign saving is negative; if it runs a deficit, foreign saving is positive. In the national income and product accounts (NIPA), $-Sf$ is listed as **net foreign investment** (NFI), which means it is also a negative number if the economy is running a trade deficit. The summary table for net saving and investment is shown in table 13.1, which shows the negative figures for NFI in recent years.

In equation (13.2), suppose domestic private saving equals total investment, which means the government deficit is equal to the current account deficit. During the 1980s, when both deficits were quite large, some economists assumed that the two deficits were somehow linked. That is not the case. In 1998 through 2000, the Federal government ran a substantial surplus, yet the current account deficit

Table 13.1   Net saving and investment, selected years

	1991	1996	2001
Total net saving	267.8	389.4	338.1
Personal	371.7	272.1	169.7
Corporate	119.2	232.7	127.7
Government	−223.1	−115.4	40.7
Total net investment	287.5	422.2	220.8
Private	192.2	460.7	484.1
Government	80.4	75.9	113.4
Foreign	14.9	−110.7	−376.7
Statistical discrepancy	19.7	32.8	−117.3

All figures in billions of current dollars
Source: Bureau of Economic Analysis website, www.bea.gov

zoomed to record levels, providing effective evidence of the decoupling of these two deficits. A more general statement linking foreign and domestic saving and investment is required.

Now suppose the public sector budget is balanced, so that $S_g = 0$. In that case, net foreign investment is equal to the difference between private domestic saving and investment. If domestic saving exceeds investment, the excess saving that is not invested in the home country is invested abroad. If investment exceeds domestic saving, the additional funds are supplied by foreign investors. The US has run a current account deficit almost every year since 1982, so we consider the case where net foreign investment is negative; i.e., domestic investment exceeds saving. That means foreign investors are providing some of the saving that is boosting domestic real growth. That could reflect either a rise in investment, or a decline in domestic saving that would allow consumers to spend a greater proportion of their current income. Indeed, the surge in the trade deficit in the late 1990s coincided with a sharp decline in the personal saving rate.

Thus NFI equals domestic saving minus investment, which can be labeled $(S − I)_D$. We next determine the slope of the NFI function relative to the exchange rate, which at this point will be represented by the real value of the dollar. As the value of the dollar increases, more foreign investment is attracted, ceteris paribus, so this curve is drawn with an upward slope relative to the value of the dollar.

The **NFI curve** is drawn under the assumption of a constant level of real income. We next examine how the curve shifts when income changes.

In terms of the IS/LM diagram, income can shift because of changes in monetary policy, fiscal policy, or exogenous changes in private sector demand. First, assume the shift is due to a change in monetary policy, which would not directly affect government saving. We showed earlier that a rise in income would boost both saving and investment, but would raise saving more than investment. Hence

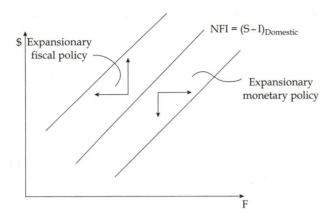

Figure 13.1

$(S - I)_D$ would increase when income rose because of easier monetary policy, which means the curve would shift out.

Now suppose, however, that income rose because of a change in fiscal policy – either a rise in government spending or a decline in tax rates. The same logic also applies to an autonomous increase in consumption or investment. In these cases, a rise in income would cause the $(S - I)_D$ curve to shift *in*, because national saving has diminished. A shift in monetary policy and a shift in fiscal policy have opposite impacts on the NFI curve; these changes are shown in figure 13.1.

One caveat at this point. We assume no changes in the rate of inflation or productivity growth in this diagram. However, a change in the value of the currency is likely to affect these variables, especially the rate of inflation. Under those changes, the NFI curve may not shift as indicated in this diagram, as discussed later in this chapter.

13.2 The basic model: joint determination of real interest rates, output, currency value, and the current account balance

We are now in a position to provide a method that will jointly determine the real interest rate, real output, the real exchange rate, and the real current account balance. For purposes of exposition we will drop the term "real" in the remainder of this section. This approach is known as the Mundell-Fleming model.

The Mundell-Fleming model was developed in the 1960s by Robert A. Mundell, often known as the intellectual father of supply-side economics, and J. Marcus Fleming, an economist at the IMF.[1] This model assumes capital mobility among countries, which is a reasonable approximation of the real world today. It can be developed with either fixed or flexible exchange rates, but since flexible exchange rates represent the dominant links among major currencies, we will concentrate on that case. Initially, this model is developed for large open economies with key currencies; the case of small open economies with little or no endogenous foreign investment is then considered as a special case.

The NFI function has already been developed. To complete the diagram for the Mundell-Fleming model, we need to add a function for **net exports** (NX). Since an increase in the value of the exchange rate boosts imports and reduces exports, NX is negatively related to the exchange rate. When domestic income rises, imports rise faster than exports, so the NX curve shifts in. Similarly, a decline in domestic income shifts the NX curve out.

In developing the IS curve, we found that an increase in interest rates boosts saving and reduces investment ex ante, yet they must both be equal on an ex post basis. Similarly, an increase in the dollar boosts NFI and reduces NX on an ex ante basis, yet they must both be equal on an ex post basis.

In developing the IS curve, equilibrium is reached by changes in income that shift the I and S curves appropriately. Similarly, changes in income shift the NX curve and changes in saving and investment shift the NFI curve, so an ex ante disequilibrium situation that arises when the value of the currency changes must always result in a return to ex post equilibrium.

At this initial stage, we consider the impact of changes in monetary and fiscal policy under the assumptions that the rate of inflation and productivity growth do not change. Also, we assume that world income remains unchanged, although a rise in US imports will generally strengthen growth in the rest of the world. Hence the initial diagram will be substantially modified later in this chapter. At this stage, however, consider a simplified model where inflation and world income are held constant. Note that when the value of the dollar changes, this represents a shift *along* the NX and NFI curves, not a shift of either curve.

The intersection of the NX and NFI curves in figure 13.2 produces the equilibrium point for the value of the currency, labeled $, and the current account balance, labeled F (for foreign trade). This NX/NFI diagram can now be combined with the IS/LM diagram to generate the joint determination of (real) interest rates, output, currency value, and net exports. For the moment, prices are assumed to be stable; since a change in the value of the currency would be likely to influence prices, that assumption is also dropped later in this chapter.

Under the assumptions of stable prices, changes in the various components of aggregate demand will have the following impact on the NFI curve; in all cases, we assume an expansion in demand.

1. An outward shift of the LM curve caused by an easing in monetary policy will raise output without any exogenous shift in the domestic saving or investment functions. As a result, the NFI curve will move out.
2. An outward shift of the IS curve caused by an increase in investment or a decline in domestic saving shifts the NFI curve in. That could stem from (a) fiscal expansion, whether through higher government spending or lower tax rates,

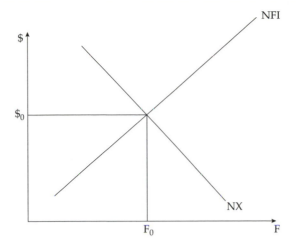

Figure 13.2

(b) an autonomous increase in domestic investment, or (c) an autonomous increase in consumption, which would reduce the personal saving rate.
3. An outward shift of the IS curve caused by an autonomous rise in net exports (probably because of faster worldwide growth) would shift the NFI curve out because income rises without any corresponding decline in the domestic saving rate.

The impact of fiscal expansion and monetary expansion using the Mundell-Fleming model is shown in figures 13.3 and 13.4. The remaining cases are left as an exercise for the reader.

Case I: Fiscal Expansion

The IS curve moves out, raising output and interest rates. The increase in real income moves the NX curve back. The NFI curve also shifts back because the drop in domestic saving caused by fiscal expansion is greater than the rise in domestic saving due to higher income. The value of F clearly declines. The change in the $ is ambiguous; depending on the relative movements of the curves, it could either rise or fall. The diagram shows no change; the important point to remember is that the higher interest rates raise the value of the $, whereas the decline in net exports lowers it.

Case II: Monetary Expansion

The LM curve moves out, raising output and lowering interest rates. The increase in real income moves the NX curve back. The NFI curve moves out because

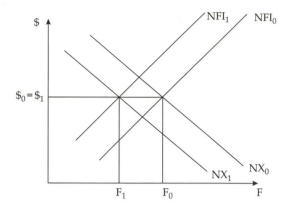

Figure 13.3 Fiscal expansion

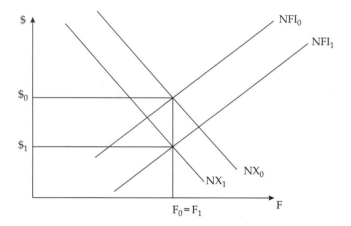

Figure 13.4 Monetary expansion

income has risen and there is no offsetting exogenous decline in saving. The value of the $ clearly declines. The change in F is ambiguous, since a decline in the value of the $ will raise F, but a rise in income will lower F. The commonsense interpretation here is that monetary expansion lowers interest rates and raises income. Since these two factors have offsetting impacts on net exports, the current account is not likely to change very much in either direction.

13.3   The Mundell-Fleming model for a small open economy

So far, our discussion concerning exchange rates has dealt with large economies and key currencies. We now consider how exchange rates are determined for small countries with underdeveloped capital markets. Usually there are few investment opportunities in such a country, and the government does not have an outstanding record of redeeming its securities. Few investors will choose to hold assets denominated in that currency; they will want to put their funds into dollars, or some other key currency, as soon as possible. It is also likely that such a country would be able to accumulate only a minimal amount of foreign reserves.

In such a situation, the amount that a country can import will essentially be limited to the amount that it can export. Suppose that current-dollar exports decline: that could happen either because of a drop in volume or a drop in price. The latter could be particularly important in monoculture economies, where the country depends on one commodity (oil, coffee, copper, etc.) as the principal source of its foreign exchange.

Such a country can always handle this situation by reducing its imports. However, that may be impractical for a variety of reasons. Imports may be necessary to produce the goods that serve as an important source of export earnings. Necessities, such as food and fuel, may have to be imported. Imports may have been ordered years ago, with severe cancellation penalties. Finally, a decline in necessity imports may lead to civil unrest.

In many cases, the initial reaction of the political leaders is to ignore the situation, hoping it will improve in the near future. Investors, however, are not willing to take this risk. Thus if they expect that imports will soon exceed exports, they will speculate against that currency, pushing its value down significantly. The country will be faced with a de facto devaluation unless it suddenly imposes currency controls. In such cases, the value of the currency is closely tied to the current account position. The relative rate of return is not important, since there are relatively few places for foreigners to invest their money in that currency.

In terms of the NX/NFI diagram, the less important the currency on world markets, the steeper the slope of the NFI curve. The economic interpretation of that result is as follows. In a small nation with underdeveloped capital markets, the rate of return on assets means little because (a) domestic investors are not permitted to invest funds in another country except when permission is granted by the government, (b) in many cases, foreign investors are not permitted to purchase these assets, and (c) the value of the currency is not freely traded but is controlled by the government.

In such a situation, the amount of foreign saving is determined by exogenous factors, such as incentives to foreign investors to build a new plant, funds made available by the IMF, or concessions to foreign investors to develop a particular natural resource of the country. It is not related to the value of the currency.

It was previously shown that the current account balance must be equal to the capital account balance with the opposite sign. Suppose exports do not change but imports rise; then the capital account balance must also rise. However, in this case, capital flows are determined exogenously. That is where the balancing item enters the picture. In order to pay for the increase in imports, small countries with weak currencies must use their holdings of foreign reserves if they wish to keep the currency from depreciating. While that may be a temporary solution for a year

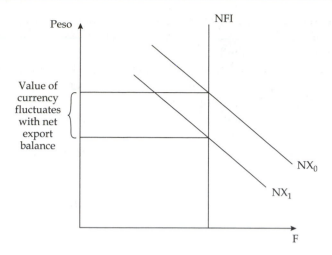

Figure 13.5

or two, it cannot continue indefinitely. Thus it is more likely that the value of the currency will decline. That will reduce the price of exports and raise the price of imports, hence bringing the current account balance back to its previous level. That is why the value of the currency for small open economies depends on shifts in net exports, as illustrated in figure 13.5.

In practice, few economies have a completely vertical NFI curve. However, except for the US, the current account balance is a significant determinant of exchange rates. That is true even for other key currencies such as the € and the ¥.

13.4   The repercussion effect in the Mundell-Fleming model

We consider two cases. The first occurs when an expansion of the US economy is accompanied by a decline in net exports, which boosts real growth in the rest of the world. The second occurs when an expansion of the US economy is accompanied by a rise in net exports, which reduces real growth in the rest of the world.

The first case is best illustrated by an expansion in fiscal policy or other autonomous shift that raises investment or consumption. The IS curve shifts out, which moves the NX curve in. Since domestic saving has fallen relative to investment, the NFI curve shifts in. So far this is the standard fiscal expansion case: the dollar remains relatively unchanged while net exports decline.

The additional factor here is that if US net exports decline, net exports for the rest of the world increase. As a result, real growth increases abroad. That boosts US exports the following year, hence shifting *both* the IS and NX curves out. Since the rise in the IS curve the second year is not due to a decline in domestic saving, the NFI curve also shifts out somewhat. Ordinarily, the NX curve would shift in when domestic income rises, but because the increase in income is due to higher exports,

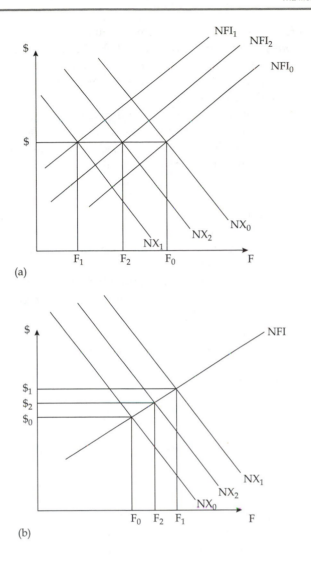

Figure 13.6

it also shifts out slightly. The net effect is that while F declines, the drop is smaller than in the first year. The dollar remains at the same level in all three years.

These shifts are illustrated in figure 13.6(a). The initial equilibrium position is assumed to occur in year 0, so all those curves are denoted with the subscript "0." The shifts in the first year – i.e., before the repercussion effect – are labeled "1," while the shifts in the second year, which include the impact of the repercussion effect, are labeled "2."

Now suppose that the IS curve initially moves out because the US government decides to subsidize exports, as shown in figure 13.6(b). That will boost interest rates and output in the first year. This time, the NX curve will shift out because the rise in exports due to the subsidy is greater than the rise in imports due to higher income. The shift in the NFI curve is ambiguous: it will shift out because of higher income, but it will shift in because of the increase in the deficit due to the subsidy. On balance, we assume the NFI curve does not shift in either direction for year 1. Note in particular that because the NX curve shifts out but the NFI does not, the value of the dollar rises.

The rise in US net exports from F_0 to F_1 will reduce real growth abroad. As a result, US exports will decline somewhat the second year, shifting the IS curve in. Ordinarily, the decline in income would cause the NX curve to move out, but because the decline is caused by lower exports, it moves in. The net result is that net exports shrink and the value of the dollar declines from year 1 to year 2. Hence the increase in net exports from the subsidy is far smaller than would be the case without the repercussion effect.

A variety of other cases could be considered: tax cuts, other changes in autonomous spending, or even a rise in tariffs or other restrictions on imports. The results are generally the same. The key factor to observe is the change in F. If net exports rise the first year, slower growth abroad will reverse part of this gain the second year, while if net exports fall the first year, faster growth abroad will reverse part of this loss the second year.

Note that if there is no change in F, there will be no repercussion effect. The key factor is not the change in real growth in the US economy; it is the change in US net exports. If they remain unchanged, there will be no repercussion effect even if the US growth rate rises or falls.

To summarize this section, a rise in world growth shifts the IS and NX curves out, while a decline in world growth shifts both these curves in. In some cases, of course, a change in world growth is caused by factors that do not originate in the US. However, to the extent that changes in world growth are influenced by the level of US net exports, the IS and NX curves will invariably offset some of the initial change in net exports. Because of the repercussion effect, the overall impact will be less than the initial change.

Yet even this is an incomplete answer because in most cases, a reduction in the value of the currency will boost inflation, hence moving the LM curve in. The effects of changes in the value of the currency on inflation, growth, interest rates, and net exports are discussed in the next section.

13.5   The depreciation effect in the Mundell-Fleming model

So far we have assumed that prices are constant when fiscal and monetary policy change. However, if the currency declines, the rate of inflation is likely to rise – especially if the currency has fallen below its equilibrium value. The next step is to show how the IS/LM and NX/NFI diagrams are affected by a change in the rate of inflation.

The case of monetary expansion has already been shown in figure 13.4. However, that diagram assumed prices remained constant, whereas a reduction in the value

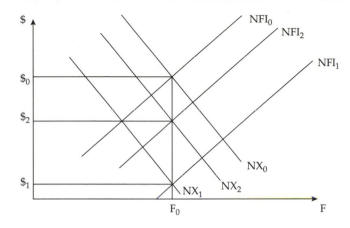

Figure 13.7

of the currency will generally raise inflation if the currency is pushed below its equilibrium level. As a result, the LM curve would move in. Figure 13.7 illustrates how this occurs. The first year is the same as shown in figure 13.4: monetary expansion reduces the value of the currency while leaving the current account balance unchanged. In the second year, the lower value of the dollar boosts inflation, so the LM curve shifts part way back. That raises interest rates and reduces income. As a result of the decline in income, the NX_1 curve moves part way out to NX_2 and the NFI_1 curve moves part way back to NFI_2. The value of net exports remains the same, but the dollar partially recovers when interest rates rise.

In the previous example, the value of the currency fell because of expansionary monetary policy. We now consider what happens when the currency declines because of a policy decision to devalue. In the case of a fixed exchange rate, the announcement is made by the Treasury; in the case of a floating exchange rate, the Treasury sells the currency in forex markets. While this may seem like a counterproductive policy, the US did so in 1973, 1978, and 1986, so the example is not far-fetched.

Assuming there has been no change in fiscal policy, monetary policy, or world growth, the first part of the diagram indicates what appears to be a disequilibrium situation, as shown in figure 13.8. The value of the currency has declined, so NX is greater than NFI. Yet we know that situation cannot exist on an ex post basis. Either the NFI curve moves out, or the NX curve moves in.

Let us review what has happened so far. Initially, a devalued dollar will boost Y by raising net exports. Note that is a movement along the NX curve, not a shift of the curve. A rise in Y will raise S more than I, causing the NFI curve to move out. Also, a rise in Y will shift the NX curve in slightly; more if the repercussion effect is important.

It is possible that these two shifts will cause the NX curve to move in far enough and the NFI curve to move out far enough that a new equilibrium point will be

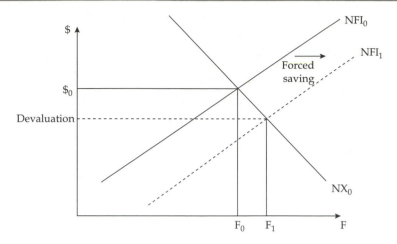

Figure 13.8

reached. Most of the time, however, that does not happen without some additional developments.

When the value of the currency declines, there is usually a rise in domestic saving because of higher inflation, and a decline in investment because of lower productivity. Both of these changes cause the NFI curve to shift out further. These shifts are shown in figure 13.8, followed by a more detailed discussion of why the saving rate often rises when inflation increases.

Just as was shown in the previous section, the repercussion effect shifts the IS curve back and higher inflation shifts the LM curve back, so, in the longer run, Y does not rise. That corresponds to common sense about the long-run impacts of depreciation, which is that it does not raise real income – just as monetary expansion, in the long run, cannot raise real income.

Yet if Y returns to its previous level, the NX and NFI curves should also shift back and the dollar would return to its previous level as well. However, we are assuming that because of policy steps taken to devalue the currency, it stays at its new, lower level. One major piece of the puzzle is still missing.

If the dollar remains at its depreciated value, ex post equilibrium can occur only if the NFI curve shifts out substantially. Yet so far we have explained that if income remains unchanged and the domestic saving and investment functions do not change, the NFI curve does not shift in either direction. Hence there must be some outward movement of the curve caused by a rise in the domestic saving rate.

The Concept of Forced Saving

The phenomenon we are looking for is known as **forced saving**. When the rate of inflation rises, the domestic saving rate tends to rise, ceteris paribus, which means holding the level of income constant (which is the case here, because $Y_0 = Y_2$). The increase in the domestic saving rate occurs for the following reasons:

1. A rise in inflation redistributes income from individuals to corporations, which save a larger proportion of their income.
2. At least in the US, a rise in the inflation rate boosts the personal saving rate.
3. For the same level of income, a rise in inflation boosts government saving because a progressive tax structure pushes people into higher income brackets, hence raising their overall tax rate. This assumes the personal income tax code is not indexed.

The concept of forced saving is usually applied to a developing country, where consumers have relatively little disposable income, so virtually all of the domestic saving is done by businesses. However, it has happened in the US as well. During the late 1970s, when Treasury Secretary Blumenthal claimed that "a weak dollar is good for America," the gross saving rate rose from 18.1% to 20.7%, and individuals saved an unusually large proportion of their disposable income because they were concerned about the impact of higher inflation on their permanent income.

We have also shown previously that higher inflation retards productivity growth and diminishes the investment ratio. Hence a decline in the value of the currency that boosted the inflation rate would also cause the NFI curve to shift out because of a decline in investment relative to GDP. It could be argued that forced saving is not an important factor in the US. However, the repercussion effect is more important in the US, which means that when the current account balance increases, growth declines in the rest of the world, hence shifting the NX curve to the left. Thus in the case of the US, the outward shift in the NFI curve would be smaller, but the inward shift in the NX curve would be larger.

13.6   Shifts in the NX and NFI curves caused by changes in inflation and productivity

In many cases, monetary easing will result in a decline in the value of the currency, which will raise the rate of inflation and diminish the growth rate in productivity. That is precisely what happened in the US economy during the 1970s, and what happens to most countries that habitually devalue their currencies.

An increase in the rate of inflation often leads to forced saving, which causes the NFI curve to shift out. In addition, a decline in productivity growth leads to less investment, which also shifts the NFI curve out (recall that NFI is the same as $(S - I)_D$). That establishes a new equilibrium point in the NX/NFI diagram. Furthermore, the increase in the rate of inflation and the decline in productivity growth offset the initial rise in Y due to higher net exports. That is another explanation of the fact that, in the long run, devaluation does not increase the level of real GDP; it only boosts inflation.

That is the normal case. However, it is also possible that monetary stimulus is a result of fiscal contraction; interest rates decline because the central bank no longer needs to fund a government deficit. In that case, a decline in the budget deficit could reduce inflationary expectations enough to stimulate the economy. Productivity would rise as resources are shifted from the public to the private sector, hence boosting investment. That would increase productivity growth and reduce the actual as well as expected rate of inflation, which would reduce private sector saving, ceteris paribus. Thus the increase in saving caused by a smaller government deficit would be offset by the decline in domestic saving, so the overall saving rate would remain unchanged. *In this case, the outward shift in the NFI curve that would ordinarily result from fiscal contraction is more than offset by the decline in inflation, which reduces private sector saving, and the rise in productivity, which boosts investment.*

This leads to an important modification in the Mundell-Fleming model rule that monetary stimulus causes the value of the currency to decline. Most of the time, that remains the case. However, if it stems from a reduction in the deficit, which boosts productivity and reduces inflation, the value of the currency need not decline as interest rates decrease.

13.7   Effects of the Reagan and Clinton fiscal and monetary policies

The original Mundell-Fleming model said that monetary expansion would reduce the value of the currency, while fiscal expansion would raise its value. Thus it would logically follow that during a period of fiscal expansion but continued tight money, the value of the currency would surge, while during a period of fiscal contraction and easy money, the value of the currency would plunge. The results since the dollar was allowed to float are summarized in table 13.2.

The Mundell-Fleming model appears to work quite well for every period except 1995 through 2001, when contractionary fiscal policy should have offset rising real interest rates and left the value of the dollar neutral. What happened?

The main answer is that the contractionary fiscal policy, which resulted in a swing in the Federal budget position from a $290 billion deficit in FY 1992 – and a $203 billion deficit in FY 1994 – to a $236 billion surplus in FY 2000, boosted real growth rather than reducing it.

This is actually a flaw in an otherwise useful tool for explaining the impact of monetary and fiscal policy on the value of the dollar and the current account balance. Mundell has claimed that the deficit doesn't matter. In particular, he stated that:

> Suppose it does mean a budget deficit in the United States – who cares? . . . I'm frankly not worried about the problem at all. I think it's a mirage, and think it's shocking that, thirty-five years after the Keynesian revolution, we should be squabbling about an issue that should have long been laid to rest.[2]

Table 13.2 Major changes in fiscal policy, monetary policy, and the dollar

Time span	Value of dollar	Real interest rates	Tax rates	Discretionary spending	Expected change
1971–1979	Down	Low	Neutral	Up	Down
1980–1985	Up rapidly	High and rising	Down	Up	Up rapidly
1986–1988	Down rapidly	Falling	Up	Neutral	Down
1989–1994	Down slowly	Low	Neutral	Neutral	Down slowly
1995–2001	Up	Rising	Neutral	Down	Neutral
2002–2003	Down	Low and falling	Down	Up	Down slowly

Mundell's point, that an increase in the deficit during recessions ought not to be considered a negative development, is well taken. However, with the increase in realization of the imprtance of expectations, particularly in financial markets, the view needs to be modified to realize that as the economy returns to full employment, a switch in the budget position from deficit to surplus will boost financial market expectations and hence raise investment. Also, a reduction in the deficit near full employment will reduce crowding out, hence providing more resources for private sector investment. Both of these changes will have the net effect of moving the NFI curve in, hence boosting the value of the dollar and reducing the value of the current account. That is precisely what did happen in the US from 1995 through 2000.

The results stemming from the Reagan changes in fiscal policy are consistent with the original Mundell-Fleming model. Expansionary fiscal policy caused the NFI curve to shift in because of a drop in the saving rate, and contractionary monetary policy caused the NFI curve to shift in because of a decline in income. The drop in income caused the NX curve to move out, but not as much as the NFI curve shifted in.

Other factors were also at work. The NFI curve also shifted in for two other reasons. A decline in inflation reduced the private sector saving rate, and a variety of factors boosted investment, including lower inflation, tax incentives for investment, and a boost in productivity growth under the Reagan Administration. Thus there was a substantial inward shift in the NFI curve because of the combined effects of (a) a bigger deficit, (b) a smaller private sector saving rate, and (c) a rise in investment. Consequently the dollar moved well above equilibrium, and the current account balance plunged. These shifts are shown in figure 13.9.

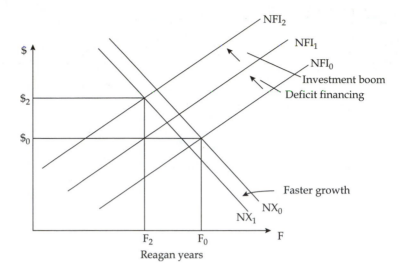

Figure 13.9

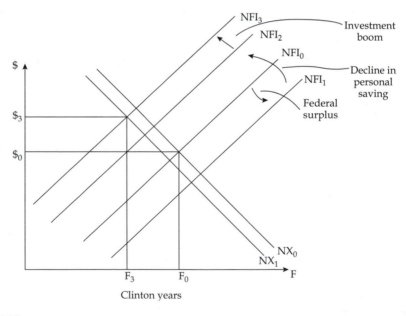

Figure 13.10

In the Reagan years, then, the NFI curve shifted in for two major reasons: less public sector saving and more investment. In the Clinton years, the NFI curve shifted for three reasons: it shifted out because of more public sector saving, but shifted in because of less private sector saving and more investment, so the net effect was an inward shift. Because of the repercussion effect, faster growth in the US also caused faster growth around the world, so the NX curve did not shift in very much even though the US growth rate accelerated. As a result, the dollar rose along with the decline in the current account balance. These shifts are shown in figure 13.10.

MANAGER'S BRIEFCASE: HOW DO CHANGES IN INVESTMENT AND SAVING AFFECT THE VALUE OF THE DOLLAR?

No one ever said predicting foreign exchange rates was easy, and one can hardly expect a highly stylized model of this sort to provide pinpoint answers. In particular, the lags can be long and variable. Nonetheless, some useful real-world lessons can be drawn from the Mundell-Fleming model, which we summarize as follows.

1. A tax cut that is designed to stimulate investment will generally boost the value of the dollar, but with some lag. Such a tax cut would reduce government saving and increase investment – after a while. If the tax cut occurs during a recession, investment probably will not respond until the economy starts to grow at above-average rates. Once that happens, however, the dollar will usually appreciate.
2. Assuming no change in fiscal or monetary policy, the dollar will usually rise during booms and decline during recessions. That is because the increase in investment is greater than the increase in domestic saving. The personal saving rate generally will not change very much, and the rise in investment will be greater than the rise in government saving.
3. The main reason that tighter money does not always boost the value of the dollar is that the increase in the rate of return, which would attract foreign investment on a ceteris paribus basis, is offset by a decline in investment and a rise in private sector saving (i.e., a decline in consumer spending). Hence the common impression that the dollar is positively related to interest rates is often mistaken.
4. All of these relationships hold under the assumption that the government makes no statement about what the value of the dollar "should" be. A statement by the Secretary of the Treasury that "a weak dollar is good for America" will invariably send the currency lower regardless of the current stance of monetary and fiscal policy.
5. In the latter stages of booms, especially those led by higher investment and increased technology, the dollar is likely to become overvalued. Before managers recommend shifting operations overseas because of the high value of the dollar, they should at least be aware that when the boom comes to an end and investment declines, the dollar is likely to follow suit a few months later.

13.8   Economic impact of an exogenous change in net exports

So far we have shown how changes in fiscal and monetary policy affect real growth, interest rates, net exports, and the value of the currency. Using the same framework, we now examine how exogenous changes in net exports and the value of the currency affect real growth and inflation. This section shows that changes in exports and imports are not necessarily symmetrical; the next section shows why countries cannot profit by depreciating their currencies. We continue to use the Mundell-Fleming model to illustrate these points.

An increase in the current account balance could occur for several reasons. First, foreign growth could rise, boosting exports. Second, domestic growth could decline, reducing imports. Third, inflation could decline, reducing the relative costs of production. Fourth, the value of the currency could decline.

A rise in consumption has approximately the same impact on real growth, employment, and inflation whether the gain is due to easier monetary conditions, a tax cut, or an autonomous shift in sentiment. In the case of foreign trade, however, the impact on real growth, employment, and inflation can be quite different depending on which of these factors caused net exports to change. Furthermore, the effect of an increase in imports is not symmetrical with a decline in exports. For this reason, each case is considered separately.

1. *Foreign growth rises*. The IS curve moves out and real growth increases. There will be virtually no impact on inflation, because the goods are being sold to export markets: if costs and prices did rise, then the gain in exports would quickly disappear. Hence inflation will not change, and the LM curve will not shift in. Foreign saving will decline by the amount that net exports rise, but the impact on the LM curve will probably be slight because the Fed is likely to accommodate the extra non-inflationary growth in exports. The value of the dollar probably will not change.
2. *Domestic growth shrinks*. This will boost net exports, but has its obvious drawbacks. The IS curve shifts back, reducing real growth; private sector agents reduce their purchases of both domestic and foreign goods and services. The LM curve will not change very much; any shift in because foreign saving has diminished would probably be offset by Fed easing because of weaker demand. Unless the economy was at overfull employment before the shift happened, inflation will be virtually unchanged. There will also be some repercussion effect; if US growth slows this year, foreign growth and US exports will decline next year.
3. *Lower inflation*. Exports will rise because the cost of production has fallen, assuming the ceteris paribus condition of no change in the value of the dollar. Since domestic goods cost less, either imports will decline, or foreign firms will have to cut their prices as well. The rise in exports will cause the IS curve to shift out. The repercussion effect is probably minimal, because lower inflation in the US

often is accompanied by lower inflation and hence lower interest rates abroad, which strengthens worldwide growth. Lower inflation may also cause the LM curve to shift out.

4. *Weaker currency.* At first glance this might seem to be similar to case (3); the cost of production declines relative to foreign countries. In this case, however, the gain in net exports is caused by devaluing the currency, which is inflationary. That would shift the LM curve back and negate much of the gain in income caused by the IS curve shifting out. Also, the IS curve is likely to shift back because of the repercussion effect, since foreign countries will initially lose market share to US firms. However, that is only a short-term development; the long-run impacts of devaluing the currency are examined in more detail in the next section.

Thus depending on the factors that cause net exports to rise, real growth may rise, fall, or stay the same; interest rates and inflation may rise, fall, or stay the same. In general we show that if net exports rise and inflation remains the same or declines, the IS and LM curves will shift out and real growth will rise. However, if the increase in net exports is accompanied by a higher rate of inflation, an inward movement in the LM curve will match the outward shift in the IS curve, so inflation will rise but real growth will not improve.

In terms of the longer-term effect on net exports, the key difference is that in cases (1) and (3), when positive developments occur – faster world growth or lower inflation – there is virtually no repercussion effect. In cases (2) and (4) when negative developments occur – lower growth or higher inflation in the US – the repercussion effect is substantial. Hence these cases reemphasize the importance of a healthy US economy for robust worldwide growth.

Higher exports are beneficial to an economy – but only to a point. By that we mean the cause of higher exports is critical. In the long run, beggar-thy-neighbor policies will never work. Export gains generated by an artificial cheapening of the currency will not boost growth in the long run. Even when export gains are due to faster productivity growth, a country cannot expect to sell more goods to its trading partners indefinitely without importing more from these countries in turn. In the case of the US, this factor is manifested in the repercussion effect: a rise in net exports in the US reduces growth elsewhere around the globe, which eventually reduces US exports as well.

The smaller long-term impact of an initial change in net exports is not just some isolated fluke; it occurs time and again. The average growth rate in the US during the massive increase in the dollar during the first half of the 1980s was just about the same as the US growth rate during the major plunge in the dollar during the second half of the 1980s. The huge trade surplus in Japan did not keep that economy from stagnating in the 1990s. During the tremendous growth spurt in Korea, its trade balance was negative in almost every year; as was also true for Thailand. Nigeria and South Africa generally have positive trade balances, but their economies are stagnating. A current account surplus alone is not a recipe for economic growth.

Changes in exports and imports are not symmetrical, especially for the US. A decline in exports will generally have a more negative impact on real growth than the same size increase in imports. Smaller countries without adequate capital markets generally can only import the same amount that they export, so there is more symmetry in these cases.

The argument for asymmetry in the US is as follows. When imports rise, consumers are usually able to purchase goods at lower prices, boosting real income and helping domestic consumption as well. Also, a rise in imports often spurs domestic producers to be more efficient, thus raising productivity. However, when exports fall, there is no corresponding gain in real income or productivity. These results are summarized in table 13.3.

Table 13.3 Economic effects of changes in exports and imports

	Value of $		Inflation	Productivity	Foreign saving	Domestic demand	Total demand
(A)	Imports rise	Down	Down	Up	Up	Up	Small loss
(B)	Imports fall	Up	Up	Down	Down	Down	Small gain
(C)	Exports rise	Up	Down	Up	Down	Up	Larger gain
(D)	Exports fall	Down	Up	Down	Up	Down	Larger loss

The direction indicated in the "domestic demand" column includes the impact of changes in inflation and productivity. If inflation falls, consumption rises, ceteris paribus, and if productivity rises, investment rises, ceteris paribus. However, these changes must be balanced against the change in net exports. When imports change, the change in foreign demand is partially offset by the change in domestic demand, so a rise in imports usually has a relatively small contractionary effect on total GDP. On the other hand, a change in exports moves domestic demand in the same direction, so there is a clear net gain in real GDP when exports rise, and a clear net loss when they decline.

Thus, in the short run, a rise in exports is almost always beneficial to the economy, and a decline in exports almost always diminishes real growth. However, the impact of a change in imports is more ambiguous. If imports rise, some consumers will have their real income increased, whereas if imports fall, consumer choice and real income are likely to be depressed. If a decline in imports reduces competition and productivity, long-run growth will be diminished. In the long run, exports are likely to remain at a higher level only if the rest of the world also grows more rapidly.

To summarize this section, countries boost their long-term growth rates by boosting exports through improved productivity, not by restricting imports. The

Japanese belatedly learned that, when import restrictions led to an extended recession throughout the 1990s. Also, as shown in the next section, trying to increase net exports by depreciating the currency, while it may generate some short-term benefits, never works in the long run.

In terms of the IS/LM diagram, a change in the trade deficit that initially moves the IS curve out will have a different impact on the LM curve depending on whether exports or imports have changed. If exports rise – assuming that change was not due to a depreciation of the currency – higher productivity should offset the decline in foreign saving, so the LM curve will either remain unchanged or shift out, enhancing the effect of higher exports. If imports decline, the combination of higher prices, lower productivity growth, and lower foreign saving will tend to shift the LM curve back in, so the rise in real output will be much smaller.

Now suppose net exports decline. If exports drop, the LM curve moves back in, so real GDP declines because both domestic and foreign demand have contracted. However, if imports rise, the IS curve moves back but real income rises, so the two effects tend to offset each other, and the decline in real GDP is much smaller. This reinforces the conclusions summarized in table 13.3.

13.9   Short- and long-run effects of an exogenous change in the value of the currency

In the previous section, we examined the impact of a shift in the trade balance caused by a change in domestic or foreign income. We now consider the impact of changing the value of the currency.

Assume a country devalues its currency by 10%, causing exports to rise 5% and imports to fall 5%. According to the $C + I + F + G = GDP$ identity, real GDP rises. If exports and imports are both 10% of GDP, real GDP initially rises by 1%.

Yet that is certainly an incomplete answer. Unlike the case where a rise in income boosts imports and the results are ambiguous, in the real world, a decline in the value of the currency hardly ever boosts real GDP in the long run. The initial gains are invariably offset by higher inflation and lower productivity, which reduces real GDP.

First consider the case where a 10% drop in the value of the currency is accompanied by a 10% increase in wage rates and domestic prices. There has been no change in relative prices and costs, and hence no effect on either domestic or foreign demand. The only significant impact is that investment is likely to rise less rapidly because of more rapid inflation, hence reducing the long-term growth rate.

Next consider the case when wages and domestic prices rise less than 10%. In that case, the cost of production has declined, so exports will increase. Also, since imports are more expensive, they will diminish. That would appear to boost real GDP. But look what has happened to the domestic standard of living. The price of imported goods has risen, which means the standard of living has declined. We thus see that *devaluations are effective only if they are accompanied by a decline in the standard of living*.

In that case, why would any country willingly devalue its currency?

1. More jobs are provided at a lower real wage. By raising the price of imports, real wages have declined, so firms are willing to hire more people at a given nominal wage rate. However, in most cases money illusion is no longer a viable explanation for employment and wage behavior.
2. Devaluation shifts real income from consumers to producers, who are now able to sell more goods because their relative price has declined. Hence it is popular with "big business" or the oligarchy. This is the phenomenon known as "forced saving," which was discussed earlier; it boosts the total national saving rate because producers save a larger proportion of their income than consumers. However, it does not boost investment and hence productivity because devaluation invariably diminishes foreign saving, so the total amount of funds available for investment usually declines.
3. If the price of the principal export declines, or the prices of key imports rise, devaluation may be the only solution, even if it is not a popular one. A country faced with a major drop in the price of coffee, bananas, or copper may have little option other than to devalue.

However, unless the underlying causes of inflation are removed, the country will soon be forced to devalue again. In fact, the answer to the question about the alleged popularity of devaluations is that countries have learned by bitter experience that devaluations do *not* work, and have gradually switched to monetary and fiscal policies that produce low inflation, a stable exchange rate, and larger increases in the standard of living. Devaluation today is no longer as popular as it was in previous generations – particularly in countries that used to have hyperinflation, notably in Latin America.

In the IS/LM diagram, when a currency devalues, the initial outward shift of the IS curve is partially offset by a reduced standard of living, which causes it to shift in again. Also, the LM curve moves in because prices have risen. Hence the initial rise in Y is offset.

In terms of the NX/NFI diagram, we have already shown that a devaluation of the currency causes an *ex ante* gap between net exports and net foreign investment. In some cases, that gap could be closed by selling foreign reserves; however, that is at best a temporary solution. More often, the lower value of the currency will boost inflation, shifting the LM curve in. Since tightening of monetary policy would offset some of the gains in Y from devaluation, sometimes the central bank will ease further. Yet such a step would just boost inflation that much more – which would continue to shift the LM curve in. Eventually, the gains from devaluation will disappear. Net exports will be higher, but domestic demand will be lower.

If devaluation does not seem to accomplish anything in the long run other than reducing the standard of living, perhaps countries should consider boosting the value of their currency, raising the standard of living. Yet here again, the argument is not symmetrical.

If the currency appreciates without a concomitant decline in production costs, exports will fall. Hence the IS curve moves back because of a drop in net exports. In the case of the US, this decline might be partially offset by a rise in the standard of living because import prices have declined. However, in the case of a small country, the amount it can import is essentially limited to the foreign exchange earned by exports. As a result, there will be no increase in the standard of living from lower priced imports; the only impact will be a decline in production that is proportional to the drop in exports.

A drop in exports never boosts economic performance. Raising the value of the currency makes sense only if it had been undervalued. Equilibrium is reached when the value of the currency appropriately reflects the costs of production relative to a trade-weighted average of other countries, and the conditions of purchasing power parity are met.

Suppose a country is already wealthy and has accumulated massive foreign exchange reserves. Then a stronger currency might benefit consumers and boost the standard of living and real growth – *but only if consumers are allowed to share in these benefits*. If a country restricts imports by imposing restrictive tariffs and quotas, an overvalued currency means consumers will not share in the benefits of lower foreign prices, and hence real growth will not increase when the currency rises. Furthermore, the monetary authorities would generally have to ease, because the value of the currency tends to appreciate as the current account surplus rises, hence increasing the probability that exports will be priced out of world markets.

We have made several qualifying statements here. However, the general thrust of this discussion can be summarized as follows:

- Devaluation of a currency may boost real growth in the short run, but not the long run. Indeed, if it is accompanied by higher import prices, the net effect is to reduce the standard of living. Even if employment rises because of higher exports, the real value of paychecks will diminish.
- If a country devalues but import prices do not rise by the same percentage, inflation will worsen and the country will be forced to devalue indefinitely. Eventually, the high rate of inflation will reduce productivity growth and the standard of living.
- Appreciation of a currency will not boost real growth unless it reflects the decline in production costs relative to other countries. Even then, it will not boost real growth unless consumers are able to share in the benefits by paying less for imports.
- If a country raises the value of its currency without any reduction in production costs, exports will fall without any offsetting benefits, hence reducing real growth and raising unemployment.

- Once again, we see that economic performance is optimized if the currency is near its equilibrium value, as measured by purchasing power parity. If it is too low, inflation will rise and the standard of living will not increase as rapidly. If it is too high, exports will suffer, and eventually firms will shift operations to other countries, hollowing out the manufacturing sector and resulting in sluggish growth and a stagnant standard of living.

The simple demand-side model indicates that reducing the value of the currency would boost exports and reduce imports, hence leading to a higher level of GDP. That is not true, because devaluation also sets in motion the following events:

1. A weaker value of the currency that moves its value below equilibrium will generally lead to higher domestic inflation, thus boosting interest rates and reducing other components of aggregate demand.
2. Lower imports could reduce foreign capital inflows, which could also boost interest rates.
3. Lower imports could result in less intensive efforts to improve productivity, hence reducing the quality of domestically produced goods as well as boosting inflation.
4. In the US, lower imports could reduce growth abroad, eventually leading to lower US exports.

After taking all these factors into account, the most likely result of devaluing the currency is inflation, and interest rates would rise but real GDP would not. If productivity growth declined, real growth would be lower in the long run than if the currency had remained stable.

If you think about it for a minute, it should be obvious that, in the long run, devaluation of the currency cannot really improve its growth rate. If it did, per capita real GDP in countries such as Brazil, which used to devalue almost every year, would have been among the highest in the world. Instead, their economies have stagnated except for those brief periods when they did *not* devalue. Even for smaller countries, where the repercussion effect is not very important, devaluation of the currency generally leads to higher inflation, tighter monetary policies, and slower growth. It is definitely not a cure-all for whatever else ails the economy. If the economy is performing poorly, the place to fix it is by improving monetary and fiscal policy, and boosting productivity growth, *not* through devaluing the currency. In the long run, economic performance is optimized if the currency remains near its equilibrium value, and is neither overvalued nor undervalued.

The last two sections showed that an increase in net exports, especially if obtained by devaluing the currency, does not boost real GDP in the long run. Yet virtually all economists agree that foreign trade benefits all countries. If it does not boost aggregate demand, the benefits must be found on the supply side: faster growth in productivity and total capacity.

Like the IS/LM diagram, the Mundell-Fleming model is a useful introductory tool but cannot be pushed beyond its limits. Nonetheless, it can be used to show that if ex ante investment exceeds ex ante domestic saving and the investment climate is strong, the value of the currency will rise and the net export balance will decline. Conversely, if ex ante investment is less than ex ante domestic saving and the investment climate is weak, the value of the currency will fall and the net export balance will rise. These situations go far to explain why the value of currencies often do not follow changes in interest rates, as used to be commonly assumed. In this sense, the Mundell-Fleming model adds to our understanding of the linkages between the domestic and international sectors.

KEY TERMS AND CONCEPTS

Forced Saving
Mundell-Fleming Model
Net Exports (NX)
Net Foreign Investment (NFI)
NFI and NX Curves

SUMMARY

- Earlier we showed that the capital account is equal to the current account with the opposite sign. Thus if a country runs a trade deficit, and its amount of foreign exchange remains constant, it has a capital account surplus. When that happens, foreign funds flow into the country, and net foreign saving rises.

- By definition, foreign saving is equal to the difference between investment and domestic saving. In a closed economy, if ex ante investment rises but ex ante saving does not, interest rates will rise; that is the principal result of the IS/LM model. However, in an open economy, an ex ante rise in investment might not be accompanied by an increase in domestic saving; instead, the gap could be filled by foreign saving.

- The NFI curve represents the amount of foreign saving, which by definition is equal to the difference between domestic saving and investment. As the value of the currency increases, more foreign saving is attracted, so the curve has a positive slope.

- The NX curve represents net exports as a function of the value of the currency. When the value of the currency rises, net exports decline, so that curve has a negative slope. An increase in income will shift the NX curve in, because imports rise more than exports.

- When deriving the IS curve, recall that investment is negatively related to the interest rate, while saving is positively related to the interest rate; yet they must always be equal ex post. Equilibrium is reached through changes in both the interest rate and income. Similarly, equilibrium between NFI and NX is reached through changes in the exchange rate, net exports, and income.

- The NFI curve does not move unambiguously when income changes. If a rise in income causes domestic saving to rise more than investment, the NFI curve shifts out, which means the value of the currency is lower and net exports are higher for an unchanged NX curve. However, if a rise in income causes investment to rise more than domestic saving, or if the rise in income occurs because the saving rate falls, the NFI curve shifts in, which means the currency value would rise and net exports would fall for an unchanged NX curve.

- Thus an expansionary fiscal policy would cause the NFI curve to shift in and to the left, because government saving has declined more than private saving rose. An expansionary monetary policy would cause the NFI curve to shift down and to the right, because government and private saving rose more than investment.

- If net exports did not change, expansionary fiscal policy would raise the value of the currency, and expansionary monetary policy would reduce it, ceteris paribus. Similarly, a decline in the personal saving rate would raise the value of the currency, as would an exogenous increase in investment. However, these changes do not take into account the change in net exports; the complete explanation must also include the NX curve.

- When shifts in both the NFI and NX curves are taken into account, an expansionary fiscal policy would reduce net exports and the value of the currency would not change very much. An expansionary monetary policy would reduce the value of the currency, and net exports would not change very much.

- These results apply mainly to countries with key currencies. In a small open economy, the NFI curve is almost vertical, so changes in income would cause the value of the currency to fluctuate, but leave net exports unchanged.

Thus, for example, if exports decline because of a drop in commodity prices, imports would have to contract by the same amount, since there would be virtually no change in the flow of foreign saving into the country.

- The repercussion effect is important primarily for the US, although it is also visible for Germany and the European economy, and Japan and the Asian economy. The net effect of the repercussion effect is to offset the effect of the initial changes in fiscal and monetary policy. Thus an expansionary fiscal policy would reduce net exports, but by a smaller amount; and an expansionary monetary policy would reduce the value of the currency, but by a smaller amount.

- Suppose the currency of a given country depreciates, either by choice or because of pressures in foreign exchange markets. A reduction of the currency represents a move along the NX curve, so net exports increase. However, if foreign saving does not change, the two magnitudes will be unequal, which cannot happen on an ex post basis. Thus some further adjustment must occur. In some cases, depreciation is accompanied by a decline in income, and hence a reduction in exports, so the NX curve shifts in. In other cases, the domestic saving rate rises by what is known as "forced saving," which shifts the NFI curve down. Depreciation of the currency raises the proportion of national income going to businesses, especially exporters, and reduces the proportion to workers, who must now pay more for imported goods. Since businesses have a higher saving rate than individuals, the overall saving rate increases, which is represented by a downward shift in the NFI curve.

- An increase in productivity is usually accompanied by a lower rate of inflation, ceteris paribus. That reduces the personal saving rate, which shifts the NFI curve in; usually it boosts investment as well. Hence higher productivity and lower inflation will generally raise the value of the currency. This can also be explained by noting that these conditions are also likely to attract more foreign capital, which would also boost the value of the currency.

- During the Reagan Administration, the Federal budget deficit increased, hence reducing the domestic saving rate; that boosted the value of the currency and reduced net exports. During the Clinton Administration, the budget position moved back into surplus, which would cause a decrease in the value of the currency, ceteris paribus; however, it rose. In this case, the increase in government saving was more than offset by the decline in personal saving, the technology-driven investment boom shifted the NFI curve in, and the rise in expectations from a balanced budget also spurred the stock market and capital spending.
- An exogenous rise in exports will boost aggregate demand and the value of the currency. It is also likely to boost productivity growth and reduce inflation. Thus GDP will rise both because of demand-side and supply-side factors. However, a decline in imports is not symmetrical. While that will also boost aggregate demand, it is likely to reduce productivity growth and raise inflation, hence offsetting some of the increase in demand.
- In the long run, devaluing the currency will retard productivity growth, hence reducing the overall growth rate in real GDP. In the short run, it is sometimes argued that devaluing the currency will boost real growth because it will raise exports and diminish imports. If the currency was previously overvalued, GDP would probably rise. If it becomes undervalued, though, the negative inflationary impacts usually overwhelm the positive demand effects. For smaller countries, a devaluation may cause foreign capital to leave the country, in which case investment would drop sharply and send the economy into a recession even if net exports were to increase.

QUESTIONS AND PROBLEMS

1. The following table shows the broad trade-weighted average of the dollar and the ratio of net exports to GDP in percent terms for each year since the US went off the international gold standard. Based on the Mundell-Fleming model, describe what the monetary and fiscal policies probably were in years when there were major changes in the value of the dollar.

Year	Value of $	Net export ratio	Year	Value of $	Net export ratio
1971	117.8	−0.3	1987	99.1	−3.0
1972	109.1	−0.6	1988	92.4	−2.1
1973	99.0	0.0	1989	94.0	−1.5
1974	95.8	−0.2	1990	91.2	−1.2
1975	95.0	0.8	1991	89.7	−0.3

Year	Value of $	Net export ratio	Year	Value of $	Net export ratio
1976	95.4	−0.1	1992	86.8	−0.4
1977	94.1	−1.2	1993	88.3	−0.9
1978	88.2	−1.1	1994	86.4	−1.2
1979	89.4	−0.9	1995	84.0	−1.1
1980	91.5	−0.5	1996	85.9	−1.1
1981	98.0	−0.5	1997	90.5	−1.1
1982	107.6	−0.6	1998	98.4	−1.7
1983	111.6	−1.5	1999	98.7	−2.7
1984	118.2	−2.6	2000	101.6	−3.7
1985	123.3	−2.7	2001	104.7	−3.9
1986	108.6	−3.0			

2. The US economy was in recession in 1974, 1980, 1982, 1991, and 2001. Based on our earlier discussion of export and import functions, net exports would be expected to increase in recession years because of the decline in imports. Yet the ratio fell slightly in 1974 and 2001, and was virtually unchanged in 1982; only 1980 and 1991 fit that pattern. Why do you think net exports continued to decline in those other recession years?

3. Several times in the last century, the UK decided to set the value of the £ above its equilibrium value. In terms of the Mundell-Fleming model, this means the value of the currency was set above the point where the NX and NFI curves would intersect in a free market. Yet we know these two magnitudes must be equal on an ex post basis, which means either the NX curve shifted out or the NFI curve shifted in. What is the economic meaning behind these shifts? In either case, what was the effect on the UK growth rate?

4. Before World War II started, the German currency, which was then the Reichsmark, was set at 2.5 to the dollar. After the war ended, the occupying forces set its successor, the Dmark, at 4.2 to the dollar. The undervalued currency was probably based on the likelihood that productivity in Germany would be much lower because of wartime destruction.

(A) By 1970, German production had made great strides, and labor costs were still fairly low, so the Dmark was clearly undervalued at 4.0 to the dollar (there had been one slight appreciation in 1961). Explain the underlying monetary and fiscal policies that would be consistent with an undervalued currency and a modest current account surplus.

(B) Over the next decade, the Dmark appreciated very rapidly relative to the dollar, reaching a value of DM1.8 by 1979. Explain the shifts in the NX and NFI curves that must have occurred to boost the value of the currency that much. What effect do you think that had on the German economy?

5. In 1961, Charles de Gaulle decided he did not want the French franc to be considered as a second-rate currency, so he chopped two zeros off the value of the franc, which meant the exchange rate was approximately FF5/$ instead of FF500/$ (he also ordered that the $ key on IBM punchcard machines be replaced by the FF symbol). This had no immediate impact on any domestic or international transactions, but was supposed to convince the French people to put inflation behind them and keep their currency in line with the Dmark and the British pound. Whether or not this change in currency values made any difference, the relative inflation rate did slow down and the value of the FF did rise relative to the dollar over the next two decades. At the same time, the current account balance improved slightly. Based on these factors, explain what happened to the growth rate, show how the NX and NFI curves must have shifted, and describe the underlying economic developments.

6. The US economy slowed down sharply in the latter half of 2000, and the actual recession started early in 2001. Monetary policy eased sharply throughout 2001, and for the first half of the year, fiscal policy did not change very much. Yet the dollar continued to appreciate in the first half of the year. It then fell sharply during the third quarter, but rebounded in the fourth quarter and returned to its highs in February 2002. It then fell 12% during the next five quarters. Why did the dollar remain strong throughout the recession, and why did it then decline sharply in 2002 even though fiscal policy became more expansive?

7. Explain how you would expect the dollar to move under the following changes in fiscal policy.
   (A) Reinstatement of the investment tax credit.
   (B) Increase in medical care benefits for the elderly.
   (C) $100 billion increase for improved Homeland Security.
   (D) Temporary tax rebate of $300 per person.
   (E) Permanent 10% cut in all personal income tax rates.
   In answering these questions, indicate how they might depend on the particular phase of the business cycle.

8. Using the IS/LM and NFI/NX diagrams, show how the following changes in the economy would affect the value of the dollar and the net export balance.
   (A) Domestic auto manufacturers offer zero-interest financing rates on new cars.
   (B) Japan changes its policy, encourages more US imports.
   (C) War in the Middle East causes oil prices to double for an extended period.
   (D) New, "thinking" computers usher in new age of technological marvels.

Notes

1. The key works are Robert A. Mundell, *International Economics* (New York: Macmillan, 1967) and J. Marcus Fleming, "Domestic Financial Policies under Fixed and Floating Exchange Rates," *IMF Staff Papers* 9 (Nov 1962). Note in particular that the model was developed while the major world economies were still on the international gold standard.
2. Hinshaw, Randall (ed.) *Inflation as a Global Problem* (Baltimore: The Johns Hopkins Press, 1972), p. 150. This book is actually the transcript of a conference held on global inflation in Bologna, Italy, in 1971.

chapter fourteen
Case studies in international trade

Introduction

The previous three chapters discussed the determinants of net exports and currency values, and the impact of changes in these variables on real GDP, interest rates, inflation, and employment. The results often differ depending on the relative importance of a given country in the world economy, the type of trade policies that are pursued, and the ongoing monetary and fiscal policy in effect. In particular, we found that in some cases, reducing the value of the currency improved economic performance; in other cases, it hampered performance.

These examples should emphasize the point that trade policy, like monetary and fiscal policy, cannot be considered in isolation: it is the interplay among these various policies that determines the behavior of the economy. To bring these factors into focus, this chapter analyzes several case studies to show how the interactions of monetary, fiscal, and trade policies – sometimes correct, sometimes incorrect – have affected the growth rate, the standard of living, and other key economic variables in countries around the globe. It also discusses the arguments for and against free trade in the current world environment. The chapter concludes with some hints about how managers can identify those economies that are likely to perform best – and worse – in the early 2000s.

14.1 International trade in the European economy

Ever since Charlemagne was crowned emperor by Pope Leo III in 800, western Europe has flirted with the idea of some kind of economic union. The move to a single currency in 2002 has convinced many economists and politicians that this time the union will be permanent. We can offer no bland assurances that the natural enmities among European nations will not erupt into war again in the future, nor that political developments will not undo the current arrangements. However, we can analyze the impact of the single Eurocurrency, indicate where theory suggests this should help, and then comment on the progress to date.

The decision of the European nations to join together using a common currency obviously involves a loss of some political sovereignty. That development by itself neither helps nor hinders economic development. If the European nations move toward leadership that reduces the growth in government spending and taxes, encourages investment and saving, and sponsors individual entrepreneurship, real output and employment will rise much faster than if the leadership tilts in the direction of bloated budgets, higher taxes, and more statism. We mention this obvious point at the outset to emphasize that the slight advantages that occur from removing all tariffs between the nations of the European Community – and the savings from not having to hedge or convert into foreign currencies – have only a second-order impact on the long-term real growth rate.

The signatories to this confederation agreed they would use their best efforts to synchronize their fiscal policies, and agreed to be governed by a single monetary policy, set by the European Central Bank (ECB). Thus countries that previously had large budget deficits, overly easy monetary policy, and high inflation would presumably benefit the most by being required to reduce the deficit, diminish growth in monetary and credit aggregates, and reduce the rate of inflation to the European average. In particular, it was thought those benefits would help previously high-inflation countries such as Italy and Spain. However, it was also hoped that larger countries such as Germany and France would be able to sell their goods and services to a wider market that was now growing more rapidly. Also, greater competition spawned by the lack of tariffs would increase efficiency and productivity, hence boosting real growth and the standard of living.

The initial decision to utilize a single currency for international transactions in 1999 – three years before the Deutschmark, French franc, and other local currencies were phased out – was widely hailed as a win-win situation for large and small countries alike, and one that would improve the economic performance of Europe. In the early years, it didn't happen. From 1994 through 1998, real GDP in Euroland rose an average of 2.1% per year; for 1999 through 2002, it rose an average of 2.1% per year. At first glance, monetary union did not improve the growth rate, although some would argue that the US recession in 2001 reduced European growth.

You can't combine a newt, a frog, and a toad and get a prince. The concept of a united Europe will not boost real growth unless improvements occur in individual countries. If the synchronization of fiscal policies results in higher taxes and bloated budgets instead of lower taxes and lean budgets, the advantages from the economies of scale, lack of tariff barriers, and ease of using a single currency would be more than offset. The European confederation will not boost overall real growth unless it boosts growth in Germany and France. While the UK has so far declined to join the monetary union, its trade relationships with Continental Europe are important enough that a stronger Europe probably cannot emerge without a robust UK economy either. Thus before returning to a more detailed analysis of the impact of a united Europe, we present individual case studies for Germany, France, and the UK, showing how suboptimal economic policies have hampered real growth at various times in the post-WWII period.

CASE STUDY 14.1   GERMANY: FROM ECONOMIC "MIRACLE" TO STAGNATION

The story of the German economic miracle after World War II is a familiar one. The Allies initially imposed strict economic controls on the economy, and many of its citizens were gradually starving to death. In April 1948, Economics Minister (and later Chancellor) Ludwig Erhard unilaterally ended price controls, and – with a very generous boost from the Marshall Plan – the economy "miraculously" recovered. By 1960, Germany had regained its rank as one of the world's leading industrial powers, and by 1973, its per capita GDP was second only to the US. Through 1973, the real growth rate in Germany continued to average about 5%.

As occurred in all other major industrialized countries, the first oil shock derailed the rapid German expansion. Yet unlike the US and Japan, Germany failed to recover. For the next eight years, from 1974 through 1982, growth averaged only 1%, although admittedly these were tough times for the US as well, with growth averaging only 2% a year. But the difference continued to widen, as growth returned to 4% in the US throughout much of the 1980s but remained at 2% in Germany.

Then the second great opportunity arose for postwar Germany. The Plaza Accord in September 1985 resulted in lower worldwide interest rates, the expanded European Common Market was poised to make Germany the economic linchpin of Europe, and the unexpected fall of the Berlin Wall and unification of Germany in 1989 lifted the Cold War burden and permitted that country to forge ahead without further Communist interference. Yet when presented with this exceptional opportunity, the politicians fumbled the ball.

The fatal mistake made by Helmut Kohl was to insist that, for political reasons, the East German Ostmark would be set equal to the DM; a more realistic estimate would have been somewhere between $\frac{1}{4}$ and $\frac{1}{2}$ of the DM. As a result, workers in former East Germany were quickly priced out of the market, and the unemployment rate soared. Manufacturing activity virtually ceased in the East.

The German government, unwilling to make former East Germans bear the burden of unification, authorized massive unemployment benefits and other transfer payments to those whose jobs had disappeared. Since the prospects for work in East Germany remained slim, and since transfer payments were generous enough to permit them to live where they desired, many former Eastern sector employees moved to the West and attempted to secure housing in that part of the country. The inevitable result was a sharp rise in rental and housing prices that boosted the inflation rate to 4%, a level that, at least by German standards, was unacceptable.

continued

CASE STUDY 14.1 (*continued*)

As an aside, we note this is almost a classic example of the conditions under which both unemployment and inflation rise at the same time. In this case, far from reducing the burden of unemployment, higher inflation exacerbated it. In this case, the culprit was the big deficit coupled with a central bank that was initially reluctant to tighten because of the changed political situation.

Eventually the Bundesbank realized it would have to step in and tighten monetary policy to defuse the rise in inflation. That medicine eventually worked, but as usual, it caused an overvalued DM and a recession, with real GDP falling 1.2% in 1993.

In the meantime, the underlying fiscal situation continued to deteriorate. While the German growth rate slowed down after 1973, the increase in social welfare spending did not; indeed, it accelerated because of the rise in unemployment. This increase in government spending boosted the deficit, which raised interest rates. That pushed the DM higher and caused slower growth, which raised unemployment and boosted the deficit further, so the vicious cycle continued. This is the structuralist school argument presented in chapter 9.

The DM peaked in early 1995, coincident with the trough in the dollar, and by mid-1997 had fallen about 30% relative to the dollar. Attempts to reduce the deficit to qualify for the common currency under the terms of the Maastricht Treaty were temporarily successful, and the government budget deficit ratio dipped below 3%. However, growth in Germany increased only moderately to 2.7% in 1998 and fell back to 2% in 1999; it then recovered to 3.2% in 2000 but fell below 1% in both 2001 and 2002, pushing the deficit ratio back above 3%. Since the decision to move to a single European currency, Germany has had the lowest growth rate of any country in Euroland.

CASE STUDY 14.2   UNITED KINGDOM: REBIRTH AFTER THATCHER

From 1950 through 1981, real growth in the UK averaged only 2.4%, compared to 3.4% in the US and 5.1% in Germany. Admittedly, Germany was more devastated by World War II than Britain, but one would have expected that the decline in British productivity during the wartime years would be quickly recovered. However, that did not happen.

Democratically elected governments tend to change after major wars. While Harry Truman won reelection in 1948, the Republicans captured control of Congress

continued

CASE STUDY 14.2 (*continued*)

in 1946 and the Presidency in 1952, and the liberal Democratic agenda of the Roosevelt years did not reemerge until 1964. In Britain, the change occurred in the opposite direction: the electorate booted out Churchill and voted in the Labour Party, which promptly proceeded to impose a welfare state in Britain, including nationalized healthcare.

Between 1945, when Clement Attlee defeated Winston Churchill, and 1951, when Churchill returned to power, the Labour Party managed to squeeze all the increase in value added out of the private sector. Punitive tax rates as high as 98% on so-called "unearned" income (interest, dividends, and rents) strangled initiative and entrepreneurship, causing an exodus of the best and the brightest. The extra money collected by the government was used to fund the welfare state. Labour also made no attempt to adjust to the realities of the post-WWII economy, instead supporting bloated payrolls in the steel, coal, and railroad industries.

Unlike Latin American nations, the British government paid for its largesse through higher taxes, so the deficit averaged only 1% of GDP in the 1950s and 1960s. Yet the cost of taxation needed to pay for these benefits was so high that private sector activity stagnated. The Tories returned to power in 1951 for 14 years but were unable or unwilling to undo the damage done by the Labour Party.

Fiscal policy, then, depressed the British economy. Monetary policy did not play much of a role; the inflation rate of 3.4% was somewhat higher than the 2.2% annual increase in Germany and the 1.8% rise in the US, but not enough to make a major difference. But what about trade policy?

Britain attempted to go back on the gold standard after World War II at a value of the £ equal to $4.03, the same as the interwar rate, but that was clearly too high, so it was devalued to $2.80 in 1949. At that time, the DM was set at 4.2/$, so the crossrate was DM11.76/£. Wages in Germany were about 22% lower than in Britain (in dollar terms), but some rough estimates suggest that productivity was at least 35% lower, so labor costs in the UK were probably slightly below those in Germany after the pound devalued in 1949. Compared with the US, both wages and productivity were about three times those in Britain, so the £ seemed properly valued in the 1950s and 1960s.

Hence the British economy did not stagnate in those two decades because of an overvalued currency. Inflation was somewhat higher in the UK, but the £ was devalued again to $2.40 in late 1967. As a result, the currency remained near its equilibrium level during those two decades, and Britain has favored a free trade policy since the 1840s. The economy stagnated in the 1950s and 1960s because of high marginal tax rates and burgeoning public sector spending.

The 1970s were a different story. While this was an unfavorable decade for inflation around the world because of the two oil shocks, it was particularly

continued

CASE STUDY 14.2 (*continued*)

unfortunate for the UK. During that decade, the inflation rate rose an average of 14.8% per year in Britain, compared to 8.4% in the US and 5.5% in Germany. Yet the £ returned to $2.40 in 1980 after having dipped lower in the late 1970s. By then, the British economy was being strangled by the overvalued pound.

The Thatcher Administration tried to reverse this stagnation by cutting high tax rates, privatization, deregulation, and encouraging entrepreneurship. How successful was this attempt?

It is a matter of perception. When Margaret Thatcher was elected Prime Minister, government spending had risen to 43% of GDP. When stepping down 11 years later amidst cries she had gutted the social welfare state and treated poor people cruelly, the ratio had declined – to 42%. Apparently the rhetoric overpowered the facts. Just as there was virtually no change in the ratio of government spending to GDP under Reagan, Thatcher was unable to make significant inroads into the relative size of the public sector.

UK growth averaged only 1.9% from 1982 through 1992 – even worse than the 2.4% growth rate during the 1950–81 period. Over the same period, the average growth rate in the US declined by $\frac{1}{2}$%, in Germany by 1%, and in France and Italy by 2%, so some of the slowdown reflected worldwide conditions. Even so, these figures do not suggest a very impressive performance. Much of the problem remained the overvalued £ during the Thatcher years.

However, that is not the end of the story because, as we have already seen, Britain was forced to let the £ float in September 1992. The turnaround was almost immediate. From 1993 through 2001, growth in the UK bounced back to 2.9% and the unemployment rate fell from 10.5% to 5.1% in 2001, even as growth in Continental Europe was stagnating. Many budding entrepreneurs from France – including but not limited to restaurateurs – departed Paris for London. Is it possible that Thatcher laid the groundwork for rapid growth but it blossomed only after her departure?

One can never answer such questions with certainty. However, it does appear that the Thatcher government kept the value of the £ too high, because the economy improved soon after Britain was forced to let the £ float freely in September 1992. In the view of many economists, it was no coincidence that the UK economy recovered the following year and has remained relatively strong. Even for the US, above-average growth also requires that, in addition to correct monetary and fiscal policies, the currency be kept near its purchasing power parity.

As of 2002, the outlook for the UK is favorable. Labor costs are about 15% below Continental Europe, the £ is fairly valued, and Tony Blair, while a member of the Labour Party, has joined with conservative leaders in Italy and Spain in favor of greater labor flexibility. Average and marginal tax rates are lower than in most other countries in Europe, and the current decision not to join the European Monetary System has apparently not dampened the growth rate.

CASE STUDY 14.3   FRANCE: THE CASE OF FAILED SOCIALISM

France deserves separate treatment because of its much greater socialist orientation. Whereas the public sector accounts for one-third to a half of total GDP in the US, UK, and Germany, the figure for France is about 55%.

France used to be a relatively high-inflation economy. From 1950 to 1965, the inflation rate averaged 5.0%, compared to 3.6% in Italy, 3.4% in the UK, 2.2% in Germany, and 1.8% in the US. The French franc (FF) was frequently devalued relative to the DM and the dollar, falling from FF3.50/$ in 1950 to FF4.90/$ in 1965 at the same time that the DM appreciated slightly relative to the dollar, rising from 4.2 to 4.0/$.

From 1965 through 1987, the disparity continued, with the inflation rate in France rising an average of 4.1% per year more than in Germany. The disparity between the currencies also widened, with the franc falling to 6/$ and the DM improving to 1.8/$. In other words, the franc depreciated an average of 4.6% per year relative to the DM. That conforms fairly closely to the PPP theory of exchange rates.

By the end of the 1980s, the burden of a large government sector and high tax rates had reduced growth in France so much that it was willing to take drastic measures to bring its rate of inflation down to that of Germany, stabilizing the FF/DM exchange rate. That goal could have been accomplished using either tighter fiscal or monetary policy. Tighter fiscal policy would have meant cutting the growth rate in government spending, which was considered but not implemented. Tighter monetary policy meant offsetting the inflationary impacts of a large government sector and big deficit ratios through higher interest rates. The latter method was chosen, with the result that real growth in France stagnated and the unemployment rate rose to 12%, the highest of any major country in Europe, although it then declined to 8.5%.

France generally failed to participate in the recent technological revolution that boosted productivity in the US, the UK, Japan, and southeast Asia. Its trade policies, while liberal on the surface, contain far more exceptions than most other countries, protecting the jobs of so-called "honest French workers," especially farmers. As a result, France did not receive the supply-side benefits of international trade that would ordinarily boost productivity.

Also, lower inflation did not boost the growth rate. That is because the major benefit of lower inflation is to spur productivity. But with the dead hand of a large government sector, those benefits were not forthcoming. Labor demanded that the government keep their full range of benefits intact whether inflation rose or fell, and whether productivity growth rose or fell. Lower inflation did not lead

continued

CASE STUDY 14.3 (*continued*)

to the creative, innovative solutions of cost-cutting in France that occurred in other countries.

France used monetary policy to bring inflation under control and stabilize the currency. Yet the anticipated pickup failed to occur because capitalism wasn't there to provide the spur for greater productivity, and archaic trade regulations reduced the benefits of international trade. This is a prime example of how monetary policy is necessary but not sufficient to spur growth and return an economy to full employment. Appropriate fiscal and trade policies are also needed to achieve that goal.

Joining more closely with the rest of Europe by itself will not help the French economy. Indeed, to the extent that trade, labor, and capital barriers are lowered, it will be even easier for resources to move outside the country. Most French political leaders understand these facts. Nonetheless, attempts to moderate excessive labor demands, particularly in the areas of early retirement and generous pension benefits, have been uniformly rebuffed. As of 2002, no solutions for these problems have yet appeared on the horizon.

CASE STUDY 14.4   THE ECONOMIC IMPACT OF THE EUROPEAN UNION

We now apply the tools developed in the previous three chapters to determine how the European Union will fare in the years ahead. First, some brief background.

In 1957, the Treaty of Rome created the European Economic Community (EEC), colloquially known as the Common Market: the original members were Germany, France, Italy, Netherlands, Belgium, and Luxembourg. In 1973, the EEC expanded to include the UK, Ireland, and Denmark. In 1979, these countries formed the European Monetary System (EMS), which was aimed at closer monetary coordination. This group was joined by Greece in 1981, and Spain and Portugal in 1986. In 1992, the Maastricht Treaty paved the way for monetary union, and the European Community was renamed the European Union (EU). These 12 countries were joined by Austria, Finland, and Sweden in 1995, boosting the ranks of the EU to 15 countries.

On May 2, 1998, 11 of these countries agreed to form a common currency that would go into effect on January 1, 1999. The UK, Denmark, and Sweden chose not to join the common currency, and Greece did not immediately qualify, since its budget deficit and inflation rates were too high, although it was permitted to join in 2001. Since a common currency meant common rates of inflation and common

continued

CASE STUDY 14.4 (*continued*)
budget policies, it was also agreed at the signing of the Maastricht Treaty in 1992 that all countries would achieve the following three goals:

- Inflation rate of less than 3%
- Ratio of budget deficit to GDP of less than 3%
- Ratio of national debt to GDP of less than 60%.

When the Maastricht goals were originally set in 1992, only one of the 15 countries satisfied all these criteria – and that was Luxembourg. The treaty appeared to be dead on arrival. However, that turned out not to be the case. The signatories viewed the provisions of the Maastricht Treaty seriously and took steps to meet at least the first two criteria (it was generally recognized that the debt ratio stipulation could only be met over an extended period of time). When the deadline arrived, Greece was the only country failing to meet these goals; as noted above, the UK, Denmark, and Sweden decided not to join the ranks of the common currency.

Thus, on January 1, 1999, these 11 countries formed the European Monetary System, using a common currency – the euro – for paperless international transactions. Domestic currencies still circulated, but starting in 2002 euro bills and coins began to circulate alongside domestic currencies. Ten years after that, plans call for all domestic currencies to be phased out, at which point all vestiges of the Dmark, franc, guilder, escudo, etc., will be relegated to coin collectors and history books.

If in fact the EU is able to end the vicious and devastating wars that have plagued the continent over the past two millennia, the union will have been an accomplishment of major proportions, even if the economy does not improve. Nonetheless, the viewpoint du jour of most economists was that a single currency, monetary policy, and fiscal policy would boost the overall European growth rate significantly. As of 2003, there has been no evidence of such a development.

The explanation of why European union should boost the growth rate depends on both demand-side and supply-side effects. On the demand side, some slight gains would accrue from removing the last vestiges of tariffs and terminating the costs associated with hedging foreign currencies. However, any such effects would be minimal, especially because most tariffs between the various European nations had already been sharply reduced in the years before 1999. Indeed, the biggest step was taken in 1958, when the original Common Market was formed; that set off an extended burst of rapid growth that lasted for 15 years. By comparison, the final tariff reductions in 1999 were of limited significance.

Thus if the EU were to boost real growth significantly, the improvement would have to occur on the supply side: gains in productivity stemming from less government spending, lower tax rates, less government regulation, and more incentives for new technologies. Also, to the extent that countries previously had large budget

continued

CASE STUDY 14.4 (*continued*)

deficits and high inflation rates, the discipline imposed by the Maastricht Treaty would boost growth in those countries by curtailing deficits and inflation.

One of the key concepts of the that Treaty was that in order for a common currency to work, all countries would need similar monetary and fiscal policies, which would lead to a similar rate of inflation. If one country had an inflation rate of, say, 2%, while another country had a rate of 7%, goods produced by the latter country would soon be priced out of European and world markets. Hence signatories of the Maastricht Treaty were required to reduce their inflation rates and budget deficit ratios. Political leaders of individual countries could then explain to their legislatures that, while such moves might not be politically popular at home, they were imposed by a pan-European authority, and were the price to be paid for receiving the benefits of greater Europe.

At first, some progress did occur. Soon after the treaty was signed, the rate of inflation fell from 4% to 2% in Germany, from 3% to 1% in France, and from 5% to 2% in Italy. The budget deficit ratios fell from 3.4% to 2.7% in Germany, 5.8% to 2.6% in France, and 10.0% to 2.5% in Italy. These are impressive gains and should not be denigrated. However, other major countries who were not signatories to the EMS also reduced their deficits sharply. Not only did the budget ratio move from a 4.4% deficit to a 2.3% surplus in the US, but it narrowed from a 7.9% to a 0.3% deficit in the UK. Faster world growth, low inflation, and declining interest rates played major roles.

Thus much of the deficit reduction in the 11 countries who agreed to a common currency was due to beneficial worldwide economic conditions, notably the US boom; when recession occurred in the US, the deficit ratios in Europe started to rise again. Furthermore, the budget-slashing moves that did occur in generating these deficit reductions were not always well received. Partly as a result of these moves, the governments in France, Germany, and Italy initially shifted to the left, not only reducing the chances for further improvements in fiscal policy but jeopardizing the existing budget cuts.

To boost productivity growth in Europe, countries must take further steps in the direction of a free market economy. In particular they need to implement the following policies:

- Hold real per capita government spending constant
- Reduce high marginal tax rates
- Provide incentives for research and development spending
- Restructure capital markets to encourage venture capital
- Reform old, outmoded business practices supported by archaic regulations
- Phase out restrictive practices by labor unions, and terminate restrictions that artificially boost wage rates above market levels.

continued

CASE STUDY 14.4 (*continued*)

Perhaps these steps will be taken in the future. However, the initial moves to reduce the deficit were not continued after 1999, and political talk centered on rolling back these steps, not extending them. As of 2003, the major improvement has occurred in the countries on the periphery – Ireland, Spain, Portugal, and Greece. Growth in the original Common Market countries was very sluggish in 2001 and 2002, although the US recession may have accounted for part of that decline.

As of 2003, the jury is still out on the effectiveness of the EU. The two basic issues are both political. First, the increased level of bureaucracy in Brussels may interfere with productivity gains. Second, citizens may decide to overrule the terms of the Maastricht Treaty and in effect vote for bigger government budgets and higher taxes, which would also retard productivity. That issue is squarely in the hands of the voters: whether they want to increase or diminish the relative importance of the government sector. Until there is more definitive movement in the direction of free market economics by individual nations and the overall leadership in Brussels, the growth rate in Euroland is not likely to improve.

14.2　International trade in the Asian economy

For many years, the Asian model of rapid growth was held up to the rest of the world as superior to the ways of the US and Europe. Japan grew at an average rate of 10% per year for two decades, then slowed down to a still-impressive 5% average growth rate. Hong Kong and Taiwan, then Korea, Singapore, Indonesia, and Malaysia, followed in those footsteps and also grew about 10% per year for two decades. Eventually, though, the parade ground to a halt. Real growth in Japan fell to 1% in 1992 and as of 2003, had not yet recovered. For the other countries listed above, commonly known as the "growth tigers," their economies plunged in 1997 and 1998, and while they have all recovered somewhat, the era of superheated growth permanently ended.

Chapter 10 showed how the Solow growth models would have predicted that the growth rate could not remain at 10% indefinitely and would eventually decline to a lower sustainable rate. However, that model would not have predicted the sudden reversal of fortune that occurred in Japan in 1992 and the other countries in east Asia in 1998. In all these cases, the disturbance occurred in the area of foreign trade, foreign capital flows, and were caused by overvalued currencies.

With some oversimplification, the Asian economic story can be summarized very succinctly. The application of capitalistic principles, coupled with initially undervalued currencies and a willingness of foreigners to invest in those countries, created unusually rapid growth rates in countries that were relatively poor. When they begin to approach the average income levels of industrialized nations and their currencies become overvalued, real growth slowed down quite rapidly. If the currency remained overvalued, sluggish growth was likely to continue indefinitely.

CASE STUDY 14.5 HOW THE HUGE JAPANESE TRADE SURPLUS BACKFIRED

The story of the rise and fall of the Japanese economy over the past 50 years is one of the most striking in economics. The principal elements of this saga are as follows:

1945–65. Devastated by losing World War II, a poor country without substantial national resources was rebuilt by saving and investing an unusually large proportion of GDP. Also, American aid was at least as important as the famed Marshall Plan for Europe, although it has received far less publicity. Growth was primarily driven by domestic demand, not exports. Japanese consumer products were then considered shoddy and low-tech, similar to Chinese goods today, although the US bought a great deal of merchandise from Japan during the years of the Korean War, giving the Japanese economy an additional boost.

1965–73. Spurred by a sharp increase in exports stemming from the Vietnam War and the undervalued yen, Japan became one of the world's leading manufacturing nations. Exports soared and the trade surplus rose – until worldwide commodity prices suddenly soared.

1973–81. Stung by the "oil shokku" and skyrocketing agricultural prices in 1973, which was exacerbated by the counterproductive US export embargo on soybeans, Japan rethought its long-term strategy. The government decided that since Japan would never have adequate supplies of food, energy, or raw materials – and since it thought that relative prices of these commodities would continue to rise – it had little choice other than to shift to the production of high-tech goods, which required far less of these inputs. The trade surplus reappeared in the mid-1970s; although it slipped back into a deficit at the time of the second oil shock, the reverberations the second time were not as severe.

1982–5. Helped by the overvalued dollar, Japan increased its trade surplus in spite of having to pay high prices for energy. The trade surplus accumulated rapidly, but the yen did not appreciate because of the intense pressure pushing the dollar higher.

1986–91. The dollar returned to normal, and oil prices fell by half. Japan now had a huge trade surplus and the yen strengthened sharply, rising significantly relative to European currencies as well as the dollar. Yet the trade surplus

continued

CASE STUDY 14.5 (*continued*)

continued to widen. In order to keep the yen from appreciating even further, Japan lowered short-term rates. That created an enormous and unsustainable boom in stock market prices and land prices. However, Japanese consumers received only limited benefits from the general prosperity, because the government refused to reduce import barriers. Archaic distribution and trade policies also kept consumer prices artificially high. Thus the growth in consumption lagged the overall gain in GDP – which was temporarily ignored because of the large gains in investment and exports.

1992–5. Finally the roof caved in. The land price and stock market bubbles burst. Not only did the Nikkei fall 60%, but it failed to recover that loss over the next six years and eventually ended up more than 75% below its peak levels. Even worse, the yen continued to appreciate. That not only reduced export growth, but gutted the manufacturing sector, as many firms moved their operations to Asian nations with lower costs. However, the trade surplus continued to widen because consumption remained weak, so the yen continued to appreciate. As a result, real GDP rose an average of less than 1% per year from 1992 through 1995. The unemployment rate failed to soar only because the Japanese count their unemployed differently than in North America or Europe.

1996–2002. The yen reached its peak in April 1995 and finally turned around. Exports and real growth rebounded, but just when it appeared that the Japanese economy was about to return to normal growth rates, the other shoe fell, which was the collapse of the growth tigers. The Japanese economy fell back into recession in 1998. Since then, real growth has averaged only about 1% per year, with yet another recession in 2001–2.

In addition, the Japanese banking system was exposed as corrupt and rotten. Most banks had "cooked the books," reporting asset levels far above reality. They did this in part by posting stock market values at the time of original purchase rather than at current market value. Banks were no longer able to extend as much credit, especially for international loans.

Several important lessons can be learned from "the story of Japan." First and most important, a huge trade surplus does not guarantee prosperity. Instead, by pushing the value of the currency well above PPP levels, Japan penalized a rapidly growing export industry and cut the growth rate almost to zero. The situation was exacerbated because of the J-curve effect, so the trade surplus continued to widen even as the yen surged, and the volume of exports grew far more slowly than the volume of imports.

Second, it is much more difficult to be a leader than a follower. When Japan was still catching up to leading-edge technology, its growth rate was phenomenal;

continued

CASE STUDY 14.5 (*continued*)

once it approached the technology frontier, its growth rate fell below that of the US.

Third, the increase in the Nikkei index to almost 40,000 in late 1989 – with many "blue chip" stocks trading at triple-digit P/E multiples – was clearly unsustainable, and the bursting of that bubble caused a major drop in capital spending. After the bubble initially burst, the Nikkei continued to decline and never recovered over the next decade.

Fourth, a well-functioning financial sector is a prerequisite for continued rapid growth. When the stock market declines by three-quarters and the capital asset base of the banking system erodes, investment falters. The problem was worse in Japan than in the US because many financial institutions continued to carry stocks on their balance sheets at the price they bought them, rather than the much lower market price. When the banking system attempts to cover up these miscues by false accounting, the ultimate result is even worse.

Yet when we strip away all the exogenous disturbances caused by recessions elsewhere in the world, the boom/bust cycle in the stock market, and the faulty financial accounting, what remains is the unmistakable conclusion that the Japanese economy initially faltered because the value of the yen was too high, and Japanese exports became less competitive in world markets, especially compared to the growth tigers.

It should be emphasized that the overvalued yen was not caused by relatively high rates of return on either physical or financial Japanese assets. The rate of inflation was about the same as in Europe and the US. Interest rates were low and falling, and after 1990, the stock market was rapidly sinking. Profit margins were also shrinking. In the previous three chapters, we saw that when the relative rate of return on financial assets and the relative rate of inflation are not influencing the value of the currency, it depends on two other factors: the current account balance and the gap between investment and domestic saving. The decline in saving helped to boost the yen higher, but even that was not the major cause. It was the ever-increasing current account balance – even though the volume of exports was only rising 1% while the volume of imports was rising 6% – that boosted the value of the yen so much. It was the J-curve come to life with a vengeance.

The Japanese government found itself in a dilemma. The economy was stagnating because the trade surplus caused an overvalued yen, yet politicians were loath to increase imports and, as they saw it, put more Japanese firms out of business. Hence the Japanese government acted in a way that most mainstream economists would have suggested, which was to employ more expansionary monetary and fiscal policies. Government spending programs, especially public works programs,

continued

CASE STUDY 14.5 (*continued*)

were greatly enlarged. Monetary policy was eased so much that the short-term money market rate fell all the way to zero by 1998. Yet this approach did not work.

If the reasoning behind the Mundell-Fleming model presented in the previous chapter is accurate, though, that should not have been such a great surprise. According to that model, the currency is related to the ex ante gap between investment and domestic saving; if saving declines, the currency rises, ceteris paribus. Hence bigger government deficits would boost the value of the currency in the absence of offsetting factors. To the extent that a lower interest rate boosts investment and reduces personal saving, it also raises the value of the currency, which is the direct opposite of the claim that a low interest rate will reduce its value.

The principal thrust of Japanese economic policy should have been to reduce the value of the yen back toward its equilibrium value. Since the ever-increasing trade surplus was driving the yen higher, that development should have been reversed by opening the door wider and encouraging more imports – *not* by the traditional methods of stimulating the economy by more public works projects and lower interest rates.

The value of the yen finally started to decline after early 1995, when its value was so far above equilibrium that the current account balance declined in spite of the J-curve effect. Largely as a result of this development, real growth rose from 0.6% in 1994 to 1.5% in 1995 and 5.0% in 1996. It seemed that the Japanese economy was back on track again.

Then the devaluation of the growth tiger currencies caused a major decline in Japanese exports, pushing the economy back into recession in 1998. Even though the value of the yen was falling sharply, it was still overvalued. Furthermore, capital spending was now declining because more and more firms chose to invest overseas, where costs were lower. The inability of many major banks to make loans because of their shaky capital position also reduced capital spending.

The Japanese government could have taken several positive steps. First, it should have reduced import barriers. That would have kept the yen from appreciating as far above PPP, which would have reduced if not eliminated the need to reduce interest rates to the point where they generated a classical boom/bust cycle. Also, that would have boosted consumer purchasing power, which would have led to more robust growth from domestic sources.

Second, Japan should have privatized and deregulated, especially in the retail sector, permitting consumers to buy goods at lower prices. In combination with the first point, that would have reduced both personal and foreign saving.

Third, it should have required that the financial sector provide timely and accurate records. The attempt to hide losses was, as usual, an even more serious mistake than the bad speculative loans in the first place.

continued

CASE STUDY 14.5 (*continued*)

Fourth, it should not have pursued the standard policies of fiscal expansion, since on balance that tends to drive the value of the currency higher by reducing domestic saving.

For a while, the export boom covered up these sins, but eventually they were all exposed. The Japanese leadership has recently begun to grapple with these mistakes and institute some reforms. However, the failure to liberalize import restrictions after 1986 caused the Japanese economy to move from world growth leader to also-ran, a mistake that can only be slowly rectified in the coming years.

Looking back with the clear vision of long-range hindsight, the seeds of destruction were actually sown in 1986, when the sudden drop in oil prices created a huge trade surplus that the Japanese did nothing to offset, and a severely overvalued yen that they tried to offset with overly easy monetary policy. The resulting bubble in stock prices and land values led to the inevitable correction, which brought the economy tumbling down. The situation was then greatly exacerbated by false accounting by both major financial institutions and manufacturing corporations. When the yen continued to increase, manufacturing firms moved to overseas locations, and the economy became hollowed out.

This section is about Japan, not the US. Nonetheless, the collapse of the stock market bubble and the revealing of the accounting frauds by Enron, Worldcom, Global Crossing, Adelphia, etc. in 2002 have raised the issue of whether the US is also heading for an extended period of stagnation. In this author's view, the differences are greater than the similarities. First, the accounting schemes, as heinous as they were, were quickly exposed and corrected. Second, financial institutions have long been required to mark to market, rather than valuing assets on their books at their original purchase prices. Third, housing prices continued to rise at above-average rates; there was no bubble in US land prices. Fourth, the US remains committed to free trade, and imports continued to rise in 2002 after a brief recession-related decline in late 2001. Fifth, once the recession got underway, the dollar quickly returned to equilibrium. The future path of the US economy remains to be seen, but the similarities with the Japanese collapse of the early 1990s are far smaller than was suggested by the popular press in 2002.

CASE STUDY 14.6   THE COLLAPSE OF THE GROWTH TIGERS

Following in the footsteps of Japan, many other east Asian countries followed suit and generated unprecedented growth rates that averaged about 10% per year.

continued

CASE STUDY 14.6 (*continued*)

Hong Kong and Taiwan were first, followed by South Korea and Singapore. More recently, Thailand, Malaysia, and Indonesia posted growth rates of close to 10%. All of these countries maintained these superheated growth rates for at least two decades.

Thus it came as a major shock to economists and investors around the world when the Thai baht uncoupled from the dollar and devalued in July 1997. The Malaysian ringgit, Indonesian rupiah, and the South Korean won quickly followed suit, with all of these currencies falling more than 50% relative to the dollar during late 1997 and early 1998. The currencies of Singapore, Hong Kong, and Taiwan also came under pressure but were not devalued.

Not only did the superheated growth rates of the growth tigers suddenly come to a halt, but these countries plunged into recession. Real GDP declined sharply in 1998 for all these countries except Singapore, although most of them recovered in 1999. Further details are given in table 14.1.

According to the simple demand-side arguments of international trade, a devaluation should boost exports and reduce imports, hence raising GDP. This is perhaps the classic example of how this relationship does not hold: a 50% depreciation was accompanied by a major recession. That should be the final nail in the coffin of the argument, if indeed any further evidence were needed, that reducing the value of the currency does not help a country boost its growth rate. Nonetheless, a devaluation does not usually cause the economy to collapse completely, so other factors must have been at work.

Korea can be considered a typical example. In the decade before the devaluation, the inflation rate in Korea was $2\frac{1}{2}$% higher than in the US: 6.1% compared to 3.6%. Because Korea was growing faster than the US, one would expect real interest rates to be at least $2\frac{1}{2}$% higher in Korea. That was in fact the case; the spread ranged from about 5% on long-term bond rates to as much as 10% for short-term money rates.

Table 14.1   Growth rates in selected east Asian countries

Country	Annual average growth rates			
	1987–96	1997	1998	1999
Hong Kong	5.8	5.0	−5.1	3.0
Indonesia	6.9	4.7	−13.2	0.2
Korea	8.1	5.0	−6.7	10.7
Malaysia	9.0	2.3	−7.4	5.6
Singapore	9.1	8.4	0.4	5.4
Thailand	9.5	−0.4	−10.2	3.3

Source: International Financial Statistics Yearbook

continued

CASE STUDY 14.6 (*continued*)

Thus Korean businesses had a choice: they could borrow money at 5% in the US, or at 10% to 15% in Korea. That sounds like a no-brainer – *as long as the won remained fixed relative to the dollar*. If it devalued, Korean companies could find themselves in the position of having to pay back twice as much (in won) as they borrowed, essentially consigning them to bankruptcy.

Thus while interest rates in Korea were correctly priced, the currency was not. If it had declined an average of $2\frac{1}{2}$% to 5% per year relative to the dollar, most of those foreign loans would not have taken place, and Korea would not have suffered such a major hit.

A country can grow rapidly only if the ratio of saving and investment to GDP is unusually high. That by itself doesn't guarantee rapid growth, but it is not possible to have rapid growth with a low investment ratio. The source of the funds for saving and investment can, of course, either be domestic or foreign.

In its most rapid growth phase, Japan relied primarily on domestic saving to boost the growth rate. The other Asian growth tigers, however, relied primarily on foreign saving. Unless the country in question has a key currency, that method of growth involves two major risks. First, exports must keep rising at an increasing rate to generate the increasing amount of foreign exchange needed to service the debt payments on foreign capital. Such countries could have a huge trade surplus but a current account deficit because of the outflow of net investment income. Second, to the extent that domestic firms borrow in foreign markets, the value of the currency must be held constant, or these firms will find their indebtedness in terms of local currency has skyrocketed. For example, suppose a firm borrows 1 billion won when the exchange rate is 5 won to the $, but it later declines to 10 won to the $; the firm would have to pay back 2 billion won, which at least in the short run would probably be impossible.

Cracks in the system began to appear as early as 1996. Because of the sharp decline in the price of semiconductors that year, the value of Korean exports declined even though volume continued to rise. The price index for Korean exports fell 4% in 1996, and the current account deficit, which had been in surplus as recently as 1993, zoomed from $8.5 to $23.0 billion. The combination of somewhat higher inflation in the growth tigers, weakness of the Japanese market, and lower export prices put downward pressure on the currencies. The only way these countries could repay these massive loans to the US and other hard-currency countries was to keep exports and real growth rising at superheated rates. Once inflows of foreign exchange diminished, the whole house of cards collapsed.

After these currencies plunged 50% or more, it became clear that loans from US, European, and Japanese banks could not be repaid on schedule. The IMF then stepped in with multi-billion dollar loans to help firms repay some of their

continued

CASE STUDY 14.6 (*continued*)

short-term obligations, and permitted the rest of the loans to be rolled over into long-term instruments, payable over the next ten years. The price the IMF exacted was an austerity campaign: slower growth, a major cutback in imports of consumer goods, and cutbacks in government spending. The former growth tigers had little choice other than to accept these terms; otherwise, their international credit ratings would have been suspended indefinitely.

When the collapse occurred, it revealed a rotten infrastructure that had heretofore been well hidden. Many of the largest firms had been losing money steadily, but were bailed out by ever-increasing loans from their cronies at the big banks, which were also technically insolvent. The infrastructure would have to be rebuilt before these countries could once again achieve rapid growth.

We can see what happened in terms of the basic growth, or supply-side, model. The sharp decline in investment and saving reduced capital stock growth, cutting the overall growth rate by more than half. Gains in technology were also reduced because firms were no longer able to borrow money to create new businesses and innovate. But what happened in terms of the basic demand-side model?

Net exports did rise slightly, although that was more through cutting imports than expanding exports. However, monetary policy became much tighter, a condition imposed by the IMF. Also, foreign investment dried up, and in some cases, domestic capital fled the country. Hence autonomous investment also declined due to worsening expectations. As a result, total aggregate demand declined – in spite of the much lower level of the currency.

Initially, even exports declined although the currencies had depreciated by 50% or more. In order to produce exports, firms first needed to import crucial parts and materials – but they could not obtain the credit to buy these goods, since the local banking system had collapsed, and no foreign banks wanted to lend money in these circumstances. Thus not only did domestic demand collapse, but exports fell as the wheels of industry ground to a halt. That particular situation was remedied within a year, which is why real GDP rebounded in 1999.

The growth tigers were living on borrowed money without giving serious consideration about how it would be paid back; implicitly assuming that a 10% growth rate would continue forever. We know from the neoclassical growth model that a 10% growth rate is unsustainable in the long run even if nothing else had gone wrong. Hence even if the currencies had been fairly valued, and if Japan had not headed into a recession, growth in these countries would have declined to about 5%.

It was also a mistake for these countries to fix their exchange rates to the dollar at the same time that the rate of inflation was substantially higher than in the US.

continued

CASE STUDY 14.6 (*continued*)

Either they should have instituted a crawling peg, or reduced the rate of inflation. These alternatives would have meant slower growth over the past few years – but would have forestalled the collapse that eventually did happen.

When any country is saddled with (a) a large budget deficit, (b) an increasing current account deficit, (c) a fall in the ratio of foreign exchange reserves to GDP, and (d) a rise in the ratio of foreign debt to GDP, it is almost certain that rapid growth cannot long endure. All these signals were present in southeast Asia, yet they were almost uniformly ignored by investors.

Superheated rates of growth can be achieved only with abnormally high rates of saving and investment. The saving may be generated from domestic sources, or it may come from foreign investors. In the latter case, these funds can quickly dry up if expectations change. At the first sign of accelerating inflation or a weaker currency, several years of rapid growth may disappear almost overnight. That is the lesson of the Asian growth tigers.

CASE STUDY 14.7   GROWTH IN CHINA: MIRACLE OR MIRAGE?

The end of communism in the Soviet Union led to a tremendous decline in economic activity in that region, with real GDP falling as much as 50%.[1] The gradual movement away from communism in China occurred under an entirely different scenario, with real GDP reportedly rising an average of 8% per year. We are skeptical of any figures from communist countries; but while growth in China appears to have been quite rapid for several years, it probably slowed down to about 3% starting in 1998, even though the government ministers continued to insist that real GDP kept rising more than 7% per year.

China accomplished its impressive growth spurt by implementing the following measures:

1. Attracting capital from overseas. In many cases, the funds came from ethnic Chinese who saw great growth opportunities in China. However, many US firms also invested heavily in the country.
2. Foreign exchange has been earned through a huge trade surplus with the US. In 2001, Chinese exports to the US rose to $100 billion, while US exports to China increased only to $16 billion. No other country or region has this great a trade disparity. That huge imbalance is accomplished in part by keeping the Chinese yuan undervalued.

continued

CASE STUDY 14.7 (*continued*)

3. China has generated internal saving by creating "capitalist zones" which permit rapid growth of free enterprise; most of the funds are then poured back into further investment.

4. While the Chinese government still rules much of the country with an iron hand and does not tolerate political dissidents, it has permitted some free market economics to operate without the dead hand of excessive bureaucracy.

5. Many foreign firms have been unable to generate profits in China. This is not because their Chinese ventures are poorly managed. Instead, many firms are required to buy raw materials and parts from the Chinese at prices set by the government. These prices are set so high that most of the profit ends up accruing to the government rather than foreign investors. While that generates increased saving in the short run, it may be counterproductive in the longer run. Recently, the Chinese have shown signs of reversing these policies.

Considering that the Chinese economy is still in the early stages of emerging from the shackles of communism, perhaps its leaders have done an outstanding job in boosting productivity and real growth. However, it is not difficult to be skeptical about many of the announced results. Foreign tourists and investors see the great progress being made in the coastal cities; they do not see the peasantry continuing to labor under conditions of near-starvation. For every new multimillionaire, there are thousands of lowly workers whose standard of living has not risen at all. That is often the case in the emerging stages of capitalism, but Chinese political officials will have to moderate their economic power to move to the next stage of economic development. It remains to be seen whether they will choose to act in that direction.

The inconvertible currency, the enormous trade imbalance with the US, and the disappearance of profit margins for foreign investors are all danger signs for the future. It is unlikely that China will be able to continue its recent growth rate without taking much bolder steps toward a capitalist economy. Recent evidence suggests, however, that they are intensifying their efforts to attract more foreign capital.

In 1998, a book by He Qinglan entitled *China's Pitfall* revealed for the first time the degree to which China was mired in corruption and cronyism; it was almost as severe as the much better-known situation in Russia. The review of this book by Liu Binyan and Perry Link, which was published in the *New York Review of Books* under the title "A Great Leap Backward," stated in part that:

> The urban "reform" amounted to a process in which power-holders and their hangers-on plundered public wealth. The primary target of their plunder was state property that had been accumulated from forty years of the people's sweat, and their primary

continued

CASE STUDY 14.7 (*continued*)

means of plunder was political power .... Only about 10 percent of GDP comes from urban private enterprise .... During 1997 and 1998 average personal income growth has fallen off sharply, and for large portions of both urban and rural poor it has reversed.

There is much more in this remarkable book that establishes how much of the so-called Chinese prosperity reported in the western press is the Oriental version of a Potemkin village.

At first glance, comments of this sort call into question the viability of investing in China. It appears that total GDP is not much above $1.2 trillion, or about $1,000 per person, compared to roughly $10 trillion and over $35,000 in the US. More to the point, if He Qinglan's estimate is correct, and only 10% of GDP comes from urban private enterprise, that would be about $120 billion, which is barely more than the $100 billion exported to the US each year. Based on these figures, it would appear that the private sector of the Chinese economy that serves domestic consumers is minuscule. It also seems likely that Chinese exports to the US cannot continue to grow exponentially indefinitely.

The information in this book strongly suggests that the initial burst of real growth, fueled primarily by imports of capital from overseas Chinese and the surge of exports to the US, foundered because the communist infrastructure was unable to support the next round of development. Labor costs in China are unquestionably very low, but they are even lower on the Indian subcontinent. Without further massive injections of foreign investment – this time from investors generally, not just overseas Chinese – and a rule of law that permits corporations to earn and repatriate profits, the outlook for the Chinese economy would not appear to be favorable.

Yet one puzzling aspect remains: why was this book published? Suppose that the top Chinese leaders surreptitiously arranged for *China's Pitfall* to be published and leaked to select members of the western Press in order to signal to the bureaucracy that major changes were critically needed. The reason for assuming that might be the case is that in September 2002, the *New York Review of Books* – which is apparently the preferred publication for leaks – summarized a rather remarkable document: an internal memorandum prepared by the current top leaders to identify and select the next generation of leadership. The purpose of making such a document available was presumably to convince investors that unlike Russia and other formerly communist countries, the mantle of leadership in China had now progressed to the point where an orderly transition could be assured, indicating that the rule of law was becoming more relevant and important – and not so incidentally, that China was now ready to welcome foreign investors on a permanent basis. If China can establish

continued

CASE STUDY 14.7 (*continued*)

its credentials and assure foreign investors they will be able to earn a normal profit and repatriate those earnings, the picture of stagnation and decrepitude so vividly painted in *China's Pitfall* could quickly be reversed.

14.3   International trade in Latin America

With the exception of Chile, per capita GDP in Latin American countries averages $5,000 or less, compared to about $35,000 in the US. The reasons for this low level of GDP ought to be one of the major puzzles of economics: the region has plentiful natural resources in terms of agricultural land, oil, and minerals; it does not have the severe problems of overcrowding that dominate many Asian economies; and European and American investors have proven to be enthusiastic about the region many times in the past. Yet it has stagnated, nowhere more than in Argentina, whose real per capita GDP has slipped dramatically relative to other countries over the past century – a century ago it ranked fourth in the panoply of nations.

One can point to bouts of hyperinflation, socialist takeovers, frequent bankruptcies, and the flight of capital back to the US and Europe when these problems erupt, but simply identifying these problems does not answer the question of why they occur. The one outstanding success story is Chile, where real GDP has increased an average of 5.0% per year since 1975, shortly after the Pinochet government introduced free market solutions – including the privatization of social security in 1981 –into the Chilean economy. By comparison, the rest of Latin America has grown at an average rate of 3% per year. Considering the rapid population growth of almost 2% per year in Latin America, that makes per capita growth 3% for Chile compared to 1% elsewhere.

It took Chile approximately 15 years to institute all the reforms that led to a democratic, capitalist society; the final link occurred in 1989, when Pinochet offered the voters a chance to decide whether he should remain in office. They voted against him, and he accepted that verdict. During this period, Chilean society suffered many unnecessary civilian deaths, which has in some minds negated the progress made on the economic front. Since 1989, though, democracy has flourished, and over the next decade, real GDP rose at an average rate of 7.5%. That performance has caused the other leading Latin American nations, notably Mexico, Brazil, and Argentina, to move in the direction of free market economics, and hopefully duplicate that stellar economic performance.

In the long run, it may turn out that these measures will be just as successful in these countries as they have been in Chile. As of 2002, however, that is not yet the case. These countries all managed to bring inflation well under control during the 1990s – but their economies did not immediately move into high gear.

Mexico had a severe devaluation and recession in 1995, Brazil faced the same problem in 1999, and so did Argentina in 2002. In the following three case studies we show how international trade restrictions and incorrect values of the currency contributed to these problems.

CASE STUDY 14.8   NAFTA AND ITS EFFECT ON THE MEXICAN ECONOMY

The North American Free Trade Agreement, signed on January 1, 1994, was designed to reduce trade barriers between the US and Mexico and, to a lesser extent, between the US and Canada, since an existing trade agreement with Canada was already in place. In particular, NAFTA included the following clauses.

• The phaseout of most tariffs and nontariff barriers for industrial products over 10 years, with specific emphasis on textiles and apparel.
• The phaseout of tariffs and nontariff barriers for agricultural products over 15 years.
• Reduction of barriers to investment in Mexican firms, particularly the petroleum industry.
• Liberalization of regulations regarding financial and telecommunications services.

NAFTA was advocated by the leadership of both the US and Mexico. The US thought it would boost exports to Mexico. Mexico thought it would boost productivity and break the stranglehold of the oligarchy, eventually resulting in a more equitable distribution of income. Implicit in the agreement was the concept that unless Mexican per capita income rose more rapidly, there would continue to be a tremendous problem of illegal immigration into the US. Besides the alleged drawbacks to the US in terms of paying for expensive social services for illegal immigrants, Mexico feared that its most productive and energetic workers would emigrate, stripping the country of its best employees. Hence both countries wanted to diminish the flow of illegal immigrants.

According to the Clinton Administration, NAFTA was one of the most important trade agreements ever signed. However, not everyone agreed with these sentiments. In the US, many voters – whose views were represented by Ross Perot and Pat Buchanan – thought US workers would not be able to compete against low-cost Mexican workers. Mexico also had its share of doubters, who thought low-productivity Mexican workers would not be able to compete against modern US methods of production.

continued

CASE STUDY 14.8 (*continued*)

Both of these arguments are fallacious if one accepts the theory of comparative advantage and the benefits of trade specialization. According to this theory, the exchange rate would move to the level where Mexico would produce those goods in which it had a relative advantage, and the US would produce those goods where it had a relative advantage. Consumers of both countries would be better off. That is precisely the argument advanced by the Clinton Administration economists.

This is, however, a fairly important example of what is wrong with the theory of comparative advantage in a real-world setting. Since Mexico had far more barriers to US imports than the US did for Mexican imports, it follows that the peso would decline relative to the dollar. That is what the theory would predict, and that part of the theory was correct.

Like many developing economies, Mexico depends heavily on foreign capital for saving and investment. When the peso started to plunge, not only was foreign capital withdrawn, but wealthy Mexican citizens transferred much of their savings to US and Swiss banks. Although the plunge in the value of the peso did tilt the trade balance in Mexico's favor, the economic situation soon deteriorated. Because of the massive flight of capital, the Mexican government was forced to institute a tight monetary policy. The economy then plunged into a sharp recession, which reduced their imports from the US. Mexican real GDP fell 6.2% in 1995, compared to a 4.4% increase the previous year. Thus instead of the US increasing its exports of goods and services to Mexico, they fell because of the collapse of the Mexican peso, a development not envisioned by either country.

In the meantime, Mexico's economic problems were exacerbated by political unrest. Part of that stemmed from what many believe were rigged elections in 1994, which the US did not denounce because the Clinton Administration wanted the PRI – the ruling party – to win reelection so that NAFTA would be implemented. The combination of alleged voter fraud and a deep recession caused civil unrest in many of the southern Mexican states, which heightened the flight of capital.

The situation would have become even more serious were it not for the fact that the US government, together with the International Monetary Fund, arranged for a $50 billion loan guarantee to the Mexican government to meet any debts owed to foreigners. As is so often the case, once the guarantee was in place, the money wasn't needed. After falling more than 50%, the peso stabilized for a while, and capital that had fled the economy began to trickle back in again. Because the 50% drop in the peso boosted inflation in Mexico, costs rose, and eventually the peso continued to move lower, but this time in an orderly fashion.

Figure 14.1 shows what happened to the trade balance with Canada and Mexico after NAFTA was signed. In both cases, there was a huge increase in the US trade deficit. While some of the change can be attributed to the stronger dollar,

continued

CASE STUDY 14.8 (*continued*)

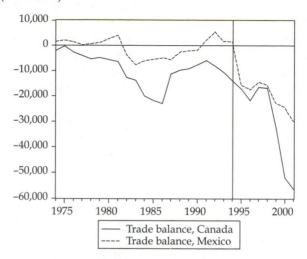

Figure 14.1 Annual US trade balance with Canada and Mexico (billions of $; 1994 is first year of NAFTA)
Source: Bureau of Economic Analysis website, www.bea.gov

most of it is due to NAFTA. Yet in spite of the big increase in the Mexican trade surplus with the US, its economy did not grow any faster. Real GDP rose 3.0% per year in the seven years before NAFTA was signed, compared to 2.9% in the first seven years after it went into effect.

The US economy did grow faster in the years after NAFTA, rising 3.7% compared to 2.7%. Maybe NAFTA did benefit the US economy in spite of the massive increases in the trade deficit with Mexico, although it is much more likely that the stock market boom and double-digit increases in high-tech investment boosted growth, and would have occurred regardless of NAFTA. Manufacturing employment declined much more rapidly after NAFTA, although some of that can be attributed to the overvalued dollar and the increase in the minimum wage. Considering that exports to Mexico grew an average of 10% per year in the first seven years after NAFTA was signed, compared to 20% per year in the seven years before that treaty was in effect, it seems unreasonable to claim that NAFTA significantly boosted the growth rate of the US economy.

NAFTA may still generate the long-run benefits that were envisioned by the Clinton Administration economists in early 1995. In its first seven years, however, the major noticeable changes have been (a) a much wider trade deficit with Mexico, (b) a sharp decline in low-paid manufacturing jobs that shifted across the border, and (c) no improvement in the Mexican growth rate. Claims that freer trade would help both countries have not yet been realized.

CASE STUDY 14.9   THE BRAZILIAN AND ARGENTINE DEVALUATIONS

In many ways the economic performance of Argentina, Brazil, and Chile have many elements in common. All three countries had relatively high standards of living in the early part of the twentieth century, but collapsed during the Great Depression. After World War II, they followed the hyperinflation route, creating full employment and the illusion of rapid growth. That illusion was soon shattered, leading to unrest in the streets. The government dared not institute layoffs among employees of the public sector for fear of exacerbating the political situation. The budget deficit ratio continued to rise, hyperinflation worsened, and productivity and the standard of living declined.

Finally, the situation became so unfavorable that drastic steps were taken. The era of easy money ended, and an austerity campaign was started. Initially, all of these countries plunged into recession, but that was accompanied by a reduction in inflation to single-digit rates. Once political credibility had been reestablished, foreign capital returned, and real growth recovered.

It is almost an economic parable. Bad economic policies lead to declining growth, economic misery, and political unrest. Good economic policies, after a period of adjustment, lead to rapid growth, economic prosperity, and political stability. However, although the experiment worked well in Chile, the success has not yet been duplicated in Brazil and Argentina. Since the lessons to be learned are thus somewhat different, each country is now considered separately.

For many years Brazil was the poster country for mismanaged economics and hyperinflation. As has often been remarked, "Brazil is a country with enormous promise . . . and always will be." For the seven year period from 1987 through 1994, the inflation rate in Brazil, as measured by the CPI, averaged 1,280% per year. Not too surprisingly, the economy was in a recession during most of those years.

Finally the government – and the voters – decided enough was enough. The Brazilian government revalued the real and set it equal to the dollar. Inflation slowed down to 6%, then 3%, and real growth rebounded to the 4–5% range. Because inflation was still slightly above the US, Brazil continued to devalue the real slightly, using a floating peg. Everything should have been fine – but it wasn't. Brazil was forced to devalue the real by another 40% in 1999, plunging the economy back into recession, and in early 2002 it was trading at approximately 2.30/$. By late 2002 that figure had fallen to 3.40/$.

The proximate cause of the Brazilian devaluation occurred when Itamar Franco, the president of Minas Gerais – who was called by another Brazilian politician "the stupidest person in Brazil" – declared that his state government would not repay

continued

CASE STUDY 14.9 (*continued*)

its debts. Naturally that alarmed investors, causing them to rush their money out of the country. Yet the alarm bells had rung much earlier. Indeed, for the previous several months, most investors were convinced that Brazil would have to devalue its currency again. The major problems were (a) its value was originally set too high when the new monetary regime was installed, (b) the trade deficit continued to increase, and (c) the government refused to take the necessary steps to reduce the growth in spending, particularly in the areas of pensions and benefits.

In the months before the devaluation, Brazil tried to hold the value of the currency by raising interest rates and restricting growth in monetary and credit aggregates. The net result was that the five-year period of prosperity came to an end and the Brazilian economy plunged back into recession in 1998. Since then, growth has recovered but at a more subdued rate.

The Brazilian story is subject to its past history of previous bursts of hyperinflation. As long as the government resolutely refused to put its fiscal house in order, and as long as the trade deficit continued to balloon, Brazil really had no choice other than to let its currency float. If the Brazilian political leaders want a stronger currency, they must balance the budget and reduce the trade deficit. So far, there is little eagerness to proceed on either of those projects. As a result, the real will probably continue to drift lower over the next several years.

After the Brazilian real failed, foreign exchange traders focused their attention on the Argentine peso. In one sense that did not seem "fair," since Argentina had tried to do everything right: it reduced the inflation rate all the way to zero, tied the peso to the dollar, and backed it with gold. Yet in early 2002, Argentina was forced to devalue the peso, pushing its level down to approximately 3.40 pesos to the $, not so coincidentally the same rate as the Brazilian real. The Argentine economy also plunged back into another severe recession, with the unemployment rate rising to 18%.

One major problem was that when the Brazilian real devalued by more than 50%, Argentinean products were no longer competitive, and their trade deficit ballooned because Brazil was able to undersell them in virtually every market where they competed. Once the real plunged, the peso was bound to sink – in spite of their stated plan to keep it equal to the dollar. The fact that the Argentine authorities kept the peso from declining for three years while investors withdrew their money from the country simply made the eventual plunge that much more severe.

By now it should be clear there are no shortcuts to economic prosperity; if there were, every tinhorn dictator in the world would have discovered them and put them to good use. Especially for smaller countries, the government budget must be balanced over the business cycle; foreign investors will not bail out the government, as they did for the US during the 1980s and much of the 1990s. Similarly, the

continued

CASE STUDY 14.9 (*continued*)

current account must be balanced over the business cycle. That in turn can be accomplished only if the value of the currency is set near its equilibrium value. Real growth will be enhanced if free trade is encouraged, which suggests working out a system with your neighbors and major trading partners to reduce trade barriers to a minimum. A common currency, such as the euro, may also help, but only if government policies switch toward those that are more free market oriented. A major devaluation by one country in a region is very likely to upset the trade balance for the entire region.

Latin America would be better off if, like Europe, it had a common currency. In fact, many economists have suggested that these countries adopt the dollar, although political pressures apparently would not permit that. If nothing is done, various currencies will continue to come under downward pressure in the future, which will cause the values of other currencies to decline even if those countries are controlling their inflation rate and keeping government spending in line. For when one country can boost its exports at the expense of its neighbors, eventually those neighboring countries will be faced with large trade deficits and downward pressure on their currencies. Thus until the Latin American nations join together in a common currency, frequent devaluations – and recessions – are likely to occur in the future.

14.4   Pros and cons of free trade in an imperfect world

Economists believe that free trade benefits all countries. Under somewhat idealized conditions that are seldom if ever met – no tariff or nontariff barriers to trade; stable, democratic governments; and free mobility of labor and capital – that is always the case.

The US probably comes the closest to satisfying these idealized conditions, yet even it does not allow unlimited immigration (free mobility of labor). Most other countries have far greater restrictions on foreign trade; in some cases, tariff rates appear to be low, but bureaucratic impediments significantly reduce the amount of imports.

We must also consider the dynamics of the situation: many theories about international trade are based on comparative statics. It may well be that in the long run, a country is better off replacing expensive domestic goods with cheaper imported goods, but if in the interim the people who lose their jobs go on a rampage and overthrow the government that introduced free trade, the desired goal will never be reached. In many cases, pro-free trade governments cannot remain in office unless they make some attempt to bend with the prevailing political winds.

Also, a serious imbalance could arise if the currency of a given country became so overvalued that none of the existing businesses could compete. According to the theory of comparative advantage, this can "never" happen; but it certainly can occur if there are barriers to trade and lack of mobility for factor resources. Gutting the manufacturing capability of an economy is certainly not in the best long-term interests of that country, even if all the canons of the comparative advantage theory are satisfied.

As a result, the optimal policy strategies for international trade are a good deal more complicated than a mere simple wave of the hand and a bland assurance that "foreign trade always benefits everyone." In this section, we discuss some of the circumstances under which this general rule must be modified.

Free trade boosts the standard of living by offering consumers the widest choice of goods, and the highest quality, at the lowest available prices. It promotes vigorous competition, prohibiting domestic oligopolies from setting prices far above costs. For smaller countries, free trade allows firms to achieve economies of scale by selling to world markets. As we have seen, free trade boosts productivity growth and reduces costs by promoting competition and encouraging the introduction of the latest available technology.

Yet in spite of these undoubted advantages, many economic agents – both business and labor – continue to push for trade restrictions for a number of different reasons. These are summarized next.

Retaliate Against Dumping

The US is empowered to retaliate against those foreign firms or industries that allegedly sell goods in the US "below cost." These firms can be fined, punitive tariffs can be assigned, or import quotas can be established. The concept is that while the steel industry (say) may be fully competitive on a level playing field, it cannot be expected to compete against foreign firms that sell at a loss.

This argument sounds fishy. Why would any firm, domestic or foreign, want to sell its output at a loss? That way, the more they sell, the more money they lose, so selling more to the US would only hasten their demise.

Of course that is not what really happens. These foreign firms are trying to broaden their market and reduce their average fixed costs, and the only way they can do so is to increase their volume of sales. When an American firm cries "foul," it generally means that foreign competitors have a lower variable cost, so it couldn't compete on a level playing field either.

Occasionally a foreign firm really does sell at a loss in order to obtain a toehold in the US market; once that has been established, it will raise prices to profitable levels. This happens far less often than the number of dumping cases brought before the tariff commission would indicate. Most of the time, "dumping" means that foreign competitors have figured out how to produce goods at a lower cost than their American competitors. "Dumping" usually means foreign firms are selling below US costs, not below their own costs.

Countervailing Duties to Offset Subsidies

If a firm really is selling below cost, that usually means the government is subsidizing its effort in an attempt to obtain scarce foreign exchange.

Here again the facts are seldom obvious. It isn't as though Japan promises its auto manufacturers an extra $1,000 for each car sold in the US. Instead, the subsidies usually occur in the form of government payments for research and development expenditures, which then reduce capital costs below what they might be in the US.

Also, the government may subsidize exports by providing low-cost, government-guaranteed loans to those companies that buy those exports. In this case, the prices of the goods are competitive, but the financing is subsidized. The US does some of this, especially for the aircraft industry, although not as much as other major industrialized countries.

There is no easy answer to this situation. If the US government imposes countervailing duties, consumers end up paying more. If the government subsidizes exports through R&D expenditures or financing, the taxpayer foots the bill. In the latter case, though, the taxes collected from an increase in employment in export industries often exceed the cost of the subsidies. In a world of compromises and second-best, subsidies are better than import duties. Furthermore, in the case of government-guaranteed financing, the "subsidy" may not end up costing the taxpayer anything.

Worldwide Monopolies

Theoretically, such a situation could arise if, for example, Boeing was so efficient that it not only drove all other passenger aircraft companies out of business in the US, but managed to drive Airbus Industrie out of business in Europe. In that case, Boeing would become a worldwide monopolist, and its drive to innovate might flag. However, the recent well-publicized woes of Boeing after it purchased McDonnell Douglas provided Airbus Industrie with a golden opportunity to gain market share. Apparently, Boeing bit off more than it could chew, and at least in the short run, lost more business from the merger than it gained.

The major example of a true worldwide monopoly has been the OPEC cartel, which unilaterally boosted crude oil prices from $3/bbl to $13/bbl in 1973, and to $35/bbl in 1979. This might seem to be an ideal opportunity for a monopolist: the world cannot function as efficiently without oil, there are no close substitutes, and hence the demand is quite inelastic. At least that is what the OPEC nations thought.

Of course, their pricing power couldn't last indefinitely; the fact that it did remain in place for over a decade testifies to the strength of their monopoly position. Above $35/bbl, all sorts of alternative energy sources – shale oil, tar sands, ethanol, recycled biomass, wind, hydrothermal, etc. – start to become viable. Also, while the short-run price elasticity for oil is quite low, the long-run price elasticity is much higher. While oil prices still fluctuate sharply in the short run, in the late 1990s, the average price of oil in real terms was about the same as it was in the early 1970s, before OPEC flexed its pricing muscle.

Infant Industry Argument

Economists have long recognized this as one of the valid reasons for imposing tariffs, providing that they are only temporary. Given sufficient time, a country may develop a world-class production and export capability; but because of start-up costs and increasing returns to scale, it cannot become competitive until a certain level of sales is reached. Yet until such domestic firms are competitive, their prospective customers will always prefer to buy imports because they are less expensive. Temporarily placing a tariff on imports will allow the domestic industry to expand to a competitive size. As soon as that happens, though, the tariff should be removed. Usually it isn't, so most infant industry arguments are spurious.

Terms of Trade for Commodities

If a country does not use tariffs to protect its newly formed high-tech industries, it may be doomed to producing only those goods based on favorable raw materials or climate (such as agricultural commodities or mining), or items such as inexpensive toys or cheap clothing. Over the long run, the terms of trade – the relative price of exports to imports – will shift against such items, and the country will forever remain poor. Except for the OPEC oil cartel, for many decades the price of basic agricultural and mineral commodities has declined relative to the price of finished goods and services.

Thus a country that relies primarily on primary sector exports will usually find the foreign exchange it receives will buy fewer and fewer finished goods and services, so the standard of living for that country will decline. Hence it will seek to develop the industrial capacity for goods and services that will at least keep pace with the overall rate of inflation by initially imposing tariffs on manufactured goods, in which case the "infant industry" argument applies.

Peril-Point Tariffs

These are initiated when a particular domestic industry, due either to dynamic changes in the world economy or an overvalued currency, is in danger of going out of business. If that were to occur, the advantage of free trade would then disappear because the competitive spur provided by imports would have no domestic counterparts. This was allegedly about to happen to Harley Davidson (motorcycles) in the mid-1980s, when the dollar was so overvalued that the company might have had to close its doors without a temporary tariff. After the dollar returned to normal levels, the tariff was no longer needed, and the company prospered.

National Defense

From a political point of view, this argument probably has the worst track record, since it has been utilized for everything from soup to nuts. Of course the US would not want to be in a position of having to buy its tanks, jet aircraft, submarines, and missiles from Germany, Japan, Russia, or China. For similar reasons, military forces in most countries are not permitted to entertain foreign bids for most of the items they purchase. However, when the argument is applied to something like candles, it is obvious that economic logic has been tossed out the window. In a well-known case many years ago, that industry actually petitioned for protective tariffs because of the vital role played by candles in national defense.

Diversification

If a country exports (say) only coffee or bananas, a sharp drop in the market prices of those commodities could wipe out the foreign exchange needed to buy energy or other food. Diversification reduces this risk, so countries will sometimes institute tariffs in order to give other industries a chance to get started.

Lower Real Wages

Even though an increase in imports does not harm the overall economy, especially in the US, it will have a negative impact on some sectors. If auto workers lose their jobs and must find alternative employment as retail clerks, taxicab drivers, or bellhops, their real income has fallen dramatically. Also, to the extent that imported clothing is made by workers with low wage rates, that reduces the wage rates of textile and apparel workers in the US.

In many cases, free trade redistributes income from the have-nots to the haves. Many people think that is the wrong direction. Yet even if one strongly believes that is a mistake, workers should still be paid their marginal product. The imbalance can then be rectified through a negative income tax, greater progressivity in the personal income tax schedule, or increased healthcare benefits to the poor.

Actually, such a situation should serve as an incentive for workers to find better-paying jobs, so in the long run, paying all workers their marginal product boosts economic efficiency and the overall standard of living. Nonetheless, an increase in imports does reduce both real wages and the returns to capital in those industries directly affected by higher imports, which often leads to intensive lobbying efforts.

Tariffs for Revenues

This doesn't apply to the US, since tariff revenues now represent only about 1% of total Federal government tax receipts. However, in developing nations where most income is still in kind and cheating is rampant, it may be virtually impossible to collect much revenue from either a sales or income tax. In that case, tariffs represent one of the few ways to collect enough revenues to keep the government functioning.

Optimal Tariff

This staple of international trade textbooks shows that under fairly general conditions, a country may place a tariff on certain goods that will increase the overall economic welfare of that nation, although not of the entire world.

The US, with its orientation toward free trade, would generally not be tempted to consider such an arrangement except for one special case: when the sellers of the good have formed a monopoly or cartel and have pushed the price of the product well above its cost of production.

The main example is the OPEC cartel. When oil prices were at their peak, if the US had applied a significant tariff to imported oil prices, that would have raised the price of oil enough that demand would have declined, which would eventually cause OPEC to lower the price of oil. The tariff would remain in place, but eventually consumers would pay no more than if there were no tariff.

Since US consumers would not end up paying more for oil, OPEC would bear the burden of the tariff. Yet although this is a sensible argument, it was never tried, mainly because some feared it would be a windfall for domestic oil producers, and politicians failed to understand that the burden of the tariff would be shifted to OPEC. Eventually the argument became moot as OPEC continued to expand production in 1998 in the face of stagnant world demand, and oil prices in real terms fell back to the level they had been in 1972, before the formation of the OPEC cartel.

Political Unrest

This case is relevant in the context of Mexico after the NAFTA agreement. In general, if free trade will cause civil unrest or a collapse of the government, steps toward reducing tariffs must be taken more gradually. Indeed, if a government that advocates free trade is overthrown and replaced by a government that reinstates high tariffs, it would be premature to move toward free trade more rapidly than political realities will allow.

While most of these arguments have some substance in the short run, they do not hold up well in the long run. Indeed, the conclusion we draw is that free trade benefits everyone in the long run – but in the short run, some caution is advised lest a country open its doors wide to free trade without having gone through a suitable transition period to make the necessary socioeconomic and political adjustments.

14.5   What factors will determine world leaders of the twenty-first century?

Students of economics presumably need little convincing that capitalism, warts and all, is superior to other forms of economic organization. However, for much of the twentieth century, that view was not shared by much of the world outside the US. Most of Europe fluctuated between socialism and fascism. Latin America preferred the route of big government and hyperinflation. India chose socialism, while the Soviet Union and China chose communism. For many years, so-called intellectuals in western democracies continued to point to managed economies as the wave of the future. In most countries, capitalism was not the preferred vehicle for growth.

The collapse of the Soviet Union showed the true face of communism to the world. European countries such as France and Sweden that had experimented with socialism became the laggards of the western world. The stark differences between the standards of living in East and West Germany, and in North and South Korea, could no longer be disguised. While North Vietnam conquered the South, the stark poverty of the nation was exposed to the entire world. The spectacular growth of the southeast Asian tigers served as a role model for many other emerging countries in the world, although in the end they tried to accomplish too much too soon.

The last decade of the twentieth century witnessed a major shift in thought among third world nations from socialism and fascism to capitalism. The major countries of Latin America reduced the deficit, privatized and deregulated, and stabilized their economies. India unlocked many of the shackles of socialism and doubled its growth rate. Eastern Europe and Russia escaped the shackles of communism, although the roots of capitalism have so far found stony soil. China discredited the reign of Mao Zedong, although it is not yet clear which direction the new leaders plan to take China in the next decade.

It would be fatuous to try and predict the course of the major world economies over the twenty-first century in any forum, let alone a textbook. Nonetheless, it should be possible, based on the points enumerated in this text, to provide a systematic approach to evaluate the long-term growth potential for various countries and regions based on the direction that certain key variables take. Such a list should contain the following elements:

- Currency correctly valued in terms of PPP
- Minimal import restrictions on trade
- Few restrictions on international flows of labor and capital
- Government that functions by rule of law
- Political freedom and encouragement of entrepreneurship and innovation
- Tolerable level of bureaucracy and minimal corruption

- Independent, credible monetary policy committed to low, stable inflation
- Full-employment balanced budget
- Relatively low marginal tax rates, especially on capital
- Less regulation and more deregulation
- High domestic saving and investment ratio
- Ability to attract foreign capital, including repatriation of foreign earnings.

As of 2002, we would rate the major world regions as follows; CH means the situation is changing for the better.

	US	WEur	EEur	Japan	China	SEAsia	India	Lat Am
Currency	Y	Y	N	Y	N	N	N	CH
Free trade	Y	Y	N	N	N	Y	N	CH
Few restrictions	Y	Y	N	N	N	Y	N	N
Capitalism	Y	Y	CH	Y	N	Y	Y	CH
Freedom	Y	Y	N	Y	N	Y	CH	Y
Laws/corruption	Y	Y	N	Y	N	N	CH	N
Monetary policy	Y	Y	N	Y	N	N	N	CH
Balanced budget	N	N	N	N	Y	N	N	N
Decl tax rates	N	N	N	CH	N	N	N	N
Deregulation	Y	N	N	CH	N	N	N	CH
High dom I/S rate	N	N	N	Y	Y	Y	Y	N
Attract foreign capital	Y	Y	CH	N	Y	Y	CH	CH
Rapid domestic growth	Y	N	N	N	N	N	Y	N
Inexpensive labor costs	N	N	Y	N	Y	Y	Y	Y
High profits permitted	Y	Y	Y	Y	N	Y	CH	Y
Score (out of 15)	11	9	3	8	4	8	6	6

This is, of course, a scorecard as of 2002 rather than a blueprint for the future. Most assuredly, many of these ratings will change in the future. For example, at the beginning of the decade, Latin America was still wallowing in huge budget deficits and hyperinflation. Nonetheless, the above scorecard provides a realistic framework in which to assess the possibilities for rapid growth in coming decades, and can be updated by managers as current events progress.

In particular, we should note that while China is the "darling" of many international investors now, the prognosis is not optimistic until it sheds more of its communist doctrines and moves closer to becoming a capitalist society. Even more to the point, countries comprising the former Soviet Union may indeed turn the corner, but they are not close to that point as of 2002.

The US, western Europe, and Japan are at approximately the same level of per capita GDP, which is well above the rest of the world. According to this scorecard, real growth in the US is likely to exceed growth in western Europe and Japan, although not by a huge margin. Of course these rankings could change; Japan could deregulate as successfully as the US, and its growth rate could rebound. Yet at the moment, few signals point in that direction.

Perhaps it is no surprise that the US, which leads all other major countries in per capita GDP by a fairly wide margin, is expected to continue its supremacy. However, this chart does provide a blueprint for how countries could improve their relative standard of living during the twenty-first century.

MANAGER'S BRIEFCASE: PICKING WINNERS IN THE TWENTY-FIRST CENTURY

The above chart shows that the US is the best place to do business. Indeed, agreement with that conclusion by many foreign investors pushed the dollar well above its equilibrium level, raising the obvious question of which other regions of the world offer enticing business opportunities, based either on rapid growth (for domestic sales) or low labor costs (as a base for export sales). Companies want to avoid the traps of excessive government regulation, but also the pitfalls of a sudden devaluation, a major slowdown in real growth, or a change in political direction. When the dollar returned to equilibrium in 2002, the major factors were the recession, the slump in investment, and the collapse of the stock market, none of which is likely to generate increased enthusiasm for foreign investors.

Based on the criteria given above, eastern Europe does not yet appear to be a very appealing area for investment. The rule of law is not yet well established, and it is very difficult to predict when the socialists will win a democratic election and put the brakes on attracting foreign investment. If one wants to take advantage of the EU market, a better idea is to locate in the peripheral countries: Ireland, Spain, Portugal, and Greece. Of course, many firms have done precisely that. These countries do not carry the risk of devaluation or rapid inflation unless the entire Maastricht Treaty unravels.

From the viewpoint of international planning by business managers, the two big questions are: what are the signs of trouble ahead in nations that appear to be on track, and what are the signs that nations currently in trouble are just about to turn around?

With respect to the first question, the recession and slowdown in east Asian countries has already occurred, and investors are now well aware of those issues. Similarly, the great hope for Latin American growth in the 1990s has largely dissipated. Since 1992, the growth express trains have been derailed in Japan, Korea, Thailand, Singapore, Malaysia, Hong Kong, Taiwan, and China. Mexico, Brazil, and Argentina have been forced to devalue their currencies, as did many of the growth tigers. The default by Russia points out the soft underbelly of all of eastern Europe, and illustrates the dangers that could arise if other countries suddenly shift into the capitalist mode – such as former countries of the Soviet Union, or China itself.

One of the two areas of the world where growth has remained rapid in recent years is represented by the peripheral nations of western Europe – Ireland, Spain, Portugal, and Greece have previously been mentioned; Finland and Iceland could also be included, although Iceland is not part of the EU, and neither are large enough to support a major local market. To the extent that these countries will continue to benefit from a common European market – and to the extent to which educated labor and capital will migrate from France and Germany into these countries – the outlook appears encouraging.

The other area is the Indian subcontinent: India, Pakistan, Bangladesh, and Sri Lanka. Their growth rates have been impressive ever since India moved closer to capitalism in 1992. On the face of it, their economic statistics do not look encouraging. All four of these countries have large government budget and trade deficits relative to GDP. The trade deficits are essentially paid for by repatriation of earnings from citizens of those countries who live and work abroad. There is no question about the huge size of the domestic markets and the rapidly growing middle

continued

MANAGER'S BRIEFCASE (*continued*)

class in India. Also, the rupee is allowed to drift lower relative to the dollar and not artificially held at overvalued levels. The problems of socialism, class discrimination, and international warfare have hardly disappeared, and building a country based on contributions of foreign workers does not seem to be particularly sturdy. Nonetheless, labor costs are among the lowest in the world. This area probably deserves a longer look from many companies than it has received. Recently India has expanded its "enterprise zones" to attract more foreign capital.

China remains the major question mark. An immediate switch to capitalism is not a viable alternative, given the current state of the country, and taking into consideration what happened in Russia. The optimists would say that the orderly transition of power in 2002 means the cult of personality has disappeared, and decisions in the future will be made on a more rational, orderly basis. The pessimists would say the underlying lack of training and experience in capitalism means the cadre of bureaucrats will impede progress even if the top leaders would like to see faster growth. The most likely alternative will probably be two steps forward and one step backward, which suggests that large companies with long-term staying power will eventually do very well with their investments in China, but those companies for which quarterly changes in earnings are important will continue to be disappointed.

Which currently depressed areas of the world are likely to turn around permanently in the next few years? Obvious interest focuses on eastern Europe and the former countries of the Soviet Union. If peace could ever be brought to the Middle East, the possibilities are very substantial, but we are not about to suggest that prediction. The sub-Saharan African economy does not yet seem ready to make its move.

A decade ago many economists and investors thought the newly liberated central and eastern European countries – Czechoslovakia (as it was then), Poland, and Hungary would be the best spots for substantial investments. In general, this area of the world has been a major disappointment, as has the former East Germany. The Germans and Japanese were able to rebound after three years of heavy bombardment from the Allied troops and massive battlefield losses; but before those reversals, these had been prosperous nations. Central and eastern Europe had been poor before the war, and for practical purposes had no investment over the past 50 years. Two generations of workers had been poorly educated, and virtually no indigenous entrepreneurs remained. It seems likely that the peripheral countries of western Europe, and the heavily populated areas of south Asia, offer better investment opportunities than the devastated lands of eastern Europe and the former Soviet Union.

Turning from the specific to the general, a country cannot expect to post above-average growth rates for an extended period of time unless it has a balanced budget, a balanced trade position, low inflation, and a high ratio of domestic saving and investment to GDP. Shooting stars that depend primarily on foreign investment usually turn out to be major disappointments when political or economic reversals suddenly spur a rush for the exits.

SUMMARY

- The UK, France, and Germany all suffered prolonged periods of sluggish economic growth in the post-WWII period. In the case of the UK, the initial problem was high marginal tax rates, followed by an overvalued pound. When these impediments were removed, the UK growth rate improved. France continues to be burdened by the dead hand of socialism. The growth rate in Germany declined when the Dmark became

overvalued and then, when it seemed as though the economy would recover, the Ostmark was overvalued after unification, hence essentially shutting down production in the former East Germany.

- The linkage of most western European nations under a common currency, fiscal policy, and monetary policy could boost productivity and the standard of living substantially if the collective governments move toward slower growth in spending, and encourage more innovation and technology. In the first three years of the common currency, that had not yet happened. The principal beneficiaries of the common European currency have been the peripheral countries that posted the largest declines in the deficit ratio and the rate of inflation.

- The Japanese economy set growth records for the first 25 years after World War II, rising about 10% per year. After that it settled down to a somewhat less dramatic but still highly respectable growth rate of 5% per year through 1991. Since then, the overvalued yen, coupled with continuing restrictions on imports, has led to a growth rate of only 1% per year. The overvalued yen, coupled with the stock market decline and the weakened conditions of many banks, also caused capital spending to shift from Japan to overseas markets.
- The east Asia "growth tigers" imitated the early success of Japan, but starting in 1997, devaluations of the currencies of Korea, Thailand, Indonesia, and Malaysia by 50% or more led to severe recessions the following year, although those economies have since bounced back. The devaluations were caused by a combination of a slowdown in the value of exports, due in part to declining prices of semiconductors, a rate of inflation higher than in the US, and excessive borrowing abroad.

- In Latin America, economic reforms have worked well in Chile, but that has not yet been the case in Mexico, Brazil, and Argentina, each of which has suffered a major devaluation in the past decade. In each case the devaluation was caused by the combination of an overvalued currency, insufficient emphasis on curbing government deficits, an increasing trade deficit, and in the months preceding the actual devaluation, a flight of capital out of the country. NAFTA resulted in a much bigger Mexican trade surplus with the US, but in the first seven years it did not boost the Mexican growth rate at all. During the same period, when the US trade deficit did increase sharply, its growth rate also appreciated.
- In the future, countries that have large government budget deficits and large trade deficits probably will not be able to maintain rapid growth rates indefinitely, and may have to devalue their currency or use contractionary fiscal and monetary policy to reduce the growth in imports. Countries that have recently devalued, or have recently moved from a totalitarian region to capitalism, are often considered superior places for investment, but that is not likely to be true unless those shifts are followed by bona fide attempts to balance the public sector and foreign trade sector over the business cycle.

QUESTIONS AND PROBLEMS

1. Recently, the US has been working with Caribbean nations to form a free trade zone similar to the NAFTA agreement with Mexico. The major industries to be affected are textiles and apparel.
   (A) How do you think this agreement would affect growth rates of Caribbean nations?
   (B) How is it likely to affect the growth rate of the US economy? The manufacturing sector? The textile and apparel industries? Growth in North and South Carolina?

(C) Would you invest in those countries if this agreement is signed? What other information would you require?

(D) Would you buy or sell stocks of major US textile and apparel firms if you knew this agreement was imminent?

2. Country N, a relatively small, impoverished country, discovers a huge reservoir of crude oil, for which the costs of lifting are less than 10% of the market price. Explain what happens to (a) the growth rate, (b) the value of the currency, assuming it is allowed to float freely, (c) the trade balance, (d) the rate of inflation. Now assume that 10 years after this initial discovery, the world price of crude oil suddenly drops by half. How do your answers to (a)–(d) change?

3. After the Korean won devalued by approximately 50% in late 1997 and the economy plunged into a severe recession in 1998, the economy rebounded strongly, with the growth rate returning to 9.3% in 2000. Without becoming an expert on the Korean economy, what do you think were the underlying factors that caused real growth to rebound so much more rapidly in Korea than in other east Asian nations that also devalued? What factors would you look at to determine whether the Korean economy would continue to outpace its neighbors?

4. Suppose you work for a large retail chain in the US that is considering expanding abroad. You are asked to determine whether the initial investment should be made in Mexico, Argentina, Brazil, or Chile. Explain which country you would select, and the principal economic reasons for that choice.

5. Now consider question 4 if you are a manufacturer of auto parts. How would your answer differ? How would it differ for manufacturing and retail firms generally?

6. Some economists and politicians have suggested that in future years, the concept of the common European currency be extended to include those smaller countries previously under Soviet domination. What would be the advantages and disadvantages to (a) the original European common market countries, (b) the peripheral countries now included in the common currency agreement, (c) the new countries that would join, (d) the UK, (e) Russia? Do you think the same arguments apply to including Turkey?

7. Under what conditions would you expect the recent rapid growth rates in the Indian subcontinent and south Asia to continue, and under what conditions are they likely to diminish in the near future?

8. India and China have roughly the same size population, and although per capita GDP in China is probably somewhat larger, the difference is not very great. Labor costs are lower in India than in China, and in spite of some socialist legacy, India is further down the road toward capitalism than China. Given these facts, why do you think so many international firms prefer to invest in China rather than India?

9. What factors would you consider when determining whether an investment in sub-Saharan Africa would be profitable for your company? Would the same factors hold for South Africa?
10. In spite of the greater emphasis on a planned economy in France than in Germany, the growth rate in France has averaged more than 1% higher than Germany over the past five years, whereas during the previous five years, the growth rates were approximately the same. Do you think the emergence of the European Union has helped France more than Germany? If so, why? If not, what other factors have depressed the growth rate in Germany relative to France? Do you expect those factors to continue in the future?

Note

1. That is, according to official statistics. However, it is more likely that GDP was overstated under the communists and understated afterwards, the reason being to avoid taxes. Even so, though, informed estimates put the decline in real GDP at 25% or more.

part V
Cyclical fluctuations

Because the US economy was subjected to only one minor recession from 1983 to 2000, the recent tendency in macroeconomics has been to ignore short-term fluctuations and concentrate, sometimes exclusively, on the factors determining long-term growth. This approach is not followed here for several reasons.

1. Business cycles not only continue to occur in the US, but in virtually every major country in the world. Real GDP declined in the UK in 1991 and 1992, and in France, Germany, and Italy in 1993. Japan has been in an extended period of stagnation since 1992, and real GDP declined in 1998 and again in 2001. Most east Asian countries plunged into a serious recession in 1998. Mexico, Brazil, and Argentina all suffered recessions during the late 1990s, with another recession in Argentina in 2002. In order to understand how the international as well as domestic economy really works, it is useful to study these cyclical fluctuations. The general shape of the business cycle, and the reasons why it occurs, are covered in chapter 15.
2. Even if the US economy does manage to avoid serious recessions in the future, explaining the cyclical swings in purchases of consumer durables, capital spending, housing, and inventory investment will enhance the overall understanding of how the macroeconomy works. In the future, it is quite possible that the manufacturing sector will exhibit all the signs of recession, but the overall economy will not actually decline. Before 9/11, it appeared that might very well be the case for the US economy in 2001. Factors leading to cyclical fluctuations in these components of aggregate demand are covered in chapter 16.
3. Financial cycle business sectors continue to be frequent even though real sector cycles are not – and can still lead to business cycles. If fluctuations in interest rates and stock prices are large enough, they may cause a recession even if no other cyclical factors are present. The links between these two sectors – and the importance of fluctuations in financial markets in cyclical behavior – are covered in chapter 17.

chapter fifteen

Business cycles

Introduction

From 1854 through 1982, a contraction in economic activity in the US occurred about once every four years. From 1983 through 2000, there was only one minor downturn. Yet the 2001 experience proved that recessions are hardly a remnant of the past, and few economists would be willing to state that they will not reoccur in the future. Moderating business cycle fluctuations should be included among the principal problems to be solved in macroeconomics, along with reducing the rate of inflation and boosting the long-term growth in productivity.

This chapter starts by recounting the long-term historical record of business cycles in the US economy. That is followed by an explanation of the typical pattern of business cycles, which are recurring, but not regular. In the post-WWII era, no downturn has lasted more than 16 months, while the length of the upturn has varied from 12 to 120 months. There is no particular method of determining in advance how long any given upturn will continue.

After reviewing the historical record, the general nature of business cycles is briefly reviewed. The length and severity of the downturn depend not only on the initial disturbance, known as impulse, but on the degree to which those effects ripple through the economy, known as propagation. The salient characteristics of each of the four business cycle phases – expansion, upper turning point, contraction, and lower turning point – are then presented. Attempts to anticipate the upper and lower turning points often rely on the index of leading indicators; yet they never miss a turning point, but they often give false signals. The reasons for this anomaly are briefly discussed.

We then turn to a more detailed explanation of the various causes of business cycles. From 1957 through 1990, each recession in the US was preceded by a substantial increase in the rate of inflation and interest rates and tighter monetary policy. However, inflation did not rise at all in the late 1990s, and long-term interest rates hardly budged, raising the question of whether the 2001 recession was due to entirely different causes than previous downturns. In fact that turns out not to be the case. The 2001 recession can be explained by business cycle theories that were developed long before the advent of Keynesian theory.

Economists generally agree that recessions can be caused by four different types of factors: exogenous shocks, changes in technology, incorrect fiscal policy, and incorrect monetary policy. The latter two are not entirely absent in the recent economic environment, but because of lessons learned in the past, they are far less common, and generally far less important. In the post-WWII period, most of the business cycle fluctuations both in the US and other major industrialized countries can be explained by the first two factors.

Until the recession of 2001, most analysis of recent business cycles focused on the confluence of higher inflation and higher interest rates shortly before the upper turning point. However, those factors did not occur in advance of the 2001 downturn. Instead, the boom was largely driven by technological advances, which eventually resulted in overcapacity in high-tech industries, a decline in profit margins, and a substantial cutback in capital spending. This theory, sometimes known as real business cycle theory, has its roots in the work of noted economists in the late nineteenth and early twentieth centuries.

The discussion of the various causes of business cycles is followed by a brief summary of the global transmission of business cycles. The question of whether the Great Depression could happen again is considered next. The chapter ends with a summary of the various exogenous and endogenous factors that determine business cycles. While many cycles are indeed caused by exogenous shocks, business cycles will probably continue even if these shocks do not reoccur.

15.1 The long-term historical record

The National Bureau of Economic Research (NBER) formally started measuring the business cycle in 1854. However, the US economy went through several cycles before then. The Cleveland Trust Company, once the leading bank in Ohio, constructed an index of economic activity dating all the way back to the beginning of the Republic in 1789. This index tells us little about what shapes the economy today, yet it is interesting to note that recessions apparently occurred back then with about the same regularity as they occurred up until 1982, namely once every four to five years. In particular, this graph shows recessions in 1793, 1797, 1802, 1807, 1812, 1819, 1826, 1833, 1837, 1840, 1843, and 1848. Most of these recessions were associated with war, the aftermath of war, or – in the case of 1837 – a financial panic caused by the closing of the Bank of the United States. Unlike other countries, agricultural shocks do not seem to have played a very important role.

The formal compilation of business cycle peaks and troughs as calculated by the NBER starts in 1854, and is shown in table 15.1. Since there is a sharp dichotomy before and after World War II, the summary statistics given in table 15.1 are listed separately for each period. In the US, the post-Civil War period was marked by a

Table 15.1 Business cycle reference dates (pre- and post-WWII)

Trough	Peak	Duration (in months)	
		Contraction	Expansion
Pre-WWII cycles			
December 1854	June 1857	–	30
December 1858	October 1860	18	22
June 1861	April 1865	8	46
December 1867	June 1869	32	18
December 1870	October 1873	18	34
March 1879	March 1882	65	36
May 1885	March 1887	38	22
April 1888	July 1890	13	27
May 1891	January 1893	10	20
June 1894	December 1895	17	18
June 1897	June 1899	18	24
December 1900	September 1902	18	21
August 1904	May 1907	23	33
June 1908	January 1910	13	19
January 1912	January 1913	24	12
December 1914	August 1918	23	44
March 1919	January 1920	7	10
July 1921	May 1923	18	22
July 1924	October 1926	14	27
November 1927	August 1929	13	21
March 1933	May 1937	43	50
June 1938	February 1945	13	80
Pre-WWII average		21	27
Post-WWII cycles			
October 1945	November 1948	8	37
October 1949	July 1953	11	45
May 1954	August 1957	10	39
April 1958	April 1960	8	24
February 1961	December 1969	10	106
November 1970	November 1973	11	36
March 1975	January 1980	16	58
July 1980	July 1981	6	12
November 1982	July 1990	16	92
March 1991	March 2001	9	120
Post-WWII average		10	57

Source: www.nber.org/cycles.html

number of severe financial panics, including those of 1873, 1893, and 1907. Each of these downturns was initiated by financial disruptions. These downturns were caused by excessive financial speculation on Wall Street, with the failure of speculators to "corner" various markets resulting in the collapse of major banks. The 1907 panic eventually led to the formation of the Federal Reserve System six years later to avoid such collapses in the future.

Yet in spite of the existence of the Fed, the US – and the worldwide – economy fell into a depression of unprecedented severity and duration in the 1930s, which almost brought capitalism to its knees and was ended only by rearming for World War II. Only in the post-WWII period have political and economic leaders learned how to avoid massive, prolonged depressions.

Since World War II, business cycles in both the US and the rest of the world have become much shorter, generally lasting only about a year, with the economy usually returning to full employment at the next cyclical peak. Although recessions are always painful to the unemployed, the post-WWII declines have been cushioned by automatic stabilizers such as unemployment compensation insurance, supplemental security income, and other forms of transfer and welfare payments available to those who have lost their jobs.

15.2   Measuring the business cycle: the indexes of leading, coincident, and lagging indicators

The seminal work on measuring and explaining business cycles in the US dates back to 1913, the publication date of the first version of *Business Cycles* by Wesley C. Mitchell. Further work by Mitchell and Arthur Burns, later Chairman of the Council of Economic Advisors and Chairman of the Federal Reserve Board, was published during the 1930s and 1940s. By 1947, the concept of a series of leading indicators was being used in an early attempt to forecast the economy.[1]

The proponents of the leading indicators approach have always made it clear that theory is not involved: they are searching for a series of economic variables that invariably lead the turning points in the overall economy. The original criteria spelled out by Burns and Mitchell were specific and complete, and since then, the widespread proliferation of computers has made it much easier to search through the thousands of economic data series to see which ones fit these criteria.

The track record of the Index of Leading Economic Indicators (LEI) will be examined in chapter 20: this section discusses the methodology used to determine that index, and the series that are currently included; a description of the coincident and lagging indicators is also presented. The LEI have received the most attention because of its alleged ability to predict recessions; the index of coincident indicators also is important because it presents the most recent and accurate snapshot of where the economy is right now. The index of lagging indicators is supposed to provide additional confirmation of whether the economy has in fact entered into a recession or recovery, but is not used much any more.

The components of the LEI have changed markedly since 1947; fewer than half of the components used then are still included. The latest major change occurred after 1995, when the Commerce Department, facing major budget cuts, decided to exit the business of keeping these indicators up to date and sold the rights to the Conference Board. One of their major changes was to include the yield spread between the 10-year Treasury note yield and the Federal funds rate as a key leading indicator; as noted throughout this text, an inverted yield curve is an important signal that the economy is about to slow down. As of mid-2002, the components of the LEI are as follows.[2]

- Length of workweek for production workers in manufacturing
- Average weekly initial unemployment claims
- New orders, consumer goods and materials
- New orders, nondefense capital goods
- Vendor performance (percentage of firms reporting longer delivery delays)
- Building permits
- S&P 500 index of stock prices
- Real M2 money supply
- Yield spread between 10-year Treasury note yield and the Federal funds rate
- Index of consumer expectations (University of Michigan).

The most important indicators are the three monetary sector indicators and are discussed in detail in chapter 20; the index of consumer expectations is also discussed there. The other components, while all qualifying as leading indicators, tend to be erratic in the sense that they give too many false signals. In fact, that is the principal criticism of the LEI: not that it misses recessions, but it too often signals a downturn when none occurs. The index also has a long and variable lead time.

The index of coincident indicators consists of the following four series:

1. Employees on nonagricultural payrolls
2. Real personal income excluding transfer payments
3. Index of industrial production
4. Real manufacturing and trade (business) sales.

The interpretation of the coincident indicators is much more straightforward. When it is rising, the economy is in an expansion phase, and when it is falling, the economy is in a contraction phase. The only ambiguity arises when the index is essentially flat; as we will see later, that occurred during much of 2001. This index is generally considered to be a better guide to the current condition of the economy than real GDP, which is available only on a quarterly basis, is subject to frequent widespread revisions, and occasionally gives misleading signals. Managers who follow the economy closely are well advised to check this index for the latest snapshot of current economic activity. These indicators are used by NBER to determine the beginning and ending dates for recessions.

The index of lagging indicators consists of the following seven series:

1. Average duration of unemployment (in weeks)
2. Inventory/sales ratio for manufacturing
3. Change in index of unit labor costs
4. Prime rate
5. Business loans outstanding
6. Ratio of consumer installment credit to personal income
7. Change in CPI for services.

This index is no longer very useful for several reasons. First, while business loans outstanding still lag the economy on the upside, they tend to lead it on the downside. Consumer credit is a coincident index. The prime rate is now equal to the Federal funds rate plus 3%; it is no longer accurate to say the Fed funds rate is a lagging indicator, since the Fed generally cuts that rate as soon as the recession becomes apparent. Even when this index is accurate, it does not greatly add to our knowledge of the economy to know that, in mid-2002, the economy had indeed been in a recession the previous year. Hence this index is not discussed further.

MANAGER'S BRIEFCASE: WHAT DETERMINES A RECESSION

We start by emphasizing that there is no one single definition of a recession: it is an empirical, rather than a theoretical, concept. Four general rules have been developed although, as we will see, none of them works all the time.[3]

First, it is often said that real GDP must decline for two consecutive quarters in order for the downturn to be a recession, but that is not a definition, and it doesn't always happen. Real GDP did not decline for two consecutive quarters in the 1960 or 1980 recessions.

Second, the unemployment rate should rise at least 2%. So far, that has been the most reliable rule. Also note that the unemployment rate is a lagging indicator, so it will often continue to rise after real growth has turned positive. That was particularly evident in the sluggish 1991–2 recovery.

Third, there should be a substantial decline in the index of industrial production, usually at least 6% – although production fell less than 4% in the 1990–1 downturn.

Fourth, inventory investment should be negative for at least two consecutive quarters – although in 1970, the two negative quarters were not consecutive, and in 1986, inventory investment fell for two consecutive quarters, yet there was no recession.

In the final analysis, the economy enters a recession when the Dating Committee of the National Bureau says it did.[4] Of course, such a distinction is not arbitrary, and is based on the behavior of the index of the leading and coincident indicators; since the dates are not chosen until several months after the actual turning points occur, the lagging index is sometimes used as an additional check.

continued

MANAGER'S BRIEFCASE (*continued*)

Table 15.2   Checklist of key measures of recession

Year recession started	Decline in real GDP		Rise in unemployment		Decline in industrial production		Decline in inventory investment		Decline in coincident indicators	
	%	Qtrs*	(a)	(b)	%	Qtrs*	(c)	Qtrs*	%	Months
1949	1.7	2	3.2	5	7.5	3	2.6	4	11.0	9
1953	2.6	4	3.4	5	8.2	3	1.6	5	9.6	12
1957	3.9	2	3.5	5	11.6	3	1.1	3	11.7	8
1960	1.6	1	1.9	5	7.7	4	1.0	2	2.4	10
1969	0.7	2	2.5	5	6.1	5	0.4	1	1.9	2(d)
1973	3.1	3	4.2	6	13.9	4	1.0	2	5.1	8
1980	2.0	1	2.0	5	5.0	2	1.2	2	2.7	6
1981	2.7	2	3.3	5	9.5	5	2.5	4	3.8	16
1990	1.1	3	2.3	10	3.7	2	0.7	4	2.2	8
2001	0.6	3	n/a		5.7	5	2.0	5	1.5	6

Quarterly data are generally not available before 1947, so the 1945 recession is not included in this table

* Number of consecutive quarters

(a) total increase during recession

(b) total increase including rise after recession ended

(c) as a percentage of total real GDP

(d) index was flat for the preceding eight months

Source: calculated by author from data on BEA, BLS, and Fed websites. The data for coincident indicators can be purchased from the Conference Board, Haver Analytics, or other data vendors.

15.3   Cyclical behavior: recurring but not regular

While the switch to more moderate business cycles after World War II has been quite marked, the post-WWII record remains irregular. From 1946 to 1960, the US economy went through four recessions in 14 years; then there were no downturns for almost an entire decade. Another bout of cyclical activity then reappeared, with four more recessions from 1970 through 1982, but there have been only two mild downturns since then. Thus the evidence suggests that while business cycles are a recurring phenomenon, there is no regular pattern of cyclical behavior.

Before World War II, a business cycle occurred on the average of once every four years, with the expansion phase lasting an average of 27 months and the contraction phase lasting an average of 21 months. After World War II, for the first 37 years, there was a business cycle on the average of once every 55 months, not much different from the prewar average, but the mix between upturn and downturn was much different. The expansion phase lasted an average of 45 months, while the contraction phase lasted an average of only ten months. Since 1982, there has been a recession only once every ten years.

These figures suggest that the increasing importance of the service sector and the decreasing importance of agricultural and manufacturing, coupled with a greater emphasis on using fiscal and monetary policy to shorten recessions, had a significant impact.[5] Few economists would disagree with that assessment. It remains to be seen whether we have made further progress in controlling the business cycle since 1982, when the frequency of cycles sharply diminished, or whether cycles will now return more often. In the late 1960s, it was often claimed that the business cycle had been conquered, yet that was followed by four downturns from 1970 to 1982, suggesting there was still much to be learned about controlling recessions.

Some economists have wondered whether the most recent business cycle was caused by different factors than its predecessors. From 1957 through 1990, every upper turning point was preceded by a rise in inflation, a decline in productivity, and a rise in interest rates. However, none of these occurred in 1999 or 2000, yet the economy headed into recession in 2001. Furthermore, there were no exogenous shocks – no wars, international incidents, or energy crises – and no fiscal contraction from raising taxes or cutting spending programs.

Before World War II, several competing strains of theories were used to explain the business cycle. Without providing a detailed description of these theories, these can be divided into two basic categories, which can be called "shortage" and "surplus" theories.[6] Shortage theories imply there is an insufficient supply of some resource, either real or financial. Once, money supply was constrained by the stock of gold; nowadays, the central bank raises interest rates and reduces credit to fight inflation. Sometimes labor shortages occur, and sometimes profit margins are squeezed, leading to insufficient funds for investment. Surplus theories, on the other hand, imply that after a long investment boom, there is so much excess capacity that firms reduce their capital spending, leading to a recession.

The one thing all these theories have in common – with the single exception of the widely discredited underconsumptionists – is that the recession is caused by a decline in investment. Yet in one case, interest rates rise, credit is diminished, and profit margins decline. In the other case, interest and credit are not restricted, but eventually excess capacity occurs.

It might appear that these theories contradict each other, but in fact they have more in common that might be initially apparent. Both have their genesis in the same phenomenon: at some point in the business cycle expansion, the cost of capital is below its equilibrium level. That stimulates aggregate demand, boosting both investment and consumption. After a while, one of two things happens. In the shortage theories, inflation starts to rise because the economy has reached full employment, labor demands bigger wage increases, productivity growth declines, and profit margins are reduced. In the surplus theories, the investment boom has been large enough that no shortages occur, and the rate of capacity utilization remains well below peak levels. In that case, interest rates remain low, and investment keeps rising as a proportion of GDP. It is also likely, although not necessary for this explanation of the cycle, that the combination of rapid growth and low inflation boosts price/earnings ratios in the stock market to unsustainably high levels, which also fuels the investment boom for a while. If that occurs, the costs of both debt and equity capital remain below equilibrium levels. Eventually, the investment boom collapses when profit margins are reduced and so much excess capacity accumulates that further expansion is unwarranted. Note that in both cases, profit margins are squeezed. That was also the central finding in the original work of Wesley Mitchell.

This latter explanation is hardly a new theory of the business cycle, and was in fact developed by Knut Wicksell almost a century ago.[7] Wicksell focused on what he called the "natural rate of interest," which he defined as the rate at which ex ante investment and saving were equal. In the early stages of the business cycle, interest rates are generally below equilibrium – independent of central bank action – so ex ante investment rises faster than saving, causing the economy to expand. After a while, interest rates rise, so ex ante investment drops below saving, causing the economy to contract.

What factors determine whether shortages or surpluses occur? The major answer is the growth rate of technology. During a technology boom, investment is likely to grow rapidly, hence boosting productivity, keeping inflation low, generating a stock market boom, and encouraging even more investment until excess capacity occurs. In the absence of a technology boom, investment will grow moderately, productivity growth will be sluggish, inflation will rise, the stock market will stagnate, and the boom will end when interest rates rise.

Seen in this light, there is an important common strand between the shortage and surplus theories. In both cases, lower interest rates stimulate demand, and higher interest rates diminish them. If the expansion is propelled by a technological shock, the surplus case is more likely to develop than the shortage case, so the results may look different in terms of inflation and nominal interest rates. However, the underlying mechanism has many similarities.

Does this mean a technology boom carries with it its own seeds of recession? In his economic classic, *Capitalism, Socialism, and Democracy* (1942),[8] Joseph Schumpeter presented just this argument, emphasizing the role of capitalism as "creative destruction." Schumpeter argued that innovations cause departures from equilibrium, leading to cyclical fluctuations as new capital replaces and destroys the old. We mention these older works to emphasize that the "new" theories of the business cycle which some have advanced to explain the 2001 downturn are in fact almost a century old.

It is common to read in the financial press that Alan Greenspan is the second most powerful man in Washington, with investors focusing on every word muttered by the Fed Chairman. Yet in many respects, the Fed simply follows forces dictated by the marketplace. During periods of economic slack, interest rates generally decline below equilibrium levels because of a lack of demand for funds, whether the Fed eases or not. During periods when ex ante investment exceeds saving, interest rates generally rise whether the Fed tightens or not.

Of course, monetary policy *can* affect expectations, and the Fed would make a mistake if it tried to keep the boom alive by reducing real interest rates and increasing the growth in monetary and credit aggregates at a time when inflation was already rising. Also, it could turn a recession into a depression by tightening policy at a time when the economy was already falling and inflation was declining, as happened during the days of the Great Depression.

However, changes in Fed policy are not the major reason that business cycles occur. As Bennett McCallum has put it, "a sizable portion of the output and employment variability that is observed in actual economics is probably the consequence of various unavoidable shocks, that is, disturbances not generated by erratic monetary or fiscal policy makers. Thus it is unlikely that many scholars today would subscribe to the proposition that all or most of the postwar fluctuations in US output has been attributable to actions of the Federal Open Market Committee."[9]

The "shocks" that McCallum mentions are of two types. One is caused by exogenous shifts in technology, as mentioned above. The other is caused by exogenous events such as energy shocks, agricultural shocks, beginnings or ends of wars, political instability, or devaluation of the currency. McCallum does not rule out the possibility that unanticipated errors in monetary and fiscal policy could cause business cycles, but he does claim that is not the major reason for cyclical fluctuations.

At this point the reader may raise a legitimate question. If business cycle fluctuations are caused primarily by exogenous factors, why study them? Even if they are very important, the events that tend to set them off are, by their very nature, largely unpredictable.

Even if the initial shock is exogenous, the impact on the economy is largely endogenous, and it is useful to understand that effect. Second, it is important to see how fiscal and monetary policies can affect the course of the economy over the business cycle, and to be able to identify when a mistake in those policies, if one does arise in the future, is likely to cause a cyclical downturn. Third, for purposes of business planning, it is important to understand how a recession can develop – as it did in 2001 – even in the absence of contractionary monetary or fiscal policy, and to be able to plan for such an eventuality.

If a major war breaks out, or if OPEC institutes an oil embargo – as opposed to merely boosting prices – those shocks will undoubtedly cause business cycle fluctuations throughout the world even if the economies of all countries were previously at equilibrium, and there is no method of forecasting such an occurrence. Yet after they do occur, it is important to understand how the economy will react.

Except for major exogenous catastrophes, there is an important underlying thread to business cycle theory, which is perhaps the most important relationship the reader should take from this chapter. When the cost of capital – both debt and equity capital – is below equilibrium, investment will increase faster than saving, lifting the economy back to full employment. By that point, the increase in ex ante investment over saving will push the cost of capital above its equilibrium level. At that point, factors will start to occur that will cause an economic downturn unless

Table 15.3 Causes of recessions

Recession	Monetary	Fiscal	Energy	Credit	Technology	Strikes	International
1945		xw					
1949		x				x	x
1954		xw					
1958	x						x
1960	x	x				x	
1970	x	x,xw				x	
1974	x		x				
1980	x		x	x			
1982	x						
1990	x	x		x			
2001					x		

Monetary contraction: rise in real interest rates.

Fiscal contraction: w = decline in defense spending after war. 1948, budget surplus ratio was 4.8% (equivalent to a $500 billion surplus in 2002 dollars); 1960, attempt to balance budget at less than full employment; 1990, Bush tax increase. Also, taxes were raised in 1968–69 in addition to the defense cutbacks from the Vietnam War.

Credit restrictions: 1980, credit controls; 1990, aftermath of S&L bailout.

Strikes: 1949, coal; 1960, steel (in 1959); 1970, auto.

International: 1949, decline in exports as Marshall Plan was phased out; 1958, decline in exports after bulge in 1957 caused by the Suez crisis, and the formation of European Common Market boosted production and diminished US exports to Europe.

the cost of capital quickly returns to its equilibrium value. If there has been no technological shock, shortages will develop, inflation will rise, interest rates will increase more than inflation, and aggregate demand will diminish. If there has been a beneficial technological shock, excess capacity will emerge and investment will decline. Understanding how these mechanisms work is critical to understanding how the economy functions, even if no one can predict truly exogenous shocks.

Keeping this fundamental underlying relationship in mind, it may be useful to identify the other factors that have caused recessions in the US economy after World War II. These factors are summarized in table 15.3.

From 1945 through 1954, three post-WWII recessions occurred before the inflation/Fed tightening link became noticeable. There was a very brief recession right after World War II when wartime production shut down, but this recession was unique. While the unemployment rose from 2% to 4%, the economy had been so far above full employment during the war that even after the recession, unemployment remained near its full employment rate. A brief recession also occurred after the Korean War ended.

The 1949 recession was not associated with any wartime activity. Once the pent-up demand following wartime shortages and the associated inflation ended, commodity prices dropped sharply and firms cut back on the inventories they had been hoarding. The backlog of demand for consumer durables was largely worked off by 1949. President Truman reduced spending but opposed the Republican plans to cut taxes, resulting in a huge budget surplus. Also, a severe and prolonged coal strike depressed the economy in late 1949. Yet even with all these exogenous factors, the decline was moderate, and the economy had started to recover even before the outbreak of the Korean War sent production skyrocketing.

In the early post-WWII period, fiscal contraction was the main exogenous factor preceding recessions, but that changed by 1960. Since then, fiscal policy has played only a minor role in downturns, and until 2001, tighter monetary policy always preceded recessions. However, that does not mean there would have been no recessions if the Fed had not tightened; it responded to higher inflation, which, if left unchecked, would have caused a recession anyhow. Paul Volcker has stated that it is "not just simplistic, but flatly wrong, to suggest that the risk of a downturn in the economy, however mild, can be laid to monetary policy."[10]

Thus it is incorrect to blame monetary policy for recessions. Interest rates don't rise just because some member of the FOMC got up on the wrong side of the bed; they rise because ex ante investment exceeds ex ante saving, and inflation increases. On the other hand, the true relationship is more complicated, for if the Fed had initially established credibility, inflation generally would not have risen very much in the first place. So in that sense, the pre-Volcker Fed helped to cause recessions by failing to establish a credible monetary policy.

The only cause listed for the 2001 recession is the technology shock, which boosted investment so much that excess capacity eventually appeared. It is generally accepted that the collapse of the stock market bubble was also a leading cause of this recession. However, that bubble occurred primarily because of unrealistic expectations that the capital spending associated with the technology boom could continue indefinitely. This episode is discussed in more detail later in this chapter.

15.4   The phases of the business cycle

Impulse and Propagation

We draw the distinction between *impulse*, which is the initial shock, and *propagation*, which is the ripple effect as this shock passes through all sectors of the economy. Although many upper turning points occur when interest rates rise in response to higher inflation, we saw in the late 1990s that full employment need not boost the inflation rate, so the theory that downturns are started by exogenous shocks can be a useful one for explaining recent business cycle patterns for several reasons:

1. It emphasizes the way in which exogenous shocks can still derail well-managed economies.
2. The 1995–2000 experience – full employment without higher inflation – emphasizes how the expansion can end because of excess capacity even in the absence of clearly identifiable exogenous shocks.

3. No matter what combination of endogenous and exogenous factors causes the upper turning point, it is important to understand the propagation of the cycle throughout the economy from an initial shock as the downturn first intensifies and then weakens.

Thus it will be useful, as we describe how the various phases of the business cycles begin and end, to keep in mind the distinction between the change that *initiates* the move from one phase to the other, and the factors that *follow* that change and determine the actual course of the economy during each of those phases.

Since the business cycle is continuous, there is no one particular place to start with its description, but the standard procedure is to begin with the expansion phase, keeping in mind the factors that caused the recession to occur in the first place.

A brief word about terminology. In the nineteenth and early twentieth centuries, downturns were often known as "panics" because of the temporary scarcity of liquidity. The term "depression" was actually coined as an antidote to "panic," trying to remove some of the pejorative connotation of that word. Nowadays, the term "depression" has taken on many of those same negative images, and "recession" has been widely substituted. It is sometimes suggested that a depression connotes a much more serious downturn, one lasting several years, in which the unemployment rate rises to double-digit levels and remains there for an extended period of time. In this material, we consider any decline in economic activity to be a recession, although the more neutral terms downturn or contraction are sometimes used as well.

Expansion Phase

Expansions usually start when the effect of easier monetary policy initially set in motion by the downturn starts to boost demand in the interest-sensitive sectors of the economy, and the negative impact of declining inventory investment is almost completed.

There is no particular time span for expansions. Most of the time, the expansion continues at least until the economy returns to full employment. If it reaches full capacity at about the same time, inflation is likely to rise, causing tighter monetary policy and leading to the next recession. If the economy is not close to full capacity, the expansion will continue until excess capacity appears and profit margins decline, which usually takes somewhat longer. Other things being equal, the further away the economy is from full employment, the longer the expansion will last, but this correlation is not very strong.

Occasionally the economy will plunge back into recession without ever having reached full employment, or without any acceleration in inflation. That occurred in 1937 and, to a lesser extent, in 1960 and 1981. The severe 1937–8 recession was due to a combination of higher taxes and an erroneous tightening by the Fed. The 1960 recession was caused by a large full-employment budget surplus, tighter monetary policy, and the aftermath of an extended steel strike; even so, it was very mild. In 1981, a recession started only 12 months after the previous one had ended, so full employment was not reached, but that was due to a surge in inflation in late 1980 and early 1981.

Other factors could also cause a recession to start before the economy had returned to full employment. Where foreign trade is an important part of the overall economy, a collapse of international markets could precipitate a downturn. An energy crisis could also occur at a time when the economy is not at full employment, although it just so happens that the first four times that energy prices have risen sharply – 1973, 1979, 1990, and 2000 – the US economy has indeed been at full employment. In countries where the farm sector is still an important part of the overall economy; the string was finally broken in 2003. crop failures could also cause recessions. While rising interest rates probably would not occur without higher inflation, other measures of credit contraction could also cause a recession, such as the collapse of the banking system.

During the expansion phase, the economy generally rises faster than its long-term sustainable rate until the economy reached full employment; if it did not, full employment would never be reached. The principal factor stimulating robust growth is the decline in the cost of capital below its equilibrium value, hence boosting investment. If that does not occur, growth would not rise at above-average rates unless the gap was filled by increased government spending.

Once full employment is reached, the ideal situation would be for the cost of capital to rise back to its equilibrium value, causing aggregate demand to rise at the same rate that total productive capacity was increasing. That would keep ex ante investment and saving in balance without boosting inflationary pressures. Historically, that has not happened very often.

To summarize the expansion phase, the economy will continue to rise at above-average rates until it reaches full employment, unless overly tight money or an exogenous shock intervenes. Once that point is reached, the economy will continue to grow at average or better rates until (a) inflation rises, or (b) excess capacity appears and profit margins decline. The mechanisms that cause this are discussed next.

The Upper Turning Point

It might not seem particularly difficult for intelligent central bankers to set interest rates at a level that equilibrates saving and investment. Since that seldom occurs, there must be something inherent in the economic system that causes interest rates and the cost of capital to differ from their equilibrium values.

Wicksell showed that in equilibrium, the cost of capital is equal to the marginal productivity of capital (MPK). Now suppose a major new innovation – improved computer technology, integrated circuitry, and telecommunications come readily to mind – boosts the MPK significantly. That happens immediately – but much of the actual investment does not take place for several years (think of the time it takes to lay fiber optic cable). For a while, the MPK has risen but ex ante investment is still below saving, so interest rates are low; stock prices are high relative to earnings, so the cost of equity capital also is low. There is a divergence between the MPK and the cost of capital.

This has little to do with central bank policy. Interest rates are below equilibrium when ex ante investment is less than saving whether there is a central bank or not, and they are above equilibrium when ex ante investment exceeds saving. Furthermore, the central bank generally is not expected to control stock market prices. Thus during the early stages of the business cycle, the cost of capital will be low, which usually boosts investment.

After a while, ex ante investment equals and then exceeds saving, so the cost of capital rises. However, as the investment from this technological innovation is put in place, the MPK falls, so now the cost of capital is higher than the MPK. Eventually this causes investment to slump.

Sometimes, however, the cost of capital does not rise. That could occur for one of two reasons, although they may be interrelated. First, the gap between ex ante investment and domestic saving could be filled by foreign investment. In the US, that would be more likely to occur if the US ran a substantial trade deficit, as was indeed the case in the late 1990s. Second, stock market prices could rise to unrealistically high levels, bolstered by what some speculators call the "new technology," keeping the cost of equity capital artificially low for an extended period of time. An increase in foreign investment may also boost stock prices for a while. The greater the technological shock that occurred in this expansion, the more likely that stock prices will rise to unsustainably high levels.

The upper turning point may then occur for several different reasons. First, there may be an exogenous shock. Second, a surge in new technology may generate an investment boom fueled by the cost of capital remaining below equilibrium, which eventually causes shrinking profit margins and excess capacity. Third, mistakes in monetary policy may boost real interest rates before the economy reaches full employment. Fourth, misguided fiscal policy could cause the economy to contract. Since the causes of the upper turning point are central to an explanation of the business cycle, all these are discussed in separate sections later in this chapter.

Contraction Phase

The behavior of the economy in the beginning of the contraction phase depends on what factors caused the upper turning point. If higher inflation and higher interest rates occur, which was typical of recessions from 1957 through 1990, the initial decline usually occurs in housing and purchases of consumer durables, which start to drop about one quarter after significant monetary tightening. New orders for capital goods are also likely to turn down quickly; purchases of some capital goods will turn down at the same time, while others will turn down with a lag. *Production* of inventories will also turn down, but because *sales* have also weakened, inventory investment may rise for a quarter or two before turning down sharply.

Thus as a general rule, overall real GDP starts to decline two to three quarters after significant tightening of monetary policy. That is slightly longer than the initial impact on interest-sensitive sectors of the economy because changes in production generally lag changes in sales. Firms usually do not cut back on their production schedules until sales have already weakened for a few months. As a result, the initial downturn in housing and consumer durables is usually offset by a rise in inventory investment. A recession generally does not get underway until both production and sales have headed down. Indeed, if production does not decline, there is a mid-cycle correction but no actual recession.

If the upper turning point has been caused by shrinking profit margins and excess capacity, the downturn is more likely to originate in a decline in new orders for capital goods, which is then translated into a decline in capital spending over the next several quarters. If interest rates have not risen and credit has not been restricted, housing and consumer durables may not turn down at all. Generally, however, there will be a large decline in inventory investment in both cases.

The Lower Turning Point

In the US economy, post-WWII business cycle expansions have varied greatly in length, ranging from 12 to 120 months. However, recessions have all been fairly short, ranging from 6 to 16 months, with most recessions lasting about 10 months.

The determination of the lower turning point is usually straightforward. It takes the Fed, as well as private sector economists, about three months to recognize that the economy is in fact in recession. When that happens, the Fed eases; or even if it does not, market rates will start to decline. It usually takes two to three quarters for lower rates to start stimulating the economy; so if the downturn has been preceded by monetary tightening which is then reversed, housing is the first sector to improve, followed closely by a rise in purchases of consumer durables. Also, inventory stocks have usually been reduced to levels compatible with the lower level of sales in less than a year, so the decline in inventory investment comes to a halt. As a result, the lower turning point usually occurs about 10 months after the recession has started.

If that is the case, why would any recession *not* last about 10 months?

1. In 1980, the credit controls were terminated and consumers responded much more quickly than they do to changes in interest rates, so the recession lasted only 6 months. Since authority for such a move has lapsed, that will not occur again.

2. The 16-month cycles for the 1973–4 and 1981–2 recessions both occurred because the Fed initially eased, but then tightened again when it saw signs that inflation had not been conquered.

In the 1973–4 recession, the Fed was as confused as anyone else about the economic impact of the oil shock. It first eased when energy prices surged, then had to tighten later, thereby postponing the recovery for an extra six months. In 1981–2, the Fed initially eased when the recession started, but it then raised rates in early 1982 even though the economy was in the depths of the recession because of continuing concerns about higher inflation, hence again postponing the recovery for an extra six months. Except for those two cases, all post-WWII recessions in the US have indeed ended in no more than 10 months.

Since the Great Depression, the Fed has always been able to jump-start the economy by easing. However, that does not guarantee that the resulting expansion phase will be robust or lengthy; that depends on fiscal policy, technology, and other exogenous shocks.

15.5   The role of exogenous shocks in the business cycle

This section examines the impact of exogenous shocks on the economy, which means changes that are not policy driven; for example, a restriction in credit availability would be considered another variant of tighter monetary policy. The most common type of exogenous shock over the past 30 years has been the change in energy prices; wars are another major example of exogenous shocks. Technological shocks are important but are considered separately in the next section.

The four major types of exogenous shocks are wars; commodity price fluctuations or shortages, mainly in agriculture or energy; international shocks, including major currency devaluations and flight of foreign capital; and political shocks, including unrest or revolution or, on a somewhat smaller scale, major strikes.

Wars

By their very nature, wars are unproductive in the economic sense. Occasionally one might argue that military developments, such as the use of atomic power, have beneficial peacetime uses, but in general the building of even more high-powered bombs which can then be dropped on enemy territory is not the sort of activity that boosts long-term productivity.

Wars can affect the economy both ways. The increase in military expenditures during World War II, the Korean War, and the Vietnam War boosted output and reduced the unemployment rate below its full-employment level; when hostilities ceased or expenditures were reduced, brief recessions followed. After the first two of these wars, shortages of consumer and producer durables during the war led to pent-up demand and economic booms following brief recessions. After the Vietnam and Persian Gulf Wars, though, the initial phases of the recoveries were unusually sluggish, due in part to a downward shift in consumer and business sentiment and in the marginal productivity of capital. In other countries, devastation during wartime can lead to a very rapid growth rate after the war ends if foreign capital is available, but can also lead to an extended period of stagnation because of insufficient saving and investment. For example, the Vietnamese economy certainly did not surge after its long war ended. Whichever pattern occurs, there is little doubt that the beginning and ending of wars have a major exogenous impact on real output and employment.

Energy Shocks

It is often thought that each of the four recessions from 1973 through 1991 was caused in part by large increases in energy prices. The standard argument states that these price increases reduce real disposable income, and since the short-run price elasticity of energy goods and services is very low, spending on gasoline and heating bills rose substantially, reducing purchases of other goods and services.

However, this argument is incomplete because it fails to consider where the extra money goes; it doesn't just disappear. If the price of energy rises from, say, $15 to $30/bbl, and the US economy uses about 6.7 billion barrels of oil per year, someone ends up with that extra $100 billion. If the US produced all the oil it used, or if it were a net exporter of oil – as was once the case – an increase in oil prices would boost the economy, as is the case in Saudi Arabia or Mexico today. Because the US economy now imports more than half its oil, the overall economic effect of higher energy prices is negative. Since Europe and Japan import almost all their oil, the contractionary impact there is even greater.

To a certain extent, OPEC nations spend some of the money they receive on US goods and services, so the rise in exports partially offsets the increase in imports. However, the net impact is to redistribute money from oil-consuming nations to oil-exporting nations.

If domestic oil producers get the money, some goes to higher taxes, some goes to more investment in oil drilling, and some goes to "greedy oil barons" who reportedly buy mink-lined Cadillac convertibles with air conditioning, or whatever else they allegedly do with their money. While that may be viewed as "unfair" by Massachusetts politicians, it still stimulates aggregate demand.[11] However, much of that increased income is taxed away – especially if excess profits taxes are enacted – so there is usually a net drain on domestic aggregate demand. Even that need not be the case if the revenues from the excess profits taxes are used to subsidize gasoline and heating oil bills in the Northeast and Midwest regions of the US.

Other factors are also involved. The energy shocks of 1973 and 1979 were accompanied by actual shortages, so production and consumption were reduced by more than the impact of higher prices. Also, to the extent that interest rates rise and the Fed tightened monetary policy, both consumption and investment declined further.

Thus higher oil prices often cause recessions not so much because of the decline in aggregate demand but because they boost inflation and are often followed by a substantial rise in interest rates. Any such situation invariably puts the Fed in a quandary. If it tightens now, a mild recession occurs soon; if it does not tighten now, a more severe recession occurs later. As seen in the following case study, though, if inflation does not rise very much, the negative impact of higher oil prices is much milder.

CASE STUDY 15.1　THE EFFECT OF FLUCTUATIONS IN OIL PRICES ON THE ECONOMY

In general we would expect higher oil prices to reduce aggregate demand, and would also expect them to have some spillover effect into the core rate, both because prices of energy-intensive goods and services (such as transportation) would rise and because labor would demand higher wages, hence boosting unit labor costs and prices. After oil prices leveled off or declined, the rate of core inflation would decline for the same reasons.

If the only effect of higher oil prices on aggregate demand is to reduce real disposable income, growth would then return to its previous levels once oil prices stabilized or declined. If, on the other hand, there were ripple effects – or if real interest rates rose – demand could remain weak in the following years. Of course changes in demand might also be influenced by factors other than the energy shock.

The figures in table 15.4 show that each successive energy shock had relatively less impact on the rate of real growth and the rate of inflation excluding energy prices; by 2000, there is very little effect. There are two reasons for this declining progression. First, the energy coefficient – the amount of energy used per dollar of real GDP – has fallen by almost half since 1973. Second, energy-using firms, such as airlines, have become proficient in hedging against major fluctuations in oil prices; for example, buying additional contracts when it falls to $10/bbl, and selling contracts when it rises above $30/bbl.

The impact on real growth appears to be mixed. We can calculate an "oil multiplier" by taking the change in real GDP as the "before" minus the "after" column and compare it with the change in oil prices as a percentage of GDP. For the first shock, the multiplier is 8.6/3.0, or almost 3. For the second and third shocks, the multiplier is about 1, which means there was very little ripple effect. In 2001, however, the multiplier apparently rises back above 3, increasing to 3.9/1.1.

continued

CASE STUDY 15.1 (*continued*)

Table 15.4 Changes in inflation and real growth when energy prices rose rapidly

Date	Oil prices 1st–2nd date	Change (%)	1 year later	Oil change as % of GDP	Change in infl rate			Change in real GDP		
					Before	During	After	Before	During	After
73.2–74.1	3.56–10.11	184	11.16	3.0	5.5	8.4	11.0	6.2	0.9	−2.4
79.2–81.1	15.64–36.54	109	33.05	4.5	9.7	10.9	8.2	2.8	1.7	−2.2
90.2–90.4	16.14–29.92	85	19.15	1.4	4.6	5.3	4.0	2.6	−0.9	1.2
99.1–00.1	11.03–27.15	146	24.50	1.1	2.2	2.2	2.7	4.4	2.8	0.5

Sources: Oil prices, Energy Information Administration website; inflation, BLS website; GDP, BEA website. Prices are West Texas posted prices for the first cycle, and the blended price of domestic and imported oil for the remaining three cycles. All prices are dollars/barrel. "Before" refers to the annual rate change in the four quarters before oil prices started rising, and "after" refers to the change in the four quarters after they stopped rising. The column "oil change as % of GDP" is equal to the number of barrels of oil used per year times the price change in $/bbl, divided by current dollar GDP for that year. The inflation rate shown here is the CPI excluding energy prices. All percentage changes are at annual rates.

However, rise in oil prices in 2000 had only a small impact on the economy; the high-tech recession occurred independently of the rise in oil prices. Nonetheless, it does seem likely that major swings in oil prices still have a multiplier of approximately 1. That is probably not enough to start a recession in the future, but it could contribute to a downturn caused by other factors.

International Shocks

If the economy of one of America's major trading partners goes into recession, US exports will decline. It is also possible that due to some disturbance abroad, other countries cannot ship as many goods, causing a large temporary increase in US exports (notably the Suez crisis in 1956–7). When exports return to normal, the drop may help to cause a recession, especially if the economy is already starting to weaken for other reasons.

An unusually clear case occurred in 1995, when the Mexican economy collapsed and suffered the biggest decline since the 1930s; this episode was discussed in the previous chapter. As a result, US exports to Mexico, which had been rising at about 20% per year, stagnated. Higher interest rates also played a major role in reducing real growth in the US; together, those factors reduced the growth rate to 1% in the first half of 1995. As it turned out, the widening of the trade deficit and weaker growth caused the dollar to decline about 10%, which boosted exports in the second half of 1995. Also, as soon as the Fed noticed that real growth was declining, it quickly reduced the funds rate.

International shocks are much more important to other countries. As discussed in chapter 14, devaluations caused recessions in Mexico in 1995, the former growth tigers of east Asia in 1998, Brazil in 1999, and Argentina in 2002. Similarly, a benign shock, such as the return of the British pound to its equilibrium value in late 1992, caused a boom to start the next year. For the US, though, the effects of change in the value of the dollar are somewhat ambiguous. An overvalued dollar clearly hurts the manufacturing sector, and an undervalued dollar helps it. However, a stronger dollar also leads to lower inflation, higher productivity, and an inflow of foreign capital that reduces interest rates and boosts stock prices, ceteris paribus. Historically there has been no significant correlation between changes in the value of the dollar and changes in the real growth rate.

Also, as discussed in section 15.9, global transmission of business cycles is still alive and well, given that a major decline in US imports causes much weaker growth abroad, so a decline in US imports will generally lead to a decline in US exports the following year. This is generally a one-way street: recessions in Europe or Japan that are not caused by previous weakness in the US generally do not have much impact.

The collapse of the international economy was one of the major factors leading to the Great Depression of the 1930s, but recent international exogenous developments are generally not powerful enough to cause actual recessions in the US, providing that monetary policy reacts quickly to offset any major loss in demand. This conclusion was strengthened by the minor impact of the southeast Asian crisis on the US economy in 1998, when the positive impact of lower inflation and lower interest rates more than offset the negative impact of lower exports.

Major Strikes

While strikes have played a role in reducing GDP during various downturns that were already underway for other reasons, they have never been the cause of recessions on their own. The 1949 recession was deepened and lengthened by a severe coal strike, but the downturn was already underway. The 1970 recession was well underway before it was prolonged by a major auto strike.

The effect of the 1959 steel strike was somewhat different. The strike lasted so long that inventories fell to unusually low levels, causing a major buildup in inventory investment in the months following the strike. When that buildup ended, real GDP headed into a mild recession, partly because purchasing power of consumers had been weakened during the strike. That was not the only reason for the recession: tight monetary policies were in effect for much of 1960, and the Federal government ran a substantial full-employment surplus. Also, many businesses never really recovered from the fairly severe 1958 recession, the first major downturn in 20 years, and hence had cut back on their capital spending plans.

Today, major strikes are not enough to cause real GDP to decline in the US. GDP is currently about $10 trillion, so a 1% drop would be equal to $100 billion at annual rates, or $25 billion per quarter. Suppose a major strike caused 500,000 employees to quit working for an entire quarter, and suppose they earned an average of $16 per hour, or $8,000 per quarter. That would be a drop of only $4 billion in personal income for the quarter; even with a multiplier of 2, that would be only $8 billion, or less than $\frac{1}{3}$% of total GDP. A change of that magnitude would hardly show up as rounding error. It now takes more than a major strike to cause a recession in the US economy – unless that strike were to lead to major supply interruptions in other sectors, such as if the entire transportation network were shut down.

As the economy becomes larger and more diversified, it takes an increasingly bigger shock in any one sector to cause an actual recession. Strikes have not played a major role in recessions since 1970, and are unlikely to do so in the future.

15.6   The role of technology in the business cycle

In the 1970s and early 1980s, a group of economists known as the new classical economists attacked much of the received wisdom of the previous three decades.[12] We have already discussed the concepts of rational expectations, the collapse of the Phillips curve, and the end of using fine tuning as a method of controlling the economy. Another development by this school is known as *real business cycle* (RBC) theory, which states that the majority of business cycle fluctuations are caused by exogenous shocks and changes in technology, rather than by switches in monetary and fiscal policy.[13] Indeed, the name itself implies that shocks that initiate business cycles are due to "real" instead of "monetary" factors.

The approach of the RBC school depends heavily on expectations, as it was developed by the economists most prominently identified with rational expectations. The approach we use, while accepting the importance of real as opposed to monetary shocks, and the role of propagation as well as impulse – another point stressed by the RBC school – nonetheless relates these contributions to those provided by business cycle theorists of the early twentieth century, and places their contributions in the overall context of the importance of the relationship between saving and investment. Hence it blends old and new approaches to business cycle theory.

As already noted, Wicksell compared the cost of capital with the marginal productivity of capital (MPK): when the MPK was greater than the cost of capital, investment rose at above-average rates, causing a boom, and when it was less than the cost of capital, investment rose at below-average rates, causing a slump.

Assume that a substantial technological innovation occurs early in the expansion phase of the cycle, so the MPK rises significantly. However, actual investment does not yet exceed actual saving for two reasons. First, many of the investment goods that have been ordered have not yet been delivered (think how long it took the internet to catch on with the general public). Second, profit margins are usually high at this phase of the cycle, boosting business saving. Hence interest rates remain low. Also, high profit margins boost stock prices, reducing the cost of equity capital.

After a while, investment plans are realized and the capital goods are delivered. Under ordinary circumstances, the economy reaches full employment, and labor compensation starts to accelerate, hence retarding the growth in profits and diminishing the saving rate. At the same time, the new investment coming on stream boosts total capacity, which lowers the rate of capacity utilization, and also diminishes profit margins. As a result of all these factors, ex ante investment now exceeds domestic saving. Ordinarily that would boost interest rates, which would reduce aggregate demand further.

However, there is no certainty that the cost of capital will rise. A booming stock market may keep the cost of equity capital low, and may attract more foreign capital, hence bridging the gap between ex ante investment and domestic saving. As a result, the investment boom could continue for several more years.

Eventually, though, the combination of excess capacity and low profit margins reduces the MPK below the cost of capital, even if interest rates have not risen. Lower profits cause stock prices to decline, raising the cost of equity capital. The investment boom thus comes to an end. Furthermore, the bigger the technological shock, the more likely that substantial excess capacity has been generated and the slump will be prolonged. Indeed, the initial phases of the following expansion may be sluggish even if the actual recession ends quickly.

That general pattern explains why the US economy failed to recover rapidly after the recessions of 1958, 1970, 1990, and 2001, all of which followed periods of extended investment booms. The economy did rebound sharply back after the 1981–2 recession, but during the 1970s, productivity growth had become been quite sluggish and there was no technology boom, and hence only moderate amounts of excess capacity.

The cost of capital – which includes the real interest rate, the price/earnings ratio for equities, and the net effective tax rate on corporate income – rises when an increase in inflation boosts real interest rates. That might occur because the central bank tightened to reduce inflationary expectations, but in the US there were many recessions before the Federal Reserve System began operations in 1913. Indeed, the main reason for its formation was to provide adequate credit during times of financial distress and hence reduce cyclical fluctuations. In the absence of a central bank, interest rates rise when the ex ante demand for investment exceeds the ex ante supply of saving.

Wicksell focused primarily on the rate of interest, but today the cost of equity capital is also important. When the stock market rises to an unsustainable price/earnings (P/E) ratio, that boosts investment enough that excess capacity soon appears. That is what happened to Japan in the late 1980s, and the US in the late 1990s. In both cases, an artificially low cost of equity capital – the result of an artificially high stock market – boosted investment to the point where the resultant excess capacity eventually caused capital spending to decline. That produced a recession even though interest rates hardly rose, fiscal policy did not turn contractionary, and no major exogenous shocks reduced aggregate demand.

Thus when investment rises too fast, it eventually turns down and causes a recession. One could argue that the job of the monetary and fiscal authorities is to try and keep the cost of capital near its equilibrium value, thus balancing ex ante investment and saving. The authorities have apparently learned from past mistakes, since recessions in the US have become milder and less frequent. Nonetheless, when the stock market gets out of hand because of what Alan Greenspan called "irrational exuberance," a recession will follow even if the Fed does not raise interest rates very much. One of the factors leading to the 2001 recession is now described in the following case study.

CASE STUDY 15.2   THE Y2K "CRISIS" BEFORE THE HIGH-TECH RECESSION OF 2001

The importance of technological change as a major cause of the business cycle was a major contribution of real business cycle theory in the 1980s. At the time this theory was not widely accepted, but it fits the facts of the 1990s much better than the monetary-based theories that dominated business cycle discussion during the previous two decades.

In the summer of 1998, when the economy was already booming and the ratio of investment to GDP was at unusually high levels, Long-Term Capital Management (LTCM) failed, and the Russian ruble was devalued. The Fed believed it was necessary to flood the banking system with liquidity to prevent a massive financial meltdown. As a result, it not only cut the Federal funds rate from $5\frac{1}{2}$% to $4\frac{3}{4}$% at a time when the economy was near full employment, but it boosted growth in the M2 money supply to an annual rate of almost 12% during the fourth quarter of 1998.

Perhaps if the Fed had not acted, the entire US banking system would have been in grave danger. Regardless of whether that was actually the case, though, many investors thought the Fed overreacted. In particular, they interpreted that easing as a message that the Fed was primarily interested in keeping the boom alive indefinitely, and would not raise interest rates even if the economy did move to overfull employment. There was a sense of diminished moral hazard, which means some investors thought the Fed would bail them out no matter what happened. That was one of the factors boosting stock prices – especially in the high-tech sector – to unsustainably high levels.

The stock market recovered quickly from the scare of the LTCM bankruptcy and devaluation of the Russian ruble, but actually remained within a normal range in the sense that the increase in the S&P 500 from July 1998 to October 1999 was a fairly modest 8%. Then it heated up to unsustainable levels.

Students of the future may look back in disbelief and wonder what all the Y2K (Year 2000) fuss was all about – after all, nothing happened. At the time, though, this

continued

CASE STUDY 15.2 (*continued*)

was another example of the accurate cliché that the American public likes nothing better than a good scare story. According to a few apparently well-meaning but totally bemused economists, the inability of computers to record information properly starting on January 1, 2000, would bring the economy to at least a temporary halt. In particular, it was rumored that ATM machines would not work, and airlines would not be able to fly safely. Some economists even predicted a 70% probability of a "major" recession starting in early 2000, although they were seldom heard from afterwards.

The issue here was not whether Y2K was a serious problem; it was. If sufficient steps had not been taken, major sectors of the economy would have indeed ground to a halt. Our point is that since the dimensions of the problem were well known in advance, it was possible to prepare adequately for the switchover. Claims that it was "unsolvable" were willful nonsense.

As someone once said, it is difficult to impart accurate information to the public when so many people believe that God is dead but Elvis is still alive. We would not even mention this particular sequence of events if it had not affected the economy significantly. In particular, the following events occurred.

1. Because of concerns that the transportation networks would be shut down, firms temporarily increased inventory stocks above normal levels.
2. Many firms stepped up their purchases of new computerized equipment to make sure it would be "Y2K" compatible, causing a temporary bulge in investment, profits of high-tech firms, and their stock prices.
3. The Fed, concerned that people would mob the ATM machines in late 1999, substantially boosted the M1 measure of the money supply. Whereas M1 had been constant at $1,097 billion from January through October 1999, it zoomed to $1,125 billion by December. The Fed pumped almost $30 billion in cash into the banking system to insure there would be no "runs" on the ATM machines.

Let's look at what happened to the key components of real GDP during this period. Inventory investment zoomed from $48 to $92 billion in 1999.4; since there was no weakness anywhere else in the economy, that boosted the real growth rate to 7.1%. The next quarter, inventory investment dropped back to $45 billion because of the excess stocks that had been accumulated the previous quarter. However, the surge in Y2K-compatible equipment delivered that quarter boosted purchases of high-tech equipment from $526 to $561 billion. Meanwhile, the extra cash the Fed had dumped into the system caused the stock market to take off like a rocket; it also boosted consumer spending. Thus the following quarter – in 2000.2 – firms rebuilt their suddenly depleted inventory stocks, boosting inventory investment from $45 to $91 billion. That boosted the overall real growth rate from 2.6% to 4.8%, but

continued

CASE STUDY 15.2 (*continued*)

the rest of the economy started to slow down, as indicated by the beginning of the bear market in stock prices, and the sluggish increase in final sales of only 2.8%.

In the third quarter, sales slumped further, real GDP rose only 0.6%, and the recession was already underway in the manufacturing sector. Purchases of high-tech equipment, which had been stepped up because of the concern about Y2K, diminished in scope, which helped burst the high-tech stock market bubble. The Fed, however, perhaps smarting from earlier criticism that it had provided unneeded liquidity to the economy, failed to ease in the second half of that year; some said it did not want to be accused of playing politics and cutting interest rates right before the presidential election. In any case, most economists now think the Fed erred by not easing in the second half of 2000.

Whether legitimate or not, concerns about Y2K temporarily boosted inventory investment and capital spending above normal levels. When combined with the Fed stance following the collapse of Long-Term Capital Management, the stock market rose to unsustainable levels. When inventory investment, capital spending, and stock prices then returned to normal levels, the resulting decline was enough to cause a modest recession. This is a clear example of how exogenous shocks that are related to each other can lead to business cycle fluctuations. While overinvestment and excess capacity were the major factors leading to the 2001 slowdown, the unnecessary fluctuations caused by the Y2K scare helped tip the growth rate into the recession column.

15.7   The role of fiscal policy in the business cycle

Fiscal policy is primarily responsible for determining the long-term rate of growth, not cyclical fluctuations. Nonetheless, major changes in the exogenous elements of fiscal policy, such as wars, clearly have a major influence on the business cycle; several downturns have followed reductions in military expenditures. In addition, discretionary fiscal policy has often been used to try and dampen booms and recessions. Finally, automatic stabilizers are an important reason why post-WWII cycles are shorter and milder. Hence fiscal policy merits a separate section in the business cycle chapter.

Automatic stabilizers, which are discussed in more detail in chapter 18, are useful in reducing the severity of recessions. If the full-employment budget remains in balance, every 1% decline in the growth rate boosts the deficit ratio by about $\frac{1}{2}$% because of lower tax receipts and higher transfer payments. Thus, for example, a switch from a 3% increase in real GDP to a 1% decline, which would represent a typical recession, would boost the deficit ratio by 2%, or more than $200 billion at 2002 levels of GDP. That is necessary and desirable; an attempt to balance the budget during all phases of the business cycle would intensify the swings in real output.

Investment always declines sharply in recessions; by definition, that must be balanced by an equal decline in saving. That could occur in one of several ways. The most sensible, and in fact what is now the most widely followed method, is for government saving to decrease sharply, which is the same thing as saying the deficit increases. Also, imports usually shrink when domestic income declines, which reduces foreign saving. Other methods could consist of reducing corporate profits sharply, hence minimizing corporate saving, or cutting personal income so much that consumers became poor and could not afford to save. Obviously these latter two methods, if tried, would magnify and prolong the downturn.

In the 2001 recession, the Federal government budget position swung from a $236 billion surplus in FY 2000 to a $158 billion deficit in FY 2002, a swing of over 4% of GDP. Admittedly, that swing was larger than usual, in spite of the mild nature of the recession, because of the massive decline in capital gains taxes and the Bush tax cut; also, investment dropped more than usual because of the high-tech collapse. Ordinarily, every 1% drop in real GDP would reduce taxes by about 1.5% and boost spending by about 1%. Since the Federal government budget is roughly 20% of GDP, that means a 1% drop in real output usually generates about a $\frac{1}{2}$% rise in the deficit ratio. As noted above, in a mild recession, the growth rate typically falls from 3% to −1%, or a 4% swing, which means the deficit ratio would increase by 2%. Typically the ratio of investment to GDP also falls about 2% in a mild recession, so that decline is fully offset by the drop in government saving. In the post-WWII era, recessions generally do not intensify from secondary effects that would be necessary to equilibrate investment and saving. In that sense, automatic stabilizers are quite important.

Discretionary stabilizers are another matter. Case study 15.3 describes in more detail how the imposition of a 10% surtax on personal and corporate income in mid-1968 had unintended results. Instead of keeping the expansion alive and reducing inflation, it boosted inflation and brought the recovery to an end.

In other discretionary fiscal policy moves, an $8 billion personal income tax rebate was distributed during the second quarter of 1975, which would be roughly equivalent to a $45 billion rate in 2002 as a percentage of personal income. The recession had already ended by the time the 1975 rebate checks were distributed, which is fairly typical of the time lag involved. The economy did grow rapidly for a year, but then stalled out again in mid-1976, so it appears the impact was only temporary. The advancement of the Bush tax cut to the summer of 2001, which had much the same impact as a rebate, probably boosted consumer spending in spite of the temporary hiatus caused by 9/11; again, though, the economy quickly slowed down again once the impact of those tax cut checks had worn off.

The long-term growth rate did improve after the 20% income tax cut in 1964–5 and the 25% income tax cut in 1981–3. In the case of the Kennedy-Johnson tax cut, the economy was already doing well; the Reagan tax cut helped pull the economy out of recession. However, both these tax cuts were designed to reduce high marginal rates as well as cut overall tax receipts, so they were more directly aimed at the long-term growth rate of the economy rather than short-term timing effects.

From the early 1960s to the mid-1980s, the rate of investment tax credit and amount of accelerated depreciation were often changed to try and stimulate or reduce the rate of economic growth. Yet for the most part, these changes were counterproductive. The institution of the investment tax credit in 1962 did not really boost investment until 1964, when the rate of capacity utilization had risen to the point where investment probably would have increased anyhow. The suspension of the tax credit in 1969 was one of the reasons a recession started later that year. The expansion of the tax credit in 1975 did not immediately stimulate investment, since it occurred at the end of the recession and the capacity utilization rate was low. The permanent cancellation of the tax credit in 1986 was part of a move to reduce marginal tax rates and was not designed to affect the short-term timing of the business cycle; the investment ratio did decline for a while, but then rose sharply during the 1990s.

In late 2001, Congress passed a bill permitting 30% "bonus" depreciation to be taken on all capital equipment ordered during the next three years. However, that also failed to stimulate capital spending in the following year.

The evidence on the success of changes in fiscal policy designed to influence short-term changes in the growth rate is not conclusive, but this review suggests these methods have not been very effective. The recoveries in 1975 and 1983 were sharper than usual, but the previous recessions had been deeper than usual. The 2001 tax cut appears to have stimulated the economy in early 2002, but then the effect quickly dissipated. Also, during all three of those recessions – 1974, 1982, and 2001 – the Fed reduced short-term interest rates substantially. In the case of the temporary tax cuts or rebates, most of the extra money appears to have been saved, so it did not boost GDP very much. The personal saving rate fell during the years of the Reagan tax cut, so it may have had a larger impact, but that was a long-term effect unrelated to the duration of the recession or the initial period of recovery.

On balance, we conclude that these discretionary tax cuts helped get the economy moving again, but not very much. In terms of their impact on business cycles, automatic stabilizers have been much more important than discretionary stabilizers. Considering the lags involved, the political log-rolling that accompanies any fiscal stimulus bill, and the resultant increase in the deficit, it would appear that short-term discretionary changes in fiscal policy do not affect economic performance except in the very short run.

CASE STUDY 15.3   THE FAILURE OF THE 1968 TAX SURCHARGE

In the mid-1960s, many economic commentators thought the US economy was heading into an era of unending prosperity. Real GDP was rising at an average of

continued

CASE STUDY 15.3 (*continued*)

almost 6% per year, yet the inflation rate remained under 2%. In 1966, however, the rapid increase in defense expenditures for the Vietnam War caused the inflation rate to rise to almost 4%. The Fed alertly stepped on the brakes, boosting interest rates and temporarily bringing real growth to a halt.

Somewhat perturbed by the slowdown in the growth rate, and prominently and publicly castigated by Lyndon Johnson, Fed Chairman William McChesney Martin quickly shifted gears. The Fed quickly eased, and both real growth and inflation started to rise again. By that time the increase in defense expenditures had generated a substantial budget deficit, but the Fed was apparently unwilling to raise interest rates enough to finance that deficit, perhaps fearing that would end the expansion, or perhaps bowing to political pressure.[14]

After much debate, Congress and the Fed finally agreed on a joint solution: a temporary 10% surcharge on personal and corporate income taxes would be put into place in mid-1968, and as a quid pro quo, the Fed would agree to hold the funds rate steady at 6% and boost growth in the money supply. The argument by government economists at the time was that the tax increase would serve as a non-inflationary way to pay for the war, while monetary easing would keep the economy from stalling out. While this agreement was being hammered out, real GDP growth zoomed to an exceptionally rapid 7.5% annual rate during the first half of 1968.

The tax surcharge was put into place, and the Fed carried out its part of the bargain: it held the funds rate at 6%, and boosted growth in M2 from 6% to 9%. However, the impact on the economy was precisely the opposite of what Washington economists expected.[15] The real growth rate sharply declined to 1%, and the rate of inflation rose from 4% to 6.3%. Eventually the Fed was forced to raise the funds rate and reduce the growth in the money supply, plunging the economy into its first recession in almost ten years by the end of 1969.

Perhaps it is easy enough in retrospect to point out that a shift to monetary ease at a period of rapid growth and overfull employment sharply boosted inflationary expectations, making it almost inevitable that the Fed would have to reverse course and tighten, causing a recession to occur shortly thereafter. Whether that is true or not, it seems clear enough that the Fed was forced to bow to political pressure: after almost bringing the economy to a halt in mid-1967, it did not tighten again until inflation was clearly spiraling out of control. Hence this program was actually a joint failure of monetary and fiscal policies. We have, however, listed it in the fiscal policy section because the surcharge was the principal mistake; without that bill, the Fed would not have been forced to hold interest rates constant and increase the growth in the money supply. Additional monetary policy errors of the 1970s are discussed in the next section.

15.8 The role of monetary policy in the business cycle

In a world without shocks, the principal goal of the monetary authorities would be to keep the real rate of interest at a level equal to the MPK. In the real world, though, several practical difficulties are immediately apparent. First, measuring the MPK is not a simple task. Second, to the extent that shocks affect the rate of inflation, the Fed must adjust nominal rates accordingly. Third, the Fed must also take expectations into account, and the perception by investors that the Fed is not vigilant enough about fighting inflation will require the monetary authorities to boost interest rates above equilibrium levels for a while. Fourth, the Fed may have to insure adequate liquidity at times of financial unrest. Fifth, large budget deficits may require the Fed to boost interest rates above equilibrium levels in order to insure that investors will purchase the additional Treasury securities.

In a world of shocks, then, the monetary authorities cannot reasonably be expected to keep interest rates at their equilibrium levels all the time. Nonetheless, that does not explain why interest rates have sometimes diverged from equilibrium for several consecutive years. Admittedly we do not know the precise value of the MPK, but as a first approximation it is not unreasonable to assume it is about the same as the growth rate in productivity. Figure 15.1 compares the real Federal funds rate with productivity growth in the post-WWII period.

During the Korean War years, the Fed was prohibited from raising interest rates, so that period can be disregarded. However, it appears that the real Fed funds rate was held far under its equilibrium value in the mid-1960s and the mid-1970s.

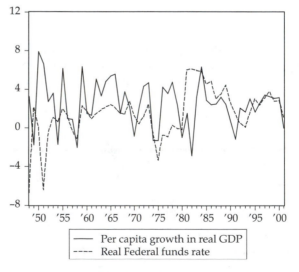

Figure 15.1 Growth rate in real per capita GDP and the real Federal funds rate (Treasury bill rate before 1955)

Both of those periods were followed by a substantial rise in inflation, and eventual recessions. Based on our analysis, it seems clear enough that the Fed should have raised the funds rate during those periods, hence forestalling higher inflation followed by an economic downturn.

This figure also suggests that the Federal funds rate was too high during the 1980s. However, that probably reflected the unusually large deficits that occurred during the Reagan and Bush Administrations. As the deficit diminished, the gap between the real funds rate and productivity growth narrowed. This comparison suggests Greenspan did a very credible job of holding the funds rate near its equilibrium value during the 1990s; the 2001 recession, which was largely caused by the stock market bubble, probably could not have been avoided, although some economists think that the Fed easing in 1998 and the excess liquidity injected into the economy in late 1999 were significant mistakes.

CASE STUDY 15.4   MONETARY POLICY ERRORS OF THE 1970S

It is sometimes claimed that the Fed cannot set interest rates by fiat, and hence cannot be accused of contributing materially to business cycle fluctuations. That is not entirely true, though, because the Fed can move the Federal funds rate far away from its equilibrium value for extended periods of time. Even more to the point, the Fed could set money supply growth by fiat in the period before banking deregulation in 1982. Thus in 1972 and 1979, Fed Chairmen Arthur F. Burns and G. William Miller bowed to political pressure and permitted the money supply to grow much faster than was commensurate with non-inflationary policy. As a result, inflation zoomed the next year, and the economy went into recession shortly thereafter.

During the first half of 1970, the growth rate in M2 had declined to 2%. As soon as the recession got underway, that pattern was abruptly reversed, and by the end of 1971, M2 was rising at a 14% annual rate. Nonetheless, the recovery in 1971 was unusually sluggish. As already described, Nixon imposed price controls on August 15, 1971,[16] devalued the dollar, instituted an expansionary fiscal program – and demanded that the Fed keep interest rates low. The increase in inflation that would have otherwise occurred during 1972 was suppressed by wage and price controls, but inflation then started to rise sharply during 1973 even though controls remained in place, and then burst into flame in 1974, rising to 12%. Eventually Burns reduced growth in the money supply and boosted the Federal funds rate to 13%, which intensified the recession. While the real growth rate would have diminished because of the first energy crisis in any case, the inaccurate policies of the Fed – including the support for controls by the Chairman – made the downturn much more severe.

continued

CASE STUDY 15.4 (*continued*)

Burns was reappointed Fed Chairman in 1974, but when his four-year term as Chairman ended in 1978, he was not reappointed by Jimmy Carter – ironically, because his monetary policy was viewed as too restrictive by the economists who advised Carter. In his place, G. William Miller was appointed to the post as Fed Chairman. In his first year, Miller did not make any unusual moves in either direction.

In early 1979, however, the economy started to slow down, and Miller decided he did not want a recession to start on his watch. As a result, he boosted money supply (M2) growth from $6\frac{1}{2}$% to $9\frac{1}{2}$%. That may not seem like a very large swing relative to the fluctuations earlier in the decade, but that increase was accompanied by a statement from Miller to the effect that he did not want Jimmy Carter to run for reelection in a recession year, and was boosting the growth in the money supply now to boost the real growth rate two to three quarters later – i.e., during the 1980 election campaign.

This time, investors did not wait so long to react, possibly because they trusted Carter less than Nixon. In any case, the *core* inflation rate (excluding food and energy) zoomed from 9% to 13%. Soon it became clear that Miller would have to be replaced. Carter first asked David Rockefeller, who declined the position but recommended Paul Volcker. Shortly after taking over at the Fed, Volcker instituted what became known as the monetary version of the "Saturday night massacre," boosting the Federal funds rate by an unprecedented 3%. Because inflationary expectations had become so thoroughly imbedded in the minds of investors, though, the inflation rate did not budge until Volcker also imposed credit controls. The economy went into a very brief recession in 1980, recovered for a year, and then plunged into a more prolonged downturn in 1981–2. It is clear that the mistakes made by Burns and Miller during the 1970s were the principal reason that real GDP was actually lower at the end of 1982 than it had been in 1979.3, before Volcker was appointed Fed Chairman.

MANAGER'S BRIEFCASE: ANTICIPATING THE NEXT RECESSION

Since the US economy just emerged from a recession in early 2002, it is unlikely that another downturn will occur in the near future. Nonetheless, it is useful to have a brief checklist that will help to identify upcoming cyclical patterns – and will also help in ignoring false signals.

1. An increase in the *real* rate of interest will slow down the economy. If interest rates rise only the same amount as the rate of inflation, a significant decline in the growth rate is unlikely. Also, a recession is likely to be preceded by a sharp narrowing, if not an actual inversion, of the yield spread.

continued

MANAGER'S BRIEFCASE (*continued*)

2. The availability of credit remains an important factor, although that has become more difficult to measure after banking deregulation. One should look at the average growth in the M2 money supply, business loans, and consumer credit. In general, a 1% change in the average growth rate of these variables will cause a $\frac{1}{4}$% to $\frac{1}{2}$% change in real GDP the following year.

3. Fluctuations in the stock market are important, but should not be overstated. Over the long run, the broad-based index of stock prices has risen about 8% per year. Relative to that growth rate, a 10% change will cause a $\frac{1}{2}$% change in the real growth rate the following year. Most of the negative impact is on capital spending rather than consumer spending.

4. Short-term changes in fiscal policy do not change the growth rate very much. A significant tax cut or increase in defense expenditures will boost real GDP with a short lag, but the impact will generally wear off after about one year. Continued deficits have an important impact on the long-term productivity growth rate, but a short-term change in the surplus or deficit will not affect the growth rate very much.

5. Fluctuations in the value of the dollar may have a very significant effect on your business if you are in a trade-sensitive manufacturing industry, but for the overall economy, there is not a very strong correlation between changes in the value of the dollar and the real growth rate. It is true, however, that a stronger dollar does reduce the ratio of manufacturing to total employment.

6. Higher inflation will generally reduce the growth rate even if real interest rates do not change. That is particularly true if food or energy prices rise sharply, since that then reduces the amount of disposable income consumers have to purchase discretionary goods and services. A 1% increase in the inflation rate tends to reduce real growth by 0.1% to 0.2%, ceteris paribus.

7. Don't overestimate the negative impact of exogenous shocks if there is no negative monetary response. As tragic as the terrorist attacks of 9/11 were, they only affected the economy momentarily. Similarly, major strikes or disruptions are generally not enough to derail the economy.

8. Offsetting impacts should always be taken into account. A major decline in stock prices that is accompanied by a sharp decline in interest rates will have a smaller negative impact on the economy than a similar decline in stock prices that is accompanied by stable or rising interest rates.

Taking all these factors into consideration, remember that recessions don't happen very often. They will invariably be preceded by a significant rise in the cost of capital, either through higher real interest rates or lower stock prices. A substantial rise in the inflation rate can also lead to a recession, although a downturn can still develop without any increase in inflation if the cost of capital rises. Exogenous shocks, international weakness, and an overvalued dollar are not likely to cause recessions unless accompanied by contractionary monetary conditions.

15.9   Global transmission of business cycles

From 1945 through 1970 the US economy went through six recessions, while most other major countries did not have any downturns at all. The cliché at the time was that when America sneezes, Europe says "Gesundheit." Accompanying this lack of cyclical activity was a certain smugness that the European way was better than the American. Later, certain political leaders suggested that the economic policies of Japan in the 1980s, and the growth tigers in the early 1990s, were superior to the American model. As it turned out, however, none of these areas have been able to avoid recessions in recent years. More to the point, when the US economy falls into recession one year, these countries are adversely affected the following year.

For a while, snide comments about the inability of US politicians and economists to manage their economy no longer seemed appropriate – although they did resurface in 2001 and 2002.

From the manager's viewpoint, the following questions are relevant. First, why is the rest of the world more recession-prone now than it was earlier? Second, to what extent will future US recessions be followed by downturns in the rest of the world? Third, to what extent will major countries outside the US suffer recessions that are not tied to fluctuations in US economic activity?

The first severe postwar US recession occurred in 1958. That year, real GNP (as it was then) in Japan rose 5.6%, down from 7.5% the previous year; the following year, it rose 8.9%. In Germany, GNP rose 3.2% in 1958, down from 5.6% in 1957; growth rebounded to 9.5% in 1959. The next serious US recession occurred in 1970, with a very sluggish recovery in 1971. Japanese GDP rose 5.3% in 1971, compared to 11.7% the year before and 9.5% the year after. For Germany, the comparable statistics are a 3.3% growth in 1971, compared to 5.9% in 1970 and 3.6% in 1972.

Averaging these figures shows that the real growth rate in Japan and Germany fell an average of 3.4% in years during or shortly after US recessions. Thus even in those earlier years, the global transmission effect of US-based recessions was significant. It was just that Europe and Japan were growing so rapidly then that a substantial slowdown still left growth rates in those countries at levels that appeared robust by US standards. However, growth in the rest of the world has since slowed down to the 3% to 4% range, so if the same marginal result occurs, those countries would be close to recession. To answer the first question, the impact of a US recession now is just about the same as it was earlier; the difference is the lower base rate of growth in the rest of the world.

The first energy shock hit Europe and Japan harder than the US because (a) they imported almost all their oil, and (b) OPEC nations spent a larger proportion of their additional oil revenues to purchase American goods than European or Japanese goods. However, since Japan switched from heavy industry to high-tech exports after the first energy shock, they were not as hard hit by successive energy crises.

In 2001, for the year, the growth rate dropped 3.5% in the US, falling from 3.8% to 0.3%. It also fell 2.9% in Canada, 2.1% in Japan, 2.4% in Germany, but only 1.1% in the UK. It fell 7.2% in Mexico and 3.0% in Brazil. Also, it fell 10.4% in Hong Kong, 7.9% in Taiwan, 5.8% in Korea, and 11.9% in Singapore. It would appear in the foreseeable future that a sharp decline in imports in the US economy, such as occurred in 2001, will cause recessions in most other countries of the world.

15.10 Could the Great Depression happen again?

For many years, the causes of the Great Depression remained a matter of dispute among economists. Milton Friedman claimed it was due to the decline in the money supply, Ben Bernanke identified the loss of credit as a major factor, Peter Temin thought high tariffs and the collapse of the European economy were a key reason, and supply-siders fingered the 1932 tax increase as a major factor.[17]

The stock market crash was the proximate reason for the downturn, but that alone would not have caused a major depression if not for errors by the Fed, a xenophobic Congress, the collapse of the European economy and foreign trade, and mistaken fiscal policy that cut spending and raised taxes during a depression. These policies all contributed to a massive loss of business confidence and virtually no net investment during the 1930s. Deflation wiped out the accumulated value of assets and cause massive bankruptcies. Consumers spent what little they had; indeed, the saving rate was negative in 1932 and 1933, but few jobs were available and the unemployment rate rose to a peak of 25%.

There is enough blame to go around for everyone. Monetary, fiscal, and trade policy were all inept. The Smoot-Hawley bill boosted dutiable tariff rates to their highest level ever, an average of 60% on dutiable imports (the figure today is less than 2%). The tax increase promulgated by Hoover in 1932 was also a serious mistake.

Having said all that, monetary policy was still the major cause of the Great Depression. That includes the errors of monetary policy, the failure of the banking system, and the unavailability of credit. From the current vantage point, it may seem incredible that the Fed actually tightened after the stock market crash of 1929, but it wanted to defend the value of the dollar in terms of the gold standard, and gold was fleeing the country. That is one of the reasons why the gold standard was substantially modified after World War II, and eventually discarded.

Until recently it was difficult to imagine how such a cumulation of errors could have occurred. However, the rash of international devaluations from mid-1997 through early 1999 offers a window to view what it must have been like. In 1997, the value of the Thai baht, Korean won, Malaysian ringgit, and Indonesian rupiah all fell by at least 50%. That was followed by the Russian devaluation of the ruble in 1998, which caught most investors completely off guard, and the devaluation of the Brazilian real in early 1999, which came as much less of a surprise.

Since the US economy continued to grow at above-average rates during and shortly after these recent devaluations, it may appear they had very little impact. However, if the Fed had tightened after each of these devaluations, hence exacerbating the stock market slump that occurred, particularly in September and October 1998, the overall result might have been quite different. Indeed, if monetary policy had reinforced instead of offset the negative impact of the devaluations, the world economy might have plunged into a prolonged recession.

We have learned much from the tragedy of the 1930s, and those mistakes will presumably not be repeated. Nonetheless, these initial errors do not explain why the economy failed to recover during the 1930s, or why the unemployment rate remaining in double digits until wartime spending started. After all, if the misguided policies of Hoover were responsible for the original downturn, why were

Table 15.5   Performance of the US economy during the Great Depression

(a) *Average annual percent change in real GDP and unemployment, 1933–44*

Period	Real GDP	Unemployment rate
1933–37	9.7	−2.7
1937–40	2.9	0.1
1940–44	11.5	−3.4

(b) *Major components of real GDP, 1929–37*

	GDP	Consumption	Housing	Capital spending	Inventory investment	Net exports	Govt purch	Private GDP
1929	182	128	9	23	3	0	19	163
1937	183	132	5	17	5	−2	26	157

All figures in billions of 1954 dollars
Source: 1960 *Economic Report of the President*

the policies of Roosevelt unable to return the economy to full employment until well after World War II started?

While this issue might seem to be of interest only to historians, Japan is now facing many of the same problems that the US did in the 1930s, with real GDP almost stagnant from 1992 through 2002. The only reason their unemployment rate has not moved into the double-digit range is that the Japanese measure unemployment differently. But there is little doubt that, as already explained in the previous chapter, a once high-flying economy has collapsed because of mismanaged fiscal, monetary, and trade policies.

Returning to the 1930s, the performance of the economy during the Roosevelt Administration can be divided into three periods. First, the economy rebounded sharply through 1937, with real growth averaging almost 10%. Second, it headed back into depression in 1938 and failed to recover until the US starting arming for World War II. Third, it moved back to overfull employment once the US entered the war. These periods are summarized in table 15.5.[18]

Based on the figures in table 15.5(b), the growth during the first four years of the Roosevelt Administration (excluding 1933), even though it averaged 9.7%, was actually an unimpressive performance. Real GDP just barely returned to its 1929 level eight years later, and private sector GDP was some 4% lower. While consumer spending was marginally higher, housing and capital spending were still 44% and 26% lower.

Investment plunged in spite of very low interest rates because of low rates of capacity utilization and business pessimism. But why did consumer spending (including housing) fail to rise at all? It wasn't that consumers didn't want to spend; the personal saving rate in 1937 was the same as in 1929, when optimism was still very high.

Employment was still lower in 1937 than in 1929, but incredibly, taxes were higher. The differences are not huge, since the average tax burden was far smaller then. Personal income taxes represented 3.1% of 1929 income excluding transfer payments; that figure rose to 4.1% in 1937. A 1% difference may not seem very large, but one can reasonably argue that, given the seriousness of the depression and the massive unemployment, tax rates should have been cut substantially during the 1930s, not raised.

The concept of the full-employment budget deficit or surplus had not yet been developed in the 1930s, but we can extrapolate back and see what it would have been. Today, a 1% rise in the unemployment rate boosts the deficit ratio by slightly more than 1%. However, taxes were only 5% of GNP then, whereas they are 20% of GDP today. Hence the appropriate figure for the 1930s would have been that a 1% rise in the unemployment rate would boost the deficit by about $\frac{1}{4}$%. Since the unemployment rate averaged 20% during the first Roosevelt term, compared to an estimated full employment rate of 4%, that means the deficit ratio was increased by 4% by the high unemployment rate. Since the actual deficit ratio for this period was 3.2%, it appears that during the first Roosevelt term, the budget position was equivalent to a slight surplus at full employment.

Perhaps the government of the time cannot be faulted for not running an even bigger deficit, since the concept of balancing the budget at full employment was not well understood then. However, given the depth and severity of the depression, more fiscal stimulus would have been appropriate. However, the Administration was associated with the slogan of "tax and tax, spend and spend, and elect and elect." In other words, the Roosevelt brain trust felt the economy would be better served by coupling increased spending with higher taxes rather than permitting fiscal stimulus.

This became particularly apparent in 1936, when Congress passed – over Roosevelt's veto – a payment to World War I veterans of $1,000 apiece, equivalent to more than $10,000 today. The total payment came to $1.4 billion, which was 1.7% of GDP; that would be almost $200 billion in terms of 2002 levels of GDP. The economy responded vigorously; real GDP rose 14% in 1936, and the unemployment rate fell from 20% in 1935 to 14% in 1937. Perhaps angered by this attempt to unbalance the budget, Roosevelt demanded – and obtained – a major increase in tax rates in 1937. As a result, real GDP fell 5% in 1938 and the unemployment rate soared back to 19%.

The memory of Roosevelt is still revered by many people. Nonetheless, it remains a fact that when the government cut taxes, real GDP rose 14%, and when it raised taxes, real GDP fell 5% the following year. Lower taxes and higher transfer payments could have ended the Great Depression many years earlier.

A deficit in the full-employment budget will eventually cause either real interest rates or inflation to increase. A surplus in the full-employment budget will either cause interest rates to fall or reduce the level of economic output. With short-term interest rates at zero, they obviously couldn't fall any further. So while the initial years of the Great Depression were due primarily to erroneous monetary policy, the 1938 depression was primarily caused by inept fiscal policy.

Today the government doesn't make those kinds of mistakes. When the economy heads into recession, the Fed eases soon afterwards; if the recession deepens, the Fed eases further. Sometimes the government cuts taxes during a recession and sometimes it doesn't, but it hardly ever raises taxes. In the post-WWII period, the only President to raise taxes in a recession was George H. W. Bush, and the voters responded accordingly.

Even though the tax increases imposed by that Bush were small and the recession was moderate, the tax hike was still enough to get him voted out of office because he violated Fiscal Policy Rule Number 1: don't raise taxes in a recession (although it obviously didn't help that two years earlier, Candidate Bush had told the nation, "Read My Lips. No New Taxes."). However, while many politicians have raised taxes after claiming they would do no such thing, few of them have prolonged an actual recession. The damage was contained by a significant easing in monetary policy – precisely opposite to the medicine administered by the Fed in the early 1930s.

The Great Depression could not recur unless the Fed tightened following severe monetary upheavals, Congress voted to restrict imports, and the government decided to raise taxes. At a minimum, these lessons from the Great Depression have been learned well.

15.11   Recap: are business cycles endogenous or exogenous?

In this chapter, we have argued that most business cycles have been caused by various types of shocks: exogenous, technological, monetary, or fiscal. For this reason it might seem that the question posed in the section heading is moot, if indeed recessions are a function of unexpected exogenous events. Yet the overall answer is more complex than that.

The argument against the exogenous case can be outlined as follows. Suppose the economy was initially in equilibrium, and no shocks occurred. Also, suppose the cost of capital was set equal to the marginal productivity of capital, and ex ante investment and saving were equal. For a while the economy would grow at its equilibrium rate.

After a while, though, there would be a decline in the perceived risk of investments, both in physical plant and equipment and financial equities. In other words, business executives and investors would start talking about "limitless prosperity" and begin to believe that "nothing could go wrong" – prosperity would continue forever. That would lead to an increase in the MPK, while at the same time the price/earnings ratio in the stock market would rise, reducing the equity cost of capital. A substantial divergence would open up between the MPK and the cost of capital, boosting the growth rate. Eventually that would lead to excess capacity, reduced profit margins, and a recession, which is not greatly different from the "surplus" theory discussed above. The major difference is that it would not take a technological shock to start this process. A change in expectations would be sufficient.

Now suppose the economy is not in equilibrium, but has just pulled out of a recession. As already shown, the MPK increases because of greater business optimism, so it exceeds the cost of capital, and after the usual lag, an investment boom starts. Interest rates could increase as soon as the MPK rises and keep the economy in equilibrium indefinitely, but that is an unlikely outcome. Most of the time, ex ante investment will exceed domestic saving, so either interest rates rise with a lag or excess capacity develops.

If the Fed follows a credible monetary policy – and is helped by a balanced budget, vigorous foreign competition, and a stable currency – business cycles will occur far less frequently, and when downturns do start, they will be short and mild. If the monetary authorities make it clear that price hikes or inflationary wage increases will not be tolerated, full employment need not be accompanied by higher inflation and interest rates. Improved methods of inventory control can help dampen the propagation effects, and the increasing ratio of imports to GDP means that an initial downturn in demand will be partially cushioned by a decline in imports. Also, greater stability in growth, inflation, and foreign exchange rates should help to stabilize capital spending. All these will reduce, but not completely eliminate, business cycles.

From time to time we can expect that genuine exogenous shocks will occur, and if they are severe enough, a brief recession is likely even if monetary, fiscal, and trade policies are all optimal. Yet the material developed in this chapter strongly suggests that even if these shocks did not occur, a mild recession roughly once every decade is a much more likely long-term scenario than no business cycles at all.

In the late 1960s, many economists thought the business cycle had been conquered. However, that turned out to be an incorrect forecast, as the US economy suffered through four recessions in the next 12 years. To a certain extent, those cycles were caused by the energy crises, but the underlying causes were policy driven: overly accommodative monetary policy, full-employment deficits that reduced productivity growth, a weak dollar that boosted inflation, and increasingly onerous and counterproductive government regulations, including the ill-fated wage and price controls.

Presumably the US will never go through another period of four recessions in 12 years. In particular, it is unlikely another series of events will cause oil prices to rise tenfold over the course of a decade. However, as shown in 1990, even a brief doubling of oil prices can contribute to a mild contraction. It would be unrealistic to predict no more energy shocks, or for that matter, no other shocks emanating from the volatile Middle East.

Part of the reason inflation rose so much in the 1960s and 1970s was that monetary policy remained too easy for extended periods of time; the real rate of interest was well below the marginal productivity of capital. Almost a century ago, Wicksell pointed out that such a situation would lead to rising inflation. We think the Fed and the politicians have finally learned that lesson. Also, counterproductive fine-tuning, such as the policy decisions of 1968 and 1969 that led to the 1970 recession, probably will not be repeated.

In spite of the occasional wobbles of the US economy in recent years, economists have learned a great deal about how to control the business cycle over the past 50 years, and for that matter over the past 20 years. After World War II, government policy makers knew not to tighten monetary and fiscal policy during a recession. After the inflation fiascoes of the 1970s, the Fed realized that the attempt to prolong the recovery with overly easy monetary policy is counterproductive in the longer run. Politicians learned that short-run fine tuning with fiscal policy usually backfires.

For this reason, we assume recessions will remain less frequent than they were during the 1970s. Assuming that oil shocks and wars do not dominate the world, and the Fed maintains its recent practice of preemptive strikes, we assume future business cycles will be infrequent and mild.

KEY TERMS AND CONCEPTS

Endogenous and Exogenous Business Cycles
Contraction and Expansion Phases
Impulse and Propagation
Index of Leading and Coincident Indicators
Real Rate of Interest
Technological Shocks

SUMMARY

- Before World War II, a recession occurred in the US economy about once every four years, and the contraction phase was almost as long as the expansion phase. From 1945 through 1982, a business cycle occurred about once every $4\frac{1}{2}$ years, but the expansion phase was almost five times as long as the contraction phase. From 1982 through 2002, there were only two mild recessions.

- From 1854 through 1954, recessions were caused by a variety of factors. From 1957 through 1990, virtually all recessions were caused by reductions in the cost and availability of credit. Invariably, these restrictions were the result of higher inflation. Sometimes the increase in inflation reflected an acceleration in unit labor costs at full

employment; in other cases, such as the energy shocks, the rise in inflation was primarily due to exogenous factors. However, none of these factors, with the exception of higher energy prices, preceded the 2001 recession.

- The variety of business cycle theories can be grouped into two main categories: theories of shortages, and theories of surplus. The shortage theories state that at full employment, the economy faces shortages of various factor resources, resulting in higher inflation and interest rates, lower profit margins, and a decline in investment. The surplus theories state that an increase in the marginal productivity of capital above the cost of capital generates an investment boom, which eventually leads to excess capacity, lower profit margins, and a decline in investment.

- Business cycles are recurring but not regular. The time between recessions varies greatly. Downturns are started by a wide variety of factors. However, once the recession has begun, the same pattern of events generally emerges, and in the post-WWII economy, recessions generally end in about one year.
- Whether endogenous or exogenous, every recession begins with one or more specific impulses. However, not every impulse leads to an actual downturn. The determining factor is the response, or the propagation, from that initial impulse.
- Every business cycle has four phases: expansion, upper turning point, contraction, and lower turning point. During the expansion phase, the economy generally grows faster than its long-term sustainable growth rate; otherwise it would never return to full employment. Once full employment is reached, the economy should slow down to its long-term sustainable growth rate. If it does not, either shortages will occur, or excess capacity will occur. In either case, profit margins shrink and investment declines, leading to a recession. Once the contraction phase has been established, the monetary authorities ease, and two to three quarters later, the economy reaches the lower turning point and is once again ready to enter the expansion phase.
- Business cycles are caused by a variety of shocks: exogenous events, a change in technological growth, errant monetary policy, and changes in fiscal policy. Exogenous events include the beginning and ending of wars, commodity shocks, changes in the value of the currency, major strikes, and political unrest. In the US, international factors are not usually large enough to cause an actual downturn, but in the 1990s, devaluations in east Asia and Latin America led to severe recessions in several countries.
- A change in technology often generates an investment boom, which occurs when the marginal productivity of capital rises above the cost of capital. That is particularly likely to occur early in the business cycle expansion phase, when interest rates are low and the price/earnings ratio of the stock market is high. That will create an unsustainable investment boom unless the cost of capital quickly rises. If it does not, excess capacity will eventually occur, which will reduce investment and diminish real growth.
- Contractionary fiscal policy can contribute to recessions, and has done so in the 1954, 1970, and 1990 downturns. In general, though, changes in fiscal policy (except for wars) are no longer a major contributor to the business cycle.
- Recent evidence suggests that while a better understanding and control of fiscal and monetary policy has reduced the likelihood and severity of business cycles, they are still expected to occur in the future even in the absence of exogenous shocks. Also, the chance of another exogenous shock causing a recession in the future, whether it be a war, energy shock, or other unforeseen disturbance, remains significant.

QUESTIONS AND PROBLEMS

1. In a typical recession, the unemployment rate rises $2\frac{1}{2}$%. Assume that at full employment, the unemployment rate is $4\frac{1}{2}$%, and it rises to 7% by the end of the recession. Typically it takes the economy about three years to return to full employment. Using the "Okun's Law" approximation, how

fast would the economy be growing during that part of the expansion phase?

2. If recessions are invariably caused by higher interest rates and reduced availability of credit, why doesn't the Fed refrain from taking those measures that apparently cause recessions?
3. What are the principal factors that determine whether inflation accelerates or not once the economy reaches full employment?
4. Explain how automatic stabilizers have reduced the length and severity of recessions in the post-WWII period.
5. Which of the post-WWII recessions in the US were caused by energy shocks? If the price of crude oil were to rise by $20/bbl next year, do you think the US economy would be plunged into recession or not?
6. Which of the post-WWII recessions in the US were caused by fiscal shocks? Which of those shocks represented declines in defense spending, and which represented increases in taxes?
7. After the world pulled out of the Great Depression of the 1930s, many forecasters expected a repeat of that decline after World War II. Now, the chances of another depression of that duration seem extremely remote. What lessons were learned from the Great Depression that presumably will not be repeated?
8. Why has the average recession in the postwar US economy lasted about ten months? Why were the 1974–5 and 1981–2 recessions about six months longer?
9. Why did the US economy go into recession in 2001 even though inflation and interest rates had not risen at all in the previous year?

Notes

1. The major research in measuring the business cycle has been done by Mitchell, Burns, Geoffrey Moore, and Victor Zarnowitz. Besides Mitchell's seminal work, which has been reprinted by the University of California Press (Berkeley), the major works are Burns and Mitchell, *Measuring Business Cycles* (New York: NBER, 1946), Moore, *Business Cycles, Inflation, and Forecasting*, 2nd edn (Cambridge, MA: Ballinger for NBER, 1983), and Zarnowitz, *Business Cycles: Theory, History, Indicators, and Forecasting* (Chicago: University of Chicago Press for NBER, 1992).
2. These lists can be found at www.conference-board.org, and may change in the future.
3. For further discussion of these points, see the NBER website given above, FAQ section.
4. The Dating Committee has been chaired since its inception by Robert Hall. As of 2002, the other members include Jeffrey Frankel, Robert Gordon, Gregory Mankiw, and Victor Zarnowitz. These five economists have sole discretion in determining when recessions begin and end.

5. Some economists have argued that the apparent increase in stability mainly reflects more accurate data. The leading proponent of this view is Christina Romer; two of her major articles on the subject are "Spurious Volatility in Historical Unemployment Data," *Journal of Political Economy* (February 1986) and "Is the Stabilization of the Postwar Economy a Figment of the Data?" *American Economic Review* (June 1986). Obviously no one is arguing that the Great Depression has been replicated in the postwar period. However, it is possible that some of the minor recessions of the previous century would not have been recorded as actual downturns with more accurate data, and in that sense the frequency of business cycles may not have diminished as much as calculated by the NBER. In this author's view, though, business cycles are generally much more moderate than they were before World War II.

6. The classic work on business cycle classification is Gottfried Haberler, *Prosperity and Depression* (reprinted by Harvard University Press, 1964, originally published by the League of Nations in 1937). Much of this material can also be found in Michel K. Evans, *Macroeconomic Activity* (New York: Harper & Row, 1969).

7. *Geldzins and Guterpreise*, translated by R. F. Kahn as *Interest and Prices*, 1934. Also see his paper, "The Enigma of Business Cycles," 1907, which appeared in translation in *International Economic Papers*, 1953.

8. Other classic Schumpeter works, where most of his ideas were originally developed, include *The Theory of Economic Development* (1911; reprinted by Harvard University Press in 1934) and *Business Cycles* (New York: McGraw-Hill, 1939).

9. Bennett T. McCallum, "Real Business Cycle Models," in Robert J. Barro, ed., *Modern Business Cycle Theory* (Harvard University Press, 1989).

10. Paul Volcker and Toyoo Gyhoten, *Changing Fortunes* (New York: Random House/Times Books, 1992).

11. Regional differences flared in the 1970s, when Texas bumper stickers read "Let the Yankee bastards freeze in the dark."

12. These views are collected and presented in Robert J. Barro, ed., *Modern Business Cycle Theory, idem.*

13. The key papers introducing this concept are Finn E. Kydland and Edward C. Prescott, "Time to Build and Aggregate Fluctuations," *Econometrica* (November 1982) (difficult to read), J. B. Long and Charles I. Plosser, "Real Business Cycles," *Journal of Political Economy* (February 1983), and R. G. King and Plosser, "Money, Credit, and Prices in a Real Business Cycle," *American Economic Review* (June 1984). Also see McCallum, *idem.*

14. According to Paul Volcker, that pressure was quite severe. "In the second half of 1965 . . . [Fed] Chairman Martin . . . broached the idea of raising the discount rate during the early autumn by half a percent, which was strongly resisted by President Johnson . . . . The Federal Reserve Board voted to increase the discount rate on December 5, 1965 . . . . I did not experience firsthand the president's explosion when he asked Chairman Martin to visit him at his ranch." Volcker and Gyohten, *Changing Fortunes, idem*, pp. 37–8.

15. Not all government economists concurred. Leonall Andersen of the St. Louis Fed correctly predicted that this strategy would result in a recession and an increase in the unemployment rate to 6%.

16. According to Paul Volcker, Fed Chairman Arthur Burns "openly called for a strong incomes policy and controls." *Changing Fortunes, idem*, p. 71.

17. These views are summarized in the symposium on the Great Depression in the Spring 1993 issue of the *Journal of Economic Perspectives*. For specific references, see Milton

Friedman and Anna J. Schwartz, *A Monetary History of the United States, 1867–1960* (Princeton: Princeton University Press for NBER, 1963); Ben Bernanke, "Non-Monetary Effects of the Financial Crisis in the Propagation of the Great Depression," *American Economic Review* (June 1983); Peter Temin, *Did Monetary Forces Cause the Great Depression?* (New York: W. W. Norton, 1976); Michael K. Evans, *The Truth About Supply-Side Economics* (New York: Harper & Row, 1983).

18. Recently the Bureau of Economic Analysis revised all the NIPA data back to 1929 using the chain-weighted deflator. While that is a useful step for current numbers, it causes gross distortions in the older data. Hence we have used the constant-dollar figures as they originally appeared, not with the erroneous corrections.

chapter sixteen

Cyclical fluctuations in components of aggregate demand

Introduction

The previous chapter examined the general patterns of business cycles. Their causes can be divided into three major categories: exogenous shocks, including defense expenditures; a tightening of monetary conditions caused by higher inflation near full capacity and full employment; and excess capacity that reduces purchases of capital goods or durable consumer goods. For the most part, however, we did not identify the cyclical characteristics of individual components of aggregate demand. This chapter focuses on monetary and stock-adjustment factors that cause cyclical fluctuations in the major components of aggregate demand; the next chapter considers financial business cycles.

Chapter 5 analyzed the principal determinants of capital spending: the cost and availability of capital and the rate of capacity utilization. To a certain extent, these variables contain some cyclical elements: the cost of capital generally increases, and the availability decreases, when the rate of inflation starts to rise and the economy is near full employment. If the rate of inflation remains stable because additional capacity is added, this capacity will eventually lead to a decrease in capital spending. This endogenous mechanism is known as the stock adjustment principle. To recap briefly, capital stock is proportional to output, so net investment is proportional to the difference between current desired and previous actual capital stock. Thus an exogenous increase in the growth rate of aggregate demand and income could result in an initial boost in investment that would be followed by successively smaller increments even if the growth rate remained at its new, higher level.

The three major components of investment in the NIPA data are capital spending, residential construction, and inventory investment. Capital spending often lags the cycle, while housing often leads it. Inventory investment generally lags the changes in final sales by one to two quarters, but usually accounts for more than half of the total decline in real GDP during recessions. Hence a separate discussion of both these components of investment expands our understanding of the overall business cycle.

The variables that determine residential construction are the cost and availability of credit, the vacancy rate – a proxy for the stock adjustment principle – and demographic factors. Inventory investment is a function of the change in sales; the stock adjustment principle is more important here than for any other component of aggregate demand. In addition, unexpected changes in sales generally produce a pattern where inventory investment initially *rises* during the first few months of recession; it then declines quite sharply. As this rate of decline diminishes, that often signals an end to the recession.

Short-term fluctuations in discretionary consumer spending are due largely to random factors such as weather conditions, fluctuations in energy prices, incentives offered by motor vehicle manufacturers, and sales by major department store chains. While most managers would find it useful to be able to predict such changes, most of them are not forecastable; even more to the point, it is important for managers not to overreact to short-term changes that will be reversed in the next month or quarter. It is more useful to understand and quantify the factors that will cause consumer demand to shift over the next several months or quarters.

The standard theories of the consumption function, as discussed in chapter 4, state that consumption is a function of average or expected income, while short-run fluctuations in actual income have only a small impact on consumption. That would mean monthly and quarterly fluctuations in consumption would be substantially smaller than the corresponding fluctuations in disposable income. However, it turns out that monthly and quarterly percentage changes in consumption are actually somewhat *larger* than the corresponding changes in income. We look past these essentially random changes in order to determine what causes endogenous economic fluctuations in consumer spending.

On an endogenous basis, discretionary consumer spending is related to current and expected levels of disposable income, plus the cost and availability of credit. The major factors causing exogenous shifts in consumption are usually lumped together under the heading of "attitudes" or "sentiment." Changes in consumer sentiment can be divided into two major categories: those that are tied to economic variables such as income, unemployment, and inflation, and those that are due to truly exogenous events.

16.1   The stock adjustment principle

The **stock adjustment principle** states that net investment (and in some cases, net purchase of consumer durables) is proportional to the difference between desired and actual capital stock. If desired capital stock is proportional to output, a given rise in output would initially result in a large increase in net investment, followed by successively smaller increments. After a while, purchases of capital goods would rise more slowly even if other output continued to rise steadily. That could generate cyclical fluctuations in the economy. This is another way of describing the concept discussed in the previous chapter, namely that if investment increases too fast, excess capacity will eventually bring the boom to an end. Symbolically, we can write:

$$K - K_{-1} = \lambda(K^* - K_{-1}) \tag{16.1}$$

where $K^* = Y^* p_w / \text{rcc}$, or

$$I_n = \lambda(K^* - K_{-1}). \tag{16.2}$$

Since replacement investment (I_r) is proportional to existing capital stock, then

$$I_g = \lambda(K^* - K_{-1}) + \delta K_{-1} \tag{16.3}$$

where Y is expected output, p_w is the price of the product, rcc is the cost of capital, K is actual capital stock, K^* is desired capital stock, I_n is net investment, and I_g is gross (net plus replacement) investment.

The principles of utility maximization state that the level of consumption[1] is proportional to some average or expected level of disposable income. However, the principles of profit maximization for the firm state that capital stock, rather than investment, is proportional to output. Thus a one-time increase in output would result in a one-time increase in capital stock. Net investment would rise rapidly for a while and then, when the desired higher level of capital stock had been reached, would level off again, ceteris paribus.

If the adjustment were immediate, investment would be proportional to the change in income. However, the desired capital goods are not all purchased immediately for two reasons. First, firms will proceed cautiously when output increases, since they are not sure whether the changes are permanent or temporary. In addition, even if all the capital goods were ordered immediately, they could not all be delivered at once (think of laying fiber optic cable or building an electricity generating plant).

Consider a scenario where the growth in income had been 3% per year, but it accelerated to 4% and stayed at that new, higher level. Assuming stable monetary conditions and expectations, the growth in permanent consumption (i.e., including the use value rather than the purchase price of consumer durables) would also shift from 3% to 4%.

However, the same claim cannot be made for investment. Suppose the capital/output ratio is steady, and growth in output is rising 3% per year, so net investment is also rising at 3% per year. Now assume the growth in output rises to 4%. Because capital stock, rather than investment, is proportional to output, the growth in investment would exceed 4% until capital stock had risen the same percentage as output, at which point it would then decline back to 4%. To a certain extent, this element of endogenous cyclicality contributes to business cycles.

The importance of the stock adjustment principle for explaining capital spending is reflected in the rate of capacity utilization. However, this principle also helps determine other components of investment. It is the single most important determinant of inventory investment. In the housing function, a higher vacancy rate will reduce housing starts, ceteris paribus. Also, an unusual surge in purchases of consumer durables may result in fewer purchases in the near future; conversely, a period during which these durables have not been readily available is often followed by a sharp increase in spending. However, in recent years this has not been a very important factor affecting purchases of consumer durables.

16.2 Empirical review: the components of capital spending

Capital spending consists of purchases of producers' durable equipment (PDE) and private nonresidential construction, most of which is buildings. PDE includes four major categories: (1) industrial equipment; (2) transportation equipment (mainly autos and trucks and aircraft, but also railroad cars and ships); (3) computers and other information processing equipment, including telecommunications equipment; and (4) other equipment, including agricultural and mining machinery, construction equipment, and office furniture and air conditioning equipment. Nonresidential construction consists of industrial buildings; commercial and office buildings, shopping centers, and hotels; nonprofit buildings such as educational and medical buildings; and a variety of nonbuilding construction such as utility lines and mine shafts. Roads, bridges, dams, and other similar structures are usually part of government spending. Currently, equipment accounts for 75% to 80% of private sector capital spending.

The major components of capital spending, together with their 2001 magnitudes, are given in table 16.1. Capital spending averages about 11% of nominal GDP, with a range of 9% to 13%. The historical proportions for each major category of PDE, which highlight the relative increase in information processing equipment, are shown in figures 16.1(a) and (b). The gain in high-tech equipment has been much more rapid in constant than in current dollars, reflecting the recent sharp declines in prices for computers.

The subtotals for all the current-dollar categories add to the totals except for rounding error. However, because of the way in which the chained deflator is calculated, that is not necessarily true for the chained dollar figures, especially for high-tech investment. Note in particular that the four subcomponents of information processing equipment sum to $586.1 billion, compared with the total figure of $548.5 billion. Hence rapid gains in these subcomponents are partially reduced in the NIPA totals. This table omits several minor categories such as scrap, used equipment, and brokerage commissions on structures.

16.3 The role of business sentiment in capital spending

The cyclical patterns of the ratios of the five major components of capital spending to GDP, all in constant dollars, are shown in figure 16.1(a) and (b). Except for 2001,

Table 16.1 Components of capital spending (fixed business investment) for 2001

	All figures billions of dollars, SAAR	
	Current dollars	Chained (1996) dollars
Equipment	877.1	988.2
Information processing	404.3	548.5
Computers	74.2	239.9
Software	180.4	182.0
Telecommunications	90.6	105.8
Other	59.2	58.4
Industrial equipment	159.0	153.8
Transportation equipment	165.8	163.6
Motor vehicles	124.1	125.9
Aircraft	33.7	29.8
Other	7.9	7.7
Other equipment	148.0	141.0
Agricultural	26.5	25.4
Mining (energy)	6.5	5.9
Construction	19.9	18.5
Office	35.7	34.0
Other	59.4	57.2
Construction	320.8	267.7
Buildings	210.1	173.6
Industrial	25.6	21.1
Commercial	118.5	97.9
Nonprofit	38.6	31.9
Other	27.4	22.6
Nonbuildings	110.7	94.1
Utilities	55.0	50.3
Farm	6.1	5.1
Mining	42.7	34.0
Other	6.8	5.9

Source: Bureau of Economic Analysis website, www.bea.gov

the high-tech equipment graph is dominated by its upward trend; excess capacity was not a significant negative factor until then. The peak of nonresidential construction occurred during the severe 1981–2 recession because of a change in tax laws that permitted faster depreciation, and a huge boom in oil-country construction that followed the increase in the price of benchmark crude oil from $13 to $35/bbl. If oil prices were to triple again and remain at those levels for an extended period of time, or if tax policies should once again change to permit investors to write off the total value of buildings in half the current time, construction would undoubtedly surge; but since those events seem very unlikely, they are mainly of

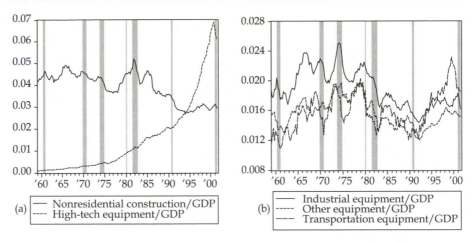

Figure 16.1 Ratios of components of capital spending to GDP, both in chained dollars (shaded areas are recessions)

Source: BEA website, www.bea.gov

historical interest. Thus we concentrate our cyclical analysis on the ratios shown in figure 16.1(b).

In addition to the expected cyclical fluctuations during and shortly after recessions, two significant patterns can be observed in this graph. First, although these components of capital spending usually rise sharply once the recovery has started, gains were quite sluggish in the early years of the upturns starting in 1961, 1991, and 2002. Second, while these investment ratios usually continue to rise until the upper turning point is reached, they started to decline in the mid-1980s, even though the economy remained robust and eventually returned to full employment in 1989. What factors caused these anomalies?

During the late 1980s, the real interest rate was unusually high, the corporate profit ratio was low, and the ratio of stock prices to GDP was low. During the early 1990s, these latter two conditions remained in place, although the real long-term bond yield had returned to normal levels (see figure 16.2). However, none of these conditions can explain the lack of investment in the early 1960s.

In the broad sense, firms postpone investment plans when executives think the return on that investment will be below the rate of return that could be earned if the money were to be invested elsewhere – including dividends to stockholders, investing in other companies, or buying back the company stock. During the late 1980s and early 1990s, attitudes about capital spending were pessimistic because of the high costs of obtaining debt and equity capital, and low profit margins. In addition, many business executives expected an extended period of subpar growth ahead because of the inability to reduce the Federal budget deficit. Even when capital spending rebounded in the 1983–5 period, those peaks were well below

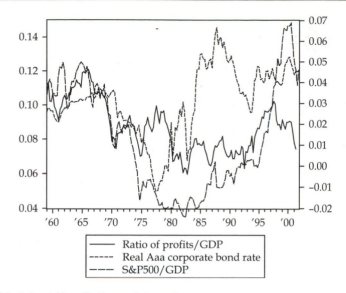

Figure 16.2   Selected variables affecting capital spending

Sources: Profits and GDP, BEA website, www.bea.gov. Bond yields and stock price indexes can be found on several sites. One convenient source is FRED, the Federal Reserve Economic Data Base of the St. Louis Fed, recently expanded to FRED II. It is at http://research.stlouisfed.org/fred

those of the 1970s. With expected sluggish growth ahead, less additional investment was undertaken.

The budget was essentially balanced in the early 1960s. Looking back at revised GDP statistics, the growth rate appears to have been above average – but that was not the view at the time. John F. Kennedy campaigned on a pledge to "get the economy moving again," which according to his economic advisors of the time, meant Keynesian stimulus. During the first two years of the Kennedy Administration, the unemployment rate remained near 6%, compared to the previous decade when 4% had been considered normal, reinforcing the underlying expectation of sluggish growth. However, that was not even the major issue. Many business executives felt that the wage/price guidelines of the time – which required major manufacturing corporations to petition the government for even modest price increases – would not permit an adequate rate of return on future investment.

The *timing* of ordering capital goods can be quite volatile, and is often influenced by sudden changes in monetary conditions, tax policies, and the change in other components of aggregate demand. However, *attitudes* affecting capital spending plans, while they can also play a major role in defining the shape of cyclical fluctuations, depend on longer range factors, namely those factors affecting the rate of return on future investment. Because most capital goods last several years, plans are based on multiyear horizons, and the amount of investment undertaken – as opposed to the timing – is not as heavily influenced by short-term cyclical factors.

MANAGER'S BRIEFCASE: WHEN WILL THE NEXT CAPITAL SPENDING BOOM OCCUR?

Over the past half-century, predicting the next investment boom has proven to be even more difficult than predicting the next recession or recovery. That is because, roughly speaking, about half the time the early stages of a business cycle have featured robust gains in capital spending, while about half the time capital spending hardly rises at all. We have presented the historical evidence above. What should managers look at in the future?

To start, you can be assured that the level of short-term interest rates has nothing to do with it. Short-term rates always decline sharply once the recession is underway. Indeed, the less robust capital spending is, the more interest rates are likely to fall. To a certain extent that also applies to bond yields, although the five-year average rate of inflation is a more important determinant.

One important factor is the rate of capacity utilization. As a general rule of thumb, if that rate is below 75%, capital spending will decline; if it is between 75% and 80%, it will rise, but at a slower rate than real GDP; if it is between 80% and 85%, it will rise slightly faster, and above 85%, a full-fledged investment boom is likely to occur, by which we mean double-digit increases.

If corporate profit margins are above average, the chances of an investment boom are much higher than if they are below average. This is particularly true in capital-intensive sectors. High profits in trade and services will not generate as much investment per dollar of profit. In the same vein, an overvalued dollar – besides reducing manufacturing profits – is more likely to convince firms to expand or move operating plants to foreign countries.

It seems logical to assume that a stock market boom will stimulate capital spending, but even that has not always been the case. The P/E ratio of the S&P 500 rose to levels in early 1962 that were almost unmatched until the 2000 blowout, yet capital spending remained sluggish. Yet when the P/E ratio was very low in the late 1970s, a major investment boom occurred because of negative real rates of interest and changes in the tax laws designed to stimulate capital spending. In the future, an investment boom is probably more likely to be correlated with rapid gains in the stock market than with the actual P/E ratio.

Taking all these factors into consideration, it is likely that in the future, investment booms will not start after recessions until the rate of capacity utilization has moved back above 80%, the stock market has risen substanstially, and real interest rates remain at low levels. The only exceptions would probably occur when the Administration and Congress jointly decide to pass changes in tax laws that stimulate capital spending, but even those changes will be ineffective as long as the rate of capacity utilization remains at low levels.

16.4   Investment in residential construction

Residential construction consists of three major components: construction of new homes, major additions and alterations, and brokerage commissions, which obviously follow new and existing home sales closely. It also includes a very small component of household appliances that are part of new apartment sales. Since major additions and alterations follow the cyclical pattern of new housing construction closely, they are not considered separately.[2]

Housing investment is a hybrid because it contains elements of consumption, the actual construction that takes place, and an investment because of expected price appreciation. Consumers maximize utility, and businesses maximize the rate of return on investment. In many cases, though, individuals buy houses for dual motives: the use of housing services and as an investment with capital appreciation. This latter factor became increasingly obvious in the 2001 recession and sluggish 2002 recovery when housing prices zoomed even as real income fell and the unemployment rate rose, as many investors transferred some of their assets from the stock market to housing.

In the long run, swings in housing starts are proportional to the percentage change in household formation, which is closely tied to the change in the population aged 20–25, and to changes in the vacancy rate. Short-term fluctuations around that trend are tied to the cost and availability of credit. As long-term trends in per capita real income increase, people tend to own more homes, but short-term fluctuations in income generally are not correlated with housing starts or sales, since they are dwarfed by fluctuations in credit conditions.

One method of explaining fluctuations in housing would be to develop a theory of the optimal housing stock comparable to the theory of optimal capital accumulation. Following that logic, the desired stock of housing would be positively correlated with income and change in net household formation, and negatively correlated with the user cost of housing, which would equal the mortgage rate plus the rate of depreciation minus the rate of capital appreciation, adjusted for tax laws. Net investment in housing would then be proportional to the difference between desired stock and lagged actual stock. The role of capacity utilization in the housing function would be filled by the vacancy rate, although obviously with the opposite sign.

There are, however, several difficulties with this approach. Suppose someone's real permanent income rises by (say) 10%. Following the same theory that was developed for optimal capital accumulation, the value of the housing stock desired by that person (or family) would also rise by 10%. But what does that mean?

There are three possible interpretations: the number of houses owned by that person rises by 10%, the physical value of the existing house rises by 10% (remodeling the kitchen, adding an extra room, etc.), or the homeowner decides to move to a more expensive house: either a bigger and fancier residence, or the equivalent home in a better neighborhood, i.e., the same amount of house with a higher land value.

The first case could represent people moving out of "doubling up" situations and buying their own housing unit, or buying a second home for investment purposes. That could depend on the expected rate of return, which may seem similar to the theory of capital spending, except that the expected change in housing prices is at least as important as the interest rate or tax rate. Many would-be homeowners face the liquidity hurdles of a down payment and qualifying for the average monthly payment; when credit conditions ease, they may purchase a house even if their income does not change.

In the second case, a rise in income might boost additions and alterations, which do have a cyclical pattern. However, the cost of capital is usually not an important consideration in these decisions. In the third case, the rise in land values is not part of GDP or NI.

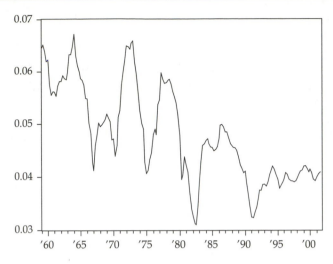

Figure 16.3 The ratio of residential construction to GDP, chained dollars, has fallen sharply over the past 40 years
Source: BEA website, www.bea.gov

As already noted, the number of housing units is closely related to the number of households. Hence there will be a bigger increase in the number of housing units if a 10% growth in real income is due to a 10% increase in the number of households rather than a 10% rise in income of existing households.

Thus trying to apply the theory of optimal capital accumulation to the demand for residential construction reveals several distinct flaws: changes in demographics, liquidity hurdles posed by the down payment, affordability, and changes in land prices instead of the value of the building. In addition, for most homeowners, the decision of whether or not to buy is independent of their marginal income tax rate.

Empirically, most of the increase in the real price of a housing unit from 1950 to 2000 reflected the rise in underlying land values – which has no counterpart in the NIPA figures, nor should it – rather than the cost or size of the house per se. The remaining increase in constant-dollar residential construction over that period was due to more expensive homes rather than an increase in the number of housing starts. For the 1994–6 period, housing starts averaged about 1.4 million per year, the same as the 1.4 million average of the 1959–61 period, even though real income had more than tripled. In the long run, there is no correlation between per capita real income and the number of houses that are built.

Figure 16.3 shows the sharp decline in residential construction expenditures as a percentage of constant-dollar GDP since 1959. The pattern of single and multifamily housing starts over the 1959–2001 period is shown in figure 16.4. Because so much of the rise in residential construction has been due to an increase in the value rather than the number of homes, most economists disregard the "optimal stock" approach and estimate the number of housing starts directly.

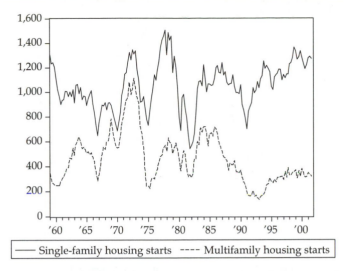

Figure 16.4   While single- and multifamily housing starts exhibit similar cyclical patterns, the rise and fall in multifamily starts relative to single-family starts primarily reflects changes in government housing programs and depreciation schedules

Source: Census website, www.census.gov

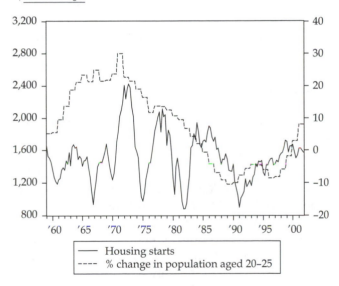

Figure 16.5

Source: Census website, www.census.gov

The positive correlation between housing starts and changes in the population aged 20–25 is shown in figure 16.5; rapid growth in this cohort resulted in a peak in housing starts during 1972–3, whereas slower rates of growth dampened housing starts for most of the 1990s. Figure 16.6 shows the correlation between housing

Figure 16.6

starts and the vacancy rate. When that rate was low in the 1970s, housing starts were high; conversely, a relatively high vacancy rate in both the 1960s and the 1990s reduced housing starts.

The big drop in housing starts in the early 1980s, however, is not explained by either of these factors; it was caused by unusually high interest rates and stringent credit conditions. The importance of monetary factors on short-run fluctuations in housing starts is examined next.

To explain the role of credit in the housing function, consider two different sets of decision-makers: builders and buyers. To a certain extent, both are influenced by the cost of borrowed money. Yet in spite of the mentality of many builders of "build them and they will buy," there is often a disparity in the marketplace that results in bulges or dips in the vacancy rate.

Anyone who has taken out a mortgage knows that the key factor the lending officer considers, assuming a clean credit rating, is the ratio of the monthly payment (including taxes and insurance) to monthly income. Based on this, the National Association of Realtors (NAR) has developed an "affordability index," which is a scaled version of that ratio. The main component of that index is the mortgage rate; the other factors are household disposable income and the price of housing. The mortgage rate is an important determinant of housing starts, and the sharp increase in mortgage rates, as reflected in that index, does explain the drop in housing starts quite closely in the 1980s. However, it does not explain the dip in the 1990s, as shown in figure 16.7 (data for the NAR index are not available before 1971). While the NAR index accurately measures the cost of a monthly

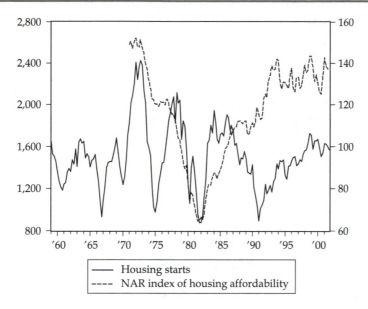

Figure 16.7

Sources: Housing starts, Census website, www.census.gov. NAR index, www.realtor.org/research.nsf/pages. NAR makes the most recent data available free of charge; historical series can be purchased from them. They can also be purchased from Haver Analytics

mortgage, it does not take into consideration the availability of credit, so some additional variables are required.

Franco Modigliani, creator of the life-cycle hypothesis for consumption, first worked on the issue of credit availability back in the 1960s, when disintermediation caused by interest rate ceilings led to nonprice credit rationing. The methods he developed then have been rendered obsolete by the removal of those ceilings and the deregulation of the banking sector, but the original idea was an important and useful one. Some variable is needed to reflect the ease or tightness of credit as well as the mortgage rate.

In fact one such variable has already been introduced: the yield spread between long- and short-term interest rates. Previously we showed that the yield spread was a useful variable for predicting dips in purchases of consumer durables the following year.

The argument for including this variable is straightforward. When the yield spread is high, banks earn a relatively low rate of return on Treasury bills, and hence are more likely to solicit real estate (and other personal and business) loans. When the spread is low or negative, the highest rate of return is often found at the short end of the yield curve, rather than bonds or mortgages. Furthermore, since an inverted yield spread usually means there will be a recession the next year, banks are less enthusiastic about loaning money to builders or homebuyers who may pose a substantial risk of default.

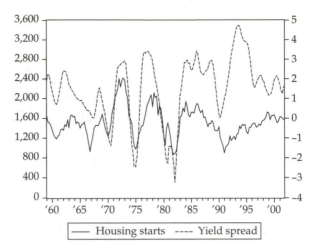

Figure 16.8 Correlation between housing starts and a four-quarter moving average of the yield spread lagged two quarters

Sources: Census website, www.census.gov, and FRED (St. Louis Fed) website, http://research.stlouisfed.org/fred

William Zeckendorf, who annoyed some New York residents with his grandiose plans to transform much of the skyline of Manhattan before he went broke, was famously quoted as saying he would "rather be alive at 18% than dead at the prime rate" (in those days, the prime rate was around 4%). Most homeowners, however, cannot qualify for a mortgage at 18%, so when short-term rates rise relative to long-term rates, lenders are more comfortable investing in Treasury securities than continuing to make real-estate loans at sky-high rates, which carry a much higher risk of default.

Nonetheless, even the yield spread does not adequately predict the decline in housing starts in 1991, as shown in figure 16.8. For that reason, a better measure of credit availability is needed. Before deregulation of the banking sector in 1982, credit availability is best measured by the percentage change in the M2 measure of the money supply; after 1982, it is represented by a weighted average of changes in M2 and in commercial and industrial loans. The correlation between housing starts and this measure of credit availability is shown in figure 16.9.

These separate graphs emphasize that fluctuations in housing starts are related to several economic factors. An easing of monetary conditions that causes builders to construct more homes than are indicated by underlying demand factors will result in a rise in the vacancy rate, which will depress housing starts in the future even if monetary conditions do not tighten. This can be seen by examining the relationship between housing starts and home sales, which is discussed in case study 16.1.

Hence housing starts are a function of the cost and availability of credit – which is measured by the mortgage rate, the yield spread, changes in the money supply, and changes in commercial and industrial loans granted – changes in population

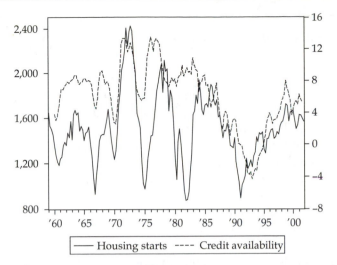

Figure 16.9 Housing starts correlated with credit availability, defined as the percentage change in M2 over the past year plus one-third of the percentage change in commercial and industrial loans starting in 1983
Sources: Census and FRED websites (www.census.gov, http://research.stlouisfed.org/fred)

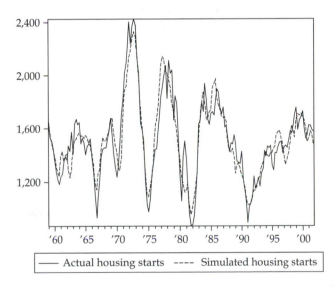

Figure 16.10 Actual and simulated housing starts, thousands, seasonally adjusted at annual rates (see text for equation)
Source: Equation estimated by author.[3]

aged 20–25, and the lagged vacancy rate. Finally, the ratio of the stock market to GDP is important; even though the stock market declined sharply in 2001 and 2002, housing starts held their own, as the P/E ratio still remained well above average historical levels. The results of the equation incorporating all these variables are shown in figure 16.10.

CASE STUDY 16.1   NEW AND EXISTING HOME SALES

Any equation used to predict housing starts always contains a combination of demand and supply factors. Builders do not start homes in a vacuum, but sometimes they become overly optimistic and build more homes than is warranted by underlying demand conditions. Sales of new and existing homes are a more accurate barometer of underlying demand for housing; yet except for brokerage commissions, those sales are not part of GDP. Nonetheless, by comparing sales of new homes, which are closely related to new single-family housing starts excluding condominiums, and sales of existing homes, which are more closely related to underlying demand, a picture emerges of the time when credit conditions caused new construction to deviate from underlying demand. The comparison is shown in figure 16.11.

During the early 1970s and again later in that decade, Fed policy held short-term interest rates below the rate of inflation, leading to an excess of housing starts. Conversely, during the early 1980s, the determination of Paul Volcker to wipe out inflationary expectations led to unusually high real interest rates for an extended period of time, hence reducing housing starts below the level of demand. In the early 1990s, the excess of bad loans made by many banks and savings and loan associations in the wake of deregulation led to much more stringent lending

Figure 16.11   Data for new home sales exclude condominiums, although they are included in single-family housing starts

Sources: Census website, www.census.gov; NAR website, www.realtor.org

continued

CASE STUDY 16.1 (*continued*)
practices, which curtailed loan demand for almost five years until the situation had been resolved. During that period, housing starts were kept below the level of demand indicated by demographic factors.

MANAGER'S BRIEFCASE: HOW WILL FLUCTUATIONS IN HOUSING STARTS AFFECT YOUR BUSINESS?

At first it might seem that the obvious answer is: it depends on what business. Presumably the answer is far different for dot.com startups or food product companies than it is for builders.

Nonetheless, the role of housing in the economy is important enough that it affects a wide variety of businesses, not just those engaged in selling to the construction trade. In particular, note that (a) stripped of the eccentricities in the monthly data, housing starts (and building permits) are an important leading indicator; (b) the depth of the recession, and the strength of the recovery, are largely determined by the percentage change in housing starts; and (c) to the extent that rising housing prices provide an increasingly important source of spendable income for many families, that has become an important determinant of overall consumer spending.

These points are illustrated in figure 16.12. Note in particular that the percentage changes in housing are larger in deep recessions and strong recoveries than otherwise. The 2001 experience might appear to be an anomaly, but in fact it should be recalled this was the mildest recession – and housing hardly declined at all. Also note the tendency of housing to lead the business cycle; since this figure represents actual residential construction, the changes in housing starts actually occur one quarter earlier.

No individual component of the index of leading indicators is as good as the composite; if it were, one would not have to follow the other variables. In particular, the 2001 recession occurred even though housing starts, and residential construction, hardly declined at all. Perhaps that would have caused some economists and managers to miss the recession completely. However, as far as consumer spending is concerned, the lack of decline in housing starts should have sent a strong signal that the decline in consumption in the forthcoming recession would be far less than usual – a much better signal than was given by the plunge in the stock market. We now explore this point further.

In the future, it is likely that changes in housing prices will have at least as great an effect on the economy as changes in housing starts. Of course the two are related: if interest rates are low and credit flows are not impeded, both variables will increase; if rates are high and credit flows are restricted, housing starts will drop sharply and housing prices will rise less than the rate of inflation, if they do not actually decline.

However, this is not a case of one size fits all. The more likely scenario during a period when interest rates are low and credit is plentiful is for housing starts to show little change, since in those circumstances they are tied primarily to demographic factors. On the other hand, housing prices are likely to rise substantially faster than inflation. For managers, the key factor to track is the difference between the average rate of appreciation in housing prices and the short-term rate at which consumers borrow. If this spread is substantially positive – as it was in 2002, when housing prices rose $7\frac{1}{2}\%$ while short-term rates ranged between $2\frac{1}{2}\%$ and 5%, depending on one's credit

continued

MANAGER'S BRIEFCASE (*continued*)

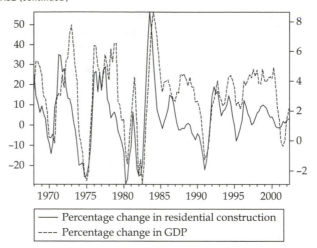

Figure 16.12 Four-quarter percentage changes in investment in residential construction and total GDP, chained 1996 dollars

rating – many consumers are tempted to cash out some of the increased equity in their homes, thus providing consumer spending with a bigger boost than expected from the change in real income and employment.

Conversely, in the future, if the increase in housing prices should decline to 5% – still a reasonable long-term gain – while the borrowing rates for consumers rose to the 4% to 7% range – that source of funding would diminish sharply. Thus even though housing starts probably would not decline because of this modest rise in interest rates, the extra boost to consumer spending due to increased liquidity from cashing out home equity would probably come to a halt, and the increase in consumer spending would be no higher than the rise in disposable income.

16.5   The role of inventory investment in the business cycle

We now turn to a discussion of the determinants of inventory investment. The short-term factors are discussed first; in the long term, the inventory/sales ratio depends on technological rather than economic factors.

The three principal reasons for holding inventory stocks are the transactions, speculative, and buffer-stock motives. The **transactions motive**, which is the most important, states that inventory stocks are proportional to expected sales, with the proportionality factor depending on technological developments. The **speculative motive** indicates that firms are likely to stockpile additional inventories when they think prices will rise rapidly or when they fear shortages; that is less important now. The **buffer-stock motive** reflects the fact that when sales change unexpectedly, in the short term production will change less than sales, with inventories serving as a buffer. This latter effect generally lasts only one to two quarters.

Using the stock adjustment formulation developed earlier in this chapter, the change between the current and lagged level of inventory stock is proportional to the change between the desired inventory stock this period and the actual stock two quarters ago. If

$$Ii^* = \alpha S^*, \tag{16.4}$$

then

$$\Delta Ii = \lambda(\alpha S^* - Ii_{-2}). \tag{16.5}$$

In this case the lags are in quarters rather than years. Ii is the stock of inventories, ΔIi is inventory investment, S is sales of goods (there are no inventories of services), and the $*$ indicated desired levels.

The first step is to determine S^*. On a quarterly basis we can write:

$$S^* = \eta_0 S + \eta_1 S_{-1} + \eta_2 S_{-2} + \eta_3 S_{-3} + (1 - \eta_0 - \eta_1 - \eta_2 - \eta_3)^* S_{-4}. \tag{16.6}$$

A four-quarter lag may seem long for an inventory investment function, but, empirically, firms do take into account changes in (seasonally adjusted) sales over the past year. Inserting that formula in (16.5) yields:

$$\Delta Ii = \lambda(\alpha[\eta_0 S + \eta_1 S_{-1} + \eta_2 S_{-2} + \eta_3 S_{-3} + (1 - \eta_0 - \eta_1 - \eta_2 - \eta_3)S_{-4}] - Ii_{-2}). \tag{16.7}$$

The treatment of λ is somewhat more complicated; it may be a constant term, or it may depend on economic variables. In particular:

- λ could depend on the percentage change in unfilled orders ($\Delta U/U$). If it were rising, firms might decide to boost their desired I/S ratio on the grounds that production levels would be rising in the near future. If $\Delta U/U$ were falling, firms might want to reduce their desired I/S ratio. This term is lagged one quarter because firms take some time to adjust to what they see happening in the market.
- λ could also represent the speculative motive. If firms thought prices of the inventories they carry were likely to rise sharply in the near future, they might boost their desired I/S ratio. They might also boost that ratio if shortages were expected. In general, though, the signal of approaching shortages would be sent through the market mechanism of higher prices, so that term should adequately represent the speculative motive. This term is also lagged one quarter.

We thus have:

$$\Delta Ii = (\beta^*(\Delta U/S)_{-1} + \gamma^*(\Delta p/p)_{-1})^* \{\lambda(\alpha[\eta_0 S + \eta_1 S_{-1} + \eta_2 S_{-2} + \eta_3 S_{-3}$$
$$+ (1 - \eta_0 - \eta_1 - \eta_2 - \eta_3)^* S_{-4}] - Ii_{-2}\}. \tag{16.8}$$

This can be linearized to:

$$\Delta Ii = a(\Delta U/U)_{-1} + b(\Delta p/p)_{-1} + c(\Delta S/S) + d(\Delta S/S)_{-1} + e(\Delta S/S)_{-2}$$
$$+ f(\Delta S/S)_{-3} + g(\Delta S/S)_{-4} + h^*S_{-2} - j^*Ii_{-2}. \quad (16.9)$$

To complete the inventory investment function, we need to add the buffer-stock motive, which says inventory investment is negatively correlated with unexpected changes in sales this quarter. Empirically, the problem is determining when changes in sales are expected and when they are not. It turns out that sales are unexpected when there are significant changes in inventory investment in the opposite direction; unfortunately, that does not provide any help in estimating inventory investment.

The most reasonable practical method is to estimate the coefficient for the difference between the change in sales this period and the change last period. The empirical equation has the same terms as (16.9) but the sign of the coefficient c on unlagged sales is likely to be negative rather than positive because of the buffer-stock motive. The empirical estimate of the equation for inventory investment shows that all of these terms are significant with the expected sign except for unlagged sales, where the coefficient is not significantly different from zero.

However, unlike most of the other empirical functions presented in this text, the results are not very satisfactory because this equation explains less than half of the variance in inventory investment. One problem is that "sales" consists of consumer durables, consumer nondurables, producer durables, housing, nonresidential construction, exports of goods, imports of goods, and defense purchases, all of which may have different adjustment lags. However, even entering all these terms separately hardly improves the fit.

The major problem turns out to be that unexpected changes in sales are not easy to measure empirically. Furthermore, when exogenous forces cause an unexpected change in sales, the resulting fluctuation is likely to be amplified for the next few quarters by changes in inventory investment. In that sense, that phase of the business cycle cannot be offset by optimal policy directives.

The fundamental cyclical pattern of inventory investment has changed over the past two decades. Before 1980, firms would tend to overstockpile inventories during periods of accelerating inflation and possible shortages. When the recession started, it would then take several quarters to work off these excess stocks.

Since then, the reemergence of a low, stable inflation rate, coupled with improved methods of inventory control described in the next section, has sharply reduced the incidence of overstockpiling. Instead, the onset of a recession causes firms to reduce inventory stocks very quickly, even if they were not excessive. That reduction in production and employment amplifies the recession until the benefits of expansionary monetary policy start to work. When final sales do improve again, firms find that inventory stocks are far too low, and a substantial rebuilding process must then occur, leading to unusually large gains in inventory investment until that rebuilding has been completed. Thus changes in inventory investment still account for most of the fluctuation in real GDP during recessions, but for different reasons.

To summarize this section, there have been three principal reasons for fluctuations in inventory investment:

1. Unexpected changes in final sales
2. Purchases of excess stocks in anticipation of price increases or shortages
3. Improper methods of inventory control (e.g., failing to measure changes in sales adequately).

Reason (1) will probably remain a part of the economy indefinitely, given the inability to predict unexpected changes in sales. Reasons (2) and (3) have become increasingly less important in recent decades. Reason (2) disappears when capacity utilization rates and inflation remain relatively low. Reason (3) is discussed in the following section, which describes some of the recent advances made in controlling inventory stocks.

If the latter two factors are omitted, major changes in inventory investment will occur only when other factors – exogenous shocks or incorrect government policies – cause final sales to fluctuate. Hence we reach the conclusion that, although inventory investment accounts for more than half of the total change in real GDP during recessions, the heart of the problem is not in inventory investment per se. It is the major changes in aggregate final sales, and throughout this text we have indicated how these can be moderated or offset.

Since fluctuations in inventory investment are quite erratic and quarterly changes are often due to temporary and exogenous effects, we do not present a graph of what would look like random numbers, but concentrate on the behavior of inventory investment during business cycle recessions, which is summarized in table 16.2.

Table 16.2 Inventory investment as a percentage of change in real GDP during recessions

Quarters of recession	Total drop in real inventories	Total drop in real GDP	Decline in inventory investment as % of GDP
1948.4–49.4	36	25	144
1953.3–54.2	22	51	43
1957.3–58.1	18	85	21
1960.3–61.1	23	75	31
1969.4–79.4	26	40	65
1973.4–75.1	71	125	57
1980.2–80.3	53	103	51
1981.3–82.4	101	144	70
1990.3–91.1	56	74	76
2001.1–01.4	158	58	272
Mean value			83
Median value			57/65

All figures in billions of chained 1996 dollars
Note: Figures start with the 1949 recession since quarterly data are not available before 1947
Source: Calculated from data on BEA website, www.bea.gov

Most of the time, inventory investment accounts for more than half of the total decline in real GDP. In two cases – the 1949 and 2001 recessions – it accounted for more than the total drop in real GDP, which means that final sales continued to rise. Both of these situations were caused by exogenous events, although they were completely different. In 1949, a severe coal strike interfered with the transportation system and caused many plants to shut down, hence sharply reducing inventories. In 2001, many firms reduced inventories sharply in the aftermath of 9/11, yet consumers actually spent more the following quarter, so inventories were then quickly rebuilt.

CASE STUDY 16.2   INVENTORY INVESTMENT DURING THE 2001 RECESSION

According to the Dating Committee of the National Bureau, the 2001 recession began in March; at the time of writing, they had not yet specified an ending date. Real GDP declined during the first three quarters of that year. During 2001, inventory investment declined from $60 billion to −$98 billion, a $158 billion drop. By comparison, total real GDP only fell from $9,244 to $9,186 billion, or $58 billion. Hence final sales rose $100 billion over that same period, or roughly 1%. That is substantially less than the average growth rate of 3% to $3\frac{1}{2}$%, but is not usually considered a recession. Hence the assumption that inventory investment is proportional to the change in final sales does not explain its sharp drop in 2001. Some other factor must have caused inventories to decline that much; if they had not, there would have been no recession in 2001.

Almost all of the unusual behavior occurred in the fourth quarter. The manufacturing I/S ratio had averaged 1.43 in the first quarter of the year, and had risen slightly to 1.45 in September; it then fell to 1.39 in the fourth quarter. The wholesale trade I/S ratio was virtually unchanged throughout the year. The biggest drop occurred in the retail trade I/S ratio; it averaged 1.60 in the first quarter and was virtually unchanged at 1.59 in September, but then dropped sharply to 1.45 in October before rebounding to 1.49 by December.

Almost all of the decline in inventory stocks was unexpected. In October, manufacturing shipments rose $7 billion, while inventory stocks dropped $3 billion. In the retail sector, the changes were even more dramatic, with an $18 billion in sales largely offset by a $12 billion decline in stocks.

Previously, the I/S ratio rose during the early stages of recession. The fact that it did not increase in the first three quarters of 2001 reflects the increasing importance of *just-in-time* and *zero inventories* that kept unwanted stocks from accumulating. In fact, the weakness in inventory investment started in 2000.3, shortly after final

continued

CASE STUDY 16.2 (*continued*)

sales started to slow down; that part of the decline was consistent with the stock adjustment principle.

To a certain extent, the unexpected surge in sales in 2001.4 represented zero-interest rate financing by the domestic auto companies. However, that was not the only factor leading to an increase in sales. Business almost came to a standstill for a few days after 9/11, as witnessed by the decline in new orders from $332 billion in August to $311 billion in September. However, they rebounded right back to $332 billion again in October, yet industrial production continued to decline, as most business executives were understandably concerned about weakening demand and chose not to restock those inventories that were depleted by the unexpected rise in sales.

Hopefully, the events of 9/11 will never happen again. Nonetheless, some useful lessons can be learned from the behavior of inventory investment in 2001. First, overstockpiling of inventories probably will not contribute very much to business cycle fluctuations in the future. Second, when final sales weaken, the lag until inventories readjust is much shorter than it was before 1990. Third, when sales do improve, inventories are likely to decline sharply for at least one quarter before production improves.

16.6   Inventory production and control mechanisms

New methods of inventory control started to be applied in the early 1980s. As shown in figure 16.13, the manufacturing inventory/sales (I/S) ratio was trendless until 1985, but then started to decline sharply, falling in almost every nonrecession year. This is due to the new methods of inventory control, commonly known as *just-in-time* and *zero inventories*. It took the retail sector somewhat longer to incorporate these new methods, but after 1990, the trend in the retail trade I/S ratio has also declined (see figure 16.14).

These new developments do not just happen because some purchasing manager decides to hold, say, 30 days' worth of inventories instead of 60. Instead, the decision to reduce inventory investment must be part of a coordinated effort to modify the method of production so materials and parts can be integrated into the manufacturing process more quickly and hence the need for excess stocks will diminish. If this is not done, firms will find themselves with shortages at critical times. Hence these new methods are closely associated with improved productivity in the manufacturing sector, much of which has been accomplished by computerization of production techniques that used to rely on manual labor.

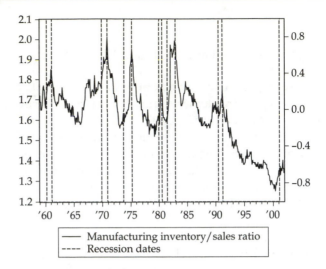

Figure 16.13 The manufacturing inventory/sales ratio

Sources: I/S ratio, Census website, www.census.gov; recession dates, NBER website, www.nber.org

Figure 16.14 The retail trade inventory/sales ratio

Sources: I/S ratio, Census website, www.census.gov; recession dates, NBER website, www.nber.org

A few comments about these new methods.

- On an individual firm basis, there is little doubt that the combination of higher productivity and lower carrying costs has resulted in lower costs.

- As a result, manufacturing prices have risen at a lower rate. Ordinarily, that would boost export growth because US firms are now more competitive in world markets, but in the late 1990s and 2000–2001, that was offset by the stronger dollar.
- Firms still have trouble predicting recessions, so in spite of these improved methods, the I/S ratio still rises during recessions. More work is needed to cure these short-term problems. However, the overall I/S ratio did fall during most of the 2001 recession, so progress is being made.
- The retail sector started to exhibit the same long-term downward trend after 1990. The vast majority of retail sales are now sold in stores with point-of-purchase computers that enable them to keep much better track of inventories, or transactions now take place over the internet.

MANAGER'S BRIEFCASE: PLANNING INVENTORY CONTROL IN THE FUTURE

This author can attest to the fact that while production managers are increasingly astute about reducing long-term trends in the I/S ratio, unexpected short-term changes in sales are still as difficult to handle as was the case in previous decades.[4] No solution to this issue is in sight; econometric attempts to measure unexpected changes in sales have also been unsuccessful. However, most problems that this author has seen have been caused by two apparently contradictory reasons: paying too much attention to erratic swings, or ignoring emerging trends. The issue is clearly to find a middle ground between these two extremes.

In our experience, these errors can be sharply reduced by augmenting various production smoothing and planning models by including relevant economic variables that affect sales in your industry. Erratic fluctuations that have no counterpart in the macroeconomic or sectoral data are likely to be due to short-term factors that will be reversed in the next month or quarter. Conversely, if orders or sales in your industry start to turn down, it is unlikely that your firm will not eventually be affected. Even if orders do not initially decline, weakness at competing firms will probably cause them to cut prices or offer better terms in order to try and maintain market share.

Managers often state that with thousands of parts or SKU items, the cost of the work involved in building econometric relationships is greater than the improvement in profits that would accrue. That is, of course, a decision to be made by each individual management team. However, the standard smoothing models provide virtually no information about turning points, and can result in substantial excess inventories for periods of several months.[5] Even a few macroeconomic variables, such as the components of the index of leading indicators that are most relevant for your business, should improve inventory control significantly.

16.7 Cyclical patterns in purchases of motor vehicles

This is an unusual section in the sense that the factors determining consumer purchases of new cars and light trucks through 2000 were apparently quite different from the ones that determined purchases starting in 2001. Hence we depart from our usual procedure and first discuss the factors that were important, then explain

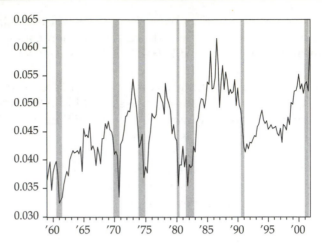

Figure 16.15 Ratio of purchases of motor vehicles and parts to disposable personal income, chained dollars (shaded areas are recessions)
Source: BEA website, www.bea.gov

what has changed. We then conclude by offering some hints about what factors might be important in the future.

Figure 16.15 shows the ratio of purchases of motor vehicles and parts to disposable income. Until 2001 this component of GDP seemed to represent the quintessential cyclical indicator. In 2001, however, the pattern was completely reversed; there was a sharp increase in this ratio during the downturn. The determinants of motor vehicle sales shifted dramatically in 2001.

Before 2001, the parameters of the equation to explain and predict motor vehicle sales were fairly straightforward: disposable income, demographic trends, the cost and availability of credit, and consumer attitudes, which can be measured either with one of the indexes for that purpose, or by including the rate of unemployment, the rate of inflation, and the stock market. This relationship is shown in figure 16.16; the equation is given in the note 6. It fits the actual data very closely except during the summer of 1985 and 1986, when incentives were first used on a large scale to clear the showrooms before the new model year vehicles arrived. As is also shown on that graph, the equation does not fit at all well in late 2001 and early 2002.

One can surmise that perhaps our equation underestimates the importance of low interest rates, but according to the data available in the G.20 series of Federal Reserve reports, the actual interest rate on new cars offered during 2001.4 fell from 6% to 3%. Sales at annual rates rose by 5 million, or roughly 31%. Based on the average length of maturity, the net effect was to reduce the average monthly payment by 2%. That implies a price elasticity of −15, which is prima facie ridiculous. Other factors must have been at work. Indeed, it is not unreasonable to speculate that if the major automobile manufacturers had simply announced a 2% price reduction – as opposed to low finance terms – sales would not have risen nearly as much as 31%.

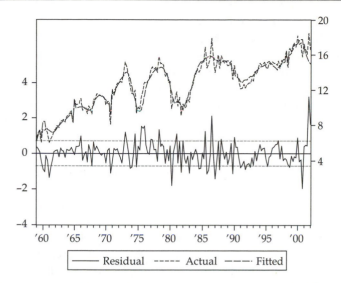

Figure 16.16   Actual and simulated values of consumer purchases of new cars and light trucks

Domestic auto manufacturers are more likely to offer attractive incentives during periods when the dollar is strong. At such times, foreign manufacturers have more flexibility in offering bigger discounts and low finance rates, hoping to gain market share. If domestic dealers do not match these offers, they are likely to lose sales not only that year but in the longer run. Thus motor vehicle sales are more likely to be countercyclical during those recessions when the dollar is strong, as in 2001, than they were in 1990–91, when the dollar was weak.

From the viewpoint of managers whose companies do business with the auto industry, the relevant question is what to expect during the next boom – and the next recession. Will auto sales return to their former cyclical pattern, or will they be driven by production, with excess vehicles sold by offering ever-increasing rebates and extremely low financing rates?

Before 2001, we found that:

1. Monetary conditions – both the cost and availability of credit – are important determinants of motor vehicle sales. Obviously auto companies are more likely to offer enticing credit terms when the Federal funds rate is 2% than when it is 15%. Furthermore, when the monetary authorities discourage lending institutions from making loans to consumers, or actually impose credit controls, motor vehicle sales will suffer. The yield spread remains important; the unusually large spread in late 2001 was a contributing factor to the rise in car sales.

    Changes in the regulations regarding the granting of credit and loans have had a major impact on consumer spending. When Paul Volcker instituted credit controls in early 1980, consumer spending fell at a record rate for the next three months until the controls were rescinded. The dip in the 1990–92 period in the debt/income ratio stemmed from the crackdown on lending practices in the aftermath of the S&L crisis; the lessened availability of credit generated sluggish growth for several years. Not until the restrictions were relaxed in 1993 did consumer spending and overall growth rise enough to propel the economy back to full employment.

2. The unemployment rate, the inflation rate, and stock prices were important; because of the importance of gasoline prices, the relative price of oil is the relevant inflation term. In 2001, the stock market plunged, unemployment rose, and consumer attitudes declined sharply, but apparently none of this affected car sales negatively.

3. Short-run changes in disposable income have a mixed track record. The fact that the ratio of car sales/income fell in every recession before 2001 indicates some short-term correlation. Also, car sales did rise in 1965, 1975, 1983, and 2001 after tax cuts or rebates occurred. On the other hand, except for 1965, all these years also featured substantial declines in interest rates and easing of credit conditions. Multiple regression analysis indicates that fluctuations in both monetary conditions and disposable income are important in determining car sales.

4. Demographic factors are important. In particular, the proportion of the population aged 16–24 is positively correlated with sales, and the proportion of the population aged 45 and older is negatively correlated with sales.

Based on this equation, we would have expected new car and light truck sales to decline from 17.1 million units in 2000 to 15.9 million units in 2001. Obviously nothing of the sort happened; they stayed at 16.9 million in the first half of the year and then rose to 17.3 million in the second half. Sales in 2002 totalled 16.7 million, about 1 million above the level predicted by this function for that year.

The "zero-interest financing," which on average worked out to about a 3% rate, cannot explain all of the discrepancy, nor can the ease of obtaining credit. In terms of the permanent income hypothesis and life cycle hypothesis theories of consumption, it would seem that consumers remained optimistic in spite of the recession in 2001 and the rise in unemployment to 6%. Even after the stock market declined sharply, most long-term investors still had substantial capital gains. Most consumers viewed the 2001 recession and the 9/11 tragedy as short-term changes that did not fundamentally affect their permanent income or wealth. Also, monetary factors continued to be of great importance. By comparison, the various indexes of consumer sentiment were not closely correlated with sales. These factors measure *short-term* changes in attitudes, whereas the modern theories of the consumption function emphasize the *long-term* expectations for income and wealth.

In the first 15 years of the post-WWII period, which included the recessions from 1949 through 1960, most consumers still vividly remembered the economic deprivation of the Great Depression, and remained concerned that any short-term decline might turn into another severe and prolonged downturn. After all, the Great

Depression started out as just another mild recession, replete with statements by business, financial, and political leaders that "a return to prosperity is just around the corner." Indeed, when a delegation came to see President Herbert Hoover in May 1930 to discuss the economic downturn, he reportedly said, "You are too late. The downturn has ended." The point of this anecdote is not to criticize politicians and economists of the early 1930s, but to indicate how the average consumer in the 1940s and 1950s might have remained worried that even mild downturns would turn into something far worse.

By the time 1970 arrived, and the economy had undergone almost an entire decade of unequalled prosperity, most of the Depression mentality had disappeared. Now, however, business cycle peaks were strongly marked by higher inflation, Fed tightening, and a reduction in credit availability. As a result, many purchases of motor vehicles were postponed. That same pattern was repeated in 1973–4, 1980, 1981–2, and 1990–91. However, there were no such restrictions or tightening in 2000 and 2001.

All these factors help determine the cyclical behavior of consumer spending. If consumers believe that their permanent income or wealth has been reduced, they will cut back on their spending; otherwise they will not, ceteris paribus. If monetary conditions restrict the degree of credit availability or raise interest rates substantially, consumers will postpone their purchases; otherwise they will not, ceteris paribus. *Temporary* increases in the unemployment rate, slower growth in real income, a setback in the stock market, or a plunge in the index of consumer attitudes will not affect patterns of consumer spending. *If you are a manager and want to know how your sales will be affected, the variables to watch are permanent income and wealth and monetary conditions, not temporary changes in short-term factors.*

Outside of those who work in New York City, or in the central business districts of Boston, Philadelphia, Washington, Chicago, and San Francisco, virtually everyone needs a car to get to and from work. Of course that does not mean they necessarily need a new car. Economists used to think that a surge in new car sales one year would result in a drop in sales the next year. Yet the last time that happened was in 1955. Most people replace their motor vehicles at regularly scheduled intervals unless they are out of work, or unless credit is restricted. A smaller percentage of people lost their jobs (as measured by the unemployment rate) in the 2001 recession than any other post-WWII downturn.

Approximately two-thirds of people who buy or lease cars use some sort of deferred payment plan – installment credit, personal leases, or leases through their place of work. Essentially the decision boils down to this: if the auto industry offers the choice between driving a 2- or 3-year-old car with a monthly payment of $400 and a new car with the same monthly payment of $400 and no penalty for early termination of the existing time purchase contract, most people are going to drive off in a new car.

The issue now becomes as much a microeconomic marketing question as it does a macroeconomic analysis: under what circumstances does it pay the auto industry to offer these incentives? The key decision factors are (a) in most cases, they must now pay production workers whether they are actually working on the assembly lines or not, (b) when the dollar is stronger, foreign manufacturers have more leeway to offer generous incentives, and domestic manufacturers do not want to lose market share, and (c) this scheme obviously makes more sense for the auto industry when interest rates are unusually low – as often, although not always, happens during and shortly after recessions.

In the future, one possibility is that "domestic" auto companies will move more of their production facilities to foreign countries, where labor laws do not require paying people for not working, and the strong dollar works to their advantage rather than their disadvantage. In that case, the auto companies might not be so anxious to offer low interest rates and large rebates in the future.

That remains to be seen. However, the lessons of the past 20 years suggest the following. New motor vehicle sales probably will not dip very much in future recessions as long as consumers remain relatively optimistic, interest rates and inflation remain low, and consumer credit is not restricted. In the same vein, increases in the unemployment rate and declines in stock markets will probably play a much smaller role in determining new motor vehicle sales in the future.

16.8   Cyclical patterns in other components of consumption

In this section we look briefly at the cyclical properties of purchases of other durable goods, and also those components of nondurables, mainly restaurant meals and clothing, which exhibit marked cyclical patterns. Both series shown in figure 16.17 have the trends removed in order to concentrate on the cyclical patterns. The trends would show a sharp increase in the ratio of other durables to income, and a sharp decline in the ratio of nondurables to income.

A detailed analysis of the cyclical factors that affect other durables and non-durables is not required here. In general, the cost and availability of credit are the key cyclical variables. Note in particular how purchases of other durables and nondurables both slumped severely during the credit squeeze of the early 1990s. Consumption of other durables turned down in every recession except the last one, when interest rates had not risen and credit was not restricted. This also suggests a significant correlation with housing starts and sales, since completion or purchase of a new house is generally followed by purchases of household furniture and kitchen appliances as well. Consumption of nondurables turned down in every recession, indicating that both income and credit variables are important cyclical determinants.

In terms of cyclical analysis, then, changes in monetary policy have a much bigger impact on short-term fluctuations in consumption than changes in disposable income, although both are important. The impact of changes in tax rates remains questionable. All components of consumption did rise following the permanent income tax cuts in 1964–5 and 1982–3. The temporary 10% income tax surcharge

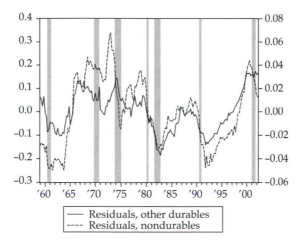

Figure 16.17   Residuals for purchases of consumer durables excluding motor vehicles and parts and nondurables relative to log-linear trends (shaded areas are recessions)

imposed in the middle of 1968 and removed in the middle of 1970 did not seem to have any measurable impact on consumption. The 1975 and 2001 rebates both occurred shortly after the Fed had eased sharply, so while consumption rose in both cases, it is difficult to assign weights to monetary and fiscal policy.

16.9   Recap: what determines cyclical fluctuations in aggregate demand

The material presented in this chapter provides a further explanation for the reasons why business cycles now occur less frequently. The endogenous stock adjustment mechanism is less important than earlier, and most of the fluctuations in the individual components of aggregate demand are due to changes in monetary conditions. If inflation does not rise near the end of the business cycle expansion, there is generally no reason for interest rates to rise, or for the Fed to restrict credit. In those cases, endogenous business cycle downturns occur only when excess capacity exists, and these cycles generally take about a decade to develop. Of course, further exogenous shocks could always cause a major business cycle downturn, but the quick recovery of the economy after 9/11 suggests that even terrorist attacks on the US will not necessarily cause an economic downturn.

The stock adjustment principle for capital spending can still cause some endogenous fluctuations if capital spending declines when the utilization rate falls, ceteris paribus. However, that is mainly the case for investment goods with long lives, while the fluctuations in capital spending are increasingly dominated by goods with short lives, such as information processing equipment and motor vehicles. Another stock market decline as severe as the 2000–2002 contraction would probably lead to another modest economic downturn, but it is unlikely that the market will become that overvalued again for several decades. Even in 1929, the peak P/E ratio was about 20, compared to 36 for the S&P 500 in March 2000 – and triple digits for those relatively few Nasdaq stocks that reported profits.

An increase in the vacancy rate would reduce housing starts, ceteris paribus, so a period of overbuilding might be followed by a decline in housing starts. That could still happen if artificial stimuli, notably government programs or interference with market interest rates, cause starts to rise well above their equilibrium level as determined by demographic factors. In the 1990s, though, cyclical fluctuations in housing starts have been much smaller, and wide swings in vacancy rates have not occurred. In 2001, housing starts hardly declined at all.

Inventory investment is likely to change significantly in response to unexpected changes in sales. However, improved methods of inventory control have reduced the likelihood that unexpected changes in sales will affect inventory investment for more than a few months at a time. Furthermore, we find that historically, most of the major swings in inventory investment reflected expectations that inflation would increase or shortages would occur, but those developments are much less likely today. Hence although inventory investment still accounts for about half of the fluctuations in real GDP during recessions, it is not the cause of economic downturns.

Finally, the stock adjustment principle does not hold for purchases of consumer durables. Instead, fluctuations in those purchases follow changes in spendable income and the cost and availability of credit. Currently, major automobile manufacturers offer rebates and other incentives to boost sales when they would otherwise be depressed by low income and high unemployment.

The permanent income and life cycle hypotheses have always needed to be modified for those consumers whose credit is restricted, have no buffer stock of liquid assets, and do not plan very far ahead. When interest rates did not rise and credit was not restricted, consumers continued to spend in spite of the recession.

Monetary policy variables clearly have an important influence on cyclical fluctuations in consumption as well as the rest of the economy. In addition, the amount of spendable income – which includes disposable income, changes in income reflecting monthly mortgage payments, and changes in income reflecting realized capital gains – helps determine cyclical fluctuations in consumption. To a limited extent, changes in the stock market may also reflect expectations, although those changes are not usually translated into consumer spending decisions; the effect is more directly felt on purchases of capital goods.

The amount banks will lend to consumers is also a key determinant of motor vehicle sales. This is measured not only by the amount of bank loans or changes in credit, but also by the yield spread. In periods where monetary policy was transmitted primarily through changes in the money supply, that variable was also important. Currently, the spread between the appreciation in home prices and the short-term rate at which consumers can borrow is probably just as important as the traditional yield spread between bonds and bills.

To conclude this chapter, business cycles will still occur when truly exogenous shocks surprise both private sector economic agents and government policymakers. Except in those cases, however, there is scant evidence that the endogenous mechanisms that used to cause business cycles are still important. Instead, most of the fluctuations in economic activity are caused by changes in the cost and availability of credit, which in turn follow major changes in the rate of inflation. If credible monetary policy can hold inflation at low, steady levels, the endogenous business cycles that can be expected to occur will be caused primarily by excess capacity after a lengthy investment boom, and hence will happen less frequently.

KEY TERMS AND CONCEPTS

Buffer-Stock, Speculative, and Transactions Motives (for holding inventories)
Stock Adjustment Principle

SUMMARY

- The principal components of capital spending are purchases of industrial equipment, high-tech equipment, transportation equipment, other equipment, and nonresidential construction. Industrial equipment generally turns down in the later stages of recessions, and generally turns up only with a substantial lag; other equipment follows the same pattern, but it turns up more quickly after recessions end. Transportation equipment follows the pattern of the business cycle more closely, and with a shorter lag. The decline in high-tech equipment was the major cause of the 2001 recession; previously it had not been a major factor. Nonresidential construction has a longer lag; it generally does not turn down until the recession is almost over, or the recovery has already started.
- Longer-term trends in the ratio of capital spending to GDP depend on the rate of capacity utilization, the ratio of profits/GDP, and the real Aaa corporate bond rate. The change in stock prices is also likely to affect

expectations as well as determine the cost of equity capital.
- In the long run, residential construction depends on demographic factors and vacancy rates. In the short run, the controlling factors are the cost and availability of credit. The cost of credit is represented by the mortgage rate; the availability of credit by changes in the money supply and loans granted. The cost of housing is not a significant variable; the increase in housing costs that might raise the barrier to home ownership is generally offset by the expectations of further capital appreciation, which increases demand. Also, when prices are rising rapidly, "creative financing" methods and shared equity mortgages can also lower the initial cost of ownership.
- The three principal reasons for holding inventory stocks are the transactions, speculative, and buffer-stock motives. The transactions motive states that inventory investment is proportional to the difference between desired stocks, which in turn are

proportional to sales, and previous actual stocks. The speculative motive reflects the increase in stocks when prices are expected to rise or shortages are likely to occur; it has become less important in recent decades. The buffer-stock motive reflects the fact that when sales unexpectedly change, inventory investment changes in the opposite direction for a few months. Thus, when a recession starts, inventory investment usually rises for a while before declining, and when a recovery starts, inventory investment usually declines for a while. The buffer-stock effect lasts for only about one to two quarters.

- Starting in 1985 for the manufacturing sector, and in 1991 for retail trade, the inventory/sales ratios have declined sharply because of new methods of inventory control and management. Before then, the manufacturing I/S ratio was trendless, while the retail trade I/S ratio exhibited a slight upward trend.

- Purchases of motor vehicles used to be the quintessential pro-cyclical indicator, but they rose in the 2001 recession. Part of that reflected the zero-interest financing options offered by the big domestic manufacturers, which in turn was implemented because most production workers in that industry are paid whether they actually are on the assembly lines or not. In addition, there was no credit squeeze or sharp rise in interest rates preceding that recession.

- Both the cost and availability of credit and disposable income are important determinants of short-term fluctuations in consumer purchases of durables and nondurables, but monetary terms are more important. Permanent tax changes appear to have a sizeable impact on consumer purchases, but temporary changes in tax rates do not. Fluctuations in consumer sentiment are not correlated with changes in consumer purchases, especially in 1991 and late 2001.

QUESTIONS AND PROBLEMS

1. The following two graphs show the ratio of consumption/income and stock prices/income, and the four-quarter percentage changes in consumption and

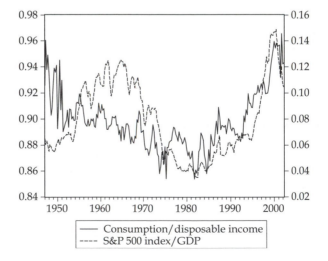

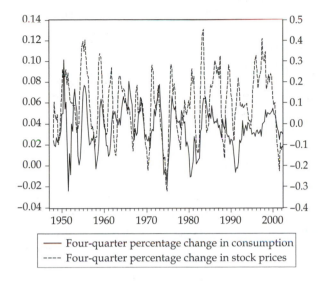

- Four-quarter percentage change in consumption
- - - - Four-quarter percentage change in stock prices

stock prices. Based on these graphs, do you think that short-term or long-term fluctuations in stock prices are the more important determinant of consumption? Why do you think the correlation in percentage changes is stronger before 1980, while the correlation with the ratios is stronger after 1980?

2. Older business cycle theories used to focus on what was called the "interaction of the multiplier and the accelerator" to produce endogenous business cycles; the accelerator said that investment was proportional to the change in output. Under reasonable empirical estimates of the underlying parameters, such a model could be shown to generate business cycles once every four to five years. Considering that the US economy has had only two minor recessions since 1982, which do you think has changed more – the multiplier or the accelerator? What are the principal reasons for that change?

3. From 1947 to 1973, the US economy went through five recessions, while Europe and Japan did not have any. Since 1982, however, cyclical downturns in Europe and Japan have been at least as frequent as in the US. What factors caused the frequency of business cycles in the US to decline, and what factors caused their frequency in Europe and Japan to increase?

4. Virtually all purchases of consumer nondurable goods do not involve extended credit terms. Yet that component of GDP exhibits a very marked cyclical pattern, always turning down during recessions. Can these declines be explained entirely by the reduction in disposable income, or are they also related to credit conditions? (Hint: what happens when consumers are forced to pay off their other loans in a more timely fashion?)

5. During past recessions, housing prices generally rose much less than usual, and fell in real terms. Yet in the 2001 recession, housing prices rose much more than average. What factors caused them to rise so rapidly during the recession? On a regional basis, the biggest price increases occurred in New York, Massachusetts, and Florida, regions whose income could generally be tied closely to the stock market (Florida representing retirees from the Northeast). What does that say about the impact of changes in stock prices on the demand for housing? Explain whether that finding is consistent with the permanent income and life cycle hypotheses.

6. Improved methods of inventory control were supposed to reduce fluctuations in inventory stocks. It is clear that these methods have helped reduce the equilibrium inventory/sales ratios in both the manufacturing and trade sectors over the past decade. Yet we find that during the 2001 recession, inventory investment accounted for more than the total decline in real GDP, the first time that had happened since 1949. Explain whether this result is due to a set of odd coincidences, or whether the improved methods of inventory control actually caused bigger fluctuations in inventory investment relative to final sales.

7. The next time the US economy returns to full employment, what factors will determine how much longer it will take for the next recession to develop? (Note: there is no "right" answer to this question; the idea is to organize your thoughts to explain under what circumstances a recession based on higher inflation and higher interest rates would occur, a recession based on excess capacity would occur, or no recession at all would occur.)

8. As purchases of high-tech equipment become an increasingly important part of total capital spending, and hence total GDP, do you think fluctuations in that category will dominate cyclical fluctuations in the overall economy? (Hint: under what circumstances will the superheated growth rate of the 1990s resume in the 2000s, and under what circumstances will these purchases grow at about the same rate as the overall economy?)

9. When inflation and interest rates rise at business cycle peaks, the dollar is likely to decline because foreign investors withdraw assets that are likely to depreciate in real terms because of higher inflation. That helps mitigate the downturn because a weaker dollar boosts exports and reduces imports. On the other hand, if the economy continues to prosper at full employment without any increase in inflation, more foreign capital is likely to be attracted, hence boosting the dollar and weakening net exports. If other sectors of the economy then weaken, that could exacerbate the recession, as occurred in 2001. To what extent do you think a stronger dollar is likely to cause cyclical downturns in the future?

10. During 2002, the Federal funds rate remained more than 1% below the rate of inflation. When that happened in 1972 and 1975, the next two business cycle peaks ended in double-digit inflation, although admittedly higher oil prices were also responsible. Do you think that the Fed decision to hold the funds rate

below equilibrium will cause higher inflation at the peak of the next business cycle? What factors would influence your answer? (Hint: besides the obvious answer that the Fed can always tighten vigorously once the recovery gets underway, consider the impact of the Federal budget position.)

Notes

1. Strictly speaking, this formulation applies to the use value of durables, not purchases.
2. It used to be claimed by some in the home improvement industry that major additions and alterations had a countercyclical pattern, on the grounds that if times were good, you sold your house, and if times were bad, you fixed it up. However, there has been no evidence of such a pattern in the past 40 years.
3. The equation is:

$$HST = -141.2 - \underset{(9.7)}{138.9} \times movavg(hvr(-5), 2) + \underset{(12.1)}{25,454} \, poprat + \underset{(8.6)}{33.9\%} chg(M2)$$

$$\times (1 - d83) + \underset{(8.9)}{24.5} \times \%chg \, (LOAN) \times d83 + \underset{(7.0)}{59.4} \times movavg(yldsprd(-2), 4)$$

$$+ \underset{(8.7)}{72.8} \times movavg(yldsprd(-6), 4) + \underset{(4.0)}{-36.9} \times movavg(rt10(-2), 4)$$

$$+ \underset{(9.2)}{6871} \, SP500/GDP \quad Adj \, R2 = 0.847 \quad DW = 0.89$$

where HST = housing starts, hvr = vacancy rate, poprat = ratio of population aged 20–25 to total population, M2 = M2 measure of the money supply, LOAN = business loans, yldsprd = yield spread between the Aaa bond rate and Fed funds rate, rt10 = 10-year Treasury note rate (a proxy for the mortgage rate), SP500 = S&P 500 stock price index. Movavg is moving average, the first number is the initial lag, the second number is the length of lag. Numbers in ( ) are *t*-ratios. After the equation is adjusted for autocorrelation (not shown here) all variables remain significant.
4. From 1993 through 2000, this author conducted a monthly survey for APICS, the American Production and Inventory Control Society, in which participating firms were requested to submit information on the percentage change in sales, orders, inventories, employment, and other key variables. An index was then constructed that would alert managers to "unexpected" changes in sales. For a while the index worked well, but when business slowed down, many staffers who filled out these reports were dismissed and not replaced, so the sample size declined and the results became more erratic, so the survey was finally terminated. APICS was not the only organization facing this difficulty; in 2001, Census announced that the monthly reports for manufacturers' shipments, orders, and inventories would no longer contain any information from the semiconductor industry because of the sharp decline in responses.
5. For some tests of this hypothesis, see Michael K. Evans, *Practical Business Forecasting* (Blackwell Publishing, 2003), chapter 7.

6. $\text{MOTVEH} = -4.93 + \underset{(7.3)}{0.52} \times \text{movavg}(\text{yldsprd}(-2), 4) + \underset{(4.3)}{0.072} \times \%\text{chg cred} + \underset{(2.5)}{0.034}$

$\times \%\text{chg lagged cred} + \underset{(4.4)}{0.0058} \text{ dstr} + \underset{(20.9)}{11.33} \times \text{poprat1645} + \underset{(10.8)}{0.0068} \times \text{SP500}(-1)$

$- \underset{(2.9)}{1.67} \times \text{relpoil}(-2) + \underset{(3.4)}{0.000401} \times \text{DI} - \underset{(5.8)}{0.473} \times \text{movavg}(\text{UN}(-1), 4)$

Adj R2 = 0.941, DW = −1.55. MOTVEH = number of motor vehicles sold, millions, cred = consumer credit outstanding, dstr = dummy variables for auto strike, poprat1645 = ratio of people aged 16–24 to people aged 45 and older, relpoil = PPI of petroleum products/CPI, DI = disposable income, UN = rate of unemployment. All other symbols and nomenclature are the same as in note 3.

chapter seventeen

Financial business cycles

Introduction

The previous two chapters described the patterns of business cycle for the overall economy and the major components of aggregate demand. This chapter discusses the cyclical patterns of (a) monetary and credit aggregates, (b) interest rates and yield spreads, and (c) stock prices. The relationship between stock prices and other monetary and real sector variables is then analyzed in detail. This completes our analysis of cyclical patterns; in the past, a chapter might have been added on the cyclical behavior of inflation rates, but whereas changes in prices used to be procyclical, they are now countercyclical because higher inflation is likely to lead to an end of the boom, whereas continued low inflation will prolong the business cycle expansion. For this reason, the procyclical nature of inflation no longer occurs.

The periodicity of US business cycle fluctuations makes it clear there is no one-to-one relationship between fluctuations in real output and financial markets. In recent decades, financial market cycles in both interest rates and stock prices have occurred more frequently than real sector cycles. This chapter discusses the nature of financial business cycles, the major factors that determine fluctuations in bonds and stocks, and the feedback between the real and monetary sectors. It examines the determinants of the difference between the return on stocks, bonds, and liquid assets, includes a few comments on the cyclical characteristics of other asset prices, and concludes with some brief remarks on asset allocation.

Cyclical fluctuations in the major components of aggregate demand are caused in large part by changes in the cost and availability of credit and equity capital. To a certain extent, changes in stock prices reflect changes in bond prices, but in recent years it has become clear that fluctuations in the stock market occur for other reasons as well. Even before the recent stock market meltdown, stock prices invariably declined during the initial stages of recessions even though bond prices, spurred by Fed easing and the expectation of lower inflation ahead, headed higher. The 2001 recession was caused in part by the sharp decline in stock prices even though bond yields had not risen much near the end of the previous business cycle expansion. An even greater divergence occurred in 2002, when stocks fell sharply during much of the year even as bond prices headed higher.

The other relevant issue is the pattern of asset allocation over the cycle: when companies should raise money, and when the choice should be short-term liquid assets, bonds, or equity investment. After the meltdown of the Nasdaq market in 2001 and the surfacing of so many scandals, it became more fashionable to refer to Wall Street as one big shell game. Yet under ordinary circumstances, financial markets perform the essential function of allocating scarce credit resources to the areas where they will generate the highest rate of return. Hence proper asset allocation over the cycle also boosts capital formation, productivity growth, and long-term increases in the standard of living. To the extent that optimal allocation does not occur, long-term productivity growth is reduced.

17.1   Cyclical patterns of monetary and credit aggregates

This section examines the cyclical patterns of three major monetary aggregates relative to GDP, all in chained dollars: the M2 measure of the money supply; commercial and industrial loans, often known as business loans; and consumer credit outstanding. These relationships are all shown starting after the Korean War; before then, the Fed was required by the Treasury to hold the price of the long bond at par, so market relationships were distorted.

Until 1982, when the banking system was deregulated, the real money supply served as an important leading indicator for the overall economy, especially for signaling recessions. As shown in figure 17.1, it turned down an average of two quarters before the economy started to decline. Furthermore, there were no false signals. After 1982, however, that relationship no longer held. Once the banking sector was deregulated, the Fed could no longer closely control money supply; changes in the monetary base diverged sharply from changes in M2. That does not mean that the availability of credit was no longer important, only that it was better measured with different aggregates.

However, real money supply growth after 1982 cannot be dismissed entirely. As also shown in figure 17.1, the decline in real money supply in the early 1990s was one of the reasons the recovery was unusually sluggish; this was reflected in a sharp decline in real business loans, as discussed below. Furthermore, the surge in the real money supply in 1998 and 1999 – the result of the Fed trying to offset any possible damage from the collapse of Long-Term Capital Management and the Y2K phantom – not only kept the economy rising at above-average rates, but was a major factor causing the stock market to rise to unsustainable levels.

Figure 17.2 shows the relationship between the four-quarter percentage changes in real business loans and real GDP. Notice that before 1982 – i.e., during the era of banking deregulation – the change in loans served as a *lagging* indicator. That reflects the fact that many loans are used for purchases of capital equipment, which is also a lagging indicator.

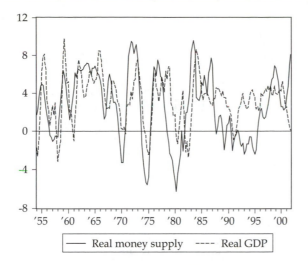

Figure 17.1   Percentage changes in real money supply and real GDP
Sources: Fed website and BEA website (www.federalreserve.gov, www.bea.gov)

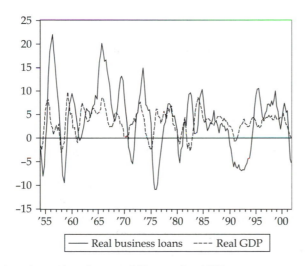

Figure 17.2   Percentage changes in real commercial loans and real GDP
Sources: Fed website and BEA website (www.federalreserve.gov, www.bea.gov)

However, after banking deregulation, the timing changed substantially. Real business loans started to decline in 1989, about a year before the 1990 recession started. As can be seen in the graph, they continued to decline for four more years. More recently, business loans started to decline in late 2000, shortly before the recession got underway, and were still declining in mid-2002 even though the recovery had started several months earlier. Thus while the upturn in

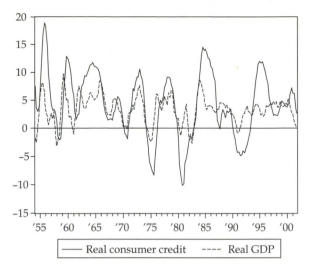

Figure 17.3   Percentage changes in real consumer credit and real GDP
Sources: Fed website and BEA website (www.federalreserve.gov, www.bea.gov)

business loans still lags the cycle, that series has also served as a leading indicator of recessions since 1982, replacing the role of the money supply.

As noted in earlier chapters, business loans continued to decline during the 1991–3 period of the upturn because of the restrictions placed on lending officers in the wake of the S&L scandals of the 1980s. That was clearly an exogenous development; yet it is one of the principal reasons why real growth was so sluggish until 1994, and cannot be ignored when explaining the business cycle history of recent years.

Figure 17.3 shows the cyclical pattern of real consumer credit. For the most part it is a coincident indicator, and in that respect is less important in explaining the business cycle than the change in business loans. Nonetheless, we discuss it briefly because of the substantial dips in 1980 and 1990–93. The decline in 1980 represented the brief imposition of credit controls, which caused the most rapid decline in real GDP ever recorded in 1980.2. The 1990–93 dip was a secondary effect of the restriction on lending activity by bank officers; while it applied mainly to business loans, granting of consumer credit was also somewhat restricted during that period.

In terms of following the monetary and credit aggregates, managers should be aware of the following considerations. First, exogenous restrictions on business and consumer credit often lead to a recession. Second, even in the absence of exogenous changes, business loans are likely to serve as a leading indicator ahead of recessions, although they continue to lag the upturn. Third, consumer credit is a coincident indicator in the absence of exogenous changes in credit regulations. Fourth, although changes in the money supply are dictated primarily by changes in the demand for credit instead of monetary policy, the Fed can still affect money supply growth – and when it chooses to implement policy in that manner, the results are still significant.

17.2   Cyclical patterns in the yield spread

The material in previous chapters has emphasized that a rise in interest rates is generally followed by a decline in the growth rate. However, a graph showing the four-quarter changes in interest rates and GDP, similar to the graphs presented in the previous section, would be inconclusive, and no stable pattern would be apparent. When the economy accelerates, interest rates generally rise, especially in the latter parts of the expansion, so the graphical correlation would contain elements of both demand and supply. Also, the real rate of interest, rather than the nominal rate, is the more important determinant of real growth. Even more to the point, though, higher interest rates are unlikely to slow down the economy very much unless those increases are also accompanied by reduced availability of credit.

In previous chapters we explained why the yield spread serves as a valid measure of credit availability. To review briefly, when short-term rates are higher than long-term rates, financial institutions are more likely to buy Treasury securities and other short-term financial instruments, such as commercial paper. Not only is the yield higher, but the market and default risks are much lower. As a result, banks reduce the amount of funds that are available to lend to businesses and consumers.

Figures 17.4 and 17.5 show the relationship of a six-month moving average of the yield spread with the twelve-month percentage change in the index of coincident indicators. The first graph shows the yield spread generally used throughout this book: the Aaa corporate bond yield minus the Federal funds rate. However, that yield spread stayed close to 2% in the months preceding the 2001 recession, so some economists, including the compilers of the Index of Leading Economic Indicators at the Conference Board, used the spread between the 10-year Treasury note yield and the 3-month Treasury bill rate, which did indeed turn negative during 2000. The only problem with this measure is that, as can be seen in figure 17.5, it did not give as clear a signal in earlier recessions.

To indicate the value of the yield spread as a leading indicator, we use the index of coincident indicators to provide a closer reading of current economic activity on a monthly basis. It consists of four components: nonfarm payroll employment, real business sales, industrial production, and real personal income excluding transfers. The properties of this index, and its comparison with the index of leading indicators, are discussed in greater detail in chapter 20; here we can say that it faithfully mirrors the turning points in all business cycles without any lead or lag, and is the main indicator used by the Dating Committee of the National Bureau to determine when business cycles begin and end.

Is the yield spread an infallible indicator of upcoming recessions? The graph suggests it failed to predict the mild 1960 recession, but in fact the yield spread was

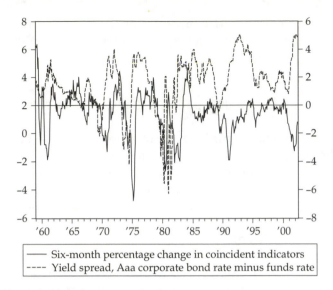

Figure 17.4 Yield spread with the Aaa corporate bond rate
Sources: Recent data, Conference Board website and Fed website (www.conferenceboard.org, www.federalreserve.gov); older data, Haver Analytics.

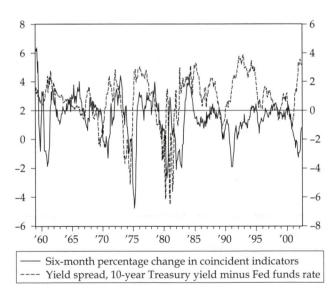

Figure 17.5 Yield spread with the Treasury note yield
Sources: Recent data, Conference Board website and Fed website (www.conferenceboard.org, www.federalreserve.gov); older data, Haver Analytics.

invested in late 1959, just not for the entire year. The yield spread turned slightly negative in 1966, yet a recession did not occur the following year because of the huge increase in defense spending during the Vietnam War. Sometimes, the lead time is longer than a full year, suggesting that the recession was caused in part by other factors in addition to the inverted yield curve. That was presumably the case in 1973 and 1979, when energy shocks intervened; in 1980, when credit controls were briefly imposed; and in 1990, when Iraq invaded Kuwait.

Most critically, though, the spread between the Aaa bond yield and the Federal funds rate provided no advance warning of the 2001 recession. However, after the Conference Board took over the stewardship of the index of leading economic indicators, they added the yield spread between the 10-year Treasury note yield and the Federal funds rate to the list of components. As shown in figure 17.5, that measure of the yield spread clearly turned negative in 2000, and can be considered a valuable signal of upcoming recessions. The only trouble with this measure is that it also turned negative for a while in 1998, yet the economy surged the following year. The inverted yield spread in 1998 occurred as part of a flight-to-safety syndrome following the collapse of Long-Term Capital Management and the devaluation of the Russian ruble; at the same time, the Fed *eased*. Hence the yield spread remains a useful leading indicator only when the spread is inverted because the Fed has tightened.

It is clear that an inverted yield spread for Treasury securities, when modified by this caveat, does signal that real growth will decline in the future. However, just as was the case for the yield spread calculated with the Aaa corporate bond rate, the lead is somewhat erratic. In general, managers are better advised to consider that while an inverted yield spread caused by Fed tightening does indicate weaker growth the following year, the decline may not turn into an actual recession unless (a) the inversion is quite marked, or (b) some other event occurs along with an inverted yield curve to reduce economic growth. That "other event" could be a major decline in the stock market, which is discussed next.

17.3   Cyclical patterns of stock market prices

We have discussed the pattern of interest rates over the business cycle at some length, but so far have not said very much about the pattern of stock prices. Many people consider the stock market to be a leading indicator because it usually turns down four to six months before recessions start, and it usually turns up four to six months before recoveries start. However, it often plunges at times when the economy is not heading into a recession, and in some cases sharp declines in the stock market have actually been followed by an acceleration in the real growth rate. In particular, it declined sharply during most of 2002 at the same time the economy was strengthening.

The relationship between the stock market and the index of coincident indicators is presented in three different graphs. During the early years, from 1947

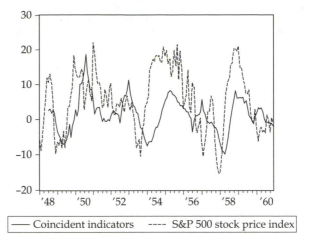

Figure 17.6 Stock prices as a leading indicator, 1947–60
Source: Haver Analytics

through 1960, the stock market was almost a perfect leading indicator, as shown in figure 17.6. It turned down before recessions, turned up before recoveries, and did not issue any false signals.

As shown in figure 17.7, the first major departure from this pattern occurred in 1962, when the market declined sharply but real growth did not slow down. The stock market also gave false signals in 1966 and 1968. It did lead the 1970 and 1973–4 recessions, but then gave another false signal in 1978. Also, it failed to predict the brief 1980 downturn.

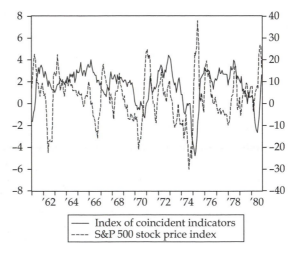

Figure 17.7 Stock prices as a leading indicator, 1961–1980
Source: Haver Analytics

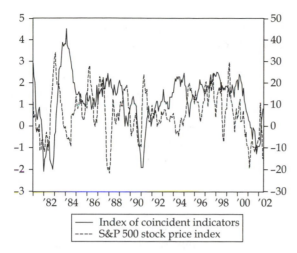

Figure 17.8   Stock prices as a leading indicator, 1981–2002
Source: Haver Analytics

Since 1982, the stock market has become almost useless as a leading indicator, as shown in figure 17.8. That statement may come as a surprise to those readers who think the great bear market of 2000–2002 signaled the 2001 recession, but that is not what happened. The stock market initially turned down because the bubble started to burst; that would have eventually happened whether or not real growth slackened. The stock market decline then caused capital spending to drop, and in that sense contributed to the recession. Also, the market did start to rebound in October 2001, about three months before the recovery began. Yet it then gave back all those gains and more in 2002, while the economy continued to expand.

The massive 40% drop of the stock market from August to October 1987 was followed by an actual increase in the rate of growth over the next several quarters. It was this disconnect that did more than any other event to sever the relationship between the stock market and the economy. However, that was not the only failure of the stock market to serve as a leading indicator: market dips in 1984, 1994, and 1998 were not followed by recessions either.

Yet in spite of this lack of apparent relationship between fluctuations in the stock market and the emergence of recessions, it would be unreasonable to claim there is no correlation between changes in stock prices and the real growth rate. On a ceteris paribus basis, a 10% change in the stock market will cause about $\frac{1}{2}$% change in consumer spending, and about a 1% change in capital spending. When the impacts on exports and imports are also taken into account, a 10% change in stock prices will cause about a $\frac{1}{2}$% change in real GDP with about a two-quarter lag. Thus, for example, a change from a 10% decline in stock prices to a 30% gain would add about 2% to the growth rate, ceteris paribus; a reversal of that magnitude would reduce the growth rate by about 2%. However, the growth rate in nonrecession years usually averages 3% to 4%. These two statements indicate that even major declines in the stock market will not cause actual recessions unless the economy is weakened by other factors.

As is so often the case, the key here is the ceteris paribus condition. Following the 1987 stock market plunge, the Fed eased so quickly that the decline in interest rates more than offset the decline in stock prices. In the early stages of recovery, rapid appreciation in stock prices is often accompanied by a reduction in bond yields, so the combined effect is quite substantial. Later in the business cycle, a decline in stock prices is often accompanied by a rise in bond yields, so here again the combined effect is quite substantial. However, there have been several times – 1987 and 2002 being two major examples – when stock prices and bond prices have moved in opposite directions.

Using the older definition of a market correction as a 10% or greater decline in the Standard & Poor (S&P) 500 index, there were four corrections from 1961 to 1970 but only one recession, five corrections from 1971 to 1982 and three recessions, and six corrections from 1983 to 2000 but only one recession. Wall Street economists who always predicted recessions in the year after a stock market correction have had an abysmal batting average. On the other hand, when the biggest post-WWII market correction did occur in 2000–2001, it helped bring about the first recession in a decade – although the economy then advanced in 2002 in spite of an even bigger market decline.

Because 10% corrections are becoming increasingly common, it has become more common to define a bear market as a correction of 20% or more. Using this more stringent definition, and taking the S&P 500 as a measure of the broad market, bear markets in the post-WWII period occurred in 1962, 1970, 1973–4, 1981–2, 1987, 2000–2001, and 2002. Besides excluding the early recessions, this list omits the downturns of 1980 and 1990–91. Also, 1962, 1987, and 2002 were not recession years. That means major bear markets have preceded only four of the eleven post-WWII recessions.

As shown later in this chapter, most of the fluctuations in the stock market can be related to the following variables: changes in bond yields, the rate of inflation, corporate earnings, the expected budget surplus or deficit ratio, and changes in the capital gains tax rate. Such a statement should not be taken to imply that any such formula would "predict" the stock market. There will always be exogenous developments – such as President Kennedy's outburst at the steel industry in 1962, the collapse of the Penn Central in 1970, the Iraqi invasion of Kuwait in 1990, the terrorist bombings of 9/11, and the accounting scandals in 2002 – that cannot be predicted by any model. Nonetheless, an understanding of the linkages between fluctuations in stock prices and the level of economic activity, and the proper positioning of asset allocation over the cycle, should help improve our understanding of how the economy functions, and prepare managers for the important task of raising capital for their own corporations and planning their own businesses.

17.4   The present discounted value of stock prices and the equilibrium price/earnings ratio

From the late 1950s to the mid-1990s, the P/E ratio of the stock market, as measured by the S&P 500,[1] during periods of average growth and relatively low inflation was about 17. By March 2000, that figure surged to a peak of 36, more than double its previous equilibrium value. Considering what happened over the next two years, it is easy enough in retrospect to identify this boom as a stock market "bubble" – however, such views were not widely held in early 2000. Some claimed the market was overvalued and about to turn down, but they had been saying that for the past several years. A few savvy analysts presumably remained bullish through March 2000 and then changed their minds right at the peak, but it has been difficult to identify them – unlike the 1987 plunge, when several analysts burnished their reputations by accurately calling the drop in advance.

One approach would be simply to dismiss the 1999–2000 bubble – and similar bubbles – as psychological aberrations and move on to other facets of financial forecasting. However, a better analytic approach is to develop a theory that explains the equilibrium value of the stock market at any given time, based on what is known about the past and expected about the future, and then explore deviations from that equilibrium value in terms of incorrect expectations.

For this purpose, we use the standard formula that says the price of any given stock is equal to the sum of all future discounted earnings:

$$P_t = \sum_{j=1}^{\infty} \left(\frac{1}{1 + \varphi_t} \right)^j E_{t+j} \tag{17.1}$$

where P = the price of the stock, E = earnings, and φ is the discount factor, which is equal to the bond rate plus a risk factor, ρ, which reflects the various risks of owning stocks relative to owning bonds. If future earnings are expected to grow at a constant rate g, then:

$$E_{t+j+1} = (1 + g_t)(E_{t+j}). \tag{17.2}$$

Substituting this in the above equation yields:

$$P_t = E_t \sum_{j=1}^{\infty} \left(\frac{1 + g_t}{1 + \varphi_t} \right). \tag{17.3}$$

Applying the usual rules for infinite sums yields:

$$\frac{P_t}{E_t} = \frac{1 + g_t}{\rho_t + r_t - g_t} \tag{17.4}$$

where ρ is the risk factor and r is the bond yield.

This formula may look unduly simple for explaining a phenomenon as complicated as the stock market, yet its power rests in the explanation of ρ, which is explored next. To provide a better interpretation of this equation, we use specific numbers. In the past, the risk factor had often been assumed to be about 6% (0.06 in this formula).[2] While the discount factor was much higher in the years following World War II because of lingering concerns about another depression, by 1958 it had declined to 6% and remained there until the early 1980s. As shown later, it then declined to an average of 3% to $3\frac{1}{2}$% in nonrecession years after 1983.

In equilibrium, the real bond rate should equal the marginal productivity of capital, which means the nominal rate would equal the underlying growth rate of the economy plus the expected rate of inflation. If inflation is steady and is expected to remain so, the nominal bond yield would be equal to the actual growth rate in nominal GDP. Over the long run, the share of profits to GDP has remained constant, so on a macroeconomic basis, the growth factor g should be the same as the long-term bond yield r under the assumptions of a stable rate of inflation, which in the long run is consistent with the forecast of a balanced budget.[3]

We first consider the case where the nominal growth rate and the bond yield are both 7%, which in fact was the average value from 1947 through 2001. Using these data in equation (17.4), P/E = 1.07/0.06 (assuming the average value of the risk factor had been 0.06), or 17.8. That might be called the "normal" or "equilibrium" P/E ratio, which is very close to the long-term historical P/E of 17 when inflation is low and stable.

Now suppose the inflation rate rises by 2%, so nominal growth and the bond yield both increase to 9%. The formula now shows that P/E = 1.09/0.06 = 18.2, almost identical to 17.8. There is virtually no change in the equilibrium P/E ratio when the bond yield rises by the same amount as the growth rate. However, that would be the case only if inflationary expectations remained stable; it is more likely that a 2% boost in inflation would boost inflationary expectations, hence lowering the equilibrium P/E ratio.

Suppose an increase in the inflation rate of 2% caused expected *real* interest rates to rise, because investors assume the Fed would eventually tighten to control the inflationary spiral. As a result, nominal GDP would not increase relative to the previous case. The real growth rate would decline by the same percentage that inflation increased, so corporate earnings would not rise any faster either (given the rise in interest costs, their growth rate might diminish). If a 2% rise in the inflation rate reduces real growth by 2% and leaves the growth rate in corporate profits unchanged, then P/E = 1.07/0.09 = 11.9. In this case, a 2% rise in the inflation rate has caused the P/E ratio to drop by about one-third.

Next consider the case where the deficit ratio rises to 4% of GDP, which occurred during the early 1980s, so nominal growth remains at 9% but the bond yield rises to 13%. In that case, P/E = 1.09/0.10 = 10.9. That is consistent with the low P/E ratios of the early 1980s.

From 1998 through 2000, the Federal budget moved into surplus. Suppose the budget ratio rises to a *surplus* of 2% of GDP, which means expected growth in profits stays at 9% but the bond yield falls to 7%. Then $P/E = 1.09/0.04 = 27.2$, which agrees with the superheated P/E ratios of 1998 and early 1999, although not the peak level of 36, which was a true bubble.

These examples suggest that both the inflation rate and the budget ratio have a substantial impact on the P/E ratio of the stock market. Higher inflation raises the concern that interest rates will rise, which diminishes expected profits both because a higher proportion of revenues must be used to repay debt and because the growth rate is likely to decline in the near future. A higher deficit is also expected to boost inflation in the future. Because of crowding out, a deficit is also likely to reduce capital formation and productivity growth. Since a budget surplus reduces the bond rate, and fewer resources are used for public sector expenditures, investment and productivity rise at a faster rate, hence boosting the stock market.

17.5   Determinants of the risk factor

The formula given in equation (17.4) is the basis of much modern capital market theory, yet empirically it does not accomplish very much unless we are able to explain what factors determine ρ.

First, however, a few comments are appropriate about what is meant by "E," the corporate earnings term. Book profits reported by corporations often include one-time adjustments; they may also include temporary gains due to inflation. Hence for purposes of analysis, most economists use the BEA definition of operating profits adjusted for IVA. For those who wish to pursue the matter further, it is a simple matter to calculate a regression equation and find that measure of profits is highly significant, whereas the book profits measure published by Standard & Poor's, even though it ought to correlate more closely with the S&P 500 stock price index, is insignificant.[4] However, as it turns out, even the BEA measure of profits is sometimes based on inaccurate reports by corporations, so most of the results presented in this chapter are based on the ratio of the S&P 500 to GDP rather than corporate earnings per se.

We now turn to the measure of g, which is the growth rate of future earnings. In deriving equation (17.4), g is assumed to be constant. That is because there is apparently no accurate way to predict growth in profits in the long run; expected earnings published by stock market analysts more than one year in the future are no better than a naive model.[5] Generally, analysts cannot predict profits accurately more than two quarters in advance. The reasons for what is perhaps a surprising lack of accuracy are discussed in chapter 20; however, we can summarize them here by pointing out that forecasts of overall real growth and inflation are generally not much more accurate than a naive model either.

Even if economic forecasts were available with perfect accuracy, though, profit forecasts might be far off the mark. In some cases, the difficulties occur because firms are corrupt, as became obvious in the aftermath of the Enron and other scandals in 2002. However, even honest firms make mistakes. More to the point, a substantial increase in sales might not boost profits if firms increased capacity and hence reduced margins. Indeed, during the impressive boom of the late 1990s, corporate profits rose an average of only slightly more than 1% per year from 1997 through 2000 – even though the real growth exceeded 4% per year and inflation was low and stable. During those years, investors routinely ignored negative profit reports.

Changes in investor perceptions about g will affect stock prices in much the same way as will perceptions about changes in ρ. If investors think earnings will grow more rapidly, they will bid up stock prices. In spite of the difficulty in predicting profits, investors are generally correct in expecting that profit growth will decline if inflation rises for several reasons. First, interest rates will rise, increasing the amount of debt repayment. Second, higher inflation is likely to result in monetary tightening, reducing the real growth rate in the future. Third, in industries that cannot raise prices very much because of market conditions, higher inflation will boost labor costs, reducing margins. Fourth, if prices rise domestically but not internationally, export sales will fall and imports will rise. Fifth, higher inflation reduces the growth rate of productivity, so the overall economy will grow at a slower rate in the future. The negative links between inflation and real growth have been amply documented throughout this text and elsewhere and do not require further extended validation at this juncture. Here we simply point out that higher inflation significantly reduces stock prices.

The second major factor influencing expectations about the future growth in earnings is the ratio of the budget surplus or deficit to GDP (hereafter, the budget ratio). A substantial deficit is likely to lead to higher inflation when the economy returns to full employment. Also, a deficit is likely to lead to crowding out, which means a decline in productive investment in the future, hence reducing the growth rate. Thus we would also expect the budget ratio to be a significant determinant of the risk factor.[6]

The third factor affecting the P/E ratio is the capital gains tax rate. Most of this represents a simple translation between pretax and after-tax yield to investors. If the average annual rate of capital gains before taxes is 12%, and the maximum capital gains tax rate is 50%, a decline to 25% would boost the after-tax rate from 6% to 9% for investors paying the maximum rate, hence boosting stock prices because of the expectations of greater yields in the future. In addition, a lower capital gains tax rate is likely to attract more venture capital, raising the growth rate of productivity and causing output and profits to grow more rapidly in the future.

The fourth factor is the dividend yield. "Growth" companies generally do not pay dividends but reinvest all of their after-tax earnings in order to expand more rapidly. Such companies invariably grow faster than companies that pay relatively large dividends, such as utilities. There is a similar effect at the macro level, so a decline in the dividend yield is likely to boost the P/E ratio of the overall stock market.

At this point there are two ways to proceed in calculating the determinants of ρ. One is to estimate the factors that determine the P/E ratio; after measuring the

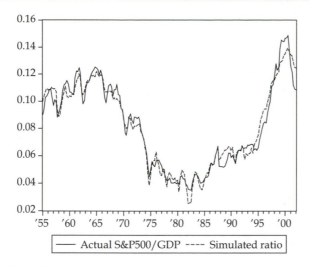

Figure 17.9   Determinants of stock prices

impact of the bond yield, the remaining variables can be assumed to influence the risk factor. The other is to re-solve (17.4) directly for ρ, and then use that constructed series in a regression equation. Both methods are presented here; the problem with the latter method, while it may seem more direct, is that it relies on the S&P measure of earnings, which contains one-time factors that are often ignored by market analysts and investors.

We first examine the results that are obtained by regressing the ratio of the S&P 500 stock price index to GDP on the ratio of profits to GDP, the Aaa bond rate, the rate of inflation, the budget ratio, the capital gains tax rate, and a nonlinear time trend, serving as a proxy for the dividend yield in order to reduce spurious correlation.[7] The sample period simulation is shown in figure 17.9. This underlying relationship identifies several key factors, which can be summarized as follows.

1. If the rate of inflation remains unchanged, bond yields and growth rates will change in opposite directions, because aggregate demand is negatively related to the real rate of interest (see point 1 in section 1.3 – the first core concept of macroeconomics). Thus if the rate of inflation is unchanged, the P/E ratio will be very sensitive to changes in bond rates.
2. A change in bond rates without any change in the underlying rate of inflation is most likely to occur when the Federal budget surplus or deficit ratio changes. In such cases, the P/E ratio is sensitive to changes in the budget ratio.
3. A change in bond rates accompanied by a similar change in the expected growth rate in profits will have virtually no impact on the P/E ratio. However, that is an unlikely combination of circumstances; it would mean (for example) that a rise in bond rates would be accompanied by an increase in the expected growth rate in profits. In fact, just the opposite is more likely to occur.

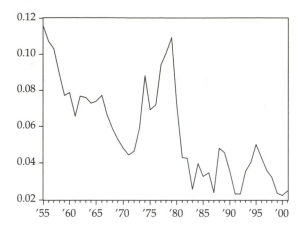

Figure 17.10   Implied risk factor for owning stocks

4. A rise in inflation will reduce expected growth in profits because higher interest rates will (a) reduce real growth and (b) boost interest costs. Hence a rise in inflation will reduce the P/E ratio.
5. A rise in the growth rate accompanied by stable inflation will boost the P/E ratio, because the growth rate for expected earnings will rise whereas bond rates will usually remain stable.

We are not suggesting that this or any other simple equation can be used to predict the stock market accurately. In particular, this equation does not track the stock market bubble of 1999–2000 very well; it also indicates that the decline in 2002 brought stock prices back below their equilibrium levels, although it is possible that expectations changed more quickly in 2001 and 2002 than in the past.

We now turn to the risk variable. Equation (17.4) can be re-solved to find the formula for ρ, which can then be calculated using the actual P/E values and the Aaa bond rate, plus the assumption that growth averages 6% per year. The annual risk premium factors calculated in this manner are shown in figure 17.10. It would be possible to use the actual annual growth rate, but the results are much less satisfactory and the resulting series jumps around in a way that is not congruent with stock market performance.

The risk factor is not shown here for years before 1955, when the Treasury/Fed accord was in effect or the country was at war. During those periods, the stock market was far below equilibrium values and those findings have little resemblance to current conditions.

During the 1960s, the risk factor calculated in this manner generally averaged about 6%, consistent with the findings of Campbell, Lo, and MacKinlay and others. It then rose back to about 10% in the latter 1970s because of concerns that double-digit inflation would increase further and wreck the US economy. Once Paul Volcker assumed command at the Fed, the risk factor dropped sharply and suddenly to about 4%, and has fluctuated between 2% and 4% since then.

Note that the risk factor apparently dropped to 2% in 1987, in 1991–2, and in 2000. The first case represented the overvaluation of the market in 1987, which did not last very long: the S&P fell 40% between late August and mid-October, culminating with the 22% drop on Monday, October 19. The low level in the 1991–2 period actually represented an increase in the expected growth rate of earnings, since they dropped to very low levels during that recession. The dip in 2000 reflected the bubble of that year, but even in 2001 the risk factor appears to have been unusually low. That once again reflects the low level of profits during the recession, and the expectation that they would grow more rapidly than usual in 2002. When that did not occur, stock price continued to drop until the risk factor returned to the 3% to $3\frac{1}{2}$% range.

One cannot really speak of an "equilibrium" value of the risk factor, since it depends on perceptions about what investors think lies ahead. However, since 1982, this factor has averaged 3% to $3\frac{1}{2}$% in nonrecession years, and is likely to continue near that range in nonrecession years under the assumption of stable inflation. If nominal growth averages 6%, profits rise at the same rate as GDP, and the corporate bond yield averages about 7%, then a risk factor of 3% would yield an equilibrium P/E ratio of $1.06/(0.03 + 0.07 - 0.06) = 26.5$, which is substantially higher than historical average values but well below peak bubble values. If the risk factor were to rise back to 0.04, which is close to the upper range in the post-1983 period, the equilibrium P/E ratio would drop to 21.2. If the P/E ratio falls below this range during periods of low, stable inflation, that doesn't mean the formula is "wrong"; it simply means expectations have shifted again.

The other notable point suggested by the risk factor premium is that it was as low in 1983 as it was in 2001. Considering that the P/E ratio was only 12.3 in 1983, compared to 24 in late 2001, that may seem to be a counterintuitive finding. The difference stems from the fact that in 1983, the Aaa corporate bond rate averaged just over 12%, even though inflation was less than 4%, compared to a 7% rate in 2001.

The risk factor has been calculated under the assumption that the expected rate of growth is held constant at 6%. Conversely, we could calculate the expected growth rate under the assumption of a constant risk factor in order to see what investors were presumably thinking about the opportunities for future growth each year. Those results are graphed in figure 17.11.

This graph suggests that when inflation is expected to rise, the expected growth rate declines; alternatively, we could say the risk factor rises. During recessions, when profits are depressed, investors generally expect they will grow faster than usual for the next few years.

We have entered the rather cryptic comment "inflation or Clinton?" by the decline in the expected growth rate – or the rise in the risk factor – during 1993 and 1994. Comments by leading Wall Street firms made it clear they disapproved of the Clinton budget priorities, especially the national healthcare plan, and advised

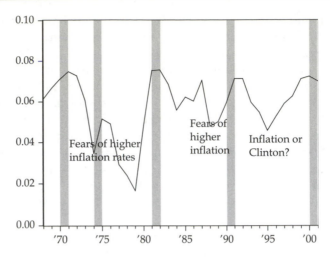

Figure 17.11   Implicit growth rate from equilibrium stock market formula

clients to avoid the stock market.[8] Inflationary expectations also rose sharply in 1994, since it was generally thought that inflation would increase as the economy approached full employment. In fact that did not happen, but bond rates rose two percentage points and short-term rates rose three percentage points, underscoring the concern about higher inflation. It is of course possible that timely action by the Fed eliminated the rise in inflation that would have otherwise occurred; but during 1994, investors did not act that way. In any case, once that inflationary threat went by the boards – and the chances of a comprehensive Clinton healthcare bill disappeared when the Republicans gained control of Congress in the November 1994 elections – the expected growth rate rose sharply, or the risk factor declined sharply. The stock market was off to the races.

Recall that the risk and growth factors are calculated after taking into account the actual bond yield, and the fluctuations shown are in addition to the changes in the P/E ratio caused by rising or falling bond yields. Thus when the threat of inflation went by the boards – or alternatively, when voters elected a Republican Congress, which pushed for a balanced budget – the expected growth rate rose back to 7%. This formula does not allow us to determine whether the improvement in growth – or decline in risk – occurred because of low, stable inflation at full employment, or because of the emerging budget surplus. Of course it is possible that the surplus itself played a major role in boosting expected growth.

Even though the P/E ratio rose to a clearly unsustainable 36 in March 2000, that valuation was not based on the forecast of an exceptionally rapid growth rate in the future, but a drop in the risk factor from 4% to 2% (0.04 to 0.02). That may not seem like a very big change, but because of how the relationship is derived, it has tremendous leverage. To see this, go back to the formula given in equation (17.4).

If g (the growth rate) equals 0.06, which is its long-term average rate, and r (the Aaa bond rate) equals 0.07, which was the case through much of this period, then a drop in ρ from 0.04 to 0.02 boosts the P/E ratio from 21 to 35. That apparently small difference was the factor behind the unsustainable bull market.

CASE STUDY 17.1   THE ENDS OF FOUR MAJOR STOCK MARKET BOOMS

Since World War II, there have been four times when the P/E ratio for the S&P 500 rose above 20: late 1961 and early 1962, late 1972, mid-1987, and the period from mid-1997 through 2000. The P/E ratio during the peak of the market in 1929, by the way, was about 19; the collapse of the market occurred because profits disappeared during the Depression, falling from $10 billion in 1929 to −$2 billion in 1932, not because the market was so overvalued based on expected earnings. All four of these periods were followed by severe declines in stock prices ranging from 30% to 50%. What caused these bubbles, and why did they collapse?

The decline in 1973 and 1974 can be explained by the normal determinants of stock prices: the inflation rate rose from 3% to 13%, bond yields rose from 7% to 9% – admittedly, not nearly as big an increase – and the economy plunged into the most severe recession of the post-WWII period. In the cases of the bear markets of 1962 and 1987, though, the economy continued to grow rapidly and the recoveries continued for several more years. The Fed tightened and bond rates rose somewhat in 1987, but not nearly enough to cause a 40% decline in the major market averages.

Folklore has it that the 1962 stock market collapse occurred after President Kennedy issued his infamous dictum that "My father always told me all steelmen were sons of bitches, but I never believed it until now." The cause of that intemperate outburst was that Kennedy thought his Administration had arranged a noninflationary pact with the steel companies in which production workers would receive a 3% wage increase, equal to the gain in productivity, so steel prices would remain constant, in line with the government-issued wage-price "guidelines." After the agreement was signed, "big steel" put through a 3% price increase, which infuriated Kennedy and the economists who advised him. Attorney General Robert Kennedy called up executives of major steel companies in the middle of the night and threatened them with the loss of Defense Department business if they did not rescind the price increase, which is indeed what happened. The entire episode was not designed to boost stock market optimism.

However, before that contretemps, the P/E ratio had risen to a rarefied level of 22; five years earlier it had been at 13. Clearly, a tremendous wave of optimism

continued

CASE STUDY 17.1 (*continued*)

had swept the investment community shortly after Kennedy had been elected, mainly on the platform to "get the economy moving again." It was believed that Kennedy was a probusiness Democrat who understood the stock market – after all, his father had been the first chairman of the SEC – and would boost real growth with stimulatory fiscal policy, notably reduction of high marginal tax rates, while keeping the budget balanced (which in fact occurred after his assassination). However, investors imagined unobtainable gains in profits from the Kennedy policies, so even if he had not fought that bruising battle with the steel industry, the market was clearly overvalued. Indeed, it had already fallen substantially in early 1962 before those comments were made, although they accelerated the decline.

The 1972 bubble was based on promises of false prosperity that would be generated by the Nixon wage and price controls. Looking back, it is difficult to think that normally savvy investors thought these controls were a good thing, but there was in fact a great deal of enthusiasm in the investment community. Many on Wall Street saw them as a scam whereby labor costs would be held down by the government while profits would be free to soar indefinitely. Here again, an exogenous event – the first energy crisis – intervened to dash those false hopes, but even before that occurred, inflation was rising and the market was weakening.

There were no golden promises of tax cuts or restraint on wages that sparked the 1987 bubble. In fact, there had been a major tax *increase* in 1986, when many of the existing tax loopholes were closed in return for reducing the top marginal tax rate to 28%; at the same time, the capital gains tax differential was eliminated, so the top rate on capital gains actually *rose* from 20% to 28%. Nonetheless, after stuttering in late 1986, the stock market took off once again in early 1987.

Perhaps some investors were encouraged by the sharp decline in oil prices from $35 to $12/bbl in 1986, even though they bounced back to $18/bbl in 1987. Earlier in the decade, it had not been uncommon to hear scenarios from normally reasonable economists about how oil prices would soon rise to $100/bbl, hence hampering worldwide growth. Also, the return of the dollar to its equilibrium value in the 1986–8 period rescued the manufacturing sector, which was being strangled by the overvalued dollar.

The main reason many people remember the Crash of 1987 was that the Dow dropped 22% on Black Monday, October 19, 1987. The major averages had already fallen about 20% from their late August highs, but a 22% decline on a single day was unprecedented even by 1929 standards. This time, however, the Fed immediately supplied the required liquidity, and while the market was extremely volatile for several weeks, it gradually moved up from those lows and rose rapidly in 1988

continued

CASE STUDY 17.1 (*continued*)

and 1989, in line with the decline in interest rates and the above-average growth in real GDP and corporate earnings.

The exogenous shock this time may have been the news that Greenspan meant business. It is likely that some Wall Street investors thought they could intimidate the new kid on the block. Alan Greenspan formally took over from Paul Volcker on August 11, 1987, but it had been known for several months that Volcker would not be reappointed to a third term, and he was not particularly anxious to take vigorous action in his last months. Many investors thought the new Fed Chairman would not have the guts to raise interest rates as long as inflation was stable. However, when Greenspan boosted the discount rate from $5\frac{1}{2}$% to 6% on September 4, 1987, investors suddenly realized he meant business. That may have been another reason why stock prices declined so quickly over the following six weeks.

The causes of these three bubbles were quite variegated, although the one common factor was the unrealistic expectation that corporate profits could grow faster than the overall economy for many more years; except for brief periods at the start of business cycle expansions, that never happens. The exogenous factors that accelerated the downturn – the Kennedy temper tantrum, the first energy crisis, and the surprise tightening by Greenspan – were all quite different, although since the P/E ratios could not continue to rise indefinitely, the market would have eventually reversed course even if none of these events had taken place.

The 1999–2000 bubble and subsequent contraction was once again built on the dreams of extraordinarily rapid profit growth indefinitely, but this time the boom was fueled primarily by high-tech stocks, and should be analyzed in somewhat different fashion, as presented in the next case study.

CASE STUDY 17.2   THE NASDAQ BUBBLE OF 1999–2000

The Nasdaq index was first compiled in 1971; before then, there was no formal measure of growth stocks, although some economists used the Wiesenberger growth funds as a proxy index. Yet while there were some excesses in growth stocks, their rise and fall had not been much different from the S&P 500 index, as shown in figure 17.12, until the 1999–2000 period, when the Nasdaq index rose so much that many growth stock valuations really did take on tulip bulb characteristics.

The foundation for the high-tech bubble was laid in late 1995, when Netscape went public, raising approximately $2 billion in its IPO and making Jim Clark

continued

CASE STUDY 17.2 (*continued*)

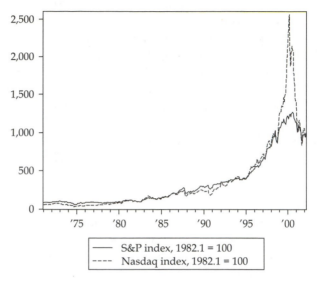

Figure 17.12   The Nasdaq bubble
Source: Haver Analytics

the first internet billionaire. Not only was that figure dramatic, but the offering broke new ground in the sense that Netscape had no earnings. In the past, P/E ratios for new companies may have been unrealistically high, but at least earnings existed. Netscape was selling only promises. Optimists pointed out at the time that Netscape had 85% of the browser market, apparently ignoring the fact that (a) they were giving the software away for free and hoping to recoup by selling servers, and (b) Microsoft would not stand idly by and fail to compete. Netscape continued to bleed red ink and eventually was purchased by AOL.

By the time of the Netscape IPO, almost every investor was familiar with the Microsoft saga, which by then had already risen from a split-adjusted price of $0.20 at its IPO to $15 per share – a 300-bagger, on its way to becoming a 1,000-bagger. The view of many eager investors was that it did not pay to wait. If Netscape and others really were the "next big thing," buy now and enjoy the ride. No reason to miss out on those instant riches.

Once other companies with no earnings, few assets, and fewer sales saw the light, investors were off to the races. Company after company was brought public without even a suggestion of positive earnings or cash flow. Yet investors continued to ask for more.

At least in retrospect, some investors said they knew the market was ready for a downturn on March 3, 2001, when Palm Pilot, a spinoff of 3Com, rose to a record
continued

CASE STUDY 17.2 (*continued*)

high of $95 per share on the opening day of its IPO. 3Com had said it would spin off 1.5 Palm Pilot shares for each share of 3Com, so even if the rest of the company was entirely worthless, the price of Palm should not have been higher than two-thirds of the closing price of 3Com that day, which was $81.81. But obviously Palm was worth a lot less than $54.54 unless you really believed the rest of the company was worthless at that point. Short sellers could have purchased the rest of 3Com at a price of −$63 per share that day, yet the negative value was not erased for more than two months. Eventually, of course, the price of Palm shares dropped substantially; in early 2002 they were selling for about $1 per share. The point is that even arbitrageurs, who could have made a killing by acting on the absurd difference in the share price of these two companies, failed to move. It was at this point that a few traders began to realize that a major selloff seemed almost inevitable – although they did not say so for several more months.

In terms of its magnitude, the Nasdaq bubble is comparable to the great bull market of the late 1920s and the subsequent crash, and the Japan Nikkei bubble in the late 1980s and the subsequent crash. The Dow Jones Industrial Average fell 90% from its peak in 1929 to its trough in 1932, but because the CPI also declined substantially during that period, that was about a 75% decline in real terms. The Nasdaq index fell 78% from its peak in March 2000 to its trough in September 2002. The Japanese Nikkei also fell more than 75% in the 1990s, although that decline occurred over an entire decade.

The 1929 crash was of course followed by the Great Depression, although as noted in chapter 15, there were many other causes. The crash of the Nikkei was followed by a decade-long recession in Japan. As of 2002, no responsible economist is predicting anything of the sort for the US economy. However, to the extent that stock market values do affect consumption and investment, the retreat of the high-tech sector is likely to reduce real growth somewhat in the next decade.

From a long-term historical perspective, the Nasdaq bubble was not just another bull market that occurs every decade or so. It was the type of event that occurs once or twice a century, and it was based on a seldom-seen phenomenon: stratospheric stock prices for new companies that had no earnings, no cash flow, and in many cases, hardly any sales. It is unlikely that such a scam will be perpetrated on the investing public again for several decades.

17.6 Impact of the budget ratio on bond and stock returns

We now return from "bubble land" to an examination of the fundamental underlying factors that cause the total returns on bonds and stocks to diverge in certain years. If nothing else changes – in particular, if the growth in profits and the perceived risk factor do not change – a 1% increase in bond prices will result in a 1%

increase in stock prices. However, that rarely happens. Usually profits are changing, and as we will see, other variables are also important.

From 1958 through 1997, the level of the Aaa corporate bond rate, unlagged and with a lag of one quarter, explained about 80% of the movement in the P/E ratio of the S&P 500. Yet if that same simple relationship is extended through 2002, the explained percentage drops to about 50%. That emphasizes the degree to which the 1999–2000 bubble, and the resultant crash, were unprecedented. The 1929–33 crash was caused by the disappearance of profits, while the 1973–4 crash was caused by a major increase in interest rates. Yet in the 2001–02 period, the P/E ratio fell by more than half even though bond yields actually declined slightly.

To a certain extent, the factors that pushed the market up to such rarefied P/E ratios were irrational. However, in the next three sections we try to identify the economic factors that helped caused this big increase: the Federal budget surplus or deficit ratio, the rate of inflation, and the maximum rate of taxation on capital gains.

It is easy enough to label the 1999–2000 bull market an irrational episode, but that does not explain why investors were so bullish. In addition to all the blather about the "new technology," the economy had been at full employment for many years without any increase in the core rate of inflation, the budget had returned to "permanent" surpluses, and there was a massive inflow of foreign capital, the direct result of the increasing trade deficit and the stronger dollar. The budget surplus has not received as much attention as the other two factors, but we think it was an important factor in boosting the stock market to unrealistically high levels; in the same vein, the return to deficit financing was one of the reasons, although obviously not the only one, that the market crashed.

When it finally became clear in late 2000 that the bull market had ended, many objective observers expected the P/E ratio to return to an average level of about 25, based on the assumption that the risk factor was about 3%. When the market rallied strongly following the shock of 9/11, that forecast was maintained. Yet the decline in the stock market during 2002 – during a period of reasonable if not overwhelming economic growth, a recovery in profits, and moderately declining bond yields – eventually brought the P/E ratio back to its longer term equilibrium values.

The equilibrium model identifies the degree to which stock prices are overvalued, but provides no hint about how long this overvaluation would last, or the peak level that would eventually be reached. By the same token, the model can identify when stock prices become undervalued, but gives no hint about how long the bear market would last, or the trough level that would eventually be reached. That model is designed to provide a reasonable determination of the equilibrium value; and then let managers make intelligent decisions during those times when the market becomes severely overvalued or undervalued.

We have prominently identified the budget surplus or deficit ratio as one of the variables that influences the risk factor, and hence the P/E ratio. Why should a reduction in the budget deficit – or an increase in the budget surplus – boost the P/E ratio relative to the bond yield? It is true that a budget surplus will reduce

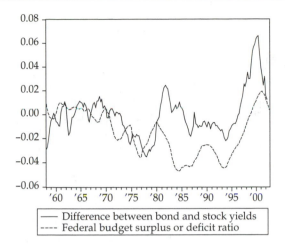

Figure 17.13   Budget ratio and difference between P/E ratio and bond prices
Source: Calculated by the author

bond yields, ceteris paribus, but that has already been taken into account; this correlation suggests there is some additional factor. Perhaps we are merely recording a spurious correlation, namely that a rise in stock price boosts capital gains tax revenues, hence raising the surplus.

Yet there are two major reasons why an increase in the budget surplus would boost the difference between the returns on bonds and stocks: one reflects the availability of funds, and the other reflects expectational factors. If the Federal government runs a surplus, that boosts saving and investment, ceteris paribus. Other things being equal, that will raise the long-term growth rate of productivity and reduce the rate of inflation. Both these factors are likely to boost profit growth in the long run. Also, a lower rate of inflation is generally expected to keep bond yields from rising in the future.

An increase in the surplus will reduce bond yields, ceteris paribus, but once again those conditions do not always hold. Suppose the surplus stems from robust growth; in that case, the Fed is likely to raise short-term interest rates, which means bond yields would not fall by the full amount indicated by the increase in government saving. In that case, the extra funds are more likely to be invested in the stock market. If the government surplus is caused by robust growth, that also means imports will rise faster than exports, so net foreign saving will increase. Those additional funds are also likely to be invested in the stock market.

Figure 17.13 shows the graph of the Federal budget ratio and the difference between the modified P/E ratio of stocks and the Aaa corporate bond yield. That difference is actually the residuals between these two variables calculated by a regression equation. The measure of the P/E ratio used here is the S&P 500 stock price index divided by GDP, rather than reported corporate earnings, because those figures tend to contain so many errors and fraudulent reporting.

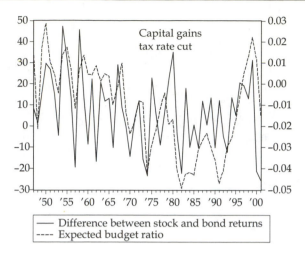

Figure 17.14 Annual changes in the difference between total return on bonds and stocks and changes in the expected budget ratio
Source: Calculated by the author

The results are instructive but not conclusive. The two lines generally tend to move together, but starting in 1983 there is a huge shift, which corresponds directly to the change in ρ described above. Hence for purposes of analysis, it is useful to present these results in an alternative format, which is the annual change in the difference between the total return on stocks – capital gains or losses plus the dividend yield – and total return on bonds – capital gains or losses plus the rate of interest. These changes are correlated with the expected change in the budget ratio, and reinforce the hypothesis that changes in the budget ratio do indeed influence the difference between the P/E ratio and bond prices.

According to these regression results underlying these graphs, a one percentage point increase in the budget ratio – e.g., from 2% to 3% – will boost the ratio stock prices to GDP by about 0.6 percentage point – e.g., from 8% to 8.6%. That would boost the P/E by about $7\frac{1}{2}$%; e.g., from 20 to 21.5. Seen in this light, the increase in the Federal budget ratio from $-4\frac{1}{2}$% in 1992 to $+2\frac{1}{2}$% at its peak in 2000 would have boosted the P/E ratio by about 10 points. Similarly, the return of the budget deficit ratio to about 3% of GDP in 2003 would then have reduced the P/E ratio by about 8 points. By comparison, the actual P/E rose from about 16 to 36 and then fell back to about 19, which means the change in the budget ratio accounted for about half of the increase and the decrease.

Since the Aaa bond yield changed very little over that decade, this suggests that the remaining fluctuations in the P/E ratio were due to (a) the expected rate of inflation, (b) further reductions in the capital gains tax rate, and (c) pure bubble mania. The next two sections explore the two economic factors.

Figure 17.14 shows the annual changes in the difference of the returns on bonds and stocks and the expected budget ratio the following year. These two curves move together fairly closely except in the years of major changes in capital gains tax rates, which is explored further in section 17.8.

17.7   Impact of changes in the expected rate of inflation on bond and stock returns

Figure 17.13 showed a one-time shift in the difference between the P/E ratio and the inverse of the bond yield in 1983. That amounts to about a 6 point increase in the equilibrium P/E ratio, which occurred because investors now believed that in the future, the Fed would act more aggressively to keep inflation under control. Investors are often criticized for not being able to foresee the future, but that prediction turned out to be quite accurate.

Nonetheless, there were occasional periods of backsliding. The core rate of inflation, which had quickly fallen to 4% once the tight-money policies of Paul Volcker were implemented, rose to 5% in 1990 (the increase in the overall CPI to 6% was caused by the spike in oil prices after the Iraqi invasion of Kuwait). That was a very small increase relative to previous business cycle peaks, but since the unemployment rate peaked at a relatively high rate of almost 6%, that left unanswered the question of whether inflation would flare up again if the unemployment rate were to fall further near the next business cycle peak.

Most of the time, in the absence of exogenous events that affect inflation such as energy shocks, the consensus forecast of the inflation rate next year is the same as the inflation rate this year. On that basis, one could use the actual change in inflation as a proxy variable for the unexpected change. Another possibility is to correlate changes in the risk factor with the difference between the consensus inflation rate this year and the actual rate last year, but the results are about the same as if the actual change in inflation is used.

In spite of this naïve method of predicting inflation, most investors used to expect the inflation rate to rise as the economy approached full employment. Or to put it another way, the myth of the Phillips curve died hard. On this basis, a decline in the unemployment rate from 6% to 4% would be expected to boost the inflation rate by 2%, ceteris paribus. In that sense, the lack of any increase in the core rate of inflation in the 1990s was enough of a surprise to boost the equilibrium P/E ratio.

Thus in the late 1990s, when a 4% unemployment rate occurred simultaneously with a core rate that remained around $2\frac{1}{2}$%, investors gradually became convinced that rapid growth and full employment need not boost inflation at all. It is more difficult to put a precise parameter estimate on this variable because the expected rate of inflation is not measurable. However, we estimate that since the core rate of inflation was expected to rise about 1% per year as a result of the economy returning to full employment, but in fact it did not rise at all, that boosted the equilibrium P/E ratio by about 3 points. That would represent a one-time shift that presumably remained in place even during and after the market crash.

17.8 Impact of changes in capital gains taxes on stock prices

Figure 17.14 showed that the difference between the total return on stocks and bonds diverged markedly in the 1979–80 period, when the maximum tax rate on capital gains was cut from $49\frac{1}{8}\%$ to 28%. Figure 17.15 shows the relationship between changes in the tax rate and changes in the difference between the scaled P/E ratio and bond prices, adjusted for changes in the budget deficit. Note in particular that this difference declined during most of the 1970s following a big increase in the maximum capital gains tax rate, and then rose sharply following the cut of the maximum rate in November 1978. In each case, the lag was one to two years.

The theoretical impact of changes in the capital gains tax rate on the stock market and the economy in general is discussed in more detail in the next chapter. We summarize these results here by noting that when the capital gains tax rate declines (say), the after-tax rate of return on stocks rises relative to the pretax rate of return even if nothing else has changed. When that happens, some investors would shift from bonds to stocks because the latter now generate a higher after-tax rate of return. That boosts the price of stocks to the point where the risk-adjusted rates of return move back to their previous relationship.

However, this adjustment does not happen instantaneously. When the capital gains tax rate is cut, some investors are motivated to sell their stock soon afterwards; initially, that would depress rather than raise the price. In other cases, stock is

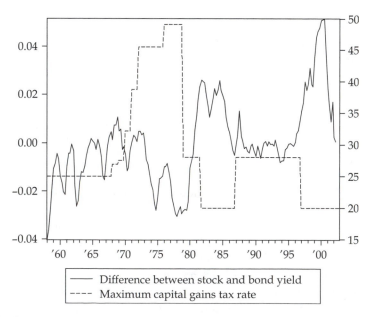

Figure 17.15   Capital gains tax rate and relative stock market performance

sold just before the rate is scheduled to increase; when the capital gains tax rate was raised at the beginning of 1987, selling pressure drove prices down in late 1986. The market then rallied sharply early the following year, but as adjustments from the higher capital gains tax rate became more important, the market began to falter. The decline in prices later that year was due in part to the higher rate of capital gains taxes, although of course that was not the only reason. The cut in the maximum tax rate from 28% to 20% in 1997 was also one of the factors pushing stock prices higher over the next two years.

On balance, we estimate that a one percentage point change in the maximum capital gains tax rate changes the S&P 500 by about 1%. Thus, for example, the rise in the capital gains tax rate from 25% to $49\frac{1}{8}$% in several stages during the late 1960s and early 1970s would have reduced stock prices by 25%; the cut from $49\frac{1}{8}$% to 28% would have boosted the market by slightly more than 20%; the rise back to 28% in 1987 would have reduced it by 8%, and the cut in 1997 would have boosted it by 8%. In each of these four cases, the actual moves in the market were substantially greater than indicated by these results, but the changes in the capital gains tax rate did contribute to each of these major moves in the market.[9]

The combination of all these factors – the Federal budget surplus or deficit ratio, the change in the rate of inflation, the maximum capital gains tax rate, and the average dividend yield, representing the decision by firms to plow more money back into the company for faster growth instead of distributing it to stockholders – can be combined to determine how much the actual P/E ratio, adjusted for the bond yield, converges or diverges from the equilibrium P/E ratio calculated by the equation given below. We have estimated such an equation, using a nonlinear time trend, instead of the dividend ratio, in order to reduce spurious correlation. The results of this regression equation are graphed in figure 17.16. The actual equation is given in the note.[10]

On a quarterly basis, this equation estimates that the 2000 "bubble" boosted the S&P 500 P/E ratio approximately 6 points above what would have been its equilibrium value based on the budget surplus, changes in the expected rate of inflation, and the rate of capital gains tax. The P/E ratio was 33 in 2000.1; this equation estimates the equilibrium level in that quarter would have been 27, which means it was about 20% overvalued for the quarter. At its peak, the P/E ratio rose to 36, so at its absolute peak the market was overvalued by 33%. At the market trough in 2002, the P/E ratio was about 6 points below what would have been expected based on these same three variables. This calculation uses the actual values of the Aaa corporate bond yield and GDP; it also assumes that actual corporate earnings are proportional to GDP; reported earnings are not considered in this approach. The equation also implies that the equilibrium P/E ratio in the future, assuming a bond yield of 7%, a balanced budget, and no change in the rate of inflation or the capital gains tax, would be about 21.

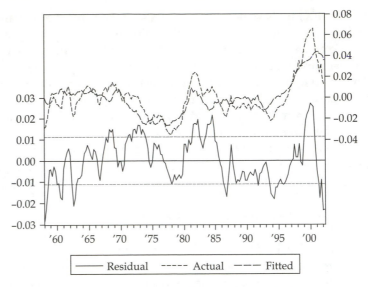

Figure 17.16 Actual and calculated performance of the P/E ratio relative to bond prices

17.9 Long-term performance of stocks, bonds, and liquid assets

We now turn to an issue that has puzzled many financial economists: why has the long-term rate of return on stocks been much higher than the long-term rate of return on bonds?

It turns out the difference is not so large as is commonly believed; the answer varies greatly depending on the time period involved. From 1947 through 1968, the total average return on stocks was 15.4%, compared to only 2.0% for bonds. However, from 1968 through 2002, the average rate of return on stocks, including reinvested dividends, was 12%, compared to 9% for bonds. Going back further, for the 1929–47 period, the average return on stocks was −0.5% (including dividends), while the average return on bonds was 5.3%. If we average these two earlier periods, the average return on stocks was 7.5%, compared to 3.6% for bonds. Since 1968 the average annual difference, in spite of the stock market rally, has been about 3% per year.

Over this 72-year period, the average difference has been 3.5%, which happens to be very close to the average over the past 20 years. Of course this "proves" nothing, but it does indicate that the huge gap between the total return on stocks and bonds in the early post-WWII years clearly represents the decline of the perceived risk premium on stocks from unusually high levels during the Great Depression and World War II. It is just as unrealistic to take the 1947–68 period as indicative of the long-term relationship between bond and stock returns as it is to take the 1929–47 period.

Table 17.1 Average return and risk for stocks and bonds (selected periods)

Period	Average annual return on		Difference	Standard deviations	
	Stocks	Bonds		Stocks	Bonds
1929–1947	−0.5	5.3	−5.8		
1947–1957	16.6	1.7	14.9	17.9	4.3
1957–1968	11.7	2.6	9.1	16.7	4.5
1968–1983	9.3	6.5	2.8	17.7	12.5
1983–2002	14.6	12.0	2.6	14.6	12.5

Source: Calculated by author, based on annual data taken from the Historical Statistics of the US before 1947 and Haver Analytics after that. "Bonds" are the Aaa corporate bond rate. Average annual returns include dividends on stock and capital gains or losses on bonds.

Is there any good reason to expect the differential between the total annual return on stocks and bonds to remain in the 3% to $3\frac{1}{2}$% range, or is this just another historical artifact? Another tenet of financial market theory says that the risk-adjusted rate of return – the return divided by the standard deviation – should be the same for all classes of assets. The standard deviations are also shown in table 17.1 and the correspondence is seen to be fairly close. However, that involves a somewhat arbitrary selection of one year as the basic time interval for measuring risk, and it also does not tell us how much the total return on bonds and stocks will fluctuate in the future.

The 3% to $3\frac{1}{2}$% risk differential is quite consistent with the calculations of the risk factor in section 17.4, which was also estimated to be 3% to $3\frac{1}{2}$% since 1982. While that does not prove anything, it does suggest that in the absence of a major change in the capitalist system as we now know it, or barring a major armed conflict, that differential will remain in place for many years. The scandals of 2002 certainly drew their share of headlines, but that is not what we mean by a major change in the capitalist system. In fact, the relatively rapid response to these scandals undoubtedly kept the market decline from turning into an even more dramatic meltdown, à la Japan.

Nonetheless, while the annual risk-adjusted return for stocks and bonds appears to be quite similar, this still raises the issue of why long-term investors – for example, people in their peak earning years putting aside retirement funds for 20 or 30 years hence – would prefer bonds to stocks. Figure 17.17 shows the cumulative rate of return on the S&P 500 stock price index, Aaa corporate bonds, and 1-year Treasury bills from 1968 through 2001; the disparity in the earlier postwar years between stocks and bonds was much greater. Yet bonds continue to be a popular investment vehicle, and not only for widows and widowers whose statistical life expectancy is measured in single digits.

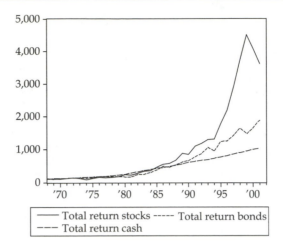

Figure 17.17   Total return on stocks, bonds, and liquid assets
Source: Calculated by the author

17.10   Cyclical fluctuations in returns on stocks, bonds, and liquid assets

We next briefly examine the returns on stocks, bonds, and liquid assets (often called cash) for each year from 1947 through 2001. "Stocks" measures the capital gains in the S&P 500 during the year, plus the average dividend yield for the year. "Bonds" measures the Aaa corporate bond yield during the year, plus the percentage change in the price of the bond during the year. "Liquid assets" is simply the yield on 1-year Treasury bills. Annual statistics are given in table 17.2.

The worst year for bonds was 1994, with a total negative return of 12.1%. That year, a "surprise" tightening by the Fed caught bond market investors off guard. However, they bounced back strongly the following year, with a total return of 31.5%, so losses were fleeting except for short-term "investors."

From 1978 through 1981, the total return on bonds was negative for four years in a row, but the aggregate decline over that period was only 7.7%, substantially less than the 1994 reduction. The biggest losses for bonds can then be compared with the 50% decline in the market during 1973–4 and again in 2000–2002. And although it doesn't show up in the average annual changes, the 40% decline from August to October 1987 was no picnic either – nor was the 30% decline in the first four months of 1962. Hence over the past 40 years, there have been four different periods when the decline in the stock market ranged from 30% to 50%. The fact that stocks have always bounced back does not disguise the fact that the perceived risk to many investors may be greater than the standard deviations shown in table 17.1.

Neither financial planners nor economists are very good at predicting recessions, yet when signs of slowdown are evident – as suggested by the leading indicators, discussed in chapter 20 – the return on bonds is far better than stocks during

Table 17.2   Total annual returns on stocks, bonds, and liquid assets

Year	Stocks	Bonds	Liquid assets	Year	Stocks	Bonds	Liquid assets
1947	5.7	−2.3	0.9	1975	37.2	14.6	6.8
1948	5.5	4.1	1.1	1976	23.8	18.7	5.9
1949	18.8	3.3	1.1	1977	−7.2	1.7	6.1
1950	31.7	2.1	1.3	1978	6.6	−0.1	8.3
1951	24.0	−2.7	1.7	1979	18.4	−4.2	10.7
1952	18.4	3.5	1.8	1980	32.4	−2.6	12.0
1953	−1.0	3.4	2.1	1981	−4.9	−1.0	14.8
1954	52.6	5.4	1.0	1982	21.4	43.8	12.3
1955	31.6	0.5	2.0	1983	22.5	4.7	9.6
1956	6.6	−6.8	3.0	1984	6.3	16.4	10.9
1957	−10.8	8.7	3.6	1985	30.5	30.1	8.4
1958	43.4	−2.2	2.3	1986	18.1	28.5	6.5
1959	12.0	−1.0	4.2	1987	5.0	−6.6	6.8
1960	0.5	9.1	3.6	1988	15.9	15.3	7.7
1961	26.9	4.8	3.0	1989	30.5	17.2	8.5
1962	−8.7	8.0	3.1	1990	−3.0	7.2	7.9
1963	22.8	2.2	3.4	1991	29.6	17.6	5.9
1964	16.5	4.8	3.8	1992	7.4	12.2	3.9
1965	12.5	−0.5	4.1	1993	9.8	22.2	3.4
1966	−10.1	0.2	5.2	1994	1.3	−12.1	5.3
1967	24.0	−5.0	4.9	1995	36.6	31.5	5.9
1968	11.1	2.6	5.7	1996	22.4	2.0	5.5
1969	−8.5	−8.1	7.1	1997	32.8	13.6	5.6
1970	4.0	18.4	6.9	1998	28.1	15.2	5.1
1971	14.3	11.0	4.9	1999	20.8	−10.5	5.1
1972	19.0	7.3	5.0	2000	−9.0	12.4	6.1
1973	−14.7	1.1	7.3	2001	−11.7	13.8	3.7
1974	−26.5	−3.1	8.2				

Source: Calculated by author

the early stages of the recession. Hence even investors who strive for the highest long-term rate of return might choose to invest in bonds during periods when the economy is heading into an economic downturn.

17.11   Recap: the importance of financial markets and asset allocation

Fluctuations in financial market prices are obviously important if your own money is at risk. But in terms of the overall economy, what are the principal lessons managers can learn from the material in this chapter?

Interest rates are the equilibrating mechanism between aggregate demand and supply. In a larger sense, that applies to the rate of return on saving and the cost of capital in general, which includes equity capital as well as short-term and long-term debt securities. In the short run, the economy functions more efficiently if money and capital markets allocate saving and investment properly. Indeed, in the days of interest rate ceilings, the artificial barrier to equilibrium in capital markets was one of the principal reasons for the frequent recessions.

In the short run, we have emphasized throughout this book how cyclical fluctuations in the principal components of aggregate demand are primarily related to the cost and availability of debt and equity capital. Hence a complete understanding of the factors that determine purchases of consumer and capital goods depends on an underlying structure that explains fluctuations in interest rates, monetary and credit aggregates, and stock prices.

In the long run, the allocation of capital to equity markets for venture capital boosts the long-term growth in productivity. Tax policies that discriminate against equity capital and lead to misallocation also reduce the long-run rate of growth. The sensitivity of asset prices to inflation provides yet another reason why higher inflation reduces productivity growth. Assets are diverted from their most productive uses to inflation hedges, which are economically sterile in the sense they do not increase the productive capacity of the economy.

From a practical viewpoint, monitoring values of the yield spread and changes in business loan demand can provide valuable clues about when the economy is about to slow down and head into a recession. The value of the stock market as a leading indicator has been called into question after it plunged so rapidly in 2002 after the recovery had already gotten underway, but no recession ever started without a warning signal from stock prices. The caveat here is that major declines in stock prices, if accompanied by Fed easing at the same time, probably will not lead to a recession.

KEY TERMS AND CONCEPTS

Equilibrium Price/Earnings Ratio
Risk Factor (of stocks over bonds)
Yield Spread

SUMMARY

• Before banking deregulation in 1982, the M2 measure of the real money supply was a key leading indicator, but that did not remain the case after deregulation. The change in real business loans now is a key leading indicator ahead of recessions, but remains a lagging indicator for recoveries. The change in real consumer credit is a coincident indicator.

- Until 2000, the yield spread between the Aaa corporate bond rate and the Federal funds rate always turned negative before recessions; however, that did not occur in 2000. The yield spread between the 10-year Treasury note yield and the 3-month Treasury bill yield turned negative in 2000, but also was negative in 1998. Nonetheless, the Treasury yield spread serves as a valuable leading indicator when the inversion is caused by Fed tightening.
- Before 1960, the stock market was an infallible leading indicator, but since then has been erratic. The stock market fell substantially in 1962, 1987, and 2002, yet in each case the rate of growth stayed the same or actually increased in the next few quarters.
- If the expected growth rate of earnings is constant, then the equilibrium P/E ratio is equal to $(1 + g)/(\rho + r + g)$, where g is the growth rate, r is the Aaa corporate bond yield, and ρ is the risk factor for holding stocks relative to bonds.
- Before 1983, ρ averaged about 0.06, but since then has dropped to about 0.035.
- The risk factor is primarily determined by the expected growth rate, the Federal budget surplus or deficit ratio, and unexpected changes in the rate of inflation. In addition, the equilibrium P/E ratio is partially determined by the capital gains tax rate and the dividend yield.
- The P/E ratio has been far above equilibrium four times in the post-WWII period: 1962, 1972, 1987, and 2000. Each time, the market subsequently declined 30% to 50%. Higher interest rates were a major contributing factor in 1973–4, but in other cases, expectations of profits were unrealistically optimistic.
- In the past, a one percentage point change in the Federal budget surplus or deficit ratio changed the equilibrium P/E ratio by about $1\frac{1}{2}$ points; a one percentage point change in the maximum capital gains tax rate changed the equilibrium P/E ratio by about 0.2 points; and a one percentage point change in the unexpected rate of inflation changed the equilibrium P/E ratio by about 3 points.
- Over the long run, the total return on stocks has been about $3\frac{1}{2}$% per year more than the total return on bonds. Most of this reflects the difference in risk, as measured by the annual standard deviations. For many long-term investors, the perceived risk in stocks remains higher than the actual risk.
- Improved asset allocation over the business cycle directs scarce capital resources to their most productive uses, hence boosting the long-term growth rate of productivity.

QUESTIONS AND PROBLEMS

1. (A) Which scenario is better for long-term economic growth: (a) the stock market grows at 6% per year indefinitely, or (b) it quickly doubles, then falls back to its previous level, and finally returns to its long-term trend rate?
   (B) Program trading was largely blamed for the unprecedented 22% decline in the Dow on Black Monday, October 19, 1987. As a result, curbs were instituted prohibiting that practice after the Dow had moved up or down a certain amount. In 2002, the market did not decline more than 5% on any

given day, but the net reduction was about the same. Which drop was least harmful to the economy?

2. The 78% drop in the Nasdaq index was actually greater in real terms than the 90% drop in the Dow from 1929 to 1932. Yet the economy suffered only a brief recession and rebounded quickly. Why did this huge decline in stock prices have such a relatively small effect on the US economy in 2001–02 relative to 1929–32?

3. If inflation rises 1%, will the bigger drop in total return occur for bonds or stocks? (Hint: was the change expected, and how did the Fed react?)

4. In the early stages of recovery, the S&P 500 and other broad-based stock market indexes generally rose at least 25%. Yet in the months of the first three quarters of 2002, these indexes dropped over 30%. Why did the market exhibit such an unusual pattern in 2002? How would you expect the stock market to behave following future recessions?

5. As CFO of your company, explain what investment strategy you would recommend in the following circumstances:
    (A) Recovery has just started.
    (B) Economy just reached full employment.
    (C) Fed just tightened.
    (D) Recession expected to start within a year.
    (E) Recession just got underway.

6. If bond prices are primarily determined by inflation, why has the total yield on bonds remained so volatile after 1983 when the core rate of inflation has gradually declined from 4% to 2%, with a peak of only 5%?

7. In mid-2002, it was announced that one of the leading bond funds managed by PIMCO now had more assets under management than the Fidelity Magellan Fund. Discuss the pros and cons of investors switching their assets from stocks to bonds in mid-2002.

8. From 1982 through 2000, the S&P 500 stock price index rose an average of 14.7% per year (all figures in this problem are annual averages). Over the same period, the Aaa corporate bond rate fell from 13.8% to 7.6%. Corporate profits adjusted for IVA and CCA grew at an annual rate of 8.5%, compared to a 6.3% average annual gain in GDP.
    (A) How much would you have expected the S&P index to rise if there were no changes in the underlying risk factor?
    (B) If in fact the risk factor dropped from 6% to 3.5%, how much of the remaining difference could be explained by that factor?
    (C) The average P/E ratio for 2000 – as opposed to peak levels – was 27.5. Based on the formulas given in this chapter, how much was that above its equilibrium level?
    (D) The P/E ratio subsequently declined to a trough of 16 before the market rebounded. How much of that change do you think was due to (a) decline

in corporate earnings, (b) change in the risk factor, (c) overvaluation of the market at its peak, (d) undervaluation of the market at its trough?

Notes

1. This index will be used to denote the "stock market" here unless otherwise specified.
2. See, in particular, John Y. Campbell, Andrew W. Lo, and A. Craig MacKinlay, *The Econometrics of Financial Markets* (Princeton, 1997), chapter 7.
3. This is not supposed to indicate that a balanced budget guarantees low, stable inflation. It is consistent with the viewpoints of US investors in the last 50 years that inflation is likely to remain stable over extended periods of time when the budget is in balance.
4. Standard & Poor's has become increasingly aware of this issue, and in April 2002 announced it would develop new "core earnings" estimated for 10,000 companies that would "provide a clearer picture of the revenues and costs associated with the companies' primary businesses." In particular, the measure would strip out capital gains from pension fund investments.
5. This finding is based on results through 1998, and hence predates the dot.com bubble, the Enron fiasco, and other willful misstatements of earnings that have since come to light. These points are discussed in Robert J. Shiller, *Irrational Exuberance* (New York: Broadway Books division of Random House, 2001), p. 253. Note that this comment is only in the paperback edition, in the section entitled "Afterword to the Paperback Edition;" the original hardcover edition published by Princeton University Press in 2000 does not contain this material.
6. Many economists would argue that it is the full-employment budget position that is important. While that has a larger impact on overall economic activity, it is the actual budget position that influences the stock market. Including the full-employment budget to explain the risk factor in a regression that already includes the actual budget ratio invariably is insignificant or has the wrong sign.
7. The dividend yield is defined as dividends per share divided by the S&P 500 index. Since that term is also part of the dependent variable, including it in the regression would essentially be putting the same variable on both sides of the equation. The dividend yield would be lagged, but even that does not solve the problem because the residuals are highly autocorrelated.
8. In 1993, Barton Biggs, chief strategist of Morgan Stanley, told clients he wanted their money to be "far away" from the healthcare scheme suggested by Hillary Clinton.
9. This is not merely an after-the-fact analysis. In 1979, this author predicted that the stock market would rise 40% over the next two years, based on the cut in the capital gains tax rate, and other factors, a prediction later praised by the *Wall Street Journal* as "uncannily accurate" (October 21, 1980, editorial page).
10.

$$DIFRET = 0.062 + 0.751 \times movavg(budrat, 4) - 0.258 \times (chginfl)$$
$$(15.4) \qquad\qquad\qquad (5.9)$$

$$- 2.34 \times 1/T - 0.101 \times lag(cgtax(-2), 6)$$
$$(12.3) \qquad\quad (10.8)$$

DIFRET is the residual calculated by regressing the S&P 500/GDP ratio on the Aaa corporate bond yield. If bond yields are unchanged, the coefficients can be converted to the standard P/E ratio by multiplying by 200.

budrat = ratio of Federal budget surplus or deficit to GDP; chginfl = % change in inflation this year minus % change last year; cgtax = maximum tax rate on capital gains income; T = time trend (to reflect decreasing dividend yield); movavg is a four-quarter moving average. The lag on cgtax is a six-quarter distributed lag. The DW statistic for this equation is very low, but when an AR(1) adjustment is used, all the terms remain significant except the time trend.

part VI
Policy analysis and forecasting

We have now presented our analysis of how the macroeconomy works. At this stage, most macro textbooks used to include a section on policy analysis, showing how the relationships that had been developed throughout the text could be used by the government to improve economic performance. Also, some macroeconomists thought that an econometric model based on these relationships could be used to provide accurate forecasts of the economy, although not everyone subscribed to that theory.

Economists in general, and macroeconomic forecasters in particular, have learned quite a bit in the last 25 years, and one of the things we now know is that models don't work as well as had once been assumed. Macroeconomic forecasts, as it turns out, are almost useless. The consensus forecast for real growth and inflation one year ahead is no better than a naive model, as explained in chapter 20, and no individual forecaster has ever been able to beat the consensus on a consistent basis. For practical purposes, there isn't a macroeconomic forecasting industry any more.

Having said that, it might seem that the last section of the book could be omitted; some may find this book too long in any case. Nonetheless, there are several salient topics that should be of substantial importance to managers. Even though fine-tuning no longer works, fiscal policy still plays an important role in determining economic performance. In the short run, automatic stabilizers keep recessions short and mild, and, in the long run, optimal fiscal policy boosts productivity growth well above the rate that would otherwise occur. In particular, we note that during periods of balanced budgets, productivity growth in the US economy has been about 1% higher than during periods of substantial deficits. These points, and some comments about "saving" social security, are discussed in chapter 18.

Monetary policy still plays a vital role in determining the performance of the economy. In the long run, it determines the rate of inflation, and, in the short run, it determines both real growth and inflation. Managers are more likely to be interested in short-term changes in Fed policy and monetary and credit aggregates, since those changes will affect their businesses directly. Any manager who prepares business plans needs to be aware of what the Fed is doing, and also realize how these plans need to be changed when the Fed institutes changes that were not anticipated. To the extent that the Fed does not change policy in a vacuum, the economic indicators that lead to changes in interest rates and other policy measure should be closely followed. These issues are discussed in chapter 19.

Finally, the overall issue of forecasting is discussed. The track record suggests that predicting the future is not something that most people do very well. This certainly applies to macroeconomists, but not only them. Financial market analysts have not done very well over the past few years either. However, to dismiss all forecasts out of hand is to admit that nothing is known about the future, and hence no business plans can be based on what is likely to occur in the years ahead. In this author's view, that does not seem to be a very profitable way to proceed either.

Hence the material in chapter 20 focuses on two main issues. The first issue is how models and other methods of forecasting can be used to determine the most likely outcome after unexpected events have happened. No one could reasonably have been expected to predict the various energy crises, the timing of various Middle Eastern wars, or the tragic events of 9/11. However, once exogenous shocks do occur, economic forecasting can still play a useful role in predicting how the economy – and sales of your own business – are likely to react.

The second issue is how some of the major economic indicators can be used to track your business. The three major indexes discussed are the Index of Leading Economic Indicators, the indexes of consumer sentiment and expectations, and the ISM Report On Business. None of these is infallible, of course, but when combined with other information about economic linkages and the reaction of the economy to changes in exogenous variables, they can be used to improve economic predictions. While there are no magic answers on how to forecast accurately here or anywhere else, an intelligent analysis of the relevant economic information should help managers improve the performance of their own businesses. It is in this spirit that the information in chapter 20 is presented.

chapter eighteen

Fiscal policy and its impact on productivity growth

Introduction

While a broad understanding of the linkages of the various sectors of the economy can improve planning skills for managers, the practical application of this knowledge often involves forecasting of capital spending, sales, costs, and other factors that directly affect the individual firm. Yet even though most managers will not be involved in policy planning, a clear understanding of what the government is likely to do – and how it will affect their businesses – should also improve operating results.

Fiscal policy plays a dual role in the economy. In the short run, it continues to reduce the impact of recessions – but mainly through automatic rather than discretionary stabilizers. In the long run, it plays a critical role in determining the growth rate of capital formation, productivity, and the standard of living. Indeed, while monetary policy is a better tool for controlling short-term fluctuations in the economy, fiscal policy is the principal factor determining whether an economy prospers in the long run.

A brief description of the short-term impact of fiscal policy is warranted for two reasons. First, automatic stabilizers are one of the major reasons why recessions have been briefer and milder in the post-WWII period than their early counterparts. Second, the issue of whether to use discretionary stabilizers to offset a recession is still very much in the news, as witnessed by the Bush Administration tax cuts in mid-2001, so we also discuss the pros and cons of those policies.

After discussing the short-run impact of changes in fiscal policy, we offer a few comments on the optimal size of the budget deficit and national debt. The chapter then summarizes a variety of fiscal policy factors that determine long-run productivity growth. The first and most important issue is the impact of fiscal policy on the rate of saving and investment, which determines capital formation. The concept of "crowding out," which occurs when government borrowing raises interest rates and reduces equity prices, is well known when the government runs deficits at full employment; however, crowding out can also occur when the economy is not at full employment, or when the budget is balanced if the government sector is expanding. That is why we also consider the optimal size of the budget itself, as opposed to the surplus or deficit.

Another key factor is the role of government regulation and deregulation, notably environmental protection. This topic is treated separately because for the most part, decisions in this area do not have much impact on the size of the budget itself. For example, the cost of complying with cleaner air and water, which costs the private sector and state and local governments almost $200 billion per year, has virtually no direct impact on the Federal budget. An important subset of this category has been the role of energy policies since 1973.

Most economists and politicians agree that three major areas of fiscal policy need to be reformed. First, the current income tax code has become so complicated that in many arcane areas, the costs of compliance far outweigh the benefits of increased revenues. In some cases, provisions of the tax code are perverse; sections designed to increase revenues actually diminish them. Second, politicians of all stripes agree that "something" has to be done about social security, otherwise it will go "bankrupt" by 2040; we examine the structure and validity of those arguments. Third, healthcare has become an increasingly large proportion of total consumer and government budgets, and the issue of how to pay for these increased costs – particularly as more new "miracle" drugs are discovered and people are able to live longer – promises to be one of the major economic issues of the twenty-first century.

Any discussion about fiscal policies of the future must take into account the fact that we live in a democracy, and the final decisions will be validated at the ballot box, so changes in fiscal policies proposed by economists must be tempered with political reality. Policies that are widely considered unfair because they favor the rich and hurt the poor generally have no chance of passage in the twenty-first century.

The key tradeoff for many fiscal policies is between equity and efficiency. If people with relatively high incomes are taxed at punitive rates, they will find ways – either legal or illegal – to avoid taxes. That could take the form of tax shelters, sheltering income in other countries, working abroad, outright cheating, or simply reducing their work effort. At the low end of the scale, overly generous benefits to those who choose not to work is not only odious to a majority of the voting public but encourages idleness. Hence any discussion of suggested reforms must also take into consideration the issues of equity as well as growth.

18.1 Automatic and discretionary stabilizers

As shown in chapter 15, one of the reasons that recent recessions are shorter, milder, and occur less frequently is the increasingly important role of automatic stabilizers; it was also suggested that discretionary stabilizers do not work very well. Both these points are expanded in this section.

When the economy falls into recession and the unemployment rate rises, the Federal budget invariably moves into a deficit. Personal and corporate income taxes fall more than proportionately, and transfer payments rise.

Consider the case of a fairly typical blue-collar worker earning $40,000 per year, including the employer-paid portion of social security. Assuming that he (most of them are still male) has a wife and two children and takes the standard deduction, his Federal income taxes would be about $2,500 per year. His social security and Medicare tax payments, including the employer-paid share, are $6,120 per year; note these are much higher than the income tax payments. In a typical state, his total state income and sales taxes would be about $1,400 per year, so total taxes paid would be about $10,000. Now suppose he becomes unemployed, and in the worst case, cannot find work for an entire year. His unemployment benefits would total about $10,000, none of which is taxed, so his after-tax income drops from $30,000 to $10,000, or a decline of $20,000. That is a serious reduction and not one to be taken lightly. Nonetheless, note that the government picks up half the tab because of the automatic stabilizers. If he has no assets and qualifies for Medicaid, or if he qualifies for food stamps and his children qualify for subsidized school lunch programs, the government tab would rise even more, generally approaching about two-thirds of his lost income.

The impact of the automatic stabilizers during a mild recession can be examined by looking at the 1990–91 experience. While these stabilizers were also at work during the 2001 downturn, the situation was complicated by (a) the tax rebate checks mailed out that summer, and (b) the increase in expenditures following 9/11. That mix of automatic and discretionary stabilizers is examined below in case study 18.1. First, however, we focus on the automatic stabilizers.

Table 18.1 shows what happened to the level and growth rate for each of the major automatic stabilizers in the Federal government budget during and after the 1990–91 recession (national defense, interest payments, and excise taxes are omitted). The drop in net government revenues (the drop in revenues plus the rise in expenditures) was $109 billion, or just under 2% of total GDP. The growth rate fell to –0.5% from an average of 3.4% for the four years before and the four years after the recession, or a drop of approximately 4%. Thus in the brief, mild 1990–91 recession, each 1% decline in real growth boosted the Federal budget deficit by an amount roughly equivalent to 0.5% of GDP. We use these figures as a comparison for the 2001 recession, when discretionary stabilizers were also at work.

The growth rate for personal and corporate income taxes in 1992–6 was slightly higher than in 1985–9, even though the growth rate of the economy was slightly lower, because of the Clinton tax increase that went into effect in 1993. Offsetting this, social security payments rose at a slower rate because of lower inflation and no increase in the base rate. However, the results would have been virtually the same if we had explicitly adjusted for these minor changes.

The 1991 recession reduced real growth by about 4% relative to its trend level, or about $230 billion at 1990 levels. Since the automatic stabilizers pumped about

Table 18.1 Automatic stabilizers during the 1990–91 recession

	Levels, billions of $					Average % change for indicated periods				
	PIT	CIT	SOC	TR	GIA	PIT	CIT	SOC	TR	GIA
1985	357	76	297	303	81					
1989	455	117	376	410	98	7.8	11.3	7.9	7.5	4.9
1990	473	118	400	445	111	4.0	0.9	6.4	8.5	13.3
1991	465	110	419	492	132	−1.7	−6.8	4.8	10.6	18.9
1992	479	118	442	549	149	3.0	7.3	5.5	11.6	12.9
1996	670	191	543	678	190	8.8	12.8	5.3	5.4	6.3
Average growth, 1985–9 and 1992–6						8.3	12.0	6.6	6.5	5.6
Percentage change, 1991						−1.7	−6.8	4.8	10.6	18.9
Difference in growth rates						−10.0	−18.8	−1.8	4.1	13.3
Change in revenues or expenditures based on										
1990 levels, billions of $						−47	−22	−7	18	15

PIT = personal income tax, CIT = corporate income tax, SOC = social security contributions, TR = transfer payments to persons, GIA = grants-in-aid to state and local governments
Source: Budget of the United States Government

$109 billion into the economy that year, these stabilizers offset almost half of the decline in economic activity that accompanied the recession. Hence the drop in real GDP might have been twice as severe – and the actual downturn might have lasted much longer – if the automatic stabilizers had not gone into effect. It is clear that these stabilizers do reduce the length and severity of recessions.

If the automatic stabilizers do such a good job, why not enhance their efficacy? Perhaps stabilizers should be utilized to make up all – or at least most – of the difference.

Most economists agree that the budget should be balanced over the cycle, rather than remaining permanently in deficit; this point is discussed below in greater detail. One advantage of the automatic stabilizers is that when the economy recovers, revenue automatically rises and the growth in transfer and welfare payments automatically declines. A permanent increase in spending or decrease in tax rates might saddle the economy with an unwanted budget deficit even at full employment. But what about temporary tax cuts – or temporary spending increases?

Economists do not agree on whether discretionary stabilizers are a good idea. However, while the consensus opinion in the 1960s was that they did improve economic performance, informed opinion has shifted to the point where most economists now think they do not benefit the economy. There are several reasons why discretionary stabilizers did not work very well.

First, according to the permanent income hypothesis, most of a temporary tax cut would be saved instead of spent, so consumption would not rise very much, but the resulting increase in the debt would still have to be funded in later years, which would raise interest rates once the economy regained its momentum. Second, a temporary tax credit for capital spending does not generate a very large increase in investment if excess capacity precluded any meaningful rise; hence the tax credit would be utilized by firms who planned to purchase these capital goods anyhow; tax credits that were not used might be turned into tax shelters. Third, an increase in government spending might cause business and investor sentiment to decline, hence reducing capital spending and stock prices.

The magnitudes of these changes are empirical questions; we raise them here not to dismiss temporary tax cuts or spending increases out of hand, but only to point out that offsetting factors do exist. If they did not, economists would recommend discretionary stabilizers during times of economic downturn.

It used to be said that by the time Congress got around to voting for fiscal stimulus, the recession would have already ended. That is what happened in 1975; the recession ended in March, while the tax rebate designed to shorten the recession was not distributed until the following quarter. The income tax surcharge, designed to offset the increased defense spending caused by the Vietnam War, should have been passed by mid-1966 for optimal impact, but did not actually go into effect until mid-1968.

However, that argument did not apply during the 2001 recession, when tax rebate checks of approximately $45 billion were distributed during the summer, and government expenditures rose sharply immediately after 9/11; both of these events occurred while the recession was still underway. At first it appeared the economy immediately rebounded, which should have been suspicious because there is usually some lag; also, the rebound was probably more closely tied to the decline in short-term interest rates that began early in the year. After rising at an annual rate of 3.8% for two quarters, real growth stumbled again after the first quarter of 2002 and declined to an annual rate of 2.2% for the rest of the year, suggesting that the impact of the temporary tax cuts and spending increases did not have many ripple, or multiplier, effects. Furthermore, the sharp decline in the stock market during the first half of 2002, which was unprecedented during the early stages of economic recovery, also retarded real growth. Thus we present these results as a case study rather than a generalized example of what might happen if discretionary stabilizers are again enacted in the middle of some future recession.

CASE STUDY 18.1   FISCAL POLICY DURING THE 2001 RECESSION

Personal income taxes were reduced by approximately $45 billion in 2001 and $100 billion in 2002 because of the changes in the rate schedule. The 10.8% annual rate rise in personal income tax receipts from 1996 to 2000 was partially due to the roaring bull market and the huge increases in stock options and bonuses tied directly to the market. Under normal circumstances, a 6% rise in nominal GDP would boost personal income taxes by about $7\frac{1}{2}$% per year,

continued

CASE STUDY 18.1 (*continued*)

Table 18.2 Automatic and discretionary stabilizers during the 2001 recession

	Levels, billions of $					Average % change for indicated periods				
	PIT	CIT	SOC	TR	GIA	PIT	CIT	SOC	TR	GIA
1996	670	191	543	692	190					
2000	1009	224	692	780	245	10.8	4.1	6.2	3.0	6.6
2001	1011	170	717	842	277	0.2	−24.1	3.6	7.9	13.1
2002	847	180	738	932	306	−16.2	5.9	2.9	10.7	10.5

taking into account the progressivity of the current tax schedule. Thus without the tax cut, on a static ex ante basis, personal income taxes in 2002 would have risen to $1,167 billion if the economy had continued to grow at its average rate. Personal income taxes that year were actually some $320 billion below that level, only one-third of which reflected the Bush tax cut.

The drop in corporate income taxes in 2001 was proportional to the drop in profits and does not reflect any change in tax rates. If there had been no recession and profits would have increased at their normal rate, corporate income taxes in 2002 would have risen to $264 billion; they fell $84 billion because of the recession. Thus total income taxes fell a whopping $304 billion because of the recession, even though it was unusually mild. Social security taxes in 2002 were $30 billion lower because of the recession.

It is difficult to identify precisely how much of the rise in transfer payments and grants-in-aid represented the recession and how much occurred because of 9/11, but we can provide some estimates based on the quarterly patterns during 2001. On this basis, we calculate that without any post 9/11 aid, transfer payments would have risen to $902 billion in 2002 instead of $932 billion, which means $80 billion of the additional rise was due to the weak economy, and $30 billion was due to discretionary spending. The quarterly grants-in-aid figures are more erratic, but we estimate they would have risen to $290 billion with the recession but no additional spending, compared to $278 billion with no recession and an actual level of $306 billion. Thus transfer payments probably rose an extra $96 billion because of the recession.

Taking all these factors into consideration, then, we calculate that net government revenues in 2002 were some $400 billion lower than would have otherwise been the case because of automatic stabilizers; with an additional $146 billion decline in revenues due to discretionary stabilizers. Thus the total swing in the Federal budget position due to the stabilizers was $546 billion, or about 5.5% of 2000 GDP. That is almost three times as big as the relative dip in net revenues in the 1990–91

continued

CASE STUDY 18.1 (*continued*)

recession. The actual change in the deficit was $394 billion because, at the same time, net interest payments plunged $60 billion instead of rising $10 billion, and under previous circumstances the surplus was rising rapidly and would have increased an estimated $82 billion if real growth had remained at 4%.

Real growth actually declined from an average of 4% in the 1996–2000 period to 0% during 2001, a decline that was very similar to the magnitude that occurred in the 1990–91 recession. However, the swing in the *automatic* stabilizers was more than 4% of GDP, compared to 2% in the previous recession, mainly because of the unprecedented postwar decline in corporate profits and stock prices. In addition, discretionary stabilizers boosted the deficit by another 1.5% of GDP to the deficit. Yet in spite of this additional stimulus, the economy did not perform very well. Real GDP did rise at a 3.8% annual rate during 2001.4 and 2002.1, but the economy then slowed down and, as noted above, rose only 2.2% during the remainder of the year, far below the average increase of better than 5% during the first year of previous recoveries; also, the stock market declined sharply during most of the year.

On balance, the evidence from the 2001–02 experience suggests that temporary discretionary stabilizers did not boost real growth very much. The strength that did occur in the early stages of the upturn was probably due more to the reduction in the Federal funds rate from $6\frac{1}{2}$% to $1\frac{3}{4}$% during the year than to the rebate checks mailed in mid-2001.

18.2   Components of the Federal government budget

Before the Great Depression, Federal government spending was about 5% of total GDP; that ratio increased to about 10% during the first two terms of Franklin D. Roosevelt. It then rose to a peak of 44% of GDP during the peak years of World War II, most of which represented higher defense spending. Shortly after the end of that war, the defense budget was sharply slashed, reducing Federal government spending to about 12% of GDP, about where it was before the war. That figure then rose to 20% by the end of the Korean War, where it is now. Over the past 40 years, that ratio has fluctuated between 17% and 23% of GDP.

However, the relative stability of this ratio since 1953 masks the major shifts that have occurred over that time period. In particular, defense spending has decreased sharply as a proportion of the total budget and GDP, while healthcare expenditures – and to a lesser extent, social security expenditures – have risen sharply. On the revenue side, corporate income tax receipts as a proportion of GDP have fallen sharply, while social security taxes have risen.

Figure 18.1 shows that the biggest changes have been the rise in social security payments, from 2% to 7% of GDP, although they have leveled off over the past decade, and the decline in corporate income tax payments from 6% to 2%. Excise

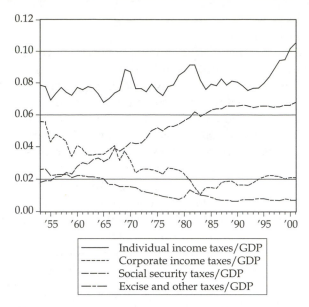

Figure 18.1 Sources of Federal government revenues as a proportion of total GDP, budget and fiscal year basis
Source: Budget of the United States Government

tax payments have declined in relative importance, falling from 2% to 1% of GDP, since most Federal excise taxes are based on the volume of transactions rather than current-dollar values. The increase in individual income tax payments from 8% to 11% of GDP during the 1990s represents the booming economy and the runaway stock market; a small proportion of that amount, probably about 0.4%, is due to the Clinton tax hikes for upper-bracket individuals. With the Bush tax cuts and slowdown in the stock market, that ratio already returned to its previous level of 8% in 2002. We do not expect any major changes in these ratios, which means individual income, corporate income, social security, and excise taxes will probably account for approximately 8%, 2%, 7%, and 1% of GDP, for a total of 18% of GDP, excluding the temporary drop in receipts due to the recession but including the permanent Bush tax cuts.

Figure 18.2 shows the major categories of Federal spending as a proportion of GDP. Defense spending has fallen from 14% to 4% of GDP since 1953, yet the overall ratio of Federal spending to GDP shows no downward trend. The 11% gap has been filled by healthcare, up from 0% to 4%; social security payments, up from 1% to 5%; and all other spending, up from 2% to 5%. Interest payments rose as a proportion of GDP during the 1970s and 1980s but have since declined to about 2%. Hence Federal spending currently stands at about 20% of GDP, excluding the one-time expenditures associated with the recession, the aftermath of 9/11, and the war in Iraq.

As the economy recovers from the 2001 recession, it is expected that the Federal budget will remain in deficit for many years, with receipts averaging about 18% and expenditures about 20% of GDP. However, that does not answer the longer term questions of how these trends will change. Assuming average growth of about

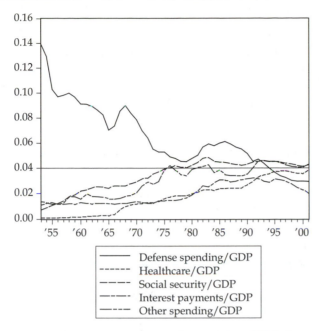

Figure 18.2   Major categories of Federal government expenditures relative to GDP, budget, and fiscal year basis
Source: Budget of the United States Government

$3\frac{1}{2}$% to 4% in real terms and 2% to $2\frac{1}{2}$% in inflation, accompanied by increases in corporate profits and stock prices that are slightly higher than GDP, the ratio of Federal receipts to GDP would rise over time from the current 18% figure *in the absence of further tax cuts* because of the progressive nature of the individual income tax rate schedule. The increase is likely to be about 0.5% per year – for example, 18.5% in 2004, 19.0% in 2005, and so on. However, under current legislation, those increases are scheduled to be offset by further income tax rate cuts; alternatively, they might be used to fund increases in the ratio of social security payments and healthcare benefits to GDP. It is also possible that if a surplus does occur again, it could be applied to reducing the national debt. Of course, some combination of these three programs could be enacted.

CASE STUDY 18.2   ON-BUDGET AND OFF-BUDGET FINANCING

In spite of the substantial Federal budget surpluses in 1999 and 2000, some politicians claimed that the "actual" surplus was much smaller because the so-called "on-budget" surplus was essentially zero in FY 1999 and rose only to $87 billion in FY 2000. The remainder of the surplus, known as the "off-budget" surplus,
continued

CASE STUDY 18.2 (*continued*)

represents the surplus that is accumulating in the social security "trust fund" and other government retirement funds in anticipation of the years when the ratio of the number of retirees to number of working people will be much higher, and that fund will start to be drawn down. The OMB figures for 1990–2002 are given in table 18.3.

Table 18.3 On-budget and off-budget components of the Federal budget

	Total surplus or deficit	On-budget	Off-budget
1990	−221.2	−277.8	56.6
1991	−269.4	−321.6	52.2
1992	−290.4	−340.5	50.1
1993	−255.1	−300.5	45.3
1994	−203.3	−258.9	55.7
1995	−164.0	−227.4	62.4
1996	−107.5	−174.1	66.6
1997	−22.0	−103.4	81.4
1998	69.2	−30.0	99.2
1999	125.5	1.8	123.7
2000	236.4	86.6	149.8
2001	127.1	−33.4	160.5
2002	−157.8	−317.5	159.7

All figures are billions of dollars for fiscal years
Source: Budget of the United States Government

The off-budget surpluses are supposed to be used to pay increased social security benefits in the years after 2020; this point is discussed later in this chapter. During the Bush–Gore debates during the 2000 Presidential election, much heated rhetoric was exchanged about "locking up the Social Security safety deposit box," the implication being that the social security surpluses would not be used to offset the on-budget deficits. Of course, as soon as the recession started, that concept went out the window.

Most politicians still like to pretend that the social security trust funds are somehow sequestered in a separate account, but economists know better. Money is fungible, and there is no real difference between money that is spent to pay social security benefits and money that is used for other transfer payments, or for that matter other purchases. In terms of the impact on financial markets, real growth, inflation, and productivity, the important number is the total budget surplus or deficit, not some subset that is artificially defined by artificially separating certain types of funds in the account books.

CASE STUDY 18.3   WHAT HAPPENED TO THE PLAN TO RETIRE THE DEBT BY 2010?

Regardless of the path of future fiscal policy, the budget outlook is not nearly as rosy as it seemed in 2000, when politicians of both parties talked about retiring all of the publicly held national debt – about $3.6 trillion – by 2010. You might wonder: just what were they smoking?

Nonetheless, that claim did not seem particularly absurd to many economists, including this author, in 2000. The arithmetic behind such a claim was basically as follows. The budget surplus had climbed to $236bn in FY 2000 and if there had been no recession in FY 2001, the figure probably would have risen to $300bn. After that, suppose that the economy grew at $3\frac{1}{2}$% per year in real terms, with inflation at $2\frac{1}{2}$%. Under that fairly standard assumption, tax receipts would rise about $7\frac{1}{2}$% per year, as explained above, and expenditures probably would rise about 6% per year. Even that figure is almost double the 3.3% annual rate gain during the Clinton Administration, but this figure allows for some rebuilding of the defense department and acceleration in medical care costs.

The FY 2001 figures were originally projected to be about $2,150bn for tax receipts and $1,850bn for expenditures. If receipts rise $7\frac{1}{2}$% per year, that would be about $161bn per year, and if expenditures rose 6% per year, that would be $111bn per year. Hence the surplus would rise to $350bn in FY 2002, $400bn in FY 2003, and so on. Doing the indicated arithmetic yields the result that the total publicly held national debt would be completely retired by 2008. These were not pie-in-the-sky projections, but just a continuation of recent growth trends, and in fact permitted some acceleration in government spending.

What happened? Primarily because of the recession, and only secondarily because of the Bush tax cuts, the deficit suddenly zoomed to what is projected, as of mid-2003, to be as high as $450bn in FY 2004. Now let's do the arithmetic again. Expenditures are likely to be about $2,350bn, with receipts around $1,800bn. If receipts then rise $7\frac{1}{2}$% per year – which, by the way, implies no further Bush tax cuts – they would increase about $135bn per year. If expenditures rise 6% per year, they would rise $141bn per year. The deficit would increase slightly for many years. And if the Bush tax cuts are enacted at a rate of about $50bn per year, the deficit would increase that much faster.

Originally, the Bush plan was to take the additional $50bn in the surplus each year and turn it into a tax cut. The alternative, of course, would have been to increase spending by that amount, which most Democrats preferred. But in either case, the original plan was based on no recession and a substantial budget surplus for many years in the future.

continued

CASE STUDY 18.3 (*continued*)

How could the surplus have cratered so completely? According to the analysis presented in this text, a 1% drop in the growth rate should reduce the surplus ratio by about $\frac{1}{2}$%. So if real growth declined from 4% to 2%, that should have lowered the surplus ratio from 3% to 1%. Instead, it plunged from 3% to −3% – *even before the Bush tax cuts are considered.*

The answer to this puzzle is found in the sharp increase in capital gains income during the 1990s. That was not only due to the record increase in the stock market, although of course that played a role. When Clinton boosted the top marginal tax rate to 50%, the statutory maximum was 39.6%, but when this figure is adjusted for the disappearing deductible, the 2.9% Medicare tax on all income, and the fact that under many circumstances, state and local income taxes and mortgage payments were no longer deductible for many high-income earners, the top rate exceeded 50%. In 1997, the top capital gains tax rate dropped to 20%. That difference encouraged many high-income earners to receive most of their compensation in stock options. In addition, the ruling by Clinton in 1993 that salaries of more than $1m could not be deducted as a business expense also accelerated the movement toward capital gains as a form of remuneration. Thus capital gains became far more important than previously, and hence the decline in the stock market had a much more severe impact on Federal (and state) tax receipts than any economist had estimated.

Will the Federal budget ever return to a surplus again? Obviously nobody can say with certainty and at this point. Nonetheless, the figures given above show that the only way to return to a surplus would be to have tax receipts grow much faster than $7\frac{1}{2}$% per year, and expenditures rise much more slowly than 6% per year, for an extended period. We do not expect another stock market boom like the 1990s, so an increase in revenues well above $7\frac{1}{2}$% appears to be extremely unlikely under any foreseeable circumstance unless a massive tax increase were instituted. The growth rate of expenditures could be cut somewhat, but increased medical care expenditures in the future, plus the increasing burden of social security starting in 2010, also make this extremely unlikely. At a minimum, then, these figures suggest that a substantial Federal budget deficit will be with us for many years.

18.3 Advantages and disadvantages of Federal budget surpluses and deficits

If you are a politician, it is very difficult not to be in favor of a balanced budget. Yet one of the primary rules of macroeconomics is that the government budget should be balanced over the business cycle for optimal economic performance, not balanced every year. Deficits should occur during times of recessions, while surpluses should accumulate during times of overfull employment. This is accomplished primarily by the automatic stabilizers.

Even given agreement on that point, budget discussions among economists can still turn contentious. After all, a balanced budget over the business cycle can be accomplished with high spending and high taxes, or low spending and low taxes. High spending can mean increased expenditures made directly by the Federal government, or the money can be funneled to state and local governments through revenue sharing. High taxes can rely heavily on tax payments from upper-income groups, or can be based on taxes that are more proportional, such as an income tax with relatively few gradations or even a national sales or value-added tax.

The evidence presented in table 18.4 indicates that a balanced budget over the business cycle boosts the real growth rate. The US budget was in deficit continuously from 1969 through 1997. If deficits hurt the economy, we would expect to find that inflation was higher, and productivity was lower, during those periods of deficits compared to periods of balanced budgets or surpluses. At the time of publication, it was still too early to draw firm conclusions about the most recent period, since the economy plunged into recession in 2001. On balance, however, the return to deficits did not seem to provide much spark to the economy in 2002.

Factors other than the budget ratio presumably influenced the growth rate, productivity, and inflation during these periods, but the evidence does strongly suggest that the budget position did make some difference. When the budget is balanced over the business cycle, the real growth rate averages about 4% (the 3.2% figure for the most recent period includes the 2001 recession); when it remains in deficit over the cycle, the growth rate drops to 3%. Furthermore, that change in the growth rate is closely mirrored in the figures for productivity growth. Inflation was substantially higher during the deficit years, and while one may assign part of the blame to the oil shocks, this period also includes the sharp decline in oil prices in 1986, when they returned almost to pre-1973 levels in real terms. The case for a balanced budget over the business cycle is strong enough that we do not press the issue further, and move to other topics.

Until 1961, political leaders of both parties paid at least lip service to the concept that the Federal budget should be balanced every year. In 1932, Franklin D. Roosevelt ran on a platform of a balanced budget and castigated Herbert Hoover

Table 18.4 Long-term trends with balanced budgets and deficits

	Real GDP	Productivity	Inflation (CPI)	Budget ratio*
1947–1968	4.0	2.8	2.3	0.6
1969–1997	3.0	1.6	5.4	−2.7
1997–2001	3.2	2.4	2.5	1.3

All figures except budget ratio are average annual percentage changes
* Ratio of Federal budget surplus or deficit, NIPA, to GDP
Source: Calculated by author

for the existing deficits. Of course the deficit ballooned during World War II, but Harry S. Truman then insisted on balanced budgets during his peacetime years, and tried to balance the budget during the Korean War years by raising taxes significantly. Dwight D. Eisenhower pushed for a balanced budget every year, although that goal was not met by a wide margin during the fairly short but severe 1958 recession.

Academic economists had been singing the praises of budget deficits during periods of economic slack for two decades, but until John F. Kennedy was elected, they had not been able to convince political leaders of the wisdom of deficit financing during years of economic slack. Simply claiming that deficits were good for the economy during recessions was not enough to do the trick. The key, then, was to estimate what the budget position would be if the economy were at full employment. The budget surplus measured by this method would then indicate the amount of fiscal stimulus that could safely be employed during a period of slack economic growth without creating inflationary pressures.

This is not quite as simple as it sounds. First, reasonable economists can disagree about the appropriate measure of full employment for any particular year. Second, the situation could be "scammed" by setting the full-employment unemployment rate so low that excessive spending increases or tax cuts would take place. Third, the money still has to be borrowed, and the cost of that borrowing always has to be weighed against the benefits of fiscal stimulus.

The concept of the full-employment unemployment rate was originally introduced by E. Cary Brown in 1956,[1] and was pushed by Walter Heller, Chairman of the Council of Economic Advisors under Kennedy (and, for a while, Johnson). It so happened that FY 1961 – the last budget prepared by the Eisenhower Administration – was unusual in the sense that the actual budget was balanced even though the economy was in recession, causing a substantial full-employment budget surplus. However, as shown below, that rarely happens. Years when the actual budget is in deficit but the full-employment budget is in surplus occur far less frequently than Heller and his colleagues expected at the time.

While the calculation of the budget surplus or deficit if the economy were performing optimally was originally known as the "full employment budget," that term was later changed to "high employment budget" in order to avoid arguments about how to measure full employment. As the full-employment rate changed markedly over the decades, that term was further modified to the "standardized employment budget," which is designed to eliminate the effect of the business cycle without identifying a particular unemployment rate as "full employment." In this incarnation it is currently calculated by the CBO and is shown in figure 18.3; these calculations were not made by the CBO before 1961.

The difference between the actual and standardized employment budget ratios is shown in figure 18.4, where it can be seen that the recession usually causes the deficit ratio to rise about 2% of GDP for mild recessions, and 3% of GDP for severe recessions. Most of the time, both the actual and standardized employment budgets are either in surplus or deficit, so arguments about the difference have lost

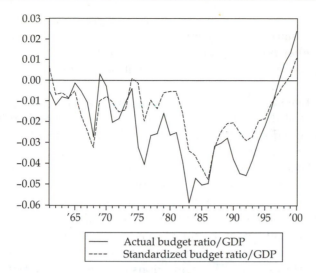

Figure 18.3   Actual and standardized Federal government surplus or deficits as a proportion of GDP, FY basis; standardized figures calculated by the CBO

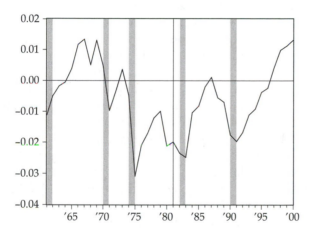

Figure 18.4   Difference between the ratio of the actual Federal budget surplus or deficit to GDP and the standardized budget surplus or deficit (shaded areas are recessions)

most of their sting. Most economists now use the rule of thumb that a recession causes a 2% to 3% increase in the deficit ratio, and take this into consideration when determining whether the actual budget position is optimal.

We now turn to the thornier question of how large the budget itself should be relative to GDP. Usually this question is couched in terms of the cliché "guns vs butter." Since defense spending now accounts for only about 15% of the Federal budget, and since such programs as social security are not seriously opposed by leaders of either political party, the argument these days has shifted to issues such as the amount the Federal government should spend on healthcare and education.

Even within that basic framework, there are still a plethora of arguments. If education is funded at the local level, students in poor neighborhoods are likely to receive an inferior education; but if it is funded at the Federal level, that increases the pressure from the morbid hand of "Big Brother." Suppose adequate funds have been set aside for old-age based on mortality tables during years when employees are normally working, but recent advances in medicine keep people alive much longer – and maintenance medicines are discovered that prolong good health but are very expensive. If the Federal government is paying the entire bill, many individuals will ignore the cost; but if they are required to pay some of the bill themselves, some people will remain in poverty for their entire lives or forgo adequate medical treatment. These questions will presumably never be answered to everyone's satisfaction, and there is no guarantee that under a democracy, representatives will be elected who can provide the optimal economic answers. The unbiased economist can simply illuminate the various issues of equity and efficiency and try to offer informed choices based on these principles.

A few examples will suffice. In 2000, according to government statistics, 6.2 million families had incomes below the poverty level by an average of $15,000 per year. Hence it would have taken some $93 billion per year to eradicate poverty in families, compared to the Bush tax cut of $100 billion per year. Was that a wise choice or not? Providing the total cost of prescription drugs to the elderly poor would cost about $50 billion per year; as of 2002, a bill to provide that aid appeared likely to pass. On a broader front, providing healthcare costs to all those under 65 who do not have health insurance would cost about $135 billion per year, hence ruling out further broad-based tax cuts for several years. At another level, healthcare advocates claim that quality care at nursing homes is approaching $100,000 per year, and as many as 5 million elderly citizens might benefit from that care, yet that would cost $500 billion per year. The voters and their elected representatives must decide which options are preferable.

Some Republicans who favor smaller government would argue that George W. Bush erred by cutting personal instead of corporate income taxes. The Federal government had a surplus of $236 billion in FY 2000. That year, Federal corporate income tax collections were $207 billion. The government thus could have completely eliminated the corporate income tax and still remained in surplus. Actually the revenue loss would have been substantially less than $207 billion because with no corporate income tax, all corporate income is passed through to the individual shareholders, who then pay taxes on that income; the main difference that would occur from eliminating the tax is to end double taxation of dividends. Some economists, and not merely conservative ones, believe that ending the corporate income tax would have kept the investment boom alive, whereas not cutting high marginal rates on personal income taxes would have had virtually no impact on consumer spending or saving. Hence the argument about what proportion of GDP should be absorbed by Federal government spending and tax revenues is far more complicated than simply debating the overall percentage.

18.4   The concept of the fiscal dividend

Under circumstances of fairly rapid growth and low, stable inflation, and without major wars to be fought, and assuming the budget is balanced in the first place, Federal government revenues generally rise faster than expenditures, so the question is whether these additional funds should be used to cut taxes, increase expenditures, or reduce the national debt. That is the real choice that voters face.

The concept of the fiscal dividend was developed during the 1960s, when real growth averaged better than 5% per year and the budget remained balanced even after personal and corporate income tax rates were cut by 20% in 1964–5. After deficits reemerged during the Vietnam War period, this theory understandably sold at a tremendous discount when the Federal government budget position remained in deficit for 28 consecutive years, but the idea itself is not far-fetched.

The general framework can be outlined as follows. Assume that over the long run, real GDP grows 4% per year, and the inflation rate averages about 2%. Because there is some progressivity in the personal income tax system, Federal tax receipts would grow about $7\frac{1}{2}$% per year. This assumes the stock market grows at the same rate as GDP, unlike the 1990s. In the absence of international conflagrations, defense spending would grow at roughly the rate of inflation, and if the budget is balanced, net interest payments would not grow at all. Using the recent level for nominal GDP of $10,000 billion, and assuming that both taxes and receipts are about 20% of GDP, that would be $2,000 billion for each category. Receipts would then rise about $150 billion per year, while expenditures for defense, net interest, social security, income security, and the cost of running the government would increase about 4% per year, or about $50 billion. That leaves almost $100 billion increase per year for a base of $800 billion on other expenditures, which would grow about 6% under ordinary circumstances. Based on that arithmetic, the Federal government generates a so-called fiscal dividend of about $50 billion per year, or about 0.5% of GDP. By comparison, during the Clinton years, when GDP averaged about $8,000 billion, the budget position improved by $546 billion, or $68 billion per year, or 0.85% of GDP. That fiscal dividend was higher because of the stock market boom, and also because of the major decline in defense spending during his two terms.

If it's so straightforward, how could the Federal budget remain in deficit for 28 consecutive years? First, the fiscal dividend in the late 1960s was spent ahead of time on the Vietnam War. During the 1970s, real growth stagnated because of double-digit inflation, so while revenues grew rapidly in nominal terms, expenditures grew even faster. Also, social welfare spending under Johnson and Nixon increased much faster than nominal GDP. The fiscal dividend of the 1980s was spent in advance on the Reagan tax cut. Thus it took from 1992 through 1997 for the fiscal discipline of the Clinton Administration – and after 1994, a Republican Congress – to bring the budget back into balance.

From 1997 to 2000, the surplus grew $258 billion over the next three years, an average annual gain of $86 billion – or 0.93% of GDP. Thus it was not surprising that politicians said the total publicly held national debt of $3.6 trillion would be wiped out by 2010, as discussed in case study 18.2. During this period, tax rates could be modestly reduced, and some spending programs could be expanded. Then the 2001 recession derailed these plans.

Yet the arithmetic presented above is just as valid in 2002 and 2003 as it was in 2000. Of course, it remains to be seen whether the economy will actually grow at an average rate of 4% once the recovery gets underway, whether defense spending will be held constant in real terms or the Bush Administration will decide to enhance its capabilities, whether planned tax rate cuts will actually be implemented, and whether increased social welfare expenditures, notably for healthcare, will return to their earlier practice of rising at double-digit rates.

A 1% shift in the real growth/inflation mix makes a great deal of difference. In particular, if real growth were to slow down to 3%, and the inflation rate were to rise to 3% – as opposed to 4% real growth and 2% inflation – the entire fiscal dividend would be wiped out. Hence adequate funding of increased social welfare spending depends largely on a rapidly growing economy. That is one of the reasons why optimal fiscal policy is so important in the long run.

Within the overall framework of the fiscal dividend, economists generally agree on a few basic principles. First, government policies that encourage people not to work for extended periods do not benefit anyone; unemployment benefits and welfare should be designed for short-term periods of recession and temporary unemployment. Second, the government should not force employers to pay employees a wage that is above their marginal product; if that does not provide enough money for workers to support themselves or their families at a minimal living standard, they should receive supplemental aid from the government in the form of food stamps, rental allowances, and medical care benefits, and a negative income tax – but a serious attempt to find employment should accompany these benefits. Third, those who receive medical care benefits from the government should pay some small proportion of the cost in order to make informed market decisions, seeking generic drug equivalents where available, and lower-cost hospitals that provide the same quality of care. All these principles are based on the concept that people are likely to work harder when they are provided with meaningful incentives, and that people are likely to spend their own money more carefully.

The impact of the overall growth rate on the fiscal dividend can be enormous over extended periods of time. If, for example, the economy were to grow at a 3% annual rate in real terms, in 40 years total Federal tax receipts in constant (2002) dollars would be about $8,285 billion. Yet if the growth rate were boosted by one percentage point to 4%, the figure would rise to $13,375 billion, a difference of over $5 trillion, or $12,000 per person per year, assuming a 1% average annual growth in population. These figures are in 2002 dollars; the difference would be much higher in current dollars. Hence many of the allegedly insurmountable fiscal problems melt away in the face of stronger growth.

CASE STUDY 18.4   THE OPTIMAL SIZE OF THE NATIONAL DEBT

While economists agree that the budget should be balanced over the business cycle, that says nothing about the optimal level of the national debt. Of course, if in fact the budget were always balanced over the cycle, there wouldn't be any debt. In the past, though, the US government and all other countries that fought major wars have generated huge increases in the national debt during periods of wartime, and then partly paid them back during peacetime. The alternative would be to finance the war on a pay-as-you-go basis, which at least in periods of all-out armed conflict would cause serious deprivation for much of the civilian population.

Figure 18.5 shows the ratio of the total national debt to GDP (GNP before 1947). The figures for GNP before 1870 are estimated by the author. The debt ratio was

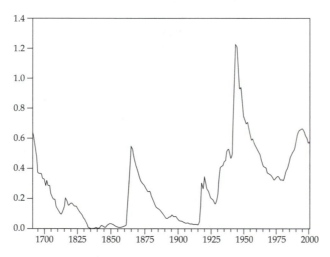

Figure 18.5   Ratio of US national debt to GDP (GNP before 1947)
Sources: National debt, Department of the Treasury and Historical Statistics of the US GDP and GNP: 1947–2001, BEA website, www.bea.gov. 1889–1946, Historical Statistics of the US 1839–1889, interpolated from five-year estimates of GNP and value added given in Historical Statistics. 1791–1839, estimated by author. Percentage growth in GNP = percentage growth in population plus percentage increases in WPI plus percentage increase in productivity. Population and WPI figures are taken from Historical Statistics; productivity growth estimates by the author

continued

CASE STUDY 18.4 (*continued*)

very high after the Revolutionary War, then declined sharply until the war of 1812, which boosted it again. The national debt was completely retired in the mid-1830s, but then rose slightly when the economy went into depression following the closing of the Bank of the United States in 1836. The debt ratio rose sharply during the Civil War, declined again, rose during World War I and fell during the 1920s, and then rose substantially during the Great Depression before zooming to an all-time peak in World War II. After that, the ratio declined fairly steadily, even during the Korean and Vietnam Wars, but rose during the Reagan years and did not turn down again until the Clinton Administration.

The burden of the debt can be measured by the cost of interest payments to the Treasury; an additional burden may be imposed on the private sector if interest rates are somewhat higher than would be the case with no debt. Net interest payments by the Treasury are currently about $200 billion, or 2% of GDP. That figure represents about a sixth of capital spending; if the debt were zero, some proportion of that money would presumably be spent on capital goods. Since the total capital stock including consumer durables and housing is approximately $20 trillion, capital stock might increase as much as 1% more per year than if the debt were zero, which would add about $\frac{1}{3}$% per year to the growth rate.

The net impact on interest rates is more problematical, since even a substantial surplus and zero debt would probably not push real interest rates below the marginal productivity of capital.[2] It is true that an increase in the *deficit* boosts real interest rates, but that has already been measured by the reduction in real growth when the government is in deficit; that effect should not be double-counted. The question here is how much a national debt that is about 50% of GDP reduces real growth when the budget is balanced; the most reasonable answer appears to be about $\frac{1}{3}$% per year. While that is certainly not zero, and the cumulative effect can be substantial, it is nonetheless a much smaller magnitude than the negative impact of deficit financing. Furthermore, if the rush to reduce the deficit resulted in substantial surpluses, the money drawn out of the economy might have a negative impact on aggregate demand, which would then slow down the increase in capital spending. For that reason, the $\frac{1}{3}$% per year is probably an upper limit.

18.5   The role of fiscal policy in determining productivity growth

The remainder of this chapter discusses offers some brief comments on how fiscal policy affects productivity growth.[3] For this purpose we will assume that the budget remains in balance over the long run, even though certain policies may generate a short-run deficit. This is not to minimize the importance of a balanced budget over the cycle, but since we have already covered this issue, the remaining topics focus on the long-term issues. Under this assumption, the ratio of the national debt to GDP would gradually decline. For example, if the actual amount of the debt remained constant while GDP grew 6% per year, the ratio of the debt to GDP would drop from its current level of about 0.5 to a minuscule 0.03 over a 50-year period. For that reason, the actual level of the debt will be ignored in this discussion.

In the long run, on a ceteris paribus basis, the economy will grow faster if the budget is balanced than if it is in deficit; it will grow faster if the ratios of spending and taxes to GDP are relatively low than if they are relatively high; it will grow faster if the tax code is more efficient; it will grow faster if the tax code encourages saving and investment instead of consumption; and it will grow faster if inflation is kept at low, stable levels. Other important goals – such as a modern infrastructure, less regulation and more deregulation, cleaner air and water, a rational energy policy, and a labor force that is well educated and remains healthy – are items that will improve the quality of life but may not boost productivity. All these are important facets of fiscal policy. We have already discussed the issue of the balanced budget, and now turn to these topics except for the role of inflation, which is more properly discussed in the next chapter on optimal monetary policy.

Short-term multiplier analysis assumes that equal-dollar tax and spending changes have the same impact on the economy.[4] However, that is true only if neither of these changes affect inflation or productivity. In general, an increase in government spending boosts inflation and reduces productivity growth, while a reduction in taxes reduces inflation and boosts productivity growth.

More specifically, a tax cut that spurs investment, increases individual incentives, or switches resources to more productive uses (e.g., out of tax shelters and into productive assets) will cause a faster growth rate in productivity over the long run. A tax cut that reduces prices – such as an excise tax cut – could have some modest positive impact because of the temporary reduction in the rate of inflation, but its long-term impact will be much smaller. Personal income tax cuts can reduce inflation because workers are more likely to accept smaller pretax wage boosts if their after-tax income has risen; but the evidence is weak showing that lower tax rates improve individual work habits. However, very high marginal tax rates do encourage the proliferation of abusive tax shelters or transference of income to offshore locations.

Some types of government spending boost productivity, such as rebuilding infrastructure and research and development on space technology. The problem with this general characterization is that many of the projects are likely to be riddled by pork-barrel politics, and the government system of bidding often insures that the work is performed by unqualified contractors. Hence the gains in productivity may be diluted by politics and bureaucracy.

If the private sector chooses not to undertake any given project, one should always try and determine whether that was because the rate of return is insufficient, or because there are significant externalities to government investment, such as space research. A better transportation system undoubtedly benefits the entire economy; in that case, the issue is how to accomplish this most efficiently. Introducing electric power to rural regions of the South certainly improved productivity and the standard of living in that region when it was first implemented. After a while, though, the heavy hand of bureaucracy reduced efficiency relative to the private sector, and what was a positive idea originally turned into a negative one.

If changes in productivity or inflationary expectations are not considered, a change in taxes and an equivalent change in government spending would generally have approximately the same impact on the economy. However, if tax cuts boost productivity while government spending increases diminish it, then a "balanced budget" program that raises taxes and spending by the same amount would result in lower productivity growth and a more sluggish increase in the standard of living, while a program that reduced taxes and spending by the same amount would boost productivity growth and the standard of living.

Suppose government spending rises by 1% of GDP, which would initially boost real GDP by about $1\frac{1}{2}$%, ceteris paribus. After considering the positive feedback effects, that boosts the deficit ratio by about $\frac{3}{4}$%, hence raising interest rates by three-quarters of a percentage point and increasing the cost of capital by about 3% (e.g., from 24% to $24\frac{3}{4}$%). That reduces capital stock by 3% in the long run, which reduces real GDP by 1%. In the long run, the decline in productivity offsets the increase in aggregate demand arising from more government spending, which means the long-term multiplier is zero.

Now suppose the government implements a tax cut equal to 1% of GDP, which stimulates investment by reducing the cost of capital. Using the same proportionality factors, a tax cut equal to 1% of GDP would boost real GDP by $1\frac{2}{3}$% in the long run.

These are long-term solutions; sometimes, short-term timing effects are also important. The Clinton tax hikes of 1993 boosted real growth because they were accompanied by spending cuts, so bond rates dropped 2% in anticipation of lower deficits in the future. In this case, the expansionary impact of lower interest rates boosted the economy in advance of the contractionary impacts of tax hikes and the cuts in government spending.

Using the above calculations as a reference point, consider what happened in 1993 when tax rates were boosted by $\frac{1}{2}$% of GDP and government spending was cut by $\frac{1}{2}$% of GDP (relative to existing trends); the deficit ratio was reduced by 1% but interest rates, because of expectations, fell by 2%. Tax rates on investment were not changed. In that case, the short-term contractionary impact from a smaller deficit would have reduced GDP by 1.5%, while the expansionary impact from a lower cost of capital would have boosted capital stock by 8%, which would have increased GDP by $2\frac{2}{3}$%. The net gain in the growth rate was thus $1\frac{1}{6}$%. The calculations are not exact because there were also some short-term increases in demand stemming from the unusually large drop in interest rates. Nonetheless, it is not far off the mark to conclude that by returning to a balanced budget, the Clinton budget package boosted the long-term growth rate of the US economy by about 1%. That is the same result we obtained earlier by looking at the long-run impact on productivity growth.

In almost all cases, we can be confident that an equal cut in taxes and government spending will boost productivity growth, whereas an equal increase in taxes and spending will diminish productivity growth. Without putting too fine a point on the empirical estimates, that general rule of thumb should help to shape optimal long-run fiscal policy.

18.6   Simplifying the tax code

The current US income tax code is a maze of complicated inconsistencies, which reduces its efficiency. The general principle of any tax code states that people with the same income and the same circumstances ought to pay the same amount of tax. The laws should not be so cumbersome that large amounts of resources are used trying to evade these regulations. Also, rich people ought to pay at least the same proportion of their income in taxes as poor people; most economists think they ought to pay a higher proportion, but presumably no one thinks they should pay a lower proportion. Also, taxes ought to be levied in such a manner that they do not distort or reduce overall economic effort and activity. One would naturally assume there would be no point in raising tax rates if that would actually diminish the amount of revenue collected.

The ideal tax is one with no distortions, which means individuals and businesses would make the same decisions with the tax as without it. However, except for a lump sum tax, no tax fits that description. Thus we try to find taxes that are (a) efficient, (b) have the least negative impact on economic choices in the marketplace, and (c) boost saving, investment, and productivity.

An efficient tax costs relatively little to collect, affects a broad class of transactions with few distortions, and cannot be easily evaded. For example, a tax on beer cans but not beer bottles would make no sense because most people would just switch to bottles. In general, broad-based taxes on sales (excise taxes) are more efficient than taxes on either labor or capital income, but it is generally agreed they are less equitable.

The worst kind of tax is one that depresses economic activity so much that the gain in revenues actually turns into a loss. Boosting marginal tax rates on personal income above 50% generally has that effect. If the aim is to stimulate saving and investment, then on strictly economic grounds, a tax on consumption rather than income is preferred. However, given that rich people save a higher proportion of their income, such a tax might be considered regressive and hence inequitable.

Theoretically, an overly complex tax scheme can reduce growth for several reasons. First, time and effort are spent trying to comply with the tax regulations that could better be spent on more productive endeavors. Second, high marginal tax rates may discourage work effort; in countries with very high marginal tax rates, the most talented employees often move to countries with lower tax rates. Third, to the extent that the tax system is widely viewed as unfair, cheating increases; even those who are usually honest seek out tax shelters of no economic merit. Fourth, scarce capital resources are not allocated properly, so the growth in capital formation and productivity is stunted.

Empirically, the effect of these factors is a matter of degree. There is little question that the highest marginal tax of 98% in Britain reduced productivity growth and caused a "brain drain." In the US, the highest marginal tax rate of 91% did not hurt the economy very much because virtually no one paid taxes at that rate; a huge loophole allowed highly paid workers and entrepreneurs to convert much of their income to long-term capital gains, which were taxed at a top rate of 25%. When the top marginal rate was dropped to 70% in 1965, the amount of taxes collected in the top brackets doubled, which should have come as no surprise.

The top marginal tax rate was dropped in several steps all the way to 28% in 1986, a low enough rate that distortions from tax shelters and cheating were minimal. However, it didn't stay there very long. The rate was quickly raised to 33%, then 36%, and then 39.6%. Several add-ons, such as the 2.9% Medicare tax paid by the self-employed, and disappearing deductions, pushed the top marginal rate to about 44% – plus the burden from state and local income taxes, which in high-tax states can push the marginal rate above 50%. When the top rate on long-term capital gains dropped to 20%, the differential became large enough that many upper-bracket individuals managed to shift most of their income back into capital gains. However, while this reduces the amount of money received by the Treasury, it is not clear how big a negative effect this has on the growth rate; shortly after Clinton raised the top marginal rate, productivity growth accelerated because of the reduced deficit and eventual return to surplus.

It is not possible to generate precise estimates of the economic cost of the USA's complicated tax structure. Accountants and auditors make up slightly less than 1% of the workforce; and of course some of these employees would prepare financial statements for public corporations even if the tax laws were very simple. The most egregious tax shelters were shut down by the Tax Reform Act of 1986. Even at a top marginal rate of 50%, the incentive for systematic avoidance or cheating is much lower than when the top marginal rate was 91%. If substantive changes were made in the tax code to boost long-term growth, given the overall constraint of a long-term balanced budget, the biggest gains would probably occur from improving the incentives for saving and investment rather than removing some of the more arcane provisions or lowering marginal rates.

In the 1996 presidential election campaign, Steve Forbes ran on the platform of a flat rate income tax. After a sizeable deductible of approximately $7,500 per person, everyone would pay the same tax rate of 17% on income from all sources. There would be no further deductions or exemptions. All income would be taxed once, including corporate income, but so would municipal bond income, which is now exempt. No deductions would be permitted: deductions for home mortgage interest, real estate taxes, state income taxes, and charitable contributions, among others, would be completely wiped off the books.

A few simple calculations by this author and others, when compared to Treasury tables showing what proportion of income was actually paid in taxes at various income levels, reveals that in fact the poor would not pay more, and the rich would not pay less. The entire benefits would occur on the supply side in terms of tax simplicity and less avoidance. However, most commentators claimed that Forbes was just trying to reduce taxes for himself and his rich friends, and admittedly he was not the best messenger. In this case, politics and emotion overwhelmed rational economic analysis – not the first, nor the last, time this will ever happen – but it certainly did discourage further discussion about radical reform of the tax system. For this reason we do not present a more detailed analysis, since it is not an issue that will face most managers during their lifetimes.

18.7 "Saving" social security and Medicare

During the latter half of the 1990s, articles frequently appeared decrying the "bankruptcy" of the social security system – and suggesting ways to stave off this dire event. Most of the solutions focused on raising taxes. Yet in fact the matter is quite different than suggested in the public and financial press. Any serious economic analysis must consider the following points:

1. What the public generally considers to be "social security" consists of several different programs. The most well-known, and also the single largest program, is indeed pension benefits for the retired. However, the formal name of the program is Old-Age, Survivors, Health, and Disability Insurance (OASHDI). In particular, disability payments have been growing rapidly as a proportion of total payments. The "health" sector, also known as Medicare, consists of two parts. Part A represents payments to hospitals, and is funded from Medicare taxes paid. Part B, which represents outpatient services, is funded primarily from general revenues; only 25% of the costs are funded by Medicare taxes. Medicaid, which consists of healthcare benefits paid to poor people, is entirely funded from general revenues and does not fall under the purview of the Social Security Administration.

2. In 1982, a blue-ribbon commission known as the National Commission on Social Security Reform, and headed by Alan Greenspan, suggested several changes in the social security system that would purportedly guarantee its solvency into the indefinite future. These changes were implemented by Congress in 1983 amidst great fanfare, yet in the following years, benefits increased much more rapidly than had been predicted by the commission and it became obvious that further modifications would be necessary. Yet their assumptions and calculations were not at fault. Instead, the increase in disability payments grew much faster than anticipated, primarily because of legislative, regulatory, and judicial action that made it easier for individuals to qualify for disability benefits.[5] Further changes in legislation could also upset current calculations for the future outlook.

3. To the extent that money is fungible, Congress can always vote to fund social security and Medicare Part A benefits from general revenues, just as is now the case for Medicare Part B benefits and Medicaid. These benefits could be paid for by higher taxes, or the government could choose to run a larger deficit. While

the latter option has several drawbacks, it has been used before and could be tried again in the future. The probability that social security benefits will not be paid in the future is zero.

4. If the government does not fund increasing social security benefits with deficit financing, many choices are available other than raising the tax rate on social security contributions. The principal options include (a) raising the retirement age, (b) tightening disability requirements, (c) taxing retirement benefits at a higher rate, or (d) raising the rate of return on invested funds. The last suggestion has received quite a bit of publicity in the wake of the stock market boom of the 1980s and 1990s – although with the major bear market that started in early 2000, the idea does not seem as attractive now.

5. Assuming that the underlying laws and regulations do not change, the key variable that determines the amount of surplus or deficit in the social security system is the productivity growth rate. If tax increases reduce the productivity growth, they could offset much of the gain in ex ante revenues that would be needed to keep the budget balanced. Thus, in performing these calculations, it is necessary to consider the long-run impact of higher tax rates on productivity.

Having cleared away some of the most popular misconceptions about the nature and funding of social security, we now turn to an analysis of the social security system in the future.

It is almost a foregone conclusion that, under current laws, OASHDI payments will continue to rise as a proportion of total personal income and GDP. The official projections of the Social Security Administration show an increase from 4% currently to about 7% under the "intermediate" case for real growth and productivity. Note that these figures exclude Medicare and Medicaid. The principal reasons for this increase are as follows:

1. A rise in the dependency ratio, which is the number of retired people divided by the number of employees. The big increase is scheduled to start in 2010, when the post-WWII baby boomers start to retire, as shown in figure 18.6. This increase is the primary reason, although not the only one, why official projections as of mid-2002 show the social security system running out of money in 2038.[6]

2. People are likely to live longer. The average life expectancy of a retired worker age 65 is now 17 years; that figure is expected to increase to 20 years by 2040.

3. The number of people receiving disability payments is likely to continue to rise faster than the overall population.

In addition to these factors, Medicare and Medicaid benefits will rise as a proportion of GDP because of the following factors:

4. Healthcare prices will continue to rise faster than the CPI.

5. The amount of per capita healthcare of the elderly will continue to rise as people live longer and more cures are found for life-threatening diseases. Also, the total

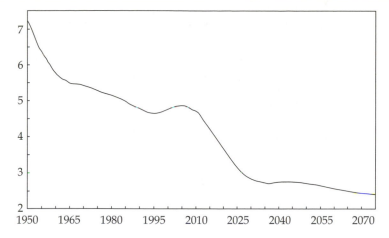

Figure 18.6   Ratio of working-age to retirement-age persons

cost of nursing homes is expected to rise sharply as the proportion of people aged 85 and older increases.

Currently, the social security system is running a substantial surplus. For FY 2002, this surplus was $160 billion. About half of that stems from the excess of current tax payments over current benefit payments; the other half stems from earnings on the funds currently invested by the Social Security Administration.

Through 2011, the unchanged dependency ratio means that the increase in benefits due to greater longevity and rising disability payments will be offset by the gain in productivity, which means wages (and tax receipts) will rise faster than prices (and benefits). As a result, surpluses in the social security system are projected to rise to a peak of $318 billion per year by 2011. After that date, though, the dependency ratio starts to rise rapidly, resulting in an eventual switch to an operating deficit and a drawdown of accumulated surplus. According to the official projections, by 2032 the drawdown of invested funds means the system will go into deficit – unless some changes are made. By 2038 it will be "out of money."

Looking at the ratio of taxes to benefits – i.e., excluding the contributions of earned interest for the moment – we find that the annual operating surplus remains at its 1998 levels of about 1% of payroll to 2010, but then starts to decline to a deficit ratio of about −2.2% by 2040. Table 18.5 shows the factors that account for this change, assuming that productivity rises at 1.5% per year; we will modify this assumption later.

It is possible that the minimum age for receiving full social security benefits, which is already scheduled to rise to 67 by 2022, will be raised further; or alternatively, that the move to age 67 will be phased in more quickly. However, as these changes have little chance politically, we turn to the economic solutions.

Table 18.5 Factors boosting social security benefits relative to tax receipts

	1998–2010	2010–40
Growth in wages minus prices (productivity gain)	1.5	1.5
Less: increased payouts		
Rise in dependency ratio	0.0	2.2
Greater longevity	0.4	0.4
Increasing disability payments	0.6	0.6
Total increase relative to payroll	1.0	3.2
Equals: change in surplus/deficit ratio from current levels	0.5	−1.7

All figures are % change per year
Source: calculated by author

By the mid-2020s, current projections call for the operating ratio to decline to zero, but the overall social security system will still have a surplus because of the interest earned on invested funds.[7] This suggests that an even bigger buildup in invested funds could keep the social security system solvent later in the twenty-first century even as the operating deficit rises. Some of the ways in which this goal could be accomplished include the following:

1. Raise the combined tax rate on social security from 12.4% to 15.4%.
2. Boost the productivity growth rate for the overall economy from 1.5% to 2.7%.
3. Increase the average rate of return on invested funds by 3%.

We do not have precise estimates of how much an increase in the social security tax rate would reduce productivity growth, but the Cobb-Douglas production function framework can be used to generate an approximate estimate. If payrolls represent roughly two-thirds of GDP, then a 2.2% increase in the tax rate would switch approximately 1.5% of GDP from investment to consumption. As a result, capital stock would grow 1.5% per year less, and total aggregate production would grow 0.5% per year less. That would reduce growth in the payroll base by the same percentage; and when we consider the additional impact of having less funds accumulate in social security during the surplus years, the net effect would be to boost the required tax rate from 12.4% to 15.4%.

The assumption of productivity growth of 1.5% represents a long-term average; it is higher in boom years and lower in years of sluggish growth or outright recession. It is also possible that the figure could be as high as 2% under alternative assumptions about the data used to calculate the real growth rate. However, an average productivity growth rate of 2.7% per year for the next 42 years appears optimistic, although that is the rate that occurred in the late 1990s. So while higher productivity growth is certainly part of the solution, it may not be the entire answer.

Another solution is to increase the rate of return on assets, so that faster growth in earned income can fill the gap caused by benefits rising faster than tax receipts. The assumptions that the social security system will run out of money by 2038 are based on a *real* average rate of return of 2.3%, which based on our assumptions of a long-term average inflation rate of 3% would be a nominal rate of return of 5.3%. Over the long run – and disregarding the phenomenal increase in the stock market since 1982, which was triggered in large part by a decline in interest rates – the annual yield on stocks can reasonably be expected to be about 3% higher than the yield on bonds. How much difference would this make?

In round numbers, total funds currently invested by the Social Security Administration are about $1 trillion. If these funds were to earn an average of 5.3% per year until 2040, the amount would rise to $8.8 trillion. If these funds were to earn an average of 8.3% per year, the accumulated funds would rise to $28.5 trillion by 2040. These assumptions and calculations are overly simplistic because the funds would build up for a while and then be drawn down, but nonetheless serve as useful approximations. In 2040, 8.3% of $28.5 trillion would provide an extra $2.4 trillion per year for social security benefits, which would be about 2.5% of GDP using the 3% real growth assumption (which is the same one we use to generate these rates of return). Since that would seem to solve the problem, why not use this approach?

That question was repeatedly raised during the 2000 presidential election campaign. When that campaign started, the S&P 500 had peaked at 1,550; a little more than two years later, it had fallen 50%, to a trough of 775. Suppose that Bush had pushed through his social security reform shortly after taking the oath of office. Total assets would have fallen almost 50%, and Congress would be under tremendous pressure to make up the difference, thereby offsetting the budget discipline that would otherwise be imposed. Consider the plight of near-retirees that saved faithfully for almost 40 years and planned to retire on a certain income based on the amount in their pension plan, only to find out that amount had fallen by 50% the two years just before retirement. The political ramifications would be most unpleasant. That is why even those who think the Social Security Administration should invest in the stock market have suggested that only a certain percentage, probably less than half, be used for equity investing.

In 1964, Barry Goldwater suggested that social security be made voluntary. The idea was not well received. Ronald Reagan, sometimes characterized as Goldwater with a smile, said that "while a President should never say never, I will never tamper with the Social Security system." It is clear that the vast majority of citizens and voters want to keep the social security system mandatory, and in a democracy, that is the overriding factor – just as other taxes are mandatory.

Social security is just another tax. Those who want to provide more generous amounts for their old age can invest in their own saving accounts, and over the past three decades, the tax laws have increasingly encouraged that alternative.

Table 18.6   Growth in aggregate social security, Medicare, and Medicaid payments

	Social security	Medicare	Medicaid
Per capita FY 1998 benefits	$381	$207	$132
Population growth[a]	2.0%	2.0%	1.5%
CPI – Inflation	3.0%	3.0%	3.0%
Increased coverage[b]	0.6%		
Additional rise in CPI – Medical care		1.0%	1.0%
Increase in longevity	0.4%		
Greater use of medical care		3.0%	3.0%
Total annual % increase	6.0%	9.0%	8.5%
Per capita FY 2040 benefits	$4,403	$7,724	$4,060

(a) aged for social security and Medicare; poor and aged for Medicaid

(b) continuing rise in disability coverage

Like any other tax, revenues received by the government will grow faster the higher the growth rate of the overall economy. The fiscal dividend on social security – the amount of taxes received minus the amount of benefits paid out – will be greater, the faster the economy grows. That is true whether the proceeds are invested in bonds or stocks.

From 1968 through 2002, as was shown in chapter 17, the average annual rate of return on Aaa bonds has been 9%, and the average rate of return on the S&P 500 – capital gains plus dividends – has been 12%. The difference is not minuscule, and over that period the total return on stocks has been 4,610%, including reinvested dividends, compared to 1,770% for bonds (both figures are before taxes). Over the next 30 to 50 years, it is likely that the same differential will continue. Even so, putting the money in stocks puts individual retirees at risk of receiving substantially less than they had expected – unless the Federal government is willing to step in and make up any losses on stocks. At least so far, no one has suggested that alternative.

We now calculate the percentage of GDP that will be accounted for by social security and healthcare expenditures by 2040. Table 18.6 shows the aggregate amounts for these categories, based on the indicated assumptions for population growth, inflation, and healthcare factors. Table 18.7 then shows what percentage of GDP will be represented by these programs under different assumptions about the real growth rate.

We see that under any reasonable set of circumstances, the percentage of GDP for social security and government-provided healthcare services will rise. However, the rate of increase varies dramatically depending on the assumed growth rate of the economy. Also, these figures do not take into account the likelihood that if the economy grows faster, the proportion of poor people, and hence the growth in Medicaid payments, will diminish.

Rather than finding new ways to increase taxes or cut benefits, it seems clear that government planning would more usefully be aimed at trying to boost the long-term productivity growth rate. Those who wish to take advantage of the superior

Table 18.7 Social security, Medicare, and Medicaid as a percentage of total GDP

Growth in real GDP	1998	2040 for differing growth rate assumptions			
		$2\frac{1}{2}$%	3%	$3\frac{1}{2}$%	4%
Social security	4.5	5.5	4.5	3.7	3.1
Medicare	2.5	8.0	6.5	5.4	4.4
Medicaid	1.6	5.1	4.2	3.4	2.8
Total as % of GDP	8.6	18.6	15.2	12.5	10.3

track record of the stock market over the long run in saving for their retirement are best advised to use private sector retirement plans, such as IRAs, Roth IRAs, 401(k), SEP, or Keogh plans.

18.8   Recap: fiscal policy and productivity growth

The topics covered here just begin to scratch the surface of the relationship between fiscal policy and productivity. Economists admit they do not have a very precise explanation of the causes of productivity. The empirical evidence strongly suggests that productivity grows faster when the budget is balanced or in surplus, the ratio of government spending to GDP is stable or declining, inflation is low and stable, and there is little or no crowding out of private investment by the public sector. There is some evidence that productivity grows faster when marginal tax rates are lower, but the relationship is not clear-cut; in general, high tax rates lead to counterproductive tax shelters in which capital is directed away from its most productive use.

The quality of life is improved when more people have access to superior educational facilities, comprehensive healthcare, safer streets and neighborhoods, less highway and airport congestion, and cleaner air and water. However, these goals are not synonymous with higher productivity. If, for example, a company uses more of its investment capital to reduce pollution, that leaves less for investment that boosts productivity. That has led some economists to argue that GDP is no longer an appropriate measure of economic well-being because it does not take into account the quality of life. In stark terms, if some employees earn a higher real wage under working conditions that are hazardous to their health, and they die earlier, is the tradeoff worth it?

Economists cannot provide definitive answers to these questions; they lie in the normative realm of economics, and in many cases are completely outside the discipline. In general, the well-informed economist can simply point out that tradeoffs are involved. Spending more money on healthcare and education means less money is spent on other consumption, and on investment. There is really no getting around the tradeoff; the "free lunch" crowd need not apply. To the extent that a majority of voters decide they are in favor of higher public expenditures on education and healthcare for the poor and needy and are willing to have their taxes raised to pay for these costs, that is a legitimate function of a democracy. In general, though, that sort of shift in priorities will tend to reduce overall productivity growth.

Assuming the productivity figures are correct – and some major questions can be raised about the government data – there have been three periods in the post-WWII US economy when productivity rose at above-average rates for extended periods. The first was 1947–55, when productivity growth averaged 3.3%; the second was 1961–6, when it averaged 3.7%, and the third was 1996–2002, when it averaged 2.7%. The first period included substantial cutbacks in government spending and tax rates after World War II, followed by a big increase in spending and tax rates during the Korean War, with another big reduction once the war ended. In general, though, all of these periods featured balanced budgets or surpluses, and (except for the Korean War) a relatively low rate of growth in real government spending. In general, they were also eras when relatively few new programs of government regulation were added. Government deregulation started in earnest in the late 1970s in the financial and transportation sectors, but the gains in productivity did not become apparent until 1996. In particular, productivity growth during the 1980s averaged only 1.4% in spite of the major reductions in tax rates and a reversal of the growing encroachment of government regulation. That was probably because of the big budget deficit.

It is clear that, from time to time, legislation will arise that could have a detrimental impact on one particular sector or region of the economy, and can reasonably be contested on realistic economic grounds. For the overall economy, though, changes in government spending plans, improvements in the infrastructure, and changes in expenditures for health, education, and welfare are best discussed on a case-by-case basis in terms of their usefulness to society, rather than couched in terms of productivity growth per se. In particular, aggressive claims that improving the infrastructure will boost the overall productivity growth rate significantly are usually grounded in pork-barrel politics rather than an unbiased examination of the impact on overall productivity growth.

For a final statement about the relationship between fiscal policy and productivity growth, we return to the framework of the Cobb-Douglas production function. If capital stock rises 3% per year, that will boost productivity by 1% per year; and if it rises as much as $4\frac{1}{2}$% per year, which is probably near the upper limit for the current-day US economy, it will boost productivity by $1\frac{1}{2}$% per year. Under ordinary circumstances, pure technology will advance about 1% per year, but during periods of major innovation that figure could increase to as much as $1\frac{1}{2}$% per year. Based on these parameters, we would expect the long-term average growth rate in productivity to remain in the range of 2% to 3%. If the ratio of government spending to GDP does not increase, marginal tax rates do not rise, the Federal budget remains balanced or in surplus, and government regulation does not become more intrusive, the figure is likely to be closer to 3%. If these factors are reversed, productivity growth would be closer to 2%. If in addition the rate of inflation were again to rise substantially, as it did during the 1970s and early 1980s, the growth rate in productivity could be expected to decline to the 1% to $1\frac{1}{2}$% range.

KEY TERMS AND CONCEPTS

Automatic and Discretionary Stabilizers
Fiscal Dividend
On-Budget and Off-Budget Components of the Federal Budget
Standardized Budget Surplus or Deficit (previously known as the high-employment budget position)

SUMMARY

- During recessions, Federal government receipts decline and discretionary expenditures rise faster than usual. As a result, a 1% drop in the growth rate reduces the surplus ratio or increases the deficit ratio by about $\frac{1}{2}$%. These automatic stabilizers have played a major role in reducing the scope and severity of recession in the post-WWII period.

- The Federal government has also experimented with the use of discretionary stabilizers to moderate recessions, but in general they have not worked very well.

- Virtually all state and local governments must attempt to balance their budgets every year. As a result, they are usually forced to raise taxes or cut spending during recessions, hence partially offsetting the expansionary impact of the Federal government.

- Since 1953, Federal government expenditures and receipts have averaged about 20% of GDP. During this period, individual income taxes and social security taxes have increased substantially as a proportion of GDP, while corporate income and excise taxes have declined. Defense spending has fallen sharply as a proportion of GDP, while expenditures for healthcare have risen rapidly.

- Most of the revenues for state and local government continue to be raised from sales and property taxes. To the extent that these taxes are proportional or regressive, they do not keep pace with increased social welfare spending, resulting either in higher tax rates or more funds from Washington.

- The Federal budget should be balanced over the business cycle, with deficits during recessions and surpluses during periods of overfull employment. The amount of the deficit during recession years should be determined based on the concept of a balanced budget at full employment.

- During periods of substantial budget deficits, productivity growth in the US economy has been about 1% per year lower than during periods of balanced budgets or surpluses.

- Because of the progressive nature of the tax system, revenues will tend to rise faster than GDP during periods of normal growth, whereas expenditures will grow less rapidly. The resulting surplus is sometimes known as the fiscal dividend: it can then be used for tax cuts, greater increases in social welfare spending, or reducing the national debt.

- The optimal size of the national debt is largely irrelevant; if the budget remains balanced over a substantial period of time, the ratio of the debt to GDP will fade into insignificance.

- Long-run productivity growth will be enhanced if the budget is balanced, if the ratio of government spending and taxes to GDP is reduced, if the tax code is more efficient, and if inflation is kept low and stable. Other goals, including modernizing the infrastructure, increasing air and water quality, and providing more educational facilities and healthcare for the aged, are likely to improve the quality of life but will not boost productivity growth.
- The social security system, which is said to be heading for "bankruptcy" around 2040, could be "saved" by raising the overall tax rate by three percentage points, boosting productivity growth from 1.5% to 2.7%, or increasing the average rate of return on invested funds by 3%, presumably by investing some of them in the stock market.
- Many fiscal policies, such as pollution abatement and control, energy policies, and social welfare spending, are designed to improve the quality of life. In some cases they might also boost productivity, but it is more likely that some tradeoff will be involved, and policies of this sort will result in a somewhat lower growth rate for productivity.
- Over the longer run, productivity growth in the US economy is likely to average 2% to 3% per year under the assumptions of a balanced budget over the cycle and low, stable inflation. If deficit financing returns for an extended period of time, and inflation rises substantially, the long-term productivity growth rate is likely to decline to the 1% to 2% range.

QUESTIONS AND PROBLEMS

1. The investment tax credit was designed to increase the ratio of capital spending to GDP and hence boost productivity growth. The credit was introduced in 1962, and although it was temporarily suspended in 1966 and again in 1969, was gradually expanded and kept in place until 1986, when it was terminated. In the decade before its introduction, productivity rose 2.6% per year. During its first decade, productivity growth increased to 2.9% per year, but during the remaining years it was in place, productivity fell to 1.5% per year. After it was disbanded, productivity growth rose slightly to 1.7% per year. Based on these figures, do you think the ITC accomplished its stated objectives? What other data would be necessary for you to make an informed judgment?
2. To solve the congestion problems of the big cities, Congress decides to increase the Federal gasoline tax by 25c per gallon, with a rebate to largely rural states; the net effect will raise approximately $20 billion per year. The money will be spent in the urban areas, but the decision has yet to be made whether the money will be used to improve the highway system or upgrade mass transit facilities. As an executive of the following affected industries, indicate which choice you would prefer.
   (A) Steel industry.
   (B) Homebuilders.
   (C) Airlines.
   (D) Construction machinery.

(E) Import/export broker.

3. In 1964 and 1965, a 20% reduction in personal and corporate income tax rates was followed by a budget surplus. In 1982 and 1983, a 20% reduction in personal and corporate income tax rates was followed by a budget deficit that rose to as much as 4% of GDP. Explain what factors caused the surplus in one case, and the deficit in the other case.

4. Suppose the capital gains tax rate were cut from 20% to 15%, which boosted the stock market by 5%. Assuming that 20% of the additional gains were realized, calculate the change in capital gains tax receipts under static ex ante assumptions. Now suppose a 5% boost in the stock market raised real GDP by $\frac{1}{2}$%. Calculate the ex post change in the Federal budget position.

5. Congress has the choice of spending $50 billion on either space exploration or increased aid to education. Outline the arguments that would lead you to conclude which type of expenditure is more likely to increase the long-term productivity growth rate.

6. You are a leading business executive for the following type of company: (A) Pharmaceutical manufacturer, (B) Airline, (C) Computer disc drives, (D) Mortgage broker, (E) Management consultant, (F) Department store, (G) Insurance agent, (H) Restaurant, (I) Farm cooperative, (J) Nonprofit museum.

   Indicate how you would instruct your Congressman to vote on the following bills.

Types of possible changes in fiscal policy

(A) One-time personal income tax rebate.

(B) Temporary reinstatement of investment tax credit.

(C) More Federal aid to education.

(D) Increase in defense spending.

(E) End of death tax (estate tax).

(F) Paid prescription drugs for all Medicare patients.

(G) $5 per ticket surcharge to pay for airport safety.

(H) Increase in social security tax rate.

(I) Improvement of Interstate Highway System.

(J) Increase in Federal excise tax on cigarettes.

(Hint: in general, you have to consider both the direct effect on your industry, and the indirect effect that will occur because of changes in economic activity.)

7. In March 2002, President George Bush signed into law a tariff increase of up to 30% on certain steel imports. Obviously the steel companies were pleased, and fabricated metal producers were displeased. Now go back to question (6) above and determine how each of the industries (A)–(J) would view this increase, if in fact it affected their business at all.

8. In an attempt to help the farm sector, Congress has several times passed legislation initiating and then extending the requirement that ethanol be blended with gasoline sold at the pump in many states. Because the cost of producing

ethanol is higher than the cost of producing gasoline, the Federal government pays a subsidy to ethanol producers. The evidence is fairly clear that the demand for ethanol boosts the price of corn. Farmers argue that they would receive a minimum price anyhow, so food costs to consumers do not rise, and the greater dependence on ethanol reduces the demand for foreign oil, hence reducing imported oil prices and the amount of money going to OPEC nations. Assuming this argument has some merit, how would you measure whether the taxpayers are essentially getting their money's worth out of the ethanol subsidy? In your answer, indicate whether that policy might have any long-term impact on productivity growth.

9. The principal economic argument for abolishing the long-term capital gains tax is that it would boost productivity, and hence pay for itself. The principal economic argument against that move is that it would encourage more people to shift their method of compensation from ordinary income to capital gains income, thereby gutting the income tax system as we know it. Under the assumption that any revisions to the tax system must generate the same amount of revenue, how would you change the capital gains tax to maximize the long-term productivity growth rate?

10. It appears that in the twenty-first century, by far the biggest increase in Federal spending will occur in increased medical care expenditures for the aged and the poor. If this does indeed turn out to be a political imperative, outline the changes you would take to keep productivity growth from declining, given these increased expenditures and the overall constraint of a balanced budget.

Notes

1. E. Cary Brown, "Fiscal Policy in the Thirties: A Reappraisal," *American Economic Review*, December 1956.
2. In the late 1990s, the reemergence of the Federal budget surplus reduced the long-term Treasury bond yield substantially, but had no impact on the Aaa corporate bond rate. This point is discussed in greater detail in the next chapter.
3. For a more detailed discussion of many of these points, see Michael K. Evans, *The Truth About Supply-Side Economics* (New York: Harper & Row, 1983).
4. Some older macro texts indicate that the long-run government spending multiplier is larger than the long-run tax change multiplier. Since that conclusion is based on the entirely unwarranted assumption that consumer saving is somehow "wasted," we do not consider that proposition further.
5. For a further discussion of this and related points, see the 1997 *Economic Report of the President*, chapter 3.
6. When the first draft of this chapter was written, the "bankruptcy" date was 2026. Large changes of this sort should make all economists skeptical about any long-term projections about the solvency of social security.
7. Current estimates of these projections, which change frequently, are always included in the Annual Report of the OASHDI Trustees.

chapter nineteen

Monetary policy and its impact on inflation and growth

Introduction

Optimal monetary policy must encompass several different goals. The first is to insure an adequate supply of liquidity for the needs of commerce and industry. Failure to observe that rule was one of the major causes of the Great Depression, and timely action by the Fed following stock market reversals in 1987 and 1998 is widely credited for keeping those expansions alive. Second, when higher inflation threatens, the Fed should tighten in a timely fashion, and when recessions occur, it should ease quickly. Third, in the long run monetary policy is responsible for keeping the inflation rate low and stable. The appropriate methods for implementing these policies are discussed in this chapter.

Why is high inflation harmful? Older arguments used to focus on the unfair nature of inflation, benefiting speculators and hurting those on fixed incomes. However, with indexing, the problems of the inequitable distribution of income can be minimized. Virtually every country that resorted to high inflation in an attempt to solve their economic problems found it actually worsened them. Most importantly, high inflation reduces productivity growth. Saving and capital formation are reduced, and investment that is undertaken is designed to benefit from higher inflation rather than increase the amount of goods and services that can be produced. Also, if it is easy to become rich simply by speculating, fewer people will work. In periods of hyperinflation, the fabric of society unravels. Even during periods of "moderately" high inflation, though, productivity growth is stunted. Hence keeping inflation low and stable is one of the key determinants of boosting the standard of living in the long run.

Throughout history, various rulers have tried to control inflation by fiat, either through outright price freezes, controls, guidelines, or income policies. All of these attempts eventually ended in failure. No government agents, even if highly intelligent and totally incorruptible, can keep track of the myriad of pricing decisions that are made every day by an efficient market. In the end, people cheat, productivity declines, and farmers end up feeding bread to the chickens instead of wheat because it is cheaper.

If high inflation is bad, and low inflation is good, then maybe zero inflation is even better, and deflation is best. However, that isn't right either. Deflation implies that asset values decline, which means debtors must pay back their loans in dollars that are worth more than when they borrowed them. The result is large-scale bankruptcy and destruction of assets. A zero rate of inflation implies that as many prices are falling as are rising. For that reason, the optimal rate of inflation is actually slightly above zero.

Since high, variable inflation reduces the growth rate, and no fiat method of controlling inflation works, we turn to the role of monetary policy in a well-managed economy. While discussion of monetary policy often focuses on moderating recessions and controlling inflation, even these goals must be subservient to the primary role of insuring adequate liquidity for the needs of commerce and industry, and take action promptly in financial crises. Even here, however, the decision is not quite as straightforward as it might seem, because of the issue of moral hazard. If investors think the Fed will always step in and bail them out, they may take undue risks that they would not otherwise take, which could encourage runaway stock market booms, followed by equally spectacular busts. Hence the Fed must determine when financial market disruptions require intervention, and when they do not.

In an ideal economic environment, there are no financial panics, the budget is balanced, no malign supply shocks occur, capacity growth keeps pace with demand, and the value of the currency is stable. Under those circumstances, monetary policy becomes a relatively straightforward and pleasant job; the Fed merely has to keep a firm hand on the tiller without changing anything. However, we all know the real world is not that ideal place. Thus the issues of monetary policy focus on what to do when (a) demand rises faster than capacity, leading to shortages, (b) exogenous shocks boost prices, (c) inflationary expectations worsen, (d) large budget deficits remain even at full employment, (e) shocks disrupt financial markets, and (f) the currency comes under severe pressure. Those are the times when central bankers earn their stripes. Each of these cases is discussed in more detail.

This chapter also focuses on the negative relationship between inflation and productivity growth, and shows how high inflation eventually reduces the standard of living. To summarize, we make the case for an actively managed monetary policy, compared to the simple rule of setting the growth in monetary and credit aggregates and never changing it, and provide some rules that central bankers are likely to follow when unpleasant surprises do erupt.

19.1 The overall goals of monetary policy: insure adequate liquidity, reduce business cycle fluctuations, and keep inflation low and stable

The previous chapter showed that the optimal fiscal policy should be directed mainly toward boosting the long-run productivity growth rate; attempts to implement short-run discretionary fiscal policy do not work very well. On the other hand, there are distinctly separate short-run and long-run components of monetary policy. In the short run, the central bank aims to reduce if not entirely eliminate recessions, while in the long run, it aims to keep inflation low and stable. To the extent that these are in conflict, a dilemma is created in which monetary policy sometimes appears to be at odds with itself.

Most macroeconomists agree that:

1. In the long run, monetary policy cannot affect the real growth rate; only fiscal policy can accomplish that. The government cannot boost the growth rate simply by printing more money.
2. In the long run, inflation is exclusively a monetary phenomenon.
3. In the short run, changes in monetary policy do affect real growth.
4. In the short run, most aggregate economic fluctuations are not due to monetary policy *shocks*.

It is important to understand what that last statement means. Monetary policy generally reacts to changes in the economy, particularly tightening during periods when inflation appears likely to rise, and easing when the unemployment rate rises substantially. However, those are not monetary shocks. Most changes that precede recessions are not due to policy shifts. If the monetary authorities tighten because inflation has risen or ease because unemployment has risen, that is not a monetary policy shock. A shock occurs when monetary policy changes in a way that is not consistent with these changes in the economy; for example, further tightening during a recession that is already well underway, or further easing when inflation is already accelerating. Monetary policy shocks do not happen very often in the US, although as we will see, they are not unknown.

In the long run, monetary policy should keep the inflation rate at a low, stable level. In the short run, though, unexpected events occasionally intrude – whether they are international disturbances, energy shocks, strikes, short-term changes in the deficit ratio, or other causes. In many cases, the Fed does not have the option of maintaining its previous policy when the economy reacts to these unexpected events. It will react to these unexpected changes in the economy. Indeed, if the Fed did nothing – if it did not raise interest rates when an exogenous shock boosted inflation – that would actually represent a policy shift, whereas raising interest rates by the amount that inflation had increased would represent no change in policy.

We discussed the **Taylor Rule** in chapter 6, which essentially said that changes in the Federal funds rate under Greenspan have been proportional to changes in the core inflation rate and the underlying real growth rate. Thus for example, if the real growth rate were 4% and the inflation rate were 2%, the funds rate would be 6%. If the economy fell into recession and the growth rate dropped to −1% while the core inflation rate stayed at 2%, the funds rate would fall to 1%, according to this rule.

Earlier we showed how the Federal funds rate frequently diverged from this simple formula. In terms of understanding how the economy functioned, we looked

Figure 19.1 The Taylor Rule during the Greenspan years (both real growth and inflation are four-quarter averages lagged two quarters; inflation is measured by the implicit consumption deflator)

for variables that explained that divergence, including the demand for capital goods and the supply of credit. In this chapter, our focus shifts in the direction of policy analysis, and the difference between the actual Federal funds rate and the values implied by the Taylor Rule can be viewed as monetary policy shocks in the sense that monetary policy diverged from what would have been expected based on underlying economic conditions. We then examine the factors that caused these shocks, and their impact on the economy.

The comparison of the actual Federal funds rate, compared to the four-quarter average of real growth plus the inflation rate over the past four quarters, is shown in figure 19.1. The inflation rate used here is the implicit consumption deflator, since Greenspan believes that measures inflation better than the CPI, which he claims overstates inflation. Because it takes the Fed an average of two quarters to react to economic data, both the growth rate and inflation rate are shown lagged two quarters.

Over the 1987–2002 period, the mean value of the Federal funds rate, and the sum of the growth rate plus the inflation rate, have been the same 5.6%. However, the two curves do not always match. Relative to the Taylor Rule, the funds rate was too high in 1989, too low in 1992 and 1993, and too low in 1999. The amount that the funds rate deviated from the sum of inflation plus real growth can be considered the exogenous component of monetary policy, or monetary shocks.

It is second-guessing the Fed to examine whether these deviations were warranted. Nonetheless, a few comments are appropriate. In the first case, overly tight monetary policy in 1989 may have contributed to the mild recession in 1990, but back then it was still widely believed that inflation accelerated substantially at full employment if the Fed did not tighten aggressively, so that increase in rates is fully understandable based on the conditions that existed then. In the second case, unusually low interest rates in 1992 and 1993 helped economic performance because it offset reductions in credit following the S&L collapse. Also, the Fed tightened with alacrity once inflationary expectations started to rise; actual inflation never did increase, and the recovery accelerated after a brief slowdown in early 1995.

The failure to tighten in 1999 remains more controversial, although many economists think it was a serious error. The "wild card" then was the uncertainty associated with Y2K. With widespread predictions of momentary failures following the switchover of computers to the new millennium, the Fed was concerned enough that it chose not to tighten in spite of unsustainable growth, and in fact pumped an extra $30 billion (as measured by M1) into the economy near the end of that year in anticipation of widespread withdrawals from ATM machines just before January 1, 2000. Of course, none of those untoward events ever happened, and economists who predicted a major recession based on that development gradually faded into the woodwork. Nonetheless, the runaway behavior of high-tech stocks in 1999 and early 2000 was due at least in part to the excessive liquidity dumped into the system by the Fed the previous year, as well as the Long-Term Capital Management bailout in the fall of 1998. If the Fed had tightened in a timely fashion in 1999, the stock market bubble would have been less severe, and the 2001 recession – which was quite mild in any case – probably would not have occurred at all.

This simple diagram indicates how excessive Fed tightening – or easing – generally moves the economy in a direction that the Fed did not desire. Given this historical pattern, few would try to deny the short-run importance of monetary policy, nor can it be claimed that the performance of the economy improves when the Fed deviates from policy indicated by the Taylor Rule.

Even under the assumption that the Fed will follow a modified Taylor Rule in the future, many economists think that monetary policy would be more effective, and inflation would be less likely to increase, if economic agents know in advance that higher wages and prices would occasion Fed tightening. Hence one suggestion is for the Fed to announce its contingency plans one period ahead (usually the time between FOMC meetings, or one every six weeks): if the economy exceeds certain parameters, then the Fed will indeed tighten. That does not put the Fed in the forecasting business. It does, however, indicate how the Fed will react if various changes do in fact occur in the economy.

Alan Greenspan appears to have taken this comment to heart. At the February 1997 Humphrey-Hawkins hearings,[1] he testified that the Fed was likely to boost the funds rate at its next meeting; previously, no Fed Chairman had ever dropped that broad a hint. The Fed has now codified this practice by publicly offering an additional statement at the end of each FOMC meeting indicating the direction of the "bias." This statement could say, for example, that although the FOMC voted to leave the funds rate unchanged, they would be likely to raise it at the next meeting if real growth and inflation continued to increase at the same pace; that would be a tightening bias. Conversely, if they said a reduction in the funds rate were likely if economic conditions continued at the same pace, that would be an easing bias. Thus the Fed now believes that clarifying its plans will disabuse economic agents of any belief that they can successfully raise wages or prices. In the absence of major exogenous shocks, that should help keep inflation low and stable for many years.

Perhaps this modus operandi will solve the short-term vs long-term dilemma of monetary policy: the Fed will not only follow a modified Taylor Rule, in which it tightens when inflation or real growth appear to be too high at full employment, but will announce such intentions in advance. In this author's view, such a procedure works quite well.

Even that rule, however, would not always determine the optimal course of monetary policy when the economy is temporarily thrown off track because of exogenous shocks. We should realize that from a historical perspective, the 1993–2000 period was an unusually calm one, similar in many respects to the 1962–6 period; the economy will not always function that smoothly. When large unexpected shocks do occur, the Taylor Rule might not function efficiently, in which case changes should be made in order to improve the performance of the economy. Before suggesting what might be done, though, we present a brief review of why high inflation should be avoided.

19.2   The negative effects of higher inflation

At one time, some economists used to claim the major problem with inflation was it redistributed income from those who could least afford it – wage-earners, pensioners, and those living on fixed income – to businesses that could raise prices quickly, and to speculators. The decrease in real income for those who could not boost their nominal incomes proportionately when inflation rose was known as an inflation tax.

If wages, pensions, and interest payments are not indexed, inflation clearly discriminates against these classes of society. However, that is seldom the case today. Most employees either have cost-of-living adjustments built into their contracts, or receive wage increases that are at least equal to the increase in the cost of living. Social security and government retirement benefits are indexed to inflation, although some private sector benefits are not. Bond yields now reflect the expected rate of inflation, so the yield includes both a real rate of return and adjustment for expected inflation. In that case, why all the fuss?

One answer is that the inflation tax remains in subtle ways even in a system with full indexation. Consider the mythical economy of Inflatonia, where all prices double each year. Interest rates are also slightly above 100%, so real rates remain positive. In addition to domestic inflation, the value of the dollar doubles each year relative to the domestic currency, known as the *worthless* (W).

This sets up a win-win situation for speculators. By buying future contracts on 5% or even 10% margin, they can receive huge gains even in real terms. Suppose, for example, someone buys W1 million of corn futures at 10% margin, thus putting up W100,000. A year later, the same amount of corn is worth W2 million, since all prices have doubled. However, the speculator's funds have risen from W1 million to W10 million, so even after considering inflation, the real value of his funds has risen fivefold. Note that in this case, the speculator is not technically borrowing the money, so the same arithmetic holds even when real interest rates are positive, which does not always occur in highly inflationary economies.

Thus high inflation redistributes income from those who "work" for a living to those who speculate. As this becomes more and more obvious, more people will start speculating and fewer will perform jobs that create goods and services. Under such a scenario, eventually the economy might come to a grinding halt – even with full indexation. Why spend eight, ten, or even twelve hours a day washing dishes or sorting chicken parts if, with one daily call to the broker, you can quintuple your money in real terms every year?

In fact, many people have neither the intelligence nor the stomach for speculation. Yet even outside of speculative activities, extremely highly inflation causes money to get redistributed in suboptimal ways. Minor public functionaries demand and receive bribes from the speculators; independent tradespeople will not perform the tasks for which they are licensed without receiving a little money "on the side." As a result, income is redistributed from the honest to the dishonest.

If inflation rages out of control, social justice demands that wage-earners, pensioners, and savers have their incomes adjusted to keep pace with infla-tion. The alternative is what occurred during the hyperinflation in Germany in 1923, when the middle class lost its savings. Hence virtually all countries with high rates of inflation now have some form of indexation. However, a much better solution is to bring inflation under control, rather than to meet the sit-uation halfway with indexation, thus encouraging graft and corruption while discouraging productivity.

As serious as these problems of lost work ethic and cheating are, the impact on capital formation and productivity is even more serious. In our mythical country of Inflatonia where the price level doubles every year, consider the opportunities facing investors. They can purchase an industrial machine for W1 million that depreciates 10% per year and is worthless after ten years – or they can buy a build-ing for W1 million whose value doubles every year and hence is worth W1 billion after ten years. Even though that represents no increase in real terms, the use of borrowed money and hedging against the drop in the worthless can gener-ate an impressive rate of return. It is clear that many buildings will be constructed as a hedge against inflation even if no one ever occupies these buildings. Investors will also purchase fine art, oriental rugs, and precious metals instead of investing in high-tech equipment that could help improve output and productivity in the economy.

Later in this chapter we will show that productivity invariably declines in coun-tries with extremely high rates of inflation, hence reducing the standard of living for all but a fortunate few. However, one does not have to reference periods of hyperinflation. During the 1973–82 decade of double-digit inflation, productivity growth in the US slumped to an average of 0.7% per year *even though the ratio of investment to GDP was unusually high.*

19.3   The optimal rate of inflation is not zero

Before turning to the methods of controlling inflation, it is useful to discuss the goal that central bankers are trying to reach. It is *not* zero inflation.

Optimal monetary policy should set the inflation rate at a level that maximizes productivity growth, not that minimizes inflation per se. Since high inflation degrades economic performance, the monetary authorities want to keep inflation low and stable. Based on the evidence presented in this chapter, it logically follows that inflation should be reduced to a low enough level that it does not interfere with economic decisions based on maximizing the real rate of return. Paul Volcker enunciated the dictum that inflation should be low enough that it does not interfere with economic decision-making, and Greenspan has endorsed that rule.

However, it does not necessarily follow from that statement that the optimal rate of inflation is zero. A level of inflation that is too high will cause individuals and firms to purchase assets that are expected to benefit from rapidly rising prices, rather than assets that will maximize the real value of production. An overly rapid rate of inflation will cause individuals to spend a larger proportion of their income now, rather than save it and earn a negative rate of return. That decline in saving will also reduce investment, ceteris paribus. Yet, a negative rate of inflation will lead to widespread bankruptcy and destruction of assets, which will also reduce saving and investment, and it will also reduce aggregate demand by encouraging economic agents to purchase later rather than now. For example, many consumers would postpone purchasing a new car if they thought the price would be 5% or 10% cheaper next year.

Having said that, it might seem "obvious" that the optimal rate of inflation is zero. However, that is not the case either, because a zero rate of inflation implies there are just as many goods and services, and by implication just as many assets, whose prices are falling as rising. Falling prices are generally inimical to optimal economic performance.

There is nothing "magic" about a zero rate of inflation. Indeed, given the government's inability to measure the inflation rate to the nearest percentage point, economists should not spend an enormous amount of effort to achieve a goal where measurement remains elusive. As long as economic agents do not base their decisions on what the rate of inflation is expected to be, it makes little difference whether the inflation rate is 0%, 1%, or 2%. It is sufficient for businesses to realize they cannot expect to raise prices in the face of stable demand and must offset cost increases with more productive methods, and for labor to realize it cannot expect wage increases in excess of productivity gains.

In that case, what factors determine whether the optimal rate of inflation should be zero, or slightly above zero?

The pricing mechanism performs a valuable function by allocating scarce economic resources. Suppose, for example, that the demand for a product or service – or for a certain type of labor – increases enough that a shortage develops.

In that case, a higher price signals product and labor markets that more resources should be devoted to the higher demand. That is the proper function of a free market pricing system. By the same token, we would expect that a decline in the demand for a product or service, or certain type of labor, would cause a decline in the price of those products or factors. However, the argument is not symmetrical.

One of the key asymmetries occurs for the price of fixed assets, especially real estate. Suppose someone buys a house for $100,000. Assume that over the next five years, the price of the house, and the overall CPI, both rise 3%. At the end of that time, the house will be worth about $116,000. The value of the house has not increased at all in real terms, but with a standard 20% mortgage, the homeowner's equity has risen from $20,000 to $36,000 in nominal terms, or from $20,000 to $31,000 in real terms.

Now suppose the same house is purchased for $100,000, but this time the CPI *falls* 3% per year over the next five years, so that the value of the house after five years is only $85,870. The homeowner's equity has shriveled from $20,000 to $5,870, or $6,836 in real terms – just about enough to cover the commission and closing costs if it were to be sold. For the average homeowner, a major portion of his wealth has disappeared. A decline in values would (a) encourage bankruptcies, making it much easier to "walk away" from a house in which one has little or no remaining equity, and (b) by the same token, make it more difficult to obtain mortgages, because lending officers would require a larger down payment precisely because of the increased risk of bankruptcy.

The third reason why a negative rate of inflation is not optimal is the likelihood of high real interest rates. In chapter 5, we explained how capital spending was a function of the real rather than the nominal rate of interest. If inflation rises from (say) 5% to 10%, and the long-term bond yield rises in tandem from 7% to 12%, the rise in nominal rates has not affected the demand for investment or the optimal capital stock. Similarly, if the inflation rate falls from 5% to 0% and the long-term bond yield declines from 7% to 2%, there is no change in real rates either.

However, long-term bond yields have never fallen as low as 2% in the US, even though there have been times when inflation has been zero or negative, including 1929–33, 1949, and 1954. There are several reasons why bond yields would not drop that low.

- *The expectational factor:* over the life of the bond, inflation will probably rise again, leading to a big capital loss or a much lower yield than could be obtained elsewhere.
- *The bankruptcy factor:* negative inflation means value of the assets declines, which increases the probability of bankruptcy and of the bonds being worth nothing. The same logic that applies to diminishing values of residential real estate also applies to many businesses.
- *The rate of return factor:* when the return on bonds is hardly higher than the return on cash, why bother to invest in bonds at all, especially in view of the market risk of falling prices?

As a result, when the inflation rate is close to zero or negative, the *real* bond yield is usually fairly high even though the nominal rate is low. Some classical economists used to talk about how at a low enough nominal rate, firms would borrow huge amounts to undertake relatively minor capital improvements, since the cost of financing was almost nil. That was a poor argument because at the same time, the real rate of interest was fairly high. Furthermore, firms would not invest if they thought the value of the assets, and the prices that could be charged for goods produced with those assets, were expected to fall over time. Thus with a negative inflation rate, real interest rates will be high and will reduce investment.

Recall that the optimal rate of inflation is one that does not influence economic decisions. If inflation is too high, people will buy now rather than later, and will purchase assets that are likely to appreciate in value rather than boost productivity. By the same token, if the rate of inflation is negative, people will buy later rather than now, and will choose assets that minimize their losses, rather than those that are likely to boost productivity; in an extreme case they will bury their money in the back yard because it will be worth more later. Thus negative inflation also reduces the growth rate.

Hence there are three reasons why a negative rate of inflation is not optimal: asymmetries in labor markets (workers will not accept nominal wage cuts), declining value of real estate and rising risk of bankruptcies, and high real interest rates. However, one could argue these do not apply to a zero rate of inflation.

Yet a zero rate of inflation certainly does not imply that no prices are changing. Instead, it means that the value of transactions for which prices are rising is equal to the value of transactions for which prices are falling. In many cases, the sectors where prices are declining face the same problems that are present when the overall inflation rate is negative.

Of course, falling prices do not always carry a negative connotation. The sharp decline in semiconductor prices has created a remarkable rise in the demand for microcomputers and telecommunications. If the price of long-distance calls had not dropped dramatically there would be no such thing as the internet. Price declines driven by technology are almost always beneficial. However, when price declines are caused by stagnant demand or overly tight monetary policy, that often results in bankruptcies and slower growth in productivity – as occurred during the Great Depression.

Thus in this author's view, the optimal rate of inflation occurs when most prices do not change, but market forces permit some prices to rise, signaling that more resources are needed in certain industries and sectors. While no pinpoint estimate of inflation is possible for this general rule – nor is it particularly desirable, given our inability to measure inflation accurately – it is probably between 1% and 2%.

The 2% figure can be justified as follows. Think of the economy as being divided into manufacturing and service sectors. In the manufacturing sector, which comprises one-third of the economy, productivity rises 4% per year, wage rates rise 4% per year, and prices are unchanged. In the service sector, wages also rise 4% per year – they cannot fall behind manufacturing wages on a long-term basis – but productivity rises only 1% per year, so prices rise 3% per year. Prices are flat in the manufacturing sector, but productivity growth and inflation in the overall economy are both 2% per year. If wages rise only 3% per year, the overall inflation rate would decline to 1%.

We thus reach the conclusion that when the economy is in equilibrium and productivity growth is maximized, the inflation rate should be between 1% and 2%, money and credit aggregates should be increasing at a rate equal to the inflation rate plus the underlying real growth rate, and short-term interest rates should be set at a level equal to the inflation rate plus the growth rate, assuming a balanced budget at full employment.

MANAGER'S BRIEFCASE: COPING WITH FALLING PRICES

From mid-1995 through mid-2002, the PPI for intermediate goods excluding food and energy fell slightly. As a result, most manufacturing firms faced declining prices during that period in spite of robust demand, which led to a sharp decline in manufacturing profits. One reason for declining commodity prices was the sharp increase in the dollar during a period when the overall inflation rate remained fairly low. But how should managers react to declining prices, especially in terms of capital budgeting?

On a variable cost basis, many firms intensified their efforts to cut costs by trimming wage gains, reducing fringe benefits, boosting productivity, and using the internet and E-sales to obtain better prices on parts and materials. These worthwhile decisions will presumably continue into the indefinite future. However, our attention here is focused on how firms should determine capital spending under these circumstances. With the Aaa bond yield near 7% but declining product prices, real interest rates for commodity-producing industries are unusually high. Also, the collapse of the stock market starting in April 2000 meant the cost of equity capital increased sharply.

Yet the decision to cut back on capital spending is counterproductive because it does not allow firms to employ the latest technology. As a result, many firms turned to outsourcing of both manufacturing facilities and services that can be undertaken more cost-effectively by outside specialists. However, that simply moves the problem back one step: how do those firms that receive these contracts manage to perform at peak efficiency when their cost of equity capital is high?

In many cases, the answer is to use overseas facilities in countries where labor costs are much lower. In addition, though, in countries with moderate inflation, it is likely that the *real* cost of capital may be much lower; the nominal rate is about the same as in the US, but inflation is rising, so debts are repaid in currencies that have declined in value. One cannot push this suggestion too far, because many emerging countries have underdeveloped capital markets and relatively few funds available for borrowing. Nonetheless, as cost pressures intensify in the US and the real cost of capital remains high, more and more firms are outsourcing part of their operations to low-cost foreign countries.

These switches need not only occur in manufacturing. In recent years, many US firms have relied on very inexpensive programming labor in India. Also, many service organizations have trained residents of India to answer questions with "American" accents; in one case, trainees were required to watch 12 weeks of *Cheers* reruns. Hence individuals calling an 800 number with a question about their bill may very well be talking to someone in Mumbai or Bangalore.

continued

MANAGER'S BRIEFCASE (*continued*)

While the search for cost-cutting benefits consumers, and permits some domestic firms to remain in business, pressures from negative inflation rates may cause the "hollowing out" of America as more firms move their operations overseas. A similar development in Japan in the 1990s was largely responsible for their decade-long recession.

19.4   The role of monetary policy in financial crises

The next six sections explore alternative situations where the economy departs from equilibrium, and assesses how the central bank should react in each case. These situations are: financial crises, excess demand, supply-side shocks, the conundrum, an increase in the budget deficit, and change in the value of the currency.

The primary reason the Fed was started in 1913, following the Crash of 1907, was a growing realization that the private sector banking system was not working well enough. The new Fed was specifically designed to be the lender of last resort and provide liquidity to avoid future crashes. Yet when the supreme test came in 1929, the Fed failed. Economists still differ about the list of reasons that caused the Great Depression and why it lasted so long, but they all agree that the Fed made things worse instead of better. After the stock market crashed on Black Tuesday, the Fed tightened instead of eased, ostensibly to protect the dollar; did nothing to help bail out domestic banks when they ran out of funds; and did nothing to stabilize the international sector.

The Great Depression was a terrible lesson, but at least it was learned well, and no financial crises surfaced for several decades. After deregulation of the banking sector, though, disruptions started to show up again. The Mexican peso collapsed in mid-1982, the victim of an overly ambitious scheme of the government to spend oil money it didn't have. The international repercussions could have been very severe if the Fed had not eased almost immediately.

In 1987, the October stock market crash might have led to major bank failures if Greenspan had not notified major financial institutions that sufficient liquidity would be forthcoming to cover failed accounts and other mismatches. Once the word was out, the market rallied and there was little need for the injection of these funds into the banking system. In the view of many economists, it was the Fed's finest hour.

As it turns out, that easing, and the extra liquidity that was pumped into the system, was one of the factors leading to somewhat higher inflation in 1988 and 1989, which may have been a contributing factor to the 1990 recession. In retrospect, monetary policy should not have remained accommodative as long as it did in 1988. However, this is a minor point compared to the havoc that could have been wreaked by a meltdown of the New York financial community.

The Fed decisions in 1998 and 1999 remain more controversial. To summarize briefly, the Fed eased in October 1998 following the collapse of the Russian ruble and the meltdown of Long-Term Capital Management, and it eased again in late 1999 to assure that Y2K would not cause havoc in the economy. Meanwhile, the Nasdaq composite index rose from a trough of 1,357 in October 1998 to a peak of 5,133 in March 2000, a 278% increase in less than a year and a half. Subsequently, it gave back all that gain, falling to a low of 1,114 in October 2002. A bubble of that magnitude probably would have not been possible if the Fed had not come to the aid of the financial sector twice in little more than one year under questionable circumstances. Players in financial markets are supposed to realize they are subject to a certain amount of risk, known as **moral hazard**; the bigger the possible reward, the bigger the risk. If the game turns out to be a one-way street, where they can win but the Fed bails them out if they lose, investors will take far greater risks than are warranted by the usual rules of finance.

When a genuine meltdown occurs that is likely to shake the foundations of financial stability, the Fed still has an ironclad responsibility to pump as much liquidity into the economy as is necessary to offset the temporary disruptions. On the other hand, when the failures do not threaten the entire financial system, the Fed is probably well advised to remain on the sidelines. These are seldom straightforward decisions, but in recent years the Fed may have erred too much on the side of active intervention when it was not really necessary.

CASE STUDY 19.1   THE COLLAPSE OF LONG-TERM CAPITAL MANAGEMENT

The full story of this saga can be found in the entertaining and informative *When Genius Failed*, by Roger Lowenstein, formerly a reporter for the *Wall Street Journal*. We provide only the outlines of this case here as they apply to the concept of moral hazard and monetary policy.

The management team of LTCM certainly appeared to have impeccable credentials, including some principals who had won the Nobel prize for developing the Black-Scholes model and its successors. Basically they traded "volatility," by which we mean the following. When the prices of various options rise sharply relative to their underlying value as calculated by the Black-Scholes model, those options should be sold, and when the prices are below their calculated value, they should be bought. This strategy does not require one to be able to predict the direction the market is heading; it is simply a variant on the oldest market rule of all: Buy Low, Sell High. But because options are so highly leveraged, the rate of return can be much greater than average long-term gains in the stock market.

The Black-Scholes model and its successors are based on the concept that market fluctuations are normally distributed. However, that is false; in fact, the Black-Scholes assumptions are never true.[2] Campbell et al. discuss several reasons why

continued

CASE STUDY 19.1 (*continued*)

that is so; one of the major reasons is that market distributions have what is collo-quially known as "fat tails," which means that very large fluctuations occur much more often than would be predicted by the normal distribution.[3] That also means that values far away from equilibrium occur much more often than predicted. Thus when options values rose well above equilibrium levels, the algorithms based on normal distributions assumed that they must soon decrease again, whereas some-times they kept rising further. Because LTCM management made increasingly large bets on these positions, they lost $4 billion during 1998 and were forced to declare bankruptcy. That meant that many large financial institutions that had loaned them money would also come under severe financial pressure. Furthermore, any attempt to liquidate these positions quickly would have increased their losses even more, because no one wanted to take the opposite side in these trades.

When small investors buy Enron, or Global Crossing, or Worldcom at its peak value, only to see their equity position complete erode over the next year or two, they have no recourse. They invested based on known information, and they lost – even if the information turned out to be faulty. Lawsuits attempt to recover losses, but since the companies in question went bankrupt, there are few assets that can be used to offset these losses due to fraudulent statements. Certainly no responsi-ble economist has suggested that shareholders ought to be compensated for their losses.

Thus when major league investors – those with hundreds of millions or even billions in assets – entrust their money to managers who make serious mistakes, why should they be bailed out?

One answer is the doctrine of "too big to fail." A series of events that caused Citicorp, J. P. Morgan Chase, Morgan Stanley, and Merrill Lynch to declare bankruptcy obviously would not be in the best interests of society, and might even lead to another Great Depression. The Fed obviously has responsibility to assure that does not happen.

Nonetheless, why were the foxes allowed to guard the chicken coop? Or in more formal terms, why did the Fed not monitor the positions of LTCM and put pressure on major financial institutions to reduce their exposure to this company when it became clear that their once-vaunted moneymaking skills had eroded? Greenspan was often asked about the increased risks involved in the expanded trading of derivatives, and his general answer was there was nothing to worry about.

Another answer is that the Fed intervention did not really cost anyone money. It can be said that the Federal government was not required to bail out bankrupt financial institutions; the problem was solved by increasing liquidity and reducing interest rates. This answer, although technically correct, rings false. The per-ceived decline in the risk of moral hazard was at least partially responsible for the unsustainable bubble in high-tech stocks over the next year and a half. In that

continued

CASE STUDY 19.1 (*continued*)

sense, the stock market – and the economy – did pay the price for the LTCM debacle.

In the future, the Fed will probably monitor more carefully those situations where massive trading in derivatives could lead to huge losses if the calculations are only slightly incorrect. If it continues to bail out those who would otherwise be big losers, financial bubbles would then probably become increasingly prevalent.

19.5   Demand-side policies: punchbowls and preemptive strikes

William McChesney Martin, who served as Fed Chairman with great distinction under five Presidents – Truman, Eisenhower, Kennedy, Johnson, and Nixon – used to say that the role of the Fed was to "take away the punchbowl just as the party is getting good." In less colorful language, this strategy was often called "leaning against the wind." When the economy showed signs of overheating, according to this philosophy, it was the job of the Fed to tighten.

Perhaps this sounds unexceptional, and at the time, it was accepted as appropriate policy. Martin left the Fed with hosannas ringing in his ears, and his performance was certainly better than that of his immediate successors, Arthur Burns and G. William Miller. Nonetheless, in retrospect, Martin's strategy was not optimal. It was replaced by the **Volcker-Greenspan strategy**, which has become known as the **preemptive strike** and basically consists, if we can use the Martin analogy, of taking away the punchbowl before the party even gets started. Or, to switch metaphors, Greenspan said it is better to be ahead of the curve than behind it.

One trouble with the Martin strategy is that once higher inflation has surfaced, it can usually be terminated only at the cost of a recession; whereas by tightening before inflation has actually increased, less monetary contraction is required, so the economy is more likely to head into a slowdown rather than an actual recession.

Nonetheless, the conflict posed here is part of the larger dilemma of monetary policy that occurs because changes in policy influence the growth rate in the short run but not the long run. If the Fed tightens too soon, it runs the risk of violating its obligations to keep the economy moving ahead in the short run. If it waits too long, it violates its obligations to keep inflation low and steady.

Under recent Fed policy, this dilemma has been at least partially solved. We have shown that in the short run, the *availability* of credit plays a more critical role than the *cost* in terms of affecting aggregate demand. Hence the Fed could use a preemptive strike to raise interest rates and send a warning to private sector economic agents that no increase in inflation would be tolerated, while at the same time leaving the availability of credit unchanged. The Fed would not have to roll out the heavy artillery, so to speak, unless raising rates had no impact on inflationary expectations. By sending a signal that it was closely monitoring the situation, the

Fed could reduce the likelihood that it would have to tighten credit availability. In particular, raising interest rates in late 1999, when both the economy and the stock market were overheating, might have forestalled the 2001 recession.

Economic agents, like everyone else, learn from their past mistakes. Suppose a firm raises prices and loses market share. A few months later, it raises prices again and loses even more market share. After a while, the firm decides it isn't a very good idea to raise prices. Similarly, labor unions push for wage increases in excess of productivity gains, and find jobs are transferred overseas. After a while they also learn their lesson.

On a macroeconomic level, if Fed policy is credible, most firms will find that every time they raise prices, the Fed implements policies that reduce real growth, which causes their sales and profits to suffer. Labor will find that inflationary wage increases cause a permanent loss of jobs. After a while they reach the obvious conclusion that it isn't worth raising prices or permitting inflationary wage gains.

Nonetheless, just as eternal vigilance is the price of liberty, the Fed must constantly remain on its guard and fight every sign of higher inflation. Otherwise business and labor might try to sneak in those price increases any time demand strengthens. Thus for monetary policy to be effective, the Fed must send a warning signal sooner rather than later. If the Fed raises the funds rate by the same amount inflation has risen, or even by the same amount that real growth has risen during periods of overfull employment, it hasn't really tightened at all, and inflationary pressures and expectations will keep building.

The risk, of course, is that by tightening too early the Fed will reduce the growth rate below its maximum sustainable rate, hence boosting unemployment and reducing growth enough to create substantial excess capacity. In general, that risk could be reduced if economists had some reasonably accurate way of determining when inflation was about to accelerate. However, to date no one has developed a reliable leading indicator for inflation.

When the economy still has excess capacity and the unemployment rate is relatively high, demand-based inflation usually does not occur, so monetary tightening is not generally required – assuming that policy has been credible in the recent past. Once the economy reaches full employment, the Fed is likely to tighten if it sees (a) real growth in excess of the long-run sustainable rate, (b) an acceleration in the inflation rate for "core" commodity prices (i.e., excluding food and energy), and (c) an acceleration in unit labor costs. Wage rates and unit labor costs usually lag the inflation cycle, so while the Fed would certainly notice if unit labor costs rose more rapidly, by then it is usually too late.

Like everyone else, the Fed doesn't know in advance when inflation is about to accelerate. As a result, the "preemptive strike" method could cause the economy to slow down because the Fed reacted to a false alarm. To determine whether this is a major risk, we examine what happened to economic activity in the years following Fed tightening that were not preceded by an actual increase in the rate of inflation.

Under Volcker and Greenspan, the Fed boosted the funds rate in 1984, 1987, 1988, 1989, and 1994. Yet the unemployment rate actually dropped in 1985, 1988, 1989, and 1995. The only time it rose was in 1990, but that increase was also caused by the doubling of oil prices following the Iraqi invasion of Kuwait and the S&L crisis as well as Fed tightening.

On the other hand, every time that the Fed tightened under Martin, the economy headed into recession next year, with the single exception of 1966, when economic activity was temporarily boosted by the Vietnam War expenditures; even then, growth slowed sharply. The institutional setting was different then, but even so it is not an outstanding record.

Thus the historical evidence indicates that credible monetary policy and the preemptive strike work much better than waiting to take the punchbowl away until the party is starting to get good. Sending a signal by raising interest rates generally harms the economy less than ignoring inflation until it is too late. There are no riskless strategies, but when the former strategy is used, the economy usually slows down but real growth remains positive, whereas when the latter strategy is employed, the economy usually plunges into recession.

MANAGER'S BRIEFCASE: HOW SHOULD MANAGERS REACT TO THE NEXT FED MOVE?

As a manager, the time will come when you will hear on TV, or read in the financial pages, that the Fed has just changed the Federal funds rate. How will that affect your business decisions?

First, while financial market conditions will change immediately, there is usually a two to three quarter lag before real GDP changes. Don't expect sales to move immediately.

Second, Fed easing will not automatically boost your sales. Housing reacts with a very short lag; most capital goods have a lag of up to one year.

It depends where the Fed is in the easing cycle. During and after the 2001 recession, it cut the funds rate at least 12 times, from $6\frac{1}{2}$% to $1\frac{1}{4}$%. In the 1990–91 recession, it cut it approximately eight times, from $8\frac{1}{4}$% to 3% (decisions were not specifically announced back then, so the number of cuts is estimated). If you plan to borrow, keep your powder dry.

Watch long-term rates to see how investors react. If the Fed tightens and bond yields rise, that means investors expect further tightening; if bond yields decline, that sends a signal the Fed probably will not tighten further. Of course, financial market investors are not always right either, but this rule of thumb works most of the time.

If the Fed tightens, the question is whether this will restrain inflation or not – and whether it will cause a recession. In this case, a quick calculation using the Taylor Rule is appropriate. Suppose, for example, the growth rate is 4%, the inflation rate is 3%, and the Fed boosts the funds rate from 4% to $4\frac{1}{2}$%. That change would probably have little or no effect on the economy, and would be followed by further increases. On the other hand, suppose it boosts the funds rate from 7% to $7\frac{1}{2}$%; that would put it above equilibrium, which probably means real growth and inflation will decline, and the Fed may not tighten much further. None of these rules works infallibly but they do provide some idea of where the Fed is in its cycle, and how the economy is likely to be affected.

Finally, stay on guard. If the Federal funds rate is well below its equilibrium value as defined by the Taylor Rule, substantial tightening will occur as soon as the economy picks up steam. In late 1993, the Fed held the funds rate at 3% all year even though the inflation rate was above 3% and the growth rate was above 4%. In retrospect, it

continued

MANAGER'S BRIEFCASE (*continued*)

seemed obvious that tightening would soon occur. Yet the Treasury bond yield fell all the way to $5\frac{3}{4}\%$, and when the Fed did tighten in early 1994, many investors were caught so far off guard that they suffered enormous losses, and even as prestigious a firm as Goldman Sachs almost went out of business.

19.6   Supply-side shocks and sticky prices and wages: how the Fed should react

The previous section discussed *demand-side* disturbances and indicated how soon the Fed should tighten when the economy is at full employment and real GDP is still rising at above-average rates. Even in that situation there remains some disagreement about when to tighten policy, although more economists now favor the preemptive strike.

However, the dilemma is much starker when the economy is subjected to a malign supply-side shock. In that case, an increase in the rate of inflation is associated with a decline in demand rather than an increase. On the one hand, the Fed should tighten in response to higher inflation, while on the other hand it should ease in response to lower growth. What is the proper strategy?

In the long run, the purpose of monetary policy is to keep inflation low and stable so that the economy can remain at full employment. However, in certain cases, such as an oil supply shock, if wages lag behind prices, the Fed will have to choose between continued full employment and higher inflation, or stable inflation but higher unemployment. We consider the case of an energy shock.

If higher oil prices decrease aggregate demand, which is likely to be the case in all countries that are net importers of oil, keeping the economy at full employment requires an increase in the price level, which in turn requires some easing of monetary policy. That is particularly true in the case of sticky wages. Since the Fed does not want inflation to encourage the ripple effects of higher prices, that always represents a short-term dilemma, which is why economists say there is no unequivocal "right" monetary policy following a supply shock when wages and prices are sticky.

We are not suggesting the Fed should necessarily favor full employment over price stability. Rather, this simplified model points out the quagmire in which the Fed finds itself. If an adverse supply shock occurs, and if in addition wages are sticky downward (which is likely to be the case), then at least in the short run, the Fed must choose. It can hold prices steady while the unemployment rate rises, or it can hold employment steady while prices rise, but it cannot maintain stability in both employment and prices.

We have seen in previous chapters that once a rise in inflationary expectations is unleashed, it usually takes several years to bring them back under control. For this reason, the preferred short-term policy of the Fed should be to try and reduce the inflationary impact of an adverse supply-side shock even at the cost of a temporary rise in the unemployment rate. Not everyone will agree with that policy prescription; we merely point out that from time to time the Fed will face dilemmas where any choice it makes will cause some economic discomfort. There is no one cut-and-dried rule of monetary policy that will work all the time. In general, though, we conclude that following a supply shock, the Fed is better off not accommodating that shock even though the short-run result is likely to be lower growth and higher unemployment. The ensuing slowdown will be less serious than if the Fed initially tries to accommodate.

19.7 Why targeting interest rates doesn't always work: the conundrum revisited

Sections 19.4 through 19.6 dealt with specific examples of how the Fed should deviate from its equilibrium rules whenever shocks affect the economy. In this section, we revisit the issue of the conundrum first raised in chapter 6.

In the absence of shocks, the Fed should set the funds rate at its equilibrium level, and keep it there as the economy returns to full employment with low and stable inflation. It should generally deviate from that rule following a shock. However, it is often the case that after a shock occurs, which necessitates a temporary deviation from equilibrium, additional complications keep the Fed from returning the funds rate to its equilibrium position. These include the following:

1. The Fed sometimes sets rates too low for political reasons, although this happens less frequently than in the past.
2. The Fed is unable to determine the equilibrium rate, because the economy responds with a longer lag than usual and declines in interest rates do not generate the desired effect in the usual amount of time. Hence the Fed eases further, which eventually turns out to be excessive.
3. Changes in inflationary expectations keep shifting the equilibrium rate.

Unless the Fed commands instant credibility, at least the first stages of tightening will produce slower growth rather than lower inflation. Suppose the rate of inflation had been 3% and the Federal funds rate was set at 4%, lower than its equilibrium level, because the economy had only recently emerged from a recession and had not yet returned to full employment. Throughout this period, assume the underlying rate of real growth is 3%. For a while, though, real growth accelerates, boosting inflationary expectations to 5%. It is unlikely that the Fed would boost the funds to 8% immediately. Instead, it raises the funds rate gradually in small steps. At 6%, that rate is still below equilibrium; that is also the case at 7%. Finally, the funds rate rises to 8% – at which point investors suddenly believe that the Fed is serious about fighting inflation, so the expected rate of inflation suddenly returns to 3%.

At that point, the real funds rate of 5% is too high, so the growth rate declines sharply; a brief recession may even occur. However, if the Fed had not boosted the funds rate all the way to 8%, it would not have regained credibility, and inflationary expectations might have risen even more.

Considering that there have been only two minor recessions since 1983, one could perhaps argue that the current set of monetary policy rules work well enough that no major changes are needed in the future. Yet before 1983, the US economy had eight recessions in the previous 38 years, plus four other periods when growth slowed almost to zero but were not officially classified as recessions, plus three bouts of double-digit inflation, plus four other times when inflation rose to 6% or more. Many economists think the Fed has learned its lessons, yet that remains to be seen.

19.8   Budget deficits and monetary policy

We have previously emphasized that the impact of short-term changes in fiscal policy cannot be determined without knowing how the monetary authorities will react. This relationship is now examined from a different viewpoint: given that the full-employment deficit has changed, how *should* the monetary authorities react? In particular, if this measure of the deficit increases, should they tighten; if it decreases, should they ease?

We focus exclusively on a change in the full-employment deficit. If the deficit diminishes because the growth rate improves, that represents no change in fiscal policy, and hence calls for no change in monetary policy. Similarly, monetary policy should not tighten if the deficit increases because the growth rate declines or the economy heads into recession. For example, raising interest rates or restricting credit during the 2001 recession just because the budget position suddenly flip-flopped back into deficit would have been a serious error, and was never seriously considered.

In determining the proper stance of monetary policy, the Fed must take into account not only the effect on the growth rate and the proximity of the economy to full employment, but the impact on inflationary expectations and productivity.

To review briefly: when the deficit increases, the central bank always has two choices. It can buy the additional securities issued by the Treasury to fund the deficit, known as monetizing the debt, which will eventually raise the rate of inflation. Or it can direct that these securities be sold to the public, which will raise interest rates, hence offsetting some of the expansionary impact of the deficit.

The evidence presented in this book suggests that short-term discretionary changes in fiscal policy do not have a very positive impact on economic performance and probably ought not to be tried except in dire circumstances. However, not everyone agrees with that sentiment, and some economists – and politicians – think the rebate checks that were mailed in the summer of 2001 helped bring the recession to a speedy end. Whether the rebate was very effective or not, it clearly was a change in fiscal policy and changed the full-employment budget position from a surplus to a deficit. Nonetheless, the Fed continued to reduce the Federal funds rate. Was that the right decision? If not, what should it have done?

We return to our two principal criteria. During 2002, productivity grew very rapidly; inflation – and inflationary expectations – did not rise at all. That suggests the Fed did indeed choose the correct policy, although the obligation to raise short-term rates in a timely fashion still remains once the economy does start to grow at above-average rates.

If the economy is not close to full employment, bond yields usually will not rise when the full-employment deficit increases even if the Fed continues to ease and monetizes most of the additional debt. Also, inflationary expectations will generally remain stable in this situation. The only significant change is that crowding out might diminish productivity growth. However, if there are still substantial excess resources, this effect is not likely to be very large either. Thus in most cases, if the full-employment deficit increases during periods of slack economic activity, the correct response of the Fed is to leave policy unchanged. Holding interest rates at their previous level will not worsen inflationary pressures if the economy has substantial excess capital and labor resources and productivity grows at above-average rates, which is usually the case in the early stages of recovery.

The more challenging policy decisions arise when the economy is at or near full employment. Suppose the full-employment deficit increases; even if the Fed does not change its policy, long-term interest rates will rise. Hence the Fed has to decide whether to monetize the increase in the deficit and hold short-term rates at their previous levels, match that increase in the bond yield with a similar rise in the funds rate, or tighten further in order to send a message to financial markets that it will not let inflationary deficit increases go unheeded.

Increases in the full-employment deficit when the economy is already at full employment are relatively rare. The major example in the post-WWII US economy occurred in the late 1960s, when government spending soared because of the Vietnam War and the so-called War on Poverty. It was clear to most economists that the increased expenditures should have been offset by contractionary policy, but there were sharp disagreements about whether that policy should take the form of a tax increase or monetary tightening.

Initially, monetary tightening was tried, and it worked; however, as soon as real growth and inflation slowed down, the monetary reins were loosened. Later, higher tax rates were coupled with monetary easing, but the result was even higher inflation and a recession the following year. This episode clearly points out the importance of expectations: they worsened when the Fed eased, so the tax hike did not have its intended consequences.

In general, if the full-employment deficit persists or even widens when the economy is near full employment, productivity growth will diminish and inflationary expectations will rise. In that case the Fed should have no hesitation in refusing to buy more government securities itself, and offer them to the public. The decision by Arthur Burns not to take that step in 1976 and 1977 led to another round of double-digit inflation by the end of that decade.

19.9   Monetary policy in an open economy

Since the severe 1982 recession, the US economy has suffered only two very minor downturns, and the core rate of inflation has changed very little. On the other hand, the value of the dollar has fluctuated very widely, rising 45% from 1980 to 1985, falling 29% by 1998 and another 10% by 1995, and then rising 33% by early 2002 before declining again.[4] How should monetary policy react to these changes?

When countries used to strive to keep the value of their currencies fixed, one of the major roles of monetary policy was to manage the value of that currency. Now, however, most countries have abandoned the gold standard and the practice of keeping their currencies at fixed rates, so they can fluctuate according to market conditions. However, the value of the currency can have a substantial impact on both real growth and inflation, with a substantial lag, so if the currency is far from equilibrium, that may require explicit monetary action even if real growth and inflation are currently at satisfactory levels.

Suppose the currency was overvalued for an extended period of time but for much of that period, real growth was robust and inflation was low and stable. However, profit margins diminished to the point where most manufacturing operations moved to other countries. By the time that caused a recession, it would be too late to undo the damage of the overvalued currency, because the firms would have already moved.

Now suppose the currency is undervalued during a period of high unemployment. For a while, inflation does not rise and growth remains robust, helped in part by the rise in net exports. When the economy finally does return to full employment, inflation starts to accelerate, and the monetary authorities have lost their credibility because they did nothing about the weak currency in previous years. It will take several years to reestablish that credibility; meanwhile, the economy is likely to undergo a series of recessions and an extended period of sluggish growth.

Central banks should intervene in foreign exchange markets under the following circumstances. First, when disorderly markets arise, the central bank should try to offset speculative fever that roils the markets. Second, even if markets are behaving in an orderly fashion, the central bank should ease when the value of the currency rises so much that it threatens to plunge the economy into a recession, and should tighten when the value of the currency is so low that it threatens to increase the rate of inflation. The Treasury and the Fed made the right decision to reduce the value of the dollar in late 1985; if the Bank of Japan had made a similar decision in 1990, it would have mitigated the severity of the decade-long recession that followed. The same comment applies to Germany in the 1990s. When Britain finally abandoned the overvalued pound in 1992, real growth finally returned to above-average levels.

To a certain extent, trying to steer the currency back toward its equilibrium value is not so different from the way that monetary policy should be implemented. When the value of the dollar continued to rise in 2001 to the point where manufacturing output declined sharply, Fed easing was clearly indicated to keep even more manufacturing firms from shifting operations to low-wage countries.

The appropriate response of the monetary authorities thus depends not so much on whether the currency is rising or falling, but its level compared to equilibrium as defined by PPP. In 1972–3 and again in 1977–8, the dollar declined sharply and fell below PPP equilibrium, causing higher inflation. On the other hand, when the dollar declined sharply in 1986 and 1987, it remained above equilibrium, so inflation did not rise and further tightening was not advisable.

Suppose the trade deficit widens; should the Fed then ease to offset this ex ante loss in purchasing power? The increase in trade deficit probably will not reduce real GDP, especially in the US, if (a) consumers benefit from lower import prices and (b) investors benefit from the inflow of foreign capital. In the era of flexible exchange rates, the use of monetary policy to affect foreign sector variables should occur only when the value of the currency moves far from its equilibrium value – not to offset a major move in the trade surplus or deficit.

19.10   Why higher inflation leads to lower productivity

By now it should be clear why high inflation impedes economic performance. Even if its negative impact on aggregate demand is mitigated by indexation, and wage-earners, pensioners, and rentiers have their incomes adjusted by the rate of inflation, the system invariably leads to a reduced commitment to improve productivity as firms seek to take the easier path of raising prices. If wage and price controls are imposed, that provides yet another reason for firms not to try to boost productivity. In such circumstances, firms find they will make just as much profit, and a higher rate of return on invested capital, if they do not reduce costs or boost capital spending but just let prices rise proportionately with cost increases. Furthermore, at a high rate of inflation, the investment decisions that are undertaken will be distorted by inflation. We have already mentioned rampant speculation. But even decisions to purchase capital plant and equipment will be distorted.

In particular, firms will invest in assets that will benefit from higher inflation rather than assets that will increase their real rate of return. During periods of relatively high inflation, for example, investors are likely to purchase buildings rather than equipment. Buildings may be constructed that remain vacant for several years, yet the owners will still earn an above-average rate of return in the long run because of capital gains. On the other hand, firms may shun investments in machinery with long lives, for after a few years, the value of the depreciation allowances will be much lower, while the price of replacing the machine will have soared. Hence the investment ratio may not decline during periods of high inflation, but the "wrong" kind of investment will be made in the sense that it will not boost productivity.

While difficult to measure empirically, it is likely that quality also deteriorates as the rate of inflation rises; this is a hidden cost of lower productivity. We have already discussed how during periods of rampant inflation, workers supplement their meager real wages through payments from graft and corruption. That sort of insidious behavior undermines the work ethic and also leads to shoddier merchandise.

Even with complete indexation, income is transferred from workers to speculators. While some speculators may also be spendthrifts, that is not always the case. It is more likely that some of their gains will be parked in "safe" currencies outside the country. As a result, much of the money that is transferred from the working class to speculators ends up leaving the country. Even funds that stay inside the country may be invested in gold coins or bullion, or other sterile assets that do not boost real growth.

However, the biggest effects are felt on the supply side. As already discussed above, higher inflation reduces the work ethic. It shifts income from investment and domestic saving to consumption and foreign saving. Also, many of the assets that are purchased do not boost productivity.

Table 19.1 shows figures for the inflation rate (GDP deflator) and real GDP for Argentina, Brazil, Chile, Nicaragua, and Peru during their bouts of hyperinflation during the 1980s and 1990s (the 1970s for Chile). In most cases, real growth was the lowest during the peak year of inflation; when inflation started to decline, real growth picked up the very same year, instead of being followed by a year or more of recession. That is most clearly the case for Argentina, but also happened in Brazil and Peru. The Nicaraguan experience is mixed. Only in Chile do we see signs that the economy plunged into recession the year after inflation peaked – and in that case the inflation rate of 695%, while gigantic, was still below the quadruple-digit rates of inflation reached in the other four countries.

Some interesting conclusions can be drawn from the juxtaposition of moderately high inflation in the US and hyperinflation in Latin America. Those economies were hurt so much by hyperinflation that real GDP declined at the peak rate of inflation, then started to improve as soon as inflation abated. In the US, on the other hand, the economy was not as severely racked by double-digit inflation, so when the monetary authorities tightened, real GDP fell for a while before recovering.

Table 19.1   Recent Latin American hyperinflations

Chile			Nicaragua		
Year	Inflation	Growth	Year	Inflation	Growth
1971	18.4	9.0	1983	11.0	4.6
1972	86.9	−1.2	1984	39.0	−1.6
1973	417.9	−5.6	1985	167.2	−4.1
1974	694.4	1.0	1986	281.5	−1.0
1975	342.5	−12.9	1987	539.5	−0.7
1976	250.7	3.5	1988	13,611.6	−12.4
1977	103.6	9.9	1989	4,772.6	−1.7
1978	56.5	8.2	1990	49,052.3	−0.1
1979	46.3	8.3	1991	376.0	−0.2
1980	29.2	2.8	1992	24.1	0.4
1981	12.2	5.5			

	Peru		Argentina		Brazil	
Year	Inflation	Growth	Inflation	Growth	Inflation	Growth
1986	74.7	9.3	75.4	7.3	146.2	7.6
1987	85.4	8.3	127.8	2.6	204.1	3.6
1988	549.8	−8.2	385.1	−1.9	641.7	−0.1
1989	2,667.1	−11.0	3,014.6	−6.2	1,321.7	3.3
1990	6,221.6	−4.3	2,023.2	0.1	2,577.4	−4.1
1991	398.0	2.8	141.0	8.9	398.0	1.2
1992	63.3	−2.3	15.3	8.7	1,032.9	−0.9

Source: International Financial Statistics Yearbook

19.11   Recap: the case for active monetary policy and optimal policy rules

In the previous chapter we argued that fiscal policies should be directed at boosting the long-run growth rate, since short-term changes in discretionary fiscal policy do not work very well. In the long run, monetary policy should be directed toward keeping the inflation rate low and stable. Yet short-term monetary policy should not be fixed; it needs to be flexible enough to adjust to unexpected shocks in the economy. In particular, a simplistic rule of thumb, such as a constant growth rate in some measure of the money supply, will not work.

The argument for holding monetary policy constant used to be that political pressures cause the monetary authorities to take steps that worsen rather than improve overall economic performance. Thus, for example, the central bank might try to prolong the recovery phase of the business cycle by keeping monetary policy easy long after it had become apparent that inflationary pressures were increasing. Then, in an attempt to rectify its earlier mistake, it might stay with an overly tight policy well after the economy had plunged into recession. Finally, an attempt to bail out large financial institutions might result in a decrease in moral hazard, thus intensifying boom/bust cycles in financial markets.

The arguments for and against a flexible monetary rule can be summarized as follows:

Arguments for:
- Hands-on management avoids financial crises and recessions.
- Serious recession could develop if policy were inflexible.
- Policy must adjust to major exogenous shocks.
- Changes in inflationary expectations caused by factors other than monetary policy require shifts in policy.

Arguments against:
- Political biases may creep in.
- Economists aren't smart enough to predict turning points.
- Tendency to overshoot targets because of variable lags.
- Steady policy will reduce unnecessary fluctuations in inflationary expectations.
- Authorities misinformed because of incorrect data.

The argument concerning political biases is important in those situations where the central bank takes its marching orders from craven politicians whose primary aim is to get reelected and line their own pockets. Under those circumstances, the results will surely be inferior to a monetary rule. However, the proper answer to that response is to insure that central bankers have political autonomy, not to place them in the straitjacket of an inflexible monetary rule. This point has gradually been recognized over the past two decades to the point where most central bankers now enjoy immunity from rash political decisions.

In spite of the increased computerization of the economy and faster flow of economic information, economists are no better at predicting recessions now than they were 50 years ago. In particular, the forecasting profession missed the recessions of both 1990–91 and 2001. That suggests the Fed should not be in the forecasting business either. Yet when the economy slows down, the Fed should act decisively and not be hamstrung by a simplistic monetary rule. Similarly, when an increase in inflationary expectations is reflected in higher bond yields, the Fed should make it clear it will tighten to keep actual inflation from rising. By sending advance signals, the Fed can tighten or ease one step at a time, and await further economic developments before taking the next move.

More to the point, it is not clear that even the ability of the Fed to make perfect predictions would necessarily improve monetary policy. Assume that the economy is at full employment and is growing rapidly, but the Fed is somehow able to divine that the growth rate will slow down sharply two quarters from now, even though the consensus forecast calls for continued rapid growth. Based on this information, the Fed eases. If major investors in the private sector do not agree with the Fed forecast, they may believe the Fed is trying to prolong the expansion at the expense of price stability, in which case inflationary expectations will rise and business and labor will push more vigorously for higher prices and wages.

The issue of long and variable lags has more cogency during recessions than booms. When the economy is growing rapidly, a rise in *real* interest rates and a reduction in credit availability has always resulted in a marked slowdown in the growth rate two to three quarters later. Yet while a significant reduction in real interest rates and a rise in credit availability often start to boost growth two to three quarters later, the strength of response has been quite variable. Hence the argument is asymmetrical in the sense that when the economy is about to overheat, the Fed needs to act quickly; when it is in recession, a little extra stimulus will not have as big a negative effect on inflation. It is the difference between trying to steer the car on a narrow two-lane road and a six-lane superhighway.

The Fed should hold the short-term interest rate at equilibrium when the economy is growing smoothly and there are no signs that inflation is about to increase. If exogenous developments push the economy into recession without any increase in inflation, the Fed should ease. However, that is usually a straightforward decision. What should the Fed do in the cases when (a) higher inflation and recession occur simultaneously, as in the case of an energy shock, or (b) the economy reaches full employment and inflationary pressures show signs of building? Surely a steady policy is not appropriate in either of these cases.

The experience of the past 30 years, plus the importance of establishing and maintaining monetary credibility, show that in both cases, the Fed is best advised to tighten, even if the short-term result is lower growth and higher inflation. When oil prices suddenly rise, there is no "best" solution; the choice is between a mild recession now or a more severe recession later. When exogenous prices are stable, the Fed has even less reason not to tighten, unless a sudden collapse in financial markets occurs, in which case the primary duty of the monetary authorities is to insure an adequate flow of liquidity. In either case, though, simply adhering to a simple monetary rule will provide suboptimal performance.

Incorrect data can be a major hazard to optimal monetary policy, so central bankers must protect themselves from acting on incorrect information. In general, the following rules can be observed. First, monthly data based on fragmentary information often contain major errors, so the Fed should not act until three consecutive months of data all exhibit the same trend. Second, if commodity prices and wage rates are accelerating but the CPI does not show any increase in inflation, the CPI is probably measuring the wrong prices. Third, if the unemployment rate and the change in employment move in the same direction, the Bureau of Labor Statistics survey data are probably faulty. Fourth, if real GDP shows big gains at the same time that production declines, the GDP data are usually inaccurate. No brief list will cover all contingencies, but a modicum of common sense in interpreting the latest economic releases will avoid the biggest snafus.

In this respect the Fed deserves credit for easing aggressively throughout 2001 even though preliminary GDP data – later revised – showed that the economy was still improving.

Any monetary rule must be flexible. Yet to the extent that private sector agents will not know the next step in monetary policy, some might argue that inflationary expectations are more likely to flare up if Fed policy is not known. That problem can be reduced if not completely eliminated by having the Fed announce its contingency planning one period in advance. If the economy overheats, or if commodity prices or unit labor costs start to rise, the Fed should make known its desire to tighten. Also, tightening should occur if the economy is at full employment and (a) a malign supply-side shock occurs, (b) the deficit increases, or (c) the dollar weakens. On the other hand, the Fed should ease if a serious financial crisis arises, because providing ample liquidity is still the primary purpose of the Federal Reserve System. This does not put the Fed in the forecasting business; it is simply reacting to economic events, and informing financial markets what is likely to happen in the near future if nothing else changes.

Even if this rule is followed, the Fed still has a balancing act to perform: nipping inflation in the bud without slowing down the economy too much. That is why we suggest the dual strategy of raising rates right away, but holding reduced credit availability in reserve. Preemptive strikes definitely are a part of this strategy. This set of rules may not be perfect, but if it sharply reduces the number of recessions, it is much better than the policy followed before 1980. Indeed, except for major shocks, this optimal monetary policy rule should allow the economy to enjoy full employment without higher inflation – and the recessions that follow – almost all of the time.

In summary, monetary policy can always perform the job of keeping inflation low and stable if that is its sole mandate. However, it is obviously beneficial to have productivity grow faster rather than slower, and to keep the unemployment rate lower rather than higher. Long-term productivity growth will be enhanced by optimal fiscal policies, as discussed in the previous chapter. Competitive pressures will boost productivity and keep inflation low when international trade is vigorous; that is promoted by keeping the value of the currency near its purchasing power parity and minimizing barriers to free trade. This combination of optimal monetary, fiscal, and trade policies should produce optimal economic performance.

KEY TERMS AND CONCEPTS

Conundrum	Preemptive Strikes
Income Policies (to reduce inflation)	Taylor Rule
Monetary Policy Shocks	Volcker-Greenspan Strategy (about low inflation)
Moral Hazard	Wage and Price Guidelines

SUMMARY

- Optimal monetary policy should include three different goals. The first is to insure an adequate supply of liquidity for the needs of commerce and industry. Second, when higher inflation threatens, the Fed should tighten in a timely fashion, and when recessions occur, it should ease quickly. Third, in the long run, monetary policy is responsible for keeping the inflation rate low and stable.

- Unlike fiscal policy, which should be used primarily to boost the long-term growth rate, monetary policy is important in both the short and long run. However, these aims may at times be contradictory. When the economy is weak, monetary policy should be stimulative, but at the same time should not set the stage for higher inflation when the economy reapproaches full employment and full capacity.

- In equilibrium, the Federal funds rate is usually set at a level equal to the real growth rate plus the inflation rate. If the funds rate changes because real growth or inflation change, that does not represent any change in policy. If the funds rate deviates from this rule, that represents a change in policy and is usually known as a monetary policy shock.

- Even with complete indexation, higher inflation reduces productivity growth because it (a) distorts capital spending decisions, (b) erodes the work ethic, and (c) breeds graft and corruption.

- However, deflation also hurts the economy because it creates destruction of wealth. Hence the optimal rate of inflation occurs when some prices are stable and some prices are rising slowly, which is usually an aggregate rate of 1% to 2% per year. A zero rate of inflation means that approximately half of the prices are declining, which could cause higher bankruptcies and a loss of assets and wealth.

- Many different versions of price freezes, controls, guidelines, and income policies have been tried in different countries throughout the ages. They have never been successful, because they distort the pricing system and reduce productivity, which in the long run raises the rate of inflation.

- Monetary policy is likely to deviate from its equilibrium position during times of financial crises, excess demand, exogenous supply shocks, change in expectations, the conundrum, increase in the budget deficit, or changes in the value of the currency.

- The first and foremost role of monetary policy is to insure adequate liquidity for the needs of commerce and industry and insure that the financial system does not collapse, as it did during the Great Depression. However, the Fed should be careful not to intervene just to bail out a few ''high rollers'' who have taken unreasonable risks because of the belief that the monetary authorities will always come to their aid in case of market declines.

- The Fed should follow the concept of preemptive strikes, announcing in advance that it will boost the Federal funds rate if it is below its equilibrium level and real growth and inflation continue at their recent rate. If the rise in interest rates does not contain inflation at satisfactory levels, the Fed should then restrict the supply of credit.

- When supply-side shocks significantly boost the rate of inflation, there is no optimal solution available to the Fed: either overall inflation will rise, or the economy will head into recession. In general, it is better to take a short recession in the near future than permit inflation to fester and have to take a longer recession later.

- If the Fed has previously established credibility, a logical pattern of preemptive strikes should be sufficient to keep inflation stable. However, it often takes several years to establish credibility. If the funds rate has been below equilibrium for some time, initial increases in the funds rate may not convince investors and other economic agents that it is serious about fighting inflation. Hence the Fed may have to boost the funds rate above its equilibrium level to reestablish credibility, in which case a slowdown or recession may result.

- If a change in the budget surplus or deficit occurs because of a major change in fiscal policy, the Fed should usually offset that with appropriate monetary policy. However, if a change in the budget position occurs because of changes in the growth rate of the economy, monetary policy should remain unchanged.

- If the value of the currency rises well above its equilibrium level as defined by purchasing power parity, the Fed should ease; if it falls below its equilibrium level, it should tighten. In an era of floating exchanges rates, though, there is no need to change monetary policy in response to major swings in the trade balance, unless those swings are caused by an overvalued or undervalued currency.

- The simplistic rule of thumb that the Fed should control the money supply by keeping it growing at a constant rate regardless of economic circumstances is completely outmoded in an age of banking deregulation. Instead, the Fed should keep the funds rate near the growth rate in nominal GDP in equilibrium, and then deviate when the economy is subjected to the type of shocks discussed in this chapter.

QUESTIONS AND PROBLEMS

1. In 1998 the Bank of Japan reduced the short-term interest rate to zero, yet the economy did not rally but remained in recession. Why did monetary policy fail to work? What else do you think the Bank of Japan could have done to stimulate real growth?

2. In mid-2002, real growth fell from 5% in the first quarter to 1% in the second quarter, and the unemployment rate continued to rise. The stock market was down over 20%. Inflation was stable at about 2%. Many people were worried about the viability of the corporate sector because of the explosion of scandals and fraud in major corporations. However, the Federal funds rate had already been reduced to $1\frac{3}{4}$%. Even if the economy limped along at a 2% growth rate in the second half, the Taylor Rule would still suggest a funds rate of about 4%. Given this information in mid-2002 – and disregarding what we know about what happened afterward – did the Fed follow the correct policy by easing further to $1\frac{1}{4}$%?

3. The banking sector was deregulated in 1982. Before then, the US economy had eight recessions in the post-WWII period, an average of one recession every $4\frac{1}{2}$ years. Since then, there have been only two recessions in over 20 years. Is it just a coincidence that the frequency and severity of recessions declined after banking deregulation and the Fed could no longer control growth in the money supply, or are there some direct linkages between deregulation and fewer recessions? If so, what are they?

4. From late 1998 to mid-2000, benchmark crude oil prices tripled, from $10 to $30/bbl. The US uses approximately 18 million barrels of oil per day, or about 7 billion barrels per year, so consumers directly and indirectly paid an extra $140 billion for oil. Yet the core rate of inflation remained virtually unchanged. To what extent was that stability due to expectations about Fed policy, and to what extent was it due to other factors?

5. Suppose during some war in the future, military expenditures increased by 3% of GDP. Describe optimal Fed policy under the following scenarios. (Hint: what happens to consumer and capital spending after the war starts?)
   (A) The government pays for the war with a tax increase.
   (B) The deficit rises by the full amount of the increase in defense spending.
   (C) Expectations decline, so the cutbacks in capital spending offset the rise in defense spending.
   (D) The war causes oil prices to double.

6. Many industries benefit in the short run from lower interest rates and an increased supply of credit availability. Nonetheless, we know from bitter experience that the attempt to hold interest rates below equilibrium for an extended period of time is likely to lead to higher inflation and an eventual credit squeeze. Few industries are more affected by credit conditions than the housing industry. As an executive of a company that supplies materials to that industry, indicate how you would adjust your business plans when the FOMC takes the following action.
   (A) The inflation rate is 3%, real growth is 4%, and the funds rate rises from 2% to 3%.
   (B) Same economic conditions, but the funds rate rises from 3% to 4%.
   (C) Same economic conditions, but the funds rate rises from 5% to 6%.
   (D) Real GDP has fallen 2% but because of an increase in the inflation rate from 8% to 10%, the funds rate rises from 12% to 14%.
   (E) Inflation rate is 2%, real growth is 4%, but because of a stock market slump, the funds rate is reduced from 2% to 1%.

7. You are a manager for a firm in an industry where prices have been flat for the past several years. The rate of inflation now rises from 2% to 4%, but the FOMC does not immediately boost the funds rate. Is this a good time to raise your prices? If so, how much should they be increased? To what extent does your answer depend on what happens to the value of the dollar? (Hint: what caused inflation to rise?)

8. In the 1970s, a big increase in the Federal budget deficit was not offset by higher interest rates, so the rate of inflation tripled. In the 1980s, a big increase in the deficit was offset by higher interest rates, so inflation declined. Suppose that Congress votes a $200 billion a year increase in medical care benefits without any corresponding increase in taxes. Explain how you would change

your business strategy if you were a company executive in the following industries:

(A) Manufacturer of railroad cars.
(B) Hardware store retailer.
(C) Stockbroker.
(D) Furniture manufacturer.
(E) Pension fund manager.

9. The US economy did not have any increase in the core rate of inflation in 1999–2000 with the economy at full employment; instead, it had a stock market bubble. Many people subsequently held Alan Greenspan and the Fed responsible for the resulting crash. Yet monetary policy is supposed to control inflation, not stock prices. What if anything did the Fed do wrong, and doesn't it deserve credit for keeping inflation low and stable? Or was low inflation due to other factors, and not the direct result of Fed policy in the late 1990s?

Notes

1. These hearings, held twice a year, are so named because they are part of the Humphrey-Hawkins legislation passed in 1978 that required the Chairman of the Federal Reserve Board to testify before Congress twice each year to discuss current Fed policy. In previous years, the Fed announced its target range for money supply growth, but these numbers have been downplayed in recent years.

2. "If the Black-Scholes formula is indeed correct, then the implied volatilities of any set of options on the same stock must be *numerically identical*. Of course, in practice they never are; thus the assumptions of the Black-Scholes model cannot literally be true ... the assumptions of the Black-Scholes model imply that options are redundant securities, which eliminates the need for organized option markets altogether." John Y. Campbell, Andrew W. Lo, and A. Craig MacKinlay, *The Econometrics of Financial Markets* (Princeton, 1997) p. 378.

3. This is not a recent point. It was originally developed by Eugene Fama in his Ph.D. thesis; the key results can be found in Eugene Fama, "The Behavior of Stock Market Prices," *Journal of Business*, 1965.

4. Recall that if the dollar were to rise 50% (say), it would return to its previous level after having fallen $33\frac{1}{3}$%.

chapter twenty

Macroeconomic forecasting: methods and pitfalls

Introduction

The viewpoint expressed in this chapter assumes that econometric models can still be usefully employed for forecasting, but not for policy analysis. Earlier it was thought that if the underlying structure were valid and stable, the model could be used for both purposes. After all, if the economy were going to follow a particular path that could be accurately predicted, and monetary or fiscal policies were then applied to change the course of the economy to a more satisfactory outcome, the model also ought to be able to predict the direction and magnitude of those changes.

Robert Lucas has famously claimed about economists that, "As an advice-giving profession, we are way over our heads." The claim that econometric models cannot be used for policy analysis, and by extension for forecasting, is sometimes known as the Lucas critique. Although Lucas overstates his case, there is much truth in that general statement. Hence whereas older macroeconomic textbooks often contained a chapter on policy analysis based on econometric model results, that material is not covered here. Instead, this chapter focuses on the usefulness of models – and other methods – for generating macro forecasts, providing managers with a list of key factors to monitor while anticipating turning points. These methods are obviously not without their errors, and we examine them, warts and all. The principal message in this chapter is that, by pointing out some of the most common errors in macroeconomic forecasting, managers are presented with a set of realistic rules and suggestions that will help them utilize forecasts to make better decisions about where their company sales and profits are likely to be heading.

20.1   Sources of forecasting error in econometric models: summary

This textbook is about macroeconomics rather than forecasting or econometrics, but since most managers will benefit from improved knowledge of future trends in sales, costs, and profits for their firms, we discuss this topic briefly. In most cases, sales and profits of individual companies are directly tied to what happens in the overall economy. Thus most managers want to be informed about the relative usefulness and accuracy of these predictions. Three key questions can be raised. First, what level of accuracy can reasonably be expected most of the time, especially when compared to simple extrapolations of existing trends? Second, since macroeconomic predictions vary widely, is there any way of determining, based on the assumptions and modeling techniques of different forecasters, which predictions are likely to be more accurate? Third, to what extent are the errors made at the macroeconomic level also relevant for determining the accuracy of forecasts for individual industries or firms?

The major sources of error in forecasting can be categorized as follows:

1. Incorrect underlying theory
2. Instability of underlying relationships
3. Errors in econometric method
4. Inadequate and incorrect data
5. Tendency to cluster around the consensus forecast
6. Inability to predict exogenous events
7. Erroneous assumptions about policy variables.

The first two topics have been covered in detail throughout this text; also, it is difficult to ascertain when the underlying models are based on faulty theory or incorrect specifications without a detailed examination of the equations. However, some of the other sources of error can be more easily explained and quantified. Hence this chapter covers the other major sources of errors in macroeconomic forecasts.

20.2 Inadequate and incorrect data and the tendency to cluster

An old saying among lawyers has it that when you have the facts, pound the facts; when you have the law, pound the law; and when you have neither, pound the table. In the same vein, when economists make inaccurate forecasts and cannot blame exogenous shocks or shifts in policy variables, they often blame inaccurate data. This author is not immune to that syndrome. Nonetheless, there have been several well-documented cases where inaccurate government data – later revised by the issuing source – has led not only to inaccurate forecasts, but to inaccurate policy recommendations. Furthermore, during the recessions and sluggish growth quarters of 1960, 1976, and 1992, a reasonable case can be made that erroneous economic data tipped the election away from the incumbent in each of these elections.

This issue has some merit, especially for short-run forecasts. For example, real growth in the first half of 1995 was originally announced as 2.0% but was later revised to 0.4%; still later, that number was raised to 1.0%. If economists had known that real growth was really that low, they presumably would have predicted a bigger drop in bond yields and hence more robust growth in 1996 than the consensus forecast. On the other hand, the average growth rate for 1995 and 1996 would not have been affected very much.

Similarly, the Bureau of Economic Analysis had a difficult time determining how much the economy declined in 2001. Originally, the data showed real GDP declining only in the third quarter of that year, but later revisions showed a decline in the first two quarters of the year as well. The sharp rebound in early 2002 was also revised down substantially.

Quarterly growth estimates of GDP are routinely revised as much as 2%. Real growth in 1993.4 was reported as high as 7.2% in early 1994; that figure was eventually revised down to 4.7%. Tables presented by the BEA in the GDP news releases show that, on average, the growth rate for real GDP is revised by 1.4% between the preliminary and final estimates. This comment is not intended as a criticism of the BEA, but it should alert managers to the likelihood that preliminary figures for real growth will be substantially revised.

Sometimes erroneous data influences the Fed to take steps that would otherwise have not occurred. In July 1995, the Fed voted to cut the funds rate by $\frac{1}{4}$% based in part on weak May retail sales of 0.2%. That figure was later revised up to 0.9%, causing then Vice-Chairman Alan Blinder to remark that if he had known May sales were that strong, he would not have voted for easing.

Earlier, the decline in real GDP in the second half of 1990 was originally pegged at about 2%, causing the Fed to move cautiously about easing. Later that figure was revised to show almost a 4% drop, at which point the Fed broadly hinted that it would have taken a more aggressive stance if it had received more accurate data. It is likely that error was one of the causes of the anemic recovery in 1991 and 1992.

The cost of bad data is inordinately high relative to the benefits. Suppose faulty data results in suboptimal monetary policy that reduces the growth rate the following year by 1%. In addition to the 500,000 people who cannot find jobs, that error costs the Federal government some $50 billion in revenues.[1] The cost of obtaining more accurate data would be far less than $1 billion. Furthermore, this is not an issue of civil liberties, government intrusion, or overly generous welfare benefits. All economists are requesting is more accurate data. Government agencies certainly cannot be blamed for producing inaccurate reports when their funding has been cut in half.

Problems also arise in trying to measure inflation; in this case, the major issue is how to treat housing prices. Theoretically, the proper way would be to employ a large enough survey to determine the rent that owner-occupied houses would receive if in fact they were offered for rent. Today, the Bureau of Labor Statistics utilizes this method, although its sample is not large enough. However, during the 1970s and early 1980s, housing prices were measured by some combination of the actual price of the house and the level of mortgage rates. Alternative calculations by the BLS have shown that, using this method, the increase in the CPI for the four quarters ending in 1980.2 would have been 11.1% instead of 14.4%.

If a better measure of inflation had been known, the Fed would not have needed to apply such crushing measures of monetary stringency, and real growth during the 1980–82 period might have been substantially higher.

Most managers do not plan to head a task force at the BEA or BLS that would improve the data, so what is the point of these comments? Especially in cyclical industries, managers who rely on bad economic data are likely to find their sales projections are far wide of the mark. Financial analysts who believed the stock market could rise at 25% per year forever got what they deserved, but to the extent that government data far overstated actual growth rates, many economists were misled.

What steps can economists, managers, and policymakers take to guard against erroneous data? First, remember that preliminary data are based on a small subsample, especially retail sales, industrial production, and new orders. Thus these advance reports should always be taken with more than the normal grain of salt until an emerging trend has been confirmed or denied by three consecutive months of data, in spite of an often hysterical response by financial market traders. Second, the Federal Reserve Board, in its industrial production release, prepares an alternative estimate of gross product originating in the manufacturing sector, which can be combined with other data to estimate GDP. On that basis, for example, real GDP in 2002.1 rose at an annual rate of only 2.7%; at the time, the BEA reported a gain of 6.1%, subsequently revised down to 5.0%. The index of coincident indicators also provides a better measure of overall economic growth than do the GDP statistics. Third, alternative measures of inflation, including the CPI, the PPI, wage rates, and total employment costs, should be compared. If one measure of inflation points to a big increase but that is not confirmed by the other measures, the user of economic data should remain wary.

CASE STUDY 20.1   HOW INCORRECT DATA INFLUENCED PRESIDENTIAL ELECTIONS

Incorrect economic data have influenced the outcome of presidential election races. In 1960, Nixon lost to Kennedy partly because of the general belief that the economy was in a recession; yet revised data showed that in 1960.3, the quarter before the election, real GDP had started to recover. In 1976, Ford lost to Carter partly because of the general perception that the economy was weak; revised figures later showed it had strengthened late in the year. In 1992, Bush lost to Clinton on the same grounds; here again, data revisions showed the economy was stronger than reported at the time.

One can of course argue that the average voter is not an eager student of the government statistics; the fact that really counts is whether the voter, or someone in his or her family, is currently unemployed, and that transcends whatever

continued

CASE STUDY 20.1 (*continued*)

the statistics show. However, with the latest economic data being broadcast at the top of the news – and with Kennedy specifically running on a platform in 1960 to "get the economy moving again" – these statistics took on increased importance.

In fact, based on these elections, some economists estimated equations to predict the outcome of presidential elections based on the growth rate, unemployment rate, inflation rate, and a dummy variable depending on whether or not the country was at war (specifically Korea and Vietnam). This equation accurately predicted every presidential election through 1996 – but then the model completely fell apart in 2000. We know now that the economy was heading into a recession, which reportedly started the following March, but that was not anticipated at the time, and in fact was not a major issue on the campaign trail: no Republican ran for office on the grounds that the economy had recently performed poorly. Of course, some people still think Gore won, but that is not the point: the election-year model predicted a landslide for the Democrats based on strong growth, full employment, low inflation, and no war, and it didn't happen.

We mention this humbling experience to emphasize that the 1960, 1976, and 1992 elections were also decided on factors other than the economic data: Nixon's unsavory reputation, Ford's inability to realize Poland was in the Communist bloc, and George Bush's infamous "read my lips" speech. Nonetheless, at the time it was generally thought that economic factors had played an important role in determining the outcome of the election, and to the extent that government data provided misleading information, the will of the voters was misdirected. Of course that can happen in elections even when economic factors are irrelevant.

Tendency to Cluster Around the Consensus Forecast

Anyone who has been in the forecasting business very long has learned not to stick their neck out so far they get their head chopped off. It is much safer to remain near the consensus – even if those forecasts are less accurate – than run the risk of being the only one predicting a downturn that never happens.

Suppose someone is the only one making a correct forecast that entails bad news – i.e., a recession will occur next year – which in fact turns out to be correct. Any such forecaster might be thought to be performing a valuable service. In fact, they are more likely to get fired.

Otto Eckstein stated publicly that he did not think the DRI model should ever predict a recession because it might convince DRI clients that a recession was imminent, so they would change their plans and the economy would actually decline. There is, of course, no evidence that a recession forecast would have caused such a change, but that decision did help to shape the consensus forecast. The forecasting field is littered with economists who correctly predicted bad news and then were fired. This doesn't excuse shoddy econometric modeling, but it may help to answer the question why the consensus forecast has never predicted a recession ahead of time.

Over time, the empirical record shows that the consensus forecast has generated more accurate results than most individual forecasts, so these comments should not be considered an attempt to denigrate the consensus opinion. However, managers should be aware that the consensus, by its very nature, will never provide accurate forecasts of major unexpected changes in the economy. If you have good reason to believe that such changes are likely to occur but others do not share this opinion, be aware of the natural tendency of forecasters to cluster around the mean as you push your own predictions. Also be prepared to lose your job if you are wrong.

Unlike theories of physics or astronomy that can be proven or disproven by actual experiments, there will never be a definitive answer to the question of how accurately econometric models predict. If macroeconomic models do better in the future, their detractors may say that was because the economy settled down and "anyone" could have predicted steady growth. If they do not improve in the future, their proponents will claim that the type of shocks that occurred could not have been predicted, and econometric models should not be singled out for having made the same mistake. We now turn to this latter topic.

20.3   Examining exogenous shocks: impulse and propagation revisited

No economist could be expected to predict the expansion of the Vietnam War, the sudden imposition of a wage and price freeze on August 15, 1971, the various energy shocks, the Iraqi invasion of Kuwait, or the terrorist bombings of 9/11. Thus, it could be argued, forecasts were wrong because of these completely unexpected events. If econometricians knew the correct values of these exogenous shocks, it is claimed, their forecasts would have been much more accurate.

Economists are not blamed for this lack of foresight. The criticism of macro models comes not from failure to predict the unforeseeable, but incorrect analysis of these events *after* they occurred. Economists failed to foresee that the energy shocks would be followed by recessions, and they also failed to foresee that the tight money policies of Paul Volcker in 1979–81 would reduce the inflation rate by almost 10% in less than two years. Models are rightly criticized for those errors, not for failing to predict that the price of oil would rise tenfold during the 1970s.

In a similar vein, most people probably did not expect Clinton to raise taxes and reduce per capita real government spending to the point where the budget position would change from a $290 billion deficit to a $236 billion surplus in eight years. However, once these changes started to occur, models failed to predict the decline in inflation and interest rates and the rise in real growth and stock market prices that followed these changes.

Econometric model forecasts can still be useful even if they are unable to predict such shocks. For example, an accurate forecast of how the economy would react to the rise in oil prices from \$3 to \$13/bbl in 1973 would have been quite useful even though the event itself was entirely unexpected. A properly structured model should have been able to provide those answers, although in this case the situation was further complicated by the end of wage and price controls in May 1974, which unleashed an unprecedented barrage of inflation.

In chapter 15 we discussed the concept of impulse and propagation of cycles; the original shock that caused a recession, and the "ripple effect" of that shock throughout the economy. The same conceptual treatment can be used for the discussion of forecasting error. Even on this basis, though, the track record of models has not been very accurate. That is because most of the time, the exogenous shocks that throw the economy off track never happened before. In the case of the first oil crisis, economists were wrong because they assumed that higher oil prices would reduce consumer spending – which was true – without realizing that the extra dollars received by domestic and foreign oil companies would boost investment and exports, hence offsetting the drop in consumption. Since the Fed made the mistake of easing, the net result was inflationary, which meant it had to reverse its policies the following year and tighten so much that a major recession ensued.

Modelers of the time could claim that since there had never been a fourfold increase in oil prices before, no one knew how economic agents would respond. However, that hardly improves the case for econometric models. Indeed, since econometric models are estimated based on historical relationships, they will probably never be useful in predicting reactions to events that have not occurred before.

A more recent example of how models failed to work occurred in 1997 and 1998. In late 1997, the Thai baht, Korean won, Malaysian ringgit, and Indonesian rupiah all fell more than 50% and those four economies headed into recession, with an average decline of 8% in real GDP for 1998. The consensus economic forecasts assumed the growth rate for the US economy would fall from 3.8% to about 2% in 1998. In fact, the growth rate rose to 4.3% (based on the change from the fourth quarter of one year to the fourth quarter of the next year). Why were the forecasts so inaccurate?

According to the analysis developed in this book, the reduction in commodity prices and interest rates, plus the concomitant gains in the stock market, boosted consumption and investment by more than the decline in net exports. Essentially, the gain in consumption added about 1% to GDP, the rise in investment added about $\frac{1}{2}$%, and the drop in net exports subtracted about 1%. Most economists focused on the drop in net exports but excluded the gains in domestic demand.

This error is precisely the sort of mistake that is being discussed here. Hardly anyone foresaw the collapse of the southeast Asian economies. However, once that did occur, the rest of the scenario should have followed logically: lower prices, lower interest rates, and higher domestic demand. Any model – or forecast – that would have predicted such results would have been considered highly accurate even if such a forecast had to be revised after the big decline in southeast Asian real GDP.

Why did almost all forecasters make the same mistake? Primarily because they focused too much on the identity $C + I + F + G = GDP$, and saw only the drop in F. They failed to take into consideration the monetary links stressed in this book, the importance of interest rates as the equilibrating mechanism, and the positive impact on C and I of lower inflation and interest rates.

Financial market participants, although initially as surprised as anyone else, recovered more quickly. As soon as investors, traders, and analysts digested the initial shock of the devaluations, interest rates started to decline. As the inflation figures continued to show slower growth in prices, interest rates fell further. Eventually that caused the Fed to ease, although the collapse of the Russian ruble and Long-Term Capital Management also hastened that decision. In the next section, we consider how markets react to economic data, and how that affects changes in interest rates and hence real growth and inflation.

MANAGER'S BRIEFCASE: REPORT CARD FOR ECONOMETRIC MODELS

Managers will have to make their own decisions about whether forecasts based on econometric models represent useful inputs into their own decision-making processes. For those who answer in the negative, the rest of the chapter focuses on alternative methods of forecasting. In making this decision, the following summary may be helpful.

1. Econometric models have never been able to predict truly exogenous shocks, nor can they be expected to do so in the future.
2. However, their forecasts can still be useful if they can explain how an initial shock will affect the economy over the next several quarters.
3. When an unexpected change in policy occurs, econometric models should be able to provide an accurate assessment of the future as long as the underlying structural relationships have not changed.
4. Even after inserting the correct value of exogenous variables, the forecasting record of econometric models is not very impressive.
5. That lack of accuracy stems partially from changed expectations, but that is not the most important factor. Structural robustness and accurate econometric method are probably more important factors.
6. In many cases, the structure of the models is defective, either because it relies on outmoded theory or because it does not take nonlinearities into account. The simultaneity problem also contributes to forecast error.
7. In the short run, erroneous government data that later are heavily revised also worsens the forecasting record, although that is not as important a factor in the long run.
8. Forecasts tend to cluster around the consensus.
9. Policy simulation analysis is often faulty not only because of structural defects in the model, but also because the initial conditions at the time of the policy change are ignored. However, models generally should not be used for that purpose.
10. The ultimate question of the usefulness of econometric models is whether they can provide better forecasts than other methods. While there are no conclusive answers, this issue is discussed in the rest of this chapter.

20.4   Market reaction to economic data

Even those who do not follow the forecasts from econometric models should not ignore the reaction of financial markets to the key economic data releases. Almost every working day of the year, the government publishes at least one, and sometimes as many as four, economic data releases. The monthly schedule appears on the first business day of each month in the *Wall Street Journal* and other sources. Various private sector firms release survey results containing consensus forecasts for these variables; these are quoted a few days ahead of time in the financial press and on the internet.

During the 1950s and 1960s, financial markets generally tended to ignore the economic data. Occasionally GNP (as it was then) or unemployment reports would catch the attention of a business reporter, but outside of the *Wall Street Journal*, they received very little coverage.

This author developed the concept of the Monthly Tracking Model in 1975 to predict the key monthly economic data series. It was a crude attempt and didn't work all the time; it is mentioned only to point out that before then, hardly anyone tried to predict the monthly data on a regular basis. Forecasting was confined to trying to predict the quarterly GDP numbers.

In the next few years, that rapidly changed. An entire industry grew up around the concept of providing economic analysis of these data. Together with on-line news and quotes, this turned out to be a much more substantial business than econometric forecasting. Dow Jones paid $1.6 billion to buy Telerate, one of the pioneer companies in this area. Michael Bloomberg, who started his eponymous firm, was said to be worth $4 billion when he ran for Mayor of New York City. Much of the growth in Reuters stemmed from their on-line analysis of economic data, although their quotes were also important. A smaller firm, Money Market Services, which offered only analysis and not quotes, was purchased by McGraw-Hill for almost $100 million. By any reasonable market test, this analysis was considered valuable information. Unlike the heyday of econometric models, which quickly vanished, many companies in this business continue to be highly profitable.

At first glance, there might seem to be very little to interpret. If the economy is growing rapidly and the unemployment rate is near full employment, the Fed is much more likely to tighten than if the economy is in the middle of a recession. However, various nuances about the data require greater skill than simply reading the reports and correlating them with historical relationships. As already noted, sometimes the data are just plain wrong, sometimes various parts of the report contradict each other (as when employment and unemployment both rise), and sometimes the reports can reveal information about inflationary pressures that are not obvious from reading the headlines.

While this text is hardly the place to analyze the nuances of the monthly economic data reports, we note that some of the most highly compensated people in the world trade financial assets based on this information. Thus watching the best and the brightest interpret this information can often provide a clue about where the economy is heading. If the collective wisdom of market-makers thinks the most recent data points to higher inflation, at a minimum that suggests that contingency plans ought to be considered.

While the Fed did not always agree with that logic, it has increasingly paid more attention to market reaction to economic data in the past few years. Indeed, if traders think the data spell higher inflation ahead, the Fed is now more likely to tighten than if traders perceive that higher inflation is not a threat.

One possible problem with this approach is that movements in the bond market could turn out to be a self-fulfilling prophecy. Bond yields rise because traders think the Fed is likely to raise the funds rate, after which the Fed raises the funds rate because bond yields rose. However, the actual risk of this circular approach so far has been minimal. From February 1996 to March 1997, bond yields fluctuated substantially but the Fed did not change the funds rate at all; that is the longest period the funds rate ever remained constant. So in spite of knee-jerk reactions to the economic data releases, the Fed does not seem to have been bullied into slavishly following the markets.

Alan Blinder, former Vice-Chairman of the Fed, has commented that the markets usually get the "sign" right – i.e., traders usually know whether a certain report is likely to lead to higher or lower interest rates – but they overreact by "a factor from 3 to 10." In other words, he thinks Fed members would be well advised to temper their reaction to market changes because they are invariably exaggerated.

Part of the reason for this exaggeration is that some traders take positions, based on the consensus forecasts, and then have to cover those positions if their guesses are wrong. It will probably come as no surprise to find out that these forecasts of monthly indicators are not any more accurate than forecasts of the economy. All one has to do is watch how the markets react when the actual number differs from the consensus to know that many of these reports come as a complete surprise. Indeed, for many years, the *Wall Street Journal* has published a compendium of interest rate forecasts six months ahead. Most of the time, less than 50% of the survey participants get the change in the *sign* right.[2]

Nonetheless, the Fed's control of the economy is undoubtedly better now that the economic data are scrutinized for their possible impact on inflation and unemployment. Even if these forecasts are not particularly accurate, to the extent that the reactions to these data provide a realistic estimate of market sentiment, including inflationary expectations, the Fed has a far better opportunity now to defuse inflationary pressures before they build to the danger point than in the days when the economic data were largely ignored. As noted in the previous chapter, preemptive strikes are a much better way to manage monetary policy than waiting until inflation has spread its roots throughout the economy. For that reason, financial market reaction, mistakes and all, has played some role in helping to stabilize economic activity. They can also provide managers with an eye on what is likely to happen in both financial markets and the overall economy in the future.

20.5   Unknown lag structures and the conservatism principle

Let's assume that eagle-eyed traders in the trading pits have spotted a significant upcoming change in inflation or unemployment, their call is correct, and the Fed decides to act on this information. That still leaves two major questions: how large a change should the monetary authorities make, and how long will it take before that change in monetary policy has its desired effect?

Many economists have noted that even if the eventual effect of a change in fiscal, monetary, or trade policy on the economy is known, the lags are long and variable. We can identify several different types of lags.

- *Data lag*. The data for any given month are released anywhere from one to seven weeks after the month has ended. Furthermore, the preliminary data often contain errors that are corrected the following month, rendering the initial reports useless. Thus the data lag is usually two to three months. However, sometimes the lag is much shorter: occasionally Fed policy changes will be based on the employment report, which appears only one week after the month has ended.
- *Recognition lag*. More often, month-to-month changes are too erratic to provide any useful information. It used to be thought that at least three months of data were needed to provide a clear glimpse of where the economy was heading. However, with market interpretation of economic data, this lag is probably shorter than it used to be.
- *Reaction lag*. How long will it take policymakers to propose the changes? The time is very short for monetary policy, although it was a year or more for fiscal policy when fine tuning was tried. The FOMC meets every six weeks but, in addition, it can take action immediately if the situation warrants. In November 1998, Alan Greenspan decided to cut the Federal funds rate from 5% to $4\frac{3}{4}$% after a telephone conference call, even though the FOMC would not formally meet again for another three weeks.
- *Legislative lag*. This applies only to fiscal policy. The political process usually takes at least another six months before the proposed change in spending or taxes is actually implemented. The Kennedy-Johnson tax cut took two years to pass, but that was a long-term change not specifically designed to affect short-term economic fluctuations. The Reagan tax cuts, by comparison, took only about six months.
- *Economic lag*. The time it takes before these changes in policy affect the economy. This lag is the most troublesome, since the economy often reacts with long and variable lags and the end result is unknown. In general, though, changes in monetary policy start to affect real growth with a lag of two to three quarters, and inflation with a lag of one to two years.

In general, the lags for monetary policy have shortened in recent years because the instantaneous reaction of financial markets to economic data means the data and recognition lags have diminished. Sometimes markets will be fooled by an erroneous data release, but most of the time, analysts are able to determine whether an economic release contains valid information about a switch in inflationary pressures or real growth. Also, the willingness of the Fed to engage in preemptive strikes has shortened the lag time.

Furthermore, the Fed now realizes that when inflation threatens, it should indeed tighten sooner rather than later. Failure to tighten when higher inflation threatens because no one knows the precise magnitude of the effect would be an egregious error. That sort of timidity increases the probability of a recession rather than reducing it.

When the unemployment rate starts to rise, the Fed should indeed ease, assuming that inflationary pressures are not worsening at the same time. However, it is far better to take several small steps at an early phase than suffer one big pratfall later, since ignoring an emerging recession invariably increases the severity of the inevitable downturn.

This commonsense logic can be bundled in some fancy terms: Alan Blinder calls it the "conservatism principle," which he in turn attributes to William Brainard. Since we don't know what the precise economic impact of a change in monetary policy will be, he argues, the monetary authorities should initially take small steps. Furthermore, the more uncertainty, the smaller the initial policy moves.

In practice this is just what the Fed has done in the 1990s. If inflation seems likely to worsen, the Fed can proceed tentatively, initially raising the funds rate $\frac{1}{4}$% and leaving credit flows unchanged. If the whiff of higher inflation turns out to be a false scent, the Fed need not change policy again, which is what happened in 1997. If it turns out that inflationary pressures are indeed increasing, the Fed can then tighten further, which is what happened in 1994, when it boosted the funds rate a total of six times.

When the economy slows down, the Fed can initially ease tentatively. If real growth then picks up again, further easing will not be necessary, as was the case in 1995. If the economy remains sluggish and the unemployment rate continues to rise, the Fed can ease repeatedly, as it did in 1991 and 1992, and again in 2001. Hence by using the so-called conservatism principle, monetary policy has worked well over the past 15 years, and especially since 1991. This method of operation is largely responsible for the combination of full employment and low inflation in the late 1990s.

The purpose of presenting this discussion of lag times and Fed response is not to offer a monetary policy manual, but to alert managers to the sort of changes in policy measures that can reasonably be expected after the economy changes. For example, suppose your business decisions are significantly influenced by (a) changes in the Federal funds rate, and (b) fluctuations in the economy following that change in the funds rate. The cycle could start in motion when, for example, an unexpected drop in the unemployment rate or rise in the inflation rate starts the wheels spinning at the Fed. If the data are not reversed the following month, the Fed is likely to tighten within one quarter. That in turn is likely to reduce many sectors of economic activity with an additional lag of two to three quarters. If you are in an interest-sensitive industry (such as housing), a report of lower unemployment or higher inflation could negatively impact your business next year.

This is an example, not a hard and fast rule. Indeed, the point of this section is to see how financial markets react to that economic information. If they dismiss it, the Fed probably will not react, and your business probably will not be affected. However, if they react with alacrity, perhaps it is time to start thinking about revising those business plans.

CASE STUDY 20.2   IS THERE A POLITICAL BUSINESS CYCLE?

Even if monetary policy follows the guidelines given above and they work out as well as can be expected, the possibility remains that optimal monetary policy could be offset by inappropriate political meddling. In particular, some have claimed that a strong President will put enough pressure on the Fed Chairman in the midst of a hard-fought election campaign that monetary policy will be temporarily derailed by political expediency. In that case, the indicators would be temporarily ignored, and the economy – and most businesses – would suffer accordingly.

A variant of this hypothesis suggests that a newly elected President will invite a recession in his first year, realizing that such a move will reduce inflation, cause the Fed to ease, and generate a booming economy heading into his reelection campaign. According to this theory, real growth would peak during the year of reelection. After the President has been reelected, it is claimed, superior economic performance is no longer of much interest.

We now examine whether any of these theories really happened on a consistent basis by calculating (a) whether the growth rate really did increase in the first three quarters of election years, and (b) whether recessions really did start more often than usual in the first year of a President's term, hence allegedly clearing the path for superior economic performance later in his term.

Since 1944 there have been eleven recessions. If they were randomly distributed, slightly less than three recessions would have occurred in each of the four years of a presidential term. As shown in table 20.1, that is not what happened. Indeed, the results in this table suggest how this rumor got started. From 1945 through 1981, there were recessions in six out of the ten first years of the presidential term of office. However, if that is the case, there must have been a shift, because there were no recessions in the first year of the next four terms. Furthermore, this hypothesis is questionable because three of the eleven recessions started in election years, which certainly would not happen if Presidents were manipulating the economy for their own gain.

continued

CASE STUDY 20.2 (*continued*)

Table 20.1   Timing of recessions in election cycles

Election	Year of election cycles			
	1	2	3	4
Roosevelt/Truman	xw	–	–	x
Truman (full term)	–	–	–	–
Eisenhower I	xw	–	–	–
Eisenhower II	x	–	–	x
Kennedy/Johnson	–	–	–	–
Johnson	–	–	–	–
Nixon	xw	–	–	–
Nixon/Ford	xe	–	–	–
Carter	–	–	–	x
Reagan I	xe	–	–	–
Reagan II	–	–	–	–
Bush Sr	–	xe	–	–
Clinton I	–	–	–	–
Clinton II	–	–	–	–
Bush Jr	x			

x = recession; w = end of a war; e = energy shock

Delving a little deeper, it turns out that five of the six recessions that occurred in the first year of the presidential term were caused by the end of wars, or energy shocks. The only endogenous recession was the downturn under Eisenhower that started in 1957. Most observers would concede that was the result of tight money policies following the rise in the inflation rate from 0.4% in 1955 to 3.0% in 1956. Indeed, as seen in table 20.2, Eisenhower is at the head of the nonpolitical list when it comes to the question of manipulating the economy for election purposes.

As can be seen, the average difference in the growth rate between election and non-election years over the past 14 election cycles has been a negative 0.5% – the economy grew somewhat more *slowly* in election years. That doesn't do much to advance the political business cycle theory. In fact, the only clear evidence of such a move was in 1972, when Nixon really did boost the economy in order to get reelected. However, he used various devices, such as wage and price controls and moving off the international gold standard, that no longer exist as policy options. Also, Fed Chairman Arthur Burns failed to withstand presidential pressure as well as Paul Volcker and Alan Greenspan, or for that matter, as well as any other Fed Chairman.

continued

CASE STUDY 20.2 (*continued*)

Table 20.2   Real growth, year before and year during
presidential elections

	Year before	Year during[a]	Difference
1948–Truman	5.4[b]	3.6	−1.8
1952–Truman*	5.0	2.3	−2.7
1956–Eisenhower	6.6	0.2	−6.4
1960–Eisenhower*	5.4	2.3	−3.1
1964–Johnson	5.3	6.5	+1.2
1968–Johnson*	2.4	5.9	+3.4
1972–Nixon	4.3	7.4	+4.1
1976–Ford	2.9	4.7	+1.8
1980–Carter	1.2	−2.6	−3.8
1984–Reagan	7.0	6.3	−0.7
1988–Reagan*	4.0	3.0	−1.0
1992–Bush	0.4	3.4	+3.1
1996–Clinton	1.3	2.9	+1.6
2000–Clinton*	4.5	2.6	−1.9
14-period average	4.0	3.5	−0.5

* Not running for reelection
[a] First three quarters of the year
[b] Last three quarters of 1947; first quarter data not available
All figures are quarterly averages of growth rates

Even though this happened once, the odds are slim today that even a strong President would be able to manipulate the economy to his election-year advantage. In this author's view, there is no evidence that any future President will tilt the economy into recession during his first year in office, or will step on the accelerator in the months before his reelection. Forecasters – and monetary policymakers – have little to fear from that option.

20.6   Summary of noneconometric forecasting methods

The forecasting record of econometric models has been disappointing. However, like the old Henny Youngman joke, the issue is "compared to what?" In particular, the issue is whether noneconometric methods provide more accurate forecasts than econometric models. We now turn to these other methods of macroeconomic forecasting, which can be grouped into three main categories.

- *Naive models and consensus surveys of macro forecasts.* Naive models state that economic variables without trends will be the same this period as last period; for those with trends, the rate of change this period will be the same as last period.[3] The consensus forecast for real growth and inflation since 1978 is discussed.
- *Leading indicators.* These always predict recessions, but also tend to predict downturns when none exist. Also, no one has found a satisfactory group of leading indicators for inflation, even though it generally lags changes in real growth in the business cycle. We examine the plusses and minuses of the leading indicator approach.
- *Survey methods for individual sectors.* The major types of surveys that are used in macroeconomic forecasting are those that measure (a) consumer attitudes and spending plans and (b) business conditions and sentiment. Other surveys that are less often used in forecasting include surveys of capital spending plans, inventories and sales, labor markets, and housing conditions.

The regional Federal Reserve Banks provide surveys of business conditions in their regions; some of these are issued on an individual basis, notably by the Philadelphia and Atlanta Feds. Furthermore, all regions contribute information that is combined in the so-called *Beige Book*, sent to FOMC members for deliberations before each Open Market Committee meeting. The Beige Book used to be scrutinized carefully for clues about how FOMC members might vote on changing the funds rate, but since there seems to be little relationship between that commentary and FOMC action, it is not followed closely any more.

20.7 Naive models and consensus surveys of macro forecasts

At first glance, a model that says this year will be just like last year may seem far too simplistic to be considered by any actual business manager or macro forecaster. On the other hand, many businesses routinely invoke such forecasts under the heading of "plans" – e.g., our plan is to increase sales 10% every year, or boost the rate of return on equity to 20%, or increase market share by 3%, or some similar exhortation. One might argue these are targets rather than forecasts, but they often serve much the same purpose in the sense that if it appears these targets are not being met, management will often devote additional resources to meeting these goals even if the result is counterproductive – too much spent on advertising, unneeded expansion, or profits "borrowed" from future years. In virtually all cases it is advisable to temper these goals with an understanding of the overall economic environment.

Naive models can also be used to determine when econometric models are useless. Over time, if a naive model has a smaller average error than the corresponding econometric model, the latter ought to be discarded without further deliberation. Some would argue that even if the average change in GDP can be explained better by a sophisticated than a naive model, changes in financial markets cannot.

Although this is true for very short changes, such as hourly or daily movements, we have tried to show in chapter 17 that quarterly and annual swings in bond and stock prices are related to economic variables.

No serious forecaster uses naïve models for prediction. However, that does not necessarily clinch the case for econometric models. We next examine the performance of consensus forecasts relative to naïve models for real growth and inflation.

Several organizations issue consensus forecasts of the US economy, including several regional Federal Reserve banks, the National Association of Business Economists, and a joint effort of the American Statistical Association and the National Bureau. However, the best known – and also best documented – source of consensus forecasts is the Blue Chip Economic Indicators Survey, originally started by Robert J. Eggert, who was Chief Economist at Ford and later at RCA. While Eggert also collected consensus forecasts at RCA, the formal Blue Chip Survey dates from 1977, so we will examine their track record since that date.

First, these consensus forecasts are compared to naïve models. Since 1977, the naïve model that says the change in real growth this year will be the same as last year shows an absolute average error (AAE) of 1.8%, compared with an AAE for the Blue Chip consensus forecasts of 1.2%. The AAE is the actual error without regard to sign, and is used because otherwise one might say a model that overpredicted real growth by 1% one year and underpredicted it by 1% the next year had an average error of zero. The AAE in this case is, of course, 1%.

This comparison would seem to indicate a clear superiority for the consensus forecast, but that statistic is misleading, as explained next.

The consensus forecasts indicate the amount that real GDP is expected to rise next year on an annual basis; that means (for example) the percentage change in real GDP from 1997 to 1998. However, what people really want to know is what will happen to real GDP over the next four quarters, usually referred to as the change on a quarterly average basis. These changes are not the same. To see that, consider the following example.

| | \multicolumn{4}{c}{Index of real GDP} | | |
	1st	2nd	3rd	4th quarter
Year 1	97	98	99	100
Year 2	101	102	103	102
Year 3	101	100	100	101

In this situation, the naïve model would assume that the growth rate from 98.5 in year 1 to 102 in year 2 would continue the following year, which means it would rise to 105.5 (excluding second order effects). Considering that real GDP actually fell to 100.5, that would be a serious error of 5%. In such situations, the consensus would probably do much better, even if it did not catch the actual downturn.

However, forecasters are likely to notice that during the second half of year 2, real GDP did not rise at all. As a result, they use that information to predict that there will be no change in real GDP from fourth quarter levels – in essence using a naïve model based on the past two quarters. That would generate a prediction that real GDP will be 102 in year 3, which would generate an error of 1.5%. That isn't very good, but it is much better than the 5% error generated by the naïve model. Thus while it appears that the consensus forecast beats the naïve model by a substantial margin, the superior performance of the consensus occurs because it incorporates quarterly data.

Using this method, we can construct a naïve model in which the change in GDP this year on an annual basis is a function of previous changes in GDP on a quarterly basis. No economic theory is involved here, only regression analysis. On this basis, such a model estimated for 1977–2002 generates an AAE of 1.0%, very similar to, although slightly less than, the Blue Chip consensus forecast.

This doesn't prove anything. However, it is consistent with the hypothesis that the consensus forecast for real GDP is the same as a naïve model that uses all the latest quarterly information.

For inflation, the naïve model that says the inflation rate this year will be the same as last year has an AAE of 1.2%, compared with an AAE for the Blue Chip consensus forecasts of 0.8%. Using the latest available information, the AAE is reduced to 1.0%, so there is some slight improvement in the consensus. However, that represents the fact that when there are big changes in oil prices one year, it is generally assumed they will not continue, whereas the naïve model doesn't know that. With that one modification, the AAEs are the same for the naïve and consensus forecasts. Thus when the naïve model is adjusted to include all the latest information, the consensus forecasts do not outperform naïve models.

It is not clear whether econometric model forecasters do better than "back of the envelope" forecasters, but no real test of this hypothesis is possible because during most of this period, the major econometric forecasts were well known, which means the remaining forecasts were not made in a vacuum. The average "casual" forecaster took one of the econometric model forecasts and "tweaked" it a little, resulting in a prediction that was similar to those of the "Big Three." The studies that have been undertaken show there is no significant difference between the average forecast error of econometric models and noneconometric macro forecasts.

No naïve model will ever predict a turning point, so the comparison is moot at those junctures. Nonetheless, it may be interesting to examine how well the Blue Chip Survey participants did at predicting recessions. We examine the record after 1977, when the Blue Chip Survey formally started. Each month's report carries a green, yellow, or red banner, which means what you would expect: green is above-average growth, yellow is below average but still positive, and red means recession ahead. The annual record for predicting real growth is given in table 20.3, the record for inflation is given in table 20.4, and the record on turning points is summarized below.

Table 20.3   Blue Chip consensus forecasting record: actual and predicted percentage change in real GDP

Forecast year	Consensus*	Actual	Actual error	Naïve error
1977	5.1	4.9	0.2	0.7
1978	4.3	5.0	−0.7	−0.1
1979	2.1	2.9	0.8	−2.1
1980	−2.0	−0.3	−1.7	−3.2
1981	0.7	2.5	−1.8	2.8
1982	0.3	−2.1	2.4	−4.6
1983	2.5	4.0	−1.5	6.1
1984	5.3	6.8	−1.5	2.8
1985	3.3	3.7	−0.4	−3.1
1986	3.0	3.0	0.0	−0.7
1987	2.4	2.9	−0.5	−0.1
1988	2.2	3.8	−1.6	0.9
1989	2.7	3.4	−0.7	−0.4
1990	1.7	1.2	0.5	−2.2
1991	−0.1	−0.9	0.8	−2.1
1992	1.6	3.0	−1.4	3.9
1993	2.9	2.7	0.2	−0.3
1994	3.0	4.0	−1.0	1.3
1995	3.1	2.7	0.4	−1.3
1996	2.2	3.6	−1.4	0.9
1997	2.3	4.4	−2.1	0.8
1998	2.5	4.3	−1.8	−0.1
1999	2.4	4.1	−1.7	−0.2
2000	3.6	3.8	−0.2	−0.3
2001	2.6	0.3	2.3	−3.5
2002	1.0	3.3	−2.3	2.8
26-year absolute average error			1.2	1.8

*Issued in early January of each year

The predictive record of Blue Chip forecasts as turning points can be summarized as follows:

- *Recession started 1/80.* Blue chip flashed the "red" banner in 10/79. Apparently a good call, but recession was actually caused by the imposition of credit controls in February 1980; if that had not happened, the recession probably would not have occurred.
- *Recession ended 7/80.* Red banner was still in place that month, and headlines said "recession is here – and with a vengeance"; "recession expected to remain through year-end." Completely missed upturn.
- *Recession started 7/81.* Green banner, headline said "economic exuberance envisioned for 1982." *Not one* out of 50 economists predicted recession. Yet the yield

Table 20.4 Blue Chip consensus forecasting record: actual and predicted percentage change in CPI

Forecast year	Consensus*	Actual	Actual error	Naïve error
1980	11.0	13.5	−2.5	−2.2
1981	11.2	10.3	0.9	3.2
1982	7.8	6.2	1.6	4.1
1983	5.0	3.2	1.8	3.0
1984	5.0	4.3	0.7	−1.1
1985	4.2	3.6	0.6	0.7
1986	3.6	1.9	1.7	1.7
1987	3.2	3.6	−0.4	−1.7
1988	4.2	4.1	0.1	−0.5
1989	4.7	4.8	−0.1	−0.7
1990	4.1	5.4	−1.3	−0.6
1991	4.8	4.2	0.6	−1.2
1992	3.3	2.9	0.4	−1.3
1993	3.1	2.7	0.4	−0.2
1994	2.8	2.7	0.1	0.0
1995	3.3	2.5	0.8	−0.2
1996	2.8	3.3	−0.5	0.8
1997	2.9	1.7	1.2	−1.6
1998	2.2	1.6	0.6	−0.1
1999	2.0	2.7	−0.7	1.1
2000	2.5	3.4	−0.9	0.7
2001	2.6	1.6	1.0	−1.8
2002	1.7	1.7	0.0	0.1
23-year absolute average error			0.8	1.2

*Issued in early January of each year

curve was clearly inverted at the time. No red banner until 2/82, seven months later.

- *Recession ended 11/82.* However, in June, the Blue Chip consensus said the recession had already ended, and predicted a 4.2% growth rate in the second half of the year. The actual growth rate was −0.6%.
- *Recession started 7/90.* Yellow banner, but once again, *not one* of the 50 participants expected a recession. Consensus forecast was for 2% growth each of the next three quarters. The actual record: −1.9%, −4.1%, and −2.2%.
- *Recession ended 3/91.* Red banner (recession expected ahead) stayed in place until June.
- *Recession started 3/01.* Red banner did not appear until September. In fairness to forecasters at the time, the BEA substantially overstated real GDP that year, so it appeared the economy was still improving whereas in fact it was declining.

- *Recession ended 12/01.* Red banner lifted two months later. A "special question" in the 12/01 issue found that 70% of the economists thought the recession would end by the following April.

While detailed records with quarterly data are unavailable before 1977, economists generally failed to predict any of the earlier recessions from 1958 through 1975. Before 1958, there wasn't a forecasting industry.

Considering how we have repeatedly shown in the text that an inverted yield spread always predicts a recession the following year, one might have thought that at least one or two intrepid forecasters would have predicted a decline under those circumstances. Maybe they told their friends about it, but not the Blue Chip Survey. We have already suggested some possible reasons for this public timidity.

The answer to the question of "how good" the consensus forecasts have been will always be subjective. In terms of advice to managers, the results given here show that the real sector forecasts are not superior to a naïve model based on quarterly data, and cannot predict turning points. The inflation forecasts have had a systematic bias over the past 20 years. Until recently, almost all of the errors have a "plus" sign, which means the predicted change in the inflation rate has been greater than the actual change. All errors were positive from 1981 through 1986, and then again from 1991 through 1995. Apparently forecasters, stung by the high rate of inflation in the 1970s, built this bias into their predictions for the next decade and a half.

Accurate forecasts are probably most important at turning points. Since the consensus forecast has been unable to predict downturns, we next turn to alternative methods that have been proposed for predicting turning points. These include the Index of Leading Economic Indicators and various private sector surveys of consumer and business sentiment.

20.8   Using the Index of Leading Economic Indicators to predict the economy

The Index of Leading Economic Indicators (LEI) has never missed a recession. Its drawback is it predicts recessions in years when the economy keeps growing. This may not be a coincidence. In particular, if the monetary authorities take appropriate action when the economy slows down, they may very well avert the recession that would otherwise have occurred. In that sense, the leading indicators did their job very well. But it raises the issue that managers must face: when the LEI declines, does that mean the economy is headed into a recession – or not?

The Conference Board purchased the rights from the Commerce Department in 1995 to publish the LEI, and also received the authority to revise the index. In response, they added the yield spread between the 10-year Treasury note yield and the Federal funds rate, which is a relevant predictor of turning points. One could reasonably argue that the efficacy of this index ought to be evaluated in terms of its most recent performance, since it has changed substantially over the past 60 years.

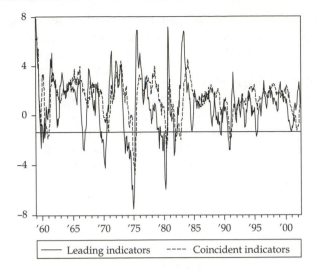

Figure 20.1 Changes in the leading and coincident economic indicators

The performance of the Conference Board-revised index in the 2001 recession is examined in case study 20.3.

The mistakes made by the LEI are all in the same direction. The index has never failed to predict an actual downturn. On the other hand, it often predicts false recessions, giving rise to such quips as "The leading indicators have predicted six of the last three recessions." That systematic bias led economists to suggest that the Index of Leading Economic Indicators be adjusted by some sort of upward trend. This was tried for several years but the results were no better than before, so the adjustment was eventually dropped.

Figure 20.1 shows the six-month percentage change in the LEI compared with the six-month percentage change in the index of coincident indicators; a graph of the levels would be dominated by the trend factor. The horizontal line at −1.4% represents the amount these two indicators fell during the 2001 recession. This graph shows that the LEI correctly predicted the recessions that started in 1960, 1970, 1974, 1980, 1981, and 1990. However, it also predicted recessions that did not start in 1967, 1985, and 1995. In all three cases, the growth rate of the economy diminished sharply but remained positive. The decline in the economy in late 1966 was offset by the surge in expenditures for the Vietnam War, which would not show up in the usual indicators. The declines in 1984 and 1994 were much milder, so if the line had been set a little lower, no recession signal would have been sent. In that case, though, the LEI would have missed predicting the 2001 recession.

To a certain extent, one could argue that if the leading indicators do their job correctly, they will end up being wrong. If the LEI signal that the economy is heading into a recession and provides a long enough lead time, that gives fiscal and monetary policymakers the opportunity to change course quickly enough that the recession would not occur. We now examine this point further in connection with the 2001 downturn.

CASE STUDY 20.3   LEADING INDICATORS AND THE 2001 RECESSION

According to the Dating Committee of the National Bureau, the 2001 recession started in March. While the events of 9/11 temporarily depressed economic activity, that particular decline was short-lived, and the recession probably ended in December. To a certain extent, the question of how well the leading indicators performed in those circumstances is unfair, since the dip in the economy in September was clearly exogenous. It makes more sense to look at the behavior of the leading indicators in July and August, and again in October to December, to see if they provided some hint that the economy was about to recover. The test for whether they predicted the initial downturn ahead of time is also relevant, since the beginning of the recession was not tied to any particular exogenous event.

At first glance the indicators seem to work well. The leaders turned down in March 2000; they had also fallen in January but then rose again in February, and the general rule calls for three consecutive months of decline to send a recession signal. The lead time was just under one year, because the recession officially started in March 2001, but based on the coincident indicators it could just as easily have been started in January. The LEI went up in May 2001, and the recession ended eight months later. It looks like a textbook example.

Nonetheless, there is something incomplete in this picture. The *coincident* indicators fell only 0.4% before 9/11; in all past recessions, they had declined at least 1.3%. Thus based on its performance through August 2001, the economy may not have really been in a recession.

After 9/11, economic activity slumped sharply for a while, and the unemployment rate quickly rose from 4.9% to 6.0%. Real GDP declined again in the third quarter, which was enough for the Dating Committee to certify the decline as an actual recession. Hence the earlier signal given by the leading indicators was validated. *Yet without 9/11 there would have been no recession. The economy was starting to pick up again because of aggressive Fed easing and the tax rebate checks mailed in the summer of 2001.* In that sense, the LEI performed well by signaling an imminent downturn, and the monetary and fiscal policymakers performed *their* duties by shifting to an expansionary policy. The recession probably would have been avoided if the terrorist bombings had not occurred. Indeed, that is the main reason the economy recovered so quickly after 9/11, hence surprising most economists.

We thus offer the following advice for how managers should use the information contained in the LEI in determining what lies ahead for their own companies. When the LEI indicate signs of weaker economic activity ahead, the Fed has to decide how much it wishes to change policy. No one knows precisely how the monetary authorities will act in the future. However, the record of the past

continued

CASE STUDY 20.3 (*continued*)

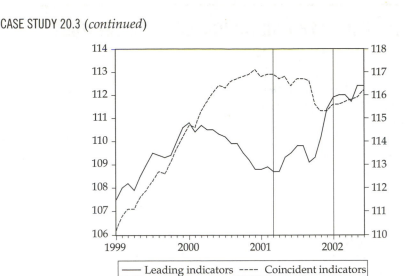

Figure 20.2 Leading and coincident indicators and the 2001 recession

20 years suggests the following rule of thumb. If inflation has been rising, the Fed will continue to tighten in spite of the forthcoming slowdown in economic activity, and an actual recession will occur. If inflation has been steady, the Fed will refrain from further tightening and, as various measures of real growth do decline, will begin to ease. In that case, no recession will occur. That is what would have happened in 2001 had it not been for the terrorist attack.

20.9 Survey methods for individual sectors

Over a dozen surveys are currently issued by private sector organizations to provide a window into the future. Naturally, each organization touts its own index as a valuable resource for managers and one that is well worth the small cost of subscription. However, rather than provide an exhaustive analysis of which indexes do and do not work well, we use Occam's razor and let the market test indicate which surveys are valuable. If a particular index has passed a market test, which means the releases are followed closely by financial market traders and featured in the business press, it is discussed here; if it is generally ignored, we assume that means potential users do not find the information helpful. On this basis, the key indexes are those for consumer confidence and sentiment published by the Conference Board and the University of Michigan, and the Report of Business published by the Institute for Supply Management (formerly National Association of Purchasing Managers).

Indexes not covered here include the NAHB index of homeowner sentiment, the *ABC-Money Magazine* weekly index of consumer sentiment, the Conference Board index on help wanted advertising, Dun & Bradstreet and Cahners indexes of business sentiment, the NFIB index of small business sentiment, various manpower surveys, various surveys of capital spending by numerous organizations, regional purchasing manager surveys, regional surveys by Federal Reserve Banks, notably Philadelphia and Atlanta, and the Beige Book. All of these are available on the internet, and managers may wish to examine them individually for specific sectors or regions of their businesses.

The Conference Board and ISM surveys have a long historical track record, are well documented, and provide a useful snapshot of what is currently happening in consumer and business spending. Both of them have passed a market test, and both can provide valuable information to managers; however, they must be used with caution.

Indexes of Consumer Confidence and Sentiment

The original index of consumer sentiment was developed at the Survey Research Center of the University of Michigan, which is staffed by economists and sociologists. Considering its location, it is not too surprising that one of the principal aims of this index was to predict auto sales.

Originally, the Michigan survey included two types of indexes: buying plans and attitudes. The buying plans asked specific questions about purchases, such as the likelihood that you will buy a new car in the next three months or six months. The attitude questions were supposed to elicit "softer" data, such as how consumers felt about the economy generally, whether they felt better or worse off, how they saw their financial future shaping up, and answers to similar questions.

At first it was assumed that the buying plans index would provide more relevant information about actual changes in consumer spending, but the results turned out to be just the opposite. Information elicited from consumers regarding their general feeling about the economy turned out to be much more useful in tracking future changes in the economy than specific questions about what they planned to buy in the near future. As a result, the buying plans index was eventually dropped. The University of Michigan index is now issued twice each month.

In 1967 the Conference Board started to publish its own index of consumer sentiment. Its index is based on a survey of 5,000 respondents undertaken by National Family Opinion (NFO). At first the index was published every other month; since July 1977 it has been published monthly. Indexes are provided for current sentiment and expectations, the latter being more useful for forecasting purposes.

The two surveys of consumer confidence and sentiment generally yield similar results. However, while the Conference Board encourages people to read their current release free of charge, the University of Michigan has chosen not to release their results to the press, claiming it would reduce their subscription base. In fact the

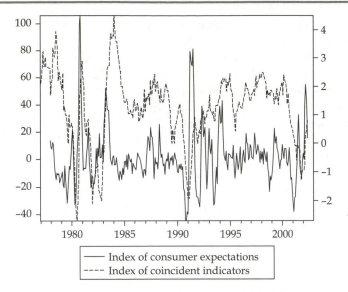

Figure 20.3 Changes in consumer expectations and the index of coincident indicators

results are "bootlegged" and appear on all the major news media within minutes of their release. However, since Michigan does not encourage dissemination of their data, we have complied with their wishes and will discuss only the Conference Board survey. Econometric examination of the two series by this author reveals very little difference.

The information in these surveys can be used in one of two ways: to predict changes in purchases of motor vehicles, or to predict changes in total GDP. As it turns out, over an extended period of time, the results are about the same for both series. Changes in the index of consumer expectations two quarters ago, which has a better forecasting record than the current conditions component, only predict about 25% of the change in either motor vehicle purchases or GDP. By comparison, single-equation regressions that use only lagged values of disposable income, unemployment, inflation, the yield spread, and the stock market predict 50% to 75% of the change in these variables, depending on the time period being considered.

However, that is not really the relevant test for the usefulness of this index. When the two approaches are combined – economic variables plus the index of consumer expectations – the forecasts for both motor vehicles and total GDP are better than when either approach is used separately.[4]

As shown in figure 20.3, the six-month percentage change in the Conference Board index of consumer expectations generally leads overall economic activity, as measured by the index of coincident indicators, by about two quarters. That lead time should be sufficient to permit managers to adjust to changing economic conditions. The problem is that the dips in 1992, 1994, and 1998 were not followed by declines in either overall economic activity or discretionary consumer purchases. Thus, for managers who want to use the index of consumer expectations as a guideline to predict changes in motor vehicle sales or changes in overall GDP, we offer the following guidelines.

1. The lag with the highest correlation is about two quarters, so changes in the index of consumer expectations are likely to affect purchases about two quarters later.
2. Changes in the index of consumer expectations themselves explain only about a quarter of the variance in either purchases of consumer durables or total GDP.
3. Changes in the cost and availability of credit – including changes in the money supply, the yield spread, and changes in the stock market – all with lags of two quarters or more, are more important than consumer expectations. Looking at this index will provide some additional information, but not as much as looking at those three monetary variables.
4. The best forecast for managers who wish to predict either purchases of motor vehicles or the overall economy can be made by combining changes in the monetary variables listed above and the information from the index of consumer expectations.

Indexes of Manufacturing Activity

The Institute for Supply Management (formerly the National Association of Purchasing Managers) has provided detailed information on manufacturing activity for over 50 years. In July 1997, this organization also added a report on the nonmanufacturing sector activity. Due to its brief track record and much lower visibility in the financial press, we do not analyze that index but confine our remarks to the manufacturing sector reports.

The most widely quoted and closely watched index on the ISM survey is the overall index of manufacturing activity. Figure 20.4 shows the comparison of this index with the index of coincident indicators. The evidence is fairly clear: the ISM index is closely correlated with the actual state of the economy, but is not a leading indicator. Nonetheless, to the extent that these figures are released on the first business day of every month, they do provide an advance estimate of what the official government statistics are likely to show. In that sense they can be quite valuable.

ISM states that approximately 250 manufacturing firms participate in the survey. They are asked to provide company information for changes in shipments, new orders, unfilled orders, delivery time of vendors, inventory stocks, employment, prices paid, export orders, and imports. At one time, the price data received a great deal of attention because (a) purchasing managers presumably have the best handle on prices they are paying and (b) it is one of the few series that provides an advance look at where inflation is heading. However, in recent years there has been no significant correlation between the ISM price component and the PPI. Considering that forecasts of inflation have not been widely followed for the past

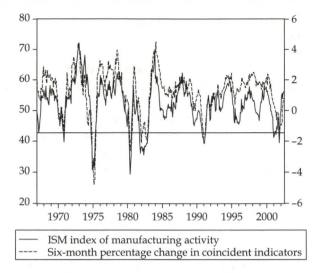

Figure 20.4   ISM index of manufacturing activity and coincident indicators

several years, we do not discuss this component of the ISM index separately. In addition to the overall index, individual data are compiled for the following nine components of economic activity:

1. New orders
2. Unfilled orders (backlog of orders)
3. Employment
4. Supply deliveries (vendor performance)
5. Production
6. Export orders
7. Imports
8. Prices paid
9. Inventory stocks.

Survey respondents are asked only to state whether these variables moved up, stayed the same, or moved down over the past month, rather than the actual percentage change. Hence these figures are not actual changes, but are **diffusion indexes**. Such indexes can be calculated two ways: the percentage of those reporting an increase plus half of those reporting no change, in which case the average value is 50; or the percentage of those reporting an increase minus the percentage reporting a decrease, in which case the average value is 0. The ISM index is based on a mean value of 50.

The horizontal line in figure 20.4 drawn at 42.7% (previously 44%) has been calculated by the ISM to show the dividing line between recessions and mere slowdowns. If the overall index falls below 42.7%, according to ISM, it means the economy is heading into a recession; if it remains above that line but below 50%, growth is below average but is still positive. On this basis, the index has identified all recessions correctly, although it usually does not give much lead time.

The advantage of using a diffusion index is that more participants are likely to respond to the survey because they do not have to provide precise estimates, or release confidential company data. The disadvantage is that a tiny change at a small firm gets just as much weight as a big change from a larger firm. As it turns out, research done by this author reveals that the overall results do not change very much regardless of which method is used, so this turns out not to be a major drawback.[5] There is one major advantage of using a diffusion index, namely that more firms are likely to agree to respond to such a survey because (a) it involves less data-crunching on their part, and (b) they do not have to be concerned about releasing confidential company information. As a result, the survey is likely to have more participants and generate more robust results.

The major complaint about the ISM index by long-time users is that the changes are not correlated with the strength or weakness of business cycle recoveries. For example, the increase in the index following the 1980 recession was much stronger than the increase following the 1982 recession, even though the 1980–81 recovery was unusually brief, whereas the 1983 recovery lasted until mid-1990 and brought the economy back to full employment. The index also overstated the strength of the 1991 recovery, which led some politicians in the Bush Administration to claim that by overstating the strength of the economy, appropriate monetary and fiscal policy actions were not taken, leading to Bush's defeat. Whether or not that index can be blamed for the misfortunes of the Bush campaign, it did overstate the expected strength of the recovery.

According to this index, the brief 2001 recession was over by June of that year. Indeed, we use this evidence to support our claim that the economy was improving and there never would have been an official recession if not for 9/11. Of course the index fell after the terrorist attacks, but that had nothing to do with the business cycle per se. On the other hand, the quick recovery of this index shortly after 9/11 should have provided forecasters with enough ammunition to predict a much quicker recovery than was shown by the consensus forecast. In that sense the ISM index was useful to forecasters.

MANAGER'S BRIEFCASE: PLANNING AFTER 9/11

As a manager for a major corporation, the CEO has just asked you for an assessment of the business outlook, and any changes in the existing business plan you recommend, following the 9/11 tragedy. Assuming your company was not directly affected by the attacks, what recommendations should you give? For background, the consensus forecast currently calls for another two to three quarters of recession, while sales in your own company suggest that business had been very weak in the first half of the year but was starting to improve. Now it is back to the drawing board.

continued

MANAGER'S BRIEFCASE (*continued*)

This actually turns out to be a clear case of how the Index of Leading Economic Indicators, and the various surveys, provided better information than the consensus forecast. In the weeks after 9/11, most economists — including this author — thought the shock to the economy would depress economic activity for several quarters, and the economy would not rebound until mid-2002. However, the leading indicators provided a different story and the two surveys discussed in this chapter indicated far different results. Indeed, by mid-December, the *Wall Street Journal* reported that Ed Hyman, who many consider the best macroeconomic forecaster on Wall Street, said all the indicators he looked at indicated the recession was ending. These indicators were available to everyone, and are reproduced in table 20.5.

Table 20.5 Leading indicators, coincident indicators, consumer expectations, and ISM survey, monthly data, 2000.01–2002.06

Month	Leaders	Coincident	Consumer expectations	ISM survey
2000:01	110.8	114.7	119.1	56.2
2000:02	110.4	114.6	114.6	56.4
2000:03	110.7	115.3	106.8	55.3
2000:04	110.5	115.7	109.7	54.7
2000:05	110.5	116.1	118.7	53.1
2000:06	110.3	116.4	111.9	52.1
2000:07	110.2	116.3	113.7	51.7
2000:08	109.9	116.6	113.9	49.9
2000:09	109.9	116.7	115.9	49.6
2000:10	109.5	116.8	108.4	48.3
2000:11	109.2	116.9	101.2	47.9
2000:12	108.8	117.1	96.9	44.3
2001:01	108.8	116.8	79.3	41.2
2001:02	108.9	116.9	70.7	41.9
2001:03	108.7	116.9	83.1	43.1
2001:04	108.7	116.7	79.1	43.2
2001:05	109.3	116.8	87.1	42.1
2001:06	109.5	116.4	93.5	44.7
2001:07	109.8	116.7	92.9	43.9
2001:08	109.8	116.7	93.7	47.9
2001:09	109.1	116.6	78.1	46.2
2001:10	109.3	115.6	70.7	39.5
2001:11	110.2	115.3	77.3	44.7
2001:12	111.4	115.3	92.4	48.1
2002:01	111.9	115.6	96.9	49.9
2002:02	112.0	115.6	94.0	54.7
2002:03	112.0	115.7	109.3	55.6
2002:04	111.7	115.8	109.6	53.9
2002:05	112.4	115.9	109.7	55.7
2002:06	112.4	116.2	106.9	56.2

continued

MANAGER'S BRIEFCASE (*continued*)

The LEI turned up very quickly in November; the coincident indicators, by comparison, didn't rise very fast. Consumer expectations also rebounded very quickly. The ISM survey of manufacturing activity not only rebounded sharply in November, recovering from the October trough, but continued to rise rapidly over the next three months.

This table also shows that by March, the gains were over. During the second quarter, the leading indicators rose only 0.3%, compared to 2.7% over the past six months; consumer expectations fell 2.2%, compared to the previous rise of 54.6%, and the ISM index rose only 1.1%, compared to 40.8%. These figures all strongly suggested that growth in the second half of the year would be slower than the 3.0% gain in the first half. By comparison, the consensus forecast, as measured by the Blue Chip Economic Indicators, called for a 3.5% growth rate, actually higher than the 3.0% gain of the first half. Based on preliminary data, the actual increase turned out to be 2.4%.

There is, of course, no guarantee that methods that have worked well in the recent past will continue to be the best choice for forecasts in the future. However, it seems clear that for the 2000–02 period of recession and recovery, the Index of Leading Economic Indicators, the index of consumer expectations, and the ISM survey of manufacturing activity provided a more accurate picture than did the consensus of economic forecasts. Managers should probably rely more on these indicators than the consensus economic forecast of the economy.

20.10   Recap: how managers should use forecasting tools

For a reality check on where the economy is right now and where it is likely to be heading over the next few months, your first step should be to look at the indexes of leading and coincident indicators, along with the index of consumer expectations and the ISM survey of manufacturing activity. However, none of these indexes provides very much information about how large the rate of advance or decline will be, or what lies ahead more than six months in the future. No one set of rules will provide infallible forecasts, but the following guidelines should help keep you away from the biggest macroeconomic forecasting errors.

Monetary Sector Variables

- The key debt market variables to watch are the yield spread and the real bond yield. An increase in the nominal bond yield accompanied by an equal increase in inflation will not slow down the economy. In general, a one percentage point increase in the real bond yield will reduce real growth by $\frac{1}{2}$%, but the lag is long and variable, often taking as much as two years. By contrast, a one percentage point change in the yield spread will change the growth rate by at least $\frac{1}{2}$% within one year.

  We have mentioned the importance of the yield spread in predicting recessions, but it should probably be emphasized that a very small negative yield spread is no guarantee of a downturn. In nonrecession years, the yield spread often averages about $2\frac{1}{2}$%. If it happens to drop to $-\frac{1}{2}$%, that would reduce the real growth rate substantially, but probably not enough to cause an actual downturn. Other factors must also be considered.

- A 10% change in the stock market will generally cause a $\frac{1}{2}$% change in real GDP over the next year, starting with a two-quarter lag. Two caveats should be applied. First, even a major stock market decline is usually not enough to cause an actual recession without further changes in exogenous or policy variables. Second, in many cases, a stock market decline will quickly be followed by a monetary easing, hence further reducing the chance of recession. Also, changes in the stock market are more likely to affect capital spending than consumer spending.
- After banking deregulation, money supply is no longer as important a determinant of economic activity, yet it should not be entirely ignored. In recent years, a 1% change in the money supply is likely to cause a $\frac{1}{4}$% change in real GDP starting about two quarters later. Furthermore, exogenous shifts in the availability of credit to either businesses or consumers are likely to cause a major change in economic activity; if such changes occur in the future, they should definitely be included in any business planning.

Fiscal Policy Variables

First, it should be emphasized that these comments do not apply to periods of all-out mobilization, such as World War II. In fact, they do not apply to *any* period where (a) massive increases in defense spending occur, (b) price controls are enacted, and (c) interest rates are artificially held at low levels. During such periods, real growth will zoom – but it will eventually be followed by massive inflation. The usual rules of macroeconomics do not apply during a period when the government is short-circuiting the pricing mechanism.

- During periods of moderate increases in defense spending, the impact on the economy will depend almost entirely on whether those increases are offset by a decline in consumer and business spending because of a decline in sentiment. During such times, the indexes of consumer and business sentiment should be watched closely to determine whether public sector spending gains will be offset by private sector spending declines.
- Substantial increases in transfer payments, such as medical care expenses, will eventually be paid for either by tax increases or through higher interest rates. In either case, there will be no long-term net expansionary impact. To the extent that the increase in government spending reduces the long-term growth rate in productivity, there will be some negative long-term impact on overall economic activity. In the short run, if the economy has substantial slack resources and interest rates do not rise when spending increases, a rise in transfer payments will boost the growth rate.
- In assessing the influence of tax cuts, one should always distinguish between the demand and supply-side effects, the latter being the impact on productivity growth. Over the period of one to two years, demand-side effects mean a tax cut

will generally boost the growth rate, while a tax hike will retard the growth rate. Different tax changes will have different impacts on the economy, but as a rough rule of thumb, the marginal coefficient for the first year is about $\frac{1}{2}$. Since the short-run multiplier is greater than 1 but less than 2, that means that in general, a tax cut representing 1% of GDP will boost the growth rate by slightly less than 1%. This is not meant to be a policy statement, but can serve as a useful rule of thumb for planning medium-term horizons. In the long run, the impact of a tax cut will depend almost entirely on its impact on productivity.

Other Factors

- Except for major shocks to the system, changes in fiscal and monetary policy generally do not affect the growth rate until two to three quarters later. Don't expect instant results, and don't conclude these policies had no effect when the results are not immediately obvious.
- Repetitive shocks have a greatly diminished impact as they reoccur. At first, the energy shock had a major negative impact on the economy, but since then, businesses have learned more effective measures for hedging against changes in prices. As a result, the tripling of oil prices in 1999 and early 2000 had very little impact on the economy.
- Don't overestimate the impact of exogenous events that are not combined with contractionary monetary and fiscal policy. That simple dictum could be applied to 9/11, but also holds in other cases.
- The economy performs best when the value of the dollar is near its purchasing power parity, but again that is a long-run statement. In the short run, an overvalued dollar hurts the manufacturing sector, but that is offset by an increase in real purchasing power and an inflow of foreign funds into financial markets. An undervalued dollar helps the manufacturing sector but is usually inflationary. In general, because the world is on a de facto dollar standard, changes in the value of the dollar do not have a very large impact on the real growth rate.

We offer the following concluding comments. Economists have learned a great deal about how to manage the economy over the past half-century. The US economy now undergoes recessions about once a decade, compared to twice a decade earlier. Inflation is much less likely to accelerate as the economy approaches full employment. Both liberal and conservative economists agree that the Federal budget should be balanced over the cycle, with deficits during recessions and surpluses during periods of overfull employment. Monetary policy has been refined to announce preemptive strikes rather than waiting for higher inflation to force its hand. Perhaps the best testimonial to the beneficial course of the economy under proper monetary and fiscal policies is that the shock of 9/11, and the explosion of fraudulent accounting cases in 2002, did not shake the essential stability of the economy; in spite of a violent downdraft in the stock market, the recovery began and continued during and shortly after these traumas. In the future, we expect business cycle recessions to be infrequent and brief.

KEY TERMS AND CONCEPTS

Diffusion Index
Index of Consumer Expectations
Index of Leading Economic Indicators

ISM Report on Business
Lucas Critique
Naive Models

SUMMARY

- Over the past 40 years, econometric models have had an undistinguished forecasting record. The principal errors made by forecasters can be divided into several different categories, including the following: incorrect underlying theory, instability of underlying relationships, errors in econometric method, inadequate and incorrect data, tendency to cluster around the consensus forecast, inability to predict exogenous events, and erroneous assumptions about policy variables.
- Some economists have argued that the underlying economic relationships are inherently unstable because economic agents learn from their past mistakes and do not react the same way to repeated changes in monetary or fiscal policy or exogenous events. While that is a valid criticism of the decision to use models for policy analysis, it does not explain why forecasts from these models have been inaccurate.
- Preliminary data are often revised; it is not unusual for the real growth rate to be revised by as much as 2% when final data are released. The preliminary or advance versions of key economic indicators such as retail sales, industrial production, payroll employment, and new orders are often substantially revised. In particular, early reports of the 1990–91 recession understated its severity.

- Most recent forecasting errors, however, stem from other reasons. Most economic forecasts tend to cluster around the consensus values, which have never been able to predict a recession in advance. Truly exogenous shocks, such as the energy crisis or the terrorist attacks of 9/11, obviously are not forecastable. To the extent that monetary policy deviates from relationships such as the Taylor Rule, or unforeseen changes occur in defense expenditures or tax policies, forecasts are also likely to be more inaccurate.
- Nonetheless, the largest forecasting errors are generally not made because of the inability to foresee these exogenous events or policy changes, but the inability to analyze them accurately once they have happened. In particular, the 9/11 attacks had a much smaller impact on the economy than most economists expected because the stimulatory monetary and fiscal policy that had already been put in place earlier in the year helped to end the recession quickly.
- The three major methods of macroeconomic forecasts that do not involve econometric models are consensus forecasts, the Index of Leading Economic Indicators, and surveys of consumer and business sentiment. Other surveys of particular sectors of the economy such as homebuilding, labor markets, capital spending plans, and surveys

of regional economic activity do not significantly improve forecast accuracy.

- Consensus forecasts of real growth and inflation provide a reasonably accurate picture of what lies ahead when the economy is growing smoothly, but have missed all the turning points in recent years. As a result, they are actually no more accurate than a naïve model.

- The Index of Leading Economic Indicators (LEI) never fails to signal a recession, but often provides false signals. However, it did provide accurate information regarding the downturn in early 2001 and the upturn in early 2002. In particular, downturns in the stock market component of the LEI are often followed by stable or even accelerating real growth.

- The index of consumer expectations generally leads changes in the coincident indicators by about two quarters, and to that extent adds to forecasting accuracy at turning points. However, it also gives false signals, and also does not provide much information about the strength or durability of an emerging upturn.

- The Report on Business prepared by the Institute for Supply Management (formerly the National Association of Purchasing Managers) is a coincident rather than a leading indicator. However, since it provides detailed data on the first business day of each month, it often provides an accurate advance snapshot of government economic data that are not released for another one to two months. As is the case for the index of consumer expectations, it does not provide much information about the strength or durability of an emerging upturn.

- The combination of the LEI, the index of consumer expectations, and the ISM manufacturing index provided much better guidance about the emergence of the economy from the 2001 recession than did the consensus forecast or predictions generated by econometric models.

- To predict the future of the overall economy, managers should rely primarily on these three indexes for predictions of up to six months. Beyond that time horizon, the basic relationships between changes in monetary and fiscal policy variables and aggregate economic activity will usually give accurate results in the absence of major changes in exogenous variables.

QUESTIONS AND PROBLEMS

1. As a manager, the following facts are in your possession at the end of "this" year and you are asked to predict the changes in the economy "next" year.
   (A) The Fed has just cut the funds rate by $\frac{3}{4}$%, but bond yields have been virtually unchanged.
   (B) The stock market has just fallen 20% over the past three months.
   (C) The Federal budget is now in surplus, and the surplus is expected to be bigger next year.
   (D) The value of the dollar has risen by 20% over the past two years.
   (E) Crude oil prices have fallen 30% over the past year.
   (F) Money supply growth has been stable at 6%.
   (G) Real growth this year was just over 4%.
   What is your forecast for real growth, inflation, and interest rates?

2. From September 2000 to March 2001, the S&P 500 index fell 27% and the US economy headed into a recession. From March 2002 to July 2002, the index fell another 27%, yet this time the recovery that was already underway continued. Based on these events, explain why you would or would not use the stock market as a leading indicator to predict a recession the next time it falls sharply.

3. The material in this chapter did not focus on different methods of predicting inflation because the core rate has changed very little since 1982. The biggest change has been 1.1%, and the average change has been less than 0.5%. Nonetheless, what factors would you look for in the future to signal that core inflation was about to rise substantially the following year?

4. The LEI, consumer expectations, and ISM (then NAPM) surveys all predicted a much more robust recovery in 1991–2 than actually happened. What factors intervened to keep real growth at an unusually low rate early in the recovery? Based on your answer, how would you adjust these series in generating forecasts for the 2002–03 recovery?

5. Suppose the dollar is overvalued by 20% and the Secretary of the Treasury announces that he hopes it will soon return to equilibrium. How would this announcement affect your sales if you were in the following businesses? (Hint: how will the stock market react to that announcement, and how will it affect oil prices?)
   (A) Motor vehicles.
   (B) Steel.
   (C) Fabricated metal products (such as heating and plumbing fixtures) for housing.
   (D) Organic chemicals.
   (E) Aerospace.
   (F) Textiles and apparel.
   (G) Fertilizer.

6. After increasing steadily for several years, the LEI turns down by 0.5% one month. What other factors would you examine in determining whether to curtail your business plans ahead of any recession, and how long would you wait before changing these plans?

7. The President of the United States decides to eliminate terrorism in the Middle East and launches a massive "first strike" against terrorist nations. Before this announcement, you had been predicting $3\frac{1}{2}$% growth and $2\frac{1}{2}$% inflation for the upcoming year. How would this announcement change your forecast? What other factors would you examine?

8. After years of smoldering unrest in southern Mexico, the rebels finally mount a full-scale attack on urban areas. Order is eventually restored, but in the meantime capital has fled the country, resulting in a 50% devaluation of the peso. You recall that there were similar devaluations in 1982, when the US economy was in a lengthy recession, and in 1995, when real growth in the US economy slowed

down to 1% before rebounding. Based on this previous information, would you expect this devaluation to reduce real growth in the US? What other economic indicators would you check before making this determination?

9. The index of consumer expectations dropped much more sharply before the brief and mild 1980 recession than it did before the much more severe and prolonged 1981–2 recession. The same pattern also occurred for the ISM/NAPM index of manufacturing activity. What other factors accounted for this anomaly? How would you take these into account when assessing the next reported drop in these indexes?

Notes

1. If that figure seems unduly high, recall that the budget position fell $400 billion in the mild 2001 recession, only a quarter of which could be tied to the Bush tax cuts.

2. In early 2002, the futures markets expected the Federal funds rate to rise to 4% by year-end. In fact, it fell further. Anyone buying December Eurodollar futures in March would have quadrupled their money by the end of the year. Even the best and the brightest are not always right.

3. This list does not include VAR and ARIMA models. Although these are useful for tracking production and implementing inventory control for companies with large numbers of individual product lines or parts, they are not used for actual macroeconomic forecasting, and in that sense have not passed a market test.

4. See, for example, Michael K. Evans, *Practical Business Forecasting* (Blackwell, 2003), chapter 8.

5. Some of this work is based on the APICS survey data, which was calculated by this author from 1993 through 1999. However, the same general result can be seen by comparing the diffusion indexes for industrial production and payroll employment with the actual changes.

Bibliography and further reading

Barro, Robert J., *Economic Growth* (New York: McGraw-Hill, 1995).

Barro, Robert J., *Getting it Right: Markets and Choices in a Free Society* (Cambridge, MA: MIT Press, 1996).

Bartley, Robert L., *The Seven Fat Years* (New York: MacMillan, 1992).

Baumol, William J., Richard R. Nelson, and Edward N. Wolff, *Convergence of Productivity: Cross-national Studies and Historical Evidence* (New York: Oxford University Press, 1994).

Bernstein, Peter L., *Against The Gods: The Remarkable Story of Risk* (New York: John Wiley, 1996).

Buchholz, Todd G., *New Ideas from Dead Economists* (New York: Penguin Books, 1990).

Dertouzos, Michael L., Richard K. Lester, Robert M. Solow, and the MIT Commission on *Industrial Productivity, Made in America: Regaining of the Productive Edge* (Cambridge, MA: MIT Press, 1989).

Friedman, Milton, *Money Mischief: Episodes in Monetary Policy* (New York: Harcourt Brace Jovanovich, 1994).

Friedman, Milton and Rose D. Friedman, *Capitalism and Freedom* (Chicago: University of Chicago Press, 1972).

Gordon, Robert J. (ed.), *The American Business Cycle: Continuity and Change* (Chicago: University of Chicago Press for NBER, 1986).

Greider, William, *Secrets of the Temple: How the Federal Reserve Runs the Country* (New York: Simon & Schuster, 1987).

Landes, David S., *The Wealth and Poverty of Nations: Why Some Are So Rich and Some So Poor* (New York: W. W. Norton, 1998).

Lowenstein, Roger, *When Genius Failed* (Random House, 2000).

Maddison, Angus, *The World Economy in the 20th Century* (Paris: OECD, 1989); also *Phases of Economic Development* (New York: Oxford University Press, 1982).

Olson, Mancur, *The Rise and Decline of Nations* (New Haven: Yale University Press, 1982).

Phelps, Edmund, *Structural Slumps: The Modern Theory of Unemployment, Interest, and Assets* (Cambridge, MA: Harvard University Press, 1994).

Prestowitz, Clyde V., *Trading Places: How We Allowed Japan to Take the Lead* (New York: Basic Books, 1988).

Roberts, Paul Craig, *The Supply-Side Revolution: An Insider's Account of Policymaking in Washington* (Cambridge, MA: Harvard University Press, 1984).

Schama, Simon, *The Embarrassment of Riches: An Interpretation of Dutch Culture in the Golden Age* (New York: Vintage Books, 1997).

Shiller, Robert J., *Irrational Exuberance* (New York: Broadway Books, 2001).

Solow, Robert M., *Growth Theory: An Exposition* (New York: Oxford University Press, 2000).

Soros, George, *The Alchemy of Finance* (New York: John Wiley, 1994).

Stockman, David A., *The Triumph of Politics: Why the Reagan Revolution Failed* (New York: Harper & Row, 1986).

Volcker, Paul A. and Toyoo Gyohten, *Changing Fortunes* (New York: Random House, 1992).

Wilson, William Julius, *When Work Disappears: The World of the New Urban Poor* (New York: Random House, 1997).

Zarnowitz, Victor, *Business Cycles: Theory, History, Indicators, and Forecasting* (Chicago: University of Chicago Press for NBER, 1992).

Index

standardized budget surplus/deficit
696–7
standard of living *see* living standards
standards *see* regulatory policy
steady state equilibrium, productivity
388
steel industry
exports and imports 174, 175, 424–7
Kennedy Administration 652, 661,
662
prices: and inflation 277, 278, 279;
sticky 330
strike (1959) 574, 581
unemployment 334–6
sticky prices
monetary policy 736–7
unemployment 327, 329–32
sticky wages
monetary policy 736–7
nominal 327, 331–2
real: efficiency wages 328, 332–4;
government restrictions 328,
337–48; insider/outsider
relationships 328, 334–7
stock adjustment principle
cyclical fluctuations 606–8, 623, 627,
635, 636
optimal capital accumulation, theory
of 192, 193
stock market
business cycles: anticipating
recessions 593; Great Depression
595; phases 575; recurrent but
irregular behavior 569;
technology 583–4, 585–6
consumption and 138: consumer
confidence 136–7; credit 120;
household net worth 130, 131–3;
marginal propensity to consume
112; taxation 117–18, 119
crash (1987) 662–3: monetary policy
203, 216, 730
cyclical fluctuations 612, 635–6,
649–52: capital spending 612;
ends of four major booms 661–3;
motor vehicle purchases 632;
Nasdaq bubble (1999–2000)
663–5; present discounted value
and equilibrium P/E ratio 653–5;
residential construction 619; risk
factor 654, 655–61
forecasting 782
foreign exchange 475

investment 168: expectations, role of
162–3; exports and imports 179;
government saving 182; optimal
capital accumulation, theory of
193; recession (2001) 169–70; tax
policy 167
IS/LM diagram 243, 260–1
Japan 529, 530
social security system 708, 710–11,
712
yield spreads 202
stocks
consumption 111
cyclical fluctuations 674–5: budget
ratio 665–9; capital gains taxes
670–2; inflation, expected rate of
669; long-term performance
672–4
Federal funds rate 212
foreign exchange rates, determination
of 464
monetary policy 221–2, 224
national income and product
accounts 53
yield spreads 202
see also stock market
strikes
business cycles 574, 581–2, 593
Reagan Administration 270, 301
structuralist school 352–6, 520
structural unemployment 79
sub-Saharan Africa 554
subsidies 547
see also trade policy
Suez crisis 580
Summers, Lawrence H. 361 n. 13
Summers, Robert 486 n. 2
Super Bowl Theory 233 n. 10
supplements to wages and salaries (S)
38
inflation 276, 286–7, 301
national income and product
accounts 37–8
unemployment 329
supply shocks *see* exogenous shocks
supply-side economics 26
surplus theories, business cycles 568–9
Sweden
European Monetary System 525
inflation 312
productivity growth 381, 384
socialism 551
unemployment 349, 350, 351